THE OFFICE

Procedures and Technology

2d Edition

MARY ELLEN OLIVERIO
Graduate School of Business
Pace University
New York, New York

WILLIAM R. PASEWARK
Professor Emeritus, Texas Tech University
Office Management Consultant
Lubbock, Texas

BONNIE R. WHITE
College of Education
Auburn University
Auburn, Alabama

Contributing Authors

Donna R. Everett
College of Education
Texas Tech University
Lubbock, Texas

Sharon Fisher-Larson
Elgin Community College
Elgin, Illinois

SOUTH-WESTERN PUBLISHING CO.

Senior Acquisitions Editor: Karen Schmohe
Senior Developmental Editor: Carol Lynne Ruhl
Production Editor: Thomas W. Bailey
Senior Designer: Elaine St. John-Lagenaur
Pagination Specialist: Timothy S. Jones
Production Artist: Steven McMahon
Associate Photo Editor/Stylist: Mike O'Donnell
Marketing Manager: Al S. Roane

ISBN: 0-538-60900-1

Library of Congress Catalog Card Number: 91-67369

3   4   5   6   7   8 D 99 98 97 96 95 94

Printed in the United States of America

CONTENTS

INFORMATION PROCESSING

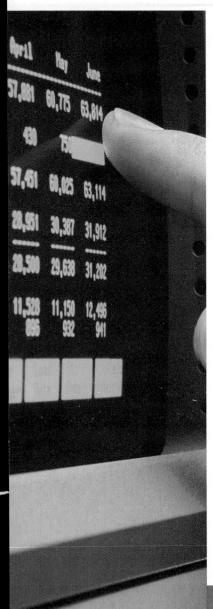

TIME AND TASK MANAGEMENT

RECORDS ADMINISTRATION AND TECHNOLOGY

Contents continues onto next page

MAIL AND TELECOMMUNICATION SYSTEMS

PERSONAL AND CAREER DEVELOPMENT

REFERENCE SECTION

TO THE STUDENT

You have a valuable learning experience ahead in your study of *THE OFFICE: Procedures and Technology*. This textbook has been written within a realistic, practical, and problem-solving framework to assure that your preparation is thorough and up to date. When you complete your study of this textbook, you will have: (1) the competence and confidence to meet the qualifications of a wide variety of office positions, (2) a firm foundation of skills and knowledge upon which to build a rewarding career, and (3) the understanding to meet the changes anticipated in business as our society moves toward the 21st Century. Learning about office procedures and technology will prepare you for career success and personal satisfaction.

AN INTRODUCTION

Secondary school office education programs are designed to develop marketable skills and understandings required for a rapidly changing workplace. *THE OFFICE: Procedures and Technology*, Second Edition, is an extensively revised textbook that reflects a thorough review of the content and accompanying materials of the previous edition. Chapters have been rewritten, content updated, and end-of-topic and end-of-chapter activities revised and expanded. New activities and a glossary have been added. The goal throughout this revision has been to provide teachers and students with a textbook focused on up-to-date procedures and the continuing impact of technological changes in the workplace.

The Challenge to Teachers

Business teachers face a two-fold challenge: to prepare students to meet the initial demand of full-time employment and to equip students with the skills to learn on the job and adapt to new ways of working. Considerable change has occurred since the first edition of this textbook was published; yet, predictions are that the rate and nature of change will continue to be significant. To help teachers successfully meet this challenge, *THE OFFICE: Procedures and Technology* provides relevant content and realistic activities organized to optimize learning.

Opportunity for Students with Varied Interests

An office education course is an important component in a secondary school curriculum. The skills and understandings developed in such a course have wide application. Students will be prepared to work in offices or to combine work and study as they further their education in postsecondary institutions. Students who aspire to professional and entrepreneurial positions will have a sound background in basic office functions, procedures, and technology that will be invaluable in meeting responsibilities of their jobs.

The Learning Objectives

The challenge to teachers and the opportunity for students are reflected in this comprehensive and up-to-date instructional package. The text and accompanying materials have been developed to assure that students:
- develop a knowledge of the role of the office and the office worker in today's constantly changing business world

- develop marketable skills in the context of efficient, effective procedures and technology
- reinforce and extend basic skills of English, math, decision making, information management, and critical thinking
- learn the importance of time management and productivity
- communicate and interact effectively with coworkers, supervisors, and customers or clients
- learn how to adjust to changing work procedures, equipment, and software
- develop an understanding of emerging technologies and their impact on how offices function
- identify opportunities for employment and professional growth in office occupations

Features that Facilitate Learning

The instructional package provides carefully organized content and numerous student activities that assure thorough understanding and realistic application of skills central to the development of key competencies. The textbook, *THE OFFICE: Procedures and Technology*, is organized into seven general subject areas and sixteen chapters. Each of the sixteen chapters is subdivided into two or three segments called *topics*. The text contains many features designed to facilitate student learning.

Chapter and Topic Objectives. Chapter and topic objectives focus on key concepts which serve as guides to students in becoming familiar with the content of each topic.

Vocabulary Reinforcement. General vocabulary terms that may be unfamiliar to some students are defined in the margin of the page on which the term is first introduced. Key concepts and terms, which appear in color and are defined in the text, are listed at the end of the chapter.

End-of-Topic and End-of-Chapter Activities. Activities to reinforce important concepts and procedures and to give students realistic experience in working on their own and in groups are included in each topic and at the end of each chapter.

Productivity Corners. The final part of each chapter is a letter and response in advice-column format which deals with a problem typically of concern to beginning office workers.

Reference Section. Commonly needed information is provided here for students' ready access as they complete activities.

Glossary of Information Processing Terms. (NEW in this edition) Selected key terms and italicized words introduced throughout the book are listed and defined.

Information Processing Activities

INFORMATION PROCESSING ACTIVITIES, an applications workbook for students, includes an activities log and working papers for completing selected text activities. Also included are:

Optional Critical Thinking Activities. (NEW in this edition) Seven comprehensive critical thinking activities related to the seven areas of the textbook are provided. The students' problem-solving skills are extended through the completion of tasks that require the application of a variety of concepts and the integration of what has been learned.

Office Simulations. Four office simulations entitled AT WORK AT DYNAMICS are briefly introduced in the text and included in their entirety in the workbook. As in an actual business office, the tasks in the simulations are integrated and interrelated. Each simulation involves decision making, activities management, and dealing with interruptions.

Optional Computer Application Activities. (NEW in this edition) Sixteen optional microcomputer activities, one related to each of the chapters of the textbook, are provided in the workbook. These activities give students hands-on experience in word processing, spreadsheet, and database applications.

Template Disk (NEW in this edition)

A template disk containing the files required to complete the optional computer application activities as well as files that can be used to complete selected text activities is available.

Printed and Computerized Tests

A printed set of tests (chapter tests, midterm examination, final examination, and performance test) is available. The chapter tests, midterm and final examinations are also available on a *MicroEXAM II* disk.

Teacher's Resource Guide

The Teacher's Resource Guide is available to teachers who adopt the textbook for class use. This manual is a comprehensive and invaluable source for practical ideas in course planning and enrichment. Topics discussed include: course design, planning for individual differences, evaluating student achievement, and supplementary instructional materials. For each chapter there are enrichment suggestions as well as solutions for all student activities. Solutions to the optional computer activities, the simulations, and all tests are included, as well as responses for the optional critical thinking activities. Transparency masters are also provided.

Acknowledgments

The authors acknowledge the contributions of thoughtful reviewers, users of the previous edition, and business people. L. Joyce Arnston, Irvine Valley College and Karen L. Duda, Youngstown State University, provided comprehensive reviews of the previous textbook. Insightful feedback from secondary school teachers and students was gratefully received. Administrative managers and business executives were queried about the learning that was most valuable for future office employees. To all these persons, the authors express thanks and appreciation.

A Commitment by the Authors

THE OFFICE: Procedures and Technology, Second Edition, has been written with unrelenting attention to the responsibilities the authors accepted: to present relevant content within a framework that assures high-level learning; to provide activities that reinforce student understanding; to help students develop a wide range of office skills; to present both contemporary and emerging office environments; and finally, to encourage the attitude that learning can be challenging, worthwhile, and enjoyable.

Mary Ellen Oliverio   William R. Pasewark   Bonnie Roe White

THE OFFICE
IN THE BUSINESS WORLD

CHAPTER 1

The Changing Office and Its Place in the Organization

The present era is often called "The Information Age." Nowhere is this more evident than in today's business office. Office workers are busy with word processing, desktop publishing, spreadsheets, databases, electronic mail, facsimiles (faxes), and graphics. Demands of companies for timely and accurate information have led to amazing innovations. Predictions to the year 2000 include even more changes. For example, telecommunication networks will transform the world into a single global community. An office worker in Emporia, Kansas, will be able to communicate with a customer in Seoul, South Korea, as easily as with a coworker in the next office.

Practically everyone at work today performs some so-called office tasks. For example, an engineer designing a machine part may photocopy the sketches being developed. A stockbroker may answer the telephone or place calls to customers.

There are, though, large numbers of workers in the United States workforce who spend full-time at tasks that are classified as office tasks. Among them are millions of word processors, clerks, and secretaries, as well as other types of office workers. Office employees provide invaluable services that contribute to achieving an organization's goals. The responsibilities of such workers are the focus of this textbook.

In Chapter 1, you will gain an overview of business offices and the environment in which office workers function. The objectives of the chapter are to:

- introduce you to the critical role of the business office

- acquaint you with the setting in which office workers function

THE CRITICAL ROLE OF THE OFFICE

When you have completed your study of this topic, you will be able to:

- describe common activities performed in business offices
- identify the technology common to many offices
- describe ergonomic concerns in the office
- explain the importance of productivity
- identify effective time management techniques

If there were no office workers, business activity would come to a standstill. Imagine organizations with no one to answer telephones, to access electronic mail, or to greet callers. Indeed, the office staff provides a critical network of human skills vital to every organization.

"Our office staff is at the heart of our company's activities," said the president of a greeting card company. The president further commented: "From preparing copy for new cards to processing payments received from our customers, we depend on well-trained, competent office workers. For example, orders must be forwarded according to the schedules set up by our customers.

Imagine what would happen if an office worker in our order department was careless about processing an order with the result that Thanksgiving cards arrived at a customer's shop in mid-December. Disappointed customers do not return for further business."

3

This company president is illustrating what is required for an office worker to be effective and efficient.

Effective: Completing a task in the proper manner

An office worker in the greeting card company processes an order so that it will be shipped to meet the customer's schedule. This office worker is effective.

Efficient: Completing a task with a minimum of time and effort

relevant: to the point

established: set up

*An office worker in the order department carefully reads the incoming order and inputs all **relevant** information at a computer terminal according to **established** procedures.*

(Note the president's comment on page 3 about the careless processing of a customer's order.)

OFFICES ARE PLACES OF ACTION

Many job opportunities are available for full-time and part-time office workers. Offices are busy places with much activity underway. The activity is varied as you see in the listing of key functions in Illus. 1-1. Here are brief discussions of job tasks of two office workers:

Illus. 1-1. Office workers perform a wide range of functions.

KEY OFFICE FUNCTIONS
keyboarding
photocopying
searching for information
composing letters and memorandums
editing and proofreading
greeting visitors
answering telephone calls
placing telephone calls
accommodating customers
arranging meetings
opening and sorting incoming communications
preparing outgoing communications
inputting data at a computer terminal
maintaining databases and files
preparing forms, including checks, orders, and invoices
maintaining financial records
using spreadsheets
maintaining a calendar
establishing priorities for tasks
managing work of assistants

promotional: aiding in achieving a goal

Karen works in the public information office of a major broadcasting company. The manager and assistants meet frequently to plan **promotional** events and announcements. Karen processes thousands of words each day as she keys drafts of reports and news releases. She also responds to numerous telephone calls. She enjoys the work in this fast-paced office; she knows she must be alert to what is going on at all times.

Christopher works in the office of the vice president of international sales for an appliance company. He is one of three office workers who perform tasks needed to keep in touch with 350 sales representatives in 28 countries around the world. Christopher helps prepare memorandums which are mailed to sales representatives; he also faxes documents to such faraway places as Sydney, Australia, and Tokyo, Japan.

Illus. 1-2. Offices are places of activity. What do you think might be the topic of discussion in this instance?

In many companies, office tasks are organized so that part-time workers can be employed. Among part-time workers are those young men and women who studied office procedures in high school so they can work part-time to help finance further education. One part-time worker who is doing this is discussed here:

> *Don studied office procedures in high school and now works in an accounting office. He also studies full-time in a local college where he is majoring in accounting. He realizes that accountants must be good office workers, too, and is grateful for the experience he is gaining as he maintains financial information through the use of a computer in the steel manufacturing company where he is employed.*

OFFICES PROVIDE VARYING SERVICES

Business offices differ one from another. Even in the same company, there may be different types of business offices. Some offices are specialized with all office workers performing essentially the same task. Others are general with each office worker doing a range of tasks. You are more likely to find more specialized offices in large companies and general offices in smaller companies.

> *A large insurance company in Hartford, Connecticut, has many specialized offices. For example, there is one office where all employees are responsible for the single task of processing **premiums** paid by millions of policyholders.*

premiums: amounts of money

> *A small advertising agency in Chicago, Illinois, has a single business office. Five office workers perform a range of tasks including answering telephones, greeting clients, preparing proposals, and arranging travel schedules. While each has specific tasks, the five assist each other. They all understand the total work of the office.*

You might ask: "Why are some offices specialized and others are not?" Offices tend to be specialized when there are large volumes of repetitive tasks. For example, an insurance company with millions of policyholders will need many employees to process premiums. An office that does that task only follows carefully designed procedures that assure effective, efficient processing of the paperwork related to the receipt of premiums.

On the other hand, when the company is small and there are varied types of activities with clients and little repetitive work, a general office is more appropriate. For example, a small advertising agency may deal with a limited number of clients who each require very different services.

**OFFICES ARE
INCREASINGLY
MORE
HIGH TECH**

transformed:
changed to a great
degree

The office continues to be a place of change. Many offices have been **transformed** in the last ten to twelve years. Typewriters were replaced with standalone word processors, which were in turn replaced by microcomputers. Now, microcomputers are being expanded to electronic workstations that are a part of a network system.

Change in the office has not stopped; it continues. New technologies are emerging constantly. Company budgets continue to provide funds for new and updated equipment. The forecasts to the next century include installation of more extensive network systems, increased use of electronic and voice mail, and computers with sufficient power for speech recognition. Company executives seek to use new equipment and methods to assure that office tasks are performed as effectively and efficiently as possible.

For example, more companies are storing information on optical disks. As you note in Illus. 1-3, a single optical disk can store approximately 25,000 letter-size documents. Imagine the difference in storage space required for a single optical disk in comparison with 25,000 paper documents in file cabinets.

Illus. 1-3. Two means for storing information.

Technology is also making it possible for office workers to work at home. **Telecommuting**, which means working at home and communicating with the office by electronic devices, is an **option** increasingly more American offices will offer.

option: choice

There are a number of ways to describe what you are likely to find in business offices you visit or in which you choose to work in the future. Possibly, the most **realistic** way is to describe the equipment that is becoming more and more common. You are likely to find the following:

TECHNOLOGY IN THE OFFICE

realistic: lifelike

- microcomputers with software for word processing, spreadsheet, and database applications
- electronic typewriters with enhanced word processing capabilities
- desktop publishing systems
- local area networks (LANs) which connect microcomputers, printers, and telecommunications devices
- intelligent copier/printers
- facsimile (fax) machines
- telephone systems with a variety of electronic features

There is frequent **upgrading** of office technology in many companies, while in other offices there is less attention to having the latest type of equipment. You will find, therefore, more advanced levels of technology in some companies than in others.

upgrading: making more up to date; improving

Some Traditional Offices Continue

Some business offices use little, if any, of the office technology developed during the past decade. You may have been in a business office recently where there are electric typewriters, a simple telephone system, and a basic copier. The records may be maintained manually and stored in file cabinets. You observed what is commonly called a **traditional** office. This style of office is becoming increasingly rare as even small organizations see the merit in newer technology. However, traditional offices can be effective and efficient in completing tasks.

traditional: from the past

OFFICE ERGONOMICS AND DESIGN

Managers are giving increasing attention to the physical and psychological environment of workers. The field of specialization related to these concerns is ergonomics. **Ergonomics** is the study of the effects of work environments on the health and well-being of employees. Relationships among biological, techno-

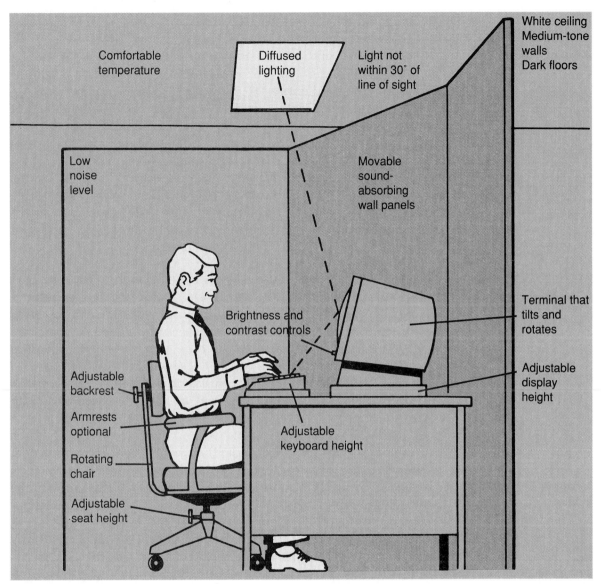

Comfortable temperature

Diffused lighting

Light not within 30° of line of sight

White ceiling
Medium-tone walls
Dark floors

Low noise level

Movable sound-absorbing wall panels

Brightness and contrast controls

Terminal that tilts and rotates

Adjustable backrest

Armrests optional

Rotating chair

Adjustable seat height

Adjustable keyboard height

Adjustable display height

Illus. 1-4. Much attention is given to ergonomic factors in offices.

logical, and psychological factors are of interest to specialists in this field.

Company executives, therefore, strive to provide a pleasant, well-designed, healthy work environment for office employees. Appealing colors are chosen for walls and floor coverings. Textured, flexible, sound-absorbing partitions that reduce noise are found in many offices. Proper lighting and ventilation are maintained. Adjustable equipment and furniture **minimize** eye fatigue

minimize: reduce

and back and neck strain. Artwork and living plants are frequently added to heighten the cheerfulness of offices.

ensure: make certain

Measures are taken to minimize accidents and ***ensure*** safety. Carpeting is installed tightly, equipment is secured to workstations, and electrical cords are concealed.

Many companies have designed offices with consideration given to physically disabled employees. Ramps and workstations are specially designed to accommodate wheelchairs; elevators have buttons low enough to be reached from a wheelchair and numbers indicated by braille symbols in addition to the standard indicators. With such facilities, physically disabled persons have far more opportunity for employment than was formerly the situation. Many states have laws requiring that facilities be adapted to meet the needs of the physically disabled.

OFFICE PRODUCTIVITY

Productivity, which means level of accomplishment, is important in business. Executives of an organization strive to encourage high-level productivity among all employees, including office workers. As costs increase, which is common in the American society, business managers strive to determine ways of improving the productivity of each unit of the organization.

Think of the difference in productivity of two office workers who prepare a report. One works at an electric typewriter; the other at a microcomputer. What happens if there are changes to be made in the report? The office worker at the electric typewriter must rekey the entire document; the one at the microcomputer, on the other hand, must key only the changes indicated.

quantified: measured in numbers

In some companies, standards for various tasks are established. Such companies have, in effect, specified the productivity expected. For example, a company may expect each word processor to produce a certain number of pages of copy per hour worked. In other companies, ***quantified*** standards are not established, but supervisors are responsible for assuring that each office worker completes a reasonable amount of work each day.

Paula is manager of the order-processing department. She has five office workers to assist her. She assigns tasks each morning. From time to time she talks briefly with each worker to see how much has been done and if there are any problems. Paula finds that the office workers are conscientious. Each follows instructions and completes assignments on schedule. Paula reminds them from time to time that she is there to be of assistance.

Illus. 1-5. Some offices can accommodate the worker who must use a wheelchair.

Rapid changes are taking place in business offices in order to improve office productivity. An overwhelming amount of activity in today's business offices motivates companies to find new equipment and procedures to reach higher levels of productivity.

TIME MANAGEMENT

Experienced office workers frequently identify good time management as one of the most important basic skills for office workers. **Time management** means planning and using the hours and minutes of a workday in the most effective and efficient manner possible to accomplish all tasks assigned.

If you cannot manage your time, your knowledge and office skills will be of little value to you or to the company in which you work. What value is it that you are able to key at a rapid rate at a microcomputer if you never complete documents by the established deadlines? What value is it that you are alert and attentive when you respond to a ringing telephone, but you are seldom at your workstation because you are chatting with a colleague in the next office?

Time management is not really a new topic for you, but perhaps you have not thought of it as a skill. For example, you have had experience in planning your time so that assignments are completed by the deadline given by a teacher. You plan your schedule so that you get to your classes on time. By now, you may have sufficient experience to evaluate how successful you are in managing time. You may be very good in this regard, or you may be like millions of others who can improve their time management skills. You will have opportunity during your study of this book to become aware of good time management attitudes and techniques.

Attitudes Are Important

There are certain attitudes that are important if you are to be an effective time manager. Among the important attitudes are these:

limitless: without an end

- Your time is valuable, and you must strive to use it wisely.
- Time is not *limitless*; therefore, you must establish priorities, which means determining the order in which you will complete the several activities you wish to do.
- Time management requires practice, and such practice can improve your skill.

Time Management at Work

Office workers, in many instances, are responsible for completing tasks without constant direction and supervision. Often the speed at which you work and the attention you give to tasks will be your decisions. For example, the rate at which an office worker prepares a second order form after completing the first one generally is determined by the office worker alone.

Most office workers have responsibility for a number of tasks, with varying levels of urgency. Therefore, they must understand their work thoroughly. Only then can they establish deadlines for jobs and the order in which the tasks will be completed.

However, you cannot always use your time as planned. There are occasions during a workday when you must be flexible and adjust your priorities. For example, there may be an interruption that may require attention to something unexpected. In such an instance, you must quickly assess the new task in relation to the one in process and make a judgment about whether to continue with the task in process or switch to the new demand.

Donna, an assistant to the manager of an electronics plant, was keying a report when a caller approached her desk. Although she anticipated having the report completed shortly, she knew she had responsibility for greeting and assisting callers. Therefore, she stopped keying and turned to the caller, greeted him and learned what he wanted. She was able to take care of the caller's request in a few minutes. Then, she returned to preparing the report.

Time Management Techniques

accomplish: reach; complete

There are techniques that will help you manage your time in order to **accomplish** your work goals. Here are some common ones for you to consider:

Plan Your Work in an Orderly Manner

For example, write down what you must do. Office workers refer to this as making a "To Do" list. Note the list shown below. In many instances office workers use their desk calendars or a small notebook for this purpose.

Illus. 1-6. Writing down your tasks helps in setting priorities.

Establish Priorities

After you know what you want to accomplish, you must determine the order in which the tasks are to be done, which is referred to as **establishing priorities**. Some tasks impose an immediate deadline while others have less pressing due dates. You will have to know the expected completion date for each task assigned to you to properly set priorities. You may need to talk with your supervisor about priorities if you encounter problems.

Assess the Time Each Task Will Require

You cannot use time wisely if you are unable to predict how much time you need to complete your tasks. Imagine an office worker asked by a manager to prepare a memorandum that is needed immediately. The office worker says: "Oh, I can do this for you in five minutes." The manager responds, "Wonderful." However, an hour later the memorandum is still in process.

The office worker failed to look at the draft of the memo. Some information was missing and had to be accessed from a database. The office worker had not considered this factor when estimating how quickly the task could be completed.

Develop Strategies for Avoiding Time Wasters

- Tell friendly colleagues that while you enjoy talking you must get back to work.
- Keep your attention and your effort on the work at hand as a way to eliminate **procrastinating** during the day. Refer to your "To Do" list, which can act as motivation to working diligently during each workday.
- Avoid false starts by first getting an overall understanding of what you are to do. It is not a time-wasting tactic to be sure you comprehend clearly what you are to do.
- Be sure you have all the information and supplies required for a task before you get underway.

The office is a hub of much activity. Its purpose is the accomplishment of tasks critical to the smooth functioning of the total organization. To do the work assigned each day requires good time management by each office worker. You will want to develop your ability to manage time; you then will possess an important skill for success on the job.

stinating:
peatedly

QUESTIONS FOR REVIEW

1. Name three tasks performed in business offices.

2. How does being effective differ from being efficient?

3. Identify three tasks in Illus. 1-1 that you believe require the most cooperation among office workers.

4. In what way does a specialized office differ from a general office?

5. What types of high-tech equipment are you likely to find in business offices?

6. Why do companies give attention to ergonomics when designing offices?

7. What types of measures minimize accidents in an office?

8. How do companies encourage high productivity among office workers?

9. What attitudes are important if you are to become a good manager of your time?

10. Describe two common techniques for good time management.

MAKING DECISIONS

Assume that you have applied for a part-time job. When you visit the office, the office manager tells you about the benefits, including wages paid. The office manager also tells you:

"We need someone who is good at keyboarding because we pre-pare many reports in this office. We will teach you the word processing software we use. Your hours will be flexible, but we would like you to work a total of eight hours each week. We expect all our office workers to be dependable, proofread their own work, and be able to work without constant direction and supervision."

Assume that the wages, hours, and type of work are satisfactory to you. What do you think about the other job requirements identified by the office manager? How do you feel about the responsibility you must accept?

What You Are To Do: Write a brief answer to the two questions raised in the preceding paragraph.

EXTENDING YOUR ENGLISH COMPETENCIES

Read the following paragraphs. You will notice that there are complete sentences as well as words that do not form a sentence.

Many new office employees attended the workshop. The program was planned to give. While employees will be in specific departments, they still have responsibilities to the total company. The company thinks its employees. If they understand what the overall goals are. Supervisors who participated in the opening discussion. The employees listened closely.

The new employees learned much from the presentations of the supervisors. The company appreciates its office workers. Examples of key tasks of office employees in the company. When the workshop ended everyone present knew a great deal about the company. It was a worthwhile experience because.

What You Are To Do: Key each group of words ending with a period. At the end of each group, key an "S" if the words form a complete sentence; key an "N" if they do not form a complete sentence.

Key a complete sentence for all groups that were incomplete. Add any words that will convey a realistic, complete thought.

APPLICATION ACTIVITIES

Activity 1

In this activity you will have an opportunity to become acquainted with what office workers are actually doing on the job. There is considerable variation in what workers do. Use this activity to develop your skill in asking questions in a friendly, relaxed manner and to develop your ability to listen to answers, and to record the answers completely or record notes that will help you to recall exactly what was said.

Word processing equipment can be used to complete this activity.

What You Are To Do: Talk with two persons who are working in business offices. (1) Ask each person the four questions shown at the top of page 17 and record the responses. (2) Write a brief report summarizing the responses.

a. Which tasks in Illus. 1-1 are the most common tasks in your job?

b. What tasks do you perform that are not on this list?

c. Which of the tasks you do require the most time during a typical week of work?

d. What equipment do you use on a daily basis?

Activity 2

Assume that you are an assistant to Mrs. Mendez, who is preparing to give a speech at a local professional organization. She hands you a draft of just one section of a speech and says, "Key a corrected copy of this draft, and please use double-spacing."

Word processing equipment can be used to complete this activity.

What You Are To Do: Key the draft shown below, making all the corrections. You may want to refer to Reference Section A for the meaning of the proofreader's marks.

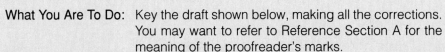

Prerequisites for Managing Time

Certainly, people who work in business should do "good" planning, but to what extent can they govern the nature of his own planning? Possibly, it is important to give some thought to some prerequisites to time management.

First, the worker must have a favorable emotional involvement in the work and its context before he can do more than a barely adequate task of time management. He must care about and take an interest in his job. If others say, "He is just right for that job," or the person feels, "I am doing exactly what I want to be doing," he is "at home" in the work situation.

Each individual should spend much time and contemplation identifying what he would like to do in his work. This should be one of the rewards of an abundant society. Man should not be trapped in unrewarding work.

Second, the worker must feel that the goals of the organization are in tune with what he believes important.

Third, the nature of the activity of the total company must be of interest to the individual.

TOPIC 2

THE OFFICE WITHIN THE ORGANIZATION

When you have completed your study of this topic, you will be able to:

- identify common types of organizations

- explain goals for different types of organizations

- explain how businesses are structured

- describe the unique role of office workers

Few, if any, activities common in organizations can be completed without some related office tasks. Office workers provide assistance through activities such as preparing documents, processing data, transmitting messages, maintaining records, and responding to customer inquiries.

To prepare for a staff meeting, the sales manager develops an agenda. The agenda is given to Elisa, an office assistant, who keys and formats it attractively and prepares multiple copies. Elisa maintains a calendar and knows when the agenda is needed; she also has a list of those who are to get the agenda so she knows how many copies to make.

To do their jobs properly, office workers need to know a great deal about their organizations, including the goals that influence what is done. In fact, you will find that you can complete a task more effectively and more efficiently if you are knowledgeable about your organization.

Brent is an assistant in the office of the executive vice president of finance. Among the tasks that Brent does is to compare actual expenditures with those budgeted for each division of the company. Brent knows the company is attempting to reduce costs. Therefore, he reads the numbers with much interest.

TYPES OF ORGANIZATIONS

Office workers are needed in all organizations. However, organizations are not all alike. In the United States, organizations are of three types:

entities: units with separate identity

- businesses
- not-for-profit *entities* (not governmental)
- governmental units

Businesses

Businesses are organized as single proprietorships, partnerships, or corporations. Laws and regulations govern business activity, regardless of the form of business. Only the corporation, though, requires a *charter* from the state. Single proprietorships and partnerships are organized without approval by any governmental agencies.

charter: written grant from a state

A **single proprietorship** is a business owned by one individual who may or may not also be the manager of the enterprise. Single proprietorships may be of any size, but many are small.

Jefferson Office Supplies

A single retail store on Jefferson Street, which is in the shopping area of a town of 43,000 residents, is owned and managed by Ted Wilson.

A **partnership** is a business that has two or more owners. Different types of partners may participate in a partnership. Some partners may provide funds only, but others may be active in managing the business. Partnerships, too, may be of any size; many are small, however.

Feldman & Quinn Interiors

An interior design studio, owned and operated by Maude Feldman and Wendy Quinn as a partnership, specializes in remodeling homes that are more than a hundred years old.

A **corporation** is a business organized under the laws of a state or the federal government. A corporation is a separate legal unit and may be privately or publicly owned. Owners have shares of stock and are called stockholders or shareholders. Most of the largest businesses in the United States are publicly owned corporations.

Privately owned: S. C. Johnson & Son, Inc., (products include cleaners, waxes, laundry aids)

Publicly owned: K mart Corporation (includes chain of retail department and variety stores and drug stores)

Professional service organizations are considered businesses, too. Medical doctors, dentists, lawyers, and accountants operate as single proprietorships, partnerships, or corporations. Laws and regulations governing a corporation of professional persons, such as doctors, are different from those which apply to a business corporation.

Not-for-Profit Entities

The United States has many organizations providing services to the people of the country. Among these organizations are associations that sponsor developmental programs for young people (4-H Clubs, Girl Scouts, Campfire Girls, Boy Scouts, and FBLA). Other common not-for-profit groups include centers for performing arts, museums, libraries, hospitals, and private colleges and universities.

Not-for-profit organizations raise funds from individual and group contributions and from fees and dues paid by participants; in some instances, limited funds are provided by governmental agencies at the local, state, or federal level.

Illus. 1-7. An office worker in a museum is explaining to coworkers the procedure for processing new member applications.

allocated: set aside for a special purpose

Increasingly, not-for-profit entities function in what is referred to as a business-like manner, which means that tasks are carefully organized and the resources are wisely **allocated** to achieve the goals established.

Governmental Units

extensive: wide; broad

In the United States, the role of government is **extensive**. There are governmental units at the federal, state, and local levels. These units are called by different names, including *agency, commission, bureau, department,* and *board.* Each unit has specific responsibilities for services considered important in the life of the citizens of the political community the particular unit serves.

> *Federal:* Environmental Protection Agency; Department of Commerce
>
> *State:* Department of Motor Vehicles; Department of Tourism
>
> *Local:* Office of Mayor; Board of Education

GOALS OF ORGANIZATIONS

Each of the three major types of organizations has different overall goals, and these goals influence the tasks performed by office workers. Businesses, including many professional organizations, seek to make a profit. On the other hand, not-for-profit entities have funds from various sources and strive to provide specified services; they do not seek to earn profits.

Goals of Businesses

revenues: total income produced from business activity

Businesses choose the activities which they assume will allow them to be profitable. When a company sells goods or provides a service, it realizes **revenues**; the costs incurred in earning revenues are called *expenses*. When a company's revenues are greater than its expenses for a given period of time, a profit is realized. Companies strive to earn profits so that they can make payments to the owners of the business. They also use profits to expand the business.

Many tasks which office workers perform relate to helping to meet profit goals. And closely tied to such goals is all the activity required to know how profitable the business actually is.

> *John works in the office of a paper manufacturing company. Each month he keys a report of sales and expenditures so management will know whether or not a profit was realized during the month.*

Goals of Not-for-Profit Entities

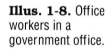

exhibitions:
showings; displays

As the name for this category implies, such organizations do not seek to make profits. The chief goal of such organizations is to provide valuable services to those who can benefit from them. Museums strive to provide interesting *exhibitions* of various types of art; libraries strive to have books, periodicals, and other media to meet the wishes of the users.

Office workers are invaluable employees of not-for-profit entities. Many activities in such entities require the skills office workers possess. Here is just one example:

> *Ruth works in a community library. One of her monthly tasks is to key a report of the number of books borrowed by patrons. The library staff encourages cardholders to borrow books. A monthly report aids in seeing if that goal is being realized.*

Goals of Governmental Units

Governmental units, in the same way as not-for-profit entities, do not strive to make a profit. These units are supported primarily with the money received from taxes. The overall goals of governmental units are related to providing the services which the citizens desire. For example, the Federal Government maintains

Illus. 1-8. Office workers in a government office.

facilitate: help accomplish; make easier

a federal highway system to *facilitate* travel throughout the country; each local governmental unit has a board of education to oversee education in the public schools.

Office workers are required throughout governmental units to facilitate the multiple tasks required to meet the needs of citizens. In fact, governmental units are one of the major employers of office workers. There are many varied types of jobs available. Here is a brief description of the duties of one worker in a federal office:

off the press: printed and available

*Nancy works in the publications office of the U. S. Department of Labor. She likes her job because she has a wide range of tasks--from answering telephone inquiries about publications to responding to letters which ask for particular lists of publications. Since new publications are coming **off the press** all the time, Nancy realizes she must keep up to date.*

TYPES OF EMPLOYEES REQUIRED

competent: skilled; capable

Organizations require many types of talented, **competent** workers, including large numbers of office workers. In your job as an office employee, you will interact with all types of employees. Understanding the general responsibilities of other employees will be helpful as you cooperate with others in getting specific tasks completed properly and promptly.

Illus. 1-9. Businesses need many types of workers as noted in headings in one newspaper's want-ad pages.

In a small company, a single person may, as is commonly stated, "wear many hats." For example, a single proprietor makes all policies for the business and at the same time manages the business on a day-to-day basis. You can imagine that an office worker who assists such an owner/manager also will do a variety of tasks in furthering the goals of the organization.

Companies beyond the very small ones require the services of several levels of managers as well as specialized technical and administrative workers. The general types of workers required in typical, large businesses in the United States are briefly described in the following paragraphs.

Board of Directors

If a company is publicly owned, a group of individuals, called the board of directors is elected by the owners. The board establishes the policies that guide senior management in directing the company. Some members of senior management are members of the board of directors, too.

Senior Management

Those persons who provide the leadership in carrying out the policies of the board of directors are referred to as **senior management**, or sometimes, top management. The chief executive officer, often called the CEO, the president, and a small number of executive vice presidents are included in this group.

The CEO and president are the persons who represent the company. In some companies, one person holds both titles. Generally, the president is considered the primary operating chief of a company.

Division Management

implement: put into effect

Companies are subdivided into units by lines of work or functions to be performed. Each unit typically is called a *division* or *department* and is run by a vice president. Persons who direct division or department operations are called **division management**. The persons at this level **implement** the policies of the executive group described earlier. You will find a wide variety of vice presidents at this level, including vice president of sales, vice president of manufacturing, vice president for product development, and vice president for communications.

Illus. 1-10. Middle managers discussing a common problem.

Middle Management

Companies may have several levels of managers and supervisors who guide operations. These employees are commonly referred to as **middle management**.

One especially important group of middle managers are those who manage administrative support services. Administrative support managers are responsible for managing and supervising the office staff in addition to other duties.

Technical Personnel

Many different types of specialized workers are required in organizations. The nature of a company's activities determines what types of technical specialists are needed. If you were to see a listing of specialists in a number of companies, you would likely find accountants, systems analysts, programmers, and economists.

Office Support Staff

As you have learned in this chapter, office workers are found in all types of businesses. Indeed, in every organization office workers are needed to implement the plans and policies of the board of directors and of management.

STRUCTURE OF ORGANIZATIONS

hierarchical:
ranked from highest to
lowest

structuring:
subdividing
responsibility

The workers to whom you have been briefly introduced are assigned responsibilities that, added together, are expected to meet the goals of the organization. The structure of an organization is formally presented in an **organization chart**. An organization chart shows positions in ***hierarchical*** order. In actual practice, the organization chart for several thousand employees will require a number of pages to show all the levels of employees.

Illus. 1-11 is a partial organization chart for a publicly owned company. Note that only the primary divisions of responsibility are shown. Note also the positions of the executive vice presidents. In Illus. 1-12 on page 28, you see the staff for one department only: customer service.

These two illustrations merely introduce the concept of an organization chart. As you proceed with your study of this book, you will become familiar with more aspects of the ***structuring*** of organizations. Knowing how an organization is structured will help you understand more clearly the duties of your own job.

Phil works in the office of the vice president of development in a cellular telephone company. He prepares many memorandums about the projects underway that are likely to lead to new products. He also plans meetings that require the participation of personnel from all divisions of the company. He knows the organization chart well since he wants to be sure the proper persons are notified about meetings and receive the appropriate materials.

UNIQUE ROLE FOR OFFICE WORKERS

As you learned from the preceding paragraphs, many employees at different levels of responsibility are required to operate a successful organization. And, at all levels of any organization there are office workers providing important information processing services. Here are just two examples:

The executive must meet with the division heads to discuss new developments for the next year. The office worker talks with each division head to determine whether the suggested date and time are convenient. When the date and time have been established, the office worker prepares an agenda and accompanying materials to be forwarded to each division head prior to the meeting.

LARSON TELECOMMUNICATIONS CORPORATION
PARTIAL ORGANIZATION CHART

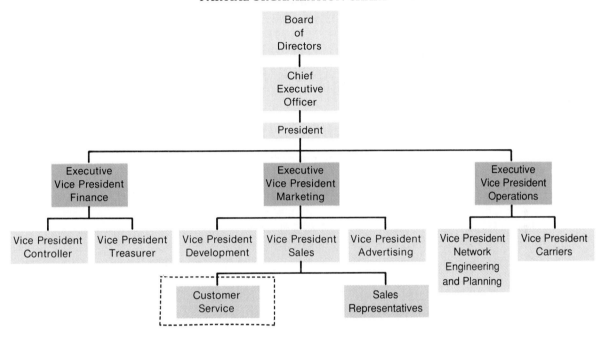

Illus. 1-11. Partial organization chart showing the primary divisions of responsibility. The organization chart for the customer service department is shown in Illus. 1-12 on page 28.

The sales representative for the Midwest Region sold a large quantity of the company's product to a customer. The sales representative called the order department to submit the order. Several office workers will become involved in preparing and processing the information required to deliver the merchandise to the customer, to bill the customer, and to record payment.

Office workers can be compared with assistants who facilitate the activities of specialists. Research associates and assistants aid scientists in carrying out experiments in the laboratory; dental assistants work with dentists in providing care to patients; legal assistants help lawyers in developing background for particular cases. Office workers assist management, as well as specialists, in performing a variety of tasks that are required to initiate, process, and maintain the facts and knowledge needed by an entity. The term *information processing* is used to describe, in general fashion, this range of assistance provided by office workers.

LARSON TELECOMMUNICATIONS CORPORATION
ORGANIZATION CHART
CUSTOMER SERVICE DEPARTMENT

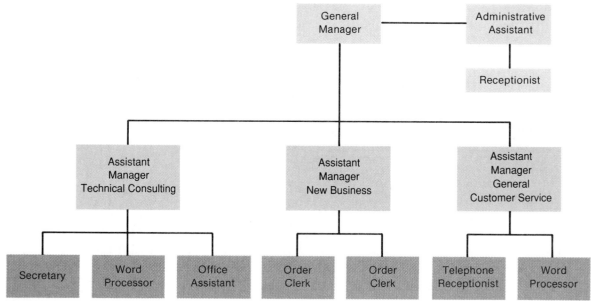

Illus. 1-12. Organization chart for a single department within a company.

Throughout all types of organizations you will find office workers. A scientist, for example, is likely to have the assistance of a laboratory associate as well as office workers. An office worker aids a scientist by filling out forms to purchase materials and supplies and by preparing reports on completed experiments.

In Chapter 2, you will be introduced to types of office positions commonly found in present-day organizations. Skills and understandings required for each type of office job are discussed. This information will help you understand the way in which office tasks are organized by types of jobs. You will then have the basis for considering your own career goals in relation to job opportunities in today's offices.

QUESTIONS FOR REVIEW

1. Why should office workers be knowledgeable about the companies in which they work?

2. Compare a single proprietorship to a partnership.

3. What is the overall goal of a business?

4. Give an example of a goal for a not-for-profit entity.

5. Give an example of a goal for a governmental agency.

6. What are likely to be the tasks of an office employee who works for an owner/manager who "wears many hats"?

7. Identify how division management differs from middle management.

8. What group of middle managers has overall responsibility for office workers?

9. What information would an office worker find in an organization chart?

10. Give an example of how office workers facilitate the work of others in an organization.

INTERACTING WITH OTHERS

Assume that you are at lunch during your first full day of work. You meet Gina, an office worker whom you first met when you were both being interviewed for jobs. Gina has just begun her job in the office of one of the executive vice presidents. Gina says to you: "I have all this material on my desk--telephone directories, brochures about the company, organization charts, and I don't know what else. I am an office assistant; I will be told what I am to do. I don't really need to know anything about this company. Can you explain to me why they have left all this information on my desk?"

What You Are To Do: Prepare the response, in written form, that you would make to Gina's inquiry.

EXTENDING YOUR MATH COMPETENCIES

An office worker's time is valuable. To give you an idea of the value of time, consider the following situation and then compute the worth of each hour, each minute, and the total of ten minutes a day for a year.

An office worker is at work for a total of 240 eight-hour days a year. The office worker wastes 10 minutes each workday.

What You Are To Do: (1) Determine how many hours are lost during the year if the office worker wastes 10 minutes each work day. (2) Compute the dollar value of the time wasted for each of the salaries shown below. (Round all figures to the nearest penny.)

Salary	Worth of an hour at work	Worth of a minute at work	Total worth of ten minutes a day for a year
$ 7,000	$3.65	$.06	$144.00
8,000	?	?	?
9,000	?	?	?
10,000	?	?	?
11,000	?	?	?
12,000	?	?	?
13,000	?	?	?
14,000	?	?	?
15,000	?	?	?

APPLICATION ACTIVITIES

Activity 1

You are an assistant to the executive secretary in the office of communications of a large wholesale food distributor. The secretary asks you to key an announcement that is to be distributed to all personnel throughout the company.

What You Are To Do: Key a copy of the announcement on page 31. Use your judgment to determine the spacing and the margins. What you prepare will be photocopied for distribution. Reference Section A may be helpful in understanding the proofreader's marks.

Word processing equipment can be used to complete this activity.

ANNOUNCEMENT

The Board of Directors at their meeting last night selected Ronald N. Tennett as chief executive officer and president of our company. Mr. Tennett will be joining us by the end of next month. Mr. Tennett is currently serving as senior vice president of Golger, Inc., which is a nation wide grocery wholesale company head quartered in St. Louis.

The Board's announcement of Mr. Tennett's hiring concludes an executive search that began five months ago with the resignation of C.W. Toles, who became president of his family's company in Sydney, Australia.

Our Board's chairperson, Florence Wills in discussing Mr. Tennett's qualifications said: "he has been a very successful manager in the field. His background in all aspects of the wholesale grocery business makes him highly promising as our head. We are confident he will find our company challenging."

Activity 2

The persons listed below are executives in the Williams Manufacturing Company. Along with other executives, these executives are shown in the organization chart of the company.

Charles A. Abelson, Executive Vice President-Finance
Roger W. Batton, Chief Executive Officer and President
George O. Egland, Executive Vice President-Human Resources
Barbara T. Gomez, Vice President-Budget
Joseph H. Lawrence, Vice President-Employment Relations

What You Are To Do: Prepare a partial organization chart with the positions and names of the persons listed above shown in an appropriate position on the chart.

CHAPTER SUMMARY

This chapter has given you an understanding of the changing office and of the setting in which office employees work. You should be able to discuss the following key points:

1. Offices are found in every type of organization because there is great need for information which is processed by office workers. To meet the needs of an organization, office workers must be both effective and efficient in their work.
2. Office tasks require skill in the use of equipment, ability to communicate with others, and understanding of how to make decisions and manage time wisely.
3. All offices are not alike. They differ in the types of tasks performed; they differ in the type of office technology available.
4. Change in the office is continuous.
5. Those responsible for designing offices give attention to ergonomic considerations so that office workers have healthy, comfortable, safe environments in which to work.
6. Office workers who know the form, goals, and structure of the organizations in which they work are likely to work more effectively and efficiently.
7. Office workers provide assistance to all types of employees so that the goals of the total organization are met.

KEY CONCEPTS AND TERMS

telecommuting	partnership
ergonomics	corporation
productivity	senior management
time management	division management
establishing priorities	middle management
single proprietorship	organization chart

INTEGRATED CHAPTER ACTIVITIES

Activity 1

Your teacher will assign you to one of these groups:

● Businesses

● Not-for-profit entities

● Governmental units

You and your classmates assigned to the group are to develop a list of at least ten different organizations located in your community or one nearby. For each organization on your list, your group should provide this information:

● Complete name and address

● General telephone number

● Brief description of the general activity of the organization

If your category is businesses, include the form of organization. If your category is not-for-profit entities, include the major sources of funds; if your category is governmental units, indicate the level at which each functions—federal, state, or local.

What You Are To Do: As a group: (1) organize the information in any easy-to-understand format. (**HINT:** You may want to design a table format.) (2) Select one member of the group to key a copy of the list. (3) Submit the list of organizations to your teacher.

Word processing equipment can be used to complete this activity.

Activity 2

Select a local business, not-for-profit entity, or a governmental unit that you know or in which you think you might like to work at some time in the future. (If you are currently working part-time, you may want to consider using the organization in which you now work.)

For the organization you select, secure the following information:

- Name, address, and form of organization.
- Types of workers employed.
- Approximate number of office employees.
- Common types of office technology in use.
- If not-for-profit or governmental, identify key goals.

Word processing equipment can be used to complete this activity.

What You Are To Do: Write a report in which you summarize the information you gathered. Be prepared to discuss your report in a class discussion.

OPTIONAL COMPUTER APPLICATION ACTIVITY
See Computer Application Activity 1
in your Information Processing Activities workbook.

PRODUCTIVITY CORNER

Kathy Malenky
OFFICE SUPERVISOR

AM I PREPARED FOR THE JOB?

DEAR MS. MALENKY:

I am a senior in high school. I have worked during the summers and after school in a fast food restaurant. Just a few days ago, I accepted a part-time job in the office of our local telephone company. I have basic keyboarding skills and I am now studying office procedures. I thought the experience would be valuable for me.

Now that I have said "yes," I wonder if I really can do all that will be asked of me. I have heard that offices expect workers to produce, yet I have much to learn. Will my supervisor be as understanding as some of my teachers? I will be working about eight hours each week, usually on Monday, Tuesday, and Thursday afternoons after my classes have ended. Am I prepared for this job?—DENISE IN NEW ORLEANS

DEAR DENISE:

You should not be anxious about the requirements of your new part-time job. Your employer knows that you are a student and do not have on-the-job experience in office skills and procedures. When you were interviewed, you certainly reflected interest in the job, ability to learn, and willingness to meet the job requirements.

Yes, your supervisor or manager likely will be as helpful as some of your teachers. Also, your coworkers will be there to assist you.

Relax! Assume that you will get clear instructions about what you are to do. Furthermore, you will be asked if you understand what you are to do. Do not hesitate to ask for additional instructions or further information.

Denise, take time to assess your own performance. Ask yourself: "How well have I done this job?" Then, check to see if indeed the job was satisfactory. Don't be disappointed if you make an error; determine its source and profit from it.

Good luck on your first office job. You will become a valuable employee through doing good work each week.—KATHY MALENKY

35

Employees at Work in Offices

Office workers are employed in all types of organizations. However, their responsibilities can vary considerably from one office to another. Consider these two advertisements listed in a newspaper:

Wanted: Travel company needs organized, detail-oriented assistant to prepare sales reports, bank deposits, invoices; must be able to work on your own.

Wanted: Secretary for electronics company; requires person who learns quickly and can work hard as a fast-paced team member. Must know full range of office procedures.

Note the differences in these two positions. One requires a person who can work alone doing specific tasks; the other requires a person who can work in a team handling many office procedures.

You must remember that there is considerable variation in office jobs. You will be able to choose one that is appealing to you.

Employers want new office workers to feel "at home" as quickly as possible. You can expect, therefore, an introduction to a new organization and a new job.

Chapter 2 provides the background for your study of succeeding chapters. You will then be able to relate office procedures to specific job opportunities.

The objectives of the chapter are to:

● acquaint you with major office job categories and related requirements

● acquaint you with the manner in which employees are introduced to their new jobs

EMPLOYMENT OPPORTUNITIES IN THE OFFICE WORKFORCE

When you have completed your study of this topic, you will be able to:

- identify major office job categories and describe related qualifications

- identify requirements for promotion

- explain the basic critical skills and qualities needed by office workers

Office workers participate in a wide range of activities related to information processing. These activities can be considered in relation to four major categories of office jobs that are open to beginning workers. These are:

- word processing

- data processing

- information management and transmission

- general assistance and customer service

Each of these categories includes jobs related to various aspects of information processing. However, some jobs include responsibilities that cut across two or more categories. For example, in a small office one person may perform a wide range of office tasks. Such a person, therefore, is responsible for tasks from all four of the categories listed above.

**WORD
PROCESSING**

Word processing is a critical task in the total information processing environment. *Word processing* is the producing of communications by trained personnel using technology and efficient procedures. If you enjoy keyboarding and preparing documents, you may find jobs in this category appealing.

Among the common beginning jobs in this category are:

● word processor
● typist
● word processing operator

Basic Skill Requirements

The proper and efficient preparation of documents using computers or typewriters requires a number of skills and abilities. Among the important ones are:

● rapid and accurate keyboarding skill
● knowledge and skill in using software
● skill in formatting and proofreading documents
● command of grammar, punctuation, and spelling
● an *extensive* vocabulary
● ability to learn *specialized* vocabularies (for example, legal, engineering, medical, or electronic)
● ability to follow instructions
● skill in transcribing from machine dictation

extensive: large, wide

specialized: related to a particular activity

Where Workers Are Employed

Word processing workers are needed throughout all types of organizations. Executives and managers who must compose many types of written communications require the assistance of office workers in this category. Word processing workers prepare drafts and final copies of letters, memorandums, and reports. Such workers may assist one manager or executive or several. Some word processing workers may assist all the staff in one department. In some organizations, there are word processing centers or clusters where workers provide assistance to several departments or to the entire organization.

Opportunities for Promotion

Beginning workers in word processing have opportunities for promotions to jobs in the same category that require more advanced skills. For example, workers who learn how to prepare complex documents with specialized formatting requirements are good candidates for promotion. Positions as manager or supervisor in departments where there is a considerable amount of word processing are frequently filled by those who began their office career in word processing. If you choose to work in a job in this category, you will learn many skills on the job which are valuable in higher-level positions. Among the qualifications required for promotion are the following:

- thorough knowledge of the range of tasks to be done
- knowledge of software *capabilities* beyond the basics
- high-level communication and human relations skills
- good judgment in formatting documents
- excellent editing and proofreading skills
- ability to manage others effectively

capabilities: what can be done

Illus. 2-1. Work in word processing requires a variety of skills and offers a number of career opportunities.

numeric: related to
figures

systematic:
established

Data processing is the collecting, organizing, and summarizing of data, generally in *numeric* form. Workers in this category prepare order forms, invoices, checks, payroll reports, and numerous other types of documents of importance to the organization. This is a category that you may want to consider if you find working with numbers interesting. Also, if you enjoy orderly, *systematic* ways of doing tasks, you are likely to find jobs in this category appealing. Organizations need conscientious workers who will follow procedures established for handling numbers.

Among the common beginning jobs in this category are:

- accounts payable clerk
- accounts receivable clerk
- stock clerk
- order clerk
- payroll clerk
- purchasing clerk

Basic Skill Requirements

Overall, workers in this category process numbers with accuracy and efficiency. To meet this expectation, there are a number of critical skills and abilities required. Among them are:

- good command of arithmetic processes
- skill in using touch-system to enter figures at a keyboard
- understanding of basic recordkeeping and accounting terms and concepts
- skill in writing legibly
- ability to check one's own work and correct errors

Where Workers Are Employed

Organizations require employees who can process figures with accuracy and interest. Many employees are needed if a company's financial activities are to be properly recorded, summarized, and reported. Employees in this category are found in order departments, accounting departments, billing departments, and in warehouses in large companies. In small companies, there may be a single accounting office where all financial data processing is done and where each employee does a variety of tasks.

Opportunities for Promotion

exceptional: not usual

Companies need persons who can handle *exceptional* problems that develop in a department as well as persons who can supervise the work of others and manage heavy volumes of activity. The increasingly complex operations in many companies mean that many companies are frequently reviewing the qualifications of persons already in their employment in order to identify candidates for higher-level positions. Opportunities for promotion within data processing are available to those who have achieved the following:

● knowledge of the complete data processing cycle and all related procedures
● understanding of the total organization so that problems that occur can be resolved properly
● ability to instruct new employees about procedures for specific tasks
● ability to give consistent attention to detail

Illus. 2-2. Data processing skills are useful in a wide range of jobs.

INFORMATION MANAGEMENT AND TRANSMISSION

Information management and transmission refers to the organized maintenance of a company's records and to the transmission of information to those within and outside the company. If you find it interesting to gather data and organize it, you may want to consider some of the positions in this category. As a worker in this category, you will be involved in assuring that information is updated on a timely basis and/or in transmitting information promptly. Among common jobs in this category are:

- data entry keyer
- database clerk
- mailroom clerk or assistant
- receiving clerk
- records clerk
- reprographics clerk
- traffic and shipping clerk

Basic Skill Requirements

Attention to detail and an ability to follow the specific procedures outlined for tasks are basic characteristics of the highly valued workers in this category. Among the skills considered important are:

- command of basic filing rules and principles
- ability to handle details without incurring any errors
- good keyboarding skills
- basic knowledge of computer functions
- ability to follow instructions for use of electronic equipment

Where Workers Are Employed

Office workers in this category are found in such places as central records departments, company libraries, mailrooms, and reprographics centers. If the structure of the organization is **decentralized**, workers from this category may be found in operating departments. For example, the human resources department may maintain its own database of all personnel in the company rather than use a central information database. Large organizations need staff who work full-time to manage the transmission of mail and other types of communications to persons within the company as well as outside the company. In a small company, an office worker may do all tasks required for maintaining records and also perform some tasks described in the other three categories.

decentralized: departments managing their own activity

Opportunities for Promotion

In some companies there is a career path in departments responsible for information maintenance and transmission, such as central records departments, management information service departments, and mailrooms. A **career path** is a clearly identified listing of positions of increasing responsibility. Because of the critical need for accurate and timely information, responsible persons are in great demand for positions at levels beyond the beginning levels. Company executives often look to office employees in the departments as a source for good candidates for promotion. Qualifications that are important for promotion include:

resolve: find a solution

- thorough knowledge of the system for maintaining information
- ability to understand problems and to *resolve* them wisely
- skill in instructing new employees
- understanding the relationship of departmental activities to the total organization's goals

Illus. 2-3. This record clerk is updating a file.

GENERAL ASSISTANCE AND CUSTOMER SERVICE

This category, **general assistance and customer service**, includes those positions where employees must perform a variety of tasks. You may find jobs in this category appealing if your interests overlap two or more categories. Also, if you are happier changing from one type of activity to another, you are likely to be suited for positions in this category. In general, the jobs require

diversified: varied

considerable interaction with people in the organization, with customers and with visitors. Common positions with *diversified* tasks include:

- administrative assistant
- customer service clerk
- general office assistant
- receptionist
- secretary

Basic Skill Requirements

The basic skills you need for positions that are diversified will vary somewhat. In general, the following are commonly listed requirements:

- good keyboarding skills
- skill in writing legibly
- ability to process information by computer
- skill in using office equipment such as calculators and copiers
- ability to manage telephone calls

simultaneously: at the same time

- ability to give attention to several tasks *simultaneously*
- ability to deal with people in a friendly, cooperative manner
- skill in establishing priorities
- ability to communicate orally and in writing

Some positions require specialized skills. The position of secretary is likely to require word processing and transcription skill. Additionally, secretaries are expected to have good judgment, organizational ability, and initiative. Secretaries for specialized offices, such as legal, engineering, and medical, must be able to use a technical vocabulary.

Receptionists must be able to meet and talk with visitors of different backgrounds, take telephone calls, transmit messages, and complete a variety of keyboarding tasks. Receptionists must know the company's personnel and schedule of activities to answer inquiries with accurate, up-to-date information.

General office assistants are required to learn about the technical details of their offices so they can aid customers. For example, office assistants in travel agencies are expected to answer questions about advance payments required for tours, penalties for canceling tours, and documents required for travel to many countries. Office assistants in banks must keep up to date with interest rates for the variety of savings accounts the bank offers customers.

Illus. 2-4. Many alert, efficient employees are needed in customer service departments.

Where Workers Are Employed

Employees in this category are found throughout every organization. A large company, for example, is likely to have a receptionist for each floor as well as a receptionist in each department. Secretaries are commonly found in executive offices. Many large companies have a department to respond to customers who telephone via 800 numbers.

In small companies, you will find that office workers who devote most of their time to word processing or data processing also are responsible for some of tasks that are described in this category of general assistance and customer service.

Opportunities for Promotion

A wide range of higher-level jobs are available to those who are able to perform their initial diversified tasks with ease and success. There are positions with more responsibility in the same department that require more independent work. There are often several levels of positions for each category.

After a year as an assistant in the customer service department of a large manufacturer of small appliances, Virginia was promoted to a supervisory position. During her first year on the job, Virginia had acquired a thorough understanding of the company policies and was able to respond to customer inquiries and complaints wisely and thoughtfully. She was able to think independently and clearly. Virginia was judged to have the abilities and skills to fill a supervisory position.

Promotional prospects are good for employees who have the following qualifications:

● are able to complete jobs with little or no supervision
● have exceptionally good oral and written communication skills
● have the ability to organize tasks and be a self-starter
● complete tasks on schedule

OVERALL QUALIFICATIONS

There are some overall, general qualifications that are identified as critical for most office employees. Among these are:

● work as a team member
● behave in a professional manner in interactions with others
● be a good listener
● possess a positive attitude toward work
● learn from observation and written instructions
● maintain an interest in an organization's goals
● be dependable

flexible: able to change

● be ***flexible*** in response to changes at work
● be able to evaluate one's own work

Office workers who reflect these basic qualifications are in demand in many communities in the United States. As technological innovations change the way office work is performed, there continues to be demand for competent office workers.

NATIONAL OVERVIEW OF THE OFFICE WORKFORCE

The largest major occupational group identified by the U. S. Department of Labor is "Administrative support occupations, including clerical." The work of employees in this category is described in these words: "[They] perform the wide variety of tasks necessary to keep organizations functioning smoothly."[1]

There are more than 21.1 million workers in this category, which is approximately 20 percent of the total workforce. The group as a whole is expected to grow approximately 12 percent,

---

[1] U. S. Department of Labor, Bureau of Labor Statistics, *Occupational Outlook Handbook*, Bulletin 2350 (Washington, D. C.: U. S. Government Printing Office, April 1990), p. 12.

to 23.6 million jobs by 2000. This is a slower projected rate than that predicted for all occupations in the workforce, which is 15 percent. [2]

Job Opportunities

Although projected rate of increase will be slower than in the past, the U. S. Labor Department predicts that administrative support occupations will offer abundant opportunities for qualified job seekers. There are large numbers employed in these occupations and there is substantial *turnover* as employees are promoted to other jobs. Office positions requiring large numbers of employees are shown in Illus. 2-5 on page 48. Prospects for job opportunities for selected positions are given in Illus. 2-6 on page 49.

turnover: people leaving and entering an occupation

Employment Requirements

For the majority of positions in the administrative support occupations, a high school education is sufficient for entry. In a number of instances, though, students are expected to have good skills in keyboarding, arithmetic, and communications. The qualifications for one position, secretary, were described as follows:

> *High school graduates qualify for most secretarial positions provided they have basic office skills. Secretaries must be proficient in typing and good at spelling, punctuation, grammar, and oral communication. Word processing experience is increasingly important and more and more employers require it. . . . Continuing changes in the office environment, many made possible by the computer, have increased the demand for secretaries who are adaptable and versatile.* [3]

Your Future Prospects

Your high school education, including your study of business subjects, provides you with the background to meet the qualifications of a variety of office positions. There continue to be many entry-level opportunities for qualified high school graduates. Furthermore, continuing education provided by employers, as well as that which you can plan for yourself in local educational institutions, will assure you of being prepared for promotions to more responsible positions.

---

[2] Ibid., p. 12.

[3] Ibid., p. 277.

Illus. 2-5.
Employment in selected
office occupations.

Category: Administrative Support Occupations

Occupation	Estimated Employment 1988
Accounting and bookkeeping clerks	2,252,000
General office clerks	2,500,000
Receptionists	833,000
Record clerks, including order clerks, file clerks, and library assistants	886,000
Reservation and transportation ticket agents and travel clerks	133,000
Secretaries	3,373,000
Stock clerks	2,200,000
Telephone operators	330,000
Tellers	522,000
Traffic, shipping, and receiving clerks	535,000
Typists, word processors and data entry keyers	1,416,000

Source: U.S. Department of Labor, Bureau of Labor Statistics as reported in *Occupational Outlook Handbook, Bulletin 2350*, (Washington, D.C.: U.S. Government Printing Office, April, 1990), pp. 244-284.

Category: Administrative Support Occupations

Occupation	Rate of Change Compared to 15 percent rate for all occupations to 2000	Job Prospects to 2000
Accounting and bookkeeping	far below average	Job openings will be numerous because of large size of the occupation.
General office	as fast as the average	Due to large number of expected job openings, primarily as a result of high turnover in this very large occupation, employment prospects should be quite favorable.
Receptionists	faster than the average	Job opportunities should be plentiful. In addition to rapid employment growth, turnover is high.
Record clerks, order clerks, file clerks, and library assistants	more slowly than the average	In all of these occupations the vast majority of the job openings will be to replace those who transfer to other jobs.
Reservations and transportation ticket agents and travel clerks	faster than the average	Applicants are likely to encounter considerable competition; supply of qualified applicants will outstrip demand.
Secretaries	as fast as the average	In addition to job openings because of growth in demand, an exceptionally large number of job openings will arise due to replacement needs.
Stock clerks	as fast as the average	Should be good because occupation is very large and many job openings will occur each year to replace those who leave for other jobs.
Telephone operators	as fast as the average, overall	There are conflicting trends; employment will increase for some jobs and decrease for others in the category.
Tellers	more slowly than the average	Qualified applicants should have good prospects, since this occupation provides a relatively large number of job openings.
Traffic, shipping, and receiving clerks	more slowly than the average	Job openings will arise due to increasing economic activity and because certain functions cannot be automated.
Typists, word processors, and entry keyers	number to decline	Despite decline in overall employment, many thousands of openings will arise.

Source: U.S. Department of Labor, Bureau of Labor Statistics as reported in *Occupational Outlook Handbook, Bulletin 2350*, (Washington, D.C.: U.S. Government Printing Office, April, 1990), pp. 244-284.

Illus. 2-6. Prospects for job opportunities for selected positions to 2000.

QUESTIONS FOR REVIEW

1. Do you agree with the statement: All office workers perform the same activities? Explain your answer.

2. What are basic skill requirements for those who have jobs classified as word processing?

3. What skills are considered important for promotion in the word processing category?

4. What are some beginning positions in the data processing category?

5. What types of skills are more important in the data processing category than in the word processing category?

6. Identify several positions that are classified as information management, including transmission.

7. What are basic qualifications for office workers in the general assistance and customer service category?

8. Identify what you believe are people-related qualities required by all office workers.

9. In which three office occupations, as shown in Illus. 2-5, are the largest numbers of persons employed?

10. By 2000, which office positions are projected to increase at a rate greater than the rate for all occupations in the society?

MAKING DECISIONS

Chris has accepted part-time work in a local bank. He will work approximately 12 hours each week. The manager said to Chris: "Would you like to be assigned to one department where you will work every week or would you prefer to work in several different departments? If you choose to be one of our roving office assistants, you will be assigned the department where you will work for a day or more when you come in the afternoon. We have both types of positions and can give you your choice." If you were Chris, which choice would you make?

What You Are To Do: Write a brief paragraph in which you indicate which type of position you would choose if you were in Chris's situation and give reasons for your choice.

EXTENDING YOUR ENGLISH COMPETENCIES

Read the text below. Note that there are several spelling errors in the copy.

When executives are asked to choose the key attributes of office employees, they frequently indentify the following:

- *strong knowledge of grammer, spelling, and punctuation*
- *accuracey*
- *capible of working under pressere*
- *ability to deel with people in a diplometic fashion*
- *punckuality and reguler attendencee*

What You Are To Do: Prepare a copy of the excerpt, correcting all spelling errors.

APPLICATION ACTIVITY

This activity will aid you in becoming acquainted with specific types of jobs in your own community or one nearby. You will be seeking answers to the question: What are the office jobs that are open to high school graduates who have studied business courses? To answer this question, your teacher will assign you to a group, which is given the responsibility to do one of the following:

1. Newspaper Search: The group assigned to this activity will read local newspapers to determine office jobs available. (The group may need to read newspapers in a local library for the period when office positions are most likely to be advertised.)

2. Overall Employment Opportunities: The group assigned to this activity will need to make inquiry of the local government employment office to learn which office positions that were listed during the past year could be filled by high school graduates with no prior full-time office experience.

3. Job Opportunities in a Particular Industry: The group assigned to this activity will need to get information from companies in the particular industry about the office positions open to high school graduates and about qualifications required of applicants.

What You Are To Do: (1) Along with the others assigned to your group, organize what you must do to get the information required for your group. (2) As a group, review the information you secured and determine the best way to summarize it for a written report and for a brief oral presentation in class. (3) Determine who will key the report, who will proofread it, and who will prepare a final draft for submission to the class. (4) Determine who will make a brief presentation to the class.

Word processing
equipment can be used
to complete this activity.

TOPIC 2

INTRODUCTION TO A NEW JOB

When you have completed your study of this topic, you will be able to:

- describe how new employees are introduced to the company and their jobs

- explain how a new employee learns on the job

- describe how new employees are evaluated

A new job means new learning. Prior to beginning a new job you will wonder about a number of matters. Among your concerns may be your specific responsibilities, your relationships with coworkers, and the work environment. Your questions may include some of the following:

- Which workstation will be mine to use?

- Where do I keep my coat?

- At what time am I expected to take breaks?

- Do I use first names when talking with supervisors and managers?

- Will I be able to ask a coworker for help if I don't know how to do something?

- Will I be expected to use software that I do not know?

- How will I know where all the departments are?

- On what basis will I be evaluated?

Employers expect new employees to have questions. In order to answer such questions, as well as to provide new employees with important job-related information, employers provide orientation programs. An orientation program will help you learn about the company, its products and/or services, your role within the organization, and how to carry out your assigned tasks.

This topic presents various types of orientation programs provided for new employees. Learning on the job and employee evaluation are also discussed. Regardless of the company for which you work, you will want to learn all you can about the company's goals, its policies and procedures, and the corporate structure. You also will want to learn the specific guidelines under which you will be expected to perform your specified duties.

ORIENTATION

Initial introduction to a new company and job is called **orientation**. Orientation programs may be formal or informal. Formal orientation programs are scheduled for a particular time and include a specified series of events. Formal orientation programs are common in large organizations where a number of new employees are beginning their jobs at the same time.

A formal orientation program for the 16 new office employees of a large bank was scheduled for the morning of their first day at work. The program began with introductions of key executives and talks by staff members from the human resources department and from key operating departments. By noontime, the 16 had learned a great deal about the company and the overall role they would have in the work of the company.

Illus. 2-7. New employees during their orientation are introduced to the equipment they will use in their jobs.

Informal orientation programs are common in smaller organizations where fewer employees are hired. An informal program is directed by the immediate supervisor of the new employee. The supervisor explains to the employee the nature of the organization as well as the specific requirements of the job.

Regardless of the manner in which the orientation is planned, the following topics are generally included:

- goals and policies of the organization
- company structure and key personnel
- employee benefits
- policies related to office safety and security
- personnel policies
- policies and procedures for office tasks
- specific procedures and schedules related to specific positions

New employees are introduced to coworkers by supervisors in most companies. Coworkers who are meeting new employees often express a willingness to be helpful if there are any questions about the work to be done.

Orientation does not always end with the initial program offered when employees first arrive at the organization. Sometimes additional orientation sessions are scheduled after workers have had two to three weeks of experience on their jobs. These sessions give the employees a chance to ask questions about the company and their jobs that have arisen since they

Illus. 2-8. A supervisor is explaining a procedure to a new employee.

began. Companies want new employees to "feel at home" as quickly as possible.

LEARNING ON THE JOB

When you begin a new job, you must remember that your supervisor realizes that you do not know everything that your new job may require. Learning on the job is expected and is considered a normal part of your orientation. Learning in the work environment is, in many ways, like learning in the classroom.

As a new worker, you can expect to be given specific information about the tasks for which you will have responsibility. A clearly stated job description may be available for your reference. Note the specific duties identified in the job description shown in Illus. 2-9.

JOB DESCRIPTION

Position Title: Junior Secretary

Division: Advertising and Promotion

Primary Functions

To help the administrative assistant to the vice president of advertising and promotion by preparing various types of communications, handling details for travel to fashion shows out of the country, and maintaining departmental files.

Detailed Duties

1. Uses a microcomputer and variety of software to prepare fashion show scripts, press releases, and correspondence.

2. Makes inquiries of hotel and travel services for forthcoming travel and follows up with reservations.

3. Helps the administrative assistant in special projects and other tasks.

4. Keys correspondence and other documents.

5. Prepares documents for filing.

6. Accesses databases.

Illus. 2-9. Job description (partial)

Equipment and Software Instruction

Generally, your supervisor will ask you if you know how to use equipment and software required to perform tasks assigned to you. If there is equipment or software that is unfamiliar to you, someone will be asked to demonstrate its use. Then, you are likely to be given time to master the operations if they are not quickly learned. Frequently, a user's manual is provided for each piece of equipment and software package. Such a manual contains detailed instructions which you are likely to find useful in becoming acquainted with the features and capabilities of equipment or software. You will want to keep manuals where you can refer to them easily.

Reference Sources

Most companies have compiled information that is of value to their office employees. You are likely to find the following references that will be helpful:

- a company manual of policies and procedures related to all employees
- an organization chart
- calendar of events and company newsletter
- *annual report*
- a company directory of all personnel with departments and telephone numbers

annual report: a
document public
companies must issue
to shareholders

You may be given personal copies of some or all of these references. You should organize them at your workstation so that you can reach them easily when you need information from them. Generally, new employees are encouraged to consult references and to ask questions whenever there are doubts about how to proceed with a specific phase of a task.

During the introduction to her new job, Paula was assured that Jill, who had been on the job for more than a year, was ready to be helpful if there were any questions. One of the first things Jill did was to show Paula where all the references were maintained and the nature of the information that could be found in each. Then, Jill said to Paula: "Don't hesitate to ask questions. Sometimes I'll be able to give you the answer; at other times, I'll be able to refer you to the right source. It will take a little time for you to know exactly what is available in written form."

EVALUATION OF PERFORMANCE

Companies require competent workers. Therefore, employees are evaluated from time to time to determine if they are performing their tasks in satisfactory fashion.

New workers are given a period of time for learning their jobs. The trial or probation period may extend over three, six, or twelve months. The length of the trial period is determined by the complexity of the job and the level of skills possessed by the employee. Companies use varying methods for evaluating workers.

Types of Evaluation

Evaluation practices vary considerably. In some companies, especially small ones, evaluation may be informal and little, if anything, may be recorded in the personnel file of the employee. In such offices, evaluations may be done at any time. On the other hand, some companies, especially large ones, often follow an explicitly stated employee performance appraisal schedule and use carefully designed evaluation forms.

Informal Observation

appraisal: judgment

You may work in a department where the manager is responsible for writing a performance appraisal on each employee at designated times. On page 59, note the *appraisal* written at the end of a new employee's probation period. In many companies, a copy of the memorandum is read by the employee. The employee, in such cases, has the right to add a comment. Generally, the employee also signs the memorandum to indicate that it was read.

Performance Appraisal Forms

In some companies, the human resources department provides an appraisal form to be used for the evaluation of each employee. Note the partial one in Illus 2-11, page 61. As you see, there are five statements for each factor evaluated. The judgments listed in the first column after the description of each factor are the most favorable evaluations; those in the column before the comment column, the least favorable.

Work Measurement

standards: expected output

Some companies have developed *standards* for specific tasks. For example, standards are based on keystrokes, lines, or pages

monitoring: keeping track of

an employee doing word processing at a microcomputer should produce. Or, standards are based the on number of invoices a billing clerk should produce. Often standards are specified per hour or per day. Devices that keep track of such factors as keystrokes and lines may allow for more detailed *monitoring* of output of office workers in the future.

In some cases, work measurement is used primarily to determine which workers need additional training and direction to improve their productivity. Also, work measurement is valuable to the manager in determining the capability of the total group.

```
     TO:   Nadja K. Thorton, Human Resources Director

   FROM:   Donald W. Rittner, WP Center

   DATE:   January 15, 19--

SUBJECT:   Performance Appraisal--Wendy E. Weber

Wendy Weber has completed her six-month probation period
in our department.  She is one of the most competent
beginners we have hired.  Although she has had an
introduction to microcomputers, she had limited hands-on
experience when she began.  However, she was an
exceptionally receptive student.  She learned quickly and
thoroughly.  Her eagerness to learn and to do each job
carefully has continued.  She is now among the three best
operators of the total group who have been at work for no
more than one year.

My overall appraisal is that her work is excellent.  I
recommend her for a maximum raise in her salary.

Comments by Employee:
```

I've had good instruction on my job; I like it!

Wendy E Weber 1/15/--
Employee   Date

Donald W Rittner 1/15/--
Department Manager Date

Illus. 2-10. An evaluation based on informal observation.

Factors Evaluated

Companies often determine what factors are of most importance in the evaluation of employees. However, there are some commonly identified factors that are used by many companies. Among the factors on which office employees are evaluated are the following:

- job knowledge
- quantity of work
- quality of work
- initiative

- cooperation
- adaptability
- judgment
- attendance and punctuality

Read carefully the appraisal form shown in Illus. 2-11. Note the description of behavior at the several levels for each of the factors considered critical in doing a satisfactory job.

Evaluating Your Own Performance

To grow in your job, you will find it a valuable practice to ask yourself from time to time: "How well am I doing my job?" To answer that question, these steps may be helpful:

1. Determine the competencies evaluated by your supervisor or manager. You may have a copy of the evaluation appraisal form used, or you may have to determine which competencies are important from what the manager says to you from time to time.
2. List the competencies in a notebook.
3. Review the list, thinking about your performance in relation to each competency.
4. Keep notes of all problems you encounter on the job. For example, a document you processed may be returned to you because it was not formatted properly.
5. Review each problem noted to determine what, if anything, you failed to do. For example, in the problem mentioned in 4, you might realize that the instructions clearly included formatting details. You had failed, however, to read the instructions carefully.
6. Analyze why you did not perform successfully. You must be honest with yourself at this point. Again, in the problem mentioned in 4, if you had clear instructions, think about the reason you did not follow them.

EMPLOYEE PERFORMANCE EVALUATION

INSTRUCTIONS:
Evaluate the employee's performance on the job now being performed by marking an X in the box above each of the following suggested statements which best expresses your judgment about the individual's capabilities. If a pre-printed statement is not an accurate description, a more applicable statement may be entered in the comments section. In order to conduct a more meaningful appraisal you should refer to the employee's job description while evaluating and discussing the employee's job performance.

Employee's Name _B. Lois Cooper_　　　Supervisor's Name _Margaret Bridges_

DEPARTMENT _Marketing_

Category						COMMENTS
A. JOB KNOWLEDGE Possession of information and understanding of the work to be performed. (how well employee knows the job)	☐ Thoroughly familiar with all phases of work.	☐ Well rounded knowledge. Requires minimum assistance.	☒ Adequate job knowledge. Requires some guidance and assistance.	☐ Limited job knowledge. Requires considerable assistance.	☐ Inadequate knowledge. Requires improvement to retain job.	Has been in complex situation for past three months. Making good progress.
B. QUANTITY OF WORK Volume of acceptable work turned out and use of working time.	☐ Rapid worker. Unusually high output.	☒ Better than average work flow.	☐ Average amount of work turned out, but seldom more.	☐ Output of work is frequently less than expected.	☐ Very slow worker. Must improve to retain job.	
C. QUALITY OF WORK Accuracy, neatness and dependability of results	☐ Consistently excellent quality.	☒ Highly accurate with few errors.	☐ Acceptable degree of accuracy. Occasional errors.	☐ Careless. Frequently does unacceptable work.	☐ Too many errors. Must improve to retain job.	Is a very good proofreader.
D. INITIATIVE Ability to originate, develop and/or carry out new ideas or methods. (amount of supervision required)	☐ Continually innovative and resourceful.	☐ Considerably resourceful. Needs little follow-up.	☒ Shows occasional initiative. Performs some assignments without much direction.	☐ Rarely shows initiative and requires frequent follow-up.	☐ Needs follow-up on all phases of work.	Has more potential than is now realized; must encourage him more.
E. COOPERATION Ability and willingness to work with others.	☒ Exceptionally good team worker. Always cooperative.	☐ Cooperative. Customarily goes over halfway.	☐ Usually cooperative. May clash occasionally with others.	☐ Cooperative only when has to be. Frequent conflicts.	☐ Very poor relationships. Must improve to retain job.	Always willing to help co-workers meet a deadline.

Illus. 2-11. Appraisal form (partial)

7. Introduce changes in your way of work. For example, if you feel you were careless in reading instructions, make a point of carefully reading every word of every instruction.
8. From time to time, review your total performance. Note if the changes in your way of work have reduced the number of errors you make or problems that arise.
9. If possible, compare your own evaluation with the one given you by the supervisor at the time your performance is appraised.

As you study the content of this textbook, you will have many opportunities to evaluate your own performance. You can develop much skill in objectively assessing how well you complete your assignments. Employers are grateful for, and usually reward, employees who can objectively review what they have done. Being able to assess your own work is often one good indicator of your interest in doing a good job. From your own personal **assessment**, you will be able to determine what you must do in order to improve your job performance.

assessment: a review and evaluation

QUESTIONS FOR REVIEW

1. What is the purpose of an orientation when entering a new company?
2. How does a formal orientation program differ from an informal program?
3. What are three topics commonly discussed during orientation periods?
4. Do supervisors expect new employees to learn on the job? Explain your response.
5. What can new employees learn from job descriptions for their positions?
6. What are some common types of references new employees find useful on the job?
7. Why is a new employee given a trial period?
8. Identify what Wendy Weber's supervisor observed that led to the statement "Her work is excellent." (See Illus. 2-10.)
9. What are three factors considered in an evaluation of an office employee?

10. How can your classwork help you in developing skill in evaluating your own performance when you are on a job?

INTERACTING WITH OTHERS

Assume that you accepted a job as a word processor. You were introduced to your tasks by the supervisor. You did not take notes while the supervisor demonstrated the use of the equipment, You thought that what was being explained would be available in an operations manual. However, at the end of the demonstration, the supervisor said nothing about a manual. The only comment of the supervisor was: "Here are some sheets of practice exercises that you may find useful in getting acquainted with the equipment. Spend the next hour getting used to this equipment."

As soon as the supervisor walked away from your workstation, you wrote some notes from memory. However, you realized that there were some initial steps in the operation of the equipment that you did not remember.

What would you do at this moment?

What You Are To Do: Prepare a brief response to the question raised.

EXTENDING YOUR MATH COMPETENCIES

You have been given the information about office positions in two cities that is shown in the table on page 64.

What You Are To Do:
1. Compute the difference (in dollars and cents) in median hourly wages for each position.
2. Compute the median salary for the total group of positions in each city. (**Hint:** Multiply number of employees for each position in each city by median salary; then add up the products computed. Finally, add the number of employees in all occupations in each city. Divide the total product by the total number of employees to get the median salary for the total group of positions in each city.)

HOURLY EARNINGS OF SELECTED OCCUPATIONS IN TWO CITIES				
Occupation	Number of Employees		Median Hourly Earnings in Dollars	
	Southern City	Northwestern City	Southern City	Northwestern City
Secretary I	69	10	$ 8.98	$ 8.08
Secretary II	60	42	12.97	10.62
Word Processors	23	34	7.32	7.47
Key Entry Operators	149	119	6.49	7.62
Receptionists	46	16	6.46	6.79
Accounting Clerks	255	268	9.42	8.24

APPLICATION ACTIVITY

Word processing
equipment can be used
to complete this activity.

You have learned that office employees are often evaluated on factors listed on page 60.

What You Are To Do: For each factor listed on page 60, describe how the activities in this course may help improve your behavior in relation to the factor. Key your responses.

CHAPTER SUMMARY

You were introduced to an overview of office jobs. Also, you learned what you can expect when you first enter the office as an employee. The points that you should understand thoroughly and be able to explain or describe include:

1. All office positions are not alike; some are specialized; others are varied.
2. The four major job categories are: word processing, data processing, information management and transmission, and general assistance and customer service.
3. Office employees have opportunities for promotion to jobs of greater responsibility that require higher-level understandings and skills.
4. All office employees are expected to be good team players; possess a positive attitude toward office work; be able to learn from observation and written instructions; and be able to evaluate their own work.

5. The U. S. Department of Labor provides information about office jobs and the prospects for employment in the future.
6. New employees are given an orientation, either formally or informally, when they begin work.
7. Evaluation of employees is a standard procedure in organizations. Employees are expected to evaluate their own performance, too.

KEY CONCEPTS AND TERMS

data processing

information management
and transmission

career path

general assistance and
customer service

orientation

**INTEGRATED
CHAPTER
ACTIVITIES**

Activity 1

You are now aware of the skills required for each of four major office job categories: word processing, data processing, information management and transmission; and general assistance and customer service. Undoubtedly, as you became acquainted with these four categories you realized that one was more appealing to you at this point than the others were. (Remember, after your study of the complete textbook, you may find your interest has shifted to another type of office job.) It is likely that you already have some skills considered important in the job category of your choice.

What You Are To Do:
- Choose the category that is most appealing to you now.
- Prepare a copy of the form on page 66 or use the one in *Information Processing Activities*. Fill in the name of your chosen job category in the blank after "for" at the top of the form.
- List on the form the skills given in the chapter for the category you select (word processing, page 38; data processing, page 40; information management and transmission, page 42; general assistance and customer service, page 43).
- Complete the form by assessing each skill according to the three factors given.

Skills required	Present skill level			Will develop in class		Some learning required on the job	
	No skill	Limited	Good	Yes	No	Yes	No
SELF ASSESSMENT FOR _____							

Activity 2

Imagine that you have completed your course in office procedures and the school year has ended. You are applying for a number of office positions. Think of a position in the job category you identified in Integrated Chapter Activity 1 which you think you would find appealing.

What You Are To Do: Compose and key a brief paragraph in which you identify the position and describe what is appealing about the position. If you wish, you may discuss the type of company to which you are applying.

OPTIONAL COMPUTER APPLICATION ACTIVITY
See Computer Application Activity 2
in your Information Processing Activities workbook.

OPTIONAL CRITICAL THINKING ACTIVITY
See Critical Thinking Activity 1
in your Information Processing Activities workbook.

Blake Williams
OFFICE SUPERVISOR

HOW CAN I BE ORGANIZED?

DEAR MR. WILLIAMS:

I took a job with a new video production company exactly a week ago. I work for a manager who has never had an office assistant. He is a very busy man and he keeps me busy. However, I must tell you I don't know what I am doing most of the time. I get assignments at any time and all the time. I'm going around in circles. My workstation is a mess.

I think I should try to get organized. I do like the place; the people are friendly and there is never a dull moment. Do you have any ideas for me?—CRAIG FROM DALLAS

DEAR CRAIG:

I am happy to hear that you do like the company where you work. You aren't frightened by the circumstances, which is good. Keep up your confidence. You are right in thinking that getting organized will help. Here are some suggestions:

- List all tasks assigned in a small notebook. Check off—and add date—as you complete each task.
- Determine the order in which all tasks you have at the beginning of the day should be done; as a new task is given to you, immediately determine where it fits into your list of tasks to be done.
- Begin a personal directory of names, addresses, and telephone numbers of all persons to whom you place calls and to whom you write letters.
- Set up your workstation with supplies that you use regularly.
- Arrange references at or very near your workstation.
- Check the arrangement of your workstation to be sure it is as efficient as it can be. (For example, is your telephone placed so that you can answer it without getting up or moving your chair?)
- Remember the questions asked you that you cannot answer; you might want to write them down. When you have a free minute, determine if you do have sources at hand for answers to such questions.
- Review all incomplete jobs at the end of the day; determine which ones should be considered first the next morning.
- Begin to draw up a calendar of tasks that must be done on a regular basis, such as weekly or monthly.

Best wishes for success in getting organized.—BLAKE WILLIAMS

THE SKILLS
OF WORKING TOGETHER

Communicating in the Office

Imagine bringing to an absolute stop all activity at 11:10 a.m. on Monday in any business organization. What do you think you would discover in progress at that instant? You would undoubtedly find conferences among executives, meetings between supervisors and office workers, office assistants reading manuals and incoming communications, administrative assistants keying messages at their terminals, executives and assistants composing memorandums and letters, customer service representatives listening to customers, tellers speaking via telephones to branch offices, and other similar activities. In short, much of the activity would involve communication of some kind. You can imagine, then, how important effective communication is in every organization.

You are familiar with communication skills. You have been studying them every year you have been in school. You use your communication skills in your everyday tasks. You also may have seen their value in part-time or summer jobs. These same basic communication skills are equally important for the business office.

This is a good time to improve any phases of your basic communication skills that you think are not as effective as they could be. In this chapter, you will find a general introduction to the usefulness of reading, writing, speaking, and listening in the office.

The objectives of the chapter are to:

- describe the reading skill that is valuable at work

- explain what effective business writing is

- demonstrate speaking and listening techniques that assure effective oral communications

READING

When you have completed your study of this topic, you will be able to:

- describe the types of reading you may do in an office job

- identify critical reading skills

- describe techniques for improving reading skills

Your reading skills will be valuable to you at work. There will be numerous occasions when you must read information quickly in order to respond to an inquiry or to determine what you should do. Few people have reached the level of reading facility where no more improvement is possible. You, too, will find it worthwhile to improve your reading skill during your study of office procedures. Studying the barriers to effective reading and carefully analyzing how you read can lead to positive changes in your reading techniques.

Although you have been reading for many years, try to step back and think about it as if it were a new process for you. Then, the information in this topic may be more useful to you.

THE READING PROCESS

You know how to read. You read textbooks in your courses. You read the local newspaper and your favorite magazines. You read instructions when you buy a new wristwatch or telephone. **Reading** is actually simple when viewed in a general sense. It is the process of translating printed information or information on a screen into useful mental impressions. What you have read becomes knowledge that influences how you think and act.

Assume you know nothing about office employment. Then, you are given an article from which you read the following: "The employment prospects of office workers are expected to remain favorable in the future. Overall, employment in office jobs will grow 6 to 8 percent in the next five years." Remember the assumption: You knew nothing about office employment.

What do you know now? How will your actions be influenced by what you have learned? Now you know that there will continue to be many job opportunities for persons like you who are studying office procedures. You may increase the attention you give to your study of office procedures because you know that you will have job prospects.

An adequate reading skill is composed of several factors. As you learned in your English courses, a good reading skill means that you:

- *read naturally*
  When you read naturally, your attention is on the meaning of what you read. It is not on the process of moving your eyes from word to word.

- *read with understanding and reasonable speed*
  You need to understand what you read in order to learn something you can use—either at the time of completing the reading or later. For example, when you finish reading the instructions for formatting a report, you are able to use the **prescribed** format.

  prescribed: ordered

  Reasonable speed means that you are not spending an excessive amount of time in reading. If you must complete a report quickly, yet you must read the instructions for the format, you will be grateful for your skill in reading quickly.

- *read with few pauses because of unfamiliar words*
  It is possible to understand the meaning of a passage when you do not know the exact meaning of every word. However, you are less likely to be **perplexed** if every word is familiar to you. Command of an extensive vocabulary is helpful.

  perplexed: puzzled

During your study of office procedures, try to use every opportunity to strengthen your reading skills. As you improve your reading skills, many tasks in your office procedures class will become easier to complete.

READING IN THE OFFICE

There are many occasions when you must read on the job. Several illustrations are discussed in the following paragraphs.

Understanding Tasks

Many policies and procedures related to your job will be available in written form. A supervisor may explain how a particular task is to be done, but you will find it helpful to read the written version of the procedures. You read to completely understand what you are to do. From time to time, memorandums related to ways of doing tasks or changes in schedules are sent to office employees. Such correspondence should be read and filed in an appropriate manner for easy reference later.

Roberto, an office assistant in the office of research and development, is responsible for ordering and maintaining all departmental supplies. Therefore, he carefully reads the memorandum shown on page 74 from the head of the Purchasing Department. He then files it for future reference.

Illus. 3-1. An office worker is carefully reading a memorandum.

Illus. 3-2. What information in this memorandum should Roberto remember?

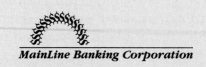

MainLine Banking Corporation

MEMORANDUM

TO: All Department Heads

FROM: Gail Atwater, Purchasing Department

DATE: October 21, 19--

SUBJECT: New On-Line System for Ordering Supplies

We are now on-line for ordering supplies. The new process is simple and, we believe, will be more efficient. The following points will be useful to you as we shift to our new system.

1. You will no longer need your hard copy of the supplies catalog. It is now out of date.

2. The supplies catalog is now in memory and ready for use. Use the command SUPCAT to retrieve the catalog. A menu-driven index will guide you through the ordering process.

3. If an item you need is out of stock, you will be given information about anticipated date of receipt. An out-of-stock item can still be ordered. It will be delivered as soon as we receive it.

4. All orders will be delivered promptly. Orders placed by 11:30 a.m. will be delivered by 3:30 p.m. Orders placed after 11:30 a.m. will be delivered the following morning.

5. If you have any questions about placing orders, please call me at extension 3612.

ts

An executive was writing an article for a professional journal. She asked a junior secretary to prepare a draft of the article following the journal's manuscript instructions. Read the excerpt from those instructions which is shown in Illus. 3-3. Then answer these questions:

● Where will margins be set for keyboarding the copy?

● Where are headings placed?

● How will you differentiate between major headings and subheadings?

```
                    GUIDELINES FOR SUBMITTING ARTICLES
                    TO THE COMPUTER MONTHLY REVIEW


   FORMAT AND LENGTH

       Manuscripts should be typed on plain 8 1/2" x 11" paper,
       double-spaced, with one-inch margins all around.  Two
       copies should be submitted.  Manuscript should not exceed
       3,500 words.

   HEADINGS

       All major headings should be flush left with the margin,
       with initial capital letters.  Subheadings should also
       be placed flush left with the margin, and underscored,
       with initial capital letters.  Usually only two levels
       of headings should be used.  However, if third-level
       headings are necessary, they should be indented the same
       as a paragraph indention, underscored, with only the
       initial letter of the first word capitalized, and fol-
       lowed by a period with the text immediately following.
```

Illus. 3-3. Instructions for preparing articles submitted to a professional journal.

Using Equipment

From time to time office employees are given new equipment to make their work easier. Sometimes demonstrations of the equipment are provided. However, workers generally find that they must read and understand the instruction manual in order to use the equipment properly.

David's office has a new telephone system—one more complex than the old system. Although he attended a demonstration of the new system, David read the brochure provided by the telephone company. He was especially interested in how to post a message. He read carefully the instructions shown in Illus. 3-4 on page 76.

Using the Posted Message Feature of your Telephone System

You can post a message at your telephone that will appear on an intercom caller's display to indicate why you are not at your telephone. You can post only one message at a time. This feature does not work when *Do Not Disturb* is activated.

To post a message:

● Press Posted Message button.
  The green light flashes.

● Dial the code for the message you want posted.
  For example, dial 11 for "Out of town for the day."
  (Note you have space for 20 prefiled messages.)

To cancel a posted message:

● Press Posted Message button.
● Dial 00.

Illus. 3-4. Instructions for using a feature of a new telephone system.

Using Forms

Businesses develop forms to simplify the task of getting appropriate and complete information. You will find forms that facilitate such tasks as recording telephone messages, requesting supplies and equipment, ordering goods, reporting travel expenses, and submitting overtime hours. It is very important that you read all instructions on forms and fill in all information requested. If some item of information is not needed in a particular instance or is not available, some comment should be added. Note Illus. 3-5, which shows a telephone message recorded on a form. What information did the person who recorded the message fail to add?

An office worker is employed by a photographic studio that specializes in food photography. She was asked to return some camera equipment that was not the type ordered. To complete this task, the office worker filled out the merchandise return form that was packaged with the camera equipment. She read each section of the form carefully and provided all necessary information.

Illus. 3-5. Can you identify what information is missing from this message?

MEMO OF CALL

To _Steve Franklin_ _____ _10/17_ ₁₉ _— —_

M s. _Gail Talbot_ _____ called from _Coleman + Perry_ _____

Telephone No.: _(212) 565-7921_ _____

I TOLD THAT PERSON YOU WERE:		THE REPLY WAS:	
Out	☑	No message	☐
Not in today	☐	See message below	☑
Not in your office	☐	Will call again	☐
Talking on telephone	☐	Answering your call	☐
In conference	☐	Please call back	☐
Out of town	☐	It is urgent	☐

ADDITIONAL REMARKS _Contract has been reviewed; there are a couple of questions about utilities. Please call ASAP._

Message taken by _____

Time _____

Responding to Inquiries

Office workers must often respond to inquiries from other departments and from customers directly. The subject of the inquiries can vary considerably. Employees are not expected to know every requested detail from memory. However, they are expected to read quickly and accurately the information needed. Increasingly, office workers are reading details on their terminal screens.

The office worker in the central reservation office for a worldwide chain of motels handles incoming calls throughout the day. She sits at a terminal where she has access to details about any location. When a prospective traveler asks: "Do you have a motel in San Diego, California?" the worker has the information on her screen only a moment after the caller has completed the question. Additional questions are answered quickly as the office worker accesses the information and reads the appropriate details from the terminal screen.

Using References/Databases

As an office worker, you will frequently need to use a variety of references. References commonly found at office employees' workstations are dictionaries, atlases, telephone directories, and procedures manuals. Some of these are likely to be books, especially atlases and telephone directories. Others may be in computerized databases maintained by your company which you can **access** at your computer terminal. Additionally, your company may subscribe to services that allow you to access specific databases as needed. You will want to become familiar with all references available, so that you will know where to search when specific information is needed. You also may want to develop references to aid you in your specific tasks.

access: to bring to the screen

> *Beth, an assistant in the international division office, found that she was constantly responsible for obtaining foreign monies from the local bank. An executive would say merely: "Beth, I must go to Milan and Munich next week. I'd like you to get me $200 in small bills and some currency for both Italy and Germany." Beth did not know the monies of all the European countries where the international managers traveled. She set up her own reference. Note it in Illus. 3-6.*

	Monies of Europe	
Austria (schilling) Belgium (franc) Britain (pound) Denmark (krone) Finland (mark)	France (franc) Germany (mark) Greece (drachma) Italy (lira) Netherlands (guilder)	Norway (krone) Portugal (escudo) Spain (peseta) Sweden (krona) Switzerland (franc)

Illus. 3-6. Beth now has a ready reference for knowing the money a manager wants.

IMPROVING READING SKILLS

impede: block

High-level reading skill will allow you to be more productive in an office position than you would be otherwise. To improve your reading skill, you must first believe that you *can* improve. "I'm not a good reader and I never will be," reflects an attitude which will **impede** your progress. You must have a positive attitude. You must believe that you can and will improve your skill. Strive for a reading skill that is so natural you need not give detailed, deliberate attention to the skill itself. Instead, you can focus on what you want to achieve from your reading. The critical skills for high-level reading are comprehension, vocabulary, and speed.

Comprehension

Comprehension is the ability to understand what you have read. To comprehend is "to know." It implies a transfer from the printed page or the terminal screen to your *mental storage* (your memory). A simple example is looking for a number in the telephone directory and keeping it in mind until you can dial it. A more complex example is reading about a supplier's new product and being able to determine whether it appears superior to the product your company is now using. Following are some techniques you may find helpful as you strive to increase your reading comprehension:

1. Put aside anything else on your mind when you begin to read.
2. Before you begin, ask yourself this question: "What do I want to know when I have completed this reading?"
3. Scan what you are going to read to get an overview of the topic.
4. Attempt to summarize as you move from one paragraph to the next.
5. After reading several paragraphs, try to put ideas or procedures in **sequence**.
6. As you read the words, attempt to draw mental pictures.
7. After reading the material, determine if you have learned what you have read. For example, if you have read instructions for processing a request for new equipment, see if you can outline those procedures without referring to the written version.

sequence: one thing following another in an orderly way

Vocabulary

A *vocabulary* is a stock of words. Having an extensive vocabulary means that you know the definitions of a large number of words. Words that are unfamiliar to you can be a barrier to your reading. There are techniques that can expand your vocabulary and help you to be an effective reader. Consider using some of these as you study the content of this book:

encounter: come upon

1. When you **encounter** an unfamiliar word, try to determine its meaning from the way it is used in the sentence. After you have a meaning you think is correct, check your dictionary. If you were right, you should have increased your confidence

inappropriate: not
suitable

in figuring out what words mean. If your meaning was **inappropriate**, try to conclude why you were not able to establish an appropriate meaning.

2. When you encounter an unfamiliar word, see if you can determine a meaning for part of the word. You see the word "rearrange," which is unfamiliar to you. You think of "re" and "arrange." You know from earlier experience that rekey means that you must do something again. You know the meaning of arrange. You then guess that "rearrange" means to put back in a new or different order. You check your dictionary and find that your guess was right.

3. While reading, have at hand a notepad and pencil to record words you don't know. Check the words on your list in a dictionary. As you read a definition, look back to the place where the word occurred. Determine from the context which definition is appropriate. *Context* refers to the parts of a sentence or paragraph around a word that can throw light on its meaning.

You may find a specialized vocabulary required in the office where you are employed. You will want to become acquainted with the specialized dictionary or other references that will help you to master that vocabulary.

Marge works in a busy software development office where terms such as bus, bugs, upgrade, and power user are common.

Speed

Another reading skill is speed. Problems with comprehension and/or with vocabulary can slow the rate at which you read. However, some people have good comprehension and extensive vocabulary, but read slowly. Some techniques to increase your rate of reading are:

deliberately: by
plan

1. Focus your attention on a whole paragraph. Tell yourself, "I want to read this paragraph as a single thought and to know what it says." By doing so, you are forcing yourself to break the habit of **deliberately** pausing at each word or each sentence. When you have finished reading the paragraph, try to summarize it in a sentence or two. If you realize that you have not grasped the meaning, read it once again as quickly as possible. Again, attempt to summarize it. You are likely to be successful on your second attempt.

passage: brief
portion of a written
work

2. Time your reading. Set a goal such as: "I will read this page, which has approximately 350 words, in 1 ½ minutes." Check to see if you reached your goal. If you did, try the same *passage* with a reduced time allowance.
3. Deliberately force yourself ahead as you read. Do not set a specific goal. Note the extent to which you return to your slower way of reading. Determine why you do not continue reading quickly.

READING AS A SINGLE PROCESS

compensated:
offset

The critical skills of comprehension, vocabulary, and speed were highlighted separately in this topic. However, when you are actually reading, these skills interact. In some cases, a weakness in one skill may be **compensated** for by strength in another. For example, you may comprehend well what you read. If you encounter an unfamiliar word, you figure out its meaning from your understanding of the rest of the sentence or paragraph. Or, you may read rapidly, but your comprehension is not good. By reading rapidly, you have time to reread the material to improve your comprehension. Ultimately, you want skill in all three areas.

You will read every day when you are working in an office. Now you have an opportunity to improve your skill so that reading will not be a barrier to your being a competent office employee.

QUESTIONS FOR REVIEW

1. Are reading skills established by the time you complete your elementary education? Explain.

2. Describe briefly the reading process.

3. Why should an office worker read a procedures manual after there has been a demonstration of the procedure to be used?

4. Which details in Illus. 3-2 do you think should be remembered by the office worker who received the memorandum?

5. What kind of information is generally provided in written form when new equipment is installed in an office?

6. What kind of information are you likely to find on forms used on the job?

7. Name two references an office worker is likely to find useful.

8. Describe one technique that you believe would help a person improve reading comprehension.

9. Describe a procedure that will aid you in adding words to your reading vocabulary.

10. Identify a technique that you believe would be effective in improving your reading speed.

MAKING DECISIONS

Mark has had reading problems throughout his school years. He knows he is a poor reader and will have to get a job where reading isn't important. At his part-time job in a small store, Mark is given oral instructions generally. Only occasionally does he have to read a memo. With some difficulty he does figure out what the memo states. Most days, though, he has no need to read anything.

Assume Mark considers you a trusted friend who will not reveal his problem. He says to you: "Do you agree with me. . . . Am I not realistic to forget about learning to read?" What would you say to your friend? How would you describe the components of good reading skill to him? What would you recommend that he do now?

What You Are To Do: Prepare a brief response to the questions raised.

EXTENDING YOUR ENGLISH COMPETENCIES

Read the following lines. Note that there are four errors in subject/verb agreement.

Employee communication were listed as one of the top priorities for good management according to corporate executives. Corporate executives, recently surveyed by Ralson Consultants, was in complete agreement about the importance of employee communications.

Based on the survey's findings, a human resources consultant recommend that efforts be made to improve the ability of supervisors to communicate on a one-to-one basis with employees.

The ability to communicate with employees on a one-to-one basis are even more important than ability to communicate to employees in groups.

What You Are To Do: Prepare a copy of these paragraphs, making the corrections required. Underscore your corrections.

APPLICATION ACTIVITIES

Activity 1

Assume that you are an office assistant in the human resources department. The manager of the department expects you to answer routine questions that are raised by employees in the company. Read the following information about vacations.

VACATIONS

Eligibility: All full-time, permanent employees are eligible for vacation time.

Vacation Length: Vacation time varies depending on years of service completed. The following vacation schedule is currently in effect:

Years of Service Completed	Vacation Length
1-4 years	10 days
5-9 years	15 days
10-15 years	20 days
16 or more years	25 days

Vacation Period: An employee may schedule vacation time during the calendar year with the prior approval of the supervisor. All vacation time must be taken during the calendar year. Unused vacation may not be accumulated and, therefore, will be forfeited at the end of the year. Exceptions are made in regard to accumulating vacation time in those cases where a department manager requests that an employee postpone vacation time until the following calendar year.

The year in which an employee is eligible for a longer vacation is the calendar year in which the relevant anniversary occurs. For example, an employee is entitled to 15 days of vacation during the calendar year in which the fifth anniversary of service occurs, without regard to the actual anniversary date.

Use of Vacation Time: All employees are encouraged to take at one time the full vacation period to which they are entitled. There is evidence that taking only a day or two of vacation at a time does not maximize the benefits to the employee of time away from work. When a half day of vacation is taken, the employee is to work 3 3/4 hours that day.

Word processing
equipment can be used
to complete this activity.

What You Are To Do: Assume that four employees in the company have called you with the following questions. Write out exactly what you would say in response to each question.

A. "I will not complete my fifth year of service until June 12. Does this mean that I cannot take the full 15 days of vacation until after June 12?"

B. "If my supervisor approves, may I take my 10 days' vacation by working only 4 days a week for 10 weeks during the summer months of June, July, and August?"

C. "I've worked here for only two years and I would like to take a long vacation next year. Would it be possible to postpone this year's vacation to next year? I would like to have 20 days for a trip to England and France."

D. "I want to take five half-day vacations the week of June 14. May I leave the office at 12 that week?"

Activity 2

Assume that you are to determine the appropriate shipping charges for packages to be sent to customers. The company for whom you are working manufactures a variety of office supplies. You have already weighed each of the following 12 packages listed on page 85.

What You Are To Do:
A. Prepare a copy of the information for the 12 packages (shown on page 85) or use the form provided in *Information Processing Activities.*

B. Use the following chart to determine the shipping and packing charge for each package. (Two-letter state abbreviations are shown in Reference Section E.) If the actual weight of the package is not an exact number of pounds, use the charge for the next higher weight. (If, for example, the package weighs 8 1/4 lbs., you would use the charge for 9 lbs.)

Package Number	Destination	Weight	Charge
1	Connecticut	8 lbs.	_____
2	Oklahoma	4 lbs.	_____
3	West Virginia	12 lbs.	_____
4	Nebraska	8 1/4 lbs.	_____
5	Kansas	11 lbs.	_____
6	Pennsylvania	9 lbs.	_____
7	Maine	5 1/2 lbs.	_____
8	Vermont	14 lbs.	_____
9	Oregon	10 1/2 lbs.	_____
10	Utah	56 lbs.	_____
11	California	10 lbs.	_____
12	Kentucky	5 lbs.	_____

Insured Shipping & Packing Charges

Find your state at right. / Shipping Weight	ME MA NH RI VT	CT NY	DE MD NJ PA VA DC WV	IL IN KY MI NC OH SC TN	AL AK FL GA IA MN MS MO WI	CO KS LA MT NE ND OK SD TX WY	AZ CA ID NV NM OR UT WA
1 lb.	$1.95	$2.04	$2.17	$2.36	$2.53	$2.71	$2.96
2 lb.	2.07	2.31	2.53	2.78	3.09	3.40	3.69
3 lb.	2.21	2.45	2.70	3.03	3.44	3.79	4.15
4 lb.	2.33	2.63	2.91	3.27	3.77	4.24	4.64
5 lb.	2.45	2.76	3.06	3.51	4.06	4.63	5.11
6 lb.	2.60	2.93	3.27	3.76	4.39	5.04	5.64
7 lb.	2.69	3.05	3.45	4.01	4.71	5.41	6.11
8 lb.	2.79	3.24	3.63	4.25	5.07	5.85	6.59
9 lb.	2.93	3.36	3.80	4.49	5.38	6.26	7.08
10 lb.	3.05	3.50	4.01	4.71	5.70	6.67	7.58
11 lb.	3.20	3.64	4.17	4.98	6.02	7.05	8.06
12 lb.	3.31	3.79	4.38	5.23	6.35	7.46	8.60
13 lb.	3.43	3.92	4.59	5.47	6.69	7.89	9.03
14 lb.	3.53	4.06	4.73	5.68	7.01	8.30	9.50
15 lb.	3.68	4.23	4.95	5.92	7.32	8.67	10.03
For each add'l. lb.	.17	.19	.23	.28	.36	.44	.54

WRITING

When you have completed your study of this topic, you will be able to:

- describe types of writing required in the office

- write letters and memorandums that reflect the qualities of good business communications

- describe a procedure for planning and completing writing tasks

Office workers have many occasions when they must communicate with others in writing. Business writing is different from social writing. When you write a letter to a friend describing a recent trip or your life at school, you are free to write as you like. Your sentences may not be complete or they might be quite long. You may write about one matter very briefly but dwell for many paragraphs on another matter. You are likely to convey your personality in your writing. Your friend knows you and will understand what you are thinking and saying.

In the business office, the situation is quite different. You may be corresponding with persons whom you do not know and who do not know you. They cannot interpret what you mean if your thoughts are incomplete. Your message must convey the total meaning. Follow up is time-consuming and expensive.

Being able to put your thoughts in writing is one of the most valued skills in business today. This skill can be developed. Attention to the components of good writing and practice is what is required. You will have opportunities for both during your study of this textbook.

The levels of responsibility which workers assume depend on two things. One is the nature of the work of the office. The other is the manner in which the executive chooses to handle writing tasks. If you were to visit several offices, you would find that office employees have varying responsibility for preparing written communications. You would find employees:

drafts: tentative
copies for review

- summarizing messages, reports, and letters
- preparing *drafts* of communications for executive review
- suggesting changes and editing
- composing communications, revising them, and then preparing final copy

Summarizing Messages, Reports, and Letters

Office workers at times must write summaries of various kinds. For example, a customer may call about a matter that requires a response from a manager who is out of the office. The office worker who talks with the customer must be able to prepare a summary which states clearly what the customer needs. Only then can the manager respond appropriately. There also may be times when a manager asks an office worker to *summarize* a letter, a report, or an article from a periodical.

summarize: state
key points in brief form

In order to do a good job at summarizing, you must listen or read attentively. Next, identify the critical points. Then write your summary as concisely as possible.

> Diana works for a major food processing company as an assistant to the president's secretary. A caller was interested in learning if the company had any copies of speeches delivered by the company founder. Diana realized she did not have the answer to the caller's question. Terry, the staff person who could be helpful, was at a meeting. Diana asked the caller several questions, including: "May the speech be on any topic?" "Why do you want such a speech?" She recorded the name, address, and telephone number of the caller, as well as notes related to the inquiry. She left a memo for Terry, who had all the information needed to respond promptly.

Preparing Drafts

Often a secretary or other office employee sees the incoming mail before it is placed on the executive's desk. In some offices, the secretary prepares a draft of a response to any letter concern-

Illus. 3-7. Office workers often assist in editing rough drafts of correspondence and reports.

ing matters that the secretary knows well. The draft, together with the letter it answers, is given to the executive for review. The executive reads the incoming letter and the suggested response. The secretary's draft may need little change to be modified quickly. Final copies then are prepared.

Editing and Suggesting Changes

Office assistants are frequently asked to review executives' written communications. Some executives like for their assistants to act as editors. An **editor** is a person who reviews what has been written and suggests changes in wording, organization, and content. Office assistants with editorial responsibility read carefully the drafts prepared by the executive. They determine whether the message will communicate clearly what the executive had in mind. Drafts which are responses to incoming letters are checked against the letters to be sure the responses are complete.

Note the draft prepared by a human resources manager shown in Illus. 3-8. Then read the revision suggested by an office assistant. What do you think are the improvements reflected in the assistant's revision?

Overtime Hours

At certain periods of the year various departments find it necessary to work overtime, and it is a condition of employment that employees work overtime if at all possible when it is requested of them. Department managers will notify those employees who are expected to perform overtime work. Employees should try to arrange personal matters so that they can work overtime when work in the department requires it. Overtime pay rules are specified in the next section.

OVERTIME HOURS

The work of most departments requires overtime hours at certain periods of the year. The willingness of employees to work overtime is appreciated. Department managers schedule overtime as far in advance as possible. However, there are times when the need to work beyond the regular hours cannot be determined in advance. Employees who can arrange personal matters so that they are able to work overtime hours will be contributing a great deal to the effective functioning of their departments. Overtime pay rates are specified in the next section.

Illus. 3-8. Handwritten draft and revision of policy statement regarding overtime hours. Why is the revision better?

Mrs. Richards, manager of human resources, discussed the role of her secretary in these words: "I must send many memorandums to our employees. These memos discuss personnel policies about vacations, overtime hours, pensions, and health insurance provisions. They must be written carefully so that no misunderstandings develop. The secretary reads what I write and then marks improvements on the copy. We review the suggestions before final copies are prepared."

Composing Messages

You one day may have to write letters and memorandums on your own. In some instances, what you prepare will be signed by the executive. In other cases, you will sign memos and letters with your own name. When you are doing the entire job of composing and signing letters, you serve as your own editor. You will want to be sure to reread carefully what you have written. If you feel it is not adequate, you may need to rewrite your message. Letters which office assistants often prepare on their own include the following:

- letters acknowledging the receipt of reports and other materials
- letters making inquiry about a particular good or service
- letters in which goods are ordered

The secretary to the director of training commented on her writing tasks in these words: "I often write letters on my own. The director may say, 'Please write to the publisher of this book to find out if we can get large quantities at special prices.' or 'Would you find out if the seminar leader we used last month will be available for another seminar next month.' The director expects me to write such letters, sign them, and send them out. As soon as I receive a response, I give it to the director."

BUSINESS WRITING HAS A SPECIFIC PURPOSE

Most activity in business is *purpose-driven.* This means that there is a practical reason for the activity. Therefore, each written communication has a purpose. Among the most common purposes are those discussed in the following paragraphs.

Seeking Specific Information

There are times when someone in the organization needs specific information in order to make a decision. Information is needed from outsiders who can provide the organization with equipment, supplies, and professional services. Also, there are times when messages are exchanged within the organization for the purpose of seeking information. Illus. 3-9 is a memorandum that seeks information from sales representatives throughout the company.

Providing Specific Information

Many written communications provide specific information. A department within an organization often provides information to other units. Customers and prospective customers make numerous inquiries that generally get prompt, courteous attention.

Laynor Pharmaceutical Corporation   **MEMORANDUM**

TO: All Sales Representatives

FROM: Gary H. Jenkins, Vice President, Sales

DATE: October 5, 19--

SUBJECT: Program for Spring Regional Meetings

The planning committee here at the home office wants to organize a program for the regional meetings that is of value to you. There are several topics that must be included in the program. But there also is time to deal with matters of primary concern to you. You will see on the attached tentative program that there are about nine hours of time yet to be scheduled.

Please give me your suggestions for topics and speakers on the attached suggestion sheet. Return the sheet to me no later than November 1. Thank you.

rp

Attachments

Illus. 3-9. Memorandum requesting information.

Following Up Oral Discussions

Much interaction among business people is oral. Discussions may be in person, by telephone, or by teleconferences. Sometimes a written communication is necessary as a follow-up to an oral discussion. The written communication may make sure everyone understood the topic in the same way, or it may serve as a summary of what happened. A written communication is a useful reference later.

The advertising director asked her secretary to attend a meeting with the company's new advertising agency representatives. The secretary's task was to record the key points of the plans developed during the meeting. After the meeting, the secretary prepared a copy of the notes for the director. The director reviewed and edited the notes. She also prepared a letter to be sent with the notes to the advertising agency representatives.

Illus. 3-10. The office assistant must record the key points of this meeting.

Sending Messages to Customers and Prospective Customers

Often, written communications encourage greater demand for the products and services of businesses. Letters, brochures, fliers, and catalogs are used to announce new products, special

delinquent: late

sales, extended hours of service, and new methods for making payments. Letters are also needed to remind **delinquent** customers of amounts still due and of the actions that will be taken if payment is not forthcoming. Office workers often assist in the preparation of such communications. The letter below is being sent to managers who are likely to have an interest in the offer.

Illus. 3-11. Why would Ms. Walters read this letter with interest?

LANHAN PRODUCTIVITY IMPROVEMENT ASSOCIATES
4679 Fourth Avenue
Pittsburgh, PA 15283-3245

October 14, 19--

Ms. Lori Walters, Director
Purchasing Department
Goodlad Manufacturing Company
367 Westport Road
Westport, CT 07079-1467

Dear Ms. Walters

Do you have purchasing assistants and other support staff that you wish were more knowledgeable about the basics of purchasing? We believe our one-day seminar is a program you will want to consider.

Our seminar has been helpful to thousands of employees. Attention is given to a range of topics including:

. mastering the purchasing function
. setting up an organized way of working
. working more wisely and effectively with vendors
. becoming a more valuable associate to your employer

The enclosed brochure gives details about locations, dates and costs, as well as registration procedures.

We look forward to seeing some of your staff at our seminar.

Sincerely yours

Jeannie Brown

Jeannie Brown, Manager
Continuing Education Programs

nh

Enclosure

Illus. 3-12. An office worker is assisting a manager in preparing a brochure.

CHARACTERIS-TICS OF EFFECTIVE WRITING

potential: to be realized in the future

Effective business writing reflects certain characteristics which you will want to understand well. Then you will know how to evaluate your own writing and its *potential* effectiveness in communicating your messages.

Clearness

Stating what you wish to communicate is what **clearness** means. To have a clear message, you must know *why* you want to communicate, *what* you want to communicate, and *who* your recipient will be. A clear message is *logically* arranged. This means the information is in an order that is easy to understand.

A clear message eliminates the need for requests for additional information. A clear letter or memorandum allows the receiver to respond immediately. The person reading a clear message need not ask when finished: "What is the meaning of this message?"

The manager of computer services in a medium-sized firm learned of a book which would be interesting to the rest of the staff. Study the following for clarity.

NOT CLEAR: *I noted in a recent copy of BUSINESS TODAY that you publish a handbook on WISE USE OF SOFTWARE PACKAGES. I would like a copy. What is the price of the book?*

> Questions raised:
> Does the writer of the letter want a copy of the book? Or, does he/she just want to know the price and will determine later whether the book will be purchased?

> CLEAR:
> In the September issue of BUSINESS TODAY, I noted that you publish a handbook entitled WISE USE OF SOFTWARE PACKAGES. Please send me one copy of the handbook and enclose an invoice. Upon receipt of the book and invoice, I shall send you a remittance.

Conciseness

Stating what you want to communicate in the fewest and most direct words possible is the meaning of **conciseness**. An efficient message gets right to the point. Conciseness in written communications means that the recipient will waste no time in reading words and thoughts that add nothing to understanding the message.

> NOT CONCISE:
> We have your letter of October 15 in which you indicate that our letter of October 4 did not include the price list as we promised. We are not sure what happened in our office. We have enclosed the price list with this note.

> CONCISE:
> Enclosed is the price list we **inadvertently** omitted from our earlier letter to you. We regret any inconvenience the omission may have caused you.

inadvertently:
accidently

Illus. 3-13.

Courteousness

A written communication reflects **courteousness** when it conforms to the expected civil, considerate behavior of the business world. Expressions such as "Thank you," "Please," and "You are welcome" are commonly used in business correspondence. As you know, most letters include a salutation and a complimentary close which are evidence of courtesy. The "you approach" is recommended for letters and memorandums. When you write from the point of view of the recipient—the "you approach"—you are likely to prepare a courteous message. Courteous letters and memorandums encourage good relations and cooperation with the recipient. Discourteous letters and memorandums create strained relations and ill will on the part of the recipient.

DISCOURTEOUS: *You write that you want a dozen packages of our file folders. However, you should know that we manufacture folders in two dozen sizes, five styles, and twelve colors.*

We have no idea what you want. You must be more specific. Read the enclosed form carefully, then fill it in precisely. When we receive the form, we will send you the file folders.

COURTEOUS: *Thank you for your Order No. 4356. However, before we can forward the file folders to you, we need to know the quantity, size, and color you desire.*

Enclosed is a brochure and order form. Please note that you are to record on the order form the quantity, size, and color for each type of file folder you want.

Your order will receive our immediate attention upon receipt of your order form.

Completeness

Completeness means providing all the information necessary for the message to be understood. Think of the recipient by asking yourself: "Are we answering all the questions the recipient might raise about this matter?"

NOT COMPLETE: *We will meet on Wednesday, November 3, at 9:00 a.m. at the Astor Hotel.*

The recipient wonders: *How long is the meeting?*
In what room will the meeting be held?
Who will be there?

COMPLETE: *Our Community Service Committee meeting will be held on November 3 from 9:00 a.m. to 3:00 p.m. at the Astor Hotel. We will meet in the Franklin Room where we will also have lunch from 12 noon to 1:00 p.m.*

Correctness

Correctness means that the information in a document is accurate and up to date. The details should be verified before the message is prepared in final form. You should not assume, for example, that a price in effect when you last wrote a letter is still in effect. Changes are common in business, and any correspondence should carry current information.

Incorrect information causes many problems in business. Further correspondence often is required; the goodwill of customers is lost; and, at times, customers discontinue their association with the organization.

Part of Kathy's job was to answer inquiries about products and prices. A prospective customer wanted a price quotation for a large volume of an item no longer in demand but still in stock. Kathy quoted a figure from an old price list. The prospective customer compared this price with those from other competitors and found Kathy's to be far out of line. What should Kathy have done before answering the inquiry?

She should have questioned the price since it was not a recent one. She should have questioned the price for a large volume.

In addition to correct content, a message should have no grammar, punctuation, or capitalization errors. Furthermore, all words should be spelled correctly. In the next section, you will have a review of the English skills that are basic to good business writing.

ENGLISH SKILLS FOR BUSINESS WRITING

Your business writing should reveal a good command of the English language. Sentences should be complete. Grammar should be proper. Punctuation and capitalization should follow standard rules. Words should be spelled correctly. You have studied these components many times during your school years.

You will now want to focus on enhancing your understanding of the rules and applying them as you complete assignments in this course.

Use Proper Grammar

cultivate: develop

Almost everyone is likely to have some uncertainties about composing a letter or memorandum. You should **cultivate** the habit of checking a reference manual if you have even a slight doubt about what is correct.

Can you identify the grammar errors in the following sentences? Can you explain what rule or rules have been disregarded? Refer to a reference manual, if necessary.

1. *A article about our company appears in today's paper.*
2. *Miss Johnson thinks that Ruth and me are not doing this project as quickly as we should.*
3. *Sally is the best typist of the two.*
4. *Do you think this job should be divided between Patricia and I?*
5. *The range of seminars are far more than the personnel director imagined.*

Follow Rules of Punctuation

You know the basic rules of punctuation. As you write or edit business documents, you will want to consider whether your marks of punctuation add to the clarity of your message. Reference Section B is a valuable source for answering many questions you may have. Can you determine where punctuation marks are needed in the following sentences? Refer to Reference Section B.

1. *Will Dr Hanley be able to meet with us today*
2. *Two years ago the ABC Company's decision was to make a considerable investment in computers*
3. *Documents are needed from our offices in Chicago Indianapolis and Kansas City*
4. *Customers always get fast accurate information*
5. *As you know the Roland Company has installed an automated tracking system*

distracting: shifting attention away from primary focus

indifference: lack of interest

Spell Words Correctly

Misspelled words are **distracting** to the recipient of your message. Such words convey an impression of sloppiness and **indifference** to quality. Your message will not be persuasive or believable if there are spelling errors. You will want to have a dictionary at hand to check the correct spelling of any word about which you are uncertain.

Can you find the spelling errors in the following lines? Refer to a dictionary if necessary. Few communications will ever have so many errors among so few words! What would be your impression of the company that sent you a letter with so many errors?

Under seperete cover we are sending you, with our complements, a copy of our latest report. We believe you will be especially interested in the questionaire used as the bases of the report. The report underscores our commitment to quality products. We will be happy to recieve your comments.

PROCEDURES FOR WRITING TASKS

Writing tasks must be managed wisely if they are to be completed successfully and on schedule. The following steps will prove useful to you whenever you are given a writing assignment:

1. Identify the reason for the written communication.
2. Secure all the information required for the message.
3. Compose a draft of your message.
   A. You may want to outline what you plan to say.
   B. You may want to key your message directly at your keyboard using your outline as a guide.
4. Review your message; make corrections, if any.
5. If required, submit your draft to your supervisor or manager for approval.
   A. If you make a limited number of changes to your initial draft, you may submit it without preparing another draft.

Illus. 3-14. An office worker's notes to guide the composition of a letter. Note how the points were reordered.

LETTER TO T.J. OLSEN COMPANY

1. *Searching for source for hand painted plates*
4. 2. *Price cannot exceed $6.50 per plate*
5. 3. *Quantity required: 1,000*
6. 4. *Can company meet delivery in February?*
2. 5. *Designs available*
3. 6. *Can we provide design? Cost?*

    B. If you made a number of changes to your initial draft, you should prepare a revised draft.
6. Prepare a final copy of your communication.
7. Proofread carefully.
8. Sign and prepare the communication for distribution or leave it for the person who is to sign the communication.

You will have numerous occasions during your study of office procedures to develop your writing skills. Use the preceding steps as a guide.

All written communications do not need to be of the same quality. For example, a memorandum to the manager of the stockroom, whom you know personally, might be written informally at a computer or typewriter. But a letter to thousands of customers might be rewritten several times before it is exactly as it should be.

With practice, you will gain sufficient facility to prepare simple messages the first time you try. Also, you will gain a sense of what a good message should be and how to prepare one.

QUESTIONS FOR REVIEW

1. How does a business letter differ from a personal letter?

2. Give an example of a situation where an office worker may need to write a summary for a manager.

3. What is the information sought by the writer of the memorandum shown in Illus. 3-9 on page 91?

4. Why might a written communication follow an oral discussion?

5. Identify three reasons why a company might send letters to customers.

6. What questions will guide you to be sure you compose a clear message?

7. Why is a concise letter considered efficient?

8. What is the meaning of the "you approach" in relation to the task of writing messages?

9. What English skills are reflected in a well-written letter?

10. What procedures should you follow in preparing a draft of a message for an executive for whom you work?

INTERACTING WITH OTHERS

Warren works as an assistant to the employment director for office workers in the office of human resources. He likes his job. He believes he has learned a great deal about how such an office should function, even though he has been at work for only three months. Warren is unhappy about one particular matter. The employment director interviews a number of beginning office workers each week; she tells each of them that she will write to them within two weeks. However, Warren spends much time on the telephone with job applicants who say, for example: "I had an interview three weeks ago; I have heard nothing from your company." Warren understands how the caller feels. He thinks there should be the follow-up promised to the applicants. Warren tells you about this situation. He asks you: "What do you think I should do about this matter?"

What You Are To Do: Prepare a list of suggestions for Warren to consider.

EXTENDING YOUR MATH COMPETENCIES

Assume that you work in the advertising department of a small garden book club. A campaign to enroll new members is undertaken through a letter sent directly to potential subscribers, classified by geographic area. You have accumulated the information about the three campaigns shown on page 102.

What You Are To Do:
1. Determine the number of letters sent for each campaign; determine the total responses for each of the three campaigns.
2. Determine the percentage return for each region and each campaign. (Example, the percentage return for Western for Campaign 1, 310 ÷ 4,000 = 7.75 percent)
3. Determine the percentage return for the total of each campaign.
4. Can you think of reasons why the response rate for the third campaign was the highest among the three?

Region	Campaign 1 February		Campaign 2 June		Campaign 3 September	
	Letters sent	Responses	Letters sent	Responses	Letters sent	Responses
Western	4,000	310	3,000	288	3,000	425
Central	2,500	180	2,000	172	2,000	269
Southern	8,000	706	7,000	687	7,000	891
Eastern	7,000	510	6,700	598	6,000	741

APPLICATION ACTIVITIES

Activity 1

Word processing
equipment can be used
to complete this activity.

Assume you are an office assistant to Peter Zinn, manager of Information Services for Malone Insurers, Inc. As Mr. Zinn was leaving the office for a meeting, he handed you several sheets of paper and said to you: "Here is a note and three listings of anticipated expenses. Please write a memo to Marge Ricardi, general manager—there are some instructions in my note. I'll initial the memo when I get back. Thanks."

What You Are To Do: Prepare the covering memorandum, following instructions given in Mr. Zinn's note on page 103. Use the memorandum provided in *Information Processing Activities* or plain paper.

Activity 2

You are an office assistant to Louis E. Valdez, director of promotion for Ridge Office Machines, 45 Ridge Road, Mansfield, OH 44904-6332.

Word processing
equipment can be used
to complete this activity.

What You Are To Do: On a plain sheet of paper, draft a letter of inquiry to Modern Video Equipment, 3912 De La Ra Road, Palo Alto, CA 94302-4567. You are to request information about small portable video screens that are appropriate for use in relatively small exhibit booths at trade conferences and shows. Then key the final document on letterhead in *Information Processing Activities* or plain paper.

NOTES FROM . . . . Peter Zinn

Anticipated expenses for three conferences are attached.

*Network Management Conference in Munich, Germany March 21-28
Computer-Based Training Conference in New Orleans, LA May 12-15
Management Information Seminar in New York, NY, September 23-26*

Please prepare covering memo for my signature — to Marge Ricardi, general manager

Tell her I'll look forward to early approval for these meetings which I want to attend next year

*Thanks
PZ*

SPEAKING AND LISTENING

When you have completed your study of this topic, you will be able to:

- describe what successful speaking is
- explain techniques that aid in active listening

The tempo of business activity would be drastically slowed if there were no oral communication. Executives know the value of oral communication in meeting the demands of business life. They provide telephones and paging equipment for employees. They expect employees to talk face-to-face about common tasks and plans for jobs to be done. Executives depend on employees who can communicate easily and effectively with each other and with outsiders.

Many problems in offices can be traced to ineffective oral communication. As you have learned, much of what happens in an office requires the cooperation of several people. You can imagine what happens when an important link in the activity is misunderstood because of incomplete or inefficient oral communication.

An executive gave an assistant oral instructions for a job. The assistant thought she had all the information required. The executive left the office for a meeting in another town. As the assistant began to do the job, she realized that there were questions about the procedures to be used. The assistant had to put the job aside until the executive returned. However, the executive assumed the job would be completed immediately.

What happened in the meeting between the executive and the office assistant that resulted in inadequate instructions? Did the executive overlook some key points? Did the assistant fail to ask appropriate questions? Did the assistant fail to listen to all the details?

UNIQUENESS OF ORAL BUSINESS COMMUNICATION

parallel: similar; comparable

You may be asking: "Aren't speaking and listening at work exactly the same as speaking and listening at home? or with my friends? or with my teacher and classmates in school? Aren't there situations **parallel** to the one described in the preceding illustration at home and school?" A quick answer to both questions is: "Yes and no." It is true that you *are* communicating orally at home and at school. It is true that misunderstandings arise in your personal communications. However, the style and rules of speaking in business are not as important in your personal communications. Oral communication in business is expected to be efficient and effective. Your family and friends probably will not impose such demands on your oral communications with them—at least, not all the time!

Personal situation:

A friend calls you on Wednesday evening to invite you to a party on Saturday night. You hesitate to give a firm answer because of some uncertainty about your Saturday plans. You and your friend talk about a number of common interests and you even talk about your hesitancy to respond to the invitation. Your friend tells you the party is informal and you can make a decision as late as Saturday afternoon.

Business situation:

You serve as a member of a company-wide employees' council. The chairperson calls to ask you to represent the council at an executive committee meeting scheduled for the following Thursday at 3:00 p.m. The chairperson is at work and expects you to look at your calendar, quickly think about your Thursday afternoon work schedule, and respond either that you can or cannot go. The person arranging the meeting

Illus. 3-15. Why would the person talking wonder about the interest of the listener? (left)

Illus. 3-16. New employees listen attentively as a supervisor explains how to use the company's computer terminals. (right)

needs to know who will be present so a list of those expected to attend can be prepared. You cannot postpone your decision. The chairperson would not expect you to spend several minutes discussing why you are not sure what your response should be.

Oral communication in business is important to the smooth functioning of every department. You will find the opportunities to personally interact with your coworkers one of the most satisfying **aspects** of your job—if you are confident of your skills. Two important communication skills are the ability to speak with ease and the ability to listen actively.

aspects: features

SPEAKING EFFECTIVELY

There are commonly accepted characteristics of successful speech in the business environment. You will want to apply these as you study and work with your teacher and classmates in your office procedures class.

Be Interested in Communicating

Being indifferent, or not caring, destroys effective communications. Have you ever listened to a speaker who seemed to be reading a speech with no understanding of the words? The speaker seemed to have no involvement with the content. Did you enjoy what you heard? Did you learn much? Probably not. On the other hand, you may have seen a demonstration of a new office machine. The demonstrator was so involved in what she or he said that your interest was captured and held throughout the demonstration. The interest of the demonstrator in communicating with the listeners **enhanced** the effectiveness of the experience for those present.

enhanced: raised; improved

When Miss Williams asked Beth, an office assistant with six months' experience, to introduce a new assistant to the staff and acquaint the new employee with the facilities, she got an immediate "Yes." Beth recalled how much she appreciated the thoughtful, careful introduction she had received. She wanted to communicate equally well with the new assistant. Would you guess that she was successful?

Speak Clearly

You will not be able to communicate if the listener is unable to hear your words exactly. Generally, you can improve the quality of your voice by deliberately speaking in a **modulated** tone which

modulated: adjusted to the situation

is pleasant and proper to the listener. If you think about the setting in which you are speaking, you then will shift from a too loud or too soft tone to one that is appropriate. When you are talking with a coworker at your workstation, for example, you do not speak so loudly that you can be heard by everyone else in the office.

Speaking clearly requires that you say each word carefully. This is referred to as *proper enunciation*. When you enunciate words properly, your listener grasps them correctly. You will find it interesting to listen for examples of poor enunciation. Two common errors are running words together and failing to sound each syllable of a word. Following are some common examples of poor enunciation:

didya	for *did you*
gimme	for *give me*
whatchagonna	for *what are you going to*
uster	for *used to*
lemme	for *let me*

Use Standard Language

Standard language is that language taught in formal English courses in elementary and secondary schools. It is the language explained in current dictionaries. Business communications should be in standard language so that your coworkers will be sure to understand you. The extent of oral communication among business people in different parts of the world reinforces the importance of using standard language. Persons who learn English as a second language while in their own country's secondary schools, for example, know only the language of the textbooks. You can imagine the difficulty they would have if American office employees used colloquialisms and slang in their conversations with them.

Colloquialisms are informal words and phrases used among persons who know each other well or among persons from a specific geographic area of the country. You will find some colloquialisms in offices among employees who know each other. Some commonly used colloquialisms are:

finish off	for *complete*
get out of line	for *fail to conform*
head up	for *serve as chairperson*
touch bases	for *discuss a matter*

Slang expressions are inappropriate in the office. You can imagine that a term such as "Awesome!" is not a standard way of communicating a thought.

Remember that slang expressions are extremely informal and often have hard-to-discover meanings unless you belong to a particular group with which the term has gained popularity.

Express Your Ideas Concisely

Thinking must precede speaking. In oral communications you must think about what someone has said to you, as well as about what you want to communicate. Much time is saved in communicating if there is thought before expression. Try asking a mental question such as, "What is it that I really need to say to communicate my meaning?" You are not likely to be misunderstood if you think about what you are saying.

> The supervisor asked an assistant: "What do you still have to complete for the Thompson report I gave you Monday?" Without a pause for thought, the assistant responded: "Not much."
>
> If the assistant had given thought to the question, the response might have been: "I only have to keyboard the conclusions, the three short appendices, and the bibliography. Then I will print the entire document." Which of the two responses do you believe the supervisor would consider more satisfactory?

Consider Your Audience

Whether you are talking with one person, several people in a small group, or with a large group, you want to consider the interests and needs of your listeners. Talking with a single person or a small group usually permits you to be more informal than you could be in a large group. You want to consider: (a) what your listener or listeners want to know; (b) what they might already know; and (c) how what you are saying can be related to their experiences. You also want to be sensitive to how listeners are reacting to what you are saying. Are they looking away with lack of interest? Do they seem impatient with the length of your comments? Are they perplexed by lack of understanding? Do they seem eager to listen? Are they seemingly ready to move away from you?

Illus. 3-17. Different audiences require different types of communication. How would communication techniques differ in these two settings?

When Karen arrived at the office one Monday morning, she encountered the manager of the department, whom she sees infrequently. The manager asked Karen: "How was your weekend?"

INAPPROPRIATE
RESPONSE:

Karen responded with a detailed account of her social activities from Friday to Sunday night, as she might do with a close personal friend in afterwork hours.

APPROPRIATE
RESPONSE:

The manager was asking a quick, friendly question. Karen's response could have been as brief as the question. Karen could have said: "I had a wonderful weekend. I hope yours was pleasant, too."

Be Aware of Nonverbal Communication

When you are talking with coworkers in person, more than your actual words are a part of your communications. Facial expressions, gestures of hands and arms, posture, and various movements of the total body also communicate.

Two office assistants are talking to one another. One is glancing at the clock frequently. The other appears to be unaware of this behavior and continues talking. What do you think the constant looking at the clock could mean?

An office assistant goes to the workstation of another employee who immediately stops working and makes eye contact with the office assistant. What do you think this immediate attention to the office assistant might mean?

You can never be sure that you are interpreting nonverbal behavior accurately. Some interpretations are not appropriate in particular cases. For example, glancing at a clock is considered evidence that a person is eager to get away. However, it might mean that the person wants to stay as long as possible before going to a scheduled appointment. Making immediate eye contact with someone who comes to the workstation may indicate a genuine interest in being helpful, or it might reveal pleasure in having an interruption from the work under way!

Facial expressions, such as a smile, can mean understanding or support for what is being said. On the other hand, a frown may convey a lack of understanding or support. Drumming the desk with the fingers often conveys uncertainty about the solution being proposed. Sitting straight while listening is interpreted to mean interest. Sitting slumped in a chair is interpreted to mean a lack of interest.

Illus. 3-18. What nonverbal communication is taking place in these two instances? What attitudes are being expressed?

Be aware of the nonverbal behavior that accompanies what you say. Make sure it agrees with the words you are using. You want your nonverbal behavior to reinforce what you are saying. You do not want to confuse your listener by saying one thing and having your nonverbal behavior communicate a totally different message.

Be Interested in the Listener's Response

feedback: response from the receiver of a message

Allow time for interaction. You will not be communicating effectively if you do not give your listeners a chance to respond. One of the major advantages of oral communication is that there can be immediate **feedback**. When you talk with others, you should be interested in getting questions, comments, and reactions to what you are saying. Actually, a person who is considered skillful in oral communication is a good listener.

UNFORTUNATE SITUATION:	*The manager of customer services called a meeting of the staff members. Without any introductory comments, the manager stated that everyone must work faster and be more productive. The manager implied that the staff were deliberately working too slowly and were not interested in working as rapidly as they could. When the announcement was completed, the manager said everyone could go back to work.*
WHAT MIGHT HAVE BEEN DONE:	*The manager should have had some introductory remarks about the purpose of the meeting. Furthermore, the problems that make it necessary to encourage higher productivity should have been discussed. There should have been time for questions and reactions. The manager could have asked the staff for suggestions to improve productivity.*

LISTENING ACTIVELY

Listening is the process of mentally participating in a conversation, a meeting, or a lecture for the purpose of comprehending what the speaker is communicating. Listening is a powerful and complex business skill. Can you imagine the breakdown in the functioning of offices if employees did not listen to each other?

in basket: desk tray for jobs to be done

*An executive asked an assistant to complete a report before a meeting at 3 p.m. the next day. The assistant was not listening and put the report at the bottom of his **in basket**. At 3 p.m. the next day, the report had not yet been started.*

The executive explained to the office assistant who in the company could provide information needed for a report. The office assistant thought he knew the person, so he didn't listen to the explanation. When he began the task, he realized that he didn't know who had the information. The executive was away from the office and the assistant had to postpone the task.

You will want to listen properly on the job. Consider the points discussed in the following paragraphs as you work to improve your listening skill.

Be Willing to Learn

optimize: to reach an effective level

Hearing, which is a physical sensation, is very different from listening. To be sure you are listening, and not merely hearing, will require the proper mental attitude. An open, confident, positive attitude will help you to **optimize** your listening power. If you are apprehensive, for example, of the person who is attempting to explain something to you, you may be unable to understand fully what is being said. Or, if you have an attitude that there is nothing further you need to know to do the job, your mind will be closed to the explanations of your supervisor. Or, if you believe that nothing useful or worthwhile can result from what you hear, you probably will have established a barrier to listening.

Focus Attention

When you deliberately focus your attention on every thought communicated by the speaker, you reinforce what you are hearing. You also ease the transfer of the speaker's thoughts to your own mental process. This technique is a form of repetition and can be effective if pursued seriously.

Ted was busily keyboarding a complex report when he was called to a meeting in his employer's office. Ted's mind was still on the report, but he knew that what his employer was telling him was important. He deliberately thought: "I must put that report aside; I must listen to what Mr. Lanz is saying to me."

Your ability to take command of yourself—to discipline yourself—will determine whether you will be successful in focusing your attention on the speaker. Focusing attention results from shifting to the back of your mind any matter that is ***preoccupying*** your thoughts. This can be done, but it may be difficult. Focusing your eyes on the speaker and refusing to move them may help you in your efforts to listen attentively.

preoccupying:
absorbing

Ted, a new employee in the sales department, found it helpful to echo mentally each statement his supervisor, Mr. Lanz, made.

Mentally Summarize

If you have some general understanding of the speaker's subject, you may be able to mentally structure an outline of the speaker's key points. For example, if you know that your supervisor gives you unexpected assignments, you may be able to set up a mental outline with the following sections: what is to be done? how long is it expected to take? and when must it be done? The as you listen to your supervisor, you can put what is said proper place in your mental outline.

Ted listened attentively to each sentence. He plac order in his mental outline. He had constructed th soon as he realized that Mr. Lanz wanted tc statistical report. His mental outline incl

What information is needed?
Where do I get the informa
How am I to organize
What must I get d
How much tir

Take No

Frequentl
cation in the
requirements
careful listening
strengthen your h

Because Mr. Lanz
found it useful to take n
him when he went into h

Illus. 3-19. You can improve your listening skills by giving attention to these points.

> ## TO LISTEN ACTIVELY, YOU MUST:
>
> - ● BE WILLING TO LEARN
> - ● FOCUS ATTENTION
> - ● MENTALLY SUMMARIZE
> - ● TAKE NOTES
> - ● ASK QUESTIONS

Ask Questions

You will find that the person talking with you is interested in your understanding clearly what is being presented. Therefore, in most cases, questions are welcomed. In a way, you are reinforcing that your listening skill was functioning properly when you raise questions. By listening carefully and raising questions, you can identify matters that were overlooked by the speaker. Your questions can also focus more clearly on the key points.

> When Mr. Lanz had completed his explanation, Ted realized that he was not sure what kind of preliminary report he was to present to Mr. Lanz. The following exchange took place:
>
> Ted: "Mr. Lanz, do you want me to organize the information I get into some type of chart or table?"
>
> Mr. Lanz: "Thank you, Ted, that's a good question. At this point, why don't you just get all the information, and then let's look it over together before we go any further."

The skills of speaking and listening are very closely related. When both skills are well developed, many problems with oral communication at work can be avoided.

There are frequent occasions at work when you must speak with others and when you must listen to what is being said. peed in accomplishing tasks and making changes in tasks or ns is dependent on many person-to-person interactions and hone conversations each day. Being responsive and atten- ill identify you as a competent employee.

QUESTIONS FOR REVIEW

1. How, in general, do oral communications in business differ from oral communications with your family and friends?

2. Why is interest in communicating considered an important aspect of effective speaking?

3. Why should an office employee modulate his or her voice in the office?

4. Why is standard language recommended for business communication?

5. Illustrate the meaning of "Think before you speak."

6. When you are speaking, whether to one person or several, why should you consider your audience?

7. Why should you be alert to nonverbal behavior when you are speaking with another person?

8. Explain what listening is.

9. Identify an attitude that is often a barrier to effective listening.

10. Identify two techniques that will help you improve your listening skill.

MAKING DECISIONS

Mrs. Aponte was called away to another executive's office. As she hurried by her administrative assistant's desk, she said: "I shall be in Jack Howe's office. I am expecting Henry Komuro in about 15 minutes. If I'm not back, please ask Mr. Komuro to wait for me." The assistant was busy preparing a report and ignored what Mrs. Aponte said.

When Mr. Komuro did arrive, Mrs. Aponte was not yet back from her meeting. The administrative assistant did not know what to suggest. She said: "My, I'm not sure where Mrs. Aponte is. She left hurriedly about 15 minutes ago; I guess you could wait, if you aren't in a hurry."

The administrative assistant had decided a few days earlier to become more efficient in her work. Therefore, she concentrated on the job she was doing and ignored everything else. Not giving attention to what Mrs. Aponte said was part of her new strategy. Do you think such a decision is likely to increase efficiency? What decision do you believe would be appropriate for the administrative assistant?

What You Are To Do: Prepare brief responses to the questions raised. Support your responses with brief explanations.

EXTENDING YOUR ENGLISH COMPETENCIES

You overheard the conversation recorded below. The two conversing have made several errors in their use of pronouns.

What You Are To Do: Prepare a copy of the dialogue between Sally and Brian, changing all pronouns used incorrectly. Underscore all pronouns changed.

Sally: "Hi, Brian. Are you going to the demonstration by Francie Hepal in the Conference Room? Ms. McClaire wants us to attend."

Brian: "No, both Lynne and me asked to be excused. We have to finish a job for Mr. Bacon this afternoon."

Sally: "That's too bad. Just between you and I, you're going to miss an important demonstration."

Brian: "Well, you'll have to tell Lynne and me what you learn. Will you?"

Sally: "Of course. It will be my pleasure to instruct you on Francie's demonstration. I won't be as good as her, but I'll try."

APPLICATION ACTIVITIES

Activity 1

Students are to reread Chapters 1 and 2. The class is divided into speakers and listeners. Then one speaker is teamed with one listener. The listener is to ask questions; the speaker is to respond. At the conclusion of three to four minutes of interacting, the listener is to record what was learned from the speaker. The speaker is to record his or her impressions of how actively the listener was listening. The questions for the interaction are:

A. What do you think would be interesting about working in a business office?

B. What would cause you to be uncertain about considering a job in an office?

C. Why is an orientation to a new job important?

D. Which office job described in Chapter 2 do you think would be the most interesting to you? Why?

E. As you think of the job requirements for the job you chose in D. above, what skills do you want to develop during the course?

Activity 2

A limited number of speakers and listeners (possibly three of each) are selected to speak to the total group from the notes they wrote for Activity 1. Students who are not participating as speakers at this point are listeners. They should take notes of what is said and be prepared to discuss the strengths and weaknesses of the presentations and of their own listening.

CHAPTER SUMMARY

The basic communication skills of reading, writing, speaking, and listening are important in the business office. You have developed each of these skills to some extent during your studies in school. However, these skills need constant attention if you are to reach higher levels of effectiveness and efficiency. These are key points you will want to keep in mind about these basic skills:

1. You will need your reading skill every day in order to understand the tasks you do, to operate equipment skillfully, to complete various forms, to respond to inquiries, and to use references.
2. Reading skills include:
   - ability to comprehend
   - an extensive vocabulary
   - reasonable rate
3. Office workers have varying responsibility for writing tasks. You may write summaries of various types of communications, prepare drafts of memorandums and letters, suggest changes and edit the writing of others, and compose messages on your own.
4. To write well, you will want to give attention to clearness, conciseness, courteousness, completeness, and correctness.
5. Oral communication will be a common phase of your everyday interactions with coworkers.
6. Speaking effectively requires that you speak clearly, express your ideas carefully, and use standard English.
7. Good listeners focus attention on what is being said and mentally summarize and understand each word. Taking notes and asking questions can enhance listening power.

KEY CONCEPTS AND TERMS

reading   completeness
comprehension   correctness
editor   standard language
clearness   colloquialisms
conciseness   listening
courteousness

INTEGRATED CHAPTER ACTIVITY

Below are listed components of the three skills highlighted in this chapter:

Reading skills   **Writing skills**
comprehend what you read   use proper grammar
understand an extensive vocabulary   use appropriate punctuation
read with considerable speed   spell words correctly

Speaking and Listening Skills
speak clearly
use standard language
express ideas clearly
focus attention on what is being said
maintain interest in what is being said

Word processing equipment can be used to complete this activity.

What You Are To Do: For each of the components listed, indicate your appraisal of your own skill. Use these categories as a basis of your evaluation: Very good, good, poor, do not know. Key a copy of the listed components and indicate your appraisal after each.

Choose two components which you would like to improve during the next few months. For each component you choose, write a brief summary of what you hope to do that you believe will be helpful in meeting your improvement goal.

OPTIONAL COMPUTER APPLICATION ACTIVITY
See Computer Application Activity 3
in your Information Processing Activities workbook.

Kathy Malenky
OFFICE SUPERVISOR

WHY DON'T I EVER DO A JOB RIGHT?

DEAR MS. MALENKY:

I work in a large company where I am an office assistant to one of the general managers. He is a very, very busy person. He calls me into his office shortly after 9:00 a.m. to give me jobs to do. He talks rapidly; he moves quickly from one job to the next. And when he's finished, he's likely to dash out of his office before I can get up to leave. I go back to my workstation and I work very hard trying to get all the jobs done. I leave them on his desk. Later, he calls me in and says: "You didn't get the information I really wanted when you called John Smith," or "You didn't set up this report as I wanted it," or "You didn't make the right number of copies of this letter." Is something wrong with me? Is something wrong with him? Is there anything I can do about this situation?—DIANE IN HUNTSVILLE

DEAR DIANE:

Communication is a two-way activity and sometimes you must step in to do what the other person fails to do. From what you describe, I'd say the manager isn't giving you complete instructions when he talks with you at the beginning of the day. However, it is possible that you are not able to write them down or you may not be remembering similar jobs that you have done. You will need to take the initiative in getting complete instructions. Here are some pointers:

1. Take notes on everything he tells you.
2. Think ahead to what you must know to do the job while you are listening and recording the instructions. Make a mental note of anything that is missing.
3. Review complex tasks by saying to the manager: "Could I just double-check that these instructions are right? I'm to call the controller at headquarters to get the November production schedule of Product XTB by individual plant?"
4. Follow your notes as you complete each task.
5. Make the best decision you can when you find specific instructions are missing in your notes and it is not appropriate to check with the manager. Base such decisions on the past experience you have had in doing similar jobs. Attach a note to the job explaining to the manager the basis for your decision.
6. Review any decisions you made (point 5) that the manager did not accept. Ask yourself why you didn't make a good decision. Try to learn from each wrong decision.

I hope you will find these pointers useful every day.—KATHY MALENKY

CHAPTER 4

Working with Others

The ability to interact well with others is a critical skill in today's office. You interact with others every time you ask your supervisor a question, coordinate your schedule with a coworker, explain a procedure to a new employee, answer a question, participate in a meeting, listen to a visitor, greet someone in the elevator, or work with others to solve a problem. The quality of this interaction affects your productivity and your level of job satisfaction.

Your attitude, actions, appearance, and voice have a bearing on your interaction with others. These factors are examined in this chapter to help you work productively with those in your office as well as with the public. You will learn specific techniques to help you interact well with supervisors and coworkers on a daily basis. Suggestions for maintaining positive interaction under stressful conditions are also presented.

The objectives of the chapter are to:

● help you understand the importance of good human relations on the job

● help you develop good human relations skills

HUMAN RELATIONS ON THE JOB

When you have completed your study of this topic, you will be able to:

- describe your role in getting along with others

- explain how your attitude influences working relationships

- explain how your actions, appearance, and voice affect human relations on the job

- describe your role in representing the company to the public

As a beginning office worker, you will need good technical skills such as keyboarding and machine transcription. An equally important skill is the ability to get along with others while on the job. The term **human relations** refers to how people interact with others—and *good* human relations improves productivity and makes the work environment more pleasant. Your ability to work well with others under a variety of circumstances is important at all times.

You may change jobs. You may lose some technical skills and gain others. Yet wherever you work—in a small bank or large insurance company, in a formal reception area or a records management center—you will always interact with people.

compatible: able to
work well together

influence: affect

The interaction among coworkers affects the tone or mood of
an office. How well you and your coworkers get along with each
other affects communication, productivity, and office morale.
When your relationships are positive, even heavy workloads or
tight schedules seem less burdensome. You and your company
profit when you and your coworkers are **compatible**.

You **influence** the office environment by your attitude (how you
think), how you exhibit your attitude, and how you look and
sound. You are not responsible for how your coworkers think,
act, look, and sound, but you are responsible for yourself. You
play an important part in making the office an enjoyable place in
which to work.

Your Attitude—Your Mental Self

self-image: your
mental picture of your-
self

nurture: help some-
thing grow and mature

Your **attitude** is your outlook on life. It includes your **self-
image** and your opinions. Attitude is guided by your mind. For
example, if you spend your mental energies worrying about what
might happen next, your outlook on life (your attitude) is probably negative. If, however, you spend your mental energies taking
each day as it comes and appreciating the people or events that
are helping you, your attitude is probably happy and healthy.

Only you can control what you think and feel. Your attitude is
your mental self; **nurture** it! Following are three elements of a
positive attitude.

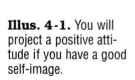
Illus. 4-1. You will
project a positive atti-
tude if you have a good
self-image.

Realize That You Are Important

Never think of yourself as *just* a billing clerk, *just* a secretary, or *just* a receptionist. Your role as an office worker is vital to the company for which you work and you, personally, make a valuable contribution to any job you hold. Without competent office workers, the entire business system would **collapse**.

collapse: fall apart

When you realize that your job is important, you can feel good about yourself—which is the first step toward achieving success in your job. When you realize that your job is important, you can go about your tasks more enthusiastically and with greater purpose. You will be happier and you will perform your job better.

Do Not Take Yourself Too Seriously

While it is very important to realize the contribution you make to the company, do not take yourself *too* seriously. Learn to laugh at yourself, and allow coworkers to laugh with you. Your sense of humor will help you **cope** with stress and get along better with others.

cope: handle well

Accept Your Coworkers

To accept others, you must believe that it is not necessary for everyone to think and act as you do. Coworkers come from different backgrounds, have different responsibilities, experience different daily pressures, and have needs and feelings different from your own. Instead of expecting that they be like you, listen to and learn from them, and respect their differences.

Illus. 4-2. "Are you sure all these cords are necessary?" This office worker's sense of humor is helping her cope with new equipment.

How You Exhibit Your Attitude

Your attitude is reflected by how you act toward others. Having a positive attitude enables you to act in a pleasant and encouraging manner. Following are some ways in which you can exhibit a good attitude.

Look for Favorable Qualities in Others

Look for favorable qualities in every person with whom you interact. When you search for good points in others, you will not be tempted to criticize them.

Be Courteous

You do not need to consider every coworker a personal friend, but you should treat all people with courtesy and respect. A good way to show courtesy is to use common-sense etiquette. For example, remember the simple courtesies of saying "Please" and "Thank you." Smile at people! Your goal should be to treat others the way you want to be treated.

Empathize with Others

Empathy is the ability to look at situations through the eyes of others and to try to understand their points of view. Empathizing helps you feel and understand what the other person is experiencing.

> *Jerri, Paul, and Luisa are coworkers in the accounting department of Tollimar & Reese, Inc. During the morning break, Jerri and Luisa were chatting:*
>
> *Jerri: Why isn't Paul friendlier? He seems nice, but he hardly talks to anyone unless he has to.*
>
> *Luisa: I used to wonder the same thing. But he is still new on the job. I think he's just nervous about doing his work correctly. He will probably relax and talk with us more when he feels more confident about his work. We'll just have to be patient and let him know he's doing a good job!*

Look for Ways to Help Coworkers

"How may I help?" is a question that workers should ask throughout the day. Of course, the best way to help is to be sure you are doing your own work completely and efficiently. Helping others while your work is left undone is not productive.

However, if you complete your work, you may offer to help coworkers finish theirs if a deadline needs to be met. Or, as you are doing your work, you may offer to help a busy coworker: "June, I'm going to the mailroom. Do you have anything you'd like me to mail while I'm there?"

Be Dependable

Accepting responsibility for your actions and carrying through is what being dependable means. If you say you will do something, do it. If you promise to be somewhere, be there. If you schedule a meeting at a certain time, be on time. If you start a job, finish it.

How You Appear to Others

Your appearance influences your working environment in much the same way as does your attitude. To an extent, it can determine how pleasant and productive your office will be.

Your Wardrobe

appropriately: properly

Even before you speak, others begin to form an opinion about you based on your appearance. If you are dressed **appropriately** for the office and take pride in your appearance, others will think you take equal pride in your work. If, however, your appearance is sloppy, it will be difficult to convince others that you are an efficient, capable worker.

Some companies have specific dress codes. Other companies allow employees to determine their attire, as long as it is appropriate. Dress attractively and in a businesslike manner. Extreme or faddish styles will detract from your professional image, so select a wardrobe with care. Your clothes should always be neat and clean. Let your appearance say to others, "I take my job seriously."

Personal Hygiene

hygiene: bodily cleanliness

Looking and feeling your best begins with good personal **hygiene**. Be sure to shower or bathe daily, and use an effective deodorant or antiperspirant. Brush your teeth regularly. You may want to keep breath mints available to use if necessary. If you enjoy wearing perfume or cologne, be sure the fragrance is not overpowering. Your hair should be clean and styled in such a way that it is not distracting to you or to others.

Illus. 4-3. Dress for success: Make a good first impression.

Remember, when you look your best, you will feel good about yourself. And when you feel good about yourself, you will be more relaxed and confident on the job.

Facial Expressions

Are you aware of your facial expressions? Do you appear to be pleasant? hostile? neutral? From a practical standpoint, it is easier for others to deal with you if you look pleasant. A smile is a simple way to put others at ease.

Annoying Habits

Habits such as twirling your hair, drumming your fingers, humming to yourself, frequently clearing your throat, and smoking can be extremely annoying to those around you. Fortunately, these habits, which look and/or sound unprofessional, can be changed. Work hard to eliminate annoying habits.

Your Voice

Often, conversations can be easily overheard in modern offices. When you are on the telephone or discussing something with a coworker, try to speak so the listener can hear you without straining. But do not speak so loudly that you disrupt other conversations around you.

If you anticipate that the conversation will be lengthy, consider going to a more private area of the office or to an area where a door can be closed. Speak at a moderate rate of speed so others can understand you easily.

The *pitch* of your voice refers to how high or low your voice sounds. When you become emotional—both happy and angry—the pitch usually goes up, and a higher-pitched voice tends to carry farther than a lower-pitched voice. You cannot change the natural pitch of your voice, but you can try to control raising it. Overall, a lower-pitched voice is more pleasant to hear.

YOUR ROLE IN REPRESENTING THE COMPANY TO OTHERS

Most jobs, some to a greater extent than others, involve dealing with the public. You may be a receptionist in a doctor's office, a customer-service worker in a large department store, a reservationist for an airline, or a teller at a bank. You are the person representing your company to the public. Your appearance and attitude are as important—if not more important—in representing your company to others as they are in influencing your office environment.

Have a Sincere Handshake

Shaking hands is a common custom that is used when people greet one another or when they are introduced to one another. How you shake hands is important in the business environment. Remember to step or lean forward slightly as you extend your hand. Shake hands firmly, and look the other person directly in the eye.

Listen Attentively

The attitude of a worker who deals with the public should be, "I want to help you in any way possible." To convey that attitude to others, you must take time to listen carefully. When you listen, your voice and body language should say, "There is nothing else to which I am giving attention now except listening to you."

impatient: restless because of delay

While you listen, look at the person. Do not check your watch, thump your pencil on the desk, think about where you will eat lunch, interrupt the speaker, or act *impatient* in any way. If you deal with the public over the phone, respond to their comments by saying, "I agree," "I understand," or other appropriate responses to let the caller know you are listening with interest. Listening attentively is the only way you can learn what the caller or visitor needs.

Be Prepared to Help

To help a caller or visitor most efficiently, you should be completely familiar with the policies and procedures of your company. You can then explain accurately and clearly the action you will take or the action the caller should take. Learn as much as possible about the services or products provided by the company. If you access information from a computer, learn to use the computer software efficiently so you can retrieve information quickly.

> *Marta works for Bachman Books, a large bookstore. During the day, Marta often receives calls from customers asking if a particular book is in stock, how long it will be before an order can be filled, and what the cost will be. She quickly accesses the needed information on the computer. When she receives new books or revised price lists, she promptly keys these changes on the computer. She knows her references must be current to give customers accurate information.*

If you do not know, or cannot find, the answer to a question, tell the caller you will ask for assistance. Most callers will wait patiently if they believe you are trying to help them. If the wait will be longer than a few minutes, don't keep the caller waiting; ask for a telephone number and call back.

Put Yourself in the Caller's Place

When you must answer the same question over and over, remember to treat the last caller as courteously as you treated the first caller. Be patient.

When you deal with the public, occasionally you will encounter an angry customer. Remember that a customer's anger is probably not directed toward you personally. Use such situations as opportunities to build goodwill between your organization and the caller.

> *Suppose you call Customer Service because you are upset that a filing cabinet was not delivered on time. Are you personally angry with the representative who answered the phone? Probably not, but you may express your frustration to the person anyway. If the representative is calm and does not respond angrily, a satisfactory solution will be reached. You will be willing to do business with that store again.*

People who call or visit your company are individuals who have differing needs. Be flexible enough to laugh with one caller one

tactful: sensitive to the feelings of others

minute and to discuss a problem seriously with another caller the next. Remember to be courteous and *tactful*—it's your job to help others.

Be Loyal to Your Goals and to Company Goals

compromise: go against

Being *loyal* to your goals means accepting jobs that help you advance in your chosen career field and that do not *compromise* your beliefs. Being loyal to your company's goals means doing your part to achieve company goals and to build a positive, professional image for the company.

When you agree with company goals, your loyalty to the organization will likely come naturally. Being loyal involves keeping company matters confidential. Just as gossiping about individuals is harmful, gossiping about your company is harmful to its image. Even in social gatherings outside the office, what you say to others about the company will affect—either positively or negatively—their perceptions of the company.

Behave in an Ethical Manner

Both employees and organizations are expected to behave in an ethical manner. **Ethics** refers to standards of right and wrong. Decisions about what is right and wrong are influenced by your family and by your spiritual and cultural value systems. Your personal code of ethics will determine your behavior both on and off the job.

Employees are acting in an ethical manner when they are always at their workstations on time and are not wasting time by talking excessively with coworkers. Employees are acting in an unethical manner when they take home office supplies or take credit for work prepared by others.

Organizations also are responsible for operating ethically, and some have adopted formal codes of ethics. Companies act in an ethical manner, for example, when they give accurate information to employees about career opportunities. Misrepresentation of goods or services to the public is an example of unethical behavior.

It is sometimes difficult to make a decision about what is right and wrong. Two guides can be used to help you make decisions about ethical issues: How would you feel if you were the receiver instead of the doer of the action resulting from the decision? What would the person whom you respect most think about your decision? You also will want to remember that while other people may influence your behavior, ultimately, you must take responsibility for your actions.

QUESTIONS FOR REVIEW

1. Define human relations. Why should office workers be concerned with human relations at work?

2. What affects the tone of an office more than workloads or schedules?

3. What is one trait that will help you not take yourself too seriously and will help you get along well with others?

4. Describe three ways in which you can exhibit a good attitude.

5. What message should your appearance send to others?

6. What is a simple way to put others at ease?

7. Name three habits that can be annoying to those around you.

8. Describe a sincere handshake.

9. Identify two ways in which you can be prepared to help a caller or visitor.

10. Define ethics. How does your personal code of ethics influence your actions at work?

INTERACTING WITH OTHERS

For the past two years you have worked in the accounting office of a department store. You and your three coworkers enjoy a friendly working relationship. Last week the store hired a new worker, Darla, to key entries into the computer. You and your coworkers have noticed that Darla only participates in conversations when she is asked a direct question. Also, she brings a lunch every day and eats in the employee lounge rather than joining all of you in the cafeteria. Your coworkers believe Darla is unfriendly and prefers to be left alone.

What You Are To Do: 1. Empathize with Darla (look at the situation from her point of view) by listing the feelings you think Darla may be experiencing.

2. What can you and your coworkers do to help Darla feel more at ease and welcome in the workplace? Prepare a list of your suggestions.

EXTENDING YOUR MATH COMPETENCIES

Melissa Johnson, office manager, is planning a speech entitled "Building Positive Work Relationships" for a Lions Club dinner. To help determine which traits to emphasize in her speech, Ms. Johnson asked four employees to rank five personal traits on a scale from 1 to 5, with 5 being the most important. The responses are shown below. Ms. Johnson has asked you to summarize the responses.

What You Are To Do: Calculate the total and average for each trait. Round the averages to two decimal places. Based on the averages, rank each trait from 1 to 5, with 1 being the most important. The higher the average, the more important the trait.

Trait	Christi	Guy	Tana	Scott	Total	Average	Rank
Accepts criticism graciously	2	3	2	3			
Practices good grooming	1	1	4	1			
Has a positive attitude	5	5	3	5			
Cooperates with others	4	4	1	4			
Has high self-esteem	3	2	5	2			

APPLICATION ACTIVITY

You are responsible for observing beginning office workers employed by Trek Tours Travel Agency. These workers are expected to interact effectively with the public as well as with coworkers. What would you expect to observe in order to give an employee a high rating for each of the following areas?

- attitude
- actions
- appearance

Word processing equipment can be used to complete this activity.

What You Are To Do: Key your response.

TOPIC 2

IMPROVING INTERPERSONAL SKILLS

When you have completed your study of this topic, you will be able to:

- describe techniques for interacting successfully with those to whom you report

- identify techniques for working compatibly with coworkers

- explain how to cope effectively with others under stressful conditions

Accomplishing company goals requires a team effort on the part of all workers. On every team there are different positions, and the people in those positions must work together in order to win. In baseball, team positions include pitchers, catchers, and outfielders. In companies, team positions include secretaries, receptionists, general clerks, mail workers, bookkeepers, and managers. Each team member must be able to interact with the other members in order to be productive and help the team reach its goals.

You will want to develop your own interpersonal skills so that you can be an effective team member. **Interpersonal skills** involve the behaviors and communication techniques that help you get along with others. In order to complete your assigned office tasks, you will be expected to interact with those to whom you report, as well as with coworkers. Effective interaction with other employees may be critical to doing your job to the best of your ability.

Interacting with others is not always easy. Deadlines, differences of opinion, and circumstances beyond your control will test your ability to interact with others. You must learn to expect such stressful situations and to handle them in a professional and productive manner.

This topic will explore the interpersonal skills you need to be successful on the job. Specific suggestions are given for interacting with those to whom you report, with coworkers, and with others in stressful situations.

INTERACTING WITH THOSE TO WHOM YOU REPORT

authority: the right to guide or direct

No matter what your position is in the company, you will have someone to whom you report—someone who is responsible for evaluating your performance. As an office worker, you may report to an office manager. The office manager may report to a vice president. The vice president will have to account to the president of the company. Even the president must act in accordance with the board of directors or laws of the state or country. Interacting with someone in **authority** is a reality of everyday business life. Interacting effectively could mean the difference between continued employment and being fired.

In this section, the term **supervisor** will be used to refer to a person who has authority over another person's position. There are many ways to improve the interaction between you and your supervisor.

Accept Work Assignments Pleasantly

How you respond to a work assignment will make a difference in how your supervisor feels about you and your work. Following are two situations where an office worker is given a task.

WRONG	Thelma:	*Ken, I'd like to have this report typed for today's meeting at 3 p.m.*
	Ken:	*All right. (Sighing and frowning, he tosses the report into his in basket without even glancing at it.)*
RIGHT	Howard:	*Jill, I'd like to have this report typed in time for my meeting this afternoon, please.*
	Jill:	*Yes, of course! (Smiles pleasantly and quickly scans the report.) Do I need to make copies of the report before the meeting?*

Both Ken and Jill agreed to type the report. What made the responses so different? What did the responses contribute to the worker-supervisor relationships? Let's examine both responses.

Ken's Response

Ken's verbal response indicated he would complete the task. But the message he sent with his nonverbal response (sigh, frown, tossing the report aside) was, "I'll do it if I have to, but I don't want to."

Thelma sensed Ken's resistance to typing the report. Becoming anxious about whether the report would be ready on time, Thelma began to remind Ken frequently about the assignment. Ken wondered why Thelma was nagging him. Ken thought to himself, "I told her I'd do it. Why doesn't she trust me?"

When the job was completed, Thelma felt as if she had to squeeze the work out of Ken, and Ken felt unappreciated. What an unpleasant cycle to experience every day on the job!

Jill's Response

Jill's response was pleasant. Unlike Ken's, Jill's verbal and nonverbal messages were consistent. Her words, tone of voice, smile, and actions all said, "I'll be glad to type the report." She stopped the task she was doing to briefly examine the report. She tried to identify questions she would have about completing it and to anticipate Howard's needs. What supervisor would not appreciate that kind of response?

diminished:
decreased

In this situation, Ken and Jill both completed the report accurately and on time. But Ken's attitude ***diminished*** Thelma's view of his work, whereas Jill's attitude enhanced Howard's opinion of hers. As a general rule, your accepting work assignments pleasantly will help make your worker-supervisor relationship productive and enjoyable.

Agree on Priorities

Setting priorities means ranking tasks in the order in which they should be completed. Assume that you must key an expense report, transcribe three letters, and make 25 photocopies of an agenda. How do you decide which task to do first? Priorities are often based on deadlines. A **deadline** is a specific time or date by which a project, task, or assignment *must* be completed. If the expense report is due this afternoon but the letters and copies of the report are not needed until tomorrow, you should key the expense report first. That is just common sense. But since priorities are not always easy to determine and sometimes change, there are times when you must discuss them with your supervisor.

Setting Priorities with One Supervisor

You may work in an office where you report to only one supervisor. To meet the demands of your schedule, you may need to prepare a written priority list. You and your supervisor may together rank the order in which you are to complete tasks. Sometimes, however, you alone may be expected to determine the order. If you are unsure of the rankings you assign, leave your priority list on your supervisor's desk for review. You want to be sure that your ranking of tasks is acceptable to your supervisor.

Setting Priorities with More Than One Supervisor

When you work for more than one supervisor or executive, establishing priorities becomes critical. Unless there is an immediate deadline, a company may adopt a "first-in, first-out" policy. Then, tasks are completed in the order in which they are received.

Work Log. There will be times when one supervisor may submit work with an immediate deadline, even though others have submitted work first. A **work log** is a record that helps you keep

Illus. 4-4. Work with your supervisor when setting priorities.

track of when work is submitted, when it is needed, and when it is completed. Illus. 4-5 is an example of a work log.

WORK LOG					
Supervisor's Name	Work to Complete	In	Needed a.m.	Needed p.m.	Out
Avery, J.	Photocopy/distribute Jenkins report	2/1		2/4	
Stewart, M.	Develop/prepare graphics for dept. meeting	2/1	2/4		
Miller, L.	Key/analyze statistical data	2/1		2/5	

Illus. 4-5. A work log helps you prioritize your work.

Notice that the work log includes a column for the supervisor's name and a column for the description of the work to be completed. You will see that J. Avery and M. Stewart both submitted work on 2/1 and that both need their work on 2/4. The a.m. and p.m. columns under "Date Needed" help you recognize priorities. M. Stewart's project should be completed first since it is due before lunch, while J. Avery's project is due in the afternoon. By frequently checking your work log, you can accurately focus on priorities.

Conflicting Priorities. When you work for more than one supervisor, there is a need for cooperation among those for whom you work because you want to do all your tasks on a timely basis. If several supervisors all want their work completed "right now," inform the supervisors of the conflicting priorities. Perhaps a meeting among the several supervisors and yourself will help you work out priorities. One supervisor may change a deadline. Or you may have to **delegate** work.

delegate: assign to someone else

By focusing on priorities, you and your supervisors work productively as a team toward finding effective ways to get the work done. Setting and communicating priorities is vital to good worker-supervisor relationships.

Suggest Solutions to Problems

After beginning a task, you may run into a problem trying to complete it. The problem may not be your fault; yet you must still deal with it by thinking of possible solutions. In the following situation, notice how differently Nina and Mark handle the same problem:

WRONG	Nina:	*Jennifer, I can't make copies of this report in time for your meeting. The copier is broken.*
	Jennifer:	*But Nina, you know I can't give my presentation without copies of that report.*
RIGHT	Mark:	*Patrick, the copier is out of order. Should I go down the street to the copy and quick-print center to make copies of the report?*
	Patrick:	*That's a good idea, Mark. Go right now and make the copies.*

The facts in the two examples above are the same: The copier is not working and the report cannot be completed without a copier. Why did the supervisors react so differently? Let's examine Nina's and Mark's approaches to the problem.

Nina's Approach

Nina began the conversation poorly by saying, "I can't . . . ." When an obstacle (the copier not working) got in Nina's way, she gave up. Jennifer was impatient with Nina for giving up so easily instead of searching for other solutions. If Nina says "I can't" enough, Jennifer will believe that Nina probably can't do her job and wonder if the company should continue to employ her.

Jennifer thinks Nina does not really care about getting the job done. Nina believes Jennifer is blaming her for the problem. Their working relationship is strained. Nina's inability, or unwillingness, to look for alternate solutions to problems *discredits* her professionalism.

discredits: takes away from

Mark's Approach

Mark's approach to the situation was both professional and helpful. First he identified the problem and then proposed an alternate method of completing the job. His approach showed

resourcefulness:
ability to find solutions

Patrick that he was dedicated to getting the job done and was willing to find another way to copy the report. Patrick appreciated Mark's professional attitude and his *resourcefulness* in solving problems.

Of course, some problems are more complex than a copier breaking down. In those situations it will take a little longer to think of alternative solutions. But when you think problems through and present alternatives to your supervisor, you save yourself and your supervisor valuable time. You are an *asset* to the company.

asset: valuable
resource

Keep Your Supervisor Informed

Supervisors need to know what is happening within their areas of responsibility. When they are informed, supervisors do their jobs better and are regarded as competent by *their* supervisors. As an office worker, you will naturally see and hear situations throughout the day that your supervisor will not. For example, an important client may unexpectedly drop in while your supervisor is out of the office. Be sure to tell your supervisor. Perhaps you are working on a project such as making arrangements for a national sales conference. Keep your supervisor aware of your progress. Advise your supervisor when circumstances arise that affect the project. For example, there may be times when differences between you and a coworker cannot be resolved without your supervisor being called in.

On a day-to-day basis, informing your supervisor means keeping the communication lines between you open so you both can do your jobs better. Informing your supervisor can happen casually throughout the day and/or at predetermined times. Some office workers have an informal, "stand-up meeting" every morning. The office worker meets with the supervisor yet remains standing. Standing encourages the participants to be brief and to the point. The office worker presents the supervisor with a short summary (either written or oral) of what was accomplished the day before, and what is scheduled for today. Priorities are confirmed.

Your Supervisor Is Human, Too

Assume that Lucy Wheeler is your supervisor. What do you expect of her? Perhaps you believe she should be competent, pleasant, understanding, easy to approach, honest, and fair.

Illus. 4-6. Remember that supervisors are human. They are trying to do their jobs to the best of their abilities.

These are worthy expectations. If Lucy Wheeler had all these traits, she would indeed be a good supervisor and working for her would be a pleasure.

But how would you react to Ms. Wheeler if she did not live up to these expectations? If you judge her too harshly, you are in essence saying, "You should be perfect!" This is an unrealistic expectation to place on anyone.

Remember that even though Ms. Wheeler is in a position of authority, she is also human. Accept her as someone who is trying to do her job the best way she can. Do not criticize Ms. Wheeler in front of others or broadcast her mistakes.

foster: encourage

Concentrate instead on Ms. Wheeler's traits that you can appreciate. Respond to her with respect and understanding. To *foster* a good working relationship with Lucy Wheeler, try to see things from her point of view. You then will enjoy a more productive working relationship.

INTERACTING WITH COWORKERS

As you learned in Topic 1, it is important to be compatible with your coworkers. If you get along with them, they can help you complete your work more effectively. If you don't get along with them, you can expect little cooperation. Coworkers who have good working relationships willingly "pitch in" to help each other. They often encourage one another, and they usually achieve more than if they had worked alone. Following are four techniques that will help you interact well with coworkers. Also see Illus. 4-8 on page 142 for helpful phrases to remember when interacting with others.

Be a Team Member

Team members often ask, "What else can I do to help?" They seldom think, "That's not *my* job!" To team members, their "job" is whatever needs to be done to complete the tasks or project. This may include helping someone else if you are available to do so, or it may mean staying a little late to help a coworker or supervisor finish a task.

Others will tend to offer you assistance when you need it if you have been helpful to them. When coworkers offer help and you need it, *accept* it. Do not try to prove you can do everything yourself. Thank them for their help and enjoy the good working relationships that result from being a team member.

You may be assigned to a work group formed to complete a large project. Three advantages of working in a group are that work is completed more rapidly because the workload is shared, each worker is assigned tasks that best utilize his or her strongest skills, and ideas for completing the project are shared.

The individual tasks required to complete a group project may be detailed on a production schedule. A **production schedule** is a listing of specific tasks to be completed, the person(s) responsible for completing them, and the dates by which the tasks must be completed. The production schedule shown in Illus. 4-7 has been created by a work group to help them prepare a 35-page report on the *feasibility* of opening an office in London. Generally, more complex projects require more detailed production schedules.

feasibility: practicality

PRODUCTION SCHEDULE New Branch Office Feasibility Study		
Completion Date	Person(s) Responsible	Task
10/1	Gary, Glenda, Jack	Planning meeting
10/16	Gary, Glenda	Gather data from cost accountants
10/23	Gary, Glenda, Jack	Develop outline
10/24	Jack	Key draft
10/26	Gary, Glenda	Edit draft; develop graphics
10/30	Jack	Revise edited draft; import graphics
10/31	Gary, Glenda	Proofread/finalize report
11/2	Gary, Glenda, Jack	Discuss report with supervisor

Illus. 4-7. A production schedule can be used to list responsibilities and deadlines for large projects.

Do Not Gossip

perpetuate:
continue

To avoid hurting others, do not start, encourage, or **perpetuate** rumors and gossip. Statements based on incomplete or false information, or based on someone's opinion about a person or situation rather than on the facts, can cause confusion and anxiety in the workplace.

You will need to be especially careful around certain people who have reputations for spreading rumors. They may try to gather bits of gossip by asking you questions or by actually reading documents at your workstation.

Express Your Appreciation

Individuals like to be recognized for a job well done. When a person's efforts are favorably recognized, that person may find new energy to continue doing the best job possible. When you express appreciation to someone, try to be as specific as possible:

Vague: *"Lee, I appreciate your help."*

Specific: *"Lee, I appreciate your handling the phone for me while I finished adding those sales figures."*

You can express genuine appreciation for others only when you take time to notice what your coworkers are doing. Be aware of things they do that make your job easier, and tell them that you appreciate it. (Supervisors enjoy being appreciated, too!) Appreciating one another's efforts contributes to a productive team spirit in the office.

Accept Responsibility for Your Mistakes

Have you ever lowered your opinion of someone who said, "I was wrong; I made a mistake"? No, you probably admired the person for being able to admit the error.

Giving excuses for your mistakes does not hide your mistakes from others—it only hides them from you. And blaming coworkers for your mistakes does not remove the blame from you. Your coworkers know who is at fault. Trying to avoid blame will cause others to resent you. When any team member makes a mistake, it affects the other team members—so you should admit your mistakes right away.

As a beginning office worker, you can expect to make mistakes because you face unfamiliar tasks. Do not let your early mistakes discourage you; instead, learn from them, and then try to do better. Recognize that mistakes can be opportunities for improvement. Your coworkers will notice and appreciate your attitude, and working together as a team will be easier.

A SHORT COURSE IN HUMAN RELATIONS

The six most important words:

"I admit I made a mistake."

The five most important words:

"You did a good job!"

The four most important words:

"What do you think?"

The three most important words:

"If you please"

The two most important words:

"Thank you."

The least important word:

"I"

Illus. 4-8. The essence of human relations from one point of view.

INTERACTING WITH OTHERS IN STRESSFUL SITUATIONS

congenial: easy to get along with

ample: enough

Your interaction with others is usually productive and enjoyable when coworkers are *congenial* and when you have *ample* time to complete your work. From time to time, however, a stressful situation may arise that tests your ability to interact with coworkers productively and professionally. **Stress** is physical, mental, or emotional tension. Stress is caused by situations such as tight schedules, unpleasant coworkers, unresolved problems, sexual harassment, and endless interruptions.

Stressful situations can actually be opportunities for you to improve your interpersonal skills and be more successful on the job. How well workers handle difficult situations often affects their chances for promotion. This section discusses practical suggestions for interacting with others in stressful situations.

Working Under Deadline Pressure

allotted: assigned

Deadlines are common in offices. Usually you know about each deadline far enough in advance for you to complete the task on time. Occasionally, however, meeting a deadline is a challenge. The time ***allotted*** for getting the job done seems short, and the pressure you feel to get the job done may cause you and others to be tense.

Work as a Team

Remember, you and your coworkers are team members working as a group to get the job done. Keep a positive attitude. Believe that together you will meet the deadline even though there may be times when you feel pressured. Concentrate on what you as a team must do and how you must do it.

Keep Your Perspective

perspective: ability to know what actually is important and what is not

It is important to keep your ***perspective*** under deadline pressure. A sense of humor will help. One employer expressed his appreciation for a worker by saying, "Her humor under fire is what helped us cope with the pressure and meet the deadline."

Coping with Unpleasant Coworkers

condescending: treating others as if they were inferior

Most of your working relationships will be good, and you will probably enjoy interacting with coworkers during the day as you go about your tasks. Occasionally, though, you may encounter coworkers who are unpleasant and uncooperative. These coworkers may be excessively critical. They may express anger quickly and harshly. Some may be ***condescending*** or rude. The human tendency is to avoid these people; but when you work for or with them, avoiding them is impossible. You must learn to deal with unpleasant coworkers professionally and effectively so that you can be productive. Here are four approaches to help you deal with difficult coworkers.

Remain Professional

Decide to act in a professional manner regardless of how your coworkers act. There are times when this is very hard to do, but it is important to try. Let's see how Tom copes with a coworker, Justin.

Justin is always rude and abrupt. Tom's reaction could be to treat Justin the same way. Instead, Tom decides to act professionally. He is pleasant and respectful. One day one of Tom's coworkers asks him, "How can you be nice to Justin? He is so rude and thoughtless!" Tom replies, "Yes, he is rude. But I'm not going to let him make me rude, too. I don't want him to be able to control me that way. If he wants to be inconsiderate, that's his decision. But I'm not going to be less of a professional just because he is. Besides, if I'm abrupt with him, I'm still angry after he leaves. As it is, after he leaves I'm able to move quickly to other tasks."

Illus. 4-9. Try to be patient and professional if you encounter a coworker who is unpleasant.

When you react emotionally to an unpleasant coworker, you usually regret it later; and you may even have to apologize. When you can act professionally towards the person, *you* remain in control of yourself. Acting professionally does not necessarily mean acting as if you have no feelings. It refers to the *manner* in which you express your thoughts and feelings.

Wait to Respond

If you are so upset that you do not believe you can respond calmly, try NOT to respond right away. Take time to collect your thoughts. If you still believe you need to discuss the issue, go to the person when *you* feel mentally prepared to talk calmly and directly.

Concentrate on Your Job

Concentrate on doing your job well, not on what others think of you personally. Trying to please people who are frequently angry or extremely critical will usually result in frustration. Instead, do your job to the best of your ability. When you have done your best, *you* can be pleased with your work. Of course, always look for ways to improve. Listen to criticism of your work even though it may be unpleasant. If a criticism is accurate, work to improve the weak area. Do so because you want to improve yourself—not because you want to please the critical person.

Be Patient

detect: notice

Remember that coworkers with whom it is difficult to interact are human, too. Many of them know that they offend and upset others. They may be trying to improve, even though you may not be able to **detect** their efforts.

Resolving Problems

From time to time a problem may arise between you and another person. You should try to resolve the problem as quickly as possible because problems that are ignored seldom disappear. Go to the person involved with the problem and discuss it with him or her *first*. Do not discuss the person and/or problem with everyone else in the office. Respect the other person's privacy and dignity.

How you approach the problem with the other person will affect how easily the problem can be resolved. Here are two approaches.

> Betty: *Stan, I can't believe you are so absent-minded. You know the mail is picked up every day at 3:30. You ignore your duties and then ask me to help you get the mail ready in a hurry, and I'm tired of it!*

> *Jack:*   *The mail hasn't been ready in time for the afternoon pickup all week. Perhaps if you began getting the mail ready at 2:45, we could avoid this frantic rush every afternoon.*

Betty's approach is harsh and critical; Jack's approach is direct, yet tactful. His approach is better than Betty's because he followed three problem-solving principles:

1. *Focus on the problem—not the person.* Betty ridiculed Stan ("I can't believe you are so absent-minded"). Jack focused instead on the problem. When people feel attacked, they will spend their energies defending themselves instead of solving problems.
2. *Describe the problem—do not evaluate it.* Jack described the problem ("the mail hasn't been ready in time"). Betty, however, gave her opinion of the problem ("you ignore your duties"). Describing the problem instead of evaluating it helps both people view the problem objectively.
3. *Courteously describe the action you want the other person to take.* Jack suggested that Stan begin preparing the mail earlier. Betty was more concerned about **venting** her anger towards Stan than she was about correcting the problem.

venting: getting rid of; expressing

Sexual Harassment

The Equal Employment Opportunity Commission (EEOC) has issued guidelines that define **sexual harassment** as any unwelcomed sexual advance that:

- is used as a condition of employment
- affects your chances for promotion
- creates an unpleasant, hostile, or offensive working environment

Sexual harassment is not present in every office, and you may never have to deal with the problem. But if it does occur, do not ignore it. Sexual harassment is illegal. To eliminate sexual harassment, you will have to take action. Reference Section G outlines specific action you should take if unwelcome advances persist.

Controlling Interruptions

One of the benefits of working in an office is that you have the opportunity to be with and enjoy people. On the other hand, people can be a source of frustration when they interrupt you often and lessen your productivity. Some interruptions are necessary—perhaps a coworker has a question or must tell you something important. Interruptions unrelated to work, however, should be controlled.

It is acceptable to have brief, social conversations with coworkers throughout the day. Lunch and breaks provide opportunities for more lengthy social conversations. But you may encounter one or two coworkers who *monopolize* your work time by talking about activities unrelated to the job. There may be times during the workday when you must tactfully communicate to a "talker" that you are busy.

monopolize: take over

Illus. 4-10. Your break and lunch time can be used to socialize with coworkers.

QUESTIONS FOR REVIEW

1. Define interpersonal skills.

2. Why is it important for you to be able to interact well with others as team members?

3. Why should you and your supervisor(s) agree on priorities?

4. What is the purpose of keeping your supervisor(s) informed?

5. What are two advantages of forming a group to complete a project?

6. Give an example of being specific when expressing appreciation to a coworker.

7. Define stress. What are two situations that can cause stress on the job?

8. What are two ways of coping with unpleasant coworkers?

9. Identify three problem-solving principles.

10. How does the Equal Employment Opportunity Commission define sexual harassment?

MAKING DECISIONS

Terri asks you to help her complete a report for Mr. Sturzenberger. You agree to prepare several charts while Terri finishes keying the report. You were under considerable pressure and you did not proofread your work before giving it to Terri.

After the report and the charts are submitted, Mr. Sturzenberger discovers errors in the charts. He points out the errors to Terri and asks her to proofread more carefully. Since your workstation and Terri's are side by side, you hear Mr. Sturzenberger's remarks. What should you do or say? Why?

What You Are To Do: Prepare a brief response to the questions raised.

EXTENDING YOUR ENGLISH COMPETENCIES

The following terms should be familiar to you from your reading of this chapter.

supervisor	interpersonal skills
setting priorities	deadlines
stressful situations	sexual harassment
team member	work log
ethics	production schedule

What You Are To Do: Compose ten sentences using these terms. Then underscore the terms within the sentences.

APPLICATION ACTIVITY

Your employer, Mr. Lechowicz, is preparing a speech titled "Working with Others and Enjoying It!" to give before the local chapter of Professional Secretaries International. He hands you the draft shown on page 149 and says, "Please key a revised draft of these ten points I plan to make in my speech. At the top of the page, center the title of the speech. Then key the ten points, making the changes I've marked."

Word processing equipment can be used to complete this activity.

What You Are To Do: Follow Mr. Lechowicz's instructions. Use plain paper. If necessary, refer to Reference Section A for a listing of Standard Proofreader's Marks.

Effective

lc 1. Interacting with others is often critical to doing your
job to the best of your ~~knowledge~~ *ability*

2. Accepting work assignments pleasantly will help make your
worker-supervisor relationship enjoyable and productive

3.4 If your supervisor is unavailable frequently prepare a
~~written~~ priority list.

4.5 Al ways keep your supervisor informed of what is
in happening with his or her area of responsibility but
do not report minor matters.

5.6 Three techniques that will help you interact well with
co workers are
Be a team member
Express your appreciation
Accept responsibility for your mistakes

6.7 Stressful situations can actually be opportunities for
you to improve your interpersonal skills.

stet *a*

7.8 When working under ~~deadline~~ pressure, ~~remember to~~ keep
ss
your perspective and work as a team.

8.3 Discuss ~~your~~ priorities with your supervisor(s) on a
day to day basis.

9. sexual harassment is illegal

lc 10. A WORK LOG helps you keep track of when work is submitted,
when it is needed, and when it is completed.

#

CHAPTER SUMMARY

In this chapter, you learned that the ability to interact well with others is a critical skill in today's office. Compatible interaction among coworkers improves communication, office morale, and worker productivity. You should be able to discuss the following key points:

1. You play an important role in making the office a pleasant and productive place by treating others with the same respect and courtesy you would like to receive.
2. To enjoy good human relations on the job, you need a positive, professional attitude.
3. Accomplishing company goals requires a team effort on the part of all workers.
4. You can improve your interpersonal skills by practicing effective techniques.

KEY CONCEPTS AND TERMS

human relations	setting priorities
attitude	deadline
empathy	work log
ethics	production schedule
interpersonal skills	stress
supervisor	sexual harassment

INTEGRATED CHAPTER ACTIVITIES

Word processing equipment can be used to complete this activity.

Activity 1

Your teachers have authority over you as a student. Teachers are in the school environment what supervisors are in the work environment. How well you are able to interact with teachers will give you insight as to how well you will probably get along with a supervisor at work.

What You Are To Do: Take time to analyze how you interact with your teachers. Describe in writing how you can apply three techniques you have learned for good human relations to the relationships you have with your teachers. As you change your attitudes and actions, see if you notice an improvement in your student-teacher relationships. You can begin practicing good human relations skills now.

Activity 2

You work for Maria Segovia in the Human Resources Department. Mrs. Segovia appoints you to a work group assigned with developing a human relations checklist to be used at in-house "teamwork" seminars for the entire workforce. She hands you the partially completed draft below.

Word processing equipment can be used to complete this activity.

What You Are To Do:

1. Your teacher will assign you and two other students to a work group. Read the partial checklist below. Then as a group, compose ten additional statements to complete the checklist.

2. When all group members agree on the statements to be included, select one person to key the entire checklist, using an attractive format. All group members should proofread and edit the draft. After all corrections/changes have been made, submit the final checklist to your teacher.

HUMAN RELATIONS CHECKLIST

DIRECTIONS: This checklist has been developed so you can assess your personality traits and work habits. Read each statement, then place a check mark in the column that best describes you. A = Always; U = Usually; S = Sometimes; R = Rarely; and N = Never. Responses will be kept confidential. Based on your responses, make an effort to reinforce your strengths and overcome your weaknesses.

	A	U	S	R	N
1. I arrive at school or work on time.					
2. I accept those who are different from me.					
3. I work effectively when under pressure.					
4. I learn from my past mistakes and mistakes of others.					
5. I show respect to people in authority.					

OPTIONAL COMPUTER APPLICATION ACTIVITY
See Computer Application Activity 4
in your Information Processing Activities workbook.

OPTIONAL CRITICAL THINKING ACTIVITY
See Critical Thinking Activity 2
in your Information Processing Activities workbook.

PRODUCTIVITY CORNER

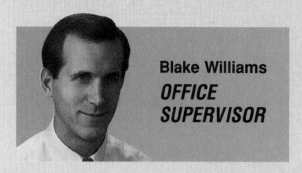

Blake Williams
OFFICE SUPERVISOR

STRESS SIGNALS

DEAR MR. WILLIAMS:

As a receptionist for a large law firm, I am very busy and always on a tight schedule. I open the mail, answer the telephone, and process legal documents on a word processor. But my primary responsibility is greeting the endless stream of clients who come to the firm each day. Most days are so busy that I don't take breaks or go to lunch!

Lately, however, I'm beginning to develop headaches—especially in the afternoon. And I'm so tired and weary at the end of the day. The people I work with are great, and I especially like what I do. I don't want to quit this job—but it's wearing me down! What can I do?—JULIE FROM ATLANTA

DEAR JULIE:

Stress can drain your energy in a hurry and cause you to become discouraged. Happily though, there are steps you can take both on and off the job to reduce stress:

● My first suggestion would be to take your scheduled breaks and lunch—even in the midst of a busy day. Taking a break will give you a chance to "re-energize" yourself.

● When you take breaks, leave your workstation. (Be sure, though, that someone is available to receive clients and answer the phone.) Take these opportunities to relax. Put aside thoughts of unfinished tasks.

● You also may want to slowly stretch your muscles, especially if you've been sitting for hours. Roll your head slowly from side to side. Stretch your arms above your head. Slowly bend down to touch your toes. All of this may not take five minutes, but you will benefit from it for hours!

● Take advantage of everyday opportunities to exercise—such as taking the stairs even when there is an elevator or walking to lunch instead of driving. You will feel more energetic during the day.

● Set realistic expectations for yourself. Trying to meet unrealistic expectations is a sure-fire way to cause stress.

● Finally, do something pleasant during your nonworking hours. Find a hobby you enjoy. Develop other interests by joining civic or service organizations. Do something helpful for someone else. And while you're at it, do something nice for you. After all, you've worked hard and deserve it!—BLAKE WILLIAMS

AT WORK AT DYNAMICS: *Simulation 1*

DYNAMICS is a manufacturer of health and fitness products, which are distributed nationally and internationally. Over the years, DYNAMICS has expanded its fitness equipment line to include sports equipment and accessories. Last year DYNAMICS initiated a company wellness program that it hopes will become a model for company wellness programs across the nation.

Last week your teacher announced that several local firms, including DYNAMICS, were hiring temporary office personnel to work after school, on Saturdays, and during the holidays. You and several of your classmates completed resumés and sent them to the firms. You were invited for an interview with Miss Amy Branigan, human resources manager of DYNAMICS. You felt that the interview went very well. Yesterday, Miss Branigan telephoned you to offer you a job. She asked that you give her an answer within a week. You liked the company, so after two days you called and accepted the job.

At your first meeting with Miss Branigan after you were hired, you learned that you would be working at the headquarters complex. This complex has approximately 2,500 manufacturing employees and 170 management and office employees. In addition, DYNAMICS employs a select group of temporary office workers to help during peak work periods and to fill in during employee vacations. Working as a "temporary" will be an excellent opportunity for you to learn about the various functions and activities of different divisions of DYNAMICS. At the conclusion of your meeting with her, Miss Branigan said, "I'm certain you will enjoy working here. We always look for responsible employees who are conscientious about completing their work assignments. I know you will do a fine job."

Your job assignments will be coordinated by Miss Branigan, who will assign you to different divisions as the need arises. Turn to your *Information Processing Activities* workbook to learn of your first assignment at DYNAMICS.

INFORMATION PROCESSING

CHAPTER 5

Information Processing Systems

Information is critical to all organizations. Effectively managed information helps an organization better serve its customers and operate more efficiently.

Managers must often use information processed by their employees in making decisions. If information is not accurate and up to date, it becomes difficult to make sound business decisions. Sound business decisions are necessary for an organization to prosper and expand.

In today's fast-paced business world, management must look for ways to keep costs low while maintaining high-quality products and services. Competition among businesses has made worker productivity a major concern of both management and employees. Information must be gathered, processed, and available at an ever increasing speed. While manual methods of processing are still in use, they are being replaced by electronic methods at a rapid pace. The computer has proven to be a fast, reliable, and economical means of processing information.

As an office worker, you will aid in tasks that help to maintain the flow of information in an organization. Understanding how the tasks you perform contribute to the total information system of an organization will make your job more interesting and more meaningful. As you study this chapter, you will learn how computer-related technology has been applied to the office.

The objectives of this chapter are to:

- acquaint you with information processing, information processing tasks office workers perform, and information processing software used to accomplish these tasks

- acquaint you with how information systems are organized and function within the office

AN OVERVIEW

When you have completed your study of this topic, you will be able to:

- explain why information processing is needed in business

- explain the information processing workflow

- describe common information processing activities office workers perform

- identify common information processing software and explain the steps you would use to learn a new software package on the job

Companies today require a great deal of up-to-date information regardless of the nature of the business:

A company manufactures automobiles and sells them through dealers in every part of the country. The headquarters office, via computer network, receives a detailed sales report from each dealership at the end of each business day. Production and regional distribution of cars are influenced by the information dealers' sales reports provide.

A large retail store maintains updated inventory reports as sales are recorded at cash registers throughout the store and transmitted to the store's computer center. Store managers use the reports to identify items that are selling rapidly and items that are moving slowly. Decisions about purchases, price markdowns, and inventory distribution are influenced by this constant flow of information.

Can you imagine how long it would take to collect and process the information needed for these two organizations' inventory reports without a computer? Before the use of computers, employees would spend days, weeks, and even months analyzing data and preparing the reports needed for decision making in business. Companies today, however, do not have weeks or months to respond to changing business markets. Information must be gathered, processed, and available for use in decision making at ever increasing speed.

Business managers, therefore, focus much attention on the need for information for decision making. As an office worker, you will assume an important role in processing accurate, concise, and timely information for effective decision making.

Illus. 5-1. This employee checks the accuracy of updated information that will be needed for decision making.

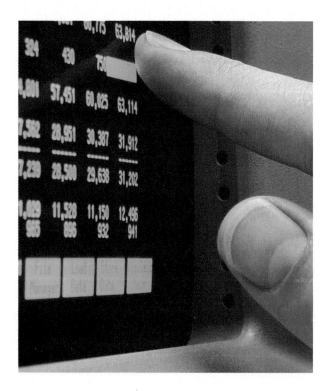

**WHAT
INFORMATION
IS**

Most of the work you perform in the office involves the processing of information. Information starts as basic facts made up of numbers, symbols, and letters. These basic facts become information when they are organized so that knowledge is gained from the facts. Information must be readily available to employees as they complete their duties:

A payroll manager prepares the weekly payroll checks. (The basic facts used include hours worked, rates of pay, and payroll deductions. When such facts are arranged by individual employees, they become information to use in preparing the payroll.)

An office worker in the shipping department answers a customer's inquiry about a shipping date. (The basic facts used are the shipping dates and invoice numbers. When the office worker locates the shipping dates for the specific invoice, the office worker has the information to answer the customer's question.)

A secretary in the sales office prepares an itinerary. (The basic facts used are flight numbers and times, travel dates, and destinations. When the secretary arranges the facts into a meaningful form, the itinerary will begin to take shape.)

In the examples above, basic facts have been organized as information for something meaningful: to prepare payroll checks, to answer a customer's inquiry, to prepare an itinerary.

Information takes many forms. The most common types are identified in Illus. 5-2. In actual usage, these individual forms of information are often ***interwoven***.

interwoven:
intermixed

COMMON TYPES OF INFORMATION	
Type	**Examples**
data	amounts, quantities, sizes, weights, capacities, ages organized to convey meaning, as in a table or listing
text	words organized to convey meaning, as in letters, memorandums, or reports
image	charts, graphs, photographs
voice	messages conveyed in person; messages conveyed by telephone

Illus. 5-2. Common types of information include data, text, image, and voice.

By processing or refining facts into a meaningful and usable form, you create information. Illustration 5-3 shows an example of how facts become information.

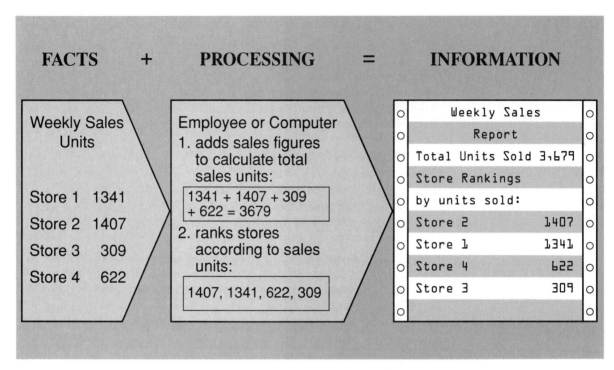

Illus. 5-3. Facts processed into a meaningful and useful form become information.

Information processing is the transformation of facts into a form that is meaningful and useful. For a business to operate effectively, it must be able to process information efficiently. Although traditional offices were able to rely on ***manual*** processing procedures and electrical equipment, more and more businesses today recognize the advantages of using electronic processing procedures and equipment. Each technological advancement seems to bring new equipment capable of increased processing speeds and, in many cases, more simplified operating procedures. When an employee is trained to use electronic equipment properly, managers expect productivity to increase.

Businesses value accurate and timely information for several reasons:

Complexity of Business

Operating even a small business can be quite complex. In a very small business, the owner may take care of all activities or have only a few office workers to handle the daily business operations. Typically, all the information needed to operate the business is in one central location, usually the business office. For a small business owner, efficient organization of information is necessary to maintain a competitive edge.

interrelated: having something in common

Efficient organization of information is even more critical in large organizations with thousands of employees. The jobs of employees in a large organization are *interrelated* in that many workers often need to use the same information. Key executives in large organizations must have information about the total organization to make decisions. Such information cannot be gained solely through first-hand observation. Executives must rely on the information provided by others.

controller: the chief accounting officer of a business

*The **controller** in the home office of a large manufacturer of household linens is responsible for all financial information management. Every week, the controller receives a report from each of the six plants in four southern states. The weekly reports give the controller a way of knowing what is being produced and the total production costs.*

Volume of Transactions

Organizations must deal with thousands of transactions each day. Consider the following examples:

- Banks process millions of checks, receive millions of deposits, and issue millions of dollars in cash each day.
- Insurance companies receive thousands of premium payments, issue thousands of new policies, and send out notices to thousands of customers each day.
- Manufacturing companies complete the production of millions of products, ship thousands of orders, and receive payments from thousands of customers each day.

Think of the problems that would occur if organizations did not maintain adequate information. The volume of transactions, for example, would be overwhelming in a bank that kept customer accounts in no particular order. Likewise, can you imagine a large, modern corporation sending a personalized letter to its 200,000 shareholders without using electronic equipment?

Demand for Timely Information

Information must be available when needed. When managers ask for information, they do not want to be told that it will be available in approximately two weeks. Customers do not expect to wait weeks for answers to their inquiries. In fact, the general public is aware of the technological developments that make possible almost ***instantaneous*** communication. People expect to receive needed information quickly and expect that information to be up to date:

instantaneous:
occurring without delay

> *Major airlines are able to maintain an international network of service because of the availability of timely information. You can request a reservation for a flight between two cities anywhere in the world and immediately receive information about the availability of seats. Customers requesting reservations are not willing to receive a response such as: "We are happy to have your reservation. We can let you know in a week if we will have a seat available."*

Value of Accurate Information

Information that is not accurate is worthless. Accurate information is required so that quality decisions can be made throughout a company. Consider the value of accurate information in the following example:

> *A manager keeps detailed information about the company's cash flow needs. The manager knows exactly how much cash is on hand.*

Illus. 5-4. Accurate information provides a sound foundation for decision making.

Therefore, cash not needed immediately can be transferred to accounts that earn interest. The company earns money because accurate information is kept about cash. If this information were not available, there would be no way to determine if some of the cash on hand could be invested temporarily.

INFORMATION PROCESSING WORKFLOW

depicted: to represent by drawing

The development and use of information in a business tends to follow a similar pattern. This pattern is frequently ***depicted*** as a workflow. **Workflow** refers to the sequence of operations followed in order to complete an activity. The information processing workflow typically consists of five operations, as shown in Illus. 5-5.

revisions: corrections and improvements

As you perform your duties, you will work sometimes in a sequence that proceeds directly through the input, processing, output, distribution, and storage operations. At other times, you may work back and forth between two or more of the operations, particularly if you are working on tasks that require ***revisions***. As shown in Illus. 5-5, information can be stored and retrieved at any point in the workflow.

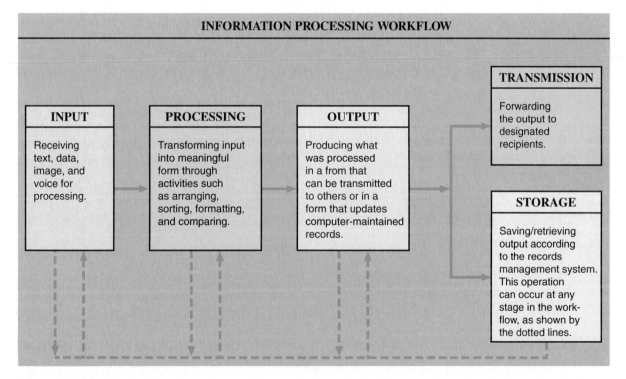

Illus. 5-5. The information processing workflow typically consists of five operations: Input, Processing, Output, Transmission, and Storage.

If you are employed in a small company with few offices, you may be allowed to determine your own workflow. If you work in a large company, your work may be concentrated in only one area with an established sequence of operations.

At this point, you will be introduced to several office activities that rely heavily on information processing. Your study of these areas will help you understand the importance of the office worker's role in the preparation of complete, accurate, and timely information. The descriptions will concentrate on the input, processing, and output of the following activities:

- document processing
- data processing
- administrative support
- records management
- transmission

Document Processing

transform: change

Office workers who are responsible for document processing **transform** what originators create (primarily with words) into output that is communicated to a wide variety of recipients. Note the sample listing of tasks performed by document processing employees in Illus. 5-6. In Chapters 6 and 7, you will learn how word processing and desktop publishing help you prepare common business documents.

ORIGINATORS	DOCUMENT PROCESSING EMPLOYEES	DOCUMENT
Create • memorandums • letters • reports • speeches • advertising copy • company newsletters • manuals • other business documents	• prepare drafts • format documents • suggest changes • verify facts • check spelling • check English usage • proofread • select typeface • layout and design	• final copy ready for reproduction, storage, or transmission
INPUT	PROCESSING	OUTPUT

Illus. 5-6. The office worker who processes documents transforms the originator's input into the finished copy.

Data Processing

Numbers are important to businesses. Transforming numbers into useful information is what office workers do in data processing departments. Such workers classify, sort, record, and merge numbers in the preparation of reports useful within the organization. Note the sample listing of tasks performed by data processing employees in Illus. 5-7. You will learn about some common data processing tasks in Chapters 8 and 9.

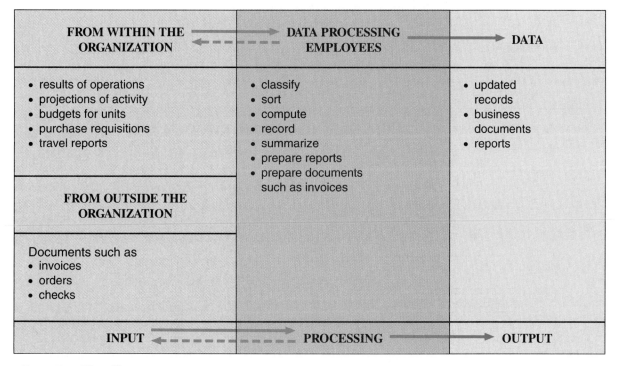

FROM WITHIN THE ORGANIZATION	DATA PROCESSING EMPLOYEES	DATA

• results of operations
• projections of activity
• budgets for units
• purchase requisitions
• travel reports
	• classify
	• sort
	• compute
	• record
	• summarize
	• prepare reports
	• prepare documents
	  such as invoices
		• updated
		  records
		• business
		  documents
		• reports

FROM OUTSIDE THE ORGANIZATION		
Documents such as • invoices • orders • checks		
INPUT	PROCESSING	OUTPUT

Illus. 5-7. The office worker who processes data transforms numbers into needed information.

Administrative Support

Businesses have long recognized that managers, in order to make the best use of their time, must have adequate office assistance. Office employees work closely with managers to assist with many management activities. Note the sample listing of activities supported in Illus. 5-8 on page 166. You will learn about some of these activities in Chapters 10 and 11.

RECEIVES REQUEST	ADMINISTRATIVE SUPPORT EMPLOYEES	COMPLETED ACTIVITY
• appointments • travel tickets • schedule meeting • copies	• schedules appointment • arranges travel and confirms reservations • contacts meeting participants and schedules meeting room • prepare multiple copies • collate copies • bind copies	• up-to-date calendar • itinerary • arranged meeting • multiple copies ready for distribution
INPUT	PROCESSING	OUTPUT

Illus. 5-8. The office worker who supports the activities of management performs a wide variety of tasks.

Records Management

Office workers who are responsible for the company's records prepare, store, and retrieve information. Note the sample listing of tasks performed by records management employees shown in Illus. 5-9. Office employees work closely with records managers who ensure that information is managed according to estab-

FROM WITHIN THE ORGANIZATION	RECORDS MANAGEMENT EMPLOYEES	DATA
• correspondence • reports • other business documents	• identify basis for storing • prepare for storage • store and retrieve information • discard outdated information	• updated records • information ready for users
FROM OUTSIDE THE ORGANIZATION		
• correspondence • reports • other business documents		
INPUT	PROCESSING	OUTPUT

Illus. 5-9. The office worker who assists with records management tasks is responsible for maintaining many of the company's records.

lished policies and procedures. You will learn about policies and procedures for records management in Chapters 12 and 13.

Transmission

Office workers who are responsible for the prompt and accurate forwarding of information to recipients perform transmission tasks. More and more, such workers use electronic means to ensure the rapid **dissemination** of information. Postal services, however, are still used for the transmission of much written communication. Note the sample listing of tasks performed by transmission employees in Illus. 5-10. You will learn more about the transmission methods and procedures in Chapters 14 and 15.

dissemination:
distribution

FROM WITHIN THE ORGANIZATION	TRANSMISSION EMPLOYEES	COMMUNICATION
• correspondence • business documents • messages	• prepare for mailing • prepare for electronic transmission • send via postal services or interoffice mail • transmit via telephone • transmit via electronic means • transmit via satellite, microwave, or radio signals • receive via the above	• forwarded communications • stored communications
FROM OUTSIDE THE ORGANIZATION		
• correspondence • business documents • messages		
INPUT	PROCESSING	OUTPUT

Illus. 5-10. The prompt and accurate receiving and forwarding of information is an important link in processing information.

SOFTWARE FOR INFORMATION PROCESSING

You will find that many businesses rely on electronic equipment for information processing. A *computer* is basically an electronic device that makes computations and logical comparisons according to the instructions it receives. Computers receive their instructions from software and use software to process information. **Software** is a set of instructions or programs that directs the computer to perform specific actions. Thousands of programs are available to today's computer users. Software may be divided into three categories: operating system software, utility software, and application software.

An end user is the person who uses computer equipment and software. As an end user, you may not know exactly how a computer works internally. Similarly, you may not know how a car's engine is constructed. However, as long as you follow the traffic laws and drive safely, you will be able to use a car to meet your transportation needs. Likewise, even though you may not know much about the internal workings of a computer, you will be able to use a computer and the appropriate software to complete certain office tasks.

Illus. 5-11. Readily available software makes the computer a versatile tool.

Operating System Software

Operating system software contains a series of programs that control the operation of the computer and provide the means for communicating with devices connected to the computer, such as a printer. When an operating system is stored on floppy disks or on a hard disk drive, it is known as a *disk operating system*, or *DOS*. When the operating system is loaded into a microcomputer from a disk, the process is referred to as *booting the system*. Computers with hard disk drives are generally set up to load the operating system automatically. In either case, you know the operating system has been loaded when the *system prompt* appears on the screen. The system prompt is the computer's signal to you that the computer is ready to run an application program or to accept commands.

Utility Software

Utility software carries out "housekeeping" duties, such as formatting a disk or making ***backup*** copies of data. Many of the utilities you will use are included with the operating system. When special features beyond those included in your operating system software are desired, utility software may be purchased separately.

Application Software

Application software directs the computer to carry out specific tasks. The application software may perform a single function, such as word processing. Other single-function application software include inventory control and database management. Software that combines several applications (such as word processing, database management, and spreadsheet) in one package, is known as **integrated software**. The **windows feature** is used to split the screen into two or more sections horizontally or vertically. This allows the user to view at the same time two or more applications or several portions of the same application. (See Illus. 5-12.)

Illus. 5-12. The windows feature lets you see several applications at one time. In this example the user can prepare a graphic as a slide for a presentation and import the same graphic into a report.

In your training for the office, you may already be familiar with at least one application package. Illus. 5-14 lists common application software categories you may encounter in an office. The wide selection of software available and the continuous **upgrading** of software have made computers increasingly popular for office use.

upgrading:
improving, adding new features

Learning New Software Packages

In modern offices, many of the activities you perform will be completed with the assistance of computer software programs. Although you may know one or more application programs, you probably will need to learn additional software packages to complete your assigned tasks. Here are several suggestions for learning programs that are new to you as well as updates to familiar programs:

1. *Open and inspect new software packages carefully.* Open the packaging carefully so as not to damage or lose any enclosures, such as disks, *keyboard templates*, and warranty cards. Compare all items in the software package against the package content listing.

Illus. 5-13. New software packages typically include program disks, user manuals, and keyboard templates (front center). Keyboard templates give you quick reference to software commands. The template is designed to fit the keyboard and identifies the actions performed by specific function keys.

2. *Review the documentation.* Take time to become familiar with the manual, also known as the *documentation.* This will help you become familiar with the program's features and gain a general understanding of where to look for answers when questions arise.

COMMON APPLICATION SOFTWARE

Software Category	Software Function
Accounting	Accounts receivable, accounts payable, customer billing, check writing, general record keeping, financial reports, financial forecasting
Administrative Support	Appointment reminders, tickler file, calendar, calculator, telephone numbers, other lists
Communications	Computer linkages to send and receive information from various communication channels
Database Management	Records creation and maintenance; records updating and editing; report preparation
Desktop Publishing	Page composition, use of features such as type style and fonts to produce high-quality documents that contain both text and images
Electronic Mail	Message transmission from one computer to another
Graphics	Translation of statistical data into graphic representation, templates, slides, clip art
Inventory Control	Inventory record creation and maintenance, status reports
Specialized	Software developed for specialized needs such as medical, law, and real estate offices
Spreadsheet	Business calculations; number manipulation via input or formulas; "what if" analyses
Word Processing	Document creation and editing, spelling and grammar checking, merging of text, data, and graphics into documents

Illus. 5-14. A wide variety of software is available to meet specific information processing needs.

3. *Use tutorials disks provided with the software.* Many software packages contain tutorials on disks. A **tutorial** is a program to help the user get started quickly and show how to use the software features. Some tutorials are divided into lessons and may include practice problems using specific software features.

Illus. 5-15. Software tutorials help you learn an application while using the actual software on your computer.

4. *Apply your previous knowledge to new or updated programs.* Use what you already know to make learning a new or updated program easier. If, for example, you learned one word processing package at school but must use another word processing package on the job, look for familiar features in the new software program. The features may have different names and require different keystrokes, but the tasks they perform are basically the same. With software updates, your knowledge of previous software editions will help you master the new version.
5. *Start with simple tasks first.* Learn the basics first, such as how to load, save, and print a file. Then, move on to the features of the software, concentrating on what you need to know to do your job. Finally, tackle the harder functions and learn how to use the software to its full capacity.
6. *Don't expect to master the software immediately.* You will make mistakes. To **minimize** those mistakes, however, write

minimize: lessen

down the answers to questions you ask of those who know the program and make notes on keystroke combinations and procedures. You will become comfortable with the program and learn its capabilities by using the software. Don't become discouraged; it takes time to master a new software program.

on-line: in direct communication with the computer

7. *Use the on-line help feature, if available.* Some application software includes an **on-line** help feature. If you do not remember how to use a particular feature, the on-line help feature will assist you.

8. *Don't be afraid to try features you have not yet used.* As your time permits, allow yourself the challenge of seeing what you can do with the software program. You will become more confident about your ability to apply the software to new tasks that may require a slightly different application of the software's features.

Caring for Disks

When at work at a microcomputer, pay particular attention to proper procedures for handling disks:

- Prepare labels before attaching them to disks. If you must mark on an attached label, apply only light pressure with a felt-tip pen.
- Insert and remove a disk carefully, limiting your touch to the edge of the protective cover.
- Never place a disk on top of heat-generating equipment. Heat will warp disks. Avoid direct sunlight.
- Never bend or fold a floppy disk or attach a paper clip to its edge. Do not place a rubber band around a group of floppy disks.
- Avoid placing a disk in close contact with magnetized objects such as a telephone or a magnetic copyholder.
- Never eat, drink, or smoke when you handle disks.
- Immediately after removing a disk from your computer, refile it properly. Replace floppy disks in their envelopes.
- Get in the habit of making backup copies of all important disks.
- Always remove your disks from the disk drives before turning off the computer.

CRITICAL ROLE OF OFFICE WORKERS

As you learned in Chapter 1, office workers play a major role in modern organizations. Now that you know what information is and how it is used by companies, you can better understand the importance businesses place on the efficient and accurate processing of information.

In today's business world, information changes constantly. Information is updated, added, or deleted on a regular basis by office workers completing information processing tasks. The increased emphasis on technology-based processing has created work environments that challenge office workers to use higher level thinking skills in completing processing tasks.

In fact, the success of a business often depends upon workers performing their information processing tasks competently.

QUESTIONS FOR REVIEW

1. What is information?
2. Describe the common forms of information.
3. What is information processing?
4. Why must a business be able to process information efficiently?
5. Why does a company need timely information?
6. Explain the five operations in the information processing workflow.
7. What is the purpose of application software packages?
8. Identify five common categories of application software.
9. Describe techniques you can use to make learning a new software program easier.
10. Describe proper procedures for caring for disks.

INTERACTING WITH OTHERS

Vickie, an office assistant in a recently established department, has had to learn much of what she does from oral instructions given by the department manager. Vicki is competent; she has been able to implement all the instructions given her by the manager. The work of the new department is done without problems.

One morning while the manager and Vicki were talking about the work for the day, the manager said: "Vicki, I just received this memo from the systems manager. We're being asked to prepare written procedures for the work completed in the department. This means we need to start recording all the procedures we have developed for all recurring activities in the office."

If you were Vicki, what comment would you make at this point in your meeting with the manager? What questions might you ask in order to clarify what you should do?

What You Are To Do: Prepare a brief response to the questions raised.

EXTENDING YOUR MATH COMPETENCIES

Assume that you are an office worker in the central office of a professional organization that sponsors seminars for various occupational groups. Recently the company completed a series of seminars in five cities throughout the United States. The standard fee for each participant at one seminar was $700. However, two of the seminars (Update on Software for Business and Assessing New Technology) had a $500 fee per participant. You were given the task of calling the manager of each seminar site and getting enrollment figures for the courses. On page 176 are the details you recorded from your telephone calls.

What You Are To Do: Using a sheet of plain paper, write the title of each of the five seminars on a separate line. Set up columns that will aid you in making the following computations:

1. the total participants for each seminar

2. the grand total of participants for all seminars

3. the total revenue earned from each seminar

4. the grand total of all revenue received

5. the total participants in each city

Then circle the title of (a) the seminar with largest total number of participants and (b) seminar producing largest total revenue.

TITLE OF SEMINAR	NUMBER OF PARTICIPANTS				
	BOSTON	NEW YORK	WASHINGTON	CHICAGO	SAN FRANCISCO
Information Processing for Small Offices January 6-10, 19--	125	245	110	117	97
Controlling and Managing Computerized Processing February 15-18, 19--	105	325	175	130	110
Security for a Computer System March 1-4, 19--	78	110	45	72	70
Update on Software for Business March 19-22, 19--	170	295	140	110	115
Desktop Publishing April 1-5, 19--	210	410	175	102	117

APPLICATION ACTIVITY

Word processing equipment can be used to complete this activity.

Assume that you are employed in the office of a monthly magazine devoted to computers. One of the reporters gives you the rough draft which follows on page 177. The notes are from an interview with Lisa Holt, Manager of Information Services at Seagrove Pharmaceutical Co.

What You Are To Do: Key a revised copy of the interview. Use your judgment with regard to line length. Make all corrections noted. If necessary, refer to Reference Section A for information about standard proofreader's marks.

Use boldface if available

INTERVIEW WITH LISA HOLT ← *line 10*

SEPTEMBER 22, 19--

REPORTER

QUESTION: What is the priority of office automation in a giant
company such as Seagrove Pharmaceutical?

LISA HOLT

RESPONSE: It's mixed. Obviously, when you have different operating companies, there are different priorities. We
started a decade ago to look at office automation and
personal computers. We actually bought our first
personal computer about nine years ago.

REPORTER

QUESTION: What services are presently available through your
system?

LISA HOLT

RESPONSE: We offer a variety of services to ~~all five~~ *four* floors of
our building. There's electronic mail and electronic
messaging. We can also transfer documents--we do a
great deal of that. *electronically*

REPORTER

QUESTION: Will you expand to more floors?

LISA HOLT

RESPONSE: As the need arises, we will respond. One of the reasons
we started slowly was to give ourselves time to learn
about local area networks and their impact upon office
automation. It was our belief early on that we would
soon *be* doing work much differently than we'd done in the
past. Things began to change as soon as we put in our
first workstations with computer capabilities. We've
learned a lot from those early pilot studies!

REPORTER

QUESTION: What have you learned? *specifically*

LISA HOLT

RESPONSE: One very important lesson is that relationships ~~between~~ *among*
people change. Let's take the case of a secretary who
works for two executives. In the past, the secretary
was directly involved in the document preparation task.
Both executives would dictate letters and memos and
the secretary would transcribe them at the typewriter.
Now that both executives have computer terminals on
their desks, they can compose documents and send them *it*
electronically to the terminal at the secretary's workstation. The secretary can either process the document and print a final copy or send the document
electronically to the word processing center for processing. We're also finding that some executives
prefer to edit and print their own documents. That
way, the secretary may not even see the document before
it is ready for distribution!

ORGANIZATION AND TECHNOLOGY

When you have completed your study of this topic, you will be able to:

- explain traditional information processing methods

- explain electronic information processing methods

- explain why maintenance and security are important considerations in electronic processing

Businesses give much attention to the processing of information. As you learned in Topic 1, the need for information processing in today's businesses is due in large part to the complexity of business, the volume of transactions, the demand for timely information, and the importance of accurate information. Attention must be given to the most appropriate technology needed for processing information. Businesses, therefore, study how to best organize people, procedures, and equipment to handle their information processing needs.

Companies also review on a regular basis the ways they process information to determine if new technology should be introduced. Often, extensive study is done before making a decision to add new technology. Such studies may involve employee participation. If, as an employee, you are involved in such a study, you may be asked to keep a complete record of what you do. Your record may include how many times you complete the same task, how often you must make judgments about how something is done, and what you accomplish during a given time period.

Computers have revolutionized the way employees process information in offices. Routine tasks that once took hours to complete manually can be completed in a fraction of the time using computers. Likewise, new and improved technology will continue to change the way we work in the future as businesses implement new equipment and procedures to better meet their information processing needs.

INFORMATION
PROCESSING
SYSTEMS

You learned in Topic 1 that putting facts into a meaningful and useful form is called *information processing.* Another term you should be familiar with is *system,* which refers to a logical structure and sequence of procedures. Therefore, **information processing system** refers to the organization and procedures used to transform facts into a meaningful and useful form.

The information processing systems found in businesses vary according to the extent to which technology is used. For example, you may work in an office where information is processed in a traditional manner with limited electronic equipment. Or you may work in an office that relies heavily on electronic processing. While traditional processing methods are still in use, they are rapidly being replaced by electronic methods.

TRADITIONAL
PROCESSING

Traditional processing relies primarily on manual processing skills of office workers rather than the processing capabilities of a computer. Office workers do much processing by hand and with limited electronic equipment. Traditional systems are found primarily in very small offices requiring few transactions, in offices where there is much variety in what is done, or in offices that require highly individualized responses to customers' needs:

> Leah and two others work in the small office of an importer of rare antique rugs. The company specializes in one-of-a-kind rugs for select customers. Leah's workstation includes an electronic typewriter, a calculator, and a telephone. She maintains the rug inventory in longhand on cards and records a telephone order by writing the information on a form. She uses her electronic typewriter to key correspondence and invoices.

Organization

Office workers are assigned clearly specified tasks. Additionally, complete instructions about each processing detail must be provided to achieve the quality of performance expected. Several positions in a small office and their corresponding duties are listed in Illus. 5-16, on page 180.

Equipment

functioning:
working

Office workers *functioning* within a traditional system usually have some basic equipment to help them perform their tasks:

HEIDI'S CHILDREN'S SWEATERS, INC.
PROCESSING TASKS OF OFFICE PERSONNEL

Mail/Messenger Clerk	Secretary	Receptionist/ Typist	Office Assistant	Bookkeeper
• opens mail	• reads incoming mail and distributes to executives	• answers telephone calls	• keeps records of inventory	• records sales
• delivers mail		• greets callers	• determines when items must be purchased	• records payments
• takes orders to wholesalers	• composes letters and memos	• makes appointments		• keeps all employee payroll records
• takes mail to post office	• types letters from machine dictation	• keeps travel schedules for executives	• files all correspondence and forms	• writes checks
• delivers packages in the city	• corrects and proofreads letters and memos	• prepares purchase orders	• makes bank deposits	• prepares bills
	• places telephone calls	• types form letters		
	• answers telephone calls			

Illus. 5-16. In a very small office, all processing tasks may be completed by one or two office employees.

Typewriters and Word Processors

Electronic typewriters and low-end word processors are common equipment in traditional offices. Electric typewriters may even be found in some offices. Typewriters and low-end word processors provide flexibility in performing a variety of processing tasks, and formatting decisions are made by the user. You will learn more about this equipment in Chapter 7.

Calculators and Photocopiers

Machines that perform calculations reduce the time needed to process numbers. Such machines help you in the basic arithmetic processes of adding, subtracting, multiplying, and dividing. Calculators have capabilities which simplify many computations. See Reference Section D, Math, for a presentation of the 10-key touch method.

Most offices have photocopying equipment. Features vary considerably on photocopiers. You may encounter a basic machine with limited features, or you may find a photocopier that can perform many copying functions. Instructions for using the features are maintained often at the machine itself. You will learn more about this equipment in Chapter 10.

Telephones and Postal Equipment

essential: necessary

Telephones are **essential** to most offices. The telephone manufacturer provides detailed instructions so that you may learn to use your telephone properly. Information about telephone systems, services, and equipment will be presented in Chapter 15.

Scales and postage meters are often provided for employees to use when preparing outgoing mail. Such equipment is relatively easy to use, and user's guides are generally available if any questions arise. Chapter 14 provides more information on this topic.

COMPUTERIZED PROCESSING

Computer-based systems are common in today's offices. Computers have many common features regardless of the specific equipment in use. In this topic you will gain a general understanding of computers. With such an understanding, you will be able to adapt to the equipment you use in your office job.

Computerized processing relies heavily on equipment (the computer) and related software as the means of transforming facts into meaningful and timely information. Most offices today have introduced some aspects of computerized processing into their information processing tasks.

Organization

restructured: organized in a different way

Information processing tasks often are **restructured** when a computerized system is installed or upgraded. The makeup and combination of the hardware and software of the computerized system is determined by the particular needs of the company. No single way of organizing computerized information processing will work for all businesses. Three common ways of organizing for computerized information processing are reviewed here.

Centralized Structure

When information processing is *centralized* by location, processing is performed in one location with specially trained staff to support the operation. (See Illus. 5-17.) The processing unit (frequently a mainframe computer), handles the major company processing tasks. Company data is stored at the central location. By keeping all data in one central location, the business is able to control access to the processing unit and control the work standards for the entire organization. Workers **upload** (transmit files to the central computer) and **download** (transmit files from the central computer) from smaller computers or remote terminals located throughout the company.

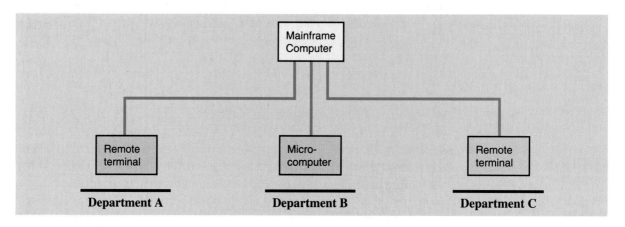

Illus. 5-17. In a centralized structure, workers access the central computer for the bulk of information processing activities.

Decentralized Structure

As the price of computers lowered and processing capabilities increased, *decentralization* began to prove cost-effective. In a decentralized structure each organizational unit is responsible for its own processing activities, and information is stored at the local site.

The standalone microcomputer is the most common equipment found in a decentralized structure. As the name implies, a *standalone* computer operates independently of other computer systems. Some standalone systems however, have been upgraded to communicate with mainframe computers, as shown by the broken lines in Illustration 5-18. The standalone computer is credited with introducing the power of computer processing to small- and mid-sized businesses.

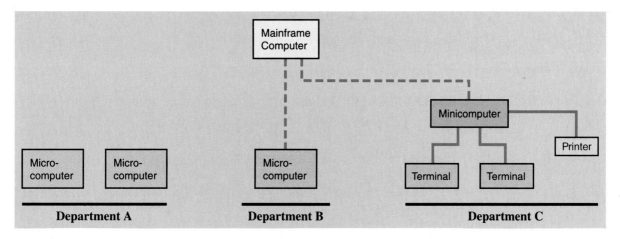

Department A   Department B   Department C

Illus. 5-18. In a decentralized structure, each department operates independently. Departments B and C have been upgraded to communicate with the mainframe computer.

Distributed Structure

The *distributed* structure has a communication link between a central computing facility and the end users. (See Illus. 5-19 on page 184.) A distributed computer system typically consists of a centralized mainframe computer linked electronically to smaller computers, such as microcomputers or minicomputers. Each department may have its own system with users connected to the departmental system. Departmental systems are capable of processing information according to departmental needs and storing selected data or passing data to the central computer to be stored. A distributed structure provides control over the network while permitting employees access to the system.

Because of the need for instant access to information, many companies today are moving to fully integrate their systems. With an **integrated electronic system**, computer-based equipment is linked electronically so that information may be exchanged between the electronically connected units. Integrated electronic systems allow not only for communication between computers but between computers and other equipment—such as linking a computer to a photocopier. An increasingly important feature of an integrated electronic system is the use of electronic mail.

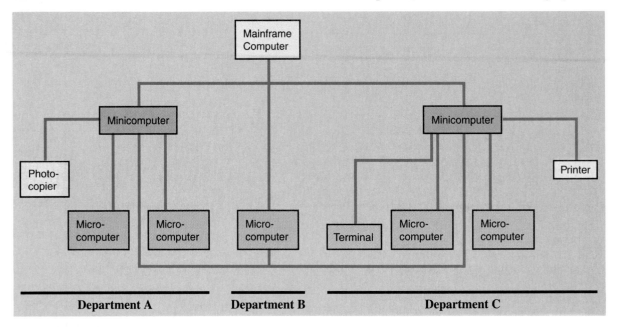

Illus. 5-19. The distributed structure enables users to have access to data at the departmental levels or at the central (mainframe) level from their individual workstations.

Since information can be transmitted electronically in seconds from one computer to another, the location of workers in the integrated system is not critical. This means that companies may transfer some office functions from a central city location, for example, to a suburban or rural area some distance from the headquarter offices.

The basic equipment for an integrated electronic system is essentially the same as that for other computer-based systems, with two exceptions: (1) how the various computer units are linked together and (2) the programs that direct the interactions among the various parts of the total system. You will learn more about such programs in Chapter 15.

Hardware

While we often speak of "the computer," many variations exist among computers. Yet, no matter the variations, the *computer* is basically an electronic device that can make computations and comparisons according to given instructions. Computers can be classified by their size, speed, and processing capabilities. With continued advancements in technology, however, the differences among computer categories have become more difficult to identify.

Three major categories of computers are used in business: mainframe computers, minicomputers, and microcomputers.

Mainframe computers are large, multipurpose machines with very high processing speeds. Mainframes can handle many users and store large quantities of data. Mainframe computers use sophisticated programs to control their operation and require specially trained employees to operate the system. The mainframe computer has traditionally done tasks such as payroll, accounting, and personnel recordkeeping for large organizations.

Minicomputers are midsized computers capable of supporting a number of users. They are less powerful than mainframe computers but can perform a wide variety of processing tasks.

Microcomputers are smaller than minicomputers. The desktop system is made up of several interacting components, such as a keyboard, a terminal, and a processing unit. Microcomputers (also called micros or personal computers) allow individual use of the equipment and are used by workers at all levels within organizations. As a business moves toward an integrated electronic computer system, the business may choose to link its microcomputers electronically.

Illus. 5-20. The portability of the laptop (left) and pocket computers (right) allows executives the freedom to work outside the office.

Other forms of microcomputers are: portable, laptop, notebook, and pocket computers. As these computers can be battery powered, they are especially helpful to employees who must work at locations where traditional computers are not available.

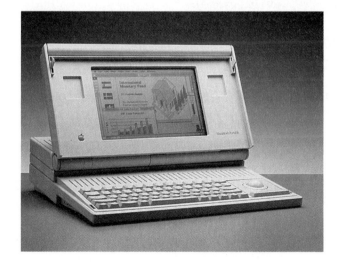

Illus. 5-21. The mainframe (top left) is a powerful computer capable of processing large volumes of information with rapid speed. The minicomputer (top right) and the microcomputer (lower right) are used throughout business. They may be connected to a company's mainframe computer.

Companies may have several types of computers to meet their processing needs. As you have learned, a computer is essentially a processing machine. To accomplish the processing tasks, every computer system includes:

devices: equipment

- ● *devices* for inputting data into the computer
- ● a central processing unit
- ● storage (memory) where data is retained for retrieval
- ● devices for outputting information

Input Devices

Data from business transactions frequently consist of handwritten, keyed, or printed facts. Before these data can be processed, however, they must be entered into the computer. Workers use input devices to enter data into computers. An **input device** is hardware that allows the computer to accept the data for processing. Common input devices include the keyboard, mouse, light pen, and optical character readers. Speech recognition is also a form of input. You will learn more about these and other input devices throughout this textbook.

Illus. 5-22.

THE WALL STREET JOURNAL

"Just act casual and try to remember which buttons you pushed."

From THE WALL STREET JOURNAL—permission Cartoon Features Syndicate.

Processor

Action, or processing, takes place in the central processing unit, which is also known as the "brain" of the computer. All computers, regardless of size, have processors. The **central processing unit** (CPU) is that part of the computer system that receives and stores instructions and data, performs arithmetic calculations and logical comparisons, and directs the actions of the input and output devices.

Within the CPU there are two types of primary or main storage: random-access memory (RAM) and read-only memory (ROM). With *random-access memory*, the processor can in random order enter, store, or retrieve data during processing. When the computer is turned off, RAM locations lose their memory. Therefore, data is stored only temporarily in RAM during processing.

The *read-only memory*, on the other hand, is permanent and contains the instructions the computer will use for performing tasks. The computer can only read data from ROM. Data cannot be written to or stored in ROM. Typically, primary memory contains enough space to allow one or only a few software programs to run at any one time.

Illus. 5-23. A computer consists of an input device, processor, output device, and auxiliary storage units.

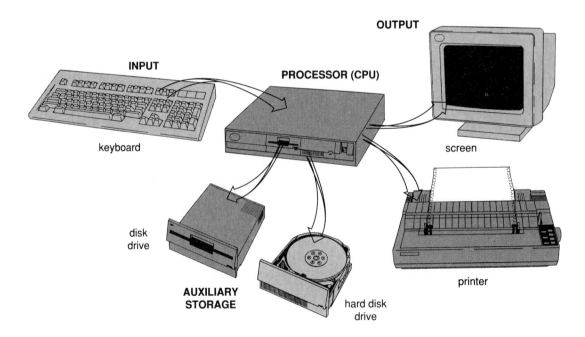

Output Devices

A computer must have at least one output device. An **output device** prints, displays, or records information. The most common output devices are display screens (display a *soft copy*) and printers (print a *hard copy*). Other output forms are magnetic or laser disks, magnetic tape, and microfilm.

Display Screens

The **display screen** or *monitor* is the most commonly used output device. The display screen becomes your window to view the input and output of the computer. Display screens are either monochromatic or color. The monochromatic (one color) screens are usually green, **amber**, or white. Color monitors are helpful for presenting and understanding graphic information. Some monitors allow the user to switch between monochrome and color modes.

amber: yellow or brownish yellow

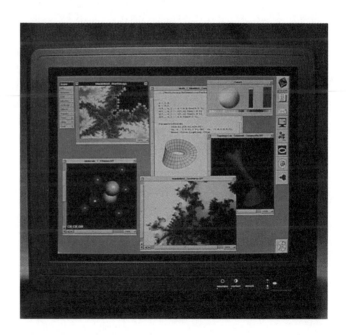

Illus. 5-24. Color monitors have increased in popularity. The graphics, text, and photography here are clear and easy to read.

Printers

Printers produce different qualities of print. Your understanding of these differences will help you select the right printer for the task at hand. *Letter-quality* print is comparable to that of an electronic typewriter. Letter quality is often the company's standard for final copies of written communication. *Near letter-quality* print is acceptable for business use but is not as high a quality as the letter-quality print. *Draft-quality* print is the lowest quality and is used often for rough drafts. On the other end of the scale, *near-typeset quality* is the highest quality print available today. Some of these printers are able to achieve almost the same quality level as professional printing. Printers are classified as either impact printers or nonimpact printers:

An **impact printer** makes impressions by the printing device striking a ribbon for each character and transferring the image onto a sheet of paper—just as a typewriter does. Impact printers are used where letter-quality copies are needed.

The *dot-matrix printer* is a popular impact printer because it is relatively inexpensive and produces copy at high speeds. The print quality, however, varies depending upon the number of pins in the print head. The 24-pin models are used to produce near-letter quality copy; the 9-pin models are used primarily for rough drafts.

A **nonimpact printer** produces output without striking images through a ribbon. Nonimpact printers are almost noise-less and are faster than most impact printers. They are often used for high-volume printing. Many nonimpact printers have exceeded the letter-quality level of the best impact printers. A variety of printing methods can be found among these printers:

- Ink-jet printers: spray a pattern of liquid ink on paper to form characters

- Laser printers: print an entire page at a time; allow both characters and graphics to be printed in near-typeset quality. Laser printers also provide easy flexibility of using different sizes and styles of type.

Auxiliary Storage Devices

Since the amount of primary storage in the CPU is limited and expensive, auxiliary storage, also known as *peripheral* or

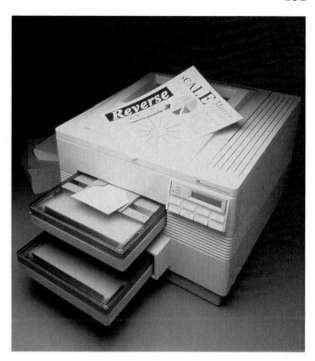

Illus. 5-25. Laser printers produce near-typeset quality printing of text and graphics.

secondary storage, is needed to store data. **Auxiliary storage** is storage that is external to the processor but that can be made available to and placed under the control of the processor as needed. Thus, large volumes of data can be stored and retrieved easily by using auxiliary storage devices.

Common auxiliary storage devices include optical storage disks and magnetic disks and tapes. Magnetic disks include the hard disk and the flexible disk. A *hard disk* is an enclosed, rigid magnetic disk with a read/write head. The *flexible disk*, also known as a *floppy disk*, is a thin, **pliable** magnetic disk. The disk may be housed in a flexible (5 1/4-inch size) or rigid (3 1/2-inch size) outer **casing**. A 2-inch disk is also becoming popular with certain types of portable computers. Magnetic tape storage may be in the form of reels and cartridges.

pliable: easily bent, flexible

casing: protective covering

RESPONSIBLE USE OF COMPUTER SYSTEMS

Office workers in a computerized processing system will have decisions to make when completing processing tasks. Such office workers need to be aware that the tasks they perform may directly affect the tasks that others in the business must complete. Office workers in computerized processing systems must monitor their own work activities to be certain they are contributing to the smooth processing and distribution of information.

As with any office equipment, you will be expected to use the computer in a responsible manner. Two important areas of responsible use are maintenance and security.

Maintenance

If you use a computer, you will want to follow proper maintenance procedures. Read and follow equipment operation instructions so that you do not accidentally cause the equipment to *malfunction*. If you are responsible for the maintenance of your computer, be sure you understand the procedures you are to follow. Suggestions for the care of your computer include:

malfunction: not function properly

- Remember that the computer is electronic equipment and should not be treated roughly. Avoid placing the computer where it can be jarred, knocked off, or dropped.

- Turn your computer on at the beginning of your workday and off at the end. Turning your computer on and off during the workday is hard on your computer because of the electrical power *surges* sent through the circuits.

surges: short, sudden rush

suppressor: a device that checks or holds the flow of power

- Use a power surge *suppressor* to protect your computer against outside power surges. Power surges can occur from electrical storms as well as from your local power company.

- If you must be away from your computer, turn off the monitor or at least turn down the monitor brightness to avoid the image *etching* onto the screen.

etching: producing permanent images

- Clean your display screen with a soft cloth dampened with a window cleaning substance or with alcohol. Do not spray the screen directly with a liquid. Some of the liquid may seep inside and cause damage. Special cleaning products are available from computer supply stores.

- Floppy disk drives collect dust over time, and the read/write head can collect dust particles, grease, and oxides. Use a drive-cleaning disk periodically to remove this buildup from around the head. Follow your computer manufacturer's suggestions for the frequency of this cleaning.

- Keep drinks away from your keyboard. If you should spill liquid on your keyboard, dry the keyboard with an absorbent cloth. Do not attempt to use the keyboard until all the liquid has evaporated.

- Keep your keyboard and printer free of dust and food particles which can interfere with equipment performance. Small cans of compressed air can be used to blow out foreign particles in the equipment.

- If you must move your computer, use cardboard packing in your floppy drives to protect the drive heads. If you have a hard disk, follow the manufacturer's directions to protect the hard disk.

- Cover your computer equipment when you leave for the day. The protective cover provides an added measure of security against mishaps such as broken water lines. Likewise, the protective covers add a barrier against dust and other foreign particles during regular office cleaning.

Security

Security for computer information systems centers around two major concerns: (1) planning for potential loss and (2) protecting against **unauthorized** access to information in computer systems.

unauthorized: not having approval or permission

Planning for Potential Loss

Many companies are careful to plan for possible disaster by instructing employees in **precautionary** measures such as making backup copies and then storing the backup copies in another location. In addition, companies instruct employees in preventive maintenance procedures. Instructing employees in these procedures helps prevent loss due to equipment care negligence.

precautionary: taken beforehand against possible danger or failure

Another potential area of loss is **unintentional** errors made by employees, such as deleting a file or incorrectly updating a customer database. Companies try to minimize potential losses of this nature through employee training.

unintentional: not planned

Assuring Authorized Access

Much of a company's information is confidential and vital to the continued operations of the organization. Companies must be careful to protect their interests. Security of computer-based information is of particular concern because an **unscrupulous** person can quickly and easily:

unscrupulous:
lacking respect for legal or moral considerations

- access information
- copy information (Hundreds of pages can be copied in less than a minute!)
- send information electronically to another location
- alter information

To avoid these and other potential security problems, companies establish security procedures and limit access to files to authorized employees who need the information to perform their jobs. For example, an employee in the inventory department would not need access to company personnel records or accounting records.

Two common security measures are access logs and access codes or passwords. An *access log* is a computer-generated record of each time an authorized user retrieves information from a file and/or completes any file processing. An access log also records any attempt by an unauthorized operator to access a file. An access code or **password** is a preassigned number or term designed to keep unauthorized people from accessing files. For example, when you enter the name of the file you want to access, the monitor may display a prompt similar to the one shown in Illus. 5-26.

If you were unable to enter the required code, you would not be given access to the file. On many systems, your attempt to enter a secured file (a file which requires a code or password to be

Illus. 5-26.
Companies frequently assign passwords or access codes as a security precaution. In order to access certain files, an office worker must enter the proper password or access code when the prompt is displayed.

```
    Enter User ID:      Bernstein

    Enter Password:   ■
```

entered) would be logged and an alert sounded at the computer center to indicate that an attempt had been made to enter a secured file.

TECHNOLOGY AND CHANGE

Modifications will occur from time to time in an organization's information flow and equipment. **Information flow** refers to the movement of information in an organization. Important considerations of an information flow are speed, geographic location, and working relationships. Changes in the flow of information may bring new procedures that you will be expected to follow. With changes in equipment, you may be given time on the job just for learning. In other cases, you may be expected to learn on your own and to continue being reasonably productive at the same time. Your willingness to learn and to adapt to the conditions under which you must learn will be a valuable attitude for you to cultivate.

If you choose an office career, you may have the opportunity to participate in this exciting office revolution. Note the changes that occurred for Brent as his company moved from a simple standalone system to an integrated electronic system:

Brent is an administrative assistant in a company that recently moved to an integrated computer system. Previously, when Brent needed sales information for use in reports he keyed for the department manager, he telephoned the sales office. A sales office employee accessed the sales department's computer to retrieve the information. Brent would wait for the employee to give him the information, take down what the sales department employee said, then enter the data into the report he was keying on his microcomputer.

When Brent's company installed an integrated electronic system, his microcomputer was linked electronically with the mainframe computer and the departmental minicomputers. Brent could then access the sales database himself. He found he saved valuable time by using his computer rather than making a telephone call and waiting for someone in another office to access the information and read it to him.

QUESTIONS FOR REVIEW

1. Describe how office workers might participate in plans for change.

2. Identify equipment you would expect to find for processing information in a traditional office.

3. How have small- to mid-sized businesses been able to consider computer systems for their companies?

4. Describe the ways in which computerized processing might be structured.

5. How do mainframe computers, minicomputers, and microcomputers differ from each other?

6. Identify the four components of a computer system.

7. Explain the importance of the central processing unit.

8. Identify and describe the two classifications of printers.

9. Give five maintenance suggestions for caring for your computer.

10. How is access to computer-based information controlled?

MAKING DECISIONS

Helen works in a medium-sized company that has been transforming noncomputerized processing tasks into computerized processing tasks. Her department, however, has not experienced as great an increase in employee productivity as was anticipated. The department supervisor has asked all office employees to keep an account of what they do each day. Employees were instructed to record what they were doing at the beginning of each 15-minute segment from 9 a.m. through 5 p.m.

Helen considered keeping such a record a nuisance and something that would interfere with her getting her work done. She decided that she would just take the sheets home with her on Thursday evening and fill them in from memory. She would fill in the form for Friday then, too, because she would have a good idea of what she would be doing on Friday. The sheets were to be given to the supervisor at the end of the day on Friday.

What You Are To Do: Evaluate Helen's decision. Would you have made the same decision in the same situation? Why? Why not? What could the supervisor have said to Helen to change her attitude toward keeping a record of her activities? Prepare an answer to each of the questions.

EXTENDING YOUR ENGLISH COMPETENCIES

The excerpt from a report relating to ink-jet printers contains a number of punctuation and capitalization errors.

What You Are To Do: Prepare a copy of the excerpt below, making all corrections required in punctuation and in capitalization. If necessary, refer to Reference Section B for punctuation guidelines and to Reference Section C for capitalization guidelines. Underscore your corrections.

We recommend the purchase of ink-jet printers for the atlanta office. This recommendation is based on certain features:

1. The high resolution printer prints 300 dots-per-inch (dpi)resolution on plain paper at two to three pages per minute ppm for black and white prints.

2. The near-silent operation will allow printers to be located at workstations without interfering with Telephone conversations or Customer inquiries.

3. The use of non-Standard paper sizes will accommodate the varied paper sizes used by different departments in the regional office.

4. An inexpensive color option costs less than $2500 for an ink-jet color printer compared to approximately $30000 for a color laser printer. The color ink-jet printer should be considered for the advertising and public relations departments.

5. The use of the ink-jet printer with desktop publishing will allow color transparencies to be made by the southeast regional office for sales representatives in that region.

If orders are placed by the end of February, delivery should be made within six weeks, by mid-april. After a six-month trial, the Managers of each department receiving an ink-jet printer will complete a printer evaluation. If satisfactory evaluations are received, we may expand the use of similar printers to all u.s. regional offices and the two south american offices.

APPLICATION ACTIVITY

Assume that you are an office assistant to Natalie B. McCardle, Information Systems Manager at Pacific-First Bank. The bank has several branches throughout the metropolitan area. Mrs. McCardle asked you to key a copy of the memo she drafted to all branch managers. On her way to a meeting, Mrs. McCardle stops by your desk and says: "Please compose a brief memo to Kenneth C. Withers, Vice President of Operations. Invite him to attend the demonstration and enclose a copy of the branch manager's memo for his information. I'll initial the memos when I return."

Word processing equipment can be used to complete this activity.

What You Are To Do: Follow Mrs. McCardle's instructions, using memo stationery from *Information Processing Activities* or plain paper.

To: All Branch Managers

From: Natalie B. McCardle, Information Systems *(Manager)*

Date: October 20, 19--

Subject: Voice Mail Demonstration

We think our experimental use of voice mail here in headquarters and at ~~one office~~ *our Seattle branch* supports its introduction throughout the organization.

A meeting *(of all branch managers)* is planned for November 14 [15] at 9:00 a.m. in the conference room here at the Embarcadero Center. We hope you can plan to attend. There will be a discussion of our experience's, a demonstration, and a tour of several offices so you can talk with ~~personnel~~ *workers* *(regularly)* who use this means of communicating. The meeting will end no later than 11:00 a.m. [30]

CHAPTER SUMMARY

Information is critical to every organization regardless of its size or purpose. Organizations give a great deal of attention to information processing and to the organization and technology of processing systems. Key points in this chapter include:

1. The most common forms of information you will find in business offices are data, text, image, and voice.
2. Information processing is important because of the complexity of business, volume of transactions, demand for timely information, and value of accurate information.
3. The information processing workflow consists of five components: input, processing, output, transmission, and storage.
4. Activities that rely heavily on information processing are document processing, data processing, administrative support, records management, and transmission.
5. Learning new software packages on the job is easier if you follow selected suggestions.
6. Equipment used to support computerized processing includes input devices, processing devices, output devices, and auxiliary storage devices.
7. Responsible computer use by office workers includes proper maintenance and security of information processing systems.
8. Equipment used to support traditional processing includes typewriters, low-end word processors, calculators, photocopiers, telephones, and postal equipment.
9. Traditional or manual processing methods are rapidly being replaced by electronic methods.

KEY CONCEPTS AND TERMS

information processing	tutorial
workflow	information processing system
software	integrated electronic system
operating system software	input device
utility software	upload
application software	down load
integrated software	central processing unit
windows feature	output device

KEY CONCEPTS AND TERMS (continued)

display screen	auxiliary storage
impact printer	password
nonimpact printer	information flow

INTEGRATED CHAPTER ACTIVITY

The company for which you work, Investments Diversified, eventually plans to acquire a microcomputer for each office employee. Although the company has been purchasing microcomputers on a regular basis, several departments still have only one microcomputer that must be shared by four to six office employees and the office manager.

With so many employees having to share a single departmental microcomputer and with the increase of information processing tasks completed by each employee, problems of congestion and misunderstandings about the use of the computers have occurred in almost every department. Since it will be several months before additional microcomputers will be purchased, the vice president of information systems has decided that guidelines should be established for the shared use of the current departmental microcomputers.

You have been chosen to represent your department in preparing guidelines. You are meeting today with representatives from other departments to establish suggested guidelines that will be forwarded to the vice president.

As a user of one of the shared microcomputers, you are aware of some of the problems:

- The first-come, first-served concept does not work. You have seen several people lined up to use the microcomputer, some with high-priority tasks. In addition to the time lost waiting in line, having people lined up around the computer puts pressure on the computer user, which results in more errors.

- Once workers get on the computer, they refuse to give it up. Workers often leave the terminal for lengthy periods of time leaving their work displayed on the computer screen.

- When users finish, they typically close the file they are working with and leave the computer in that software program. When the next user sits down at the microcomputer, that person must decide which software program is active and figure out how to get out of the program so that he/she can access the software program he/she needs to use.

- If the computer user has had to leave the terminal even for a short period, some employees will remove the work of the user so that they may have access to the computer. This has caused the loss of several hours of work and is seen by all employees as a very dangerous situation.

- Some employees freely copy software they know should not be copied.

Since you are familiar with this situation, you have some ideas that you think would help correct this situation:

- Have each office manager meet with the office employees at the beginning of each workday to decide priorities.

- Post a computer log and have each person record his/her beginning and ending times.

- Prepare an "in use" sign for use if a worker must leave the computer for a short time.

- Establish time limits as to how long employees can be gone from a computer before their work can be removed.

- Do not allow employees to remove other employees' work without permission from the office manager.

- Return the computer screen to the system prompt when finished.

What You Are To Do: In your meeting with other departmental representatives, determine if there are any additional problems beyond those you have already identified (pages 200-201). Write each problem your group identifies, including those problems listed on pages 200-201, on a separate sheet of paper. The problem statements should be in complete sentences.

Next, develop guidelines to solve these problems identified. You may want to use the suggested ideas listed above as a starting point. Word your guidelines carefully. Use complete sentences so that your coworkers will understand exactly what is expected of them in each situation.

Word processing equipment can be used to complete this activity.

Next, key a final copy of your identified problems and solutions to be forwarded to the vice president. Decide the format you will use and determine an appropriate title.

OPTIONAL COMPUTER APPLICATION ACTIVITY
See Computer Application Activity 5
in your Information Processing Activities workbook.

PRODUCTIVITY CORNER

Kathy Malenky
OFFICE SUPERVISOR

WORKING WITH YOUR COMPUTER

DEAR MS. MALENKY:

For the past four months, I've been working as a roving assistant to several secretaries and administrative assistants. I like the work and have learned a great deal about the company. But I'd like something permanent.

Just yesterday I was asked to consider a permanent data entry position in the Customer Service Department using a microcomputer. I think I would like the work—and I've even had some training on computers in high school—but I'm hesitant to take the job. I've heard so many stories about health problems related to using micros. I'm only 18 and maybe it's silly to think about such problems—but I do.—PAUL IN MINNEAPOLIS

DEAR PAUL:

You are not silly to be thinking about health problems. In becoming adjusted to using new technology, many workers have failed to take account of where and how they work. You can reduce the possibility of developing health problems. Here are a few suggestions:

- Adjust the placement of your terminal for comfort—you don't want to be stretching to reach the keyboard or hunching over the keyboard to depress keys.
- Move your keyboard toward you to avoid being immediately in front of the screen. This will reduce your exposure to any low-level radiation that may be emitted by the screen.
- Adjust your chair height for comfort.
- Check that you have sufficient lighting.
- Plan for brief pauses in your work at the computer from time to time:
  - Take your eyes off your work; look away; close your eyes momentarily.
  - Drop your arms and move your body while sitting.
  - Drop your neck slowly to the left and to the right; return to normal position.
  - Raise your arms and stretch them, then return to normal position.
  - Clasp your hands behind your neck and press your elbows back as far as possible; return to normal position.

What I am suggesting, Paul, is that you want to be sure your workstation is comfortable and that you learn to use brief pauses to relieve tension and to relax.

I am sure you will enjoy your new assignment. Best wishes for success.—KATHY MALENKY

203

CHAPTER 6

Word Processing: Formats for Business Documents

Word processing is an important part of a company's information processing system. Company executives and managers must communicate with each other as well as with outsiders such as customers and suppliers. Office employees responsible for word processing tasks provide valuable assistance to executives and managers.

If you choose a position in word processing, you will be participating in a key function of any business. Common business documents such as letters, memorandums, reports, and tables are the primary forms of written communication in an office. Often equipment is used to compose and process these documents.

The impact of computer technology on written business communications has led to simplified document formats. Using simplified document formats saves time and reduces formatting errors in documents.

You must remember, though, that format variations exist among organizations for common business documents. Some variations are the result of the different word processing equipment used by companies. You can adjust quickly, however, to equipment variations when you know the basic formats commonly accepted in the business community.

You already have acquired some keyboarding skills. You also have some understanding of the formats for common business documents. This chapter builds upon and helps extend the knowledge and skills you have acquired to this point. You will have an opportunity to learn how written documents are formatted in business offices. In this chapter you will learn also about the procedures and equipment used for originating documents.

The objectives of this chapter are to:

- acquaint you with the parts of and common formats for business letters, memorandums, reports, and tables

- acquaint you with procedures and equipment used for originating documents

FORMATTING LETTERS

When you have completed your study of this topic, you will be able to:

- list the characteristics of a letter that conveys a good impression
- describe the basic parts of a business letter
- prepare letters that are formatted according to commonly used business standards

Letters are extremely important to the total communications of American business. Each day millions of letters are processed by office employees. Many companies strive to provide the latest equipment for word processing because letters are so important. Features of modern word processing equipment make it easier for employees to apply their knowledge of formats to complete letters attractively and speedily.

Your knowledge of the parts of the business letter and of acceptable letter formats contributes to your productivity as you prepare letters. As you study Topic 1, take time to learn the letter parts and standard formats thoroughly. By doing so, you will reduce the occasions when you must check references to review how you should format a particular letter part.

recipient: receiver

A standard format for a business letter increases efficiency. Both the person who prepares the letter and the **recipient** of the letter gain from a standardized format. You, as an office worker processing letters, will not need time to decide how to set up the letter. You will use a standard format that your company has established. And, when the recipient receives the letter, the task of reading and comprehending is simplified because the format is basically familiar.

Walter works as a word processing operator for a large insurance company. During a typical day, he processes many business letters. Walter discovered very quickly that his knowledge of basic letter parts and their correct placement increased his efficiency in keying the documents.

A LETTER'S INITIAL IMPACT

The primary purpose of a business letter is to convey a message. However, even before the message is read, the recipient is likely to make a judgment about the letter and its sender. An attractively formatted letter on quality paper will encourage the recipient to read the message with care. On the other hand, a carelessly formatted letter on smudged paper may result in a negative attitude toward the sender and may fail to get close attention.

A letter gives a good first impression if it has the following characteristics:

- The margins, indentions, and spacing are pleasing to the eye.
- Each letter part is correctly placed within the letter.
- Appropriate stationery is used.
- There are no obvious corrections or strikeovers.
- The print is neat, clear, and of uniform darkness.
- There are no smudges or fingerprints.

Make your letters as attractive as possible. If the appearance of the letter is pleasing to the eye, the receiver will want to read the letter.

PARTS OF A BUSINESS LETTER

In Illus. 6-1 you will find all the parts that could be included in a business letter. Of course, few letters will include all these parts. Some parts are included in most letters, while other parts are included only when needed.

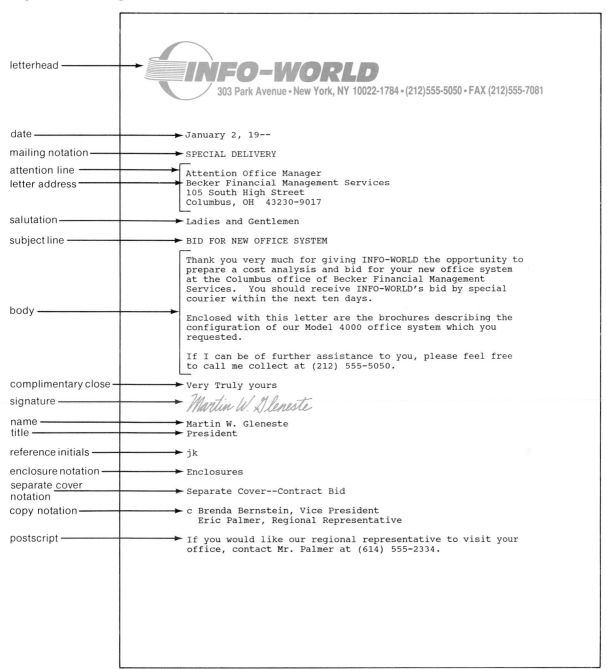

letterhead

INFO-WORLD
303 Park Avenue • New York, NY 10022-1784 • (212)555-5050 • FAX (212)555-7081

date ———— January 2, 19--

mailing notation ———— SPECIAL DELIVERY

attention line ———— Attention Office Manager
letter address ———— Becker Financial Management Services
105 South High Street
Columbus, OH 43230-9017

salutation ———— Ladies and Gentlemen

subject line ———— BID FOR NEW OFFICE SYSTEM

body ———— Thank you very much for giving INFO-WORLD the opportunity to
prepare a cost analysis and bid for your new office system
at the Columbus office of Becker Financial Management
Services. You should receive INFO-WORLD's bid by special
courier within the next ten days.

Enclosed with this letter are the brochures describing the
configuration of our Model 4000 office system which you
requested.

If I can be of further assistance to you, please feel free
to call me collect at (212) 555-5050.

complimentary close ———— Very Truly yours

signature ———— *Martin W. Gleneste*

name ———— Martin W. Gleneste
title ———— President

reference initials ———— jk

enclosure notation ———— Enclosures

separate <u>cover</u>
notation ———— Separate Cover--Contract Bid

copy notation ———— c Brenda Bernstein, Vice President
Eric Palmer, Regional Representative

postscript ———— If you would like our regional representative to visit your
office, contact Mr. Palmer at (614) 555-2334.

Illus. 6-1. Business letter shown in block format with open punctuation.

Parts Generally Included:	Parts Added When Appropriate:
printed letterhead	mailing notation
date	attention line
letter address	subject line
salutation	enclosure notation
body	separate cover notation
complimentary close	copy notation
signature	postscript
name	second-page heading
title	
reference initials	

Printed Letterhead

Business letters typically are keyed or printed on stationery with preprinted headings. This stationery is called *letterhead*. A letterhead generally gives the company name, street address, city, state, ZIP Code, telephone number, and sometimes a facsimile (FAX) number. Some companies also include a company slogan or logo. A **logo** is a letter, symbol, or sign that identifies the company. Can you locate the INFO-WORLD logo in Illus. 6-1 on page 207?

The letterhead should be easy to read, attractive, and representative of the company that sends it. For example, notice the positive impression created by the INFO-WORLD letterhead. The large letters slanting to the right give a sense of forward motion. The placement of the street address, city, state, ZIP Code, and telephone and FAX numbers gives a sense of horizontal balance to the letterhead.

Plan the placement of your letter so that the combination of the printed letterhead and the typewritten or printed message will form an attractive letter.

Date

The date indicates to the reader when the letter was prepared. The complete date (month, day, and year) is used as the dateline. Abbreviated forms of the date are not acceptable in business writing, and *st, nd, rd,* or *th* is never used in the dateline of a business letter.

Proper:	Not Proper:
January 2, 19--	1/2/--
	2nd of January, 19--

Military offices (and offices where military style is used) key the date as follows: *2 January 19--*. Notice that the order is day, month, and year. Notice also that punctuation is not used.

Many companies have adopted standard formats for letters and other business documents. **Standard format** refers to the layout pattern of a document on a page. Standard letter format often specifies that the date should be entered or keyed on a specific line (line 16 is a common placement) for all letters. Formatting documents and common letter and punctuation styles will be discussed later in this topic.

Mailing Notations

Mailing notations are used when the letter requires some type of special postal service. Mailing notations on the letter provide a record of the specific mail service used. Special services include *certified mail, registered mail, special delivery, insured mail,* and *air mail* (for overseas mail). When using a special mailing service, identify that service by keying the appropriate notation a double space below the dateline. Use all capital letters for the mailing notation.

Other notations, such as *PERSONAL* or *CONFIDENTIAL*, should be shown between the date and the letter address. These notations remind the reader of the nature of the letter's content. Such notations also appear on the envelope to inform the mailroom staff that the envelope is to be delivered to the addressee without being opened.

Letter Address

Complete information about the addressee is given in the letter address. The **addressee** is the organization or the person to whom the letter is directed. The envelope matches the information on the letter address, which includes:

- name
- title (if appropriate)
- department or division (if appropriate)
- company name
- complete mailing address

By including the complete address on all letters, you will have a file copy that serves as a good reference for the organization's or person's address.

A common practice is to begin the letter address on the fourth line space below the date. If a mailing notation is used, the letter address is keyed a double space below it.

Name and Title

The name of the addressee is keyed on the first line of the letter address. If the letter is addressed to more than one individual, each name should be keyed on a separate line. When more than one name is included in the address, the names are placed either in alphabetic order or in order of ***prominence*** (for example, Vice President before Office Manager).

prominence: importance

```
Mrs. Janet L. Gollmar        Mr. Samuel F. Kusnerak
Mr. Kenneth G. Stewart       Vice President
                             Mrs. Martha A. Rutkowski
                             Office Manager
```

A courtesy or personal title generally precedes each name. Commonly used courtesy titles are *Mr., Ms., Mrs., Miss, Dr., Professor, The Honorable, Sister,* and *The Reverend*. When known, use the courtesy title the addressee prefers. If a woman's title ***preference*** is not known, use *Ms.*, which is an acceptable title for either a single or married woman. Also be careful to spell the addressee's name correctly. A misspelled name creates a negative impression for the reader. If you are unsure of the appropriate courtesy title or the correct spelling of a name, check previous correspondence received from that individual. As a last resort, call the individual's company and inquire about the courtesy title or the correct spelling of the name. Some companies omit courtesy titles from all correspondence. This means that the addressee would be identified simply as *Patrick L. Plizga* or *Betsy J. Wells*.

preference: one that is liked better

Business titles (Sales Manager, Human Resources Director, Vice President) may be keyed either on the same line as the person's name or on the next line. The length of the business title will determine on which line it will be keyed. You want to achieve a balanced look within the lines of the letter address:

```
Ms. Maryann C. Appelt, Treasurer          Mr. Alfred L. Vinci
Amalgamated Plastics & Supply Co.         Advertising Manager
921 California Avenue                      Leisure Sports
Pittsburgh, PA   15202-9481               5110 Transit Boulevard
                                          Buffalo, NY   14221-3741
```

Company Name

The name of the company should be keyed exactly as the company name appears on the letterhead. For example, if the letterhead shows Reynolds, Frazier, & Crum, you would not use Reynolds, Frazier, *and* Crum. The company name follows the individual's name, unless a department or division is included in the address. If a department or division is used, the company name follows it.

```
Mrs. Kiki Komura, Auditor          Mrs. Kiki Komura, Auditor
Reynolds, Frazier, & Crum          Internal Audit Department
                                   Reynolds, Frazier, & Crum
```

Delivery Address

digit: figure

When the name of the street is a number from one through ten, the street name is spelled out (2819 Tenth Avenue). Use figures for street names that are numbers above ten (127 East 15th Street). When house or building numbers consist of the **digit** 1 (one), spell out "One." Use figures for other single digits (3 Waycross Road).

Some companies use a post office box number as well as a street address. The post office box is added for correspondence. The street address only is used for shipments of products or supplies made to a specific location. Other information, such as an apartment number or suite number, generally is keyed after the delivery address and on the same line.

For Correspondence: For Shipments:

```
Craftmaster Lumber Company          Western Wildlife Publications
31 Duck Creek Road                  One Park Circle, Suite 119
P.O. Box 779                        San Marcos, CA   92069-9703
Berwick, ME   03901-9142
```

City, State, and ZIP Code

The last line of the letter address contains the city, state, and ZIP Code. The United States Postal Service has designated two-letter standard abbreviations to be used with the ZIP (Zoning Improvement Plan) Code. A list of two-letter standard abbreviations is provided in Reference Section E. The ZIP Code appears on the same line as the city and state. Use of the expanded ZIP Code (ZIP + 4) reduces mailing costs and speeds mail deliveries by allowing the Postal Service to use automated equipment to sort the mail. The last four digits of the expanded nine-digit code allow faster and more accurate sorting of mail to small geographic segments, such as city blocks, single buildings, or a group of post office boxes.

Foreign Addresses

subsidiaries: a company controlled by another company

Many companies have customers in foreign countries. Likewise, a company could have **subsidiaries** in several countries. If you prepare correspondence to a foreign country, key the name of the country in all-capital letters on a separate line:

```
Horiuchi International          Sr. Pablo Blanco
18-5, Azukimochi 2-chome        Princesa 5, Torre de Madrid
Higashi-ku                      Planta 10, Oficina 5
Osako 541                       Madrid 28007
JAPAN                           SPAIN
```

Attention Line

Frequently, when a letter is addressed to a company, an attention line is used to direct the letter to a particular person (office manager, for example) or department within the company. The attention line is keyed on the first line of the letter address. The word *Attention* should not be abbreviated. The following styles are acceptable:

```
ATTENTION OFFICE MANAGER
Attention Office Manager
Attention:   Office Manager
```

When an attention line is used, the addressee is the company and not the person or department in the attention line.

Salutation

greeting: expression
of good wishes

The **salutation** is a *greeting* to the addressee and should, therefore, be appropriate for the addressee. If the addressee is a company, use *Ladies and Gentlemen* as the salutation. If the addressee is an individual, the salutation may be as informal as *Dear Jack* or as formal as *My dear Mr. Sharp*. Often the salutation the letter originator chooses is determined by the relationship with the recipient. The following are acceptable salutations:

FOR MEN

FOR WOMEN

Commonly Used:

Commonly Used:

```
Dear Brian
Dear Mr. Bennington
```

```
Dear Margaret
Dear (Ms., Mrs., Miss) Fagerstrom
```

Less Commonly Used:

Less Commonly Used:

```
My dear Brian
My dear Mr. Bennington
```

```
My dear Margaret
My dear (Ms., Mrs., Miss) Fagerstrom
```

Sometimes the name of the addressee is not known. For example, you may have only a title, such as *Sales Manager*. An acceptable salutation is *Dear Sales Manager*. Salutations may also reflect the nature or name of the group, such as *Dear Colleagues, Dear Stockholders,* or *Dear Global Agency*. The salutation is keyed a double space below the letter address.

Subject Line

The writer of a letter may include a subject line to highlight the main topic of the letter. Key the subject line a double space below the salutation (see page 207). A common format is to key the line in all capital letters and omit the word *Subject*. The following styles are acceptable:

```
BID FOR NEW OFFICE SYSTEM
SUBJECT:   BID FOR NEW OFFICE SYSTEM
SUBJECT:   Annual Automation Conference
Subject:   Annual Automation Conference
```

Body

The message of the letter is referred to as the **body**. The message begins a double space below the salutation. If a subject line is used, the message begins a double space below it. Strive to have at least a two-paragraph message. Paragraphs are usually single-spaced with a double space between paragraphs. Avoid paragraphs that are either too long or too short. If the message is brief, you may double space the entire body. Be alert to keeping the right margin as even as possible.

Complimentary Close

farewell: a wish of well-being made at parting

The **complimentary close** is the *farewell* of the letter. Like the salutation, the complimentary close can be informal or formal. The complimentary close and the salutation should convey the same degree of informality or formality. Use an informal complimentary close with an informal or friendly salutation. Use a formal complimentary close with a formal salutation. The following complimentary closings are listed in order from informal to formal:

Commonly Used:	Less Commonly Used:
Cordially	Cordially yours
Sincerely	Yours cordially
Yours truly	Sincerely yours
	Yours sincerely
	Yours very truly
	Very truly yours
	Yours respectfully
	Respectfully

The complimentary close is keyed a double space below the last line of the body. Capitalize only the first letter of the first word of the complimentary close.

Signature, Name of Originator, and Title

All letters should be signed before they are mailed. The handwritten name of the originator is called the *signature*. Because handwritings vary, the signature may not be read easily. The keyed name below the signature simplifies the reading of a poorly written signature. The originator's name is keyed on the fourth line space below the complimentary close. It may be followed on the same line or on the next line by a business or professional title such as *Manager, Vice President,* or *CPA.*

Yours truly   Very sincerely yours

Renaldo E. Lopaz   *John R. Ruel*

Renaldo E. Lopaz   John R. Ruel, CPA
Claims Adjuster

Personal titles, such as Mr., Ms., Mrs., or Miss, are not generally used before the keyed name. If a name could be that of a man or woman, (Robin or Leslie, for example), then it is appropriate to add a personal title so that the receiver knows how to address the writer if a response is needed. The use of parentheses around such titles is optional.

Robin M. LaFabre   *Leslie W. Webster*

(Mr.) Robin M. LaFabre   Ms. Leslie W. Webster

Some women prefer to indicate their personal title preference. This preference can be indicated as part of the keyed or handwritten name. Examples of how a woman's name might appear follow:

Joanna Manjerovic   *Claudine A. Reynolds*

Mrs. Joanna S. Manjerovic   Miss Claudine A. Reynolds

Ruth P. Bezdek   *Ms. Donna C. Antonacceo*

Ms. Ruth P. Bezdek   Donna C. Antonacceo

If the person for whom you prepared the letter is not available, you may be asked to sign the letter. To do this, sign the writer's name in your own handwriting and place your initials after the signature.

Michael B. Gillespie

Michael B. Gillespie   *CR*

Sometimes the name of the company is keyed as part of the closing lines. This practice is unnecessary if the company name appears on the letterhead. If used, the company name is keyed in all capital letters a double space below the complimentary close. The originator's name and title then are keyed four lines below the company name.

Sincerely yours   Yours respectfully

DATA SYSTEMS SPECIALISTS   GLOBAL TRAVEL INCORPORATED

Alan F. Conrad   *Judi R. Bronstein*

Alan F. Conrad   Judi R. Bronstein
Regional Vice President   International Consultant

Reference Initials

The **reference initials** identify the person who keyed the document. These initials are placed at the left margin a double space below the writer's name and title. The writer's initials are not necessary if the name is keyed. If you are the writer as well as the person who keys the document, no reference initials are needed.

Marybeth is a staff assistant to the public information director of a large communications company. The director has delegated to Marybeth the task of getting up-to-date reports in a wide range of fields. Marybeth writes many letters requesting reports. She writes such letters, keys them, and signs her own signature; therefore, no reference initials are added to her letters.

Enclosure Notation

Items included in the same envelope with a letter are **enclosures**. The enclosure notation is a reminder to you to include the items in the mailing envelope. The enclosure notation is keyed a double space below the reference initials. (See page 207.)

One enclosure is indicated by the word *Enclosure*; more than one, by *Enclosures* with the number of enclosures optional. For the reader's convenience or for important documents, the enclosure notation may identify the enclosed items.

```
Enclosures 2                              Enclosures
Enclosures: Sales Catalog                    Sales Catalog
            Order Form                       Order Form
```

Separate Cover Notation

If a letter refers to items sent in another envelope or package not included with the letter, you should include a separate cover notation. This notation is keyed a double space below the last enclosure line if one is included. One item is indicated by the words *Separate Cover*; more than one item, by either of the following:

```
Separate Cover 2
Separate Cover: Cost Analysis Printouts
                Annual Report
```

The separate cover notation alerts the office assistant to expect in the mail additional items related to the correspondence. In Chapter 14, you will learn how to keep a record of such items.

Copy Notation

A copy notation indicates that copies of the letter have been sent to individuals other than the addressee. This notation is keyed a double space below the separate cover notation. The copy notation is indicated by the letter *c*.

```
c Lee Ann Cloonan
```

When copies are sent to several individuals, a check mark often is placed beside the name of the individual to receive each copy. This procedure aids you in preparing envelopes for all who are to receive copies. If the writer wishes to add a handwritten comment on one of the copies, the check mark lets the writer know which copy will be sent to which individual.

```
c Alan Oldsfield ✓
  Wesley Schmidt
  JoAnne Winiarski
  Jessica Ziobro
```

The notation *bc* is used to indicate a blind copy. A blind copy notation refers to the practice of omitting the copy notation on the original copy. It is used when the sender does not want the addressee to know to whom a copy of the letter is being sent.

```
bc Geraldine O'Conner
```

The blind copy notation should appear only on the copies of the letter. On photocopies, the blind copy notation can be keyed on one photocopy which can be photocopied again to produce as many copies as are required.

Postscript

Some writers include a postscript. A **postscript** is a short message at the very end of the letter. It usually is used to add information omitted from the letter or to add special emphasis to an important point. The postscript is keyed as a separate paragraph and placed a double space below all other notations. (Refer to page 207.) Notice the initials P. S. are not used.

Second-Page Heading

Occasionally, a letter will require more than one page. In such instances, each page except the first page is numbered. The second-page heading should include the name of the addressee, the page number, and the date. The second-page heading is blocked at the left margin as shown in Illus. 6-2.

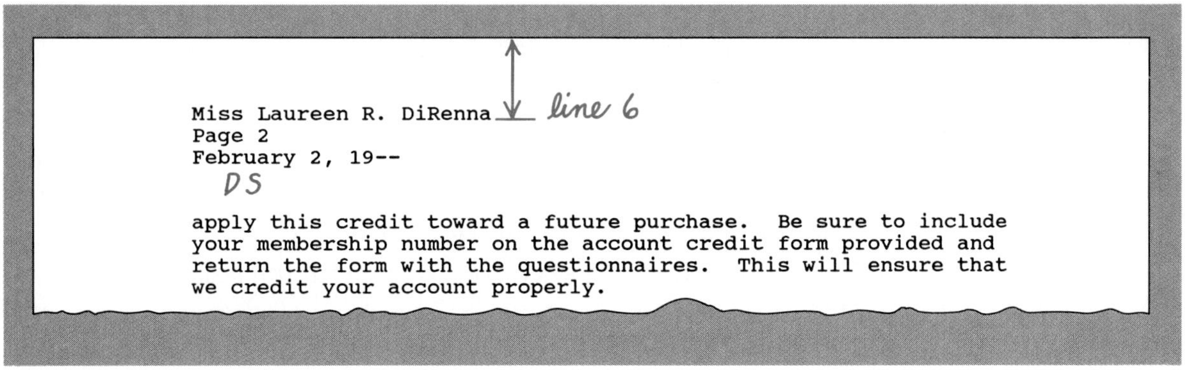

Miss Laureen R. DiRenna   *line 6*
Page 2
February 2, 19--
DS

apply this credit toward a future purchase. Be sure to include
your membership number on the account credit form provided and
return the form with the questionnaires. This will ensure that
we credit your account properly.

Illus. 6-2. Second-page heading

LETTER FORMATS

Letters are formatted in several different ways. The most commonly used formats are *block*, *modified block*, and *simplified block*. As you read about each format, locate the appropriate sample letter on page 221. The first line of a letter, like the first line of all documents, is keyed on an even-numbered line (12, 14, 16, or 18, depending upon the letter length and the type of envelope used).

Block

All lines in the **block format** begin flush with the left margin. The popularity of this format is due to the ease of keying all the special lines. Block format is highly efficient because it saves time in moving from one part of the letter to another.

Modified Block

The **modified block format** has two variations. In the first variation all letter parts are keyed exactly as they are in block style except for the dateline and the closing lines. These two parts begin at the horizontal center of the page rather than flush with the left margin. In the second variation, paragraphs are also indented.

Simplified Block

The **simplified block format** has the following characteristics:

- All letter parts begin at the left margin.
- The date is keyed on line 12.
- The address is keyed in all capital letters with no punctuation.
- The subject line replaces the salutation. Double space above and below the subject line.
- The complimentary close is omitted.
- The writer's name is keyed on the fourth line below the body of the letter.
- The writer's title or department name, if used, may appear on the same line as the writer's name or on the line below it. Strive for balanced line lengths.
- The signature block (writer's name, title, department) may be keyed in all capital letters or in upper and lowercase letters.
- A standard-length line is used. The six-inch line is common: 60 pica or 10-pitch spaces; 72 elite or 12-pitch spaces.

Keying the dateline on line 12 allows the letter address to show through the window portion of a window envelope.

Supporters of the simplified block letter format believe it is more appropriate for modern communications than the other formats because it is streamlined. Supporters are especially ***vocal*** about eliminating salutations and complimentary closes, which they believe are now outdated.

vocal: inclined to talk freely

PUNCTUATION STYLES

Two punctuation styles are commonly used in the special lines of business letters. These are open punctuation and mixed punctuation. As you read about each style, locate the appropriate sample letter shown in Illus. 6-3.

Open Punctuation

Open punctuation means no punctuation marks are used after the salutation and the complimentary close. Open punctuation is considered a time-saving style, and it often is used with a block format letter. See Illus. 6-3 for an example of a block letter with open punctuation.

Mixed Punctuation

When the **mixed punctuation** style is used, the salutation and complimentary close are followed by punctuation marks. The

Block/open punctuation

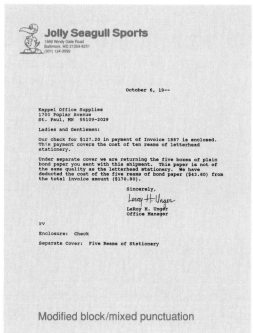

Modified block/mixed punctuation

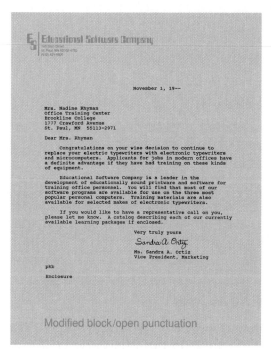

Modified block/open punctuation

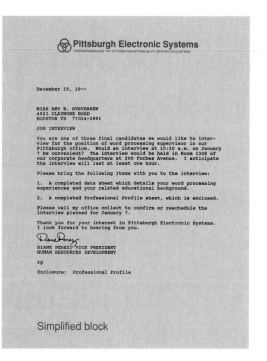

Simplified block

Illus. 6-3. Commonly used business letter formats.

proper punctuation with this style is a comma after the complimentary close and a colon or a comma after the salutation:

Formal: Informal:

Dear Mr. Nassar: Dear Mark,

Ladies and Gentlemen:

Refer to Illus. 6-3 for an example of a modified block letter with mixed punctuation. The persistence of the use of this punctuation style reflects the belief of many business people that some punctuation should appear after salutations and complimentary closes. Business letter writing traditions last a long time!

ENVELOPE FORMAT

A parallel exists between specific parts of a business letter and the information that must be included on an envelope. To be informative to postal workers and to recipients, envelopes must include the following information:

- the return address
- special address notation, if any
- special mailing notation, if any
- the recipient's name and address

The Return Address

Most companies have printed return addresses on their envelopes similar to the letterhead of the company. If no return address is printed on the envelope, key the return address a double space from the top of the envelope and three spaces from the left edge.

Special Address Notations

Special notations, such as CONFIDENTIAL, PERSONAL, or HOLD FOR ARRIVAL, that do not affect the cost of mailing are keyed in all capital letters a double space below the return address and three spaces from the left edge of the envelope.

Special Mailing Notations

Special notations, such as REGISTERED MAIL or SPECIAL DELIVERY, that affect the cost of mailing are keyed in all capital letters below the area where the stamp will be placed.

Recipient's Address

If mail is to be handled efficiently by postal workers, the address on the envelope must be accurate, complete, and easy to read. The envelope address should include the same information given in the letter address.

If you are using a No. 10 envelope (9 $\frac{1}{2}$″ by 4 $\frac{1}{8}$″), begin the address on about line 14 and about five spaces to the left of center. If you are using a No. 6 $\frac{3}{4}$ envelope (6 $\frac{1}{2}$″ by 3 $\frac{5}{8}$″), begin the address on about line 12 and about ten spaces to the left of center. Addresses should be single-spaced and in block format, as shown in Illus. 6-4. If an attention line is necessary, always place it first.

The United States Postal Service recommends that all words in the address be keyed or printed in capital letters and no punctuation marks be used. The only exception is the hyphen within the ZIP Code. Keying the address in this manner facilitates the handling of envelopes by automated postal equipment such as *OCR's* (optical character readers).

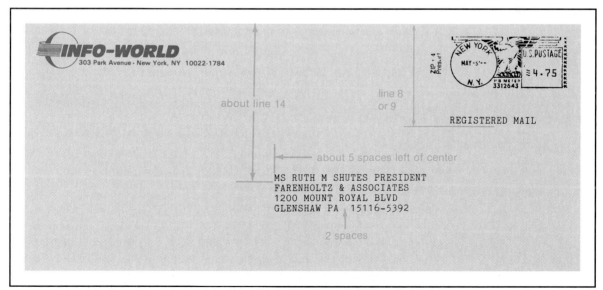

Illus. 6-4. United States Postal Service (USPS) recommended envelope format.

In many companies where office assistants use electronic word processing equipment, customers' letter addresses (which include each customer's name and address) are keyed in the format recommended by the Postal Service and stored for use later. The names and addresses can be recalled and printed automatically on envelopes or mailing labels. The names and addresses can also be merged with a standard letter body to produce original letters for large mailings. The simplified block letter format is particularly suited to this purpose.

QUESTIONS FOR REVIEW

1. How does a knowledge of letter parts and formats contribute to productivity?

2. Why is a standard format used for business letters?

3. What parts of a letter always will be included in any letter?

4. What information generally is included in a company's letterhead?

5. Where should a mailing notation appear on a letter?

6. Describe what generally is included in a letter address.

7. Why do you include the ZIP Code in a letter address?

8. In what ways does the block letter format differ from the simplified block letter format?

9. Where are punctuation marks required when you are using mixed punctuation?

10. What information shown on a letter must also be shown on the envelope?

INTERACTING WITH OTHERS

Brenda is a new office worker at Capital Distributors. Three other employees work in the same office. The first day Brenda reports to work, her supervisor, Ms. DeAngelo, tells her to take time to become acquainted with the office equipment and the company procedures manual. While she is studying the procedures manual to see how various company documents are prepared, Ms. DeAngelo interrupts her and says, "I have drafted several letters which I would like you to prepare for my signature. I will be out of the office for about three hours. I'll sign the letters when I return."

Brenda took the letters from Ms. DeAngelo and placed them in her in basket until she finished studying the procedures manual. Later, when Brenda began to process the documents, she found that Ms. DeAngelo did not include the recipient's full name and address on any of the letters. Since each salutation identified the recipient by last name only, Brenda felt that she had no way of locating the missing information. Therefore, she went back to the procedures manual to review some sections and did not key the letters. When Ms. DeAngelo returned, she approached Brenda and said, "I'll sign those letters now."

If you were Brenda and you were not able to complete the letters before Ms. DeAngelo returned, what would you say to her when she asked for the letters? What might Brenda have done when she discovered that complete names were missing?

What You Are To Do: Prepare a brief response to the questions asked.

EXTENDING YOUR MATH COMPETENCIES

Assume that you are an office worker in the Accounting Department of The Computer Depot, a small retail computer store. Your supervisor, Mrs. Lowell, hands you the report shown on page 226 and asks you to determine the total sales, the cost of units sold, and the gross profit on the sales of each product. "I'll need this information to fill in the figures on the draft of my letter," Mrs. Lowell said.

What You Are To Do: Write the headings *Product No., Total Sales, Cost of Units Sold,* and *Gross Profit* across the top of a sheet of plain paper. Then list each product by its product number. Compute the total sales for each product. (Multiply units sold by the selling price.) Compute the cost of units sold for each product. (Multiply units sold by the wholesale price.) Compute the gross profit for each product. (The gross profit is the difference between the total sales and the cost of units sold.) Add the gross profit column to determine the total gross profit figure. Finally, refer to your figures to determine the information Mrs. Lowell needs to complete the portion of the draft shown on page 226. Write the information at the bottom of your paper. Save your work; you will need it to complete an assignment in Topic 2.

PRODUCT EARNINGS REPORT

Product Description	Product Number	Units Sold	Wholesale Price	Selling Price	Total Sales	Cost of Units Sold	Gross Profit
Monitor	M2021	15	$173.90	$ 248.50	$?	$?	$?
Keyboard	K001	5	126.18	180.25	?	?	?
CPU	C3011	82	995.60	1,422.32	?	?	?
Disk Drive	D8929	111	145.55	207.93	?	?	?
Computer Desk	K3723	15	134.40	192.00	?	?	?
Diskettes (box)	T5221	722	20.65	29.50	?	?	?
Computer Paper (box)	P0010	57	13.30	18.98	?	?	?

TOTAL GROSS PROFIT..$?

List all products by product number

Our gross profit for this earning period was
$_____. The three products (by product number)
that produced the highest total sales are
___?___ ($?), ___?___ ($?), and ___?___ ($?)
the three products that produced the greatest gross profit
for the store during this period are ___?___ ($?),
_____ ($_____), and _____ ($_____).

APPLICATION ACTIVITY

Word processing equipment can be used to complete this activity.

Assume that you are an office worker for Pfeifer Office Furniture. The letter, which follows, originally was prepared by a temporary office employee and is not mailable. Your supervisor, Louis Nicolas, asks you to key a corrected copy of the letter. "Some of the required letter parts are missing and other letter parts are keyed incorrectly," he says. "Please use block format with open punctuation."

What You Are To Do: Use letterhead in *Information Processing Activities* or plain paper. If necessary, refer to Illustration 6-1 on page 207.

PFEIFER OFFICE FURNITURE

2700 West Haddon Avenue Chicago, Illinois 60622-9022

April 21st, 19--

Special Delivery

Wolff Pharmacies
1192 Goshen Street
Attention Accounting Department
Hartford, Ct. 06106-9202

Sir

    Enclosed are the price list and catalog you requested in
your letter of April 5. As you will notice, we stock over fifty
different workstations, each designed to accommodate different
configurations of computer equipment.

If your company decides to stock five or more of our computer
workstations, we can offer you an additional 5 percent discount
off the list price.

Thank you very much for your interest in Pfiefer Office Furniture. If you need additional information, please feel free to
call me collect at 312-555-2987.

Yours Truly

Louis W. Nicolas, Sales Manager

ly

TOPIC 2

FORMATTING MEMORANDUMS, REPORTS, AND TABLES

When you have completed your study of this topic, you will be able to:

- format formal and informal memorandums and explain how memorandums differ from letters

- format informal (unbound) reports and tables and identify their parts

- describe the ways in which documents are originated and identify effective transcription guidelines

Letters are used for communicating with people outside the company; memorandums are used for communicating with people within the company. As you can imagine, there are numerous occasions when persons within a company must write to each other. Personnel directors send memorandums to all employees informing them of vacation and holiday schedules. Payroll department managers send memorandums to employees informing them of new social security rates or income taxes. Credit managers send memorandums to sales representatives describing new terms for extending credit to customers.

Regardless of the department you choose as your place of employment, you undoubtedly will aid in the preparation of many memorandums, reports, and tables. For example, it is not uncommon for managers of departments to report on a regular basis to top management. Such reporting is done in written form.

Additionally, managers are responsible for suggesting changes in company procedure. Often such suggestions must be reviewed by top management, who expect to read a report as a part of the review process. Company managers, with the aid of office workers, produce many reports and tables for both external and internal purposes.

Often internal communications must be developed and prepared under considerable pressure because of the need for prompt decisions. In such an environment, you can imagine how your skills as a word processing worker become critical. An alert, competent office worker is an important partner in getting memorandums and reports done promptly and properly. Many office workers find the preparation of communications under pressure one of the most challenging jobs they face. You, too, may enjoy such a challenge.

Jill is a word processing worker in the office of the director of product development. A new product that was being sold on an experimental basis in only seven cities across the country was received by the public with far more enthusiasm than anticipated. Sales were beyond projections; stock was insufficient to meet demand. It became clear that new production facilities were required. The entire department moved into high gear as plans were developed for increasing production. Jill was invaluable in preparing drafts of reports as they were being developed. Several workdays extended well into the night. However, Jill worked the additional hours willingly because everyone was so cooperative and all were contributing to doing an exceptionally good job. She liked being a member of such a hardworking team.

MEMORANDUMS

streamlined: containing only the essentials

A **memorandum** is a *streamlined* business document used to communicate with an individual or a group of individuals within an organization. Memorandums (also called *interoffice memos* or *memos*) do not contain all the parts used in letters. For example, the salutation, complimentary close, and signature are omitted. Many offices use full- or half-sheet preprinted memorandum forms that contain a printed memorandum heading. Memorandums prepared with a memorandum heading, whether on preprinted forms, letterhead, or plain paper, are *formal memorandums.* (See page 231.) Memorandums typed or printed on plain paper or on letterhead without a memorandum heading are *simplified memorandums.*

Many offices store forms in computer memory and recall them as needed. For example, the basic memorandum form with its margin settings, line spacing, and printing requirements can be stored electronically in computer memory. The office worker recalls the memo to the screen (refer to Illus. 6-5, page 230) and begins keying immediately. The keyed memorandum can be printed on plain paper or letterhead or sent electronically to another computer.

```
                    UNITED TECHNOLOGIES
                       MEMORANDUM


    TO: Department Heads

    FROM: Amy Johnson, Director Human Resources

    DATE: November 15, 19--

    SUBJECT: Annual Leave Carryover Requests

    Please remind your employees that requests for annual leave
    carryover must be returned to this office by December 15.  We
    will begin adjusting annual leave accruals at that time.
    Employees with five or fewer years of service as of December 31
    may carry forward up to 80 hours of annual leave.  Employees
    with six to ten years of service as of December 31 are eligible
    to carry forward up to 120 hours.  Employees with over ten
    years of service as of December 31 may carry forward their
    annual leave balances up to 320 hours.
```

Illus. 6-5. Using forms stored in computer memory increases worker productivity.

Illus. 6-6 shows the various parts of a memorandum on a preprinted form. Refer to this illustration as you read about the purpose and proper placement of each part.

Heading

constitute make up; form

The guide words TO, FROM, DATE, and SUBJECT *constitute* the **heading**. The guide words should be printed to allow for double spacing between the lines of the heading and to allow for approximately a 1-inch left margin. Note that in Illus. 6-6 the guide words are placed so that the same margins may be used throughout the keying process. Set your left margin to key the heading information two spaces to the right of the printed heading.

If you prepare a formal memorandum without a preprinted form, use 1-inch side margins throughout. Block the guide words in the heading one inch from the left edge of the paper to avoid resetting margins, as in Illus. 6-5.

A memorandum may be sent to more than one individual. The following formats are acceptable when you prepare such a memo:

```
TO:  Adam Brown, Kim Ling, and Carole Matthews
TO:  All Regional Vice Presidents
TO:  See Distribution List Below
```

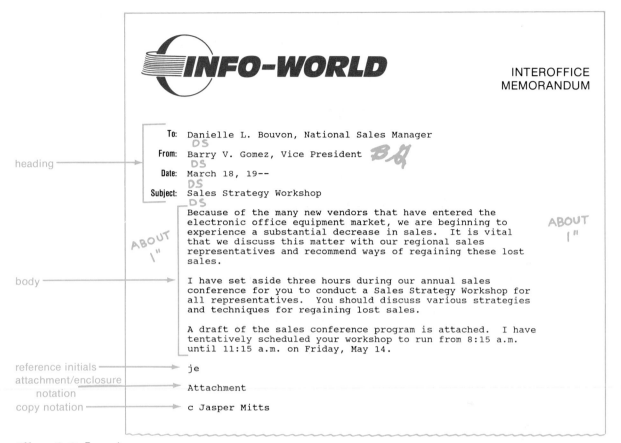

heading

body

reference initials
attachment/enclosure
notation
copy notation

Illus. 6-6. Formal memorandum format

The distribution list mentioned in the heading in the last example would be keyed a double space below the reference initials at the end of the memo. This procedure aids you in making sure that all intended recipients receive a copy of the memo.

```
cd

Distribution List:
Alson, T. F.
Balsas, Richard
Cantwell, Mary Sue
Dodwell, Winter
```

Personal preference will determine whether or not handwritten initials are included after the sender's name in the heading.

Body

The body begins a double space below the last line of the heading. Paragraphs may be blocked at the left margin or indented five spaces. Use approximately 1-inch side margins.

Reference Initials

Reference initials identify the person who keyed the document. These initials are keyed at the left margin, a double space below the last line of the body.

Attachment/Enclosure Notation

When an item is attached to a memorandum with a paper clip or a staple, an attachment notation is used. When the item is placed in an envelope with the memorandum, an enclosure notation is used. The notation is placed a double space below the reference initials. More than one attachment or enclosure may be indicated in any of the following ways:

```
Attachments
Attachments 2
Attachments:  Flextime Policy
              Vacation Schedule


Enclosures
Enclosures 2
Enclosures:  Software Price List
             Order Form
```

Copy Notation

Key the copy notation c a double space below the enclosure notation or a double space after the reference initials if there is no enclosure.

```
              c  Steinfield
```

**THE
ENVELOPE**

If the person receiving the memo is located nearby, the memo may be placed in the person's in basket. In this case, an envelope may not be needed. However, if the receiver is in a different part of the building or in a different building altogether, the memo typically is sent in an interoffice or intra-company envelope or in a plain color envelope used only for intra-company mail. A confidential document always is placed in an envelope and the envelope is marked CONFIDENTIAL.

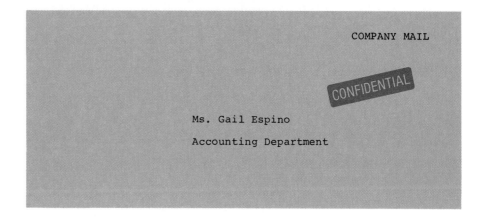

COMPANY MAIL

CONFIDENTIAL

Ms. Gail Espino

Accounting Department

Illus. 6-7. An envelope marked "CONFIDENTIAL" should be opened only by the addressee.

THE SIMPLIFIED MEMORANDUM

The **simplified memorandum** is an example of a popular format. Omitting the heading words TO, FROM, DATE, and SUBJECT eliminates unnecessary keying and aligning with pre-printed headings. Standard format for a simplified memo often specifies that the date be keyed on a specific line (line 10, for example) or a double space below the letterhead, if letterhead is used.

As you look at Illus. 6-8 on page 234, note the following characteristics of this format:

- One-inch margins are used and memo parts are blocked.
- Only single, double, or quadruple spacing is used, which works best with electronic processing equipment.
- The name of the addressee is keyed on the fourth line space below the date.
- The subject line is keyed in all capital letters.
- The writer's name and title are keyed on the fourth line space below the body of the memo.
- All notations after the reference initials are double-spaced.

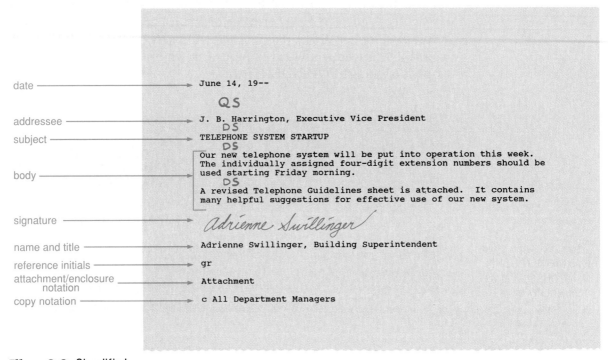

date ——————→ June 14, 19--

QS

addressee ——————→ J. B. Harrington, Executive Vice President

DS

subject ——————→ TELEPHONE SYSTEM STARTUP

DS

body ——————→ Our new telephone system will be put into operation this week.
The individually assigned four-digit extension numbers should be
used starting Friday morning.

DS

A revised Telephone Guidelines sheet is attached. It contains
many helpful suggestions for effective use of our new system.

signature ——————→ *Adrienne Swillinger*

name and title ——————→ Adrienne Swillinger, Building Superintendent

reference initials ——————→ gr

attachment/enclosure
notation ——————→ Attachment

copy notation ——————→ c All Department Managers

Illus. 6-8. Simplified
memorandum format

INFORMAL, BRIEF REPORTS

A business **report**, whether formal or informal, is written to convey information in a clear, concise manner. You probably know something about reports in general if you have written such documents as assignments in school.

Reports include both a main heading (or title) and text, called the body of the report. Informal, brief reports also may include the following additional parts:

- secondary heading
- reference list (or bibliography)
- side headings
- title page
- reference citations
- abstract

The number of additional parts included will depend upon the nature of the report and the subject matter covered. Essentially, reports are organized to communicate the intended message or information quickly and clearly.

Informal, unbound reports of no more than five to six pages will be discussed here. You will learn about long reports in Chapter 11.

PARTS OF INFORMAL REPORTS

Illus. 6-9 on page 236 shows an informal, unbound report. The unbound report may fit on one sheet of plain paper or it may require several sheets of paper. If the report requires several sheets, it is stapled in the top left-hand corner. Unbound reports do not have extra space left in the margin for fastening the pages together.

Because these documents are informal, they do not require all the parts of more formal reports. In this topic, you will learn about the main heading, the secondary heading, the body, and side headings. Other report parts will be discussed in Chapter 11.

Main Heading

Standard format for an informal, unbound report specifies that the main heading or title be entered on a specific line (line 10, pica; line 12, elite). The main heading is centered and keyed in all capital letters. If two lines are required for the heading, the lines may be either double-spaced or single-spaced. To take full advantage of automatic word processing features, however, the main heading is often double-spaced.

Secondary Heading

Some reports require a secondary heading. The secondary heading is centered a double space below the main heading, but only the first letters of key words are capitalized. The body of the text begins a quadruple space below the secondary heading. When word processing software is used, alternating between single and double spacing frequently requires the user to change line spacing codes. To save processing time, standard format users place a quadruple space between the last line of the heading and the body of the report when the report is double-spaced. (Refer to Illus. 6-9 on page 236.)

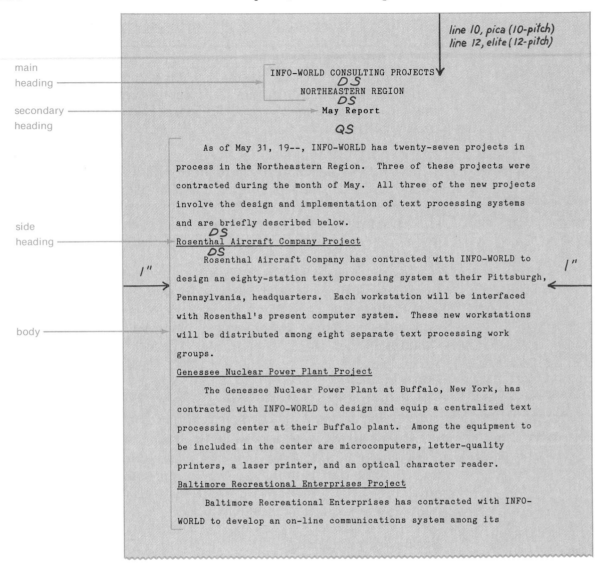

line 10, pica (10-pitch)
line 12, elite (12-pitch)

main heading

secondary heading

side heading

body

INFO-WORLD CONSULTING PROJECTS
DS
NORTHEASTERN REGION
DS
May Report
QS

As of May 31, 19--, INFO-WORLD has twenty-seven projects in process in the Northeastern Region. Three of these projects were contracted during the month of May. All three of the new projects involve the design and implementation of text processing systems and are briefly described below.
DS
Rosenthal Aircraft Company Project
DS
Rosenthal Aircraft Company has contracted with INFO-WORLD to design an eighty-station text processing system at their Pittsburgh, Pennsylvania, headquarters. Each workstation will be interfaced with Rosenthal's present computer system. These new workstations will be distributed among eight separate text processing work groups.

Genessee Nuclear Power Plant Project

The Genessee Nuclear Power Plant at Buffalo, New York, has contracted with INFO-WORLD to design and equip a centralized text processing center at their Buffalo plant. Among the equipment to be included in the center are microcomputers, letter-quality printers, a laser printer, and an optical character reader.

Baltimore Recreational Enterprises Project

Baltimore Recreational Enterprises has contracted with INFO-WORLD to develop an on-line communications system among its

1"   1"

Illus. 6-9. Informal, unbound report format

Body

The **body** of the report presents the information that the sender wants the reader to have regarding the subject of the report. The body may be double-spaced or single-spaced. Double spacing is used between paragraphs whether the paragraphs are single-spaced or double-spaced.

Side Headings

emphasis: highlighting something of importance

A side heading is used to divide a main topic into subdivisions. Side headings are keyed in capital and lowercase letters at the left margin and are underscored for **emphasis**. Use a double space before and after all side headings.

Page Numbers

succeeding: to come next after another

A report frequently has more than one page. In such instances, each page except the first is numbered. The page number is placed at the right margin on line 6. If a heading is used on the second and **succeeding** pages, the page number is part of that heading. The heading may be blocked at the left margin or placed horizontally across the page, as shown in Illus. 6-10. The text continues a double space below the heading and/or page number.

Features of word processing equipment and software contribute to an office worker's efficiency by automatically printing the heading at the top of succeeding pages. You will learn more about this feature in Chapter 7.

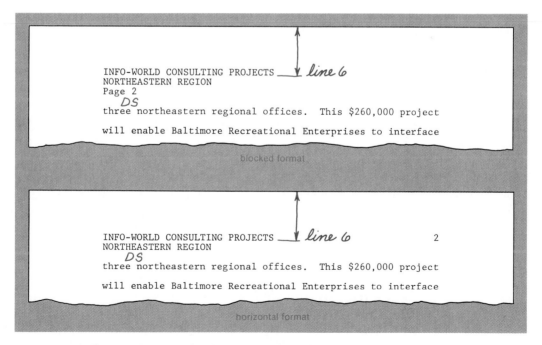

Illus. 6-10. Formats for second and succeeding page headings

accompany: go with

A **table** is a systematic arrangement of facts, figures, and other information. A table should be self-explanatory and not require referring to any text that might ***accompany*** the table. Tables summarize information and often are used to make comparisons. Look at the table in Illus. 6-11. Which employee received the highest commission? How much were his or her total sales for the first quarter? Which employee received the lowest commission? How much were his or her total sales for the first quarter?

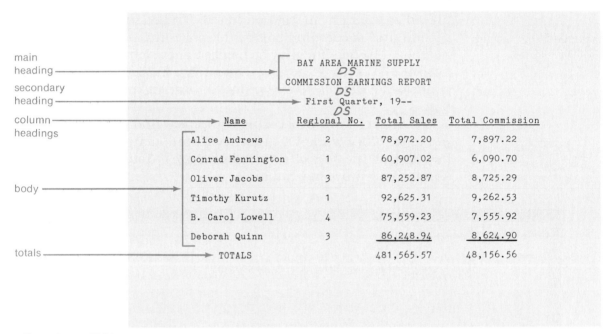

main
heading

secondary
heading

column
headings

body

totals

BAY AREA MARINE SUPPLY			
DS			
COMMISSION EARNINGS REPORT			
DS			
First Quarter, 19--			
DS			
Name	Regional No.	Total Sales	Total Commission
Alice Andrews	2	78,972.20	7,897.22
Conrad Fennington	1	60,907.02	6,090.70
Oliver Jacobs	3	87,252.87	8,725.29
Timothy Kurutz	1	92,625.31	9,262.53
B. Carol Lowell	4	75,559.23	7,555.92
Deborah Quinn	3	86,248.94	8,624.90
TOTALS		481,565.57	48,156.56

Illus. 6-11. Table format

Illus. 6-11 shows the standard parts of a table. Some simplified tables will not include all these parts. More complex tables will include other parts such as a source note, ruled lines, and leader dots. Refer to the illustration as you read about standard table parts.

Main Heading

The main heading is the title of the table and describes its overall content. The main heading of a table is treated in the same manner as the main heading of an informal report.

Secondary Heading

Some tables require a secondary heading such as the one shown in Illus. 6-11. The secondary heading is centered a double space below the main heading, and only the first letters of key words are capitalized. The column headings begin either a double or a triple space below the secondary heading. In order to take advantage of the automatic features of word processing equipment, standard format may call for the column headings to begin a double space below the secondary heading, if there is one.

Column Headings

Column headings are used to identify the information provided in particular columns. A column heading is centered above the longest line in that column and is keyed in capital and lowercase letters. Column heads may be underscored in order to set them off from the body of the table. A double space precedes and follows the column heading.

Body

aligned: lined up

The **body** of the table contains the information indicated by the column headings. You may either double-space or single-space the body. Unless a table is very long, it usually will be double-spaced. When the table is part of the text of a letter, memorandum, or report, the spacing of the table will be determined by the space available on the page. Notice in Illus. 6-11 that word columns (such as Name) are *aligned* at the left and figure columns (such as Total Sales) are aligned at the decimal point.

Totals

The last entry in a column is underscored in order to indicate that figures in the column have been added to obtain a total. The word *Totals* is indented and keyed a double space below the last entry in the body of the table.

ORIGINATING DOCUMENTS

A common responsibility of managers is to originate letters, memorandums, and reports. As an office worker, you may be asked to assist managers with this task. Likewise, you may be asked to prepare common documents to send out under your own signature.

Managers differ in the ways they originate their written communications. Equipment availability and personal preference generally will influence how a manager prepares documents. However, even one manager may use several methods, choosing the one best suited to the particular writing task at hand.

Marian Yanlow is responsible for writing many letters, memorandums, and reports in her position as vice president for systems engineering for a large manufacturing company. If she has a letter to write which she thinks is difficult to compose, she begins by making notes in pencil on a yellow pad. However, for the many relatively straightforward letters she composes, she uses the company's centralized dictation system. She also uses her laptop computer at home or while traveling to draft documents.

Traditional Methods

Some managers think best with a sheet of paper and a pencil when they must compose a letter or report. So they prepare drafts of all, or at least some, correspondence in longhand. Other managers like to think without having to worry about writing down their thoughts, so they choose to dictate to an office worker with shorthand or alphabetic writing system skills. These are both examples of manual methods of composing documents.

If you consider only the time involved, manual methods are not likely to be as economical as machine methods. However, since companies care about the quality of written communications, managers are often free to use the method that helps them do the best job possible.

Illus. 6-12. Methods of originating documents vary according to the available equipment and the executive's preference. This executive is using a portable dictation unit while traveling.

Machine Dictation Methods

Equipment for recording dictation ranges from small, portable units that fit easily into briefcases to units that are components of a centralized dictation system.

Portable and Desk-Top Units

Portable and desk-top units are designed to meet a variety of dictation needs. Portable units vary in size—some lightweight units are smaller than a three-by-five-inch card. Some portable units are battery operated only; others use either electric current or battery power. Portable units are used often when dictation is done away from the office.

Desk-top models vary. A desk-top unit may be a simple dictation machine or a combination dictation/transcription machine. Some units have built-in sensitive microphones, visual displays to indicate instructions and length of each dictated item, and telephone answering capability. Instead of a visual display, other models provide an index slip on which the dictator indicates instructions and length of each dictated item.

Illus. 6-13. Portable and desk-top machine dictation units.

Centralized Dictation Systems

A **centralized dictation system** is a system in which all dictation is recorded in a central location but the managers dictate from remote locations such as their offices. Managers either use their telephones to connect with dictating units in the recording center or they use hand microphones (kept at their desks) that are components of the dictation station.

Guidelines for Effective Machine Transcription

Use the following suggestions to increase your productivity when you transcribe recorded dictation:

- Adjust the machine controls (volume, tone, and speed) for your comfort.
- Check the indicator slip or the lighted display to help determine the length of the dictation.
- Listen to the instructions given by the dictator, such as number of copies and enclosures.
- Be alert to spellings and directions given by the dictator.
- Listen ahead, then key what you have heard. Repeat this procedure until you complete the dictation. As you improve your skill, strive to continue keying at all times.
- Remember to include the proper name and title of the dictator as well as the appropriate closing notations.

Direct-Entry Methods

Some managers have replaced the pad and pencil for producing first-draft copy of memorandums, letters, and reports with direct-entry methods of originating documents. *Direct-entry methods* involve keying or dictating first-draft copy into the computer and storing the copy for later editing by the assistant. The direct-entry method can save managers much time. As the office assistant, you will be expected to retrieve, edit, format, and prepare the manager's direct-entry documents into final copy. Chapter 7 deals with processing documents electronically.

Illus. 6-14. This manager is keying a draft of a report directly into the computer.

QUESTIONS FOR REVIEW

1. What is the purpose of a memorandum? How does it differ from a letter?

2. How does a simplified memorandum differ from a formal memorandum?

3. A list of catalog descriptions is to be stapled to a memorandum. What notation is added to the memorandum?

4. Describe the envelope that generally is used for memorandums.

5. Identify the most commonly used parts of an informal, brief report and explain the placement of each part.

6. What is the purpose of a table?

7. Explain the meaning of the statement: A table should be self-explanatory.

8. In what ways are the heading of a report and the heading of a table similar?

9. Describe the ways in which documents are originated.

10. Why may a manager wish to use a direct-entry method of originating a document?

MAKING DECISIONS

Liza works for Mr. Lawrence Remington, merchandising manager for a large department store. Mr. Remington gives Liza a handwritten table to key for an important meeting later that day. He asks her to verify the accuracy of all column totals before keying the table. He tells her that he needs ten copies "in the standard format" and that he will be preparing notes for the meeting so he does not want to be disturbed.

Liza immediately starts to verify the column totals. She cannot, however, read some of the handwritten figures nor does she know the standard format. Mr. Remington already is working in his office with the door closed.

Explain what you would do if you were in Liza's situation. Describe how Liza can determine what the numbers should be and what format she should use to prepare the table.

What You Are To Do: Prepare a brief response.

EXTENDING YOUR ENGLISH COMPETENCIES

As part of an employee development plan, you are working your way through a business communications training program developed by your company to improve the communication skills of its employees. Below is an excerpt you see on your computer screen from a draft of a letter from Computer Corner Furniture. Notice the antagonistic tone of this response to a customer who was having difficulty assembling a computer workstation.

What You Are To Do: Revise the excerpt, making any changes necessary to prevent the response from conveying a negative or hostile attitude on the part of Computer Corner Furniture.

```
You obviously did not read the instructions which accompanied
the computer desk, Model 122, which you purchased from our
company.  In case you misplaced or lost your instructions, I
have enclosed another copy for you.

The instructions clearly state that you must assemble the
base of the desk first, then the electrical wiring is inserted
through the left front leg of the desk and through the slot in
the top of the table.  Obviously, it's too late to insert the
electrical wiring once you have assembled the entire desk.
You'll have to take the desk apart and start all over.  This
time, follow the instructions.

If you have any more problems with this desk, we do have a
branch office in Independence.  Please contact them; you
should have sent your complaint to that office in the first
place.
```

APPLICATION ACTIVITIES

Activity 1

Assume that you are the office assistant to Marie Sanchez, vice president of personnel for Western Security Systems. Mrs. Sanchez finishes her telephone conversation and calls you into her office. "I've just received word that our transcription machines will arrive next Friday," Mrs. Sanchez said. She continued: "Please send a memo to the departmental secretaries telling them when the equipment will arrive. Tell them that we will begin delivery to individual offices the first of next week. Oh yes, also include the guidelines they should use for effective machine transcription."

Word processing
equipment can be used
to complete this activity.

What You Are To Do: Compose and key the memo. Provide the appropriate heading information. Use next Friday's date. Send the memo to "All Departmental Secretaries." Provide an appropriate subject line. If necessary, refer to Illus. 6-6 on page 231. Refer to page 242 for machine transcription guidelines. Use the memorandum form in *Information Processing Activities* or plain paper.

Activity 2

Refer to the Extending Your Math Competencies exercise on pages 225-226. You previously completed the Total Sales, Cost of Units Sold, and Gross Profit columns for your supervisor, Mrs. Lowell. She has been working on the earnings report and has asked you to prepare a table for the report using your computations.

"Please include the Product Description, Units Sold, Total Sales, and Gross Profit columns," Mrs. Lowell said. "We also need a secondary heading to identify the reporting period. I suggest you use 'Reporting Period January 1-March 31.'"

Word processing
equipment can be used
to complete this activity.

What You Are To Do: Refer now to your computations. If you did not complete the exercise before, do so now. Key the table on plain paper using the columns Mrs. Lowell requested. Use correct table format.

Activity 3

Assume that you are an office assistant at Brown-Corwin International. Harold Owens, your supervisor, has made some minor revisions to a one-page informal report he needs for a meeting tomorrow. He asks you to key a revised copy of the report shown on page 246.

Word processing
equipment can be used
to complete this activity.

What You Are To Do: Use plain paper and key a corrected copy of the report. Be sure to follow all handwritten directions. If necessary, refer to Illus. 6-9 on page 236.

Please use standard format. H.O.

Document Storage

The diskettes used with our system are the 5 1/4 inch, double/density, ~~single/sided,~~ soft-sector type. With this type of diskette, as many as 100 documents can be stored on a single diskette. The diskettes used to store our processed documents represent the paper less files of our company.

The *external* storage medium used with our *computerized* document Processing System is the diskette. It is very important that each processed document be copied onto a diskette and deleted from the *computer's* internal memory. ~~of the text-editing system.~~

Formatting *Diskettes*

Before a new diskette *can* be used to store documents, it must be formatted. Formatting gets the diskette ready to recieve and store documents. When you format a diskette, the *disk* operating system will check the diskette for bad spots, it will *set up* make a directory for the document identification you assign to each document stored, and it will delete (erase) ~~or wipe off,~~ documents already stored on the diskette.

It is only necessary to format a diskette once. The format procedure should only be used when you are using a new diskette or when you wish to erase all of the documents stored on the diskette. If you format a diskette on which documents are already stored, those documents will be deleted.

CHAPTER SUMMARY

Office workers who are responsible for word processing must have a thorough understanding of commonly prepared written communications such as letters, memorandums, reports, and tables. In this chapter, you were introduced to the parts, standard placements, and acceptable formats for business documents.

1. Although standard formats exist, you may find variations in the way companies format letters and other documents.

2. Memorandums are used for internal communications.

3. Reports are written to convey information in a clear, concise manner. Short reports often have fewer parts than long reports.

4. Tables are a systematic arrangement of facts, figures, and other information. Each table should be self-explanatory.

5. Managers can prepare their communications by writing, dictating, or entering copy directly into the computer.

6. Equipment used for machine dictation includes portable units, desk-top units, and centralized dictation systems.

7. Your transcription productivity will be increased if you follow the guidelines for effective machine transcription.

KEY CONCEPTS AND TERMS

logo	modified block format
standard format	simplified block format
addressee	open punctuation
salutation	mixed punctuation
body (letter, report, table)	memorandum
complimentary close	heading (memorandum)
reference initials	simplified memorandum
enclosures	report
postscript	table
block format	centralized dictation system

INTEGRATED CHAPTER ACTIVITY

You work for the general manager of Dibert Real Estate Company. The manager likes the way you compose responses to incoming letters. He gives you the letter which follows, and says: "Please draft a response to this letter from Professional Office Equipment. I've made some notes in the margin that should be of help to you."

**Word processing
equipment can be used
to complete this activity.**

What You Are To Do: Compose a letter to Professional Office Equipment, to be signed by the general manager of Dibert, Kenneth L. Breman. Use modified block format with mixed punctuation. If necessary, refer to Illus. 6-3 on page 221. Use plain paper.

Professional Office Equipment

974 Hudson Avenue　Pontiac, Michigan　45058-8409

June 27, 19--

Dibert Real Estate Company
700 South Washington Avenue
Lansing, MI　48933-9012

Ladies and Gentlemen

It has been nearly three months since we delivered and installed your new copy machine, Model No. 1022. Payment for this machine was due within 30 days after delivery.

We have sent you three statements, but you have not forwarded your payment.　Please send us your payment today so that it is not necessary for us to take legal action.

Yours truly

Christine M. Latkovic

Christine M. Latkovic
Credit Manager

lp

*The copy
machine has
not worked
properly
since it
was installed.*

*We sent
Professional
a letter on
April 2 indicating
that we would
not submit a
payment until the
machine was
repaired or replaced.*

*Called Professional
on May 22 and
explained the
problem to a
Mrs. Thomas.*

OPTIONAL COMPUTER APPLICATION ACTIVITY

See Computer Applications Activity 6 in your Information Processing Activities workbook.

PRODUCTIVITY CORNER

Blake Williams
OFFICE SUPERVISOR

WHY CAN'T THERE BE ONE SET OF RULES?

DEAR MR. WILLIAMS:

My first full-time job is that of an office assistant in the accounting department of our local college. I like my work, but I do have a major problem: I key documents for eight different professors who don't seem to want their letters prepared in the same way!

Just last week, I did some letters for the first time for one professor. He returned them to me, asking me to add "Ph.D., CPA" after his name. He was very nice about it, and it was easy enough to add these letters. Then yesterday I did some letters for another professor. I checked her credentials in the college catalogue, and I saw that she was also listed as Ph.D., CPA. So I typed these initials after her name. She, too, was nice; but she said, "Under no circumstances are you ever to type those initials after my name. Simply type 'Department of Accounting' after my name." I've also learned that some professors want block format for their letters, while other professors prefer modified block with five-space paragraph indentations.

What am I supposed to do to keep track of *what* to do?—TRACY IN TRENTON

DEAR TRACY:

Unfortunately, there isn't one set of rules anywhere. Individuals have different opinions about identifying their credentials. There is nothing wrong with listing such credentials as Ph.D. and CPA. However, many individuals are more comfortable when they do not include such information in their correspondence.

Some organizations have established format guidelines, yet you may still find individual variations within these guidelines. Therefore, it's wise to ask about format preferences before preparing any correspondence so that rekeying is not necessary.

You might find it helpful to set up your own reference manual—possibly a loose-leaf notebook. You could have a section for each of the eight professors for whom you are likely to prepare written correspondence. When you prepare the first letter properly, make an extra copy (unless the subject matter is confidential) and put it in your notebook for future reference.

Good luck in your new job!—BLAKE WILLIAMS

CHAPTER 7

Word Processing: Processing Business Documents

Preparing written communications is a critical task in today's offices. Conveying accurate and appropriately worded messages is the concern of executives and administrative assistants as they compose letters, memorandums, and reports. Processing these business documents in proper form with no errors in spelling, grammar, or punctuation is the concern of office workers. Thus, your command of English will be invaluable as you process documents.

The preparation of business communications is a high-volume task in many offices. Millions of letters and memorandums are composed, processed, and mailed each business day. Over 70 billion document pages (other than letters and memorandums) are prepared, processed, and distributed yearly. Therefore, many competent office workers are required to process this volume of written communications.

As discussed in Chapter 5, word processing is a critical function within an organization's information processing system. As an office worker responsible for word processing tasks, you will play an important role in helping your company maintain its standard of high-quality written communications.

The objectives of the chapter are to:

- describe the environments in which documents are processed and the equipment office workers use to process documents

- develop your understanding of word processing functions

- introduce you to advanced word processing features and give you an overview of desktop publishing

WORD PROCESSING ENVIRONMENTS AND EQUIPMENT

When you have completed your study of this topic, you will be able to:

- describe how word processing tasks are organized in multipurpose and specialized environments

- describe equipment used for word processing and identify nonkeyboard input methods

- explain how technology impacts the way in which office workers complete word processing tasks

In offices where few written communications are processed, any office assistant might be given the task of preparing the occasional letter or memorandum. The office assistant may be given oral instructions or may be expected to determine on her/his own what to do. In companies where many documents are processed, however, carefully established procedures enable workers to perform word processing tasks with high-level productivity.

You will find that word processing tasks are performed in different settings or environments. In an office where word processing tasks are limited, you may not find the most advanced processing equipment. In offices where word processing tasks are performed in volume, the most sophisticated equipment is likely to be used.

open: willing to
consider

New and advanced technologies continue to bring about changes in today's offices. When new equipment or software is purchased, you may experience changes in how you complete work assignments. By being flexible and **open** to change, you will be able to adapt to different work settings and with a variety of equipment and software.

WORD PROCESSING ENVIRONMENTS

Word processing tasks are organized differently in different offices. The organizational structure, equipment available, types of documents, and employees' skills are all factors in determining how word processing tasks are completed. As you study this topic, give attention to how these four factors affect an organization's procedures for processing business documents.

Multipurpose Environments

Many offices are *multipurpose.* If you choose to work in such an office, you probably will perform many different tasks, including word processing.

> Beth works in an office where each employee has a computer and software for performing word processing, database, and spreadsheet functions. She is pleased she knows all these functions and can switch from one application to another, depending upon the work she is completing.

Policies and Procedures

specialization: to
direct one's efforts in a
particular area

Word processing in a multipurpose office is guided often by informal policies and procedures. Instructions may be given orally for each job, and some task **specialization** may develop naturally—even in a multipurpose office. Certain office workers may develop better skills than others and prefer certain tasks. Therefore, selected word processing tasks may be assigned to those individuals who have both the skill and the desire to complete them.

In such an environment, there may not be a procedures manual to guide you in completing tasks. You will be expected to determine the most appropriate format for a document and the best way to organize a task in order to meet a specified deadline.

prior: previously
written

The files of **prior** correspondence will help you become familiar with how similar documents have been formatted in the past.

You may also need to determine the individual preferences of the executives for whom you process documents. One executive,

Illus. 7-1. Workers in a multipurpose office perform a variety of tasks, including word processing.

complex: made up of a number of parts

for example, may prefer to see drafts of all documents. Another executive may request drafts of *complex* documents only. Likewise, one executive may prefer to have all letters keyed using block format while another may prefer the simplified block format. You may find it helpful to record preferences of executives in a notebook to which you can refer.

Shared Equipment

Sharing equipment is common in offices where word processing tasks are not performed with great frequency. In an office where few documents are input into the computer using a scanning device, for example, all workers in the office may share a single scanner. You will find also that printers are frequently shared.

The cooperation of all employees is needed for efficient use of shared equipment. Each worker assumes certain responsibilities in using the equipment. As a minimum, you are expected to learn how to operate the equipment properly and to report to the appropriate person any difficulties you experience with the equipment. You also will need to know how priorities for use are established.

Range of Responsibility

An office worker may be given the responsibility of composing responses to certain types of letters and memorandums. In some offices, the office assistant may sign such letters and memorandums. In other offices, the executive will review what the office assistant prepared and sign the final copies. In addition, the office assistant may make copies for distribution and storage. In fact, the entire document process may be completed by a single office employee, especially in small offices. If you are given responsibility for the entire process, be certain you understand the deadlines that must be met.

Mike works in the business office of a small plastics company. When the company president learned that Mike understood the business thoroughly, he was given the task of preparing responses to most letters and memos. The president reads what Mike prepares and then signs all outgoing copies. Mike has learned how to individualize responses to most letters by selecting appropriate paragraphs from paragraphs stored in memory on his computer. Since Mike works primarily on his own, he assumes full responsibility for making sure that all letters and memos requiring responses are answered as soon as possible.

Specialized Environments

Some businesses have established formally organized units that specialize in preparing documents. The most common forms of organization are *decentralized* and *centralized* units. Both types of units often are referred to as *WP centers*.

Decentralized Units

Many companies find that their word processing needs are best served by decentralized units, commonly known as *satellite clusters*. Such units generally are located throughout the company near the department or departments served. The departments provided with word processing services are called *user departments*. Note in Illustration 7-2 how the departments within the human resources division share a satellite cluster, as do the departments within the marketing division.

Centralized Units

In some companies, all departments use the services of a centralized unit. Centralized WP centers may be found in various

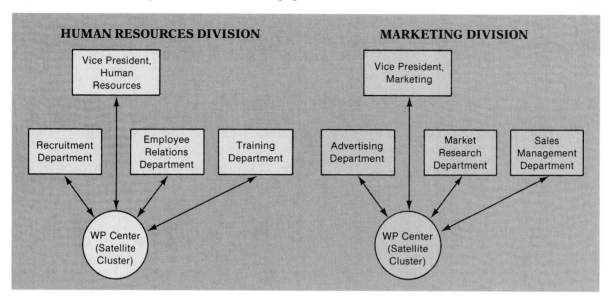

Illus. 7-2. Decentralized WP centers meet the needs of several user departments.

organizations such as government bureaus, hospitals, and educational institutions. The size of the center will depend upon the nature and volume of documents processed, the equipment and software available, and the services the center provides. Some centralized units are relatively small; others are quite large. Generally, carefully established procedures are communicated in writing to all user departments.

By centralizing the processing of documents, companies may be able to purchase better equipment. For example, an expensive high-speed laser printer may not be **justified** for an individual department. By sharing equipment in a centralized location with trained personnel, however, more expensive equipment that produces higher-quality documents can be purchased.

justified: economically reasonable

Specialized Services and Job Titles

Some degree of specialization among workers occurs in both centralized and decentralized settings. Depending upon the nature of the organization, some workers develop **expertise** in processing specific documents, such as financial or legal documents, complex research proposals and reports, or company newsletters. Positions you may find in WP centers include:

expertise: skill or knowledge

- Manager/Supervisor/ Coordinator of WP
- Electronic Publishing Specialist
- Word Processing Specialist

- Word Processing Operator
- User Support Specialist
- Transcriptionist
- Page Composition Specialist

enhance: improve quality

Some WP centers **enhance** their services by using the latest technology and by becoming the software training and support resource for the company. A WP center with sophisticated desktop publishing capabilities can offer services once performed only by outside printers. Word processing specialists who know specific software packages thoroughly can provide training assistance to less experienced users throughout the company. In addition, the WP center can provide final document processing for rough drafts prepared electronically, usually on floppy disks.

Illus. 7-3. This page composition specialist is using desktop publishing software to prepare a newsletter to be distributed to all company employees.

WORD PROCESSING EQUIPMENT

The major categories and features of word processing equipment will be highlighted in this section. Generally, newer equipment means that tasks will be automated rather than performed manually. Tutorial disks and/or user manuals accompany most equipment models. Such references are especially useful in acquainting you with equipment capabilities. Learning and using equipment features that aid you in completing tasks will enhance your productivity.

Electric Typewriters

Electric typewriters continue to be used in some offices for word processing. This equipment is most appropriate where there is not a high volume of word processing tasks.

Many electric typewriters have a correcting feature. A special cover-up or lift-off tape installed in the machine simplifies error correction. The typist depresses the correction backspace key and strikes the incorrect letter. Correction tape either covers up the error or lifts it off the paper.

Electronic Typewriters

Electronic typewriters are important processing tools in many offices. Electronic typewriters have text entry and editing capabilities beyond those of electric typewriters. *Microprocessors* (small electronic chips) used in electronic typewriters make possible the many automatic features that increase worker productivity. Electronic typewriters are not as complex as personal computers, so it is easier to learn how to use all the features.

Electronic typewriters are not all alike. *Low-end* models have limited features beyond those found on electric typewriters, while *high-end* models have many features similar to those found on personal computers. Common time-saving features found on many electronic typewriters are shown in Illus. 7-5.

Illus. 7-4. A low-end electronic typewriter with one-line display.

COMMON TIME-SAVING FEATURES OF ELECTRONIC TYPEWRITERS	
Automatic carriage return	Machine returns automatically to the beginning of the next line.
Automatic word wrap	Machine automatically determines if the next word will fit on the current line and, if it will not, places the word on the next line.
Automatic decimal tab, center, and underline	Machine automatically aligns columns of numbers at the decimal point, centers text between margins, and underlines a specified segment of text as it is being entered at the keyboard.
Automatic relocate	Machine returns to the point where keying was interrupted to allow the operator to correct an error.
Index/Reverse index	Machine can space down (indexing) or up (reversing) without first returning to the left margin.
Correction memory	Machine holds a specific number of characters in memory for the user to return from the current keying position to correct an error. A cancel key is used to lift the incorrect character off the page. The user then keys the correct character.

Illus. 7-5. Common time-saving features enhance the capabilities of electronic typewriters.

Text Memory

capacity: amount of space

If you use an electronic typewriter, you will need to know the *capacity* of its text or document memory. **Text memory** is internal memory that is erased once the typewriter is turned off, unless the model has a battery to provide current to maintain the memory. A typical page of text (30 lines of 60 characters each) requires approximately 2,000 characters of memory including keystrokes for spaces, paragraph indentions, and carriage returns. Thus, if a machine has a 10,000-character memory, you would be able to store a document no longer than approximately five pages in the machine's memory for playback. Internal memory ranges from less than two pages on low-end models to well over 300 pages on high-end models.

User Considerations

Electronic typewriters provide a number of advantages including:

- *Letter-quality documents.* The use of carbon ribbons produces clear, easy-to-read documents.
- *Flexibility.* Various processing tasks can be completed with ease, including preparing envelopes and labels and completing forms.
- *Learning and operating ease.* An electronic typewriter is easy to operate mainly because of its keyboard. Special keys found on the keyboard allow you to take advantage of many time-saving features. With only a few hours' training, you can learn to operate most models.
- *Low maintenance.* The automatic features of electronic typewriters are built into a microprocessor. Therefore, there are few moving parts, which reduces maintenance cost and time.
- *Communications networking.* Information can be received and transmitted electronically. Electronic typewriters can be connected to other electronic typewriters, word processors, microcomputers, or local area networks.
- *Upgradeable models.* A business may start with a low-end model and **upgrade** its equipment capabilities as needs change.

upgrade: improve with additional capabilities

Word Processing Systems

All word processors, regardless of the equipment used, have five basic components: keyboard, display screen or terminal, logic or intelligence, storage media, and printer.

Screen-Based Electronic Typewriters

Electronic typewriters, as previously discussed, range in capabilities and features from low-end machines with few features and limited capabilities to high-end machines with many features and greatly expanded capabilities. Some high-end machines now include the five basic components of word processors and have capabilities that closely resemble those of microcomputers. High-end models that have the basic components plus high processing features and capabilities are often called word processors or word processing systems by their manufacturers.

Illus. 7-6. This high-end electronic typewriter has expandable memory, a 70,000 word spell corrector, a calendar feature, and an electronic telephone message pad.

Display screen. Display screens of high-end electronic typewriters are similar to computer screens. These screens use a full 80-character horizontal line. Display screen sizes range from a typical 14-line display to a full-page WYSIWYG display. **WYSIWYG** ("What you see is what you get") means that the document shown on screen appears the same as it will on the printed page. Most screen-based electronic typewriters use cursor control keys to control the movement of the cursor on the screen.

Auxiliary storage. In addition to text memory, electronic typewriters may have external, or auxiliary storage. Screen-based electronic typewriters frequently have one or two disk drives built into the machine. Storing documents to disk expands the storage capabilities of electronic typewriters. Some electronic typewriters have hard disk drives. A hard disk drive increases storage capacity and allows expansion to other functions, such as spreadsheets, graphics, data management, and various administrative applications (calculator, telephone book, messages).

In the coming years, you will continue to see electronic typewriters with new or improved features and capabilities.

Dedicated Word Processors

Equipment designed solely for word processing is referred to as a *dedicated word processor*. Dedicated word processors, which were common in the 1960s and 1970s and continue to be used in some offices today, are limited primarily to text processing.

Microcomputers

The microcomputer is fast becoming the most popular system for completing word processing tasks. Because of their speed and versatility, microcomputers increase employee productivity while maintaining quality output. A typical microcomputer workstation consists of input device(s) (keyboard and mouse), central processing unit (CPU), monitor (screen), storage (floppy disk drive or hard disk drive) and a printer, as shown in Illustration 7-7.

Illus. 7-7. The processing power of the microcomputer makes it easy to combine word processing with other applications, such as database management and graphics.

Keyboard

The keyboard of a microcomputer looks much like the keyboard of a typewriter with additional keys. A typical microcomputer keyboard is shown in Illus. 7-8. *Function keys* (identified by #3) perform editing and formatting functions such as inserting and moving text. You must learn the uses of the function keys as they relate to each software package you use. Learning the function keys is an important step to using the full power of the software.

Cursor control keys (identified by #10) are generally marked by arrow symbols. These directional keys move the cursor up, down, to the left, and to the right. Although keyboards vary slightly from one computer system to another, you will be able to adapt quickly to new keyboard arrangements.

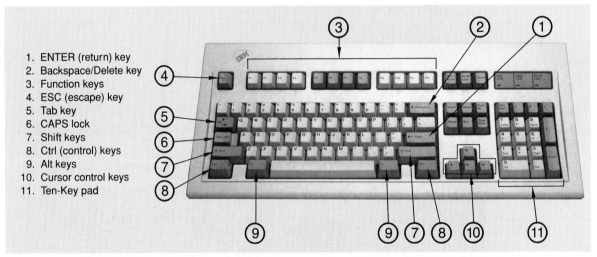

1. ENTER (return) key
2. Backspace/Delete key
3. Function keys
4. ESC (escape) key
5. Tab key
6. CAPS lock
7. Shift keys
8. Ctrl (control) keys
9. Alt keys
10. Cursor control keys
11. Ten-Key pad

Illus. 7-8. The IBM PS/Model 30 keyboard. IBM is a trademark of International Business Machines Corporation.

Software for Word Processing

sophistication:
capability

Software packages are available at varying levels of **sophistication** to fit specific processing needs. Basic packages are relatively inexpensive and enable you to complete processing functions such as justifying the right margin and searching for and replacing words. More sophisticated packages offer features such as automatic footnoting and text merging.

You may already be familiar with at least one word processing software. Although software programs differ, there are many similarities among them. You will be able to apply your knowledge of one program to learning additional software. You will learn more about word processing software in Topics 2 and 3.

Office workers do not always use a keyboard for entering text. You may find one or more of these alternate input methods in the office where you work:

Scanners

Scanners are input devices that convert characters, images, and printed code into a form the computer can process. By scanning the shape of characters, an *optical character recognition* (OCR) device reads typewritten, computer-printed, or hand-printed copy. The OCR device converts the characters into electronic signals that are recorded on a magnetic medium, usually a floppy disk. OCR devices range from the small, hand-held wands to large machines capable of reading thousands of documents a minute.

A page scanner quickly converts a page of printed text into electronic copy for processing. Some page models may be limited in the number of typefaces they can scan. On the other hand, advanced character recognition scanners are capable of converting varied typefaces and formats. Depending upon the equipment and the condition of the original copy, you may need to make some correction to the scanned electronic copy.

Illus. 7-9. The hand-held scanner (left) and the page scanner (right) are popular input devices that speed text entry.

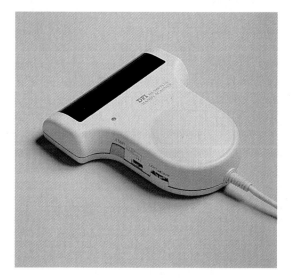
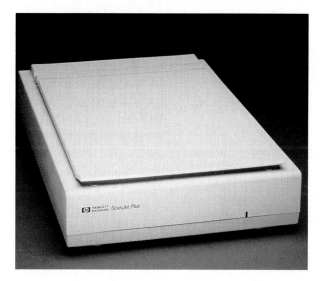

Mice and Trackballs

A **mouse** is a small input device designed to fit in the palm of your hand. As you move the mouse across a flat surface, you control the movement of the cursor on the computer screen. Once the cursor is in the desired screen location, you can perform such actions as making menu choices or selecting application functions by depressing one or more of the buttons on the top of the mouse.

stationary: remains in the same position

A **trackball** performs the same functions as a mouse without being moved across a surface. The trackball is *stationary*. Simply move the ball in the desired direction to operate the trackball.

Illus. 7-10. A mouse (left) moves across a flat surface; the trackball (right) remains stationary.

Touch Screens and Special Pens

A **touch screen** allows you to select functions or to enter limited amounts of text by merely touching areas of the screen. Small tablet-like computers, called **Pen PCs**, can recognize words and numbers written by hand on a screen and instantly turn them into computerized data. This system is particularly helpful to workers who must fill out forms away from regular workstations. Predictions are that this radically different computer will appeal to even the *PC-phobic*.

PC-phobic: someone afraid of computers

Voice Input

Voice input, also known as *speech recognition*, allows you to enter data and direct the computer by speaking the words. Most voice input systems have a designated vocabulary or memory limit. When the system is set up, the user generally pronounces

digital: in numbered form

the words several times to allow the program to recognize the voice and words. The system recognizes the words by breaking them down into *digital* patterns that can be stored in the computer. Later, when the user speaks the words, the computer compares the digital pattern of the spoken word to that of the digital pattern of words in computer memory. When a match is found, the word is displayed on the screen. Some personal computers can recognize up to 30,000 words, and the vocabulary size is expected to increase. Despite being able to recognize a large vocabulary, many computers understand you only if you speak slowly and distinctly.

TECHNOLOGY AND CHANGE

Change is an accepted part of today's office scene. As new technologies evolve and word processing becomes integrated with other information processing tasks (including data processing, records management, and reprographics), workers will need to adapt to new procedures and equipment. When you find yourself faced with change, remember that you have a basic understanding of word processing. This background will serve as a foundation for developing new skills and understandings. If you are flexible and willing to learn, you will have no difficulty working in a changing environment.

QUESTIONS FOR REVIEW

1. What policies and procedures are likely to be found in a multipurpose word processing environment?

2. When equipment is shared in an office, what guidelines should be followed?

3. Describe the two organizational units in specialized word processing environments.

4. Identify five job titles of workers in word processing centers.

5. What is the importance of text memory in an electronic typewriter?

6. Identify six advantages of electronic typewriters.

7. Why are some screen-based electronic typewriters called word processors?

8. Why are microcomputers popular for completing word processing tasks?

9. How do mice and trackballs differ?

10. How does a basic understanding of word processing help you to adapt to change in the office?

MAKING DECISIONS

Andrea is an office worker who has excellent keyboarding skills and enjoys her work very much. She has been on the job for less than three months and has received a number of compliments from her supervisor. Andrea feels that she would be able to do a much better job if two problems were resolved. She finds the lighting at her workstation is inadequate. She also finds the music that is constantly provided in the office is distracting.

One day at lunch Andrea mentioned these two problems to a coworker. Her coworker quickly responded: "I think the lighting is fine, and the music is very relaxing. If you complain, there will be changes that the rest of us won't like." Later that same day, Andrea's supervisor stopped at her workstation and asked, "How are things going?"

What You Are To Do: Prepare a response to the question raised.

EXTENDING YOUR ENGLISH COMPETENCIES

You are the office assistant to B. J. Jeffreys, sales manager of Hollingsworth Book Distributors. Ms. Jeffreys hands you a memo (page 268) and says, "I barely had time to draft this. Please change or add to the wording to make it complete. I'm sure there is a memo in the files on meeting times that will be helpful. I'll sign the memo when I return." When you check the files, you find a keyed memo (page 268) on meeting times.

What You Are To Do: • Read the memo draft. Prepare a list of questions you will want to ask Ms. Jeffreys when she returns.
  • Use the information in the file memo to gather the details you need to complete the memo Ms. Jeffreys left with you.
  • On a sheet of plain paper, key the memo in final form. Use the simplified format shown on page 234.

APPLICATION ACTIVITY

You are a word processing operator in a new satellite WP center. The manager of the center is in the process of developing a manual to be sent to

Word processing equipment can be used to complete this activity.

everyone who will use the services provided by the center. The manager has given you a draft of one page entitled "Responsibilities of Originators." The draft appears below.

What You Are To Do: Key the copy attractively on a single sheet of plain paper. Use your own judgment with regard to line length and spacing.

Responsibilities of Originators

1. Clarity--the originator of ~~an assignment~~ a job must examine
   before submission the copy, ~~in advance,~~ for clarity. ~~An assign-~~
   ~~ment may~~ be typed, handwritten, or a combination ~~of both. Most importantly, assignments~~ The copy must be ~~jobs~~
   in legible form to be acceptable for processing
   in the ~~(WPC).~~ Word Processing Center

2. Completeness--~~assignments~~ jobs must be presented in complete
   form for processing. Jobs submitted in a
   "piece-meal" fashion are excessively time-
   consuming and ~~delay the completion of assign-~~
   ~~ments~~ cannot be completed efficiently.

3. Correctness--~~when an originator receives a completed~~
   ~~assignment from the WPC, it becomes the~~
   ~~responsibility of the originator for the~~
   ~~accuracy and format of the assignment.~~ The
   WPC is not responsible for input control
   problems resulting from a failure to correctly
   interpret illegible handwriting or scribbling,
   inaccurate data, etc. Although all completed
   ~~assignments~~ jobs are scanned in-house for grammar,
   spelling, and punctuation discrepancies, the
   final approval of ~~an assignment~~ a job remains the
   sole responsibility of the originator.

4. Revision--if ~~an assignment~~ a job requires editing, it is
   recommended that standard proofreading symbols
   be used to specify all revisions. As a convenience, a chart of standard proofreading
   symbols ~~has been~~ is included in this manual.
   Insertions of additional text must be clearly
   stated and legible.

5. Priority Processing--~~assignments~~ jobs requiring special
   handling must be approved by the ~~Director~~ of Manager
   Word Processing. Logical and valid reasons
   must substantiate such requests. Originators
   are urged to keep special requests for priority
   processing of ~~assignments~~ jobs to a minimum.

6. Advance Notice of Large Projects--if an originator is
   aware of an impending project that will require
   an unusual amount of processing assistance from
   the WPC, it is imperative that the Center be
   notified as soon as possible. ~~Wherever~~
   ~~possible, all originators are requested to~~

The meeting should not last more than two hours.

From: B. J. Jeffreys, Sales Manager

Date: March 22, 19-- Stet 22

Subject: New Meeting Date

The meeting of sales representatives scheduled on for 9:00 A.M. Tuesday, March 26, 19--, in Conference Room B has been changed. The meeting will be held on March 27.

If you are unable to attend this rescheduled meeting, please call Kenneth Derby.

Hollingsworth Book Distributors

January 14, 19--   MEMORANDUM

All Sales Representatives

SCHEDULED MEETINGS

A sales meeting will be scheduled each Tuesday morning at 9 a.m. in
Conference Room B. All sales meetings will last one hour. Please
schedule the weekly meeting time on your calendar. If you are
unable to attend, please call Kenneth Derby at Extension 3567. If
changes are necessary to this schedule, you will be notified.

B J Jeffreys

B. J. Jeffreys, Sales Manager

bb

TOPIC 2

HOW DOCUMENTS ARE PROCESSED

When you have completed your study of this topic, you will be able to:

- explain word processing workflow and describe the basic tasks of word processing

- identify word processing aids and explain procedures for proofreading electronic documents

- explain procedures for managing electronic files

Technology has changed dramatically how documents are prepared in offices. In most offices, the task of keying entire documents over and over again has been eliminated. With electronic word processing, an office worker can make changes quickly and easily.

In this topic, you will learn about the basic workflow of word processing. This workflow follows the same pattern as the information processing workflow you studied in Chapter 5. With a thorough understanding of this process, you will be able to adapt to the variations you may find in offices.

As you perform word processing tasks in the office, you will find that certain processing tasks are repeated for most documents you prepare. These tasks include entering text, formatting, editing, and printing the document. The use of word processing software helps to assure that these basic tasks are completed efficiently.

In most offices, you will be expected to use electronic word processing. Aids such as tutorials, on-line help menus, prompts, messages, and user's manuals will help you learn and adjust to different word processing systems. Likewise, electronic dictionaries, thesauruses, and style and grammar checkers will aid you in producing error-free copy.

When documents are completed, they must be stored and/or transmitted to the intended receiver. Therefore, your processing duties will include storing and retrieving documents. Learning to use electronic file management procedures will prepare you to complete this responsibility.

WORD
PROCESSING
WORKFLOW

Five basic steps are completed each time a document is prepared. A typical workflow for a document requiring revisions by the originator is shown in Illus. 7-11. Note that the word processing workflow includes the basic steps of the information processing workflow: *input, processing, output, transmission,* and *storage.*

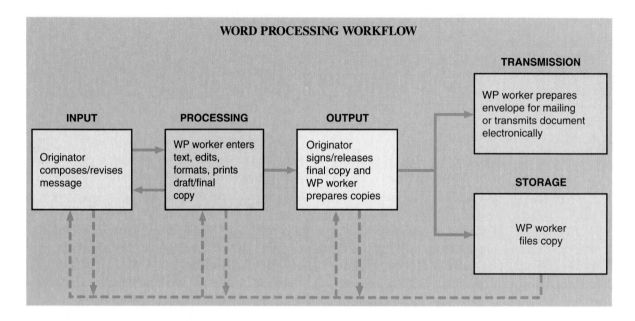

Illus. 7-11. A typical workflow for a letter requiring revisions by the originator (solid lines). Note that the document can be stored and retrieved at any point during the input, processing, and output steps (broken lines).

**BASIC WORD
PROCESSING
TASKS**

In the word processing workflow above, the originator composes and revises documents for processing by the assistant. The material prepared by the originator is known as *input.* Executives use different methods to compose documents. Many executives prefer to handwrite their drafts. Others prefer to dictate their drafts to a recording device for transcription later by the assistant. Still others prefer to compose their documents at the computer, which is an effective method for executives with good keyboarding skills. The executive keys a draft, saves the draft to disk, and gives the disk to an assistant for processing. The assistant then retrieves the document file the executive created and edits, formats, and prints the document.

*Janice is the assistant to the manager of operations in a large textile company. The manager composes many letters, memorandums, and reports. He writes some in longhand and uses a dictation machine for others. Janice knows the manager must **adhere** to a strict schedule, and she is aware of all deadlines. She checks the manager's out basket frequently for new jobs and completes them promptly.*

adhere: hold firmly to

Illus. 7-12. This office assistant is retrieving a document that an executive created for formatting and printing.

Processing the document includes all activities from the time you receive the input until a completed document is ready for the originator's signature or ready for multiple copies to be made of the final document. Basic processing activities for preparing documents typically include entering text, formatting, editing, and printing. For example, the tasks you would complete to prepare a letter from a handwritten draft include: keying and formatting the letter following company guidelines for correspondence, editing the letter, and printing a final copy for the executive's signature.

Entering Text

Input, as you know, can take different forms. Documents can be input by scanning, voice recognition, keying rough drafts at the computer, dictating to a machine or a person, and handwriting copy. When you receive the document you are to prepare, you may use a combination of methods to enter the text. Much of the copy you prepare using word processing involves the input you receive from dictated or handwritten copy.

Word processing software used with microcomputers and some high-end electronic typewriters simplifies the task of entering text. Figure 7-13 highlights common text entry features of word processing software.

Illus. 7-13. Common word processing software features for entering text.

COMMON TEXT-ENTRY FEATURES OF WORD PROCESSING SOFTWARE

- Cursor movement (left or right) by character, word, or beginning/ending of line
- Cursor movement (up or down) by line, screen, page, or beginning/ending of document
- Cursor movement to specified page or previous location
- Scroll (up or down) by line or screen

- Automatic word wrap
- Automatic pagination
- Automatic file backup
- Word count
- Table of Contents
- Footnotes

Formatting

The arrangement of the text is referred to as its *format.* Determining the desired layout or arrangement of text on the page is called **formatting**. Many companies have procedures manuals which contain standard format instructions and examples for frequently prepared documents. If format examples are not available, you will be expected to make formatting decisions. These decisions should reflect your desire to produce attractive, easy-to-read documents.

Formatting on Electronic Typewriters

Automatic formatting features on electronic typewriters may be selected by depressing specific *code* keys. For instance, you may select an option that will allow the typewriter printhead to move automatically to a new writing line as you continuously key copy. This feature frees you from having to use the return key.

The return key would be used only for short lines, such as the letter address. Code keys enable other functions to be performed automatically, such as centering a word or phrase, decimal alignment of numbers in columns, and indenting lines.

Formatting on Microcomputers

Formatting procedures differ according to the word processing software package and the processing capability of the computer. Word processing software programs come with preset format settings called **default standards**, frequently referred to as *defaults*. Defaults represent commonly used format settings. Preset defaults include line length, top margin, bottom margin, line spacing, tabs, page length, and pitch. If you do not change the defaults, the preset standard will be used. Defaults are easy to change, and users often change them to suit the requirements of the document.

On some systems, format lines are automatically displayed at the top or bottom of each page on the screen. This format line, however, will not appear on the printed page. Illus. 7-14 is an example of how formatting decisions are displayed in one system. A status line precedes the format line and includes the identification of the document (0311), the storage location (Drive B), and the cursor location (page 1, line 1, position 1). Immediately below the status line is the format line, which shows the formatting choices: single spaced lines, tab set locations, and left and right margins.

Illus. 7-14. The status and format lines provide valuable information to the office worker using word processing.

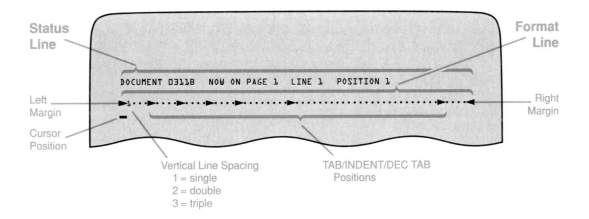

DOCUMENT 0311B   NOW ON PAGE 1   LINE 1   POSITION 1

Status Line

Format Line

Left Margin

Right Margin

Cursor Position

Vertical Line Spacing
1 = single
2 = double
3 = triple

TAB/INDENT/DEC TAB Positions

The user's manual that accompanies the software will have complete details for all keying and formatting possibilities. You should become familiar with the procedures for choosing the options appropriate for your word processing tasks.

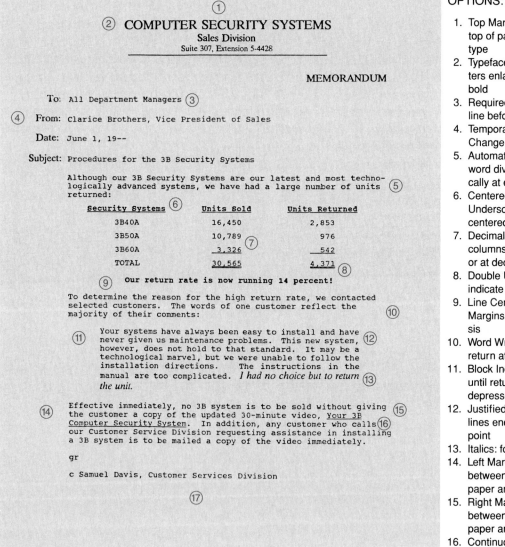

COMMON FORMATTING OPTIONS:

1. Top Margin: space from top of page to first line of type
2. Typeface Change: characters enlarged, centered, bold
3. Required Return: to end line before right margin
4. Temporary Margin, Change Typeface
5. Automatic Hyphenation: word divided automatically at end of line
6. Centered Headings, Bold, Underscored: headings centered over columns
7. Decimal Tabs: numbers in columns aligned at right or at decimal point
8. Double Underscore: to indicate totals
9. Line Centered Between Margins, Bold: for emphasis
10. Word Wrap: automatic return at end of line
11. Block Indent: indents text until return key is depressed
12. Justified Right Margin: lines end at the same point
13. Italics: for emphasis
14. Left Margin: space between left edge of paper and the line of type
15. Right Margin: space between right edge of paper and the line of type
16. Continuous Underscore: to underline titles
17. Bottom Margin: space from last line of type to the edge of paper

Illus. 7-15. Common software options for formatting text.

Editing

Many business documents are changed one or more times between the time they are composed and the time they are printed as final copy. The process of making changes is known as editing. Editing refers both to changes the originator makes and to changes the office assistant makes in producing a new draft of a proposed document. To make editing changes that can be understood easily, originators often use standard proofreader's marks. (Commonly used proofreader's marks are listed in Reference Section A.)

Steve works as a word processing specialist for an engineer who prepares many reports. Steve has been instructed to prepare rough drafts of all reports. The engineer edits the drafts using standard proofreader's marks. After the engineer gives Steve the revised copy, Steve makes all text and formatting changes indicated. The director may revise complex reports several times. Steve's knowledge of the features of his word processing software allows him to make changes easily and quickly.

Illus. 7-16.
Formatting and editing changes can be accommodated with ease using word processing software.

If you use word processing software to process documents, you must learn the basic editing features of that software. Word processing software is designed to ***facilitate*** editing changes common to the preparation of business documents, such as inserting or deleting text and moving or copying text from one location to another in the document. While specific procedures will vary

facilitate: make easy

Illus. 7-17. Common word processing software features for editing text.

according to the equipment and software you use, you will find that electronic editing will help you produce desired changes quickly and accurately. Illus. 7-17 is a listing of common editing features available with most word processing software.

COMMON EDITING FEATURES OF WORD PROCESSING SOFTWARE

- Insert/delete: characters, words, lines

- Delete: paragraph, block, to end of page/document

- Restore deleted text

- Insert/typeover mode

- Automatic paragraph reformatting

- Line/paragraph numbering

- Block: mark beginning/end; find beginning/end; move or copy; hide; delete

- Search: for string of characters forward/backward

- Replace: string with/without verification

- Global replace: with/without verification

- Search and delete

- Windows

Printing

Some processing decisions are made at the point of printing. If you select the print option from the *main menu*, a *submenu* for printing (such as the one shown in Illus. 7-18) will be displayed.

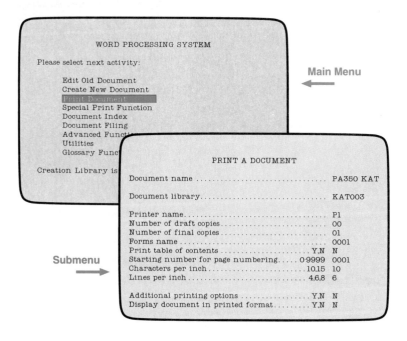

Illus. 7-18. This submenu lists options for printing the document. Assuming the user prints the document with the options selected, how many copies of the document will be printed?

WORD PROCESSING SYSTEM

Please select next activity:

    Edit Old Document
    Create New Document
    Print Document
    Special Print Function
    Document Index
    Document Filing
    Advanced Funct
    Utilities
    Glossary Func

Creation Library is

Main Menu

PRINT A DOCUMENT

Document name . . . . PA350 KAT

Document library. KAT003

Printer name. P1
Number of draft copies. 00
Number of final copies 01
Forms name 0001
Print table of contents . . . . Y,N   N
Starting number for page numbering. 0-9999   0001
Characters per inch 10,15   10
Lines per inch 4,6,8   6

Additional printing options . . . . Y,N   N
Display document in printed format. . . . . Y,N   N

Submenu

If you do not change the submenu, the document will be printed according to default printing instructions. Changes are made to the defaults by rekeying the numbers.

Depending upon the software and equipment you use, special print commands can be inserted in the document copy as you key the text. These special print commands, such as bolding or italics, may be considered formatting features as well.

Print commands are usually inserted within the text by depressing a specific code key, function key, or a combination of keys for the specific print feature you want to use. Once the print control is **activated**, it remains active until you turn it off, usually by repeating the same combination of keys. Using the same code to turn a function on and off is known as a *toggle switch*. If you want to bold a heading in a report, for example, you would: (1) depress the code or function key(s) needed to start the bold feature, (2) key the heading, (3) then turn off the bold feature by depressing the same code or function key(s) again.

activated: put into operation

COMMON PRINTING FEATURES OF WORD PROCESSING SOFTWARE

- Pitch control: 10, 12, 15
- Pagination
- Hyphenation
- Superscript, subscript
- Headers, footers
- Elimination of orphan and widow lines

- Proportional spacing
- Print interrupt
- Print: specific page(s), page on which cursor located, multiple copies
- Screen print
- Binding offset

Special Print Features:

- **Bold**
- Underline
- Double Underline
- *Italics*
- Shadow

- SMALL CAP
- Redline
- Strikeout
- Superscript Example
- Subscript Example

Illus. 7-19. Common word processing software features for printing text and special printing features to enhance text.

**WORD
PROCESSING
AIDS**

Illus. 7-20. At the main menu bar (1), the user of this pull-down menu would move the cursor right from File to Edit to select the Edit submenu (2). From the Edit submenu, the user would choose the Select option (3). The user would then be ready to choose an option from the Select submenu (4).

Manufacturers of word processing equipment and software have introduced a number of aids to assist users in processing text efficiently. The amount of assistance varies from one product to another, but some basic aids are commonly available.

Menus

A listing of available options is called a **menu**. **Submenus** are more detailed listings under each of the options in the main menu. You select the option by moving the cursor to the desired position. Illus. 7-18, page 276, is an example of one format for menus and submenus.

Another menu format is the *pull-down menu* as shown in Illus. 7-20. At the main pull-down menu, you choose the submenu for the desired function generally by one of three procedures: pressing the letter that appears in bold, such as E for Edit; pressing

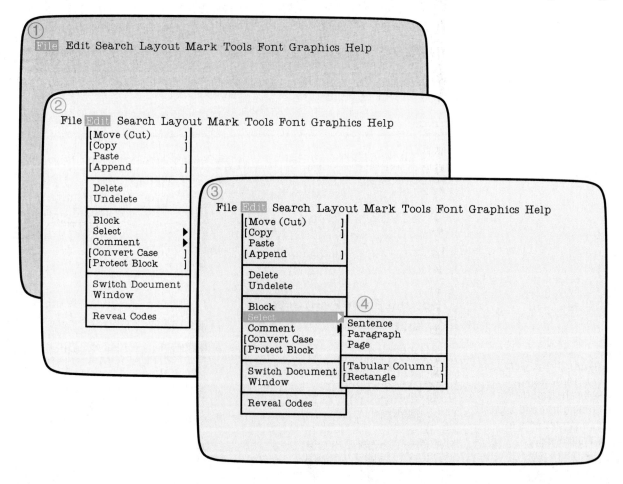

the return key to select the function; or placing and clicking the mouse pointer on the function name.

Prompts and Messages

Prompts and messages appear on your monitor at appropriate times to help guide you through the processing tasks. **Prompts** are usually one-line statements or questions that provide additional instructions or request specific detail before the next step can be completed. Typical prompts include:

- Copy What?
- Delete What?
- File Exists, Overwrite it?

- Page Length:
- End of Edit?
- File Open, Quit Anyway?

Messages are generally self-explanatory statements that guide you in completing the task or acknowledge that the task is being performed. Typical messages include:

- Looking Up
- Disk Full
- Execute or Cancel

- Please Wait
- End of Document
- Invalid Length

Illus. 7-21. Using this electronic dictionary, the user would depress the enter key to correct the misspelling.

Dictionaries and Thesauruses

The electronic dictionary and thesaurus are two aids that will increase your processing accuracy. The electronic dictionary, sometimes called a spell checker, contains a list of correctly spelled words. A spell checker, as shown in Illus. 7-21, finds

CUSTOMER SERVICES

We are happy to provide customized research and publication srvices These include market research studies, comprehensive data bases and technology position papers, and in-depth competitive analyses.

Esc	Exit the spelling checker	<⏎	Replace the word
F1	Ignore	F2	Suspend CORRECTing
F3	Add word to Temporary	F4	Add Change to Temporary
F5	Add word to Personal	F6	Add Change to Personal

Select an alternate, or type a replacement after the "?"
?:srvices
services, vices

keying and spelling errors. The effectiveness of the dictionary is limited by the number of words it contains.

synonyms: words of like or similar meaning

antonyms: words of opposite meaning

The thesaurus displays the **synonyms** and **antonyms** of highlighted words. A thesaurus is helpful if you find, for example, that one word is repeated frequently. You should exercise careful judgment in selecting synonyms or antonyms.

Grammar and Style Checkers

Electronic grammar and style checkers help find grammatical errors and check the style of writing. A style checker, for example, will highlight the use of negative words in a document, thus alerting the writer to a negative writing tone.

PROOFREADING ELECTRONIC DOCUMENTS

Regardless of the electronic aids used, you are responsible for evaluating completed documents. Use the spell checker first. Then complete a detailed manual proofreading. Remember that spelling packages are limited in the errors they can catch. Errors such as "there" for "their" and grammatical errors, for example, will not be detected.

Illus. 7-22.
Proofreading guidelines provide a checklist for the careful proofreader to follow.

Proofreading requires your complete attention. You must proofread carefully to produce error-free documents. Move the cursor through the document as you proofread. Check all numbers and unusual spellings against the original document. Proofreading guidelines are shown in Illus. 7-22.

PROOFREADING GUIDELINES

1. Is the document technically correct? Check the following:

   _____ grammar   _____ number usage
   _____ punctuation   _____ capitalization
   _____ spelling   _____ word division
   _____ word usage

2. Is the document content accurate? Check the following:

   _____ data accurate and complete   _____ mailing notations followed
   _____ directions followed   _____ enclosures assembled
   _____ all totals verified   _____ photocopies made

3. Is the document appearance professional? Check the following:

   _____ stationery appropriate   _____ clean and smudge free
   _____ copy placement appropriate   _____ type easy to read
   _____ format consistent   _____ copy error free

**STORAGE
AND
TRANSMISSION**

Two important steps in the word processing workflow are the storage and transmission of documents. A document loses its usefulness if it becomes lost and cannot be retrieved or if the recipient does not receive it on time.

Electronic File Management

The following guidelines will help you manage electronic files more effectively:

1. Develop a plan for naming document files. If such a plan is already in use by the firm, you will be expected to follow the established naming *convention* (procedure for naming files).

framework: basic structure

2. Keep a record of the file naming plan. Use it as your guideline to name files and to keep your naming **framework** consistent.

back up: duplicate

3. Prepare **backup** files on disks to protect against file loss. Documents that would require considerable time and effort to reconstruct should be backed up frequently.

4. Archive hard disk files. Archiving is a means of reducing disk storage space by compressing files. Compressed files may also be copied to off-line disks for backup copies.

fragmented:
in separate parts

5. Clean up the hard disk. Establish a schedule for deleting unneeded documents. As documents are created, revised, and deleted, the document files become **fragmented**. Fragmented files reduce computer operating efficiency. Follow the system manual procedures for backing up and restoring files to the hard disk.

6. Follow security procedures consistently. Departing from security procedures can cause loss of data and lead to tampering of data by unauthorized users.

Electronic Document Transmission

Businesses use various means to distribute and transmit documents. Some offices transmit communications electronically:

Jamie works as an office assistant in a branch office of a large bank. She prepares many reports using word processing. Once the reports are approved, she transmits them electronically to the main bank. Although the main bank is 20 miles away, Jamie's reports reach the bank in seconds.

The speed with which documents can be transmitted electronically is very appealing to business people. You will learn about storage and transmission of documents in Chapters 12, 13, 14, and 15.

QUESTIONS FOR REVIEW

1. Identify the steps in the word processing workflow.

2. What are the four basic word processing tasks?

3. What are default standards and how are they used?

4. Describe five common formatting features of word processing software.

5. Describe five common editing features of word processing software.

6. Identify three common word processing aids and explain their functions.

7. What is a menu? What is the relationship of a submenu to the main menu?

8. What is another name for an electronic dictionary?

9. What guidelines should you follow when proofreading a document?

10. What is the importance of document storage and transmission?

INTERACTING WITH OTHERS

Ted is one of three office assistants in the small legal firm of Breece and O'Malley. Each office assistant has a workstation with a microcomputer and a dot matrix printer. All three assistants share one laser printer. Ted feels that his coworkers monopolize the use of the laser printer because they use it to print nearly all the documents they process. Every time Ted tries to use the equipment, his coworkers say that they are working on a "rush job" that must be completed immediately. Ted frequently has no choice but to use his dot matrix printer to print the final copy of reports. Yet, he often must reprint the entire report on the laser before his manager will consider it a final copy.

If you were Ted, how would you approach this problem with your coworkers? What would you say to them?

What You Are To Do: Prepare a response to the questions raised.

EXTENDING YOUR MATH COMPETENCIES

You work as an office assistant to the sales manager of Tidewater Computer Stores. You are helping to prepare a report comparing income earned through the first six months of this year with income earned during the first six months of last year. You are asked to complete the computations required on the report (on page 284) before it is keyed.

What You Are To Do: Use the form in *Information Processing Activities* or plain paper and compute the missing totals. Then determine the percentage change from the prior year to the current year. Refer to Reference Section D for information about percentages.

APPLICATION ACTIVITY

Tanya is the office supervisor in a small office. She is responsible for delegating tasks to the office employees. The office is equipped with two electronic typewriters (one with no text memory and one with 10,000-character, or 10K, text memory), three microcomputers with word processing software, a laser printer, and a scanner. The following tasks are typical of those Tanya assigns:

1. 2 envelopes
2. a 10-page report requiring minor revisions
3. a 3-paragraph letter
4. a 2-page report
5. a 1-page final agenda for a meeting
6. individualized letters to 20 sales representatives
7. a 500-name mailing list which will be used monthly
8. file folder labels for 3 new clients
9. a general memorandum to all employees (photocopies to 25 persons)
10. an 8-page statistical report requiring extensive revision
11. text copy for the company newsletter
12. update of a 20-page report prepared 2 years ago on an electric typewriter

Word processing equipment can be used to complete this activity.

What You Are To Do: On a plain sheet of paper, set up three column headings: *Task, Equipment,* and *Rationale.* Considering equipment capabilities, determine the appropriate equipment (electronic typewriter—no memory, electronic typewriter—10K memory, microcomputer, or scanner) to use for each task. Then under the appropriate heading key the task number, the equipment you would use, and your reason for your choice.

Gross Income by Types of Products and Services
Comparison of Six-Months Results
(Dollars in Millions)

	Current Year (6 months)	Prior Year (6 months)	Percentage Change from Prior to Current Year
Processors:			
Sales	282	303	?
Rentals	72	173	?
Total	?	?	?
Peripherals:			
Sales	3055	2507	?
Rentals	613	97	?
Total	?	?	?
Office Systems/Work Stations:			
Sales	2828	2707	?
Rentals	244	444	?
Total	?	?	?
Program Products	1088	854	?
Maintenance Services	1833	1553	?
Other:			
Sales	447	381	?
Services	99	83	?
Rentals	89	126	?
Total	?	?	?
Grand Total	?	?	?

(Refer to this report when completing "EXTENDING YOUR MATH COMPETENCIES" on page 282.)

TOPIC 3

ADVANCED ELECTRONIC DOCUMENT PROCESSING

When you have completed your study of this topic, you will be able to:

- describe advanced word processing features

- describe desktop publishing features and procedures

- explain the basic procedures of user support systems

Most word processing software will perform the basic applications of creating, formatting, editing, and printing documents. In many offices today, however, more advanced applications are needed. Therefore, office workers with advanced document processing skills are in increasing demand. If you have a solid background in basic word processing fundamentals, as shown in Topic 2, you will be prepared to master advanced document processing features.

In this topic, you will be introduced to several advanced word processing features. Such features are useful, for example, when preparing multipage documents or repetitive documents. Word processing makes a significant contribution to office productivity when repetitive documents are prepared.

Perhaps one of the most exciting aspects of advanced document processing is that of desktop publishing. The user of desktop publishing can produce a wide variety of high-quality publications. Many businesses now prepare their own professional-looking publications, such as brochures, catalogues, and newsletters. Before desktop publishing, only a printing company would have been able to produce such documents. In this topic, you will learn how desktop publishing works by studying the fundamental guidelines and procedures of desktop publishing.

Many software manufacturers offer user support services, such as telephone support. In this topic, you will learn how to gain the most help from this important resource.

ADVANCED WORD PROCESSING FEATURES

Many word processing software packages offer features that add to greater efficiency and flexibility when preparing documents. The features described in this section are helpful to workers who prepare multipage documents and repetitive documents and who use other advanced word processing features.

Preparing Multipage Documents

extensive: much, broad

Preparing lengthy documents often involves ***extensive*** editing as the document goes through several revisions. Working with blocks of text and paging the document are common tasks you will encounter when processing multipage reports.

Blocks of Text

Major changes can be made to a document using the *block* command. Follow the appropriate procedures to highlight the text to be blocked, then select the function to be performed, as identified in Illus. 7-23. What happens when the move command is used on a blocked (highlighted) portion of text is shown in Illus. 7-24.

Illus. 7-23. The Block command identifies a segment of text in order to perform selected activities on the identified text.

COMMON BLOCKED TEXT FUNCTIONS	
Delete	Removes highlighted text from the document
Move	Deletes highlighted text from its current position and moves it to a different place in the document
Copy	Leaves highlighted text in its current position and also copies it to a different place in the document
Append	Copies highlighted text to the end of another document

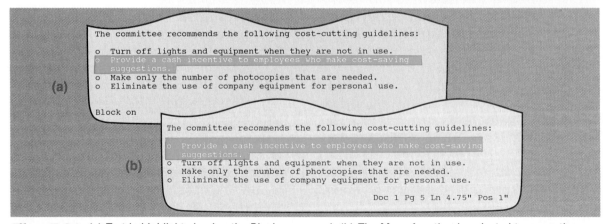

Illus. 7-24. (a) Text is highlighted using the Block command. (b) The Move function is selected to move the highlighted text to its new location in the report.

Pagination

Pagination is the process of dividing the document into individual pages for printing. *Page breaks* are determined by (1) the word processing software inserting an *automatic page ending* as the page is filled or (2) the user entering the command for a *forced page ending.* The automatic page numbering feature of the word processing software accurately records each page number. When revisions change the page endings, the *repagination* feature adjusts the text automatically and renumbers the pages.

Additional pagination features help you move efficiently through the initial keying as well as later revisions of documents:

Headers and Footers. The *header* command places the same information above the text at the top of every page of a document. Page numbers and abbreviated report titles are frequently used as headers. The *footer* command places the information below the text at the bottom of the document pages. Page numbers are common footers. Once activated, header and footer text will appear on every page of the document unless instructions are given to **suppress** its printing on a specific page.

suppress: keep from happening

Widows and Orphans. Because pagination merely counts lines before dividing a page, some paragraphs may be divided inappropriately. Paragraphs divided between pages should contain at least two lines on each page. A first line of a paragraph printed by itself at the bottom of a page is a *widow line.* The last line of a paragraph printed by itself at the top of a page is an *orphan line.* Word processing software can adjust the lines on a page to avoid widows and orphans.

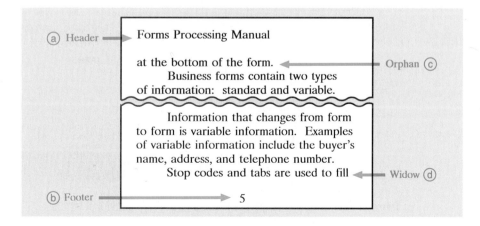

Illus. 7-25. Examples of a (a) header, (b) footer, (c) orphan line, and (d) widow line.

Footnotes. The footnote feature automatically places footnotes at the bottom of the proper page. If a text segment that has a related footnote is moved to another part of the document, the footnote will also be placed on the new page and renumbered automatically.

Preparing Repetitive Documents

Most word processing programs contain features that enable you to prepare repetitive documents quickly. These features also can be used to keep the document style uniform. Several time-saving features are available for processing repetitive documents:

Mail Merge

variables: items that change

The **mail merge** feature is used to prepare individualized copies of form documents. A *primary document* (skeleton) is prepared with appropriate codes placed where **variables** are to be inserted. Next, the *secondary document* (variable list) is created which contains the listing of the variables to be inserted in each letter. The two documents are merged at printing.

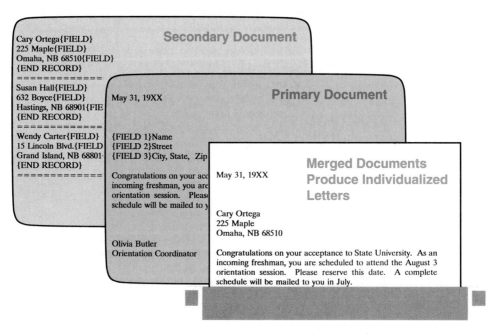

Cary Ortega{FIELD}
225 Maple{FIELD}
Omaha, NB 68510{FIELD}
{END RECORD}
=============
Susan Hall{FIELD}
632 Boyce{FIELD}
Hastings, NB 68901{FIE
{END RECORD}
=============
Wendy Carter{FIELD}
15 Lincoln Blvd.{FIELD}
Grand Island, NB 68801
{END RECORD}
=============

Secondary Document

May 31, 19XX

Primary Document

{FIELD 1}Name
{FIELD 2}Street
{FIELD 3}City, State, Zip

Congratulations on your acc
incoming freshman, you are
orientation session.   Pleas
schedule will be mailed to y

Olivia Butler
Orientation Coordinator

May 31, 19XX

**Merged Documents
Produce Individualized
Letters**

Cary Ortega
225 Maple
Omaha, NB 68510

Congratulations on your acceptance to State University. As an incoming freshman, you are scheduled to attend the August 3 orientation session. Please reserve this date. A complete schedule will be mailed to you in July.

Illus. 7-26. The merge feature is used to prepare individual letters.

Form Letters and Paragraphs

Some word processing software allows you to place stop codes in a skeleton (primary) document. The user fills in each variable, moving from code to code through the document. This feature is useful if you prepare a standard form or letter only occasionally.

Prestored sentences and paragraphs are another form of individualizing repetitive messages. Prestored text combined to form a finished document is known as **boilerplate** text, as shown in Illus. 7-27. To assemble a document, you may combine any custom text (such as the individual's name and address) with selected prestored sentences and paragraphs. Document assembly occurs at text entry. Once you have assembled the document, you would save and print it in the same manner as other documents.

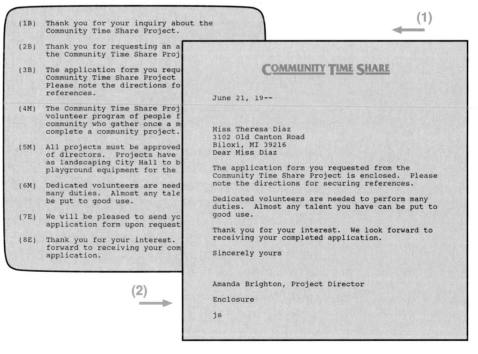

Illus. 7-27. (1) The office worker selected paragraphs 3B, 6M, and 8E from this boilerplate text to prepare (2) an individualized response.

Stylesheets

Stylesheets can reduce formatting time and retain consistency within documents. **Stylesheets** are preset formats used to automate document formatting. Once developed, you may save and retrieve stylesheets for future documents. Thus, when a standard report is to be prepared, you would retrieve the appropriate stylesheet file with the format decisions already determined.

Macros

A **macro** is a file created to represent a series of keystrokes. Once the macro has been created, you key the macro name rather than the series of keystrokes. Any combination of key strokes that is used repeatedly can be placed in a macro. Macros not only save you keying time but assure that the repeated keystrokes are accurate.

> *Amy started with simple macros. The first macro she created printed the closing lines of a letter: complimentary close, space returns, name, and title of her supervisor. Whenever she keyed a letter for her supervisor, she recalled the macro by depressing the two-key identification she had assigned to it. The closing lines appeared automatically on her computer screen. Amy learned quickly that macros streamline keying, editing, and formatting of many documents she prepared on a regular basis.*

Using Other Advanced Features

Other advanced features are available that are helpful in preparing a wide variety of documents:

Columns. Two column styles, newspaper and parallel, are commonly available. *Newspaper columns* are read from top to bottom. As the operator keys the copy, text automatically flows, or snakes, from the bottom of one column to the top of the next column and from page to page. *Parallel columns* are read across the page from left to right. Parallel columns are used when the information in the columns must be kept in line across the page such as in listings, schedules, or resumes.

Math Functions. Common math functions include addition, subtraction, multiplication, and division. Numbers in the rows or columns can be calculated as they are entered. One use of the math feature is to verify totals.

Table and Alignment Features. The manner in which tables are developed depends upon the features available. If features are limited, you will need to calculate the table layout. Some **alignment** features may be available to assist keyboard entry: decimal tab (aligns the figures at the decimal point); flush right text

alignment: to bring into line

(aligns text to the right with an uneven left margin); and center text (centers on line of writing or within a defined text column). Some word processing software has a table-generating feature that automatically determines column spacing and prepares the table layout, as shown in Illus. 7-28.

Illus. 7-28. The table-generating feature automatically determines column spacing and table layout. Totals were calculated automatically using the math feature.

COMPUTER TIME ALLOTTED AND USED BY DEPARTMENTS

DEPARTMENT	HOURS ALLOTTED	HOURS USED
Accounting	25.00	15.45
Administration	17.00	7.30
Human Resources	10.00	12.25
TOTAL	52.00	35.00

DESKTOP PUBLISHING SYSTEMS

distinction: difference, contrast

enhanced: to make greater in attractiveness

Desktop publishing is the creating of computer-generated publications that appear to have been professionally typeset. Desktop publishing (DTP) allows the user to combine both graphics and text on the computer screen. Word processing, on the other hand, is used primarily to create and edit documents containing only text. You will find this *distinction* blurred as some high-level word processing programs add graphic features.

A business has more control and greater flexibility in preparing documents when those documents are produced in-house. Workloads do not have to be coordinated with outside printing firms, and in-house schedules can be adjusted to meet deadlines.

A primary reason for using DTP is the *enhanced* appearance of finished documents. Almost anything that can be typeset by a professional printer can be produced using a DTP system:

- annual reports
- announcements
- catalogues
- brochures
- business cards
- directories
- letterheads
- newsletters
- transparencies

Organizations that produce extremely complex, multi-colored documents may use mini or mainframe computer systems or special workstations and high-volume printers to produce magazines, newspapers, and technical documents. This more advanced level of publishing is referred to as corporate electronic publishing. Corporate electronic publishing involves higher levels of equipment and operator skill than does DTP.

System Components

Desktop publishing combines text and graphic elements to produce a document. *Page composition software* is the tool you would use to bring text and graphic elements together to create the desired document.

The more sophisticated the desktop publishing software, the more computer memory and speed are required for efficient operation. In addition to a computer, other hardware components frequently used include: laser printer, page-size monitor, scanner, and mouse.

Illus. 7-29. Desktop publishing brings document enhancement to small businesses and to the departmental level of large companies.

Using Desktop Publishing

Desktop publishing involves these basic steps, as shown in Illus. 7-30:

1. Key, proofread, and edit the document text using word processing software.
2. Scan, select, or develop graphics to be used in the document.
3. Plan the page layout.
4. Merge text and graphics. Print the final document.

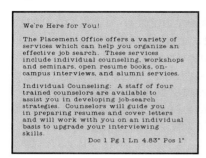

Step 1. Use word processing software to prepare the text.

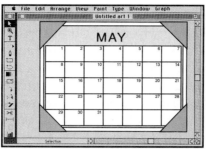

Step 2. Prepare document graphics.

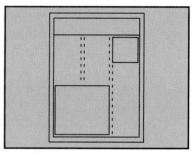

Step 3. Plan the page layout.

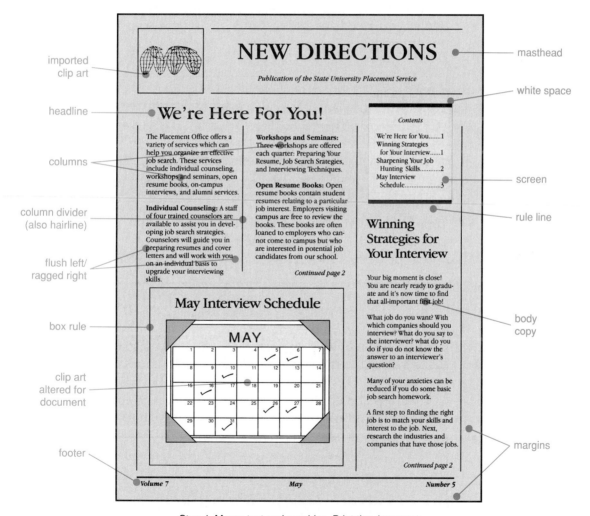

Step 4. Merge text and graphics. Print the document.

Illus. 7-30. Basic steps in desktop publishing and related terminology.

From your previous studies, you know how to prepare text using word processing software (Step 1 of desktop publishing). Additional steps are completed (as shown on page 293) to combine text and graphics to produce a finished document. To help you to understand desktop publishing terminology, typographic elements are discussed in this section. Guidelines are presented for using graphics (Step 2) and page layout and design (Step 3).

Typographic Elements

Typography refers to the style, shape, or appearance of printed alphabetic and numeric characters. To use DTP effectively, you need to understand basic typographic concepts and terminology:

Illus. 7-31. Basic typeface elements.

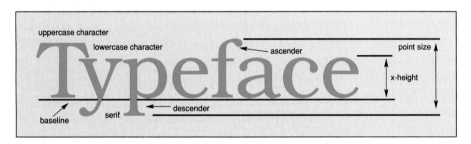

Type. Type is the basic element of DTP. In DTP, *type* refers to the characters of an alphabet used for printing. A **typeface** is a specific type design, such as *Helvetica* or *Times Roman:*

Illus. 7-32. Hundreds of typefaces are available, and each has its unique name.

A **font** is the complete alphabet (upper and lower case), numbers, and symbols of one typeface in one size and one style:

Illus. 7-33. This font shows the Dutch Roman typeface in one size (14 point) and one style (italic).

ABCDEFGHIJKLMNOPQRSTUVWXYZ
abcdefghijklmnopqrstuvwxyz
1234567890 ! @ # $ % ^ & * ( ) - = + \ ?
< > , . ; : { } '

Size. Type size is expressed in points. A *point* measures $1/72$ of a vertical inch. The point size of a typeface is determined by measuring from the top of an *ascender* (such as a *b* or *t*) to the bottom of a *descender* (such as a *p* or *y*):

8 points   10 points   12 points   24 points

Style. Typefaces are printed in different sizes and in different type styles. In addition to *Plain Print*, Bold Print and Italic Print are common typeface styles. *Bold print* is often used to emphasize text. *Italic print* is not as legible as bold print but can be used effectively for contrast and emphasis:

Plain Print   **Bold Print**   *Italic Print*   ***Bold Italic Print***

Line Length. Line length is measured in picas. A *pica* measures $1/6$ of a horizontal inch. Thus, a line length of 30 picas is five inches long.

Spacing. Line height is measured from the base of a character on one line (baseline) to the base of a character on the next line (baseline). *Leading* is the insertion of extra space between lines of type. Kerning refers to the horizontal spacing between characters. Characters such as *i* and *t* do not require as much space as *M* and *W*, for example. *Kerning* is the reduction of space between combinations of letters so as to use only the required space for each character. These concepts are illustrated in Illus. 7-34.

Illus. 7-34. Leading (left and center) and kerning (right) affect the readability of copy.

Leading is used to adjust the space between lines by small amounts. (.20 inch space)	Leading is used to adjust the space between lines by small amounts. (.15 inch space)	To Unkerned type To Kerned type

Graphic Elements

Graphics are used to further explain text and to make a document more appealing. Graphic elements include anything on the page that is not text, such as figures, charts, drawings, and photographs. Graphics can be imported into the DTP document by scanning the desired image or by using graphics software to develop and import the image into the document. A popular form of graphics software is electronic clip art. **Electronic clip art** is predrawn art available on disk. Most clip art contains an assortment of images, borders, and letters. Electronic clip art allows you to include graphics without preparing the artwork yourself. Enlarging and shrinking the graphics is easily done in some programs. Guidelines for using graphics include:

- Keep graphics simple and legible; avoid too much information.
- Use professional looking graphics, such as clip art.
- Use graphics that relate to or clarify text.
- Make the graphic a *focal point* on the page.
- Use color carefully if a choice of colors is available.

focal point: center of attention

Page Layout and Design

The purpose of *page layout* (page composition) is to determine the placement of text and graphics on a page. These general design guidelines will help you produce attractive, easy-to-read documents:

1. Prepare a sketch of the page layout before working with the DTP software to help clarify the placement of elements on the page.
2. Avoid using more than two typefaces within a document. Choose the most readable typefaces and be consistent in their use.
3. Use type styles effectively: bold styles for main headings and subheadings; italic styles for emphasizing words, titles and quotations. For easy reading, avoid underlining blocks of text.
4. Use appropriate point size: 10 to 12 point sizes for easy text reading; headings two to four point sizes larger than the text.

	Design 1	Design 2
Main Heading	12 point bold	14 point
Subheading	10 point bold	12 point
Text	10 point	10 point

5. Avoid crowding the page. Allow ample white space (blank space between the text and graphics) on each page to balance the page layout and to guide the reader's eye movements. Leave more space above a heading than below the heading.

6. Give consideration to side and top margins. Leave slightly more space at the bottom of the page than at the top.
7. Assess the overall appearance and readability of the page.

USER SUPPORT SYSTEMS

As you learn more advanced software packages, you may need help beyond that available to you in a manual or a tutorial. Many software manufacturers provide telephone user support. This support is a valuable resource. To take full advantage of user support:

1. Know the support level you are eligible to receive. Different classes of service may be available for different prices. Much user support, however, is free to software purchasers. Have your user identification number available when you call.
2. Be prepared to report your hardware configuration. This information may be important to solving the problem.
3. Be prepared to explain the problem clearly and specifically.
4. Be prepared to work at your terminal during the call. Often, the support operator will work through the problem with you.

QUESTIONS FOR REVIEW

1. Identify and describe four blocking functions.

2. What is a widow line? an orphan line?

3. Explain the mail merge feature.

4. How can a macro increase your productivity?

5. Identify three alignment features that assist keyboard entry.

6. Why do businesses use desktop publishing?

7. Identify the desired hardware components of a desktop publishing system.

8. What are four guidelines for using graphics in a document?

9. Identify six page layout and design guidelines to help produce quality documents.

10. What is a user support system and how can you take full advantage of it?

MAKING DECISIONS

Candy received a telephone call at 9:10 a.m. from Tony, a coworker: "Candy, I'm in trouble. Mr. Ganster was really upset with me yesterday for being late, and today I've overslept! I won't be there for another hour! I know Mr. Ganster is out at the plant, but he may call me within the hour. Please, please tell him I've gone to the stockroom for supplies. Bye; I must hurry!" Tony hung up before Candy could respond. At 9:25 a.m. Mr. Ganster called.

What You Are To Do: What decision would you make in response to Tony's request? What would you say to Mr. Ganster?

EXTENDING YOUR ENGLISH COMPETENCIES

You have been given the paragraph below, which is an excerpt from a memo. It contains four errors in the agreement of subject and verb.

What You Are To Do: Key a copy of the excerpt, making all corrections required so that subjects and verbs are in agreement.

Each of the buildings are in need of considerable repair. Four architects from the Pyramid Architectural firm is certain that the work can be completed within one year. However, the owners' assessment are that the work will require an additional six months. So we must get another estimate. Do you think one of your staff architects are available to do this job for us?

APPLICATION ACTIVITY

Assume you are the secretary to Mrs. Dorothy E. Meyers, Human Resources Director, at Three Rivers Realty Co., One Point Park Plaza, Pittsburgh, Pennsylvania, 15230-8372. Mrs. Meyers has revised the text of the letter sent to applicants for administrative assistant positions. She asks you to make the marked changes and to send the letter to three recent applicants.

What You Are To Do: Depending upon your equipment capabilities:

1. Prepare the letter text as a primary document. Place the applicants' names and addresses in a secondary document for merging (See Illus. 7-26 on page 288).
2. Print a letter to each applicant.
3. Use the letterhead provided in *Information Processing Activities* or plain paper. You may also develop your own letterhead.

Word processing equipment can be used to complete this activity.

Please revise this text and send letters to the applicants below.

Dear

Thank you ~~very much~~ for your inquiry concerning a position with our company as an administrative assistant. ¢

Our administrative assistants are promoted to those positions after they have worked in our company for a ~~number of~~ years. They must demonstrate their ability to work efficiently within ~~the~~ office *(at least)* system. I think you will find similar hiring ~~practices~~ in most companies. ¢
our *policies*

We ~~do~~ have several openings for word processing operators in our headquarters office. If you would like to be considered for one of these positions, please complete the enclosed application and return it to James Baker, Human Resources Division. ¢

If you decide to pursue a position with our company, ~~I think~~ you will find that we have an excellent promotion policy. ~~for qualified employees.~~
very attractive working conditions and

Yours truly

Mr. Phillip H. Tobin	Ms. Yasuko Higuchi	Mrs. Cathy Crane
714 Garden City Drive	Two Oliver Plaza	344 Orchard Lane
Monroeville, PA 15146-4792	Pittsburgh, PA 15222-4842	Mt. Lebanon, PA 15228-1442

CHAPTER SUMMARY

In this chapter, you learned about word processing concepts and procedures for preparing business documents:

1. Word processing is performed in multipurpose and specialized environments using electric typewriters, electronic typewriters, word processing systems, and microcomputers.
2. Text input methods include the keyboard, scanners, mice, trackballs, touch screens, pen PCs, and voice input.
3. Basic word processing tasks involve entering text, formatting, editing, and printing.
4. Word processing aids include menus, prompts and messages, dictionaries and thesauruses.
5. Special procedures are used by office workers to proofread electronic copy and to manage electronic files.
6. Advanced word processing features are often needed to prepare multipage documents and repetitive documents efficiently.
7. Desktop publishing is used by many businesses to enhance documents. DTP skills are becoming valued office skills.
8. User support services offered by many software manufacturers are a valuable resource.

KEY CONCEPTS AND TERMS

text memory	submenu
WYSIWYG	prompts
scanners	messages
mouse	pagination
trackball	mail merge
touch screen	boilerplate
pen PCs	stylesheets
voice input	macro
electronic clip art	desktop publishing
formatting	typography
default standards	typeface
editing	font
menu	

INTEGRATED CHAPTER ACTIVITIES

Activity 1

You are an office assistant to Renee V. Bentley, director of administrative services for a major insurance company. She also serves as president of the National Administrative Services Association. The insurance company encourages Ms. Bentley's active involvement in this professional organization. Ms. Bentley has asked you to key a final draft of a letter and an accompanying enclosure.

What You Are To Do:
- Key a final copy of the letter on page 301. Make all changes indicated on the draft. Use the letterhead provided in *Information Processing Activities* or plain paper. (The National Administrative Services Association is located at 3033 Finley Road, Downers Grove, IL 60515-3278.)

- Key a final copy of the enclosure on plain paper. Use word processing features (if available) to enhance the enclosure.

Word processing equipment can be used to complete this activity.

Mr. Willard L. Shapiro, President
Shapiro Electronics Corp. SP.
5791 Ghirardelli Square
San Francisco, CA 94132-4291

Dear Will

At the Board meeting following our annual convention in
Boston last week, we voted unanimously to invite you to be
the general program chairman for our annual meeting
scheduled for San Francisco next year's

You have had considerable experience in our organization, and you
know what is required to handle this job properly. We have
no question about your ability to do so. You will, of
course, have the support of our staff. At our meeting, we
determined that there should be approximately 43 sessions
during the convention. On the enclosed sheet, we have
identified the general topics that the Board believes must
be covered by the programs. Also indicated are levels and
formats that are to be included.

As you know, three members of this year's committee will
continue as members of next year's committee. The three who
are continuing are as follows: Amy Sweeney of Sacramento,
Donald Wohland of Palo Alto, and Roger Mitliff of Berkeley.

The Board and I hope that you will accept our invitation to
assume this important job for the Association.

Sincerely yours

National Administrative Services Assoc. SP.

Program Notes -- San Francisco

The subject areas to be covered include:

- Technology
- Management
- Software
- Training
- Productivity
- Professional Development

- Office Automation
- Ergonomics
- Quality Circles

Session levels should include:

- Basic
- Intermediate
- Advanced

Formats for sessions should include:
- Workshop (Hands-On)
- Lecture
- Roundtable Exchange
- Panel Discussion

Use your own judgment in regard to arranging this on a full sheet of paper. RB

Activity 2

You work in the WP center at Current Enterprises. Bradley L. Levine, Manager of Computer Services, is developing new procedures for acquiring software. The center supervisor assigns you the task of preparing the final copy.

What You Are To Do: Key a final copy of the memo using the current date. If your equipment permits, develop a Computer Services memorandum form (See page 274 as an example). Otherwise, use the memo form in *Information Processing Activities* or plain paper.

Word processing
equipment can be used
to complete this activity.

~~We believe~~ we can handle software requests in a more efficient manner if all requests within your department are approved by you before they are forwarded to my office.

To assist both you and Central Computing in requesting and evaluating software, a software Request Form has been attached to this memorandum. ~~As you will note,~~ Part A ~~of this form~~ contains the minimum information that must be known about a product in order for it to be ~~investigated.~~ considered. Part B contains questions of a more technical nature which (can usually be answered by the vendor or by information *contained in software* (~~secured from~~ the ~~product~~ installation manual.)

Please send this memo to all Department Managers. The subject is requesting New Software. B. Levine

Remember that acquisition of software packages is based on technical/support considerations. Once a ~~product~~ *package* has been approved, an implementation schedule will be drawn up by our office, *working with* ~~and~~ the staff member who requested *the package* ~~it.~~ Dates will be set for initial installation, full testing, and production. ~~date.~~ The test period will require your full cooperation, ~~since this is the period when~~ *as* you ~~can~~ learn how to use the product, ~~noting~~ *and note* any "bugs" that need to be eliminated.

During the test period, we will develop documentation and support materials for users.

OPTIONAL COMPUTER APPLICATION ACTIVITY
See Computer Application Activity 7
in your Information Processing Activities workbook.

OPTIONAL CRITICAL THINKING ACTIVITY
See Critical Thinking Activity 3
in your Information Processing Activities workbook.

PRODUCTIVITY CORNER

Kathy Malenky
OFFICE SUPERVISOR

NEW JOB JITTERS

DEAR MS. MALENKY:

I definitely am doing something wrong! I'm embarrassed to admit that although I've been working in an office for almost a month, yesterday I didn't key one document that wasn't returned to me for corrections. As I made the corrections, I realized that I should have caught the errors—but I didn't. I have a very understanding supervisor; she thinks I can do the work but feels I'm too nervous and am not concentrating. I *am* nervous. I want to do a good job, but I keep asking myself, "*Can* I do this job?"

Is there any hope for me? I don't know where to begin. Can you help me?—BEVERLY IN BALTIMORE

DEAR BEVERLY:

You seem sincere about wanting to be a good worker. It takes courage to admit that every document required corrections. You also realize that you do not proofread as you should. You are facing the situation in an honest manner, and that is a basic require-

ment for solving any problem. Here are some suggestions:

1. Try to put aside the constant questioning of how well you are doing.
2. Begin acting like a competent worker by giving full attention to the job at hand. Make sure what you are keying makes sense. If you have a question, ask your supervisor.
3. Practice being calm. Take care not to put too much pressure on yourself to complete the job too quickly.
4. Carefully proofread what you have keyed. Ask questions like: "Is the grammar of each sentence correct? Is the punctuation correct? Are the words spelled correctly?" Imagine that there must be a mistake somewhere in what you have keyed. Inexperienced proofreaders often assume that there aren't any mistakes in the copy. Such an attitude leads to overlooking errors.

Yes, there is hope for you. The fact that you want to improve is the first big step.—KATHY MALENKY

303

CHAPTER 8

Data Processing Systems: Common Applications

Can you imagine a business that needed no numeric information? Of course not. Numbers are important to practically every aspect of any business activity. How many orders do we have for Product X? What is the price we must pay for our next purchase of fabric? How many items remain in our inventory of Y raw material? Will this expenditure exhaust our budget allowance? What is the amount owed us by customers?

Again and again during the workday questions arise that require up-to-date information in numeric form. You may have a job where you will have the numbers at hand to answer questions.

Many office workers are required for processing figures, commonly called data processing. In more and more companies such workers use electronic methods for completing tasks. To perform tasks properly, regardless of the processing method, workers must have a good understanding of what they do. Timely, accurate information is the output of the thousands of data processing workers in American companies.

As you know, not all companies are alike. Therefore, the numbers that are critical to companies are likely to differ, too. But there are some similarities among many companies. In Chapter 8, you will be introduced to three common tasks of data processing workers: processing orders, processing purchases, and maintaining inventories.

The objectives of the chapter are to:

- acquaint you with the office tasks related to processing orders from receipt to shipment

- introduce you to effective and efficient purchasing and inventory maintenance procedures

CUSTOMER SERVICE

When you have completed your study of this topic, you will be able to:

- identify the different systems for processing orders

- explain how an office worker prepares an incoming order for processing

- describe the several departments that participate in processing orders

Customers are important to companies. Orders for goods are given prompt attention because companies believe that satisfied customers are likely to place orders in the future. Companies inform prospective customers about their policies regarding orders. How promptly orders will be filled and what guarantees are offered are matters of interest to customers.

A sports clothing company sells through catalogs. Orders by telephone are received by clerks at computer terminals. The details of each order are keyed, the availability of the items is automatically checked, and the shipment date given to the customer.

You understand why companies must carefully organize their order processing procedures. You will find that more than one department participates in the task of responding to the requests of customers promptly. This means that each

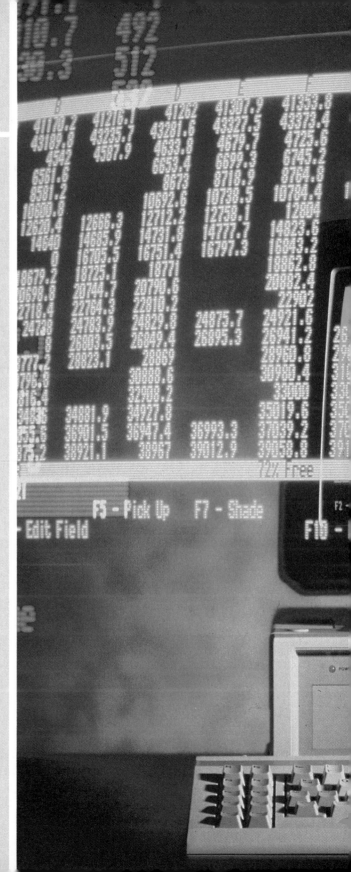

department must give immediate attention to the steps for which it is responsible. The order processing tasks reflect the need for team effort. The company or individual ordering goods is dependent on the team effort. Goods ordered are frequently needed on the scheduled delivery date if the work of the buying company is to progress smoothly.

A manufacturer of cellular telephones uses parts produced by other companies. Parts must be on hand when needed. Suppliers of parts must be dependable. An executive of a parts supplier stated: "Our business is successful because we never delay a shipment. If we promise to ship on the 12th, we ship on the 12th."

Varying Systems for Processing Orders

If you were to visit several companies, you would likely find that orders are not processed alike in all the companies. You would find that some companies use a noncomputerized system; others use a computerized batch system; and still others use an on-line interactive system. The differences relate to the following:

- the nature of equipment used
- the procedures for preparing order-related documents
- the methods of distributing documents

Note these differences summarized in Illus. 8-1. You must remember that what is to be accomplished does not change as you consider one system in relation to another. Companies take advantage of more advanced technology for one or more of the following reasons:

- to achieve a higher level of accuracy
- to process at a faster rate to provide better service to customers and to handle larger volumes of orders
- to reduce the number of office workers who perform manual operations

You might well ask: "Why do I need to learn how to do tasks in a noncomputerized system when the company in which I accept a job probably will have employees doing such tasks electronically?"

That is a reasonable question. The basic reason for introducing you to noncomputerized order processing is to give you clear and complete understanding of each phase of the processing.

VARIATIONS IN ORDER PROCESSING SYSTEMS

System	Processing	Preparation of Documents	Distribution of Documents
noncomputerized	by office employees with the aid of typewriters and calculators	by office employees	by interoffice mail or messenger
computerized batch	by computer in data processing center	by computer in data processing center	by interoffice mail or messenger
computerized on-line, interactive or noninteractive	by computer at terminals in offices through-out the organization	by computer in department where needed	by computer

Illus. 8-1. Variations in order processing systems.

Then, if you work in an office where there is an on-line, interactive electronic system, for example, you will know what the computer is doing—the action of the computer will not be a mystery to you. Knowing what is being done by the computer will be useful as you respond to inquiries from customers or are asked to take care of an order-related problem.

Illus. 8-2. An order clerk accepting a telephone order.

Noncomputerized procedures are still in use. A company may be small and the volume of orders does not warrant the installation of a computer system. Also, a company may ship large orders to a limited number of customers. Again, such a company may not need a computerized system.

The departments that participate in the processing of orders are shown in Illus. 8-3. The flowchart for order processing is shown in Illus. 8-5. A **flowchart** is a diagram showing step-by-step progress through a system. Note that specific symbols are used for documents and processes. (Some are identified in Illus. 8-4.) As each department which participates in the process is discussed, return to Illus. 8-5 to see the relationship of the specific step to other steps.

ORDER PROCESSING TASKS BY DEPARTMENT	
Department	**Key Task**
sales	orders are received and processing begins
credit	credit checks of prospective customers are made
warehouse	place where goods are maintained
packing and shipping	goods packed and forwarded to customers
billing	invoices for goods ordered are prepared

Illus. 8-3. Can you identify what an office worker in each department does?

Receiving Orders

Orders are commonly received by telephone and by mail. Of course, many customers buy goods in retail stores where orders are placed in person. Our discussion, however, will not consider retail order processing.

If you have responsibility for accepting orders, you will have the following information at hand:

● an up-to-date listing of all goods for sale
● current price lists

- shipping charges
- company policies related to discounts, returns of goods, payment dates, shipping dates, and related matters
- a standard procedure for preparing sales order forms or coding incoming orders.

Illus. 8-4 Commonly used flowchart symbols.

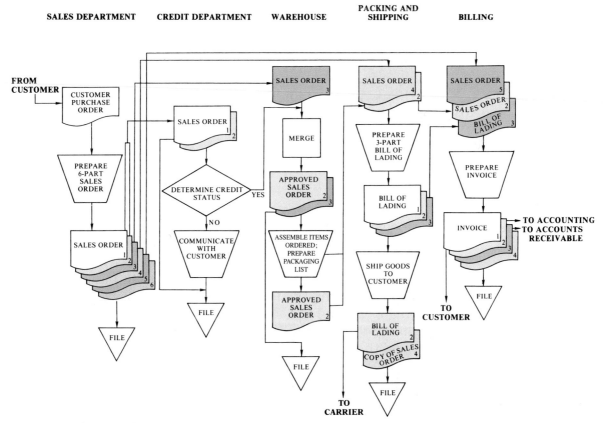

Illus. 8-5. Can you follow the route of sales order copy 2?

You will want to organize these materials so that you can refer to them quickly and easily. Furthermore, you will want to read the materials so that you are thoroughly familiar with the products of your company and the policies under which orders are accepted and processed.

Telephone Orders

Many sales representatives and customers find it convenient to place orders by telephone. If you have the task of receiving orders by telephone, you will find the following procedures helpful:

1. Be prepared by having the appropriate form at hand so that you can record all information directly on the form.
2. Record the information in legible handwriting so that no problems arise in determining what you wrote.
3. Check your form to see that the caller has given you all the information you need to have a complete order.
4. Repeat to the caller all important details, including what was ordered, quantities, style or color choice (if applicable) and prices. You will also want to verify the customer's name and address.
5. Thank the caller for the order.

Mail Orders

You may find that orders in the company where you work are primarily mail orders. If your tasks include handling incoming mail orders, you will find the following general steps useful:

1. Open the envelopes carefully, if orders are delivered to you unopened.
2. Check to see if the order letter or order form gives complete information about the name and address of the sender before you discard the envelope. Where in Illus. 8-5 is the order from the customer shown? What document does a customer send to a seller?
3. Stamp the current date on the letter or form.
4. Read the contents to determine that all details are included.
5. Verify
    *   prices (if included in the order)
    *   that the customer is on the approved credit list
    *   that all details pertaining to the goods ordered are included

6. Follow up, according to the company's procedures, on any information you were unable to verify. For example, if the customer was not on the approved credit list, you would send a copy of the order with a request for review of the customer's credit standing to the credit department.

7. Prepare carefully any forms required for further processing. In many companies, you will prepare a sales order form. See Illus. 8-7 on page 312 for an example.

8. Proofread your work.

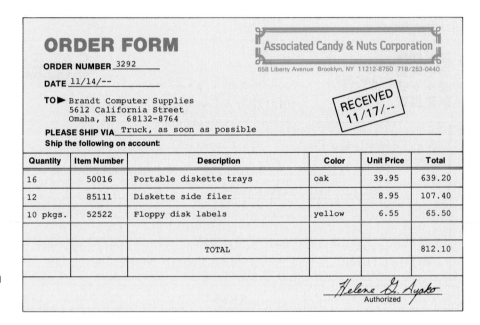

ORDER FORM

Associated Candy & Nuts Corporation

658 Liberty Avenue Brooklyn, NY 11212-8750 718/253-0440

ORDER NUMBER 3292

DATE 11/14/--

TO ▶ Brandt Computer Supplies
5612 California Street
Omaha, NE 68132-8764

RECEIVED 11/17/--

PLEASE SHIP VIA Truck, as soon as possible

Ship the following on account:

Quantity	Item Number	Description	Color	Unit Price	Total
16	50016	Portable diskette trays	oak	39.95	639.20
12	85111	Diskette side filer		8.95	107.40
10 pkgs.	52522	Floppy disk labels	yellow	6.55	65.50
		TOTAL			812.10

Helene G. Ayako
Authorized

Illus. 8-6. Order form received in the mail from a customer.

Establishing Credit

In many companies goods are sold on credit to most, if not all, customers. To be sure customers are likely to pay their obligations, companies investigate the credit standing of ***prospective*** customers. The credit department has the task of checking the credit rating of new customers. If you choose to work in a credit department, you are likely to perform tasks such as the following:

prospective: future

- Receive inquiries from the sales office about companies or individuals who are placing orders for the first time.

- Search department files to learn if the credit standing of a company or individual had been reviewed earlier.

- Prepare forms for a credit check from a credit agency and/or bank.
- Place all the documents related to the prospective customer on the desk of the credit manager, who is responsible for deciding whether or not to grant credit.
- After a decision is made by the credit manager, send the original order form to the sales department for proper processing.

Illus. 8-7. Where did the order clerk get the information for this sales order form?

BRANDT COMPUTER SUPPLIES

SALES ORDER

5612 California Street Omaha, NE 68132-8764

SEND TO
Associated Candy & Nuts Corporation
658 Liberty Avenue
Brooklyn, NY 11212-8750

Sales Order No. 568730
Customer's Order No. 3292
Date 11/17/--

INSTRUCTIONS Ship via truck as soon as possible.

QUANTITY	ITEM NUMBER	DESCRIPTION	COLOR	UNIT PRICE	TOTAL
16	50016	Portable diskette trays	oak	39.95	639.20
12	85111	Diskette side filer		8.95	107.40
10 pkgs.	52522	Floppy disk labels	yellow	6.55	65.50

Ray Brinkman — Order Clerk

ORIGINAL
(ORIGINAL AND COPY 2 TO CREDIT DEPARTMENT)
(COPY 3 TO WAREHOUSE)
(COPY 4 TO PACKING AND SHIPPING DEPARTMENT)
(COPY 5 TO BILLING DEPARTMENT)
(COPY 6 IS FILED IN SALES DEPARTMENT)

Assembling Goods

warehouse: place where goods for shipment are stored

The copy of the order form prepared in the sales office that is forwarded to the **warehouse** is the basis for gathering all the goods ordered. The task of filling an order requires attention to *every* detail shown on the order form. You will find that every company has established some means of verifying the accuracy of the goods assembled for each order. You will also find procedures to follow when the goods ordered are not in stock.

> Maria works as an order clerk in the stockroom of a manufacturer of costume jewelry. Orders are received in large numbers from small specialized shops and department stores. Maria assembles all the items for a particular order. She is careful and does not make mistakes. She knows customers must receive exactly what they ordered.

In some companies, an office worker prepares a packing list that accompanies the goods forwarded to packing and shipping. A **packing list** is a document on which each item and the quantity being shipped is listed. A copy is generally enclosed in the shipment.

Preparing Invoices

Invoices are prepared in the billing department. An **invoice** is a statement sent to the customer that indicates the goods ordered and their total price. Page 314 shows an invoice ready for mailing.

Before an invoice is prepared, the billing department generally has a copy of the sales order completed in the sales office as well as a document from the warehouse. You will find the following are common procedures for preparing invoices:

1. Compare all details given on the forms received from the sales department and the warehouse. If there are any discrepancies, follow up with the departments to determine what corrections are needed.
2. Prepare the invoice, giving special attention to assure that
   - the address is correct.
   - payment terms are appropriate for the customer.
   - prices are correct and current.
   - computations are accurate and shipping and related charges are included.
3. Forward copies of the invoice to proper offices after your work has been reviewed by your supervisor.

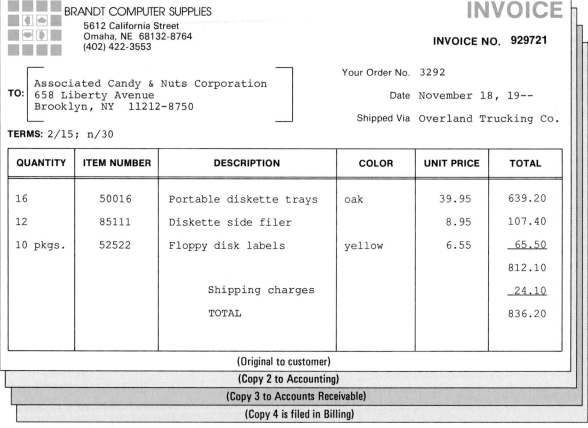

Illus. 8-8. In what department was this document prepared?

Packing and Shipping

Assembling all the needed forms and preparing bills of lading are the key office tasks in packing and shipping departments. Employees, of course, also must be sure that the actual goods being shipped are the ones shown on the original orders.

A **bill of lading** is a form that shows exactly what goods are being shipped. (See example of a bill of lading in Illus. 8-9.) The bill of lading is prepared in triplicate and signed by the representative of the *carrier* at the time the goods are released to the carrier. The carrier gets two copies and the shipper keeps one copy. One copy which the carrier gets is signed by the customer upon receipt of the goods. The employee of the carrier then forwards the copy signed by the customer to the company from which the goods were shipped.

carrier: an organization that transports goods

STRAIGHT BILL OF LADING – SHORT FORM – Original – Not Negotiable

SHIPPER'S NO. 929721
AGENT'S NO. 2552

RECEIVED, subject to the classifications and tariffs in effect on the date of the issue of this Bill of Lading.

Carrier _Overland Trucking Co._

SHIPPER _Brandt Computer Supplies_ Date _11/18_ 19 _--_

Consigned to _Associated Candy & Nuts Corporation_

Destination _658 Liberty Ave._ Street _Brooklyn_ City _NY_ State

Routing

Delivering Carrier _Overland Trucking Co._ Vehicle or Car Initial _J_ No. _89_

Subject to Section 7 of conditions of applicable bill of lading, if this shipment is to be delivered to the consignee without recourse on the consignor, the consignor shall sign the following statement.
The carrier shall not make delivery of this shipment without payment of freight and all other lawful charges.

(Signature of Consignor)

If charges are to be prepaid, write or stamp here, "To be Prepaid."

to be prepaid

Received $ _____
to apply in prepayment of the charges on the property described hereon.

NO. PACKAGES	DESCRIPTION OF ARTICLES	WEIGHT
1	16 Portable diskette trays	
	10 pkgs. Floppy disk labels	
	12 Diskette side filers	18 lbs.

Agent or Cashier

Per _____
(The signature here acknowledges only the amount prepaid.)

SHIPPER _Brandt Computer Supplies_ Per _NC_

SHIPPER'S ADDRESS _5612 California St. Omaha, NE 68132-8764_

Agent _Overland Trucking Co._ Per _AG_ _11/18_ 19 _--_

Charges Advanced $ _____

†Shipper's imprint in lieu of stamp not a part of Bill of Lading approved by the Interstate Commerce Commission.

†"The fibre boxes used for this shipment conform to the specifications set forth in the box maker's certificate thereon; and all other requirements of Uniform Freight Classification."

ORIGINAL (given to carrier; signed by buyer; returned to shipper)

SHIPPING ORDER (retained by carrier)

MEMORANDUM (filed in Shipping)

Illus. 8-9. What company will receive the goods listed on the bill of lading?

Lauren works in the packing and shipping department of a large paper manufacturing company. Her department is a busy one, but it is well organized because the company's policy requires prompt shipment of all orders. Lauren prepares bills of lading, checks packing slips against the copy of the order received from the sales department, and inserts the packing list in the outgoing package. She files memorandum copies of bills of lading promptly.

Following Up Orders

Customers are likely to call or write the sales department if they have any problems with their orders. One of your tasks as an office worker may be to check the records relating to orders in response to customer complaints and inquiries. From time to time, all office workers who participate in some aspect of order processing are required to get information about what actually happened to orders. You will want to keep any records for which you are responsible in proper order. That way you will be able to locate the record you need when a customer inquiry is assigned to you for a response.

If goods are damaged or lost, the customer is granted a reduction in the amount owed. If you are working in the department that handles returns and reductions, you may have the task of preparing credit memorandums. A **credit memorandum** is a form that shows the amount by which a customer's account balance has been reduced. The credit memorandum in Illus. 8-10 shows that Associated Candy & Nuts Corporation returned one defective portable diskette tray and therefore is entitled to a credit of $39.95. At least two copies of the form are made. One copy is mailed to the customer. The other is retained by the accounting department.

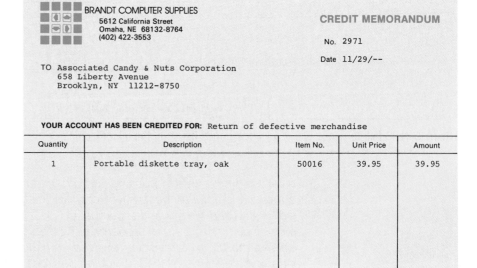

BRANDT COMPUTER SUPPLIES
5612 California Street
Omaha, NE 68132-8764
(402) 422-3553

CREDIT MEMORANDUM

No. 2971

Date 11/29/--

TO Associated Candy & Nuts Corporation
     658 Liberty Avenue
     Brooklyn, NY 11212-8750

YOUR ACCOUNT HAS BEEN CREDITED FOR: Return of defective merchandise

Quantity	Description	Item No.	Unit Price	Amount
1	Portable diskette tray, oak	50016	39.95	39.95

Illus. 8-10. Whose balance was reduced based on this credit memorandum?

COMPUTER-IZED ORDER PROCESSING

Many companies process orders by computer. Now that you understand common noncomputerized procedures for processing orders, you will have an introduction to how such procedures are done with the use of computers. Two variations of computer methods will be discussed.

Batch System

In some companies, orders are processed using the batch system. After an office worker in the sales department has determined that orders are from customers who have satisfactory credit ratings, the orders are prepared for forwarding to the data processing center. The **volume** of orders determines whether a batch is made up of orders for several hours or for an entire day.

volume: number or amount of a certain type of item

Tasks in the Order Department

If your responsibilities include receiving orders by telephone or by mail, to some extent your tasks are those described for the manual system. However, you will find there are differences from the manual system in the way you prepare sales orders for further processing. You are likely to follow steps such as these:

batches: collections of the same kind of item

1. Assemble orders in **batches**. For example, you may be instructed to include in one batch all orders received by noon each day; all other orders received that day will be included in a second batch.
2. Compute the total number of orders in each batch.
3. Compute the dollar value of orders in each batch.
4. Compute a hash total for the batch. A *hash total* is a number that has no value except as a check that all items are actually processed. For example, the total of the order numbers is a common hash total. If the orders in a batch are numbered 111 through 134, the total of 111 + 112 + 113 + ... + 134, which is 2940, is a hash total. The hash total on the report from the computer center should agree with the hash total computed in the order department.
5. Prepare a control sheet. A *control sheet* is the cover sheet that lists all orders and accompanies the batch. The control sheet shows the computations identified in earlier steps. (See Illus. 8-11 on page 318.)
6. Place each batch with its control sheet in the proper place for pickup by messenger for delivery to the data processing center.

Tasks in the Data Processing Center

Office workers in the data processing center will use what you prepared in the order department as their input. These office workers will input the details of the orders at terminals.

```
CONTROL SHEET

                                  BATCH NO.    2732
     DATE:    11/12/              DOCUMENTS:   Sales Orders


     A/R CODE          CUSTOMER          DOCUMENT NO. AMOUNT

        4197    R.M. Lawrence & Sons        79214    $ 3795.50
        3271    Dierbeck Manufacturing Co.  79215      5211.00
        1718    Kimura Import-Export Co.    79216      4798.00
         687    Manglo Universal Corp.      79217      1890.70
        4321    Gietz Communications Co.    79218      2750.50


        1212    Marshall Leather Co.        79251      7324.60


                                           3010835   $131351.50
```

Illus. 8-11. A control sheet must accompany a batch of orders.

valid: correct

exceptions: deviations that prevent processing from progressing

The input will be verified electronically through the use of an edit program. *Edit program* software determines that order data are **valid**, computes batch totals, and processes a list of the results, including **exceptions**, if any. An office worker in data processing will have the task of investigating and correcting all exceptions listed.

Also in the data processing center, an office worker at a computer terminal prepares packing slips, invoices, and bills of lading. Another office worker will have the task of reviewing the documents outputted, assembling them in proper order, and forwarding copies of the documents to the appropriate departments.

Tasks in Billing, Warehouse, Packing, and Shipping Departments

As noted in the preceding paragraphs, it is possible in a batch system for the data processing center to process documents formerly prepared manually by office workers in a number of departments. These departments may no longer prepare the documents, but office workers continue to have some important tasks. Office workers in departments that receive computer-prepared forms perform tasks such as the following:

- reviewing the documents received from data processing to be sure all information is included
- matching all related documents for each order
- identifying documents to be included with the shipment
- filing departmental copies of documents properly

On-Line System

An on-line system permits you to input and to retrieve data at a computer terminal. If the system with which you are working is *interactive*, the computer essentially is carrying on a ***dialogue*** with you. Note the difference:

dialogue: two-way conversation

> *TASK: You want to determine if the customer who has sent an order is on the approved list of customers.*
>
> *If you are at a terminal that is <u>on-line, but not interactive</u>, you will use your terminal keyboard to retrieve the list of approved customers. You read the list to find the customer's name. Once you retrieve and read the list, you can answer the question: "Is the person who sent this order on our approved customer list?"*
>
> *If, instead, you are at a terminal that is <u>on-line and interactive</u>, you will use your terminal keyboard appropriately to ask: "Is Royce Corporation an approved customer?" Almost instantly you will be able to read on your screen the response: "Yes, Royce Corporation is an approved customer," or "No, Royce Corporation is not an approved customer." What you have been able to do is ask a question which is answered directly by the computer.*

You may be working in the department that receives the initial orders electronically from sales representatives in various locations. In such an office, you are likely to follow these steps if your system is on-line and interactive:

1. Identify yourself at your terminal by keying in the security ID assigned to you. Also key in the password for order processing. This is a very important step and is necessary to ensure that only persons authorized to process orders actually do so.
2. Access the orders received. For each order, determine that the information the sales representative transmitted is complete.
3. Follow the prescribed format for entering the sales order

data. The prescribed format must be followed to allow for review and acceptance by the computer. Your input will be processed immediately, unless all lines are in use. Often the wait is merely seconds. (The first step in the processing done by the computer will be a credit check. The computer will let you know if the order can be accepted, which means that the order does not exceed the credit allowed, or credit limit.)

4. If the order is rejected, you will want to follow company procedures in such circumstances. You may have to prepare a letter to be sent to the customer or a memorandum to be sent to the credit department.

5. If the order is accepted, input the proper commands for completion of the processing. At this point the computer will perform all calculations required and will simultaneously transmit the necessary information to the terminals in the warehouse, the billing department, and the packing and shipping department. In each of these departments, there are printers for outputting the documents needed for completing the order processing tasks.

```
THE BLACKSTONE
MANUFACTURING COMPANY


4578 Blaine Street
Fairmont, WV  25664-6143
Balance Outstanding..4,500
Credit Limit .......20,000
```

Illus. 8-12. Before an order is processed further, a credit check is made.

QUESTIONS FOR REVIEW

1. Why do companies organize their order processing system carefully?

2. Describe briefly the systems that may be used for processing orders.

3. For each department identified in Illus. 8-3, indicate what documents are prepared for noncomputerized processing.

4. What information should you have at hand in order to effectively receive telephone orders from customers?

5. How does a packing slip assure that the goods ordered are actually the ones being shipped?

6. What information do you need to prepare an invoice?

7. Identify how each copy of a bill of lading is used and to whom copies are provided.

8. If a computerized batch system is in use for processing orders, what documents is an office worker in the data processing department likely to prepare?

9. Explain how you would get information about the credit standing of a customer from an on-line, not interactive system.

10. Explain how you would process an order if you were using an on-line, interactive system.

INTERACTING WITH OTHERS

Gail works in the order department of a company that has an on-line, interactive system for processing orders. Her company produces small scale appliances for kitchens. Gail accesses the orders sales representatives have transmitted via electronic mail. Orders from first-time buyers must be accompanied with information required for a credit review. Gail noted that an order from a new customer did not have the required credit-related information. She, therefore, transmitted a message to this effect to the sales representative, Richard Wallen. Soon she had a telephone call from Richard who said: "Why are you not cooperating with me? This customer is opening a large housewares store; I promised him that there would be no problem in filling this order immediately. I don't see why a customer with an order as large as this one has to submit information for a credit check. Take my word for it, this man is going to have a successful business."

Gail knows that the processing of an order without credit approval will not be completed—that is standard procedure. She knows also that the credit approval process is completed quickly by an efficient credit department.

What You Are To Do: Be prepared to discuss what Gail's response should be to Richard.

EXTENDING YOUR MATH COMPETENCIES

Many companies encourage their customers to pay invoices promptly by allowing a cash discount if payment is made within 10 or 15 days of the invoice date. Assume that you are determining if customers have written checks for the correct amounts. The invoices you are checking show the details provided on the printout below. Note that 2/10, n/30 means that a 2 percent discount is allowed if payment is made within 10 days of the invoice date. The total owed is to be paid within 30 days.

What You Are To Do: Compute the amount that should appear on the check received from each of the ten customers.

Customer	Invoice date	Amount	Terms	Date payment made	Amount of check
E. G. Jay and Co.	11/29/--	$ 9,785.75	2/10, n/30	12/8/--	?
Johnson and Sanders	11/30/--	4,750.25	2/10, n/30	12/9/--	?
Lannon and Sons	11/30/--	21,560.59	2/15, n/30	12/14/--	?
Littleston Corp.	11/30/--	8,350.00	2/15, n/30	12/17/--	?
Marsdon & Marsh, Inc.	11/30/--	24,540.00	2/15, n/30	12/14/--	?
Paulson & Co.	11/30/--	17,459.46	2/15, n/30	12/14/--	?
Ramez Brothers	11/30/--	8,900.25	2/15, n/30	12/13/--	?
Richards, Inc.	11/30/--	12,459.80	2/10, n/30	12/9/--	?
Salerno & Ku	11/30/--	5,400.90	2/10, n/30	12/9/--	?
Wallberg Co.	11/30/--	14,657.86	2/15, n/30	12/9/--	?

APPLICATION ACTIVITIES

Activity 1

You work in the sales order department of Wyland Fabric & Wallcovering Company, 14 Hoosier Street, Adams, MA 01220-4351. Orders are received by letter and by telephone. Two telephone orders and two order letters follow. (**Note:** Qty. refers to *yards* in all cases.)

Word processing equipment can be used to complete this activity.

What You Are To Do: Complete a sales order form for each of the four orders. Use the forms in *Information Processing Activities* or prepare forms similar to the one shown in Illus. 8-7 on page 312. Number the sales orders consecutively, beginning with 5021.

☎ TELEPHONE ORDER

Date _October 11, 19--_

Received by _Karen_

Company _Victorian Styles_

Shipping address _197 North Ave._
Dallas, TX 75203-4792

Special instructions _Customer order No. 3211_
Ship via truck

FABRIC NAME	NUMBER	COLOR	QUAN-TITY	PRICE PER YARD
Gene	73-351	Ocher & Blue	20	12.50
Lottier Lace	73-410	Coral	15	11.75
Petit	73-343	Expresso	21	13.50
Ferndale	73-372	Orange	26	25.00

☎ TELEPHONE ORDER

Date _October 11, 19--_

Received by _Karen_

Company _Leslie's Interiors_

Shipping address _296 Corbit St._
Newark, Delaware 19711-8146

Special instructions _Customer order No. 52911_
Ship via air express

FABRIC NAME	NUMBER	COLOR	QUAN-TITY	PRICE PER YARD
May Flowers	38-450	Peach & Rouge	15	21.50
Rosalie	38-810	Pastel	12	36.75
Hampton	38-884	Blue	18	23.25
Colette	39-044	Delft Blue	8	45.00

CURTIS FURNITURE MANUFACTURING COMPANY
461 Garrison Street High Point, NC 27260-8491
(919) 422-8080

October 9, 19--

RECEIVED
10/11/--

Wyland Fabric & Wallcovering Company
14 Hossier Street
Adams, MA 01220-4351

Ladies and Gentlemen

The following fabrics are needed for a special upholstery order:

    45 yards of Danube (A76-520, Multi) at $13.25 per yard
    19 Yards of Narta (A76-511, Multi) at $13.50 per yard

If you cannot ship the fabrics by truck by October 15, please let me know immediately. This is our order No. 9321.

Sincerely yours

Sandra Swartz, Manager

lc

Modern Day
Decorators   1519 Ridge Drive
                  Philadelphia, PA 19121-7482
                  (215) 821-5500

October 9, 19--

Wyland Fabric & Wallcovering Company
14 Hossier Street
Adams, MA 01220-4351

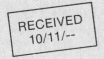

RECEIVED
10/11/--

Ladies and Gentlemen

Please ship the following fabrics on our order No. 1299:

Melinda   73-390   Winter Blue 25 yards at $12.00 per yard
Corabelle 73-311   Apricot   40 yards at $13.00 per yard
Nostalgia A73-531 Pastel   35 yards at $10.25 per yard

We understand that these fabrics are in stock and that you
can ship them promptly by truck. Thank you for taking care
of this order.

                              Sincerely

                              George H. Jason

                              George H. Janson, Manager

CW

Activity 2

Assume you work in the billing department. All orders given in Activity 1 were shipped. You have checked the prices shown on the orders; all were correct. Additional information you have includes:

Shipping Charges: Victorian Styles; by truck; charges, $28.50

Leslie's Interiors; by air express; charges, $36.50

Curtis Furniture Mfg. Co; by truck; charges, $19.60

Modern Day Decorators; by truck; charges, $21.50

Terms: All customers are given terms of 2/10, n/30.

What You Are To Do: Complete an invoice for each of the four orders given in Activity 1. Use the forms in *Information Processing Activities* or prepare forms similar to the one shown in Illus. 8-8 on page 314. Number the invoices consecutively beginning with 6121 and use the date October 18 for all the orders.

Word processing equipment can be used to complete this activity.

TOPIC 2

PURCHASING AND INVENTORY MAINTENANCE

When you have completed your study of this topic, you will be able to:

- describe why purchasing and inventory maintenance are important activities in many organizations

- explain the procedures for processing purchases

- explain good inventory maintenance procedures

Companies must purchase a wide variety of goods to meet their business needs. Buying and keeping track of what is bought require the services of many employees, including office workers.

A chain of 400 men's and boys' sports clothing stores has a central buying office where all purchases of goods for resale are initiated. Keeping the stores properly stocked requires a staff of 60 office workers. These office workers assist buyers in preparing purchase orders, maintaining catalogues of suppliers, maintaining up-to-date files of purchase orders, and getting information from vendors.

The hotel division of a large company has one purchasing department that devotes full time to buying furnishings needed for new hotels and for replacement purposes. Four office workers assist in this major activity.

If you were to visit a number of businesses, you would learn that purchasing and inventory maintenance functions differ from company to company. But you also would learn that common attention to basic principles assures wise use of a company's resources. These principles are:

- high-quality goods should be purchased at the lowest price possible

- no more goods should be purchased at one time than are required to meet the needs of the company's production or selling schedule

To be sure these principles are functioning in the organization, all those who work in the purchasing or inventory departments must perform their tasks promptly and accurately.

The overall goal of the purchasing function in any organization is to have on hand all goods needed for the smooth operation of the business. To fulfill this goal, companies organize purchasing in a number of ways. In general, these are the forms of organization you are likely to find in companies:

- Centralized: All purchasing for the total organization is done through a single purchasing office or department.
- Decentralized: Goods are purchased by each department requiring them.
- Mixed: Purchasing is divided between a central office and departmental offices. In such a plan of organization, there are clear-cut policies about which types of goods are to be purchased centrally and which types are to be purchased by the departments.

ORGANIZATION OF THE PURCHASING FUNCTION	
Type	**Example**
Centralized **The Children's Corner**	A chain of 15 small stores in four states in the Northeast has a central buying office in New York City. All merchandise for the 15 stores is purchased through the central office.
Decentralized **TEL-COM**	A medium-sized telecommunications company that manufactures a variety of equipment has factories in several cities throughout the country. Each factory has its own purchasing office. The headquarters office in St. Louis purchases no materials or components for the factories.
Mixed *The Crab's Claw*	A chain of restaurants in six southern states has a central purchasing office for purchase of all equipment and furniture as well as all staples needed for food preparation. However, each restaurant has a local purchasing office where fruits, vegetables, seafood, meat, and bakery goods are ordered.

Illus. 8-13. The purchasing function is organized in different ways.

For purposes of introducing you to the office tasks related to purchasing, we will focus on the centralized office. The discussion that follows, therefore, will assume that you are at work in such an office. The same tasks also would be performed in companies organized differently.

Requisitioning Purchases

If you work in a central purchasing office, you provide a service to all the departments which require goods or supplies for their

initiated: begun; gotten underway

operations. Purchases are actually *initiated* by the various departments. An office worker in one of the departments that needs goods or supplies will fill in a purchase requisition. A **purchase requisition** is a form that describes what is to be bought. The department manager is authorized to approve purchases and to forward the forms to the purchasing department for processing.

In Illus. 8-14 you see a purchase requisition prepared for submission to the purchasing department. You will find there are variations among different companies in the information provided.

Lehigh Community Hospital ✚   **PURCHASE REQUISITION**

Date ___November 17, 19--___   Department ___Central Food Services___

From ___Steven Zabitz___   Location ___Ground Floor, Room 310___

Date Required ___Within 6 weeks, if possible___   Charge to Account No. _____
                                      (Accounting Use Only)

Quantity	Description	Unit Price	Total
12 doz.	Heavy white stoneware plates	4.79	689.76
12 doz.	Heavy white stoneware soup bowls	4.40	633.60
12 doz.	Heavy white stoneware mugs	3.10	446.40
			1,769.76

NOTE: I've made some inquiries and I think these are the best prices available. Suggest you buy from Baum Chinaware at 17 East 26th Street, New York, NY 10010-4557.

Deliver to ___Steven Zabitz___   Department ___Central Food Services___

Approved for Purchase by ___*Emilio Ramos*___
                              Department Manager

Illus. 8-14. Who initiated this purchase requisition?

If you have the responsibility for receiving purchase requisitions, you will have to:

● Review the purchase requisition to see that all the information needed is provided.

verify: check the accuracy of

- **Verify** that the signature is that of the person in the department who is authorized to approve such requisitions.
- Check items listed in catalogues maintained in the purchasing department to be sure all details, including item identification number, size, and price, are correct.

Preparing Purchase Orders

If you work in the purchasing department, you will find that purchase requisitions are reviewed before you are asked to prepare purchase orders. A **purchase order** is a form used to secure products from a supplier. The purchasing agent may have to make a decision about the best source for the product being ordered.

After the review by the purchasing agent, you probably will have the task of preparing purchase orders. You will find that it is common practice to use purchase order forms that are *prenumbered*, which means the numbers are printed in sequence on the supply of forms. Prenumbered forms are used so that all purchase orders can be accounted for as related to the company's business. You may be in an office that processes orders manually or one which processes them electronically.

Illus. 8-15. What is the name of the company that placed this order?

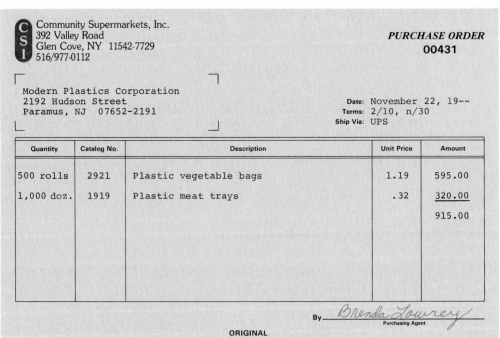

Noncomputerized Preparation

If you are working within a noncomputerized system, your tasks generally will require that you follow steps such as these:

vendor: supplier of goods needed

1. Establish the accuracy of the name and address of **vendor**, if not checked at the time of receipt of the purchase requisition.
2. Verify the details of each item ordered.
3. Compute extensions and totals.
4. Prepare multiple copies. Copies are needed for the:
   - vendor from whom the goods are being purchased
   - department that submitted the purchase requisition
   - receiving department where goods will be delivered
   - accounting department where payment will be made
   - purchasing department (so that a complete file of all goods ordered is maintained)
5. Proofread your work.
6. Place copies on manager's desk for review and signature, if required.
7. When the manager returns the purchase order, mail original to vendor and forward copies to the appropriate departments.
8. File departmental copy according to purchase order number.

Computer-Assisted Preparation

As you learned in the preceding topic, processing of orders often is done with the assistance of computers. You may find that some purchasing tasks also will be done by computer.

Illus. 8-16. Many office workers are needed to process purchases for a large company.

The company in which you choose to work may use a batch system for processing all purchase orders. With such a system, you will have the task of preparing the information required by the data processing center where the actual purchase orders are produced. The multiple copies of each order produced will be returned to you. You then will verify the accuracy of each purchase order and distribute copies to the proper parties.

If your company has an on-line, interactive system, you will be able to input at your terminal the information required for each purchase order. Then you will be able to get printouts of computer-generated purchase orders for transmission to vendors and to departments requiring copies.

Following Up Purchase Orders

You will find that vendors generally send confirmations when they receive your orders. A **confirmation** is a form or a letter that acknowledges that the order was received. The date the goods will be shipped often is included on the form or in the letter. (See an example of a confirmation in Illus. 8-17.)

You may be assigned the task of maintaining the records for all purchase orders for which the goods are yet to be received. Such records often are arranged according to the date on which goods are to arrive. You may keep such a record in your files or on a computer. If you find that you have not received notice of shipment by the anticipated shipment date, you may have to make an inquiry by telephone, letter, or electronic mail.

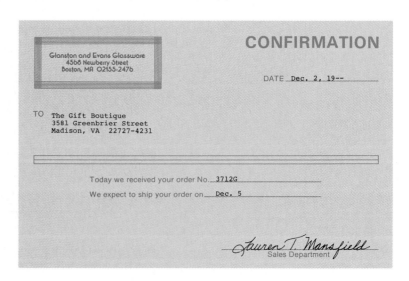

Illus. 8-17. What is being acknowledged in this confirmation?

Receiving Goods

In some companies, receiving goods is under the supervision of a separate receiving department. If you have the task of receiving goods, your primary responsibilities can be described in these steps:

retrieve: secure; get

1. Establish that the goods received were ordered. **Retrieve** the related copy of the purchase order; note the order number on the invoice and on your purchase order.
2. Compare the goods received with the goods listed on the purchase order, noting the quantity and description of each item.
3. Open the goods and note their general condition.
4. Prepare a receiving report, if one is required.
5. Follow up on any problems such as incomplete shipment or damaged goods.

THE INVENTORY MAINTENANCE FUNCTION

Goods maintained in quantity to meet the demands of an organization are referred to as **inventories**. Much attention must be given to procedures that assure that inventories are adequate to meet business needs. Office workers make valuable contributions to the maintenance of inventories.

Where Inventories Are Maintained

You will find that the places where inventories are maintained are referred to as *stores, stockrooms,* or *warehouses.* In the discussion here, the term *stockroom* will be used to refer to the place where inventories are maintained. The term **stock** is used to refer to the quantity of a particular item that is on hand in the stockroom.

Receipt of Goods in Stockroom

If you work in a stockroom, you may assist in receiving goods. Although the goods were counted and inspected when received by the receiving department, you must verify that what you get is what is recorded on the receiving form. The employee who delivers the goods to the stockroom must get a signed copy of the receiving form of his/her department. You must check all goods against the receiving form list before signing the form. New technology, such as **bar coding**, is being used to assure accurate

bar coding: a means of scanning information by marks on each package

Illus. 8-18. This worker is counting goods received. A hand-held scanner reads the information represented by the bar codes printed on the incoming merchandise.

counting of goods. Note Illus. 8-18 which shows an employee counting by bar coding.

In some companies goods are received directly by the persons responsible for maintaining the stockroom. In such a situation, the second verification of the goods received is eliminated.

Sonya and Roy work in one of several large stockrooms of a mail-order company. Large quantities of goods arrive daily and are quickly transferred to a stockroom in the company. Sonya and Roy are responsible for verifying that the goods belong in their stockroom and that the quantities actually received match the quantities on their copy of the purchase order.

Michael is an office assistant in the stockroom of a shoe manufacturing company. Raw materials, including several types of leather, are received right at the stockroom. Michael does the initial checking of the incoming materials against the purchase order copy he has and then follows through with other tasks.

Records Maintained in Stockroom

Records are important in a stockroom. They may be maintained in loose-leaf notebooks, on cards, or in computer memory. There are basically two systems for records: the perpetual inventory control system and the periodic inventory control system.

Perpetual Inventory Control System

instituted:
established

Procedures ***instituted*** to keep continuous records of both incoming and outgoing goods in inventory is called a **perpetual inventory control system**. When goods are received, an office employee records quantities received. Then, as goods are taken or released from the stockroom, an entry is made to the records.

A perpetual inventory control system provides information quickly about the status of any item. Therefore, it is relatively easy to know when reordering is required. In fact, the record indicates the level of stock at which an order for additional units should be prepared. This level is referred to as the **reorder point**. Note the record shown in Illus. 8-19 with the reorder quantities indicated.

```
                    WESTERN HILLS AUTO SUPPLY CO.
                              INVENTORY
                            AUGUST, 19--

PAGE 2
                                        Quantity   Reorder       Cost per
       Item No.    Description           on Hand    Point    Unit {Average}

      261 3957   Dent Pullers              150        24            9.88

      261 3958   Body Fender Repair Kit    258        20           16.70

      261 3959   Body Repair Kit           212        20           88.00

      261 3960   Airless Paint Sprayer     119        36           19.99

      261 3961   Car Roof "Rack" Bar Kit    94        30           14.88
```

Illus. 8-19. How many body repair kits can be released from inventory before the reorder point is reached?

Periodic Inventory Control System

A **periodic inventory control system** is a series of procedures used for recording receipt of incoming goods only and for counting goods on hand at regular intervals. Companies that use such a system do not think that the time and cost of recording the release of goods from stock is justified. Such companies believe they have sufficient control of inventory if counts are taken ***periodically***.

periodically: at
established intervals

A major manufacturer of men's and boys' sports shirts maintains a sizable inventory of fabrics for shirts. When the cutting department needs fabric, the inventory clerk cuts the length of each fabric requisitioned, but the inventory card for the item is not updated. At the end of each four-week work period, the inventory clerks take a physical count of the fabric on hand. The inventory cards then are brought up to date with the current stock quantities.

A very large hardware store maintains an orderly stockroom for the thousands of items sold. Records are updated with new arrivals of stock, but items are transferred to the selling floor without updating the records. Every two weeks, inventory clerks take a count of each item and at that point the records are updated. The constant flow of items out to the selling floor makes it difficult to update records on a continuous basis.

Requisition of Goods

If you are an office assistant with inventory control responsibilities, you will be given a list of specific procedures that are to be followed whenever goods are released. Common procedures include these:

- Release goods only on receipt of a requisition signed by an authorized person.
- Review the requisition to be sure all details are accurate and an appropriate budget code (if needed) is provided.
- Gather the goods requested.
- Check the goods against the listing on the requisition, giving particular attention to quantities, item number and type, and similar details.
- Ask the person receiving the goods to sign the requisition.
- Give a copy of the requisition to the person requesting the goods.
- Make entries on inventory records, if a perpetual system is in use.
- File in the proper place the copy of the requisition maintained in the stockroom.

Physical Count of Inventory

From time to time, a count of the actual goods in the stockrooms is taken, regardless of the inventory system in effect. This task is referred to as the **physical count**. If the company in which you work uses the perpetual inventory control system, the physical count is used to determine if the records are accurate. If the periodic system is used, the physical count is needed to determine the value of inventories so that financial statements can be prepared. You will learn about financial statements in Chapter 11.

If you are to participate in the physical count of inventory, you will find that you are assisting in the following:

- helping to put the stockroom in good order through checking to be sure items are in proper places
- counting goods and recording on specially designed forms quantities of and details about each item (See Illus. 8-20 for an example of a typical inventory count sheet.)
- organizing the sheets on which the counts are recorded
- computing the value of the goods in the inventory

INVENTORY COUNT SHEET   HERMITAGE HARDWARE CO.

COUNT TAKE on ___2/31/--___

BY ___Mercina Simeonidis___

STOCK NO.	DESCRIPTION	QUANTITY ON HAND	COST PER UNIT	TOTAL VALUE
247 1191	THREE-FOOT HOUSEHOLD LADDER	21	8.95	187.95
247 1134	FOLDING STEP STOOL	17	9.15	155.55
248 3566	TRASH CAN CART	27	12.99	350.73
248 3582	HEAVY-DUTY STOOL	19	9.88	187.72
653 9951	THREE-TIER METAL SHELF	12	18.55	222.60
			TOTAL	4,639.27

Illus. 8-20. Computer-generated inventory count sheet.

Computerized Systems

You have just learned how inventories are maintained in a manual system. In many organizations, inventories increasingly are maintained with the use of computers. In some companies, updating inventories is done in the data processing center, which receives copies of all requisitions for goods from stockrooms where inventories are maintained. Once the inventories are updated, a printout of current inventories is prepared and forwarded to the stockroom.

If you are working in the data processing center, you will use a terminal to input the details required to update inventory records. If you are working as an office employee in the stockroom, you will be responsible for preparing the requisitions for **submission** to data processing. A procedure similar to that described for preparing orders for the data processing center is commonly followed.

submission:
forwarding; sending

> *Rachel works in the central stockroom for a chain of women's specialty shops. The stores are located in shopping malls in a three-state area. Managers at the stores call Rachel's department frequently to learn if the goods they need are in stock. At her computer, Rachel accesses the stock record and is able to give the caller an immediate response.*

Some companies have developed a complete inventory control system with the use of an on-line, interactive application program. If you work in a stockroom where such a system is in use, you may use a terminal to input data about incoming stock as well as data about all items released from the stockroom to other departments. In such a system, all records are kept in computer memory.

Illus. 8-21. A worker maintaining inventory records with the help of a computerized system.

If your computer system is on-line, but not interactive, you will be able to access the up-to-date listing for any item. Then you can determine what the quantity on hand is. If, on the other hand, your computer system is on-line, interactive, you will merely input your question about the particular item: "What is quantity on hand for Item No. 4567?" Then you will find printed on your screen the up-to-date quantity on the item.

If Rachel were at work in the central stockroom for a company that had an on-line system for its total company (including the stores at the malls), managers would no longer need to call her. Instead, they would use terminals at the local stores to access information needed.

QUESTIONS FOR REVIEW

1. What two principles are considered important in purchasing goods and maintaining inventories?

2. How does centralized purchasing differ from decentralized purchasing in a company?

3. Who in a company initiates a purchase requisition?

4. How does a purchase requisition differ from a purchase order?

5. For what purpose would purchase orders be prenumbered?

6. Company A sends a purchase order to Company B. For what reason does Company B send Company A a confirmation?

7. Why is a copy of a purchase order sent to the receiving department?

8. Describe the procedures an office worker in a receiving department is likely to follow.

9. Identify the information maintained in a perpetual inventory control system.

10. How does a periodic inventory control system differ from a perpetual inventory control system?

MAKING DECISIONS

Ed, who works in the stockroom of a large department store, was surprised to see a department manager coming toward his workstation. Someone had left the door unlocked, even though the stockroom was to be locked at all times. A buzzer must be pressed to gain entrance. The manager said to Ed:

"I need stock in a hurry; our sales are higher than usual today. Let me take what I need; I'll make a list of the items as I put them on the shelves; I'll send you a copy of the list."

Ed is new in the position. He recalled that during his orientation, the supervisor had stated repeatedly how important it was that no merchandise leave the stockroom without a record being made on the spot. The supervisor also said that the requisition must be signed by the person taking the goods.

What You Are To Do: Be prepared to discuss Ed's responsibility in this situation. What do you think Ed should say to the manager?

EXTENDING YOUR ENGLISH COMPETENCIES

The excerpt below is from a report about a purchasing and inventory control system. The excerpt has six errors in the use of plurals and four errors in the use of the possessives.

What You Are To Do: Prepare a copy of the excerpt, correcting all errors. Underscore the words you changed.

```
     We found the visit to Gondale Corporation informative.
One of the companys problem with its micro-to-mainframe
setup is slow response when there are many user on the
system.  One of the managers comments to us was:  "Sometimes
there are a couple of second between the time you hit a key
and the time something happens on the screen."

     Some micro-to-mainframe linkes have alleviated the
problem by taking advantage of the personal computers
processing power.  With the micro, user select a database
and choose the fields to be retrieved while still off-line
with the mainframe.  This system eliminates much of the
users on-line interaction with the mainframe, which in
turn keeps the computer from bogging down.  Also, some
links allow tasks to be prioritized according to the size
of the search, urgency, and other feature.
```

APPLICATION ACTIVITIES

Activity 1

You work in the centralized purchasing department of the Regency Hotel. The manager has given you the purchase requisition which was received from the housekeeping department. Notes on the requisition below were made by the purchasing manager. When you check the catalogs for the linen and towel manufacturing companies, you find the information shown below the requisition.

Word processing equipment can be used to complete this activity.

What You Are To Do: Prepare purchase orders for the goods listed on the purchase requisition from housekeeping. Use the forms provided in *Information Processing Activities* or prepare two forms similar to the one shown on page 328. Request that goods be shipped via truck.

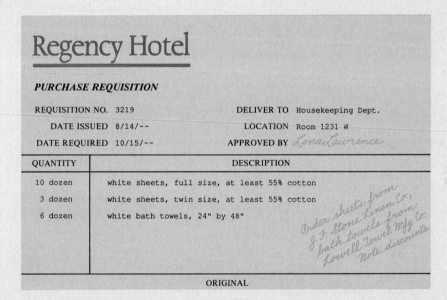

Regency Hotel

PURCHASE REQUISITION

REQUISITION NO. 3219   DELIVER TO Housekeeping Dept.

DATE ISSUED 8/14/--   LOCATION Room 1231 W

DATE REQUIRED 10/15/--   APPROVED BY *Lena Lawrence*

QUANTITY	DESCRIPTION
10 dozen	white sheets, full size, at least 55% cotton
3 dozen	white sheets, twin size, at least 55% cotton
6 dozen	white bath towels, 24" by 48"

Order sheets from J. F. Stone Linen Co.; bath towels from Lowell Towel Mfg Co. Note discounts.

ORIGINAL

CATALOG INFORMATION

Stone Linen Company
9321 Highland Avenue
Greensboro, NC 27403-3445

White Sheets, **$6.50** each full size, 60% cotton; **$4.25** each, twin size, 60% cotton; 10% discount on purchases of 3 dozen to 9 dozen; 20% discount on purchases of 10 dozen or more; goods sold on account, 2/10, n/30

Lowell Towel Manufacturing Co.
139 Blain Street
Winston-Salem, NC 27101-4657

White Bath Towels, **$3.19** each; 15% discount on purchases of 6 dozen or more; goods sold on account, 2/10, n/30

Activity 2

You work for a company that sells a wide range of items. Twice a year there is an actual physical count of all goods in inventory. Your company has a computerized inventory system. For the physical count, you are given print-outs which show for each item in stock, the stock number, description, and cost. At this point, you have completed the count of the items shown on the printout below and you have recorded the quantity in stock for each item.

What You Are To Do: First compute the total value for each item in stock. Then compute the total value of all items listed. Use the form in *Information Processing Activities* or prepare a copy of the printout below.

```
                        HADDEN HALL DISTRIBUTORS
     12/31/--              INVENTORY COUNT SHEET                    00:04 PAGE 1
                    USING DISK:  HADDEN HALL      INVEN08-17
```

ITEM CODE	DESCRIPTION	QUANTITY ON HAND	COST PER UNIT	TOTAL VALUE
2253T	INFRARED HOME INTRUDER ALARM	10	79.15	?
2379T	SCULLING CYCLE	15	410.50	?
2572T	DIGITAL TWO-SCREEN TV	6	659.25	?
2301T	PERSONAL COPIER	20	151.70	?
4321T	FOUR-STAGE AIR PURIFIER	10	141.20	?
3192T	FOLDING ARCHITECT'S TABLE	14	75.00	?
2192T	LIGHT SOCKET FAN	10	25.90	?
2147T	PORTABLE BUTANE STOVE	25	33.75	?
2139T	COUNTERTOP WATER FILTER	10	102.50	?
2271T	CARD TABLE EXTENDER	14	24.50	?
2511T	ELECTRONIC THERMOSTAT	15	42.80	?
2501T	GIANT-SCREEN SLIDE VIEWER	20	131.50	?
2617T	ELECTRONIC CAT/DOG FEEDER	6	77.20	?
2611T	SQUIRREL-RESISTANT BIRDFEEDER	10	21.75	?

CHAPTER SUMMARY

Information in numeric form is vital to business activity. Such information is provided through data processing. Companies have developed efficient procedures so that numeric information is processed properly. Some of the most common data processing tasks—processing orders and purchases, receiving goods, and maintaining inventories—are the topics of this chapter. You have learned these key points:

1. Although varying systems are in use for processing data, the end result is essentially the same.
2. Orders require activity in several departments including: sales, credit, warehouse, packing and shipping, and billing. Specific documents relate to the work of each department.
3. The processing tasks related to purchasing goods and to maintaining inventories involve several departments, also.
4. Office workers must understand the responsibilities of the several departments participating in the processing discussed in this chapter. Furthermore, all tasks must be performed accurately and on a timely basis.

KEY CONCEPTS AND TERMS

flowchart	confirmation
packing list	inventories
invoice	stock
bill of lading	perpetual inventory control system
credit memorandum	reorder point
purchase requisition	periodic inventory control system
purchase order	physical count

INTEGRATED CHAPTER ACTIVITY

Word processing equipment can be used to complete this activity.

The manager has edited a draft of a memorandum to all domestic plant managers about the forthcoming inventory observation to be done by the outside auditors.

What You Are To Do: Prepare a final copy of the memorandum, making all changes indicated by the manager. Correct two keyboarding errors that the manager overlooked. Use the form provided in *Information Processing Activities* or plain paper.

TO: Plant Managers, (U.) (S.) Factories   *sp*

FROM: Estelle Liebruder, Inventory Control, Home Office

DATE: December 9, 19--

SUBJECT: Inventory Observation, December 31, 19--

Our auditors, Weckfield and Goddard, *will* have ~~scheduled~~ staff to be in *at* each of our 14 plants on Thursday, December 31. Their their purpose is to observe the physical count of ~~all~~ our factory inventory. It is very important that each plant be prepared for an efficient, complete count on that date.

We are requesting that there be no movement of goods in or out of the finished goods wearhouse during December 31. Activity ~~in process~~ should cease at noon, so that our own staff can count all work in process. *The count will be observed by the Weckfield and Goddard auditors.*

~~Prior to the 31st,~~ you will want to be sure that all items in the warehouses are properly organized so that the count can be made as quickly and as accurately as possible *on December 31.*

It will be necessary (also) to have *ready* all information about goods in transit ~~that belong to us~~ so that these goods can be added to the actual physical inventory on hand.   *stet*

OPTIONAL COMPUTER APPLICATION ACTIVITY
See Computer Application Activity 8
in your Information Processing Activities workbook.

PRODUCTIVITY CORNER

Blake Williams
OFFICE SUPERVISOR

HOW DO YOU LEARN A "FOREIGN" LANGUAGE?

DEAR MR. WILLIAMS:

I was elected by my two friends to ask you how we can learn a "foreign" language—the language used in the offices where we work.

My two friends and I began our first full-time jobs about a month ago. Wendy works for the chief economist at a large bank in the Wall Street area; Debbie is at a large advertising agency on Madison Avenue; I'm at the headquarters office of a brokerage house. We were together Friday night. We all said that we are stumped again and again by the language used all around us. We all decided that we could overcome this problem. We think we should understand what is going on so we can do our jobs more intelligently. Do you have any hints for us?—KATHI, FOR WENDY AND DEBBIE, TOO, FROM NEW YORK CITY

DEAR KATHI, WENDY, AND DEBBIE:

I like your spirit. Of course, you can learn the new languages you face at work.

There are a number of ways you can gain command of the new language each of you hears. Additionally, there are some sources for assistance.

1. Listen attentively to the context in which an unfamiliar word appears to determine if you can guess what the word represents.
2. Write down *every* word that is puzzling to you.
3. Think of the new words you have added each day and use the following sources to see if you can discover the proper meanings:
   - memos and other correspondence where what you heard might appear in written form and provide some clues to you
   - reference materials available to workers (magazines related to the specialization or even a dictionary)
   - specialized columns in newspapers such as the *Wall Street Journal* and *The New York Times*
4. Take time to think about the new words as you encounter them in your daily work. Don't hesitate to use the words as you discuss matters with your coworkers and supervisor.

Best wishes in gaining command of your "foreign" languages.—BLAKE WILLIAMS

Data Processing Systems: Financial Applications

Financial information is critical to the successful functioning of all organizations. Checks received from customers must be recorded as receipts in cash accounts and as payments in customers' accounts. Records of sales must be maintained so that monthly statements can be prepared for customers who have balances outstanding. Invoices for goods and services purchased from other companies must be recorded and paid on a timely basis.

The accounting system that provides the needed financial information is based on principles accepted by the accounting profession. Companies adhere to these principles so they can process financial transactions efficiently and can compare the results of their operations and financial position with the results of other companies.

In this chapter, you are introduced to several specific components of financial accounting systems and to the data processing procedures related to each. Remember that the size of an organization will influence how financial data processing tasks are organized. For example, in a small business one office employee may take care of all financial transactions, from recording them to preparing reports. In a large business, many employees are needed to process just one type of transaction, such as recording sales to customers' accounts or preparing payroll for employees. The method of processing—whether noncomputerized or computerized—will influence the way in which you perform tasks in financial data processing. If you are using a noncomputerized system, payments from customers will be recorded with pen on a card or sheet. If you are using a computerized system, those same payments from customers will be recorded by keying the payment at your computer keyboard.

The objectives of this chapter are to:

- introduce you to common record keeping procedures related to cash and accounts receivable

- help you develop an understanding of procedures for processing payments

CASH AND ACCOUNTS RECEIVABLE

When you have completed your study of this topic, you will be able to:

- explain the value of internal control for cash handling procedures

- prepare a deposit slip

- prepare entries for a petty cash fund

- prepare a bank account reconciliation

- describe procedures for maintaining accounts receivable

In the business world, *cash* refers both to actual cash (coins and bills) and to funds in checking accounts in banks. While some companies, such as supermarkets and retail stores, may handle large volumes of currency, in other companies virtually all transactions are paid by checks. The treasurer of the company and the departments that report to this executive are given the responsibility for managing all activities related to cash.

If you work in a small office, you are likely to have some responsibility for cash-related transactions. If you work in a large company, you may work in a department where many cash-related transactions are processed. You will find that you will comprehend your tasks if you thoroughly understand the safeguards for cash and procedures for processing cash.

As you learned in Chapter 8, many sales are made on account with payment made at some future time. The amounts of money owed a large company at any one time can be considerable. Office workers are needed to take care of customer accounts. In fact, in large companies there is an accounts receivable department. **Accounts receivable** refers to the amounts owed by customers for goods or services provided. You will find it useful to understand the basic noncomputerized and computerized procedures for handling accounts receivable.

SAFEGUARDS FOR CASH

negotiable: transferable from one person to another

fraud: an act of misrepresentation

assets: resources available for use

misappropriated: used for purposes other than those authorized

Businesses use the term *cash* to mean currency, bills, and checks. Currency and bills are easily transferred without identifying the owner. Checks can be transferred with some ease because they are **negotiable**. Therefore, businesses must carefully guard the flow of cash, regardless of its form, through their organizations.

You will find that companies organize tasks to minimize the possibility of **fraud** and theft of cash. For example, in a small company, the owner may open all incoming mail, remove all checks and cash, and make all deposits at the bank. The owner also may personally sign all checks issued. Furthermore, the owner may directly supervise all the employees. This provides additional assurance that company **assets**, including cash, are not being **misappropriated**. The overall organization for safeguarding assets is a component of a company's *internal control.*

Division of Responsibility

Of course, in processing cash transactions in large organizations, direct supervision by the owner-manager is not possible. You will find, therefore, that companies beyond those classified as very small have instituted procedures to safeguard cash and other assets. In Illus. 9-1, note the separation of tasks that aids in insuring that all checks received by the company are actually added to the company's cash account.

Internal Audit Function

audits: examinations to verity the facts reported

In some companies, an *internal audit department* establishes and oversees the system for safeguarding assets. Staff in such a department performs **audits** to determine if the procedures for control are actually being followed.

PROCESSING OF INCOMING CHECKS (Noncomputerized System)

Mail Clerk

- opens and sorts mail
- places checks in one pile
- stamps endorsement on checks
- prepares multiple copies of a listing of all checks
- forwards checks and a copy of listing to the cashier
- forwards a copy of the listing to accounts receivable or the accounting office
- files one copy of the listing

Cashier

- receives the listing of checks prepared by the mail clerk
- verifies the listing by comparing each check with the listing
- prepares deposit slip
- makes deposit in person or by mail
- receives a copy of receipted deposit slip from bank
- forwards a copy of receipted deposit slip to accounting office

Accounting Clerk

- receives the listing of checks prepared by the mail clerk
- receives copy of the receipted deposit ticket prepared by the cashier
- verifies the listing prepared by the mail clerk by matching each check with the deposit slip received from the cashier
- makes entries in customers' records

Illus. 9-1. Separation of duties assures internal control of incoming checks.

Jill, a staff member in the internal audit department, was assigned the task of determining the efficiency of the mail procedures. She arrived unannounced early in the morning just as the mail was being opened. She observed the work of two office assistants, Tom and Rica, who had the task of recording all checks received. Tom and Rica knew the procedures they were expected to follow. They followed the procedures at all times, so the audit revealed no problems.

As an office worker, you at times will help the personnel responsible for internal auditing. Such employees perform a valuable service. They determine if resources are being used as planned, and they determine how well the operations of the company are functioning. Your cooperation with such personnel is critical in meeting the overall goals of the internal auditing function and, ultimately, the goals of the organization itself.

Bonded Employees

adhere: stick to

To further safeguard resources, companies strive to hire persons of integrity, which means honest persons who will **adhere** to the policies and rules pertaining to their jobs. As further assurance that losses of assets will not be a financial loss to the company, employees are bonded. **Bonding** is insurance for financial loss due to employee theft or fraud.

By securing references, the insurance company makes a search of the employee's past behavior. This search, which is generally more thorough than that done by the company at the time employees are hired, is considered another advantage of bonding.

Illus. 9-2. As an office worker in the internal audit department, this employee is assisting an auditor in the preparation of an analysis of sales.

COMMON TASKS OF OFFICE WORKERS

Office workers perform many tasks in aiding executives and managers responsible for cash. Two of these tasks are preparing bank deposits and reconciling a bank account balance.

Preparing Deposits

It is a common policy to deposit all checks and cash in a bank as soon as possible. In some organizations where many checks and cash are received, deposits are likely to be made several times a day. In other companies, a deposit is made on any day when cash and checks are received.

endorsed: signed

If you have the responsibility of preparing a bank deposit, your first task will be to see that all checks are properly **endorsed**. This means that the person authorized to endorse checks has made the appropriate endorsement. In many companies, office workers who prepare deposits also endorse the checks using a stamp.

Common Endorsements

An **endorsement** is a signature, and at times instructions, stamped or written on the back of a check. An endorsement is required before a check is transferred from the company or person to whom the check is written to another person, company, or bank. Endorsements vary. Some provide more protection than others; some provide more instruction about the disposition of the check. The most commonly used forms of endorsements are *blank*, *restrictive*, and *special*. Look closely at Illus. 9-3 as you read about each form of endorsement:

Illus. 9-3.
Endorsements can be stamped or handwritten and provide varying levels of protection.

ENDORSE CHECK HERE

Sean Burns

Blank endorsement

Only the signature is used. The signature must be in ink. This endorsement provides little protection, since anyone who gains access to a check with a blank endorsement can readily transfer it to another person or to a bank. Generally, you will not want to use this endorsement unless you are in the bank and will be depositing the check immediately.

ENDORSE CHECK HERE

**For Deposit Only
The Appliance Store**

Restrictive endorsement

The purpose of the transfer of the check is indicated in the endorsement. Note in the illustration that the check is marked *for deposit only*. Restrictive endorsements are often made with a rubber stamp or a stamping machine.

ENDORSE CHECK HERE

Pay to the Order of Baylor Florists Drew L. Westwood

Special endorsement

The signature of the endorser is preceded by the name of the person or company to whom the check is being transferred. In some instances a special endorsement is referred to as an *endorsement in full*.

To prepare checks for endorsement, be sure they are all in *reading position* when face up. Then turn them over, with the left edge at the top. Carefully stamp or write each endorsement in the appropriate endorsement area. The legal endorsement area on the back of a check can be no more than 1 1/2 inches from the left top edge of the check. The area immediately below the legal endorsement area is reserved for the bank stamp.

Deposit Slip

A **deposit slip** lists all cash and checks to be added to a bank account. You will need to prepare such a form for all cash and checks that are to be deposited in the bank. As you see in Illus. 9-4, you will have to record the following details:

Illus. 9-4. If you have a number of checks, they are listed on the back of the deposit slip and then the total is written on the front beside the words TOTAL FROM OTHER SIDE.

- the date on which you are recording the items.
- each item to be deposited by amount. For each check, you will need to identify the bank on which the check is drawn. You do this by recording the bank's number, which is the upper portion of the fraction noted on each check.
- the total amount to be deposited. This amount includes all checks listed on both the front and back of the deposit slip.

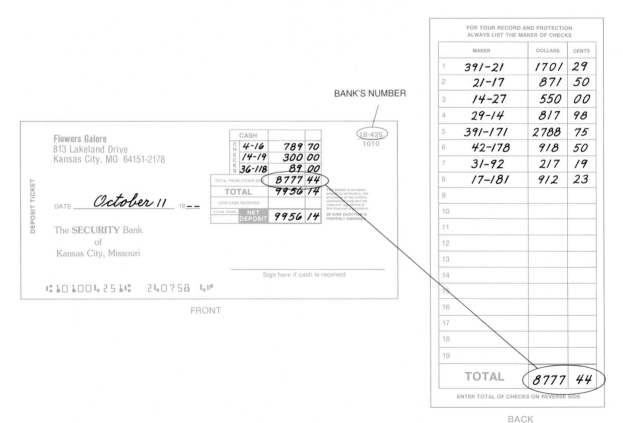

To verify the accuracy of the total deposit, compute the total by going through the actual items and adding them up. Check to see if this total is exactly the same as that which you computed for the total listing on the deposit slip. If the two totals are the same, you are assured that your listing is correct and includes all items.

Inez works as an office assistant to the cashier in a large company. One of Inez's daily tasks is preparing deposit slips for all items to be taken to the local bank. Inez works in a systematic fashion so that she makes no errors. She verifies that each deposit slip is correct by totaling the actual checks. She is proud that the bank has never sent the cashier a notice that an error had been made in a deposit!

Making Deposits

Office workers may have the task of making deposits in local banks on a regular basis. If your tasks include going to the bank with deposits, you want to be sure all checks and deposit forms are in proper order and in an envelope before you leave the office.

Deposits can be made electronically at automatic teller stations at the bank and at other convenient locations. If you make this type of deposit, follow instructions and get a receipt. Verify that the receipt shows the amount of your deposit.

In many companies, payments from customers are made directly to a bank **lockbox**, a postal address maintained at the company's bank to collect checks. A worker in the bank's office typically uses a computer to process the checks and automatically update the company's bank balance. If there is a computer

Illus. 9-5. This worker is making a deposit at an automatic teller machine conveniently located near the office.

network, the bank employee will transfer updated information to each company for which lockbox payments are received.

Reconciling a Bank Account Balance

reconciling: bringing into agreement

Companies need to be sure that receipts and disbursements shown in their records also are reflected in the bank's records. If you have the task of comparing these records, you will need a bank statement as well as your own company's records. This task is called **reconciling** the bank balance with the company's cash account.

Bank Statement

Banks send statements that show the activity in each account on a regular basis. Businesses that have many transactions receive such statements weekly or biweekly; others receive such statements monthly. As you will note in Illus. 9-6, a bank statement gives the following information:

- the balance as of the opening date of the statement
- a listing of all checks by number and amount that the bank has received and **honored**

honored: accepted and paid

- automatic teller transactions and miscellaneous charges
- a listing of deposits
- the balance of the closing date of the statement

canceled: paid by the bank

scanned: "read" by electronic equipment into a computer's memory

In addition to the bank statement, the bank returns all **canceled** checks and any *advices* reporting increases or decreases in the bank balance. (Some banks only provide the statement and copies of checks which have been **scanned** by an *optical scanner.*) The advice on page 354 reports that a check deposited was returned by the bank on which it was drawn. Because the person writing the check did not have sufficient funds to cover the amount of the check, the check was not honored. Such checks are referred to as *NSF* (not sufficient funds) checks. Illus. 9-6 shows that Adler Knitting's balance was reduced by the amount of the check that was not honored. Generally, there are no documents included that relate to **automatic teller machine (ATM) transactions**. These are deposits and withdrawals made at electronic machines. You must be sure to keep the slips provided at the time these transactions are made.

ПECHEƧ BANK
Cincinnati, Ohio

ADLER KNITTING MANUFACTURING CO
658 TEAKWOOD AVENUE
CINCINNATI OH 45224-4578

CHECKING ACCOUNT NUMBER
32921-6

08/31/--
DATE OF STATEMENT

BALANCE FROM PREVIOUS STATEMENT	NUMBER OF + CREDITS	AMOUNT OF DEPOSITS AND CREDITS	NUMBER OF DEBITS	AMOUNT OF WITHDRAWALS AND DEBITS	TOTAL ACTIVITY CHARGE	STATEMENT BALANCE
22,890.75	4	26,962.10	20	29,255.96	25.00	20,596.89

DATE	CODE	TRANSACTION DESCRIPTION	TRANSACTION AMOUNT		ACCOUNT BALANCE
07-22	AW	0248 634	200.00		22,690.75
07-23		DEPOSIT	6,790.40		29,481.15
		CHECK 187	3,750.00		25,731.15
		CHECK 189	1,890.25		23,840.90
07-27	AW	0248 634	2,500.00		21,340.90
07-28		CHECK 190	6,590.70		14,750.20
07-29	PD	RAE'S SWEATER CORNER DEPOSIT	7,980.70		22,730.90
08-03		CHECK 191	3,875.00		18,855.90
08-04		CHECK 192	1,870.70		16,985.20
		CHECK 194	580.90		16,404.30
08-05		CHECK 193	450.00		15,954.30
08-06	AC	OWL DEPOSIT	4,280.90		20,235.20
08-09	AW	0248 634	1,000.00		19,235.20
08-10		CHECK 197	2,975.25		16,259.95
		CHECK 195	1,800.00		14,459.95
08-11		CHECK 196	290.20		14,169.75
08-12	PD	RAE'S SWEATER CORNER DEPOSIT	7,910.10		22,079.85
		CHECK 198	378.28		21,701.57
08-16		CHECK 202	150.50		21,551.07
		CHECK 201	95.70		21,455.37
		CHECK 199	110.98		21,344.39
08-17		CHECK 206	525.00		20,819.39
08-18		NSF CHECK	197.50	NSF	20,621.89
08-19		SERVICE CHARGE	25.00	SC	20,596.89

Illus. 9-6. Can you find the beginning and ending account balances on this bank statement? Automatic teller transactions are coded AW (ATM withdrawal) and AC (ATM deposit/credit); preauthorized electronic deposits are coded PD. Can you find the monthly service charge (SC) for maintaining the account?

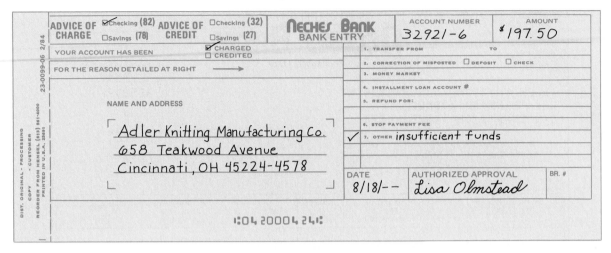

Illus. 9-7. This advice informs the depositor (Adler Knitting) that a customer's check in the amount of $197.50 was returned by the bank because of insufficient funds.

The Company's Records

To complete the reconciliation, you will need the checkbook or check register which records all checks written and all deposits made. You also will need last month's reconciliation. You then are ready to undertake the reconciliation. What you will be doing is finding the reasons for the difference, if any, between the ending balance shown on the bank statement and the balance shown in your checkbook or check register.

Purposes for Preparing a Reconciliation

Cash is a valuable resource for all business organizations. From time to time, therefore, it is important to know the exact status of the cash account. A monthly reconciliation is completed for the following purposes:

- to determine that all deposits made actually have been recorded by the bank, as indicated on the bank statement
- to be sure that all the checks that cleared the bank are actually checks written by authorized persons in the company
- to determine which checks have not yet cleared the bank
- to know what additional bank charges, as indicated on the bank statement, need to be recorded in the books of the company
- to determine the actual cash balance as of the date of the bank statement

Steps in Preparing a Reconciliation

You will find that the company in which you work has an established procedure for preparing bank reconciliations. You will want to learn the specific procedures you are to follow. Assume that you are working in an office where a bank statement is received monthly and a reconciliation is prepared at that time. The steps described here are likely to be similar to the ones you will learn on the job:

1. Compare the ending balance on last month's bank reconciliation with the beginning balance on this month's bank statement. Under normal circumstances, these two balances will be identical. If there is a difference, record the two figures on a sheet of paper. You will need to investigate this difference before you complete your reconciliation.
2. Record on your reconciliation worksheet the balance in your check register as of the last day of the month. (See Illus. 9-8.)
3. Record the ending balance as shown on the bank statement.

Illus. 9-8. Bank reconciliation worksheet.

Adler Knitting Manufacturing Co. Reconciliation of Bank Statement August 31, 19__				
Balance in check register August 31, 19__	18711 50	Balance on bank Statement, August 31, 19__		20596 89
Deduct:		Add:		
Service Charge 25.00		Deposit in Transit		
NSF 197.50	222 50	August 30, 19__		2851 10
		Total		23447 99
		Deduct:		
		Outstanding Checks		
		No. 188 198.70		
		No. 200 110.10		
		No. 203 347.29		
		No. 204 82.50		
		No. 205 4220.40		4958 99
Adjusted check stub balance, August 31, 19__	18489 00	Adjusted bank balance August 31, 19__		18489 00

4. Compare each deposit shown on the bank statement with the deposits recorded on the check register.
   A. Mark with a small check mark both places if the amount and date agree.
   B. Record on your worksheet any deposits shown in the check register that are not on the bank statement. Deposits made near the end of the month are not likely to have been processed by the bank by the date of the statement. Such deposits are referred to as *deposits in transit.*
5. Arrange in numeric order the checks returned with the bank statement. (You will skip this step if it is not the bank's policy to return checks.)
6. Compare the amount of each check with that shown on the bank statement. Use small check marks by the items on the statement to show that there is agreement. Record any differences noted. You will want to follow up on these discrepancies before preparing your final reconciliation.
7. Compare each canceled check with related information in the check register. Place a small check mark in the register if there is agreement. (See Illus. 9-9.)

ITEM NO.	DATE	PAYMENT ISSUED TO OR DESCRIPTION OF DEPOSIT	AMOUNT OF PAYMENT	√	AMOUNT OF DEPOSIT OR INTEREST	BALANCE FORWARD	
		PLEASE BE SURE TO DEDUCT ANY PER CHECK CHARGES OR MAINTENANCE CHARGES THAT AFFECT YOUR ACCOUNT				28681	15
187	7/17	To Taylor Brothers / For	3750 00	√		Payment or Deposit 3750 00	
						Balance 24931 15	
188	7/18	To Elman and Stone Co. / For	198 70			Payment or Deposit 198 70	
						Balance 24732 45	
189	7/18	To Marshall Gomez / For	1890 25	√		Payment or Deposit 1890 25	
						Balance 22842 20	
190	7/25	To Leitz Mfg. Co. / For	6590 70	√		Payment or Deposit 6590 70	
						Balance 16251 50	
	7/29	To Deposit / For		√	7980 70	Payment or Deposit 7980 70	
						Balance 24232 20	
191	8/1	To Yarns, International / For	3875 00	√		Payment or Deposit 3875 00	
						Balance 20357 20	

Illus. 9-9. One item on this check register does not have a checkmark. What is the status of check #188?

8. Record on your worksheet the number, date, and amount for each check that was written but had not cleared as of the date of the bank statement. Such checks are referred to as *outstanding checks.* The total of such checks will be subtracted from the bank statement balance.

9. Review last month's outstanding checks as listed on the bank reconciliation to determine which ones are still outstanding. Also list these on your worksheet.
10. Record on your worksheet any charges shown on the statement that are not recorded in your company's records. For example, any checks returned for insufficient funds (NSF checks) must be subtracted from the balance in your check register. Bank charges also must be subtracted.
11. Complete the computations required on your worksheet. Note that the two balances are the same in the reconciliation shown on page 355. Having the same balances means that your cash account has been properly reconciled.
12. Prepare your final copy of the bank reconciliation. Use a sheet of plain paper or the reconciliation form provided on the back of the bank statement.

When you have completed a bank reconciliation, you will submit it to your supervisor for review. Once it is approved, you will want to file it in the proper place so that it can be readily retrieved. When you receive the next bank statement, you will refer back to this completed reconciliation to determine which checks were outstanding and should be in the next batch of canceled checks.

Computer-Generated Bank Reconciliation Statements

You know that in many offices recordkeeping tasks are computerized. Therefore, you may use a computer and spreadsheet software to prepare a bank reconciliation worksheet. The advantage of an electronic spreadsheet is that the program automatically makes all calculations. Your understanding of the purpose of a bank reconciliation and your skill in using the spreadsheet software will aid you in completing the task properly.

Maintaining a Petty Cash Fund

There are occasions in many offices when cash is needed to pay for small expenditures, such as delivery services, postage due, and taxi fares. To facilitate such payments, departments are given a small sum of money, which is called a **petty cash fund**. Amounts in such funds can range from $20 to as much as several thousand dollars.

In the office of a small insurance broker, a petty cash fund of $75 is maintained to pay for taxis and special delivery services needed from time to time.

The sales office of a women's fashion manufacturing company has a petty cash fund of $3,500, primarily to provide money for lunch ordered at a local coffee shop for visiting buyers and for late dinners when staff members must work or entertain major buyers from around the world.

Establishing the Fund

petty cashier:
person in charge of petty cash fund

The department head establishes the amount of cash that is to be maintained in the petty cash fund. Once this amount is approved by the officer responsible for payments, a check is written payable to **Petty Cashier**, the person in charge of the petty cash fund. This check may be cashed by the company cashier in the treasurer's office or at the bank. The petty cashier will keep the cash in a locked cash box. Only the petty cashier has access to the key.

In some organizations, petty cash funds are maintained in a separate checking account. However, our discussion here will be limited to a cash box system only. Regardless of the petty cash system used, the petty cashier must adhere to the highest ethical behavior as he or she makes payments from the fund and maintains appropriate records.

Making Payments

disbursements:
money paid out

To assure control of funds, records must be maintained for all **disbursements** from petty cash. As a petty cashier, you will need to keep a complete and accurate record for every payment you make from the cashbox. You should be supplied with petty cash receipt forms which you will fill out each time you give out cash. Here is a procedure that is commonly followed in offices:

reimbursement:
payment for an outlay of cash already made

1. Ask each person who seeks **reimbursement** to submit to you a sales slip, statement, or receipt that indicates what was purchased, what the price was, and that payment was made. Generally, reimbursement should not be made without some kind of document. Occasionally, cash payments are made even though no sales slip, statement, or receipt is provided. On such occasions, the employee being reimbursed should present a brief memo describing what was spent and the purpose of the expenditure.

2. Prepare a petty cash receipt for each reimbursement and ask the person who will receive the cash to sign the receipt. Note the receipt shown in Illus. 9-10. It indicates the amount paid out, to whom payment is made, and the purpose of the payment.

3. Attach the sales slip or other document to the receipt and place these papers in the cash box.

PETTY CASH RECEIPT

HARDESTY SECURITY SYSTEMS

No. _42_   Date _November 17,_ 19 _--_

                                 Amount $ _10.75_

Ten and 75/100 _____ Dollars

For _Postage_ _____

_____

                        Received by _Wanda J. Davis_

Illus. 9-10. A petty cash receipt is issued for each reimbursement from the petty cash fund. What is the value of such a record?

Keeping a Record

In some offices many transactions require petty cash. An organized record is, therefore, justified. In some departments, a *petty cash book* is maintained for recording receipts and disbursements. A page from such a record is shown on page 360. Note the headings of the columns under which the expenditures are recorded. In each office the same types of expenditures are likely to occur again and again. Therefore, the column headings for your office may be different from the ones shown here. By classifying the expenses as indicated on page 360, the task of preparing a report at the end of the month or at the point when the fund must be **replenished** will be simplified.

replenished: restored to original level

Replenishing the Fund

You will need to note the amount of cash in your cashbox and to replenish your fund according to established company procedures. In some offices, the fund is replenished when a certain

MONTH OF *November, 19__* **PETTY CASH RECORD** PAGE *12*

Date	Explanation	Petty Cash Vchr. No.	Receipts	Payments	Art Supplies	Books/Other Publications	Messenger Services	Office Supplies	Taxi/Bus Fees	Postal Services	Miscellaneous
Nov. 1	Balance		25000								
6	Books	39		1295		1295					
8	Taxi	40		850					850		
8	Office Supplies	41		770				770			
11	Postage	42		1075						1075	
14	Messenger	43		645			645				
17	Art Supplies	44		1250	1250						
18	Art Supplies	45		3015	3015						
19	Books	46		1875		1875					
19	Messenger	47		1420			1420				
20	Office Supplies	48		1050				1050			
20	Art Supplies	49		660	660						
21	Taxi	50		2190					2190		
21	Office Supplies	51		970				970			
21	Messenger	52		1455			1455				
22	Taxi	53		1040					1040		
23	Taxi	54		1170					1170		
24	Taxi	55		1635					1635		
24	Postage	56		1145						1145	
27	Miscellaneous	57		1210							1210
	Totals		25000	24720	4925	3170	3520	2790	6885	2220	1210
	Cash Balance			280							
	Totals		25000	25000							
30	Cash Balance		280								
30	REPLENISHED FUND # 3721		24720								

Illus. 9-11. In the petty cash record pictured here, what was the purpose for the expenditure reimbursed most often?

balance is reached. In others, the fund is restored to its original amount at the end of each month regardless of the level of funds. In the process of replenishing the fund, you also will prepare a summary report of the expenditures. Here is a procedure that is commonly used in offices:

1. Total the columns in the petty cash book. (See Illus. 9-11.) If you are not using a petty cash book, add the amounts given on all the receipts in the petty cash box.

2. Add the amount of the petty cash receipts to the amount of petty cash remaining in the cashbox, as in the following example:

Petty cash on hand	$ 2.80
Petty cash receipts	247.20
Total of petty cash fund	$250.00

3. The total, in this case $250, should equal the amount of petty cash you had when you last balanced and/or replenished the petty cash fund. If the figure you arrive at does *not* equal the amount you had in the petty cash fund when you last balanced or replenished it, you have a ***discrepancy***.

discrepancy:
difference

4. Investigate any discrepancy. Careful attention to managing the petty cash fund will result in few, if any, discrepancies. If, after your investigation, you find that you are over or short by a few pennies, note this difference in your calculation. For example, if in Step 2 you found only $2.75 in cash, your calculation would indicate:

Cash on hand	$ 2.75
Receipts	247.20
Cash short	.05
Total	$250.00

You also will indicate the shortage (the missing amount for which there is no explanation) in your summary report.

5. Prepare a report of the activity in the petty cash fund for the period beginning with the last replenishment or the last time you balanced the records. Note the portion of the report shown in Illus. 9-12 on page 362.
6. Prepare a request for a check for the amount of the receipts plus any shortage (or minus any overage).
7. Submit your report, the accompanying receipts, and your request for a replenishment check to the manager for review.
8. When the manager returns the documents to you, follow up by sending a copy of the report to the accounting department and by sending the request for a check to the proper office.
9. Exchange the check for cash in the treasurer's office or at a local bank. Immediately place the cash in the cashbox.

Computerized Petty Cash Records

You may work in an office where all petty cash records are stored in computer memory through the use of spreadsheet software. You would enter the beginning balance when the fund is established, funds paid out, explanation of expenditures, and petty cash receipt numbers. When a summary report is needed, you will be able to generate one by using the appropriate software commands. Attention to detail and keying all data accurately are critical competencies needed when maintaining petty cash records.

```
            PETTY CASH SUMMARY REPORT
          November 1 to November 30, 19--

   Balance, November 1                              $250.00
   Expenditures:

      Art Supplies                    $49.25
      Books/Other Publications        $31.70
      Delivery Services               $35.20
      Office Supplies                 $27.90
      Taxi Fees                       $68.85
      Postal Services                 $22.20
      Miscellaneous                   $12.10

   Total Expenditures                              $247.20
                                                   -------
   Balance, November 30                              $2.80
                                                   =======
```

Illus. 9-12. This petty cash summary report answers the question: "For what purposes were funds used?"

From your study of Chapter 8, you will remember that a copy of the sales invoice prepared in the billing department is forwarded to the accounts receivable department. Also, copies of credit memorandums are routed to the accounts receivable office. In this chapter, you learned that a listing of all checks received from customers also is forwarded to the accounts receivable department. The listings of checks and the copies of credit memorandums are two primary sources of information that must be included in the records maintained on customers.

If you work in an accounts receivable office, you will be responsible for recording:

- all sales to customers on account
- all payments received from customers on account
- all adjustments required in customer accounts

Recording Charges to Customer Accounts

A common procedure for recording charges to customers' accounts follows. In this example, assume that you have been given copies of invoices.

1. Arrange the invoices in alphabetic order so that you can go through the customer cards efficiently.
2. Search for the card for the customer listed on the first invoice. On the card, record the date, invoice number, and invoice total. If the customer has a balance outstanding, add the new figure to the balance shown by using a calculator and record the new balance on the card. On page 364, note the invoice and the amount recorded on the customer's account card. Note that the columns for amounts are headed "debit" and "credit." These are accounting terms which you may already know. As you see on the card for Marsden Manufacturing Company, a *debit* increases the balance owed, while a *credit* reduces the amount owed. An invoice for goods shipped to a customer will result in a debit to the customer's account.
3. Continue with the preceding step until you have recorded all the invoices.

Using a Computer to Record Charges

access: locate stored data and bring to the screen

If the company's accounts receivable are maintained in computer memory, you should (1) *access* the account (either by customer number or customer name) and (2) key the charges to the customer's account. As you input the charges, the new total for each account will be automatically calculated. Your understanding of the company's accounting procedures and accounting software will insure that the information is debited or credited properly.

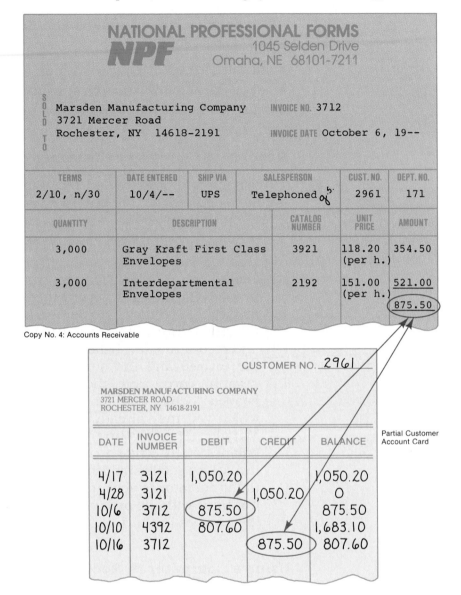

Illus. 9-13. (Top)
The accounts receivable
department's copy of an
invoice sent to Marsden
Manufacturing Company.
(Bottom) Note the two
entries for $875.50
made in Marsden's
customer file. Does the
debit entry increase or
decrease the amount
owed?

Recording Payments Received from Customers

A common procedure for recording payments received from customers on account follows. In this example, assume you have been given listings of checks from the mail clerk.

1. Record each of the amounts given on the listing of receipts on the appropriate customer's account card. Also record the

date of the check and number of the invoice paid, if indicated. Subtract the amount of the invoice paid from the balance owed (using a calculator).

2. On the listing of receipts, indicate with a check mark your completion of each entry in the appropriate customer's account. (See Illus. 9-14.)

On the listing of receipts shown in Illus. 9-14, note that the accounts receivable clerk has placed a check mark beside the receipt from Marsden Manufacturing Company. The check mark indicates that the amount has been recorded in the customer's account.

Illus. 9-14. Listing of receipts for October 17.

Receipts for October 17, 19--					
Check Date	Customer Name	Invoice Number	Amount Owed	Discount Taken	Payment
Oct 15	Lansdem	2932	10 000 00 ✓	200 00	9800 00
14	Wilson ✓ Brothers	3219	895 00 ✓	—	895 00
15	Ahath ✓ Co.	2171	1295 00 ✓	25 90	1269 10
15	Marsden Mfg. Co.	3712	875 50 ✓	17 51	857 99

As you study the entries in the customer file for Marsden Manufacturing Company on page 364, note that Marsden made a payment for Invoice No. 3712 (dated October 6) in the amount of $875.50 on October 16. This payment reduced the account balance to $807.60. In this instance, Marsden paid within the discount period and was entitled to $17.51 reduction in the amount owed. Therefore, the amount recorded as paid (credited) on Marsden's customer account in Illus. 9-13 is the total amount that was owed ($875.50), not the net amount after the discount ($857.99).

Using a Computer to Record Payments Received

In a company where accounts receivable are stored in computer memory, you will use a keyboard to input amounts paid. The computer system compares the data keyed for each customer with that customer's account number and outstanding balance. If all the data are correct, the computer system automatically updates the account.

Some large organizations receive many checks in the mail on a daily basis (for example, banks, gasoline, and utility companies). These companies may use a **magnetic ink character recognition (MICR)** machine. A data-entry clerk keys the amount of each check into the MICR machine. The MICR machine reads and prints the amount under the signature line, prints the company's endorsement on the back of the check, and converts the characters into electronic signals to be recorded on magnetic tape or entered directly into computer memory.

Recording Adjustments

Any adjustments in the amount owed will be noted on a *credit memorandum* and customer accounts will show these adjustments. For example, if goods are returned, a credit memorandum will be the basis of reducing the amount owed. You would record on the customer's card the amount shown on the credit memorandum and subtract that amount from the balance. Information from credit memorandums will be entered at your computer if the company's records are computerized.

QUESTIONS FOR REVIEW

1. What is included in the general category referred to as *cash*?
2. In processing incoming checks, what tasks generally are handled by the cashier?
3. Explain why a company might bond an employee.
4. How does a blank endorsement differ from a restrictive endorsement?
5. Why is a deposit slip prepared?
6. What information is included on a bank statement?
7. Why is a bank account reconciliation completed?
8. Why are departments given petty cash funds?
9. Describe how charges to accounts receivable are recorded using a non-computerized system and a computerized system.
10. What information is given on a credit memorandum?

INTERACTING WITH OTHERS

Assume that you are the cashier for the petty cash fund in your department. The fund is maintained at $1,000 because of the many small payments that must be made during the month. One Wednesday, shortly after the fund had been replenished, one of your friends in the department says to you: "I certainly didn't budget my money very well this week; I'm down to my last $5. You know that I'm dependable. Would you let me borrow $25 from the petty cash fund? You have almost $1,000 just lying there! And if I had only $25, I'd be able to take care of my expenses until Friday, which is payday."

You wonder why your friend didn't plan better. You know that you can depend on him/her to repay the fund as soon as paychecks are distributed in two days.

What You Are To Do: Explain what you would do if you were faced with the situation described above.

EXTENDING YOUR MATH COMPETENCIES

Your tasks include opening the mail and making a list of all checks received. Below is the listing of checks you made as you opened the mail. These checks will be deposited later in one of two banks. The checks from Mills, Olsen Corp., Yaroff Bros., Susi & Karlin, Rice Corp., Caputa & Zinn, and Prevetti Co. are deposited at the Penn Avenue Bank; the remaining checks are deposited at the Smithfield Bank.

What You Are To Do: (1) Find the total of the amounts of all checks received. (2) Determine what the total deposit would be at the Penn Avenue Bank. (3) Determine what the total deposit would be at the Smithfield Bank.

```
RECEIPTS 10/15/--

L.T. Mills            4200.50    Rice Corp.            781.18
Olsen Corp.           7592.70    Rabinowitz & Sons    2768.71
Mars, Linwood & Co    2540.15    Caputa & Zinn         848.88
Gomes & Co.            985.40    Beilens, Lutz & Co    129.50
Yaroff Bros.          1975.95    Prevetti Co.         8912.50
O'Brien & Wickes      3791.21    Jay F. Sterling       819.19
Susi & Karlin         7297.45    W. N. Neeley         7819.12
```

APPLICATION ACTIVITY

You work in the office of the cashier. You have been given the form below and the bank statement for the month ending October 31. (Note that your company uses a form different from the one on page 355.) You have checked all the deposits and all the checks shown on the statement. You also have compared the checks returned with your check register. Your worksheet shows the following information: The bank statement balance is $4,467.03. The check register balance, before adjustment, is $3,560.58. One deposit is in transit for $1,256.50. The following checks are outstanding: #457 for $356.76, #481 for $125.00, #482 for $890.65, and #483 for $790.54.

What You Are To Do: (1) Prepare the bank reconciliation using the form provided in *Information Processing Activities* or copy the form below. You will find variations in the forms used in business offices. (2) If spreadsheet software is available, use it to prepare and print the bank reconciliation again. Note the time it takes you to prepare the bank reconciliation using each method.

RECONCILEMENT OF STATEMENT

TO RECONCILE YOUR CHECK BOOK WITH THE BANK STATEMENT, WE SUGGEST THE FOLLOWING STEPS:

1. Arrange the paid drafts in numerical order and check them off against your check book register.

2. Be sure that all charges or deductions have been subtracted and interest credits added to your check book balance.

3. List all your outstanding drafts (those not yet paid by the Bank) on the back of the statement in the space provided. Add all the drafts and arrive at a total.

4. Complete the reconciliation form, as shown alongside.

EXAMPLE: Statement Balance .... $ -500
Add Deposits in Transit .... +100
Total .... -400
Subtract Outstanding Drafts .... -300
Check Book Balance .... $ -700

DRAFT(S) OUTSTANDING (ISSUED BY YOU BUT NOT YET INDICATED AS PAID ON ANY STATEMENT)

NO. OR DATE	AMOUNT

1.	Statement Balance	
2.	Add Deposits Recorded in Your Records But Not Shown On This Statement	
3.	Total	
4.	Subtract Total "Drafts Outstanding"	
	Balance (This Should Equal Your Check Book Balance)	

TOTAL

PAYMENTS AND ACCOUNTS PAYABLE

When you have completed your study of this topic, you will be able to:

- explain the purpose of an accounts payable department
- describe the procedures for processing payments for goods
- describe the procedures for processing payroll payments

Companies buy goods and services on account in much the same manner that they sell on account. Therefore, at any given time a company has obligations to make payments in the future. Obligations for future payments are called *liabilities*. Liabilities which are to be paid in the normal period for common costs are referred to as *current liabilities*. Companies have developed efficient procedures to assure that all payments are made on time. Naturally, vendors will not want to do business with companies that do not pay their obligations on schedule. Many companies make all payments within the specified discount periods so that they are entitled to discounts.

In a small office, one person is likely to process all payments in addition to doing other tasks. On the other hand, in a large organization, where there are large volumes of payments each month, you will find an office devoted entirely to processing payments. This office is referred to as the *accounts payable department*. Although the specific procedures in one company may differ somewhat from those in another company, the overall objectives of every accounts payable office are the same. These objectives are to:

- assure that all payments are for purchases actually received by the company
- keep accurate records of all obligations according to the date payment is due
- process all payments accurately and on a timely basis

In this topic, you will be introduced to common procedures for handling typical current liabilities for goods. The procedures for services are handled differently in some cases. Additionally, you will learn about special considerations in handling payments for wages and salaries.

The discussion of payments will assume that you are working in an office that has responsibility only for processing accounts payable. **Accounts payable** refers to the amounts owed by a company. The focus will be on noncomputerized and computerized accounts payable systems.

Documents Reviewed

goods: raw materials, merchandise

As you have already learned, companies want to be sure that payments are made only for *goods* actually purchased and received. The task of the accounts payable department is to review all the documents for each purchase made. Therefore, copies of purchase documents are forwarded to this department. The documents and their usefulness in the accounts payable department are as follows:

- Purchase requisition: Shows that the request for what was purchased was authorized by someone who had been delegated such responsibility

- Purchase order: Shows exactly what was ordered and to what address it was to be shipped

- Receiving report: Shows that goods were actually received by the company

- Invoice from vendor: Shows what is owed for the purchases

- Credit memorandum, if any: Shows the reduction in amount owed due to return of goods or to allowance for goods not received or of poor quality

The review is essentially a task of determining if all these documents are present for each purchase and that all the details on the several documents are the same.

You will not arrange for payment until all documents are accounted for and agree with each other or until there is a reasonable explanation for missing documents or discrepancies in information. You should talk with your supervisor to get a judgment about what should be done, even if you think an explanation is reasonable.

Illus. 9-15. As a member of the accounts payable department, this office worker has responsibility for reviewing documents related to purchases made by the company.

Preparation of Vouchers

In many offices a voucher system is used for payments. This system requires the preparation of a voucher before a check is written. A **voucher** is a document that records the name of the vendor, the date of the invoice, the terms, and the amount owed. (See page 372.) If you have the responsibility for preparing vouchers, you generally will follow these steps:

1. Check to be sure that all the documents related to the purchase are present. Often an envelope-type file folder is used to collect all the documents for a payment. On the outside of the folder there is a listing of the documents that are included.
2. Prepare the voucher, being sure to check every detail required on the form.
3. Leave the vouchers on the manager's desk for review and signature.
4. File the vouchers appropriately. Vouchers typically are filed by the dates on which they must be processed in order to meet the payment due dates. Filing vouchers in this way creates a **tickler file**—a file that is reviewed daily for the purpose of taking action to clear the items from the file. In companies where the policy is to take all cash discounts allowed,

VOUCHER

The Lampshade Store
426 Monroe Street
Cedar Falls, IA 50613-3467

VOUCHER NO. <u>4379</u>

DATE: <u>October 17, 19--</u>

PAY TO : <u>Just Shades</u>

<u>135 Greene Street</u>

<u>New York, NY 10003-4689</u>

For the following: (All supporting documents are attached.)

INVOICE DATE	TERMS	INVOICE NUMBER	GROSS AMOUNT	DISCOUNT	NET PAYABLE
October 17	2/10, n/30	5479	$4,560.90	$91.22	$4,469.68

PAYMENT APPROVED

Helen Northcutt

Illus. 9-16. Can you name the documents that are needed before this voucher can be written?

the date on which payment must be made to meet the deadline for a discount determines where the voucher is filed in the tickler file.

Preparation of Checks

If you are responsible for preparing checks for payments due, you generally will check your tickler file daily to retrieve all vouchers for which checks are to be prepared. As you know, a *check* is a written order to a bank to make payment against the depositor's funds in that bank.

Ordinary Checks

In some offices, especially small ones, a checkbook that is similar to one that an individual uses for personal check writing is the source of checks for paying business obligations. If you are responsible for writing checks using such a checkbook, these suggestions will be helpful:

1. Read carefully the name of the company or individual to whom payment is to be made as well as the amount of the check. If you are writing a check in time to take advantage of a discount, you should compute the discount using a calculator.
2. Fill in the checkbook stub or the check register. (See Illus. 9-17 for the way in which an item is listed in a check register.)
3. Prepare the check at a typewriter or with a pen. (See Illus. 9-17.) Note that the amount is written in numbers as well as in words. Notice how the space between the name and the dollar sign and between the amount in words and the word "dollars" is filled in. This is done so that changes cannot be made easily. Notice that the purpose of the payment is shown on the face of the check on the Memo line.

Illus. 9-17. (Top) Check register. (Bottom) Check prepared at a typewriter.

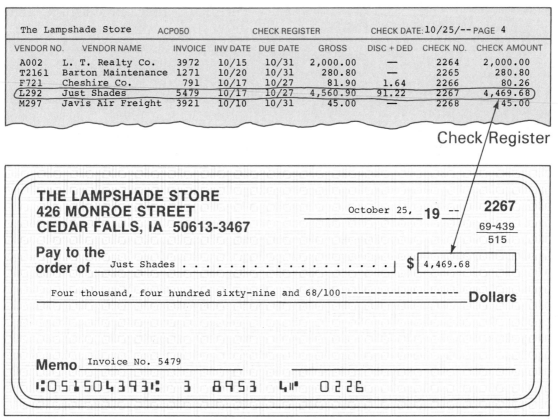

VENDOR NO.	VENDOR NAME	INVOICE	INV DATE	DUE DATE	GROSS	DISC + DED	CHECK NO.	CHECK AMOUNT
A002	L. T. Realty Co.	3972	10/15	10/31	2,000.00	—	2264	2,000.00
T2161	Barton Maintenance	1271	10/20	10/31	280.80	—	2265	280.80
F721	Cheshire Co.	791	10/17	10/27	81.90	1.64	2266	80.26
L292	Just Shades	5479	10/17	10/27	4,560.90	91.22	2267	4,469.68
M297	Javis Air Freight	3921	10/10	10/31	45.00	—	2268	45.00

The Lampshade Store   ACP050   CHECK REGISTER   CHECK DATE: 10/25/-- PAGE 4

Check Register

THE LAMPSHADE STORE
426 MONROE STREET
CEDAR FALLS, IA 50613-3467

October 25, 19 --   2267
69-439
515

Pay to the order of   Just Shades . . . . $ 4,469.68

Four thousand, four hundred sixty-nine and 68/100-------------------- **Dollars**

Memo Invoice No. 5479

⑆051504393⑆ 3 8953 4⑈ 0226

Ordinary Check

Voucher Checks

perforated: having a row or series of holes through

Voucher checks are ordinary checks with an additional portion that gives a description of the payment. The two parts are **perforated** so that they can be separated easily. The voucher is detached before the check is deposited.

The procedures for preparing voucher checks are the same as those for ordinary checks, except that you also fill in a voucher instead of merely indicating the purpose of the check as you would on an ordinary check. You will want to be sure that all details shown on the voucher are accurate.

Special Checks

From time to time, you may find that special checks which provide guarantee of payment are needed in your office.

- certified check: An ordinary check which the bank marks "certified" after establishing that the funds are in the account of the party drawing the check. The funds are immediately subtracted from the depositor's account.
- cashier's check: A check written by a bank on its own funds. Such a check can be purchased with cash or with an ordinary check.
- bank draft: An order drawn by one bank on its deposits in another bank to pay a third party. Such a draft can be purchased with cash or with an ordinary check.

Computer-Generated Checks

Workers in many companies use computers to prepare checks. If you are authorized to prepare checks, you likely will be issued a password to access the company's accounts payable system. Security measures must be taken to safeguard both the information used to prepare the checks and the printed checks.

You will refer to each vendor's file in the accounts payable system to obtain information needed to complete the checks, such as vendor name and address, amount to be paid, and the purpose of payment. Then, by selecting a menu option such as PRINT CHECKS, checks will be printed as shown in Illus. 9-18.

Illus. 9-18. Computer checks shown here are ready to print.

The Use of Electronic Funds Transfer

Payments, as well as deposits, can be made electronically, where there is no physical exchange of cash or checks. **Electronic funds transfer (EFT)** is the use of a computer and a telecommunications network to transfer funds from one party to another. In some companies, magnetic tape generated by the company's computer is used by the bank to electronically transfer the specified amount of money to the vendor's bank. The vendor's bank electronically processes the deposit and credits the vendor's account. Also, many companies electronically deposit wage and salary payments to employees' designated banks where the funds are credited to the employees' accounts.

PAYMENTS FOR WAGES AND SALARIES

You will find that companies have carefully designed procedures for payroll. Employees expect to be paid on time and for the proper amount. To meet the expectations of all employees, office employees in payroll-related jobs keep accurate records and do their tasks on a timely basis.

The payroll in many companies is processed by computer systems. However, you will want to understand basic procedures and typical pay methods used in modern businesses.

Methods of Payment

If you choose to work in a payroll department, you will learn the method or methods used for paying employees. In some companies, all employees are paid by the same method. However, in other companies several different methods may be used for varying groups of workers. Increasingly, payroll procedures are being computerized. However, in order for you to fully understand what is required in processing payments to employees, you first will be introduced to noncomputerized procedures.

Salary

Under this method, the employee is paid an amount that is quoted on a weekly, monthly, or yearly basis. The *gross salary*, which is the salary before any deductions, is the figure quoted. A salary quoted on a yearly basis is **subdivided** into the number of pay periods per year. A person who earns $16,500 yearly and is paid twice each month will have a gross salary of $687.50 each pay period.

subdivided: separated into several parts

Hourly

wage: payment based on number of hours worked

In some positions, employees are paid on the basis of a **wage** rate per hour. The hourly rate applies to the hours considered standard. The standard work week may be 35, 37½, or 40 hours. When workers paid on an hourly basis work more hours than those specified as standard for their work week, they generally earn a higher rate for the **overtime** hours. It is common for overtime rates to be 1.5 to 2 times the standard hourly rate. Many factory workers, as well as part-time and temporary office workers, are paid on the basis of an hourly rate.

overtime: hours worked over the standard work week

Illus. 9-19. This office assistant works a standard 40-hour week. She is paid an hourly rate and receives a payroll check at the end of each week.

Commission

Some workers' earnings are based on a percentage of the value of what they sell or process. The percentage may vary by volume of sales or of production. This method is commonly used for the payment of salespersons and sales representatives. For example, sales representatives of a computer supplies company are assigned territories which they are to service. Since their earnings depend on the sales they generate, they are motivated to work with attention and considerable effort.

In some jobs, you will find a combination of methods used. For example, a commission, referred to as a *bonus*, may be given to employees who are successful beyond some established standard. Such a bonus is often a percentage of additional sales or production.

Deductions from Earnings

deductions: items which reduce gross pay

As you have learned, salaries and wages are quoted at their gross figures, which is before any *deductions* are considered. The earnings actually received generally will be less than the wages or salaries quoted. Some payroll deductions are required by law; others are optional, or voluntary.

Deductions Required by Law

Deductions required by law include the following:

- federal income tax
- Federal Insurance Contributions Act tax (referred to as *FICA* or as *social security tax)*
- state income tax (where applicable)
- city income tax (where applicable)

exemption: a withholding allowance

Federal income tax deductions vary depending on level of wages or salary and on number of *exemptions* claimed. Each employee must complete a Withholding Allowance Certificate (referred to as a W-4 form), which is kept on file by the employing company. The employee is responsible for notifying the human resources department of any changes in the number of exemptions. The deduction for federal income taxes is based on the number of withholding allowances claimed by each employee.

FICA deductions are a percentage of gross wages or salary, up to the maximum amount of wages or salary taxed. The employee's contribution to social security is matched by the employer. Each year the rates are reviewed by Congress. Congress has the authority to change the rate as well as the maximum amount taxed. The payroll office in your company can provide you with the up-to-date percentages for deductions and the amount of earnings subject to FICA tax. This information also is available from your local office of the Social Security Administration.

State and local government units that tax the earnings of citizens issue instructions for the computation of taxes to be withheld. Your office will have such information on file for your reference.

Cut here and give the certificate to your employer. Keep the top portion for your records.

Form **W-4**	**Employee's Withholding Allowance Certificate**		OMB No. 1545-0010
Department of the Treasury Internal Revenue Service	▶ For Privacy Act and Paperwork Reduction Act Notice, see reverse.		

1 Type or print your first name and middle initial	Last name		2 Your social security number
Jeffrey C. Hunter			*321-22-4697*

Home address (number and street or rural route)	**3 Marital Status**	☐ Single ✔Married ☐ Married, but withhold at higher Single rate.
45 Newland Place		
City or town, state, and ZIP code		**Note:** If married, but legally separated, or spouse is a nonresident alien, check the Single box.
Matawan, NJ 07747-6321		

4 Total number of allowances you are claiming (from line G above or from the Worksheets on back if they apply)	**4**	*I*
5 Additional amount, if any, you want deducted from each pay	**5**	$ —

6 I claim exemption from withholding and I certify that I meet **ALL** of the following conditions for exemption:
- Last year I had a right to a refund of **ALL** Federal income tax withheld because I had **NO** tax liability; **AND**
- This year I expect a refund of **ALL** Federal income tax withheld because I expect to have **NO** tax liability; **AND**
- This year if my income exceeds $500 and includes nonwage income, another person cannot claim me as a dependent.

If you meet all of the above conditions, enter the year effective and "EXEMPT" here .... ▶ | **6** | 19

7 Are you a full-time student? (**Note:** Full-time students are not automatically exempt.)..................................... | **7** ☐ Yes ☐ No

Under penalties of perjury, I certify that I am entitled to the number of withholding allowances claimed on this certificate or entitled to claim exempt status.

Employee's signature ▶ *Jeffrey C. Hunter*	Date ▶ *July 5*	, 19 — —

8 Employer's name and address (Employer: Complete 8 and 10 only if sending to IRS)	9 Office code (optional)	10 Employer identification number
Modern Software, Inc. 29 Exchange Place New York, NY 10038-0630		

Illus. 9-20.
Employee's Withholding Allowance Certificate (W-4 form). How many deductions does Jeffrey Hunter claim?

Voluntary Deductions

Voluntary deductions vary considerably. In some companies, employees voluntarily make deductions for health insurance, savings plans, retirement plans, and other purposes.

If you are working in a payroll office, you may have the responsibility of keeping the records up to date for individual deductions. You will be given information on the procedures you are to follow and the references you will need to use as you complete your tasks.

Records for Payroll

Companies maintain careful records of all payments made to employees. In fact, many companies issue payroll checks that have an attached voucher. This voucher shows the payments made to date as well as all the deductions to date. At the end of the year, the company is responsible for issuing to each employee a Wage and Tax Statement (commonly called a W-2 form) for the calendar year. Additionally, the company makes monthly or quarterly reports to government agencies of taxes withheld and taxes the employer must pay. Periodically, the company makes deposits of the amounts withheld and the taxes owed.

Illus. 9-21. (Top) Computerized employee earnings record. (Bottom) Computerized payroll record. What are Jeffrey Hunter's net earnings for the year?

Basic records for payroll include an individual employee's earnings record and a payroll register which records all the payments for a payroll period. Note Illus. 9-21.

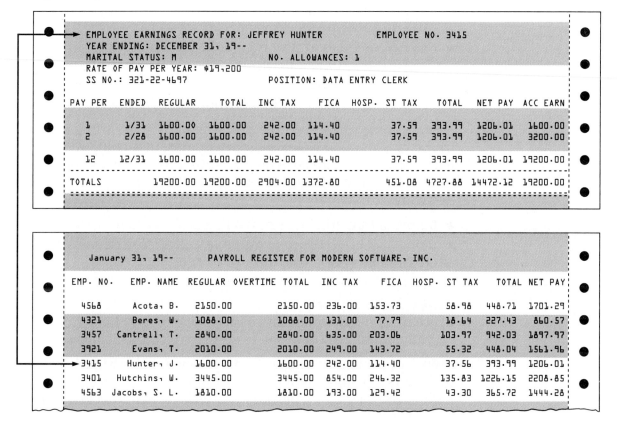

EMPLOYEE EARNINGS RECORD FOR: JEFFREY HUNTER   EMPLOYEE NO. 3415
YEAR ENDING: DECEMBER 31, 19--
MARITAL STATUS: M   NO. ALLOWANCES: 1
RATE OF PAY PER YEAR: $19,200
SS NO.: 321-22-4697   POSITION: DATA ENTRY CLERK

PAY PER	ENDED	REGULAR	TOTAL	INC TAX	FICA	HOSP.	ST TAX	TOTAL	NET PAY	ACC EARN
1	1/31	1600.00	1600.00	242.00	114.40		37.59	393.99	1206.01	1600.00
2	2/28	1600.00	1600.00	242.00	114.40		37.59	393.99	1206.01	3200.00
12	12/31	1600.00	1600.00	242.00	114.40		37.59	393.99	1206.01	19200.00
TOTALS		19200.00	19200.00	2904.00	1372.80		451.08	4727.88	14472.12	19200.00

January 31, 19--   PAYROLL REGISTER FOR MODERN SOFTWARE, INC.

EMP. NO.	EMP. NAME	REGULAR	OVERTIME	TOTAL	INC TAX	FICA	HOSP.	ST TAX	TOTAL	NET PAY
4568	Acota, B.	2150.00		2150.00	236.00	153.73		58.98	448.71	1701.29
4321	Beres, W.	1088.00		1088.00	131.00	77.79		18.64	227.43	860.57
3457	Cantrell, T.	2840.00		2840.00	635.00	203.06		103.97	942.03	1897.97
3921	Evans, T.	2010.00		2010.00	249.00	143.72		55.32	448.04	1561.96
3415	Hunter, J.	1600.00		1600.00	242.00	114.40		37.56	393.99	1206.01
3401	Hutchins, W.	3445.00		3445.00	854.00	246.32		135.83	1226.15	2208.85
4563	Jacobs, S. L.	1810.00		1810.00	193.00	129.42		43.30	365.72	1444.28

Payroll Check Distribution

Procedures in distributing paychecks will vary from company to company. One company may distribute checks in person by the paymaster or a member of the paymaster's staff. Other companies electronically deposit wage and salary payments to employees' designated banks where the funds are credited to the employees' accounts. The company provides the employee with a voucher that details the salary paid and all deductions, and the bank sends the employee a notification of the deposit.

Computerized Payroll Tasks

You may work in a payroll department where the processing of earnings is computerized. The procedures used will vary depending upon the size of the workforce and the degree to which the record keeping is automated. However, typical tasks you may be asked to complete include the following:

- inputting attendance information for each employee from time cards or time sheets using special software
- reconciling the hours worked with the hours reported
- updating employee files due to changes in salary status or payroll deductions
- processing, printing, and distributing paychecks

Some companies use time and attendance recording systems where employees register their attendance at a computer terminal. Attendance data goes directly into the company's computerized payroll system. In this office, your duties may include the following:

- insuring that employee payroll records are kept up to date
- using special software to automatically figure deductions and changes in salary, overtime, or commission
- updating vacation and sick leave data
- printing paychecks
- creating weekly, monthly, quarterly, or yearly tax reports which must be submitted to state and federal agencies

Whatever tasks are assigned to you, you must remember that it is extremely important to be accurate and to keep salary information confidential. Following procedures, carefully verifying all your work, and maintaining orderly records will insure high-quality performance.

QUESTIONS FOR REVIEW

1. What is a liability?

2. What documents are forwarded to an accounts payable department?

3. What would you want to verify when reviewing a purchase order and an invoice related to the same purchase of goods?

4. What does a voucher include?

5. Describe how you would prepare an ordinary check to be sent to a vendor using a noncomputerized and a computerized system.

6. How does a certified check differ from an ordinary check?

7. How does the hourly method of payroll payment differ from the salary method? How does the salary method of payroll payment differ from the commission method?

8. What deductions from earnings are required by law?

9. Describe the information recorded in a payroll register.

10. Identify five tasks you might perform in an office where the processing of earnings is done on a computer.

MAKING DECISIONS

One office worker, Valerie, has responsibility for filing all vendor invoices and purchase orders in the accounts payable department. Janie's job is to check the accuracy of vendor invoices against purchase orders. From time to time, Janie must retrieve such documents from the files. Recently, Janie has had difficulty in locating specific documents. Often she must search through practically an entire file drawer to find what she needs. Janie noted that others seem to be spending much time looking through the files, too.

Janie has no authority to supervise Valerie. The supervisor has said nothing about the matter as far as Janie knows. "Since the supervisor doesn't use the files, the supervisor may not be aware of this problem," thinks Janie. Janie believes the work of the department would be far more efficient if the filing were done carefully.

What You Are To Do: Describe your decision at this point, if you were in Janie's position.

EXTENDING YOUR ENGLISH COMPETENCIES

One of the staff members of a professional publication for accountants prepared the following very rough draft of an announcement planned for a forthcoming issue of the magazine. There are five misspelled words in the rough draft.

What You Are To Do: Prepare a copy of the announcement, making all corrections required in spelling. On a separate sheet of paper, give an appropriate definition for each of the six words that are circled.

The Business Accountants Association has formed a new (advisory) group on small businesses which will (fund) independantly any of the Board's specific (projects.) It will help the Board indentify the (implications) of Board decisions to small businesses. Also, it will help identify any (implementation) problems small businesses may have with those decisions. The executive director of the Association is one of the members of the new panal. Any member who wants to coment on an (issue) envolving small business may write to the national office.

APPLICATION ACTIVITY

You are an office employee in a retail furniture company store in a suburban mall. You have been given the following schedule of salaries of employees. You have been told that employees are paid twice monthly, on the 15th and on the last day of the month.

What You Are To Do: Determine the gross salary for each of the employees for the period ended November 30. For employees who receive commission, the commission earned is based on their net sales for the two-week period preceding the current pay period. You have been given this information.

Administrative and Office Employees	Salary	Basis
Agins, Richard	$18,000	Annually
Birin, Otto	1,400	Monthly
Dalla, Sarah.............	19,500	Annually
Flynn, Julia	34,500	Annually
Kramer, Elsie............	1,200	Monthly
Phillip, Michael..........	1,550	Monthly

Sales Employees	Monthly Salary	Net Sales November 1-15
Chase, Eric	$ 600 plus 6% commission	$16,000
Hayward, Louise	1,000 plus 6% commission	21,000
Majia, Dora	1,000 plus 6% commission	15,560
Myers, James	600 plus 6% commission	12,436
Pedro, Silvia	1,000 plus 6% commission	10,500
Saha, Eunice............	1,000 plus 6% commission	17,540

CHAPTER SUMMARY

Chapter 9 has given you an understanding of three critical components of any organization's accounting system. Although procedures may vary from company to company, office employees have responsibility for maintaining accurate, up-to-date records at all times. You should be able to discuss the following key points:

1. Companies generally separate responsibility for tasks in processing cash, and they also bond employees in order to have good internal control.
2. Office workers assist in the processing of cash by seeing that checks are endorsed properly, by filling in deposit slips, by preparing bank reconciliations, and by maintaining petty cash funds.
3. Keeping records of customers' obligations is the primary task of office workers in accounts receivable departments. The accounts receivable department gets copies of invoices, credit memorandums, and listings of customers' checks.
4. Vendors must be paid within the discount period, if that is the company's policy. Otherwise, vendors must be paid within the total period allowed for payment.
5. Payroll-related tasks must be performed in time for checks to be issued on regular paydays.

6. Increasingly, cash records, accounts payable, accounts receivable, and payroll-related tasks may be performed using computers and specialized software.

KEY TERMS

accounts receivable	MICR
bonding	accounts payable
endorsement	voucher
deposit slip	tickler file
lockbox	voucher checks
ATM transactions	EFT
petty cash fund	

INTEGRATED CHAPTER ACTIVITIES

Activity 1

You have been given invoices that are to be paid within the discount period. The figures shown below have been taken from the invoices. Also, the terms for payment are given.

Vendor	Amount Owed	Terms
Jim's Imports	$ 2,345.00	2/10, n/30
Premier Associates	5,678.50	3/15, n/30
Poteet Stationers	3,450.00	2/10, n/30
C.M. McDougal & Co.	10,650.65	3/15, n/30
Handex Corporation	12,450.00	2/10, n/30
Meyer & Sons	9,456.43	1/10, n/30
Caprock Spas	7,789.42	1/10, n/30
CCC Cotton Co-Op	4,569.23	2/10, n/30
Mullenax, Inc.	5,908.00	2/10, n/30

What You Are To Do: Compute the amount that should be sent to the vendor in each instance. **NOTE:** Do you remember how to compute discounts? Example: 2/10, n/30 means that a 2 percent discount is allowed if payment is made within 10 days of the invoice date. If not paid within 10 days, the total due is to be paid within 30 days of the invoice date.

Activity 2

You are an assistant in the office of the director of accounting systems for Allied Chemical. The director hands you the rough draft shown below and says, "Please key a final copy of these responsibilities for processing incoming checks. Better read through it one more time to make sure I caught all errors. Use your own judgment with regard to format."

Word processing equipment can be used to complete this activity.

What You Are To Do: Key a final copy of the new procedure, making the corrections noted. Use boldface for the job titles if your equipment permits.

WORKFLOW OF INCOMING PAYMENTS (Computerized System)

Mail Clerk

1. Opens mail and places checks in separate batches
2. Prepares a listing of all checks
3. Stamps endorsement on back of each check
4. Forwards checks to cashier with a copy of listing
5. Forwards 1 copy of listing to data entry

Data Entry Clerk

1. Recieves checks from mail clerk
2. Accesses each customer's account for which a check has been ~~been~~ received
3. Keys the amount of payment indicated on listing
4. Prepares summary of all payments recorded
5. Forwards copy of summery to General Accounting Office

Cashier

1. receives checks, and a copy of listing from mail clerk
2. Compares each check with the amount on the listing to see that the amounts are the same
3. Prepares deposit slip
4. Makes deposit in person or by mail
5. Receives copy of receipted deposit slip from bank
6. Files a copy of the receipted deposit slip.

OPTIONAL COMPUTER APPLICATION ACTIVITY
See Computer Application Activity 9
in your Information Processing Activities workbook.

OPTIONAL CRITICAL THINKING ACTIVITY
See Critical Thinking Project 3
in your Information Processing Activities workbook.

PRODUCTIVITY CORNER

Kathy Malenky
OFFICE SUPERVISOR

WHY CAN'T I USE A CALCULATOR PROPERLY?

DEAR MS. MALENKY:

I don't understand how I can make so many math errors—and I *am* using a calculator!

I took a job that requires me to use a calculator a great deal of the time. Why do I get halfway through a column of figures and make an error—such as adding the same number twice?

I have an understanding supervisor, but I think she will be disappointed with me if I don't learn to operate this calculator more efficiently. I've been on the job for three weeks. Any suggestions?—STEVE IN ST. LOUIS

DEAR STEVE:

Your willingness to face your weakness straight on is to be commended. You must realize, though, that there is no reason why you cannot become absolutely accurate in all your computations.

You want to improve. Now you must develop a strategy for improvement. Try the following:

- Focus on the specific task at hand by reading *each* number exactly as it is recorded.

- Develop your skill in striking keys by the touch method.

- Think about the magnitude of the numbers you are striking and attempt to estimate the result. Check your actual result against your estimate.

- In the early stages of your improvement efforts, redo each computation. If you are adding a column of numbers, add from the bottom to the top after adding from the top to the bottom. When you compute a quotient, follow up by multiplying the quotient by the divisor to see if your result is the dividend. When you compute the product of two numbers, follow up by dividing the product by the multiplier to see if you get the multiplicand.

- Keep a record of *all* mistakes you make in a day. Analyze them to see what *types* of errors you are making.

- Think of what will help you overcome the types of errors you make. For example, if you often transpose digits, you probably are reading the numbers carelessly. Focus *directly* on each number to help you reduce the instances of such errors.

Best wishes for correct computation.—
KATHY MALENKY

AT WORK AT DYNAMICS: *Simulation 2*

Miss Branigan telephones to say that your next assignment will be in the Sales and Marketing Division of DYNAMICS. Several full-time employees are on vacation, and you are needed as a substitute for one of these employees. "I think you will enjoy working in this division," Miss Branigan says. "There's always such a bustle of activity."

Miss Branigan proceeds to give you a preview of what you will encounter in the Sales and Marketing Division. Since this division handles the sales and marketing functions, the major focus is the presentation and selling of products to potential customers. Here, plans are made for national advertising on television and radio. Catalog copy and newspaper and magazine advertisements also are prepared here. Each year DYNAMICS has a new clothing line of warm-up suits and action sportswear. This year's line will soon be marketed nationwide.

An important function of this division is to provide customer services. For example, if a problem (such as the receipt of damaged merchandise) arises with an order, the Customer Services Department takes the call, determines the problem, and then proceeds to complete immediately all follow-up actions required. "We strive to keep our customers satisfied with our products and our service," says Miss Branigan. "Naturally, the Customer Services Department prepares many letters to be sent to our customers, and the Word Processing Center processes these letters."

Turn to your *Information Processing Activities* workbook to learn more about your assignment in the Sales and Marketing Division of DYNAMICS.

TIME AND
TASK MANAGEMENT

CHAPTER 10

Activities Management

Most office workers want to be good at their jobs and be recognized as being good at their jobs. However, you don't become a valued, respected worker by chance. Good office workers must apply all the skills they have learned:

- technical skills and knowledge, such as keyboarding documents in the approved company format

- communication and behavioral skills, such as working cooperatively with others and displaying proper work attitudes

- activities management skills, such as planning the order of completing tasks

What you actually do in your office job will depend in large part on the nature of the business for which you work, the size of the business, and the geographical location of that business. You will find, however, that your job fills a specific need in that business organization. In meeting the requirements of your job, you may be called upon to do many different kinds of tasks. Therefore, you will need to plan and organize your work activities carefully in order to perform efficiently and on time. You will need to effectively use the resources which support your work activities: your time; your workstation; office manuals; reprographic services; and the office supplies, forms, and equipment.

To work effectively and efficiently, you must have a safe environment. You will want to be acquainted with the critical concerns for safety and security that are the responsibility of all office workers. The objectives of the chapter are to:

- assist you in developing your understanding of the importance of an organized workstation and the management of your time

- identify frequently used office reprographic equipment and procedures

- describe important safety and security procedures for the office

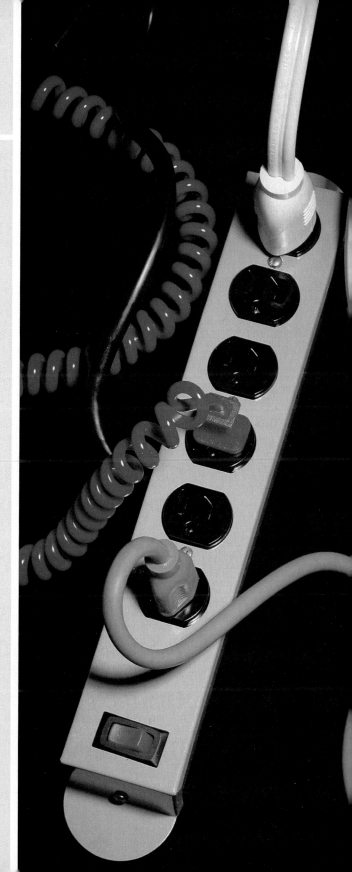

WORKSTATION AND TIME MANAGEMENT

After you have completed your study of this topic, you will be able to:

- identify the function of your office workstation

- identify common office workstation equipment, supplies, and accessories

- arrange your workstation to increase productivity

- identify common office time wasters

- apply basic time analysis procedures to help you better manage your time

As an office worker, you must be able to manage your work effectively to become productive. Proper lighting, control of sound and climate, and the arrangement and design of your workstation contribute to your productivity. Most companies strive to provide physically comfortable and safe environments for their office employees. It becomes your responsibility to keep your work area well organized.

Time management is also a major factor which contributes to your productivity. Managing your time at the office is a process of choosing the most effective way to do your job. The creative use of techniques to manage time will enrich your work life.

**THE WORK-
STATION**

Ergonomics, as you have learned, is the study of the effects of the work environment on the health and well-being of employees. Your workstation is a key component of your work environment. A **workstation** is the physical area in which a worker performs his or her job. A typical workstation provides a work surface and space for equipment and supplies.

Your workstation should be organized so you can work efficiently and productively throughout each workday. For example, the workstation shown in Illus. 10-1 is arranged so that the worker is within easy reach of frequently used items such as the computer keyboard and telephone.

Illus. 10-1. Many companies provide flexible workstations that can be arranged to meet specific user needs.

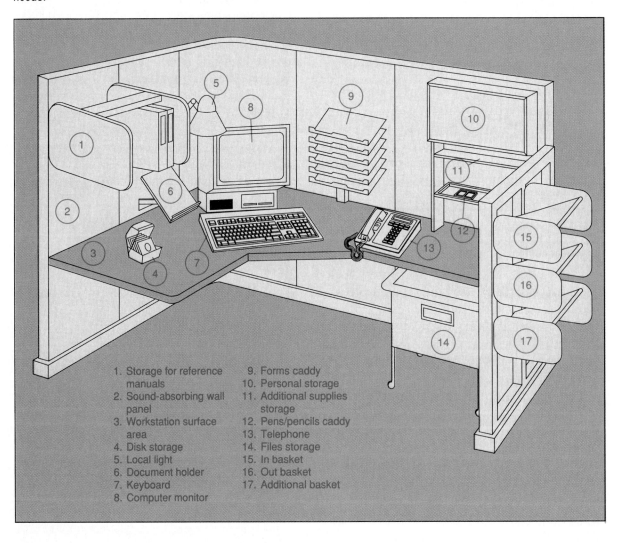

1. Storage for reference manuals
2. Sound-absorbing wall panel
3. Workstation surface area
4. Disk storage
5. Local light
6. Document holder
7. Keyboard
8. Computer monitor
9. Forms caddy
10. Personal storage
11. Additional supplies storage
12. Pens/pencils caddy
13. Telephone
14. Files storage
15. In basket
16. Out basket
17. Additional basket

Modular Workstations

components: parts or units

Modular workstations are made up of standard, interchangeable **components** such as sound-absorbing wall panels, storage areas, and a work surface. Interchangeable components permit the workstation to be arranged to meet a worker's individual needs. For example, many of the components can be adjusted by height and angle.

Many businesses prefer modular workstations because of their design flexibility. A modular workstation, as shown in Illus. 10-1, can be moved easily from one place to another in order to meet the changing needs of the office. Modular workstations are generally used with the open office plan; however, they can be adopted for use with any office plan.

Ergonomic Seating

sedentary: sitting

A well-designed chair is essential since many office workers spend much of their time in **sedentary** positions. However, ergonomic seating involves more than just a quality chair. An ergonomic chair must be adjustable, like the one shown in Illus. 10-2. Each office worker should be able to adjust his or her chair to fit individual physical requirements for comfort and good posture.

Illus. 10-2. Some authorities believe the chair is the most important component of the workstation.

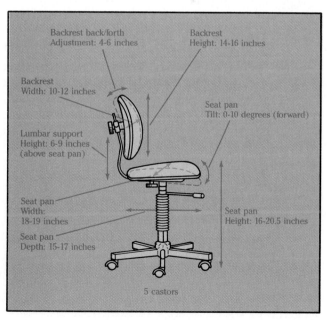

Backrest back/forth
Adjustment: 4-6 inches

Backrest
Height: 14-16 inches

Backrest
Width: 10-12 inches

Seat pan
Tilt: 0-10 degrees (forward)

Lumbar support
Height: 6-9 inches
(above seat pan)

Seat pan
Width:
18-19 inches

Seat pan
Height: 16-20.5 inches

Seat pan
Depth: 15-17 inches

5 castors

Organize your workstation (both the surface areas and the drawers) so that the arrangement of equipment and supplies increases your efficiency. Stock only the items that you need for daily or frequent use. Supplies, reference materials, and equipment such as terminals and transcription units should be arranged to provide a functional work area. A **functional work area** is an area that is well maintained, well equipped, well organized, and efficiently managed.

Workstation Surface Area

Keep your workstation's surface clear. Clutter on your workstation's surface can cause unnecessary delays as you search for papers or objects. Remove materials that do not relate to your current project. Label file folders with descriptive labels, and place documents that are not needed in the folders. Place the folders in your file drawer.

Illus. 10-3. Keep your workstation surface free of clutter.

Arrange your equipment and supplies to allow easy access so that you avoid making needless movements. Keep frequently used supplies such as pencils and paper clips in a caddy on the surface of your work area. Reaching for the caddy is more efficient than opening and closing a drawer each time you need an item.

Center Drawer and Top Side Drawer

Reserve your center drawer for frequently used supplies that are not needed on the surface area, such as a letter opener, scissors, and paper clips. Arrange the contents of the center drawer so that the most frequently used supplies are toward the front where you can reach them easily.

Illus. 10-4. Top, side drawer with stationery separator (left). Center drawer (right).

The top, side drawer is often equipped with a *stationery separator*. This device provides convenient slots in which to store frequently used items such as letterhead and plain paper. Place the items you use most frequently in the separator slots near the front.

File Drawer or Lower Drawers

A desk may contain either a file drawer or additional side drawers. A file drawer can be used to store work in progress as well as files that are referred to frequently. Other drawers can be used for less frequently used supplies and a few personal items.

Reference Books

The nature of your job will determine which references you will use most often. Frequently used references should be located at your workstation and may include a dictionary, telephone directory, and an office reference manual. References used less frequently should be **accessible** but need not be located at your workstation. These may include an almanac, atlas, **thesaurus**, and equipment and software manuals.

accessible: easy to locate

thesaurus: book of words with synonyms

Office employees use a variety of equipment, supplies, and accessories to do their jobs. In fact, the right resources help you perform your job properly. What you need at your workstation will depend on your particular job. Also, electronic offices will have some equipment, supplies, and accessories that will differ from those used in traditional offices.

comprehensive:
completely covering

Some of the more common equipment, supplies, and accessories are shown in Illus. 10-5. Although this is not a *comprehensive* list, it's typical of what you may find at an office workstation.

WORKSTATION EQUIPMENT, SUPPLIES, AND ACCESSORIES		
	workstation equipment	typewriter, microcomputer or computer monitor and keyboard, printer, transcription unit, electronic calculator, telephone
	basic supplies and accessories	calendar, scissors, paper clips, stapler and staple remover, pencils, pens, tape and tape dispenser, notepaper and message pads, in and out baskets
	communication-related supplies	date stamp and ink pad, stationery, envelopes, forms, correction supplies, typewriter ribbons, printwheels or elements, reference books
	information processing supplies	diskettes, diskette file, printwheels, software manuals, computer paper, data binders, printer ribbons

Illus. 10-5. Shown here are some of the more common pieces of equipment, supplies, and accessories often kept at a workstation.

Using Office Equipment

Office equipment can be an investment in reducing labor costs. Since the quality of your work often depends upon the condition of your equipment, you will want to keep your equipment in top working condition. To get dependable service from your equipment, you will need to practice preventive maintenance. **Preventive maintenance** involves servicing equipment and replacing parts while the equipment is functioning properly in order to prevent the equipment from failing. Fewer repairs are necessary when equipment is cared for properly on a daily basis. By practicing preventive maintenance, you can help equipment perform well over a longer period of time. You will want to follow these three maintenance guidelines:

1. Learn how to use and care for the equipment properly. Read and understand the manufacturer's operating instructions.
2. Inspect and clean equipment regularly. Know the basic care routines your equipment requires. Establish a regular inspection schedule. **Adhere** to the preventive measures (such as oiling and cleaning) recommended by the manufacturer.
3. Report problems immediately. When you spot a potential problem, report it to your supervisor. Many minor problems can be corrected before they become serious and require costly repairs.

adhere: follow closely

Using Office Supplies and Accessories

An adequately stocked workstation is essential to your productivity. If you run out of supplies in the middle of a critical task, you could lose valuable work time in trying to replenish needed supplies. Also, you run the risk of not completing the task on time.

One of the best ways to save money for your company is to use supplies properly. Here are three guidelines to follow:

1. Select the quality of the supply according to the nature and importance of the task. For example, if you are preparing a rough-draft copy of an important letter, don't use expensive letterhead paper. Use a lower quality paper for the rough draft and the letterhead paper for the final copy. Learn to read product labels for the correct use of a product.
2. Look for ways to conserve supplies. For example, reuse file folders by placing new file folder labels over the old ones.
3. Do not **hoard** supplies in your workstation. It is a work area, not a storage area. Check your workstation periodically. If you have not used a supply item in several weeks, perhaps it should be returned to the supply cabinet.

hoard: collect in great number

Illus. 10-6. To perform your duties efficiently, keep adequate quantities of needed supplies at your workstation.

TIME MANAGEMENT

You learned that time management is the process of planning your activities to gain better control over your time. Managing your time effectively is critical to your success on the job. You will want to learn how to eliminate time wasters and handle time obligations efficiently. Analyzing how you spend your time will help you become more effective in managing your work. One of the first steps in learning how to use your time is recognizing how your time can be wasted. In the office setting, you will need to learn to *distinguish* between time obligations and time wasters.

distinguish: to know or perceive a difference

Common Time Wasters

Often not all time spent "at work" is productive. You can waste time without realizing it. Following are some common time wasters you may encounter, along with suggestions for overcoming them.

Unnecessary Telephone Conversations

To the office assistant, the telephone can be either a time saver or a time waster. Often, a telephone call that starts out as a time saver can become a time waster. For example, if an office worker takes ten minutes to verify information on a price list and five minutes to discuss the latest episode of a favorite television program, a conversation which started out as productive ends up being a time waster. If this happens two or three times a day, the time lost can add up rapidly.

Frequent Interruptions

barriers: anything that serves to block entrance

Interruptions in your work can come from drop-in visitors and even your supervisor. Discouraging the drop-in visitor may involve building **barriers** against interruptions. If you have a door, close it. If possible, turn your workstation so that you do not face an open door or common passageway. If you do not need an extra chair by your workstation, remove it.

Excessive Socializing

abuse: improper use

Although some socializing will help you maintain good working relations with your coworkers, too much socialization is an **abuse** of company time. Some workers may socialize too much, and you will be wise to avoid engaging in long conversations with them. When a *talker* tries to involve you in idle conversation, offer a simple response like: "I really must get back to work. Maybe we could discuss this at lunch." You will maintain good working relations while excusing yourself to continue your work. If you are consistent in your responses, the talker will soon learn that you are not distracted easily from your work.

Also, be careful not to mistreat your lunch time and your break times by extending them beyond the approved time periods.

Illus. 10-7. Lunch is an ideal time to socialize with coworkers.

Ineffective Communication

You will be expected to follow both written and oral instructions from your supervisor and coworkers. You will also be expected to give clear written and oral instructions to others. As you learned in Chapter 3, if the information given or received is inaccurate or incomplete, much time can be lost in doing a task wrong and correcting it. Be certain the instructions and directions you give are specific and accurate. Likewise, be sure that you understand any instructions you receive.

Disorganization

Being disorganized can be a major time waster. Searching for the paper you just had in your hands, missing important deadlines, and shifting unnecessarily from one project to another are all signs of a disorganized person. Take the time to organize your work area and prepare a daily plan for your work. You should think through and thoughtfully plan complicated jobs before starting them. Group similar tasks together and avoid jumping from one project to another before finishing the first task. Do not **procrastinate**. If unpleasant or difficult tasks are left for later, they can become potential crises just waiting to erupt.

procrastinate: delay intentionally

Orderly Approach to Work

Using time efficiently involves developing an orderly approach to your work. Following are some suggestions for handling your time obligations more effectively.

Use a Calendar as a Work Management Tool

Your desk calendar or a wall calendar can become a useful work management tool if you use it to record task deadlines and reminders. A calendar can not only help you organize your daily work but also help you identify **peak** and **slack** work periods.

peak: a period of increased work activity

Once you know when to expect peak and slack work periods, you can plan your work to allow for more productive use of your time as well as for a more even workload. To accommodate a peak period, think ahead to determine what jobs could be completed prior to the peak period. Then, the peak period will not impose undue pressure on you.

slack: a period of decreased work activity

Planning for the slack periods is equally important. During slack periods, you can catch up on those tasks that do not have deadlines but nevertheless must be done.

Illus. 10-8. A calendar can help you plan and organize tasks.

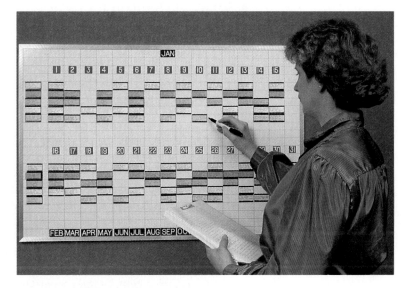

Plan Your Work Activities

Planning your daily work activities will help you avoid forgetting tasks that need to be completed. Take five or ten minutes either at the beginning of the work day or at the close of the previous work day to plan the coming day's work. Prepare a "To Do" list similar to the one shown in Illus. 10-9 on page 403, and complete the tasks according to their order of importance. Keep the list accessible as you work. Check your list frequently. This list should guide you through your daily activities. As tasks are completed, cross them off. Tasks not completed can be carried over to the next day's "To Do" list. Be alert, however, to any item that seems to be carried over too many times. Perhaps such an item should be broken down into smaller segments or perhaps you are procrastinating in completing the task.

Set Priorities

Once you know what tasks you are facing for the day, rank the items on your "To Do" list and complete the most important tasks first. To determine the priority of the tasks, ask yourself these questions:

- How much time will the task require?
- By what date (time) is this needed?
- Are others involved in completing the task?
- What will happen if this task is not completed on time?

At times you may need to discuss your priorities with your supervisor to be certain that you both agree on the order for doing tasks. Once you set your priorities, finish the tasks in their priority order. Remain ***flexible***, however, to revising your priorities as circumstances change.

flexible: able to adapt or change as necessary

*Before Ana Maria left work, she jotted down the tasks she needed to complete the next day at work. She checked her "To Do" list for any uncompleted tasks to be carried over to the current list. She also checked her calendar and her supervisor's calendar for any **pertinent** notations. Her calendar contained a reminder notation that the national sales meeting would be held three weeks from tomorrow. Jim McPheeter, a regional sales manager, is to accompany her supervisor to the meeting. Both her supervisor and Mr. McPheeter are to present a revised version of the standard sales contract at the meeting. Ana Maria must prepare a draft of the revised version for review within the next 24 hours.*

pertinent:
significant; important; to the point

Ana Maria's "To Do" list for tomorrow is shown in Illus. 10-9. Notice that she has identified the tasks as A, B, or C. The A-level tasks are those tasks that need immediate attention or completion. If the item is a long-term project, the portion of the task that should be finished that day is listed. B-level tasks are those that can be done once the A-level tasks have been completed. C-level tasks have no specific deadline, but can be done when the A and B tasks have been completed.

Control Large Projects

Sometimes it is difficult to get started on a large project even though that project may be very important. Smaller tasks can be checked off your "To Do" list with ease, whereas a large task may seem too ***formidable***. Do not let the size of a project keep you from getting the project under control and moving toward satisfactory completion of the task. Here are several suggestions for handling a large project:

formidable: causing dread or fear

- Break the large project into smaller tasks.
- Determine the steps to be taken in each of the smaller tasks.

TO DO

<u>Thursday, January 13</u>

Priority		Completed
A-2	Prepare minutes from 1/10/-- regional sales meeting; distribute to participants	
A-1	Prepare and distribute memo announcing a staff meeting for this Monday, 1/17/--	
B-3	Key rough draft of revised sales contract for national sales meeting	
B-4	Call Karen to get tentative dates from company calendar	
B-1	Call McPheeter's assistant to coordinate travel date to national sales meeting	
B-2	Call travel agency for flight times on travel date	
C-1	Delete last year's backup copies of short-term sales agreement with vendors	

NOTES: Karen is taking half of a vacation day. She'll be in at 1:00 p.m.

Illus. 10-9. Ana Maria's "To Do" list.

- Establish deadlines for each section or smaller task and stick to those deadlines.
- Look for ways to improve your procedures and simplify the completion of the project.
- If the large project is one that will be repeated periodically, record your procedures including suggestions you want to follow in the future for improvements.

Simplify Your Work

Work simplification is the process of improving the procedures for getting work done. It often involves streamlining, or simplifying, some steps and eliminating others. You are striving to improve the way you work by using the most efficient way to do an essential task or series of tasks. As you complete a task, be aware of the steps you are going through. Eliminate any unnecessary steps and/or details.

Here are four suggestions to help you simplify your work:

- Group and complete similar tasks together. For example, if you are to make photocopies of the letters you are preparing, make them all at once rather than making several trips to the copier. If you have several phone calls to make, try to make them in sequence.
- Be alert to combining tasks if doing so will increase your efficiency. For example, if you are to deliver a letter to the mailroom and the supply store is near the mailroom, pick up the office supplies you intended to get the next morning.
- List the procedures you use to complete a large task. For example, if you are preparing a large mailing, divide this large task into smaller tasks by listing the major procedures involved, such as printing mailing labels, attaching labels, stuffing envelopes, and mailing envelopes. Then, if necessary, list the steps in each major procedure. Be alert to any sequence of steps that does not seem logical. Study your listing carefully to determine if any steps can be combined.
- Determine how to best organize and arrange the equipment and supplies you use to complete a task. For example, if you cross a room several times to use a calculator in the completion of a task, you need to reorganize the placement of the equipment to provide a smoother flow of work.

BASIC TIME ANALYSIS PROCEDURES

Your time is a valuable resource that you should use wisely. Time cannot be replaced. In the preceding sections of this topic, you learned some of the ways in which you can better use your time on the job. You now know some good time management procedures, as well as some of the common ways time can be wasted. You can now analyze how you spend your time on the job.

Time analysis aids you in determining how effectively your time is used. By keeping a written account of what you do, you can determine whether or not you are using your time effectively. With this information you can then develop a plan of action to correct or redirect the use of your time.

Keep a Time Inventory

Start by keeping a written record of what you do and how much time is used. Record all activities in a time-use log: telephone calls, meetings, discussions with coworkers, and so forth.

You may choose to keep a time-use log for a day, for several days, or even a week. The longer you keep your time-use log, the more representative it will be of how your time is spent. A partial time-use log is shown in Illus. 10-10 on page 406.

Analyze How You Spend Your Time

When you have completed your time-use log, you are ready to analyze the results. By studying your time-use patterns, you will be able to spot problem areas quickly. Be alert to the following points as you analyze your time-use log:

- During what time of the day was I most productive? When was I least productive? Why?
- How did I lose (or waste) my time? Was it because of unnecessary interruptions, visitors/socializing, crises, telephone? Who and what was involved in each case?

Develop a Plan of Action

After you have analyzed how you spend your time, determine how well the tasks you complete contribute to meeting your work goals.

TIME-USE LOG

Name _Michele Fitch_

Day 1 _Monday_ Day 2 _Tuesday_ Day 3 _Wednesday_ Day 4 _Thursday_ Day 5 _Friday_

	Day 1 _Monday_	Day 2 _Tuesday_	Day 3 _Wednesday_	Day 4 _Thursday_	Day 5 _Friday_
8:45 a.m.	arrived early opened office	arrived early opened office	arrived early opened office	arrived early opened office	arrived early opened office
9:00 a.m.	checked calendar, tickler & To Do list	checked calendar, tickler & To Do list	checked calendar, tickler & To Do list	checked calendar, tickler & To Do list	checked calendar, tickler & To Do list
9:15 a.m.	met with supervisor	met with supervisor	keyed meeting notes and report	met with supervisor	met with supervisor
9:30 a.m.	keyed report	keyed letter		organized trip reports	memo to staff
9:45 a.m.		took notes at meeting		keyed trip expense forms	made copies and distributed
10:00 a.m.					
10:15 a.m.			coffee	handled phone call	coffee
10:30 a.m.	coffee break		checked supplies and completed requisition form	coffee break	talked to Nancy
10:45 a.m.	telephone call to confirm Wed. travel	mail arrived	mail arrived	mail arrived	filed
11:00 a.m.	mail arrived	opened/sorted/ distributed	opened/sorted/ distributed	opened/sorted/ distributed	
11:15 a.m.	opened/sorted/ distributed	coffee	talked to Nancy	keyed report	mail arrived
					opened/sorted/

Illus. 10-10. Michele's record of how she used her time each day for one week.

For each activity you have listed in your time-use log, ask yourself if that activity contributed to the satisfactory completion of your job requirements. If not, you need to develop a plan of action to **maximize** the effective use of your time. Use the techniques discussed in this topic as a basis for increasing your time-use effectiveness and as a foundation for developing a systematic approach to your job.

maximize: to increase to the greatest extent possible

QUESTIONS FOR REVIEW

1. Define ergonomics.

2. What is the function of the office workstation?

3. What is the guiding principle you should follow in planning the arrangement of any workstation?

4. Define the term "functional work area."

5. Describe how you can organize your workstation (both surface areas and drawers) to increase your productivity.

6. Discuss the guidelines an office worker should follow when using office equipment, supplies, and accessories.

7. Define time management. Why is time management important to the office worker?

8. Identify and describe common time wasters in the office.

9. Describe the procedures you can use to handle your time obligations effectively.

10. What steps do you take to complete an analysis of how you spend your time?

MAKING DECISIONS

Ana Maria arrived at the office a few minutes early and began to review her "To Do" list for the day. (**Note:** Take time now to review Ana Maria's "To Do" list on page 403.) Her supervisor, Mr. Baldwin, arrived and asked her to come into his office. Ana Maria picked up her notepad and her "To Do" list and followed Mr. Baldwin into his office.

Mr. Baldwin told Ana Maria he had received a call at home last night that the sales meeting scheduled three weeks from today at national headquarters had been moved to the day after tomorrow because of an emergency.

Mr. Baldwin will need to fly to the sales meeting tomorrow and will need 20 copies of the new sales contract form to take with him.

Ana Maria took notes as her supervisor discussed these changes. She also added making the 20 copies of the sales contract form to her "To Do" list. Ana Maria said to Mr. Baldwin: "This definitely changes the priorities for today."

What You Are To Do: Your teacher will divide you into groups to discuss the changes Ana Maria needs to make in her priority list. As a group, decide the new order of priorities needed to reflect the change in her supervisor's schedule. Use a sheet of plain paper to prepare a revised "To Do" list.

EXTENDING YOUR ENGLISH COMPETENCIES

You work in the Human Resources Department of Raleigh Corporation, a manufacturer of modular business furniture. Your supervisor, Florita Langford, has prepared a punctuation test to be administered to job applicants. She asks you to complete the punctuation test (shown on page 409) to make sure the instructions are clear before she has large quantities of the test printed.

What You Are To Do: Follow the instruction on the test. Use a plain sheet of paper. If necessary, refer to Reference Section B, Punctuation.

APPLICATION ACTIVITY

As you have learned in this topic, managing your time on the job and developing an orderly approach to your work are important elements in your job productivity. You can begin now to develop the habits of proper time management and orderly arrangement of your work. This will be beneficial to you as you continue your education and also will be helpful in any occupation you choose. In this activity you will complete a daily time log. When you have charted your activities, you will use your chart to help you determine your most and least productive time periods.

What You Are To Do: ● Use the Time-Use Log in *Information Processing Activities* or prepare a time-use log similar to the one shown on page 406 using a sheet of plain 8 $\frac{1}{2}$″ x 11″ paper. Use 15-minute time intervals, and prepare the chart to cover your entire waking day; for example, 6:30 a.m. until 11:00 p.m.

- Complete your time-use log. If you start Day 1 on Monday, for example, write *Monday* in the blank following Day 1. Try to record your activities every 15 minutes as you progress through your day and evening. Record all your activities: studying, attending class, watching TV, talking on the telephone, eating, and so on.
- Analyze your time log and then summarize your analysis.
  Analyze: Identify the hours where you used your time most productively as well as those hours where you wasted your time. During what hours of the day do you get the most accomplished? During what hours of the day do you tend to waste your time?
  Summarize: Write a two- or three-paragraph summary of your analysis of your time-use log. Use your comments from your analysis above as a starting point for your summary.

Punctuation Test to be used with EXTENDING YOUR ENGLISH COMPETENCIES

PUNCTUATION TEST

Each of the following statements is a sentence. Key each sentence and insert appropriate punctuation mark(s).

1. A workstation should be arranged to meet each workers needs
2. Modular furniture is made up of standard interchangeable modules for example sound absorbing wall panels
3. Modular furniture is usually used with an open office plan however it can be used with any office plan
4. Keep the following general reference sources available at all times dictionary telephone directory and office reference manual
5. When preventive maintenance is practiced quality work often depends on the condition of your equipment you can expect your equipment to perform well over a long period of time
6. While at work do you use your time effectively
7. Completing a monthly marketing report should become a high priority if your supervisor says please have the final draft of this report ready in two hours
8. Proper lighting sound and climate at your workstation contribute to your productivity
9. Its wise to periodically ask yourself How do I waste my time
10. Socializing occasionally will help you maintain good working relations socializing excessively is an abuse of company time

TOPIC 2

REPROGRAPHIC SYSTEMS AND PROCEDURES

When you have completed your study of this topic, you will be able to:

- explain how office copiers are classified

- identify common copier features and operating procedures

- explain how to control copier supplies and operating procedures

- prepare materials to be copied

- describe phototypesetting/imaging and its uses

Reprographics is the process of making copies of documents and other items. Businesses have different needs for reprographic services, depending upon the size of the business and the types of documents to be reproduced.

Large organizations frequently have a reprographics center where materials are sent to be reproduced. In this setting, you would prepare the original from which the copies are made. You would also use special forms to give detailed instructions to reprographics personnel. Organizations often have a minimum number of copies that will be made by the reprographics center. Smaller copy-

ing jobs are handled by individual employees using *convenience copiers* located throughout the business.

Small organizations do not usually have a reprographics center. In this setting, you would be responsible not only for preparing the original but also for making the copies.

No matter the size of the organization, you need to know the capabilities of reprographic equipment you are likely to find on the job. You should also be familiar with advances in reprographics technology, including phototypesetting/ imaging and desktop publishing.

**OFFICE
PHOTO-
COPIERS**

Photocopiers, also called *copiers*, are types of reprographic equipment that produce copies directly from an original. The original can be handwritten, keyboarded, printed, or drawn. You can produce copies quickly using a photocopier, and the quality of the copy is excellent if the machine is in good condition.

Photocopiers are found extensively in business offices today, and they are used by almost all employees. You will find that much of the activity in the business office centers around preparing, distributing, and storing copied materials. Photocopiers like the one shown in Illus. 10-11 are found in many offices because they are convenient and versatile. For example, many models reproduce onto one or both sides of a sheet of paper and can copy onto letterhead paper, mailing labels, bond paper, and colored paper.

Electrostatic Copying Process

photoconductive:
sensitive to light

The most commonly used copying process is the **electrostatic process**. The electrostatic process involves copying the image of the original onto paper by means of an electrical charge to a ***photoconductive*** surface. The electrical charge produces a magnetic field which attracts an image of the original.

Illus. 10-11. Many businesses have convenience copiers located throughout the business for employee use.

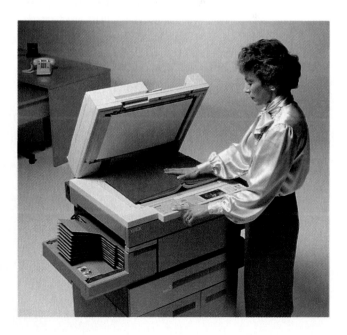

Reprographic Technology

Advances in technology continue to improve the reprographic process. Advances include optic fibers, laser beams, and microprocessors. Optic fibers are thin glass rods that transmit light. Laser beams are highly focused streams of red light. In both processes, the light is used to transfer the image of an original onto a photosensitive surface and, finally, to paper.

Microprocessors select the sequence of operations and proper paper arrangements based on the copier function chosen by the machine operator. Microprocessors also perform **diagnostic** functions such as alerting the machine operator to paper jams and low levels of paper.

diagnostic: determining the nature of a problem

ELECTRONIC COPIER/ PRINTERS

Electronic copier/printers, sometimes called *intelligent copiers*, can receive, transmit, store, print, and copy data. Microprocessor technology enables these copier/printers to produce copies from sources such as word or data processors, graphic scanners, or even pictures. For example, you may key material at your computer terminal, proofread the copy, and then transmit it electronically to the copier/printer in a reprographics center where the copies will be printed.

Electronic copier/printers can easily be commanded to use specific print fonts, justify lines, number pages, or insert graphics within the text material. Electronic copier/printers are available with speeds ranging from 10 to 200 pages a minute. Companies that **generate** reports and forms in large quantities find the electronic copier/printer to be cost effective.

generate: produce

Illus. 10-12. Electronic copier/printers can produce large quantities of copies at very high speeds.

COPIER CLASSIFICA-TIONS

Copiers can be classified according to their capacity: low, mid, high, and duplicating (see Illus. 10-13). Copier capacity is usually determined by two factors: speed (copies produced per minute) and volume (copies produced per month). As an office worker, you should know the capacities of your company's copiers so that you can select the best copier for the task at hand.

Kevin is a new employee at Textron, Inc. His supervisor, Paula, is explaining the features and capacities of each copier available for Kevin's use. Paula emphasizes that choosing the most appropriate copier for each copying job is an important step. She hands Kevin two copying jobs. One is a 10-page proposal requiring one photocopy. The other is a 55-page report requiring six photocopies. Paula asks Kevin to choose the copiers that will complete each job most efficiently. Based on what Kevin has learned about the company's copiers, he knows it is most efficient to copy the 10-page proposal on the low-capacity copier and the 55-page report on the high-capacity copier.

Illus. 10-13. Select the most appropriate copier for the task at hand.

COPIER CAPACITY	SPEED	VOLUME	COPIER USAGE
	Copies a Minute	Copies a Month	
Low	up to 20	up to 20,000	Low-capacity copiers are frequently the desk-top convenience copiers located close to the employees who use them. A low-capacity copier may be the only copier needed by a small business.
Mid	between 21 and 50	up to 60,000	The trend in mid-capacity copiers is to allow companies to select those features that meet the needs of the work group. Thus, by using a modular approach, a company can develop a custom-copying system by selecting from a group of available special features.
High	between 51 and 90	between 50,000 and 100,000	High-capacity copiers typically are found in centralized locations such as reprographic centers. The copiers are floor-console models and generally have a full range of special features as standard components.
Duplicating	over 90	between 50,000 and 200,000	Copier/duplicators produce excellent copies and do not require the specialized labor that the more traditional processes require. As with high-capacity models, special features are standard components to reduce labor needs and to increase productivity.

**COPIER
FEATURES**

Special features designed to meet specific copying needs and to increase the user's productivity are available on many copiers. Most of the copiers you will use will offer several of the following features, which are only a few of the many features available. The symbols in Illus. 10-14 are standard symbols used on copiers to represent a specific function or activity.

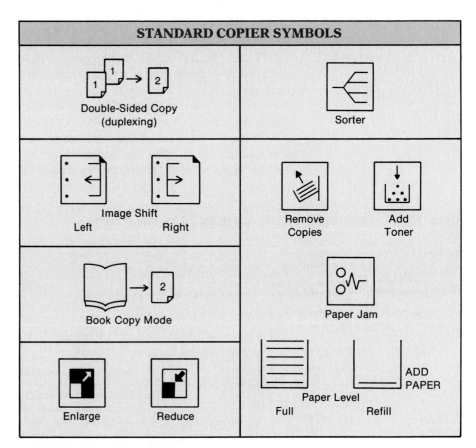

Illus. 10-14. You will quickly learn to interpret these standard copier symbols.

Automatic Duplexing

The duplexing feature allows you to copy on both sides of the paper. This feature saves paper and lessens the weight and, therefore, postage costs of mailings.

Automatic Image Shift

This feature creates a margin on one or both sides of the copy paper to allow space for three-hole punching or for binding the copies (both single-sided and duplexed copies). For example, if you have a letter that needs to be copied and included in a bound report, the automatic image shift feature will provide the space for the extra left margin without losing any portion of the letter.

Book Copy Mode

The book copy mode allows you to copy both pages of an open book or magazine onto the front and back of a single sheet of copy paper. This feature allows rapid copying of bound material and saves paper.

Image Enlargement and Reduction

Some copiers allow you to make the print size of a photocopy larger or smaller than the print size of the original document. For example, some copiers are capable of 102 to 140 percent enlargement, which produces a copy 2 to 40 percent larger than the original. A range of 66 to 88 percent reduction produces a copy 12 to 34 percent smaller than the original.

Sorter

The sorter feature enables the copier to automatically collate the copies. *Collating* is the process of integrating or arranging the copies in order. Copiers with 10-, 15-, or 20-bin sorters are typical. Using a copier with a sorter to collate 10 copies of a 50-page report is much more efficient than collating the copies by hand.

Automatic and Semiautomatic Document Feed

On some copiers you must lift the copier lid, place each original on the glass surface, close the lid, and instruct the copier to make the required number of copies. With automatic document feed, you place the stack of originals in the receiving tray, and the copier automatically feeds the originals into the copier. With semi-automatic document feed, you feed one original at a time through the receiving tray. However, the copier lid can still be lifted for easy copying of books, three-dimensional objects, and oversized originals.

Self-Diagnosis

Most copiers can self-diagnose common technical problems. When a problem occurs, a symbol or message indicating the nature of the problem is displayed. For example, if copy paper jams as it feeds through the machine, the copier may display a paper jam symbol similar to the one shown in Illus. 10-14 on page 414. Or if the paper supply drawer is not closed properly, the copier may display a message similar to the shown in Illus. 10-15. With the self-diagnosis feature, the operator knows immediately the cause of a problem and does not waste time *troubleshooting*.

troubleshooting:
determining the cause of a problem

Illus. 10-15. The message displayed tells the office worker to please close the upper paper supply drawer. Then the copier will be ready to make the three copies requested.

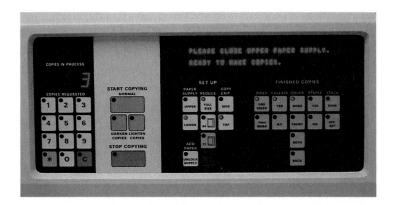

Color

Some copiers can make color copies using removable toner cartridges of different colors. Color copiers can prepare colorful graphs, charts, brochures, and transparencies. Some advanced color copiers can produce high-quality copies from photographs, slides, film negatives, and transparencies.

Image Editing

The image editing feature allows you to change images on a photocopy without permanently changing the original document. You can select a block of text or an illustration and highlight it, add color to it, or delete it. These modifications will appear in the photocopy only; the original will remain the same. Image editing uses digital technology to electronically "cut and paste." Cutting and pasting is the process of manually cutting a block of text with scissors and pasting it with tape or rubber cement to the desired location on the page. A photocopy is then made of the page to get a clean copy.

CONTROLLING COPIER SUPPLIES

Office employees need to be knowledgeable about the proper use and selection of reprographic supplies. You will find that the selection of paper, toner, and other supplies can significantly affect the per-copy price of reproduction. All employees are expected to follow closely the recommendations of the vendor or manufacturer when using copier supplies in order to control costs.

Various kinds of paper can be used in the photocopier. Copier paper typically is purchased by the *ream* (500 sheets of paper), and it is good to keep several reams on hand. You will need to know the proper paper to use for the copiers you have in your office and for the particular copying job you need to do. Instructions for using special-purpose paper products, such as address labels, reinforced binder paper, and non-tear sheets, are provided with the product. Follow these operating instructions to achieve maximum effectiveness when using any special-purpose, paper-copying product.

Most copiers display a message when it is time to replace supplies such as the toner cartridge or developer cartridge. For supplies such as these that are replaced infrequently, a general practice is to keep only one or two of each type on hand. That way, valuable storage space can be used for more frequently used supplies such as various sizes and colors of paper that are used in larger quantities.

Illus. 10-16. Use copier supplies that are recommended for your type of copier.

**CONTROLLING
OPERATING
PROCEDURES**

Without adequate controls, copying costs can rise dramatically. If a company has convenience copiers located throughout the building, it is easier for copy misuse to occur. Employees who do not know how to operate the equipment properly may damage the copier or misuse supplies.

> *When Larry found that there was no paper in the copier, he added two reams to the paper bin. Before he had run off three copies, the machine was jammed. He was upset and sought help from Robin, a coworker. When Robin checked the paper bin, she said, "You haven't inserted the paper under the guides correctly." Larry responded, "Oh, is there a special way to place the paper in the bin?" Robin then showed Larry how the paper should be placed in the bin so that it will be guided into the copier correctly.*

Management often takes steps to control operating procedures. The steps most often instituted are the use of centralized copying, monitoring devices, a copy log, or individual user guidelines.

Centralized Copying

Companies with large reprographic needs will centralize the reprographic equipment to control the number of copies made and to make the best use of the equipment. Companies provide guidelines for using centralized reprographic services to assure quality production, proper equipment use, and economy of use.

allocate: assign

Companies often use a chargeback procedure to **allocate** copying costs to the individual or department responsible for the copying. If you have the task of submitting items to a central reprographics center for copying, you may be required to complete a reprographic request form similar to the one shown in Illus. 10-17.

Monitoring Devices

To gain better control over their copying equipment and to reduce the number of unaccountable copies, management will place monitor devices on their convenience copiers. You cannot operate the copier without the monitoring device. Various types of monitors are available from simple mechanical counters to electronic recorders.

Illus. 10-17.
Companies with centralized reprographics centers may require you to fill out a form to request reprographic services.

REQUEST FOR REPROGRAPHIC SERVICES

DEPARTMENT _Advertising_

ACCOUNT CODE _341_

SUBMITTED   Date _3/16/--_ Time _10:00_

NEEDED   Date _3/18/--_ Time _3:00_

JOB NO._____

TOTAL ORIGINALS_____

TOTAL COPIES_____

TOTAL CHARGE_____

(For Reprographic Center Use)

SUBMITTED BY _Amy Santos_ ____ ROOM NO. _418_ EXT. _5174_

APPROVED BY _Cory Roe_

Number of Originals	Description	Paper Size		Duplex	Tot. Copies Per Orig.	TOTAL COPIES
		Letter	Legal			
1	Letter	✓			150	150
12	Report	✓		✓	150	1800

_____ Colored Paper: _____ Canary _report only_ ✓ _____Buff _____Blue _____Green _____Pink

_____ Colored Cover Stock: ✓ _____Buff _____Blue _____Green

✓ Collate _report_

✓ Staple No._1_ ; Location_____ _upper left corner_

✓ Call when ready for pick-up

_____ Return by interoffice mail

_____ SPECIAL INSTRUCTIONS _Use buff cover stock for front and back covers of the report._

Copy Log

A common copier control procedure is the copier log book. When a copier log book is used, you are expected to record information ***pertaining*** to your copy job in a log similar to the one shown in Illus. 10-18 on page 420. To complete the log, you would:

pertaining: relating to

1. Record your name as the person making the copy.
2. Record the name of the person/department for whom the copies are being made.
3. Record the number of originals.
4. Record the number of copies per original.
5. Record the total copies made.
6. Record any special features used.

Illus. 10-18. Copier logs help control costs.

COPY LOG

Machine _Copier 2_

Name	Person/Department	Number of Originals	Number of Copies Per Original	Total Copies	Special Instructions
J. Talbert	Customer Service	4	5	20	collate
J. Talbert	Customer Service	20	10	200	duplex collate
C. Krane	Accounting	1	23	23	shift left
K. Lyle	President Votaw	2	25	50	book mode

User Guidelines

Another way to control copying is to establish guidelines for employees who use copiers. As a responsible employee, you should follow these five general guidelines:

1. Follow company policy regarding the maximum number of copies to be made at convenience copiers. Large copier needs are best handled through centralized reprographic services, when available.
2. Be cost conscious when planning to use the copier:
   - Use the economy features of the copier, such as duplexing, to save file space, postage costs, and work time.
   - Never run off more copies than you need or rerun copies to see if you can get a better one.

explicitly: clearly

3. Comply with copyright laws. Copyright laws list ***explicitly*** those documents that cannot be copied. These documents include money, postage stamps, United States securities, birth certificates, passports, draft cards, drivers' licenses, automobile registrations, and certificates of title.
4. Do not make copies for personal use.
5. Practice good housekeeping rules and common courtesy when using the copier. Always clean up the area after you have completed your copying project. If you have a long copy job and another worker needs a priority copy, stop at a convenient point and let the other person have access to the machine. If you need a few copies and someone else is near

the end of a long copying job, wait until the other person is finished to make your copies.

To obtain attractive copies, care must be taken when preparing documents to be reproduced. The following guidelines will help you achieve professional-looking copies.

Originals/Masters

Even the most attractive format can be ruined if you do not give attention to the actual preparation of the original on your typewriter or word processor. The print wheel, printing element, or keys should be clean to produce clear, sharp characters. Use white bond paper with a dark ribbon (preferably a carbon ribbon). Handle your original carefully. Smudges and smears can show up on the copy. Unless your copier reproduces to the edge of an original, leave at least a one-fourth-inch margin on all sides of your original.

Correction Techniques

Proofread the original carefully. One mistake on an original from which you make 100 copies magnifies that mistake a hundred times. If you do not have electronic equipment or a typewriter with a correction ribbon, make corrections using white-out or correction tape. When using liquid white-out, make sure the fluid is thin enough that it will not mound up when it dries. Allow the fluid time to dry before making the correction. Correction tape can be used to cover entire lines of copy and can be typed upon immediately after its application.

Equipment Checks

To achieve excellent copies, you must keep the equipment operating at peak performance. Know your copier and follow the directions for using it. If the copies are too light or too dark, adjust the exposure control. If your copier does not have an automatic feed, position the original carefully so that copies do not appear to be run at an angle. If spots appear on your copies, check the glass surface to see if it is clean. Do not remove paper clips and staples over the machine, because they may fall into a machine opening.

Illus. 10-19. An occasional paper jam is easily remedied by an employee knowledgeable about the equipment.

Do your share to keep the copier in excellent condition. If the *add paper* indicator comes on, fill the paper bin properly before leaving. If you use special paper, remove your special paper before leaving. Return the regular paper to the paper tray. If you have a paper jam and are not authorized to remove or troubleshoot the equipment, get the key operator (person knowledgeable about the equipment). Do not leave the copier in a *down* condition without informing the key operator or your supervisor.

TYPESETTING

Phototypesetting is a photographic process used to set text and art into special columns and widths. Businesses use phototypesetting to create items such as newsletters, pamphlets, and advertisements.

A phototypesetter workstation looks much like a word processor, as shown in Illus. 10-20. The operator keys in copy and uses command keys and codes to input format instructions. The document is printed, then cut and pasted into the desired arrangement. The final document is then printed. This cutting and pasting process is called *page composition*.

Newer phototypesetters, called *photocompositors*, can complete the page composition process electronically, eliminating the need for manual cutting and pasting. Photocompositors have both photographic typesetting and text editing capabilities.

Illus. 10-20. Phototypesetting combines text and art to produce items such as pamphlets and advertisements.

As an office worker, you may have an opportunity to use a phototypesetter to help prepare documents for your company. There is much room for creativity when preparing these types of documents.

Imaging

Imaging is a new, general term that refers to the process of reproducing the image of a page. It is replacing the specific term phototypesetting, which is one type of imaging process. This new wording is an example of how modern technology creates changes in terminology.

Desktop Publishing

Businesses that have large printing jobs, such as newspaper or magazine publishers, usually have their own phototypesetters or photocompositors. Businesses that have occasional typesetting jobs may use commercial services or *in-house* desktop publishing systems.

in-house: within the company

As you have learned, documents can be prepared on microcomputers using desktop publishing software programs. Companies are finding that desktop publishing is an economical way to create a variety of documents, including letterhead, forms, and newsletters (see Illus. 10-21 on page 424). The cost of desktop publishing is low compared to traditional phototypesetting, and interest in desktop publishing is increasing rapidly as costs decrease. Also, using desktop publishing to create, arrange, and print documents in-house is much faster than using commercial services.

Illus. 10-21.
Newsletters are a common desktop publishing application.

QUESTIONS FOR REVIEW

1. What is reprographics?

2. Explain the electrostatic copying process.

3. Name two technological advances which have improved the reprographic process.

4. Copier capacity is usually determined by what two factors?

5. Identify and describe five common features found on office copiers.

6. Explain how you would photocopy a thirty-page document using a copier with automatic document feed.

7. Describe two methods of controlling copier operating procedures.

8. Identify and describe two user guidelines you should follow to help control copying operations.

9. Describe the phototypesetting process.

10. What are advantages of using desktop publishing rather than commercial services or traditional phototypesetting?

INTERACTING WITH OTHERS

Theresa McAuliffe, office manager, is concerned about the large increase in copier expenses. She asked her administrative assistant, John, to determine the reasons for the increase.

For several weeks, John observed the traffic flow to the copier and the types of documents being copied. He found that employees were making more copies of documents than were actually needed. They were also copying on only one side of the paper when duplexing could have been used. Also, some employees were using the more expensive colored paper when white paper would have been sufficient. John also discovered that employees were making copies of personal documents.

To overcome these problems, Ms. McAuliffe suggested and the president agreed that everyone, including the president, should bring all copying jobs to you, the newly hired reprographics clerk. You are instructed by Ms. McAuliffe to record on a copy log the date, the number of copies made, and the person for whom copies were made. All of the employees except Susan Franklin, vice president, now follow this procedure. Mrs. Franklin walks past your desk directly to the copier and makes her own copies. Sometimes she records the information on the copy log and sometimes she does not.

You realize that at the end of the month the number of copies on the copier counter will not be the same as the number of copies on your copy log. What factors should you consider in attempting to correct this situation? How will you handle this situation?

What You Are To Do: Prepare a brief response to the questions raised.

EXTENDING YOUR MATH COMPETENCIES

You work in the reprographics center of Livingston Productions. Management is in the process of preparing a budget for the upcoming year. Your task is to provide data regarding the operation of the office copiers. This information will be useful in determining next year's budget for the reprographics center.

Livingston Productions bought the copiers five years ago. During that time, 763,978 copies were made at an average cost of $.043 per copy.

What You Are To Do: Calculate the average copies made per year, month, and day. Then calculate the average copying costs per year, month, and day (round your answers to two decimal places). Finally, determine the total costs since the copiers were purchased. Record your answers on a sheet of plain paper.

AVERAGE NUMBER OF COPIES

Total Copies in 5 years   =   763,978

Average Copies per Year   =   _____
   (Total Copies ÷ 5 years)

Average Copies per Month   =   _____
   (Total Copies ÷ Number of months in 5 years)

Average Copies per Day   =   _____
   (Total Copies ÷ Number of days in 5 years,
   assuming there are 30 days in each month)

AVERAGE COST OF COPIES

Average Cost per Copy   = $.043

Average Cost per Year   =   _____
   (Average Cost per Copy ✕ Average Copies per Year)

Average Cost per Month   =   _____
   (Average Cost per Copy ✕ Average Copies per Month)

Average Cost per Day   =   _____
   (Average Cost per Copy ✕ Average Copies per Day)

TOTAL COST OF COPIES

Total Cost Since Copiers
Were Purchased   =   _____
   (Average Cost per Copy ✕ Total Copies)

APPLICATION ACTIVITIES

Activity 1

Schools, as well as companies, have reprographic equipment to help employees complete tasks efficiently. For example, your school administration may prepare a packet that explains school regulations, class registration procedures, and school holidays. The packet would be reproduced for each student. A letter announcing an open house at your school may be photocopied and mailed to your home. A schedule listing school activities, such as student council meetings and sporting events, may be photocopied and posted in each classroom. Also, teachers may use reprographic equipment to reproduce student handouts and tests.

Word processing
equipment can be used
to complete this activity.

What You Are To Do: Prepare a one-page report about the reprographic equipment available in your school. For each piece of equipment, include the brand name, location, features, and controls and procedures used (such as monitoring devices and copy logs).

Activity 2

You are an office assistant to Jane Hisle, manager of reprographics services for Intercontinental Insurance. Ms. Hisle has been working all morning on a draft of a memo to be distributed to all department managers regarding changes in reprographic services. She hands you the draft and says: "I've finally finished it! Please key this memo and run off enough copies for all department managers in our headquarters building. On second thought, you'd better let me review the memo before you photocopy it."

You key the memo and hand it to Ms. Hisle as directed. A few minutes later, she returns the memo and says: "It's a good thing I asked to see this memo one more time. I've found a few changes that need to be made before it's photocopied and distributed." You then use correction procedures to make the necessary changes before the memo is photocopied.

Word processing
equipment can be used
to complete this activity.

What You Are To Do:
- Key a copy of the memorandum on page 428 *without* making the changes noted. Use memo stationery in *Information Processing Activities* or plain paper. This document now represents the memo you handed to Ms. Hisle for review. Assume that she then edited the document and returned it to you.
- Revise the memorandum, incorporating the changes marked by Ms. Hisle.

TO: All Department Heads (Headquarters Building)

FROM: Jane V. Hisle, Manager, Reprographic Services

DATE: November 11, 19--

SUBJECT: ~~Changes~~ *Improvements* in Reprographic Services

The Reprographic Center is planning some changes which will be of
interest to you and your staff. New equipment is being procured
to improve the services available and to make ~~reductions in cost~~ *cost reductions*
possible:

1. Copy services are being expanded to provide a greater selection.

The mid-capacity copier is being replaced with a high-capacity
model. This machine will provide high-quality copies. It will
provide reduction capability, duplexing (front and back), and collating with the push of a button. The price for copies will
remain the same until we have an opportunity to complete the actual cost comparisons. We do, however, anticipate ~~reduction in~~
~~costs shortly~~ *cost reductions soon*

Legal papers can be printed as letter size on the high-capacity
model. Computer printouts can be reduced to legal size, and two
letter-size originals can be reduced to one letter-size copy.
This reduction capability, along with the ability to print two
originals on one sheet, should not only reduce costs but should
reduce printing time.

One or two low-capacity, convenience copiers with control monitors
will be added in the reprographics center. The chargeback price
per copy will be $.04 for letter size and $.05 for legal size.
Copies on these machines should be limited to no more than ~~20~~ *15*
copies per original.

2. An added service will be equipment to make 16-mm microfiche
frames from originals. Each microfiche will hold up to 64 pages.

Most of the changes listed above will be in effect by January 1.
We would be happy for you and/or your staff to visit us and let us
show you some possible uses of this new equipment.

xx

*Some convenience copiers will be retained
in selected locations at the same chargeback
price for quick, readable copies.*

TOPIC 3

OFFICE SAFETY AND SECURITY

When you have completed your study of this topic, you will be able to:

- describe positive safety attitudes important for office employees

- identify ways to make your workstation safer

- describe emergency safety procedures

- explain how you can assure your personal security on the job

- describe how building and office security measures contribute to the security of all employees

Most of us think of the office as a safe place to work. Office workers are not required to use heavy equipment or power tools. Office workers are not exposed to poisonous chemicals or dangerous working conditions. Yet thousands of office workers have disabling accidents each year. Falling, tripping, or slipping account for more than half of all office accidents. Common causes of falls include drawers partially open, slippery floors, torn or loose carpeting, obstructions on stairs or in walkways, and dangling telephone or electrical cords.

Other causes of office accidents include faulty or poorly maintained equipment, collisions and obstructions, falling objects, fire and electrical hazards, and human carelessness. Potential safety problems can exist in any office. With knowledge of correct safety procedures, however, you can learn how to correct potential safety problems and prevent injury to yourself and your coworkers.

The purpose of office security is to provide protection for office workers and office property. The degree and form of the security will depend on such factors as the nature of the business and building location and design.

The effectiveness of a company's program for security depends on the cooperation of all employees. You will want to understand the procedures used in the company where you choose to work so that you will contribute to the safety and security of everyone.

Accident prevention in the office depends on knowledgeable and responsible office employees. Employees who develop positive safety attitudes are able to detect potential safety problems and take steps to eliminate them.

You can develop a positive safety attitude if you understand that you, as an employee, are largely responsible for your safety. Excuses are not acceptable explanations for accidents.

Awareness/Knowledge

To many people, the office seems to hold little danger. Becoming aware of the potential safety hazards in an office is the first step to gaining control over unsafe procedures and conditions. Increasing your practical knowledge of preventive measures will give you specific techniques for eliminating safety problems in the office environment. A safe and secure office environment is important to the physical and mental well-being of all workers.

Accident Prevention Approach

Unfortunately, accident control often is imposed only after an accident occurs. However, attention is needed *before* accidents occur so emphasis will be on preventing the undesirable incident from occurring in the first place. This is an accident prevention approach.

Molly came around the corner with her arms full of supplies for the supply cabinet. She could not see very well where she was going since her arms were loaded with supplies. She should not have been trying to carry so much, but she was trying to save a few steps and not have to make a second trip.

Laverne looked up from the phone to see Molly just a few feet from her open file drawer. When Laverne realized that Molly could not see where she was walking, she called, "Watch out!" Too late—Molly fell with a loud crash over the bottom file drawer. X-rays showed that Molly had broken her wrist when trying to catch herself in the fall. Molly was unable to resume her full duties for eight weeks.

This accident could have been prevented if Molly and Laverne had acted responsibly. Laverne should have closed the file drawer, and Molly should have carried the supplies in two trips rather than in one.

Most office employees spend the majority of their working time at their workstations. The wise safety practices you use at your own workstation will repay you in personal safety benefits. As you begin your office career, start immediately to practice the following safety pointers.

Surface Areas

As you work, you will occasionally use scissors and other sharp objects. Place these objects away from the edge of your workstation so they will not be knocked off easily. Avoid eating or drinking at your desk. An overturned drink can ruin hours of hard work! Pencils stored on the top of your desk with the sharp points up are dangerous. Pencils are best stored flat or with points down.

Use a staple remover, rather than your fingernail, to remove staples. Never examine a jammed stapler by holding it near your eyes or testing it over your finger.

Workstation Drawers

accumulate: collect

Keep your workstation drawers neat. Do not allow papers to *accumulate* to the point of clutter. If the drawers are cluttered, your hands could easily be punctured by hidden scissors, pins, or pencils. Sharp objects such as pins and thumbtacks should be placed in closed containers.

Even with these precautions, never reach blindly into a desk drawer or file drawer. This can happen easily if you are rushed or are talking to someone.

Close workstation and file drawers by the handle. Don't push a drawer shut by placing your hand at the top or side of the drawer. You may lose a fingernail or suffer a crushed finger or hand.

Chairs

Most office chairs have *casters*, which are small wheels that provide ease of movement for the worker. This same ease of movement can produce painful injury unless you look at the chair and hold onto the chair arms or seat as you sit down. When seated, be careful not to lean too far forward or backward so that you will not flip out of the chair.

Illus. 10-22. How many potential safety problems can you identify?

Chair Mats/Static Control Mats

A *chair mat* is a vinyl pad placed underneath the chair to eliminate wear on the carpet from the rolling back and forth of the chair. Static control mats are designed for use on floors underneath workstations and computer monitors. The purpose of the static control mat is to safeguard valuable computer data and electronic equipment from possible harm from a charge of static electricity.

Chair mats and static control mats can cause you to trip, particularly if the edges are beginning to curl. Replace worn mats when they become a hazard.

WORK AREA SAFETY

In addition to your workstation, other objects in your immediate work area can either add to your comfort and work productivity or become a source of injury.

Office Furnishings

Learn how to use small furnishings such as a step stool and paper cutter. In using a step stool with casters, step firmly in the middle of the stool. Never step to the side because this can cause the stool to slide out from under you. When using the paper cutter, keep your fingers away from the blade and never leave the blade up. Furniture with rough or sharp edges should be sanded or taped to prevent injury to employees and to prevent clothing from being torn.

conversely: reversed in order

File drawers should be filled beginning with the bottom drawer of the cabinet and moving to the top drawer of the cabinet. **Conversely**, file cabinet drawers should be emptied beginning with the top drawer of the cabinet and moving to the bottom drawer of the cabinet. When working with file cabinets, pull out only *one* drawer at a time so that you do not change the cabinet's center of gravity and cause the cabinet to tip over.

Electrical Equipment

proliferated: grown rapidly

The number of small electrical appliances and equipment has **proliferated** in many of today's business offices. Business equipment such as electric staplers, electric pencil sharpeners, electric hole punchers, deskside paper shredders, and electric copyholders adds to the convenience of office workers.

With the increase in small electrical equipment and computer equipment in the office, many cords and cables become a safety hazard. Cables and cords should never extend into traffic areas. Do not overload electrical outlets. If necessary, purchase a device made specifically for multiple plugs. An extension cord should be used only to extend the position of the electrical appliance, not to increase the power load.

General Office Equipment

You will want to keep the following safety procedures in mind when you use office equipment:

- When operating office equipment, follow the manufacturer's directions for safe and efficient equipment usage.
- If you are operating equipment, avoid other activities, such as talking, which will distract you from the operation of the equipment.

- If you have a tingling sensation, notice smoke, or smell something burning while you are operating the equipment, turn the equipment off and report the problem to your supervisor immediately.
- Know where the power switch is located on the equipment in your general area.

Computer Monitors

Working safely and comfortably at your computer monitor depends in large part on how you care for your vision. Common symptoms of eyestrain are teary or burning eyes, blurred vision, and headaches. Learning proper eye-care habits can help reduce eyestrain as you work at your monitor.

Place antiglare filters similar to the one shown in Illus. 10-23 over the monitor screen. Filters reduce glare, static electricity, and dirt and smudge buildup on the screen. Adjust the screen brightness to a contrast level that is comfortable for you. Adjust the screen angle so that it is at eye level or slightly lower. Also, minimize the glare on the monitor screen by placing your monitor away from windows or other bright light sources. Remember to occasionally clean the screen with an antistatic cloth to remove dust, dirt, and fingerprints.

Illus. 10-23.
Antiglare filters reduce the glare and reflection that cause eyestrain.

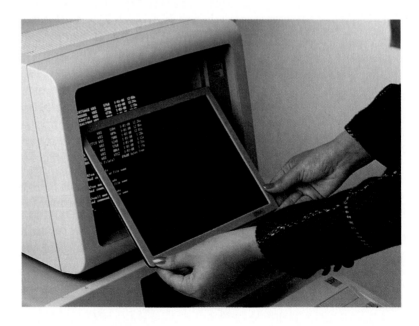

EMERGENCY PROCEDURES

Learn emergency procedures immediately upon beginning a new job. If your office does not have established procedures, do what you can to help initiate practices such as those described in the following paragraphs.

Emergency Telephone Numbers

Emergency telephone numbers are used to seek help for an immediate, dangerous situation. The primary emergency telephone numbers are the police department, fire department, ambulance, operator and, where available, a general emergency number such as 911.

Emergency telephone numbers should be posted beside each telephone or, ideally, stored in each telephone's memory. The memory feature saves valuable time in an emergency. You press only one or two buttons, and the telephone automatically dials the number.

First Aid Procedures

First aid kits should be located conveniently within the office. They should be inspected frequently and restocked whenever supplies are used from the kit.

Some firms will send an employee from each floor or work group for first aid training and/or CPR (cardiopulmonary resuscitation) classes. These courses are given periodically by the American Red Cross. Each employee should know who has completed first aid training and who is qualified to help in the critical

Illus. 10-24.
Everyone in the office should know which employees are trained in first aid and CPR.

first minutes of an emergency. First aid posters can be put in **conspicuous** places to further assist employees.

Fires

Some companies prohibit the use of appliances such as cup warmers and space heaters because of their potential fire hazard. If appliances are allowed in your office, always unplug them when they are not in use and before leaving the office. Know the locations of the nearest fire exit, fire alarm box, and fire extinguisher. Large office buildings generally have the fire alarm boxes and fire extinguishers in the same location patterns on each floor. Learn how to use the fire extinguisher and know the type of fire it is intended to put out. Never attempt to fight a fire alone. Always have someone report the fire to the proper agency.

Building Evacuation Plans

Learn the established escape routes and **evacuation** procedures. Emergency exit routes should be posted in conspicuous places throughout the building. Employees should know their individual responsibilities during a drill or evacuation. Who, for example, is responsible for checking conference rooms, rest rooms, and other areas where the alarm may not be heard?

PERSONAL SECURITY ON THE JOB

Protection of yourself and your property requires a continuous **vigil** on your part. Most businesses strive to provide a safe and secure work environment for their employees. To **complement** the company's effort in providing for your safety and security on the job, you should always use good common sense.

Protecting Personal Property

A purse left at a workstation, a jacket slung over the back of a chair or left in an unoccupied office, cash left out in plain sight—all are invitations to a would-be thief. Keep personal belongings out of sight and locked up in a drawer, file cabinet, or employee locker or closet. The key to this drawer or other receptacle should be issued only to the employee who is assigned its use.

Working Alone

Sometimes you may find it necessary to stay late at the office or to come in early. If your company has established security measures, follow the company procedures for being in the building during non-working hours.

abide: stick to it

If no after-hours procedures exist, establish your own security routine and ***abide*** by it. Follow these security procedures when you work alone:

- Always work near a phone and keep emergency telephone numbers handy.
- Lock all doors to your work area. Do not open the door to anyone you are not expecting or cannot identify.
- Get to know the cleaning staff and when to expect them.
- If you use the elevator to leave the building, do not enter the elevator if anyone is in it whom you have reason to suspect.
- Avoid using a rest room that is located away from your work area.
- When working late, phone home before leaving the office to let someone know what time they can expect you. If you live alone, call a friend before leaving the office and again when you get home to let her or him know you've arrived safely.
- Park your car near the building entrance and/or near a parking lot light. Check the parking lot visually before leaving the building. Have your car keys in your hand and ready to use. In some organizations, security personnel are available to escort you to your car.

BUILDING AND OFFICE SECURITY

safeguards: protection

Building and office security measures are necessary ***safeguards***. Casual consideration of security measures today has been replaced by a more serious approach to planning and analyzing security needs. Crime and fire are the two major security concerns of a business.

Controlling Outsider Access

Although businesses cannot operate without being open to the public, the public does not need open and uncontrolled access to all parts of most office buildings.

Businesses use varied security means to safeguard their personnel and assets. In large metropolitan areas, for example, the presence of a highly visible, centrally located security station with personnel in the lobby has proved effective.

Some companies have security personnel who make sure each visitor signs a log and gives his or her name, address, and the name of the person or office being visited. (See Illus. 10-25.) Other companies find it more convenient to send an employee to the lobby to escort the visitor back to the office. In smaller offices, the receptionist may be the controlling agent simply by being present in the front office.

Illus. 10-25. The purpose of office security is to provide protection for office workers and office property. This security guard makes sure all visitors sign the visitors' log.

Controlling Employee Access

Many medium- and large-sized businesses gain positive identification of those employees who should have access to the buildings and grounds through the use of *identification (ID) cards*. Photo ID cards, like the one shown in Illus. 10-26, are issued by many companies. Your cooperation in wearing your ID helps assure your personal safety and security on the job.

Businesses which must restrict employee entry to selected areas of a building often use magnetically coded cards as a substitute for keys. A magnetically coded card carried by the employee can be inserted into a magnetic card reader to gain access. If the card is authorized for entrance, the door opens.

Some companies use magnetically coded badges that can be sensed by electronic readers, referred to as *proximity readers*. As the wearer approaches a controlled access point, the electronic reader reads the code on the badge and transmits the information to a computer. This information provides a record of who entered and left designated areas, the time of entry, and in some instances, the time of exit—all valuable security information.

Illus. 10-26. Some companies issue ID cards or magnetically coded access cards to their employees.

Olivia looked up to see a repairperson coming through the doorway. "I'm here to check your computer. Apparently, you had a large electrical surge last night. Here's the order," he said as he flashed a copy of a repair order in front of Olivia. "This will take a few minutes—why don't you just take a short break."

Olivia got up from her terminal, but she was puzzled. She hadn't heard that an electrical surge had occurred. "Besides," she thought, "we have surge protectors for the equipment." Olivia felt she should check this with her supervisor, Ms. Calibre.

Ms. Calibre was not aware of an electrical surge occurring either. "Let me check on this before we do anything," she said.

Olivia stepped back into her office to see the repairperson disconnecting the computer:

Repairperson: Looks like I'll have to take your computer back to the shop for repairs.

Olivia: You'll have to wait until my supervisor authorizes you to take the computer.

Repairperson: Well, I have several other computers to check. Why don't I just come back after I've checked them and pick this one up.

The repairperson left hurriedly, and a minute or so later Olivia's supervisor appeared at the door: "No one authorized a computer repair check. We had better report this."

Ms. Calibre called the police immediately to report the incident. The police sergeant told her that several businesses had recently lost computers and typewriters in this manner. "You're lucky to have an alert employee," the sergeant told Ms. Calibre. "None of the others questioned an unexpected repair check. When the employees returned from their 'little breaks,' their equipment was gone."

Detection Systems and Alarms

After a detailed study of security needs and an analysis of the building and the surrounding area, firms often choose a combination of approaches to secure their facilities. In addition to the methods discussed previously, detection systems and alarms help complement a firm's security measures. A *detection system* consists of **monitoring** devices and alarms that sense and signal a change in the condition of an area being protected. Some detection systems detect entry into the area while others are designed to detect movement in the area.

Detection systems and alarms are designed to reduce a firm's reliance on an on-site security guard. Even if a firm has security officers, the officers cannot be at all stations at once. Closed-circuit television, as shown in Illus. 10-27, can be used to provide continuous monitoring of corridors, entrances, or other sensitive areas. When used with a video tape recorder, closed-circuit television provides the firm with a record of significant events for review.

monitoring:
warning; watching

Illus. 10-27.
Closed-circuit television provides continuous monitoring of the premises.

QUESTIONS FOR REVIEW

1. Describe how an accident-prevention approach can help control office accidents.

2. What are the safety practices you should follow in maintaining your own workstation?

3. What are the safety practices you should follow with regard to office furnishings and electrical equipment?

4. What are the safety practices you should follow with regard to general office equipment and computer monitors?

5. Describe the emergency office procedures you should learn immediately upon starting a new job.

6. Describe some of the precautions you may take as an office worker to protect your personal property on the job.

7. How can you help assure your personal security when you are working alone?

8. How can a firm control an outsider's access to the business?

9. Explain some of the procedures businesses use to control employee access.

10. Explain how detection systems and alarms complement a firm's security measures.

MAKING DECISIONS

Your supervisor, Mr. Petersen, is reading a memo when you enter his office. He shakes his head and says: "This is the second memo the managers have received about security leaks. One of our competitors has just introduced a new product, and it's identical to a product we have been working on. Apparently they discovered our plans. The president wants our thoughts on how to improve our product security. In addition to the main shredder in the reprographics center, he is suggesting a shredder for each office. Well, I'm just glad everyone on *my* staff can be trusted."

As you hear this, you remember several situations you have observed in the office:

● You have seen poor photocopies—even photocopies of confidential material—discarded in the wastebasket.

● Computer printouts with product-testing results are left stacked next to the filing cabinets rather than being locked inside them.

- Workers often talk about current projects during their breaks.

- Workers have a habit of using the offices of other workers who are out of town or on vacation.

- Workers too freely give out unnecessary information to callers, such as telling a caller exactly where the individual is.

"Tell me," Mr. Petersen says, "Do you think we need a shredder?" How do you respond to him? Do you tell him what you think he wants to hear, or do you use your observations as a basis for your response? How can you use this question as an opening to discuss security procedures in your office? What suggestions can you make for tightening general office security?

What You Are To Do: Prepare a response to the questions.

EXTENDING YOUR ENGLISH COMPETENCIES

In this exercise, you will practice spelling correctly some frequently misspelled words. Use a sheet of plain paper.

What You Are To Do: Set your margins for a 70-space line. Set your first tab 19 spaces from your left margin. Set the second tab 38 spaces from the left margin. Set your third tab 57 spaces from the left margin. Leave a 2-inch top margin and double-space the entire exercise. On a sheet of plain paper, center the title: FREQUENTLY MIS-SPELLED WORDS.

Key the word as shown at the left margin. Tab to the second column and key the word again while looking at the correct spelling in your textbook. Tab to the third column and key the word without looking at the word either in the textbook or from your keyed copy. Tab to the fourth column and repeat the spelling practice. After you have practiced each word following this procedure, remove your paper and use standard proofreader's marks to correct your copy. Refer to Reference Section A for standard proofreader's marks. Give your corrected copy to your teacher.

Word processing equipment can be used to complete this activity.

absence	absence	absence	absence

accommodate

applicable

bankruptcy

bookkeeping

calendar

committee

convenience

definitely

efficiency

eligible

foreign

grammar

judgment

knowledge

occurred

privilege

receipt

separate

thoroughly

APPLICATION ACTIVITY

Word processing equipment can be used to complete this activity.

Your supervisor, Mr. Petersen, is concerned that each employee take an active interest in good safety practices. He is considering an employee's suggestion that a safety committee be formed for each floor of the building. He would like you to develop a safety guidelines checklist for the committee members to use as a starting point in their discussions.

"This is just a suggestion," he says as he hands you the format sample which follows. "If you can think of a better format, try it. We will refine the checklist later. At this time, I need about 15 to 20 safety guidelines we can use as the basis for our first discussions."

What You Are To Do: Use your textbook, magazine articles, or safety hand-
books as your source. Compose a listing of 15 to 20
office safety guidelines. Then key a draft of the safety
guidelines checklist for Mr. Petersen's review.

Fifth Floor Safety Guidelines			
Safety Guidelines	Practiced	Not Practiced	Location/Comment
1. Keep your workstation surface free of sharp objects, such as scissors, when they are not in use.			
2. Pull open only one drawer of a filing cabinet at a time to avoid tipping the file cabinet.			
3. Post emergency telephone numbers on or beside your telephone.			

CHAPTER SUMMARY

In this chapter you learned the importance of managing your time and
workstation effectively. You also learned that reprographics technology is
continuously advancing. The roles of both employee and employer in establishing and following office safety and security procedures were also discussed. You should be knowledgeable about the following key points:

1. Activities management is a vital key to your success on the job. Although
   what you actually do in your job will depend upon the nature of the business for which you are employed, you will need to be able to plan and
   organize your work activities, whatever they may be. You will need to
   manage effectively the resources that support your work activities.

2. The basic resources that support your work activities are your workstation and your time. Your workstation provides the physical space for you to do your job. By correctly organizing the equipment and supplies at your workstation, you can increase your productivity. Your time on the job must be channeled to assure that time obligations are handled effectively and that time wasters are eliminated.

3. The typical office employee uses a variety of office supplies and equipment. Correctly selecting, using, and caring for office supplies is an important cost reduction factor in an office. Office workers are expected to learn how to use office equipment properly and to do their part in keeping equipment properly maintained.

4. The primary reprographic equipment used in most offices today is the photocopier. Most office copiers contain features such as enlarging or reducing from the original, duplexing (copying front and back), and sorting the copies. As an office worker, you are expected to help control copier costs and to prepare materials correctly to be copied.

5. Organizations strive to maintain a safe and secure environment for all their employees. As an office worker, you will want to adhere to safe practices at your workstation. You will also want to understand and abide by all security measures established by the company in which you work.

KEY CONCEPTS AND TERMS

workstation	photocopiers
functional work area	electrostatic process
preventive maintenance	phototypesetting
work simplification	imaging
reprographics	

INTEGRATED CHAPTER ACTIVITIES

Activity 1

In this chapter you learned the importance of effectively managing your time and work activities in order to increase your on-the-job productivity. You learned that reprographics supports the completion of many work tasks. You also learned that office supplies and equipment are the means which help you complete your work.

Word processing
equipment can be used
to complete this activity.

What You Are To Do:
- Key a one-paragraph response of several sentences to each of the four open-ended statements below. Do not limit your comments entirely to what you have learned in this textbook. Include your own ideas and feelings about each statement.
- Use standard proofreader's marks to edit your statements. Key a final copy of your responses.

1. Time management is a cooperative effort between the supervisor and the office assistant. Each must respect the other's time. Effective use of one's time means...

2. Companies are concerned about controlling copier costs. Many companies rely on the honesty of their employees in using office copiers appropriately. Appropriate use of the office copier means...

3. Without proper supplies and equipment, office workers could not do their jobs. As a future office worker, I plan to use supplies and equipment...

4. Organizations try to provide a safe and secure working environment. As an office worker, my responsibilities are...

Activity 2

You are an office worker whose tasks include ordering copier supplies when the inventory is low. Every six months you call several office supply stores to be sure you are buying the least expensive, highest quality supplies for the company's copiers. This is called comparison shopping. The supply of toner is low, and your comparison shopping has revealed the following information: Store A sells 120 grams of toner for $23.16; Store B, 270 grams for $40.00; Store C, 275 grams, $46.25; and Store D, 240 grams, $37.09. Which store will give you the most toner for your money? (**Note:** The toner that will give you the most for your money is the toner with the least expensive cost per gram.)

What You Are To Do: Calculate the cost per gram for each toner by dividing the cost by the number of grams (round your answers to three decimal places). Record your answers on a sheet of plain paper.

OPTIONAL COMPUTER APPLICATION ACTIVITY
See Computer Application Activity 10
in your Information Processing Activities workbook.

PRODUCTIVITY CORNER

Blake Williams
*OFFICE
SUPERVISOR*

SAFETY FIRST—ALL THE TIME!

DEAR MR. WILLIAMS:

My supervisor arrived this morning and found the coffeepot left plugged in. Last week, someone forgot to lock up an expensive calculator at the end of the day. My employer is becoming concerned that the safety and security practices of our office are too lax.

Although we have no formal safety program, we do try to practice good work habits. We are all very busy and we won't have a lot of time to listen to lectures on safety and security. Do you have any suggestions for us?—FRED IN TULSA

DEAR FRED:

Safety and security instruction should not be left to lectures alone. Try the following ideas:

- Establish a safety committee. Rotate membership to get maximum involvement from all employees. Get first aid training for committee members to increase their value to the employees.

- Use bulletin boards, posters, brochures, booklets, films, checklists, and the company newspaper to communicate safety messages.

- Use a checklist with specific safety and security pointers so that employees know exactly what is expected of them.

- Assign particular duties, such as unplugging the coffeepot or locking up the calculator, to specific individuals. Post the list of assignments.

- Hold periodic fire drills. With over 18,000 office fires a year, according to the National Safety Council, this can be time well spent.

- Designate specific employees to help handicapped workers in an emergency. Devise an evacuation plan and practice it together.

- Write the National Safety Council, P.O. Box 11933, Chicago, IL 60611, for information on office safety and security.

Good luck in developing a sound program for your office.—BLAKE WILLIAMS

CHAPTER 11

Administrative Support Functions

Today's office assistant provides valuable aid to management. Much of the decision making and processing of information required of business executives is based upon the input they receive from their staffs. Likewise, many of an executive's business responsibilities, such as conducting a meeting or traveling, are facilitated by the executive's staff. Tasks supporting the executive's activities often are delegated to responsible and trustworthy assistants. As an office worker, you may be involved in a wide range of support activities which facilitate executive decision making and aid in completing tasks.

In this chapter, you will learn about the administrative support activities which you as a future office worker may be assigned. You will learn about reminder systems, such as calendars and tickler files, that are used to schedule office activities. You will also learn to apply correct procedures for maintaining these systems.

Assisting with meetings and making travel arrangements are two important support activities. Your knowledge of how to handle these activities will contribute significantly to a smoothly operating office.

One of the more challenging support activities is assisting with business reports. Your responsibilities may vary from gathering information to formatting and keying the reports.

Administrative support activities provide you with an opportunity to use your creativity and resourcefulness in the office. As you perform these duties successfully, you demonstrate that you are a responsible assistant—and an important aide to management.

The objectives of this chapter are to provide you with the background and skills to:

- use common reminder systems, assist with business meetings, and make travel arrangements

- assist in the preparation of business reports

REMINDER SYSTEMS, BUSINESS MEETINGS, AND TRAVEL

When you have completed your study of this topic, you will be able to:

- identify proper procedures for maintaining calendars and tickler files

- explain the office assistant's duties in helping with business meetings and preparing documents related to business meetings

- describe the major forms of business travel and identify proper procedures for completing business travel arrangements

Knowing what to do, when to do it, and how to do it are important factors in your ability to be of assistance to executives or managers. The more knowledgeable you are about the details of calendars, tickler files, business meetings, and travel, the more help you can provide the executive or executives for whom you work.

Reminder systems such as calendars and tickler files are used in offices to assist you in scheduling office activities. **Reminder systems** consist of devices designed to bring to mind events, tasks, and other office-related activities. The purpose of reminder systems is to allow scheduling these activities for the most efficient use of time and resources.

Business meetings bring people together to communicate information and make decisions. Increasingly, however, more meetings are not face to face. Technological developments allow executives or managers in different locations—even on different continents—to conduct meetings without leaving their offices. Well-organized meetings, whether face to face or by electronic means, are necessary if businesses are to function smoothly.

Because a significant portion of an executive's time during the day may be spent in meetings, most executives recognize the importance of meetings that are well planned. In this topic, you will learn how to help your employer plan and conduct meetings efficiently and effectively.

Some executives must travel to meet their business responsibilities. As an assistant to a traveling executive, you will be expected to be knowledgeable about the major methods of business travel. In this topic, you will also learn proper procedures for completing basic travel arrangements.

REMINDER SYSTEMS

As an office assistant, you may have the responsibility for keeping track of appointments, meetings, travel dates, and deadlines. Perhaps the most widely used device for keeping track of such items is the calendar. The tickler file (so named because it "tickles" your memory) is a companion to your calendar because it provides a convenient place to keep notations of tasks to be performed on specific dates.

Calendars

Typically, you will have your own calendar to maintain, as well as that of any manager for whom you make appointments and schedule meetings. To maintain the calendars properly, clarify the following points with the manager:

- To what extent do you have authority to make appointments?
- When should you check with the manager before making appointments?
- Are there regular times when appointments are not to be made, such as the first half-hour of the day?
- To what extent will the manager make appointments without checking with you?

Illus. 11-1. Since a calendar on your desk can be viewed by others, avoid writing confidential entries on it.

The extent of authority delegated to you for making appointments will depend in great part on the nature of the business. For example, if you were keeping the appointment book for a doctor, most of the appointment requests would be from patients. You would be expected to schedule appointments without having to verify each appointment with the doctor. On the other hand, you may work in a general office where both you and the executive make appointments. You both must agree on procedures which will allow you to operate effectively.

Appointment Guidelines

1. Do not schedule overlapping appointments. Try to determine the amount of time needed for each appointment. Also, the executive may prefer that some time be left unscheduled to return telephone calls or prepare for the next appointment.
2. Keep a complete calendar. Record names, telephone numbers, and other *pertinent* information.

pertinent: related to the point at hand

3. Use legible handwriting to record entries on handwritten calendars. Avoid crossing out and rescheduling over scratched-off entries. To make changes easily, many assistants keep their appointments in pencil.
4. Determine a symbol to designate confirmed appointments. As appointments are confirmed, record the symbol. Such commonly used symbols include a check mark, an asterisk, or an underscore of the individual's name. (See page 452.)

Illus. 11-2. An office assistant responsible for scheduling appointments for more than one executive often uses a group appointment calendar, like the one shown here. What symbol has the assistant used to indicate confirmed appointments?

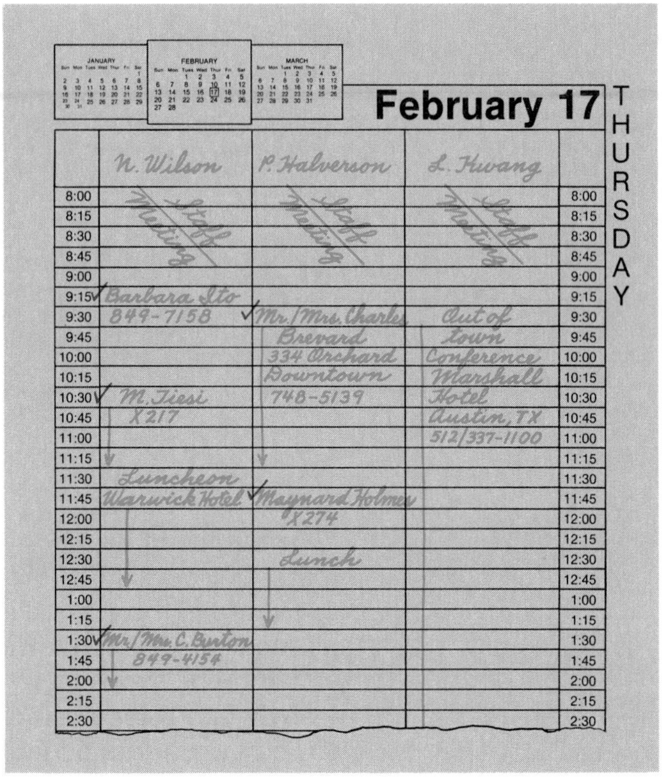

5. If the executive does not keep a calendar of appointments, provide a daily listing of appointments and reminders at the beginning of the workday. Show the appointments for the day in **chronologic** order, as in Illus. 11-3.
6. Keep the previous year's appointment calendar. Many assistants have found it necessary to refer back to a calendar to reconstruct needed information. If you use an electronic calendar, print a copy of the calendar before deleting the data.

chronologic: arranged in order by time

Entering Recurring Items

Some meetings and tasks are performed periodically, perhaps weekly, monthly, quarterly, or annually. As you set up your calendar at the beginning of the year, enter the **recurring** meetings and tasks on both your calendar and the executive's calendar. If you block out the times for these recurring items, both you and the executive will know what time is available for scheduling other appointments.

recurring: happening again

NATHAN WILSON

SCHEDULE FOR MONDAY, MARCH 28, 19--

NO	START	FINISH	LENGTH	WITH	REMARKS
1	08:00	08:30	30	Staff	Meeting to discuss week's priorities; Conference Room A.
2	08:30	09:00	30	Nancy	Initial budget review planning session to determine documents needed for 1:30 meeting.
*	09:00	10:00	60	FREE	Reminder: Check with Dave(x2211) about trip to Simms Plant.
3	10:00	12:00	120	Blondelle_ Webb (555-5667)	Meeting to discuss system designs for Simms Plant.
*	12:00	01:30	90	FREE	
4	01:30	03:30	120	Mat Hastings (x5321) John_ Baker (x3444) Nancy	Meeting to discuss quarterly budget review; Marketing Department. Conference Room C.
*	03:30	04:00	30	FREE	Review management articles.
5	04:00	05:00	60	Dave Tokuda (x2221)	Planning session for trip to Simms Plant, Conference Room B. Check with Nancy for backup materials.

Illus. 11-3. An office assistant who maintains an electronic calendar provides an executive with a printout of the day's schedule. Notice that all appointments have been confirmed (confirmed appointments are underlined).

Illus. 11-4. This medical assistant uses a computer to maintain a listing of appointments.

Responding to Appointment Requests

People request appointments in different ways: in person, by telephone, by letter or memorandum, or by electronic message. Although the manner in which you respond to these requests changes slightly according to the ***medium*** of communication used, the basic information you need will be the same:

medium: means or system

- WHO: name and telephone number of the individual requesting the appointment
- WHEN: date, time, and approximate length of appointment
- WHERE: location, if other than the executive's office

When you receive a request for an appointment, check your calendar to determine that the date and time requested are available. If the requested time is not available, you may suggest alternative appointment dates and times. If requests for appointments have to be approved, obtain the executive's approval before confirming the appointment. In some instances, the executive may also ask you to determine the purpose of the meeting and identify all ***backup materials*** needed.

backup materials: related or supporting documents

Coordinating Desk Calendars

If both you and the executive schedule appointments using desk calendars, you need to coordinate appointment calendars so that they are consistent and up to date. Adjustments to schedules are made by the executive and the assistant usually at the beginning of the workday or at the end of the previous workday. Such adjustments include confirming tentative appointments, rescheduling appointments, deleting canceled appointments, and changing time allotments.

Coordinating Electronic Calendars

networked: interconnected electronically

An **electronic calendar** is a calendar maintained in computer memory. An electronic calendar ***networked*** between the assistant and the executive can be updated by either party. This means changes made by the executive are reflected instantaneously at the assistant's workstation. Instead of receiving a printed copy of the day's schedule as shown in Illus. 11-3, Mr. Wilson would check his electronic calendar at the beginning of the day, as shown in Illus. 11-5.

minimal: small or
least possible

Electronic calendaring systems have different features. Some electronic calendars allow only **minimal** information and minimal line length. Others provide for recording additional notes regarding the appointment or current projects. Some electronic calendaring systems use sound, such as a bell or a buzzer, to remind executives of their specific engagements.

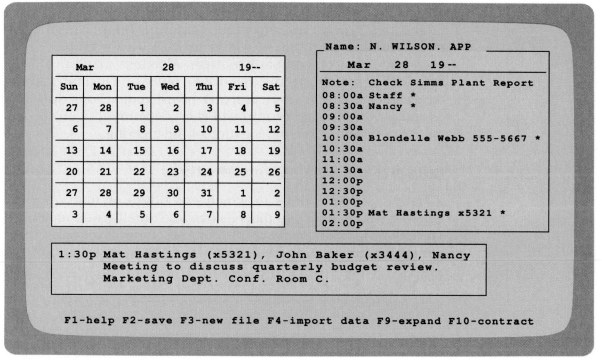

Illus. 11-5. An electronic calendar with confirmed appointments shown with asterisks.

Tickler File

A **tickler file** is a chronologic system for keeping track of future actions. Such a file is divided into 12 monthly divisions with 31 daily parts for the current month. Tickler files can be set up using cards, a pocket file (an accordion-like file), or a file drawer with file folders. A tickler file also can be maintained on a computer.

Store in a tickler file items requiring future action. Assume your employer says to you, "Please call a local restaurant on Monday and make a luncheon reservation for a party of two for next Friday." You would prepare a reminder to make the reservation and place it in your tickler file under next Monday's date.

As soon as you become aware of a deadline or of a detail that needs to be checked again in the future, place a notation in your tickler file under the relevant day. Check your tickler file each morning and remove those items requiring attention on the current day. Complete the appropriate action for each item. Between your tickler file and your calendar, you will be aware of what must be done to keep the office functioning smoothly.

BUSINESS MEETINGS

Meetings provide an important communication link in business. Without meetings, it would be difficult for employees to keep up to date on company matters. Meetings may range from an informal meeting in the executive's office to a formal board of directors' meeting in the company board room. Your duties in assisting with these meetings will vary, depending upon the formality, function, size, and location of the meeting.

Informal and Small Group Meetings

Many of the meetings in which executives or managers are involved will be informal discussions and small group meetings. The following example shows how one office employee carried out her responsibilities for setting up a meeting:

> *The manager called Jana on the intercom. "Jana, see if you can get the four Hansville Project engineers together tomorrow at three o'clock for about an hour...and see if the conference room is available." As the manager spoke, Jana wrote down the instructions. She noted the materials she had to prepare for the meeting, as well as the arrangements she needed to make for special equipment. Immediately after taking all of the instructions, Jana verified the availability of the conference room and telephoned each of the engineers. She told them the time, place, and approximate length of the meeting. She then arranged for the necessary equipment and photocopied the materials needed for the meeting. The next day, Jana checked the conference room before the meeting to see that everything was in order.*

Formal Business Meetings

A formal meeting follows a definite order of business, which is called an agenda. An **agenda** is a list of the topics to be discussed during the meeting. You may have responsibilities before, during, and after a formal meeting.

Illus. 11-6. Informal, small group meetings are held frequently in many organizations.

Before the Meeting

The following suggestions will be helpful to you in your planning. You may not use all the suggestions for each meeting. However, these guidelines will be helpful to you as you assist with the planning for most business meetings.

Establish a Meeting Folder. Once you are aware that a meeting will take place, set up a folder for that meeting. Use this folder to collect items related to the meeting, such as the list of attendees, the agenda, notes, and copies of materials to be distributed.

Reserve the Meeting Room. When you are given the date, time, and location of the meeting, check immediately to see if the desired meeting room and time are available.

Notify the Meeting Participants. Notify the participants as soon as possible of the time, place, approximate length, and purpose of the meeting. Identify any materials or supporting documents they should bring to the meeting.

Use Your Reminder Systems. Mark your calendar and the executive's calendar with the meeting time and place. Use your tickler file to help you control the preparation details. For example, if you must prepare 20 copies of a report for the meeting, place a note in the tickler file to remind you of this responsibility.

Key the Agenda. All participants and the recording secretary should receive a copy of the agenda prior to the meeting. An agenda typically contains many of the items shown in Illus. 11-7.

Obtain Equipment. The manager will determine what equipment is needed and expect you to follow through by arranging for the equipment.

Organize Meeting Materials and Handouts. You may be expected to gather certain materials such as extra notepads, pencils, file folders, and courtesy identification badges. Also organize any materials and handouts such as reports, letters, and statistical data, that will be distributed at the meeting.

Illus. 11-7. An agenda is a list of the topics to be discussed during a formal business meeting.

AGENDA

RIVERTON IMPROVEMENT COUNCIL

June 30, 19--

1. **Call to Order:** Nancy Hollingshead, Improvement Council President

2. **Roll Call:** Troy Canfield, Secretary

3. **Reading of the Minutes:** Troy Canfield, Secretary

4. **Treasurer's Report:** Shawn Petersen, Treasurer

5. **Committee Report:**

    Recognitions Committee: Harold King, Chairperson

6. **Unfinished Business:**

    Telecommunications Improvement Project

7. **New Business:**

    East Riverfront Drive Improvement Project

8. **Date of Next Meeting**

9. **Adjournment**

Prepare the Meeting Room. The room temperature should be comfortable and the room arranged to fit the meeting style. Check that requested equipment is in the room and is working properly.

Illus. 11-8. If a meeting is to run smoothly, a lot of planning and organization must be done before the meeting begins. Here, the office assistant is preparing the meeting room.

During the Meeting

The degree to which you assist the executive during the meeting will depend upon where the meeting is held and the tasks to be done. You may be responsible for the meeting minutes.

Minutes are the official record of a meeting. The minutes detail the action taken by the group, and they provide the reader with a concise presentation of factual information about the meeting. The minutes should not be a **verbatim** transcript of the meeting, but you must record all pertinent information. Thus, the minutes must give a clear, accurate, and complete accounting of the happenings of the meeting. Although various reporting formats are acceptable for recording minutes, the following items appear in most minutes:

verbatim: word for word

- name of group, committee, organization, or business holding the meeting
- time, date, place, and type of meeting (for example, weekly, monthly, annual, called, special)
- name of presiding officer
- members present and absent (In a large organization, only the number of members present needs to be recorded to verify that a **quorum** was present.)
- reading and approval of the minutes from the previous meeting

quorum: minimum number of members necessary to conduct business

- committee or individual reports (for example, treasurer's report, standing committees, special committees)
- unfinished business (includes pertinent discussion and action taken)
- new business (includes pertinent discussion and action taken)
- time, date, and place of next meeting
- time of adjournment
- signature of the secretary/recorder or individual responsible for the minutes

The following suggestions will be helpful to you when it is your responsibility to prepare the minutes of a meeting:

1. Have at the meeting a copy of the meeting agenda, a copy of the minutes of the previous meeting, and a copy of any report or document that might be referred to during the meeting.

parliamentary procedure: guides for conducting meetings

2. If you record and transcribe minutes frequently, a ***parliamentary procedure*** reference source (such as *Robert's Rules of Order Revised*) will help you better understand the meeting proceedings and the correct terminology to use when taking and preparing minutes.

3. Record the important points of discussion during the meeting and identify the individual making a comment. Often, only the action taken or the conclusion reached is recorded without identifying the persons involved.

4. Record the name of the person making a motion and the name of the person seconding the motion. Motions should be recorded verbatim, and a statement should be made in the minutes as to whether or not the motion was adopted.

5. Correct minutes of the previous meeting. Sometimes at the following meeting, corrections must be made to the minutes before they can be approved. If only a few words are affected, lines may be drawn through the incorrect words and the proper insertions made above them. If more than a few words are affected, lines may be drawn through the sentences or paragraphs to be corrected and the corrections written on a new page. The page number of each correction should be indicated on the original minutes. The minutes should not be rewritten after they have been read and approved at the meeting.

```
                    RIVERTON IMPROVEMENT COUNCIL
                          Meeting Minutes
                           June 30, 19--
```

Time and Place of Meeting

The regular weekly meeting of the Riverton Improvement Council was held on Tuesday, June 30, 19--, in the Meeting Chambers at City Hall. The meeting was called to order by President Nancy Hollingshead at 7:30 p.m.

Attendance

Present were Improvement Council members: Elizabeth Clark, Roger Addock, Douglas Ivey, Laura Johnston, Steve Munesada, Harold King, Shawn Petersen, Troy Canfield, and President Nancy Hollingshead. Absent was Emily Pierce.

Approval of Minutes

The minutes of the June 23, 19--, meeting were read and approved.

Treasurer's Report

Treasurer, Shawn Petersen, reported that with the receipt of the State Improvement Funds check, the Improvement Projects account has a balance of $359,450.

Report of Recognition Committee

Harold King, chairperson, submitted the committee report (attached to the minutes) recommending that the name of Jane Ann Adams be submitted to the City Council as a candidate for Employee of the Month. Ms. Johnson moved and Mr. Munesada seconded that the committee report be accepted. President Hollingshead directed the secretary to prepare the Resolution of Recognition for submission (attached to the minutes).

Unfinished Business

President Hollingshead reported that the three recorded bids for the Telecommunications Improvement Project have been forwarded to the city engineering department for evaluation.

New Business

East Riverfront Drive Improvement Project. Purchase of the Martin Victor Wolfe property at 1232 Riverfront Drive.

City Manager, John Byrd, reported that the city has negotiated with the property owner to acquire the property as part of the East Riverfront Drive Improvement Project for the sum of $150,000. The property has been

profits from the resell of the house be returned to the Improvement Project Fund. Mr. Addock seconded the motion. All members voted aye. President Hollingshead directed the treasurer to prepare a check to the City of Riverton for $150,000 for the acquisition of the property.

Date of Next Meeting

President Hollingshead declared the next regular meeting of the Improvement Council of Riverton to be held on July 7, 19--, at 7:30 p.m. in the Meeting Chambers at City Hall.

Adjournment

Mr. Ivey moved and Ms. Johnston seconded the motion that the meeting be adjourned. The motion carried, and President Hollingshead declared the meeting adjourned at 8:45 p.m.

Troy Canfield
————————————————
Troy Canfield, Secretary

Nancy Hollingshead
————————————————
Nancy Hollingshead, Improvement Council President

Illus. 11-9. Minutes are the official record of a meeting.

After the Meeting

Your work does not end when the meeting ends. Once the meeting is over, you will need to complete certain follow-up activities. Calendar notations should be made for any item from the meeting that will require future attention.

Prepare and Distribute the Minutes. Prepare the minutes as soon as possible. Preparing the minutes will be easier if you do it while the details of the meeting are fresh in your mind. Use examples of previous minutes for appropriate format. The chairperson will proofread the typed minutes before they are distributed to be sure there are no omissions or errors.

Complete Related Correspondence. Complete any correspondence associated with the meeting, such as thank-you letters to speakers or resource persons or letters requesting information. All these letters will be signed by the executive, but you may prepare them.

TELECONFER-ENCES

audio: sound

video: picture images

A **teleconference** is a meeting of people in different locations connected by a telecommunications system. The telecommunications system may involve only ***audio*** exchanges among the participants, as in a telephone conference. Or it may be more sophisticated, as a ***video*** exchange system. *Videoconferencing* permits people to meet at two or more locations with visual and audio contact (through television cameras, microphones, and monitors) almost as if they were in the same room. Time for teleconferences is expensive and should be used wisely.

Often, much assistance is necessary in preparing for a teleconference. Your role may include the following duties:

1. Reserve the conference room and necessary equipment.
2. Notify the participants of the date, time, length, and purpose of the meeting. Include a telephone number and the name of a contact for participants in the event of technical difficulties.
3. Prepare and distribute any related materials well in advance of the meeting. If several documents are to be sent, use different paper colors to copy different reports. That way, it will be easy to identify reports during the teleconference.
4. Prepare and distribute to the participants the on-line agenda well in advance of the teleconference. The **on-line agenda** is a listing of the events and topics of discussion planned for the teleconference, with the estimated time for each item.

Illus. 11-10. A tele-conference is a meeting of people who are geo-graphically separated but who are connected by a telecommunications system. This video conference permits voice and video communication.

BUSINESS TRAVEL

Travel arrangements are made in accordance with company policy. Large firms may have a travel department to handle travel arrangements. Smaller firms, however, may rely on the services of a travel agency or the office assistant to make the travel arrangements. In addition, some companies have special agreements with travel agencies, hotels, and transportation companies for designated services. You will be given instructions to follow in completing any travel arrangements you are assigned.

To complete such arrangements, you will need to be knowledgeable about the major forms of business travel. There is frequently some opportunity to choose the **mode** of travel, the time of departure and arrival, and the kind of accommodations. When such choices are available, you will need to know the executive's personal preferences in order to make travel plans effectively.

mode: manner or way of doing something

Commercial Air Travel

Time is money for the busy executive, and the popularity of air travel among business people reflects this point. Often, the only way to manage a tight schedule is by air travel. In the United States, an extensive network of airline routes is provided by national, regional, and commuter airlines.

Schedules and Flight Information

If the manager is a frequent flyer on one particular airline, an updated airline timetable provides a convenient way to determine travel information such as:

- arrival and departure times
- flight numbers
- days of the week the flight is available
- services offered (meals, snacks, movies)
- toll-free reservation numbers

Airline schedules are available free of charge at ticket counters in airports, at airline offices in major cities, at large hotels, and from travel agents.

If the manager uses several airlines, you will find the *Official Airline Guide* (OAG) a valuable source of flight information and schedules. The company for which you work may have a copy of this publication for your reference. If not, a travel agent can provide you with the same information.

Reservations and Tickets

You may make reservations by calling a travel agent or an airline directly. While you are on the telephone, the agent or airline representative will access a computer and tell you if seating is available. If seating is available on the flight(s) you request, the reservations can be confirmed at that time.

Airline tickets most frequently are printed electronically. If you use the service of a travel agent, a computerized printout schedule of the flight itinerary, invoice, and boarding pass may be received with the airline tickets.

Some businesses subscribe to the OAG's Electronic Edition, an on-line service. The assistant making the travel arrangements can scan various airlines' accommodations, make the selections, and have the tickets prepared for pickup at the airport.

Other Forms of Business Travel

The rental car and train provide alternative forms of executive travel. You may have occasion to make travel arrangements for the executive using one of these forms of transportation.

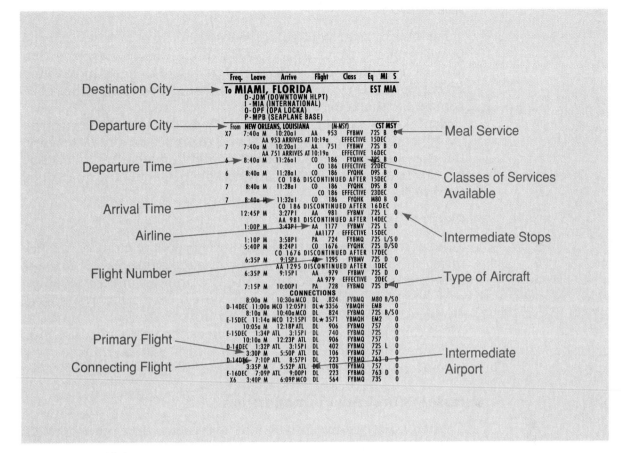

	Freq.	Leave	Arrive	Flight	Class	Eq	MI	S
To MIAMI, FLORIDA							**EST MIA**	

Destination City →
Departure City →
Departure Time →
Arrival Time →
Airline →
Flight Number →
Primary Flight →
Connecting Flight →

Meal Service ←
Classes of Services Available ←
Intermediate Stops ←
Type of Aircraft ←
Intermediate Airport ←

Illus. 11-11. Listing from the *Official Airline Guide.* If you departed from New Orleans on the 7:15 p.m. flight, at what time would you reach Miami's International Airport? Did you have any intermediate stops?

Illus. 11-12. Some businesses prefer to have all travel arranged through a designated travel agency.

Rental Car

For short trips, particularly in a local area, many business people prefer to rent cars. A rental car may also be suitable when an executive flies into a city and has appointments in outlying areas. Rental cars are available at most airports and other convenient locations for the traveler.

Rental cars vary in price according to the size of the car, the length of time the car is needed, and the miles driven. Determine the executive's preference before contacting a car rental agency or your travel agent. Follow any established company guidelines for renting a car.

Train

Train travel is popular in some sections of the country, particularly in areas with high population concentrations. Train stations are located in the centers of cities and can provide an alternative to air travel on certain rail routes. Overnight trains have sleeper services which allow the executive to sleep and eat on the train. Check with a travel agent or check the yellow pages of your telephone directory for information on the railway lines serving your area.

Hotel/Motel Accommodations

When traveling executives stay overnight, they need hotel or motel accommodations. The executive may specify a particular hotel or motel, especially if he or she is familiar with the city or if a convention or meeting is being held at a specific hotel. In other cases, the executive may rely on you to select the lodging.

The OAG's *Business Travel Planner* provides names, addresses, telephone numbers, room rates, and other information about hotels and motels throughout North America. For oversees travel, consult the OAG's European and Pacific/Asia editions. The company for which you work may have a copy of these publications. If not, a travel agent can provide you with the same information.

Procedures for Arranging Travel

Traveling executives must be able to meet their business obligations scheduled away from their offices. They must arrive at meetings on time and with the necessary supporting materials.

You will find that carefully planned travel arrangements are crucial to the success of the business trip.

Trip Planning

As soon as you learn that the executive is making a trip, you probably will become involved in the planning of that trip. As an office assistant, you will be responsible for gathering accurate and timely information on details relating to the trip.

Prepare a Travel Folder. A travel folder (or trip file) will help you organize the details of an upcoming trip. A folder should be used to collect background information and details about the trip, such as notes on reservations, tickets, accommodations, and meeting or appointment confirmations.

Plan the Trip. Planning for the trip probably will revolve around meetings already scheduled and around meetings which the executive needs to schedule during the trip. If you are responsible for scheduling the meetings, you will need the names and titles of the persons to be scheduled as well as the company names, addresses, and telephone numbers of the individuals.

Completing Travel Arrangements

Once the travel plans are approved, you may be expected to confirm appointments and make travel and lodging reservations. In addition, you may assemble the travel documents and related business materials for the meetings.

Illus. 11-13. At large airports, rental car agencies provide shuttle service to and from car rental lots and the airport terminal.

Confirm Appointments. Call each individual with whom the executive plans to meet and confirm the appointment time, date, place, and purpose.

Make Reservations. If you make the reservations yourself, contact the airline, car rental agency, and hotel or motel directly to communicate the travel details. When you make reservations by telephone, use toll-free telephone numbers whenever possible. Write down the names of the persons who make and confirm reservations. Always make a note of the rates you are quoted.

Many reservations are in the form of a confirmation number. Record the confirmation number and repeat it to the reservation agent to assure the accuracy of the number. The confirmation number should be included on the executive's itinerary. The executive also may wish to have written confirmation if there is enough time to receive such a confirmation before the trip.

You may also make reservations through a travel agent or through the travel department within the firm. If you make reservations in this way, you will give the travel details to the travel agent or appropriate travel personnel who will make the reservations for you. You will be notified once the reservations have been made and confirmed. In addition, you may receive a computer printout that details the travel arrangements as well as the confirmation numbers.

alternative: another choice

If the plans for a trip change, check with the executive prior to canceling any travel reservations. The trip may be postponed and may require that **alternative** travel arrangements be made. The alternative arrangements generally can be made at the time you cancel the first trip. Have your confirmation numbers and other pertinent reservation details available when you place such a call.

Prepare an Itinerary. The **itinerary** is a detailed plan of a trip that serves as a guide for the executive while he or she is away from the office. The itinerary includes travel arrangements, appointments, hotel or motel reservations, and reminders or special instructions. Allow enough travel time between appointments so that the executive does not have to rush to make the next appointment. The itinerary should be in an easy-to-read format which gives the executive his or her day-by-day schedule for the complete trip, as shown in Illus. 11-14.

```
              ITINERARY FOR CHARLES R. STAFFORD
                   May 17 to May 19, 19--


WEDNESDAY, MAY 17      Atlanta to Dallas

  9:43 a.m.            Leave Hartsfield Atlanta International
                       Airport on Delta Flight 17.  Breakfast
                       served.

 10:50 a.m.            Arrive Dallas/Ft. Worth International
                       Airport.  Pick up rental car keys at Sun
                       Rentals Counter; Confirmation Number:
                       3840576.

                       Hotel reservations at Fairmont Hotel,
                       1717 N. Akard St. (214-555-5454).
                       Confirmation Number:  3K4895F.

  2:30 p.m.            Meeting with Mr. Thomas Thatcher, Vice
                       President Marketing, Fabric Wholesalers,
                       1314 Gaston Avenue, 214-555-1958, to
                       discuss fabric purchase agreement.

  7:00 p.m.            Dinner with staff at hotel to review
                       plans for Apparel Fair.


THURSDAY, MAY 18       Dallas to San Diego

 12:02 p.m.            Leave Dallas/Ft. Worth International
                       Airport on Delta Flight 443.  Lunch
                       served.  Drop rental car keys at Sun
                       Rentals counter at airport.

 12:55 p.m.            Arrive at Lindbergh Field International
                       Airport.  Mr. Stanley (619-555-6687) will
                       meet you at the airport and drive you to
                       the Naples plant for the tour and return
                       you to your hotel.

                       Hotel reservations at the Seven Seas
                       Lodge, 411 Hotel Circle South, 619-555-
                       1302.  Confirmation Number:  38T2684.


FRIDAY, MAY 19         San Diego to Atlanta

  7:55 a.m.            Leave San Diego Lindbergh Field
                       International Airport on Delta Flight
                       860.  Breakfast Served.

  3:52 p.m.            Arrive Hartsfield Atlanta International
                       Airport.
```

Illus. 11-14. A comprehensive itinerary contains relevant travel details, as shown here.

Check with the executive to determine to whom copies of the itinerary are to be sent. The executive will need several copies: a copy to carry, an extra copy to be carried in the baggage, and possibly a copy for family members.

Gather Supporting Items. The following items represent various supplies, documents, and supporting materials the executive may expect you to assemble:

- travel tickets, itinerary, and travel funds
- hotel/motel and car rental confirmations
- supporting correspondence, speeches, reports, and files for each appointment/meeting
- forms for recording expenses

While the Executive Is Away

formidable: hard to handle

Keeping the office running smoothly while the executive is out of town may seem like a ***formidable*** task for the beginning office worker. However, you can do much toward meeting this responsibility by following these suggestions:

- Keep up your regular duties and use your time wisely.
- Keep an itemized listing of incoming mail.
- Answer any routine mail that you can.
- Keep a log of telephone calls and office visitors.
- If possible, avoid making appointments for the first day the executive is back in the office.
- Keep notes of matters you will want to discuss with the executive upon his or her return.

When the Executive Returns

Certain follow-up activities should be completed as soon as possible after the trip. A common follow-up activity is processing the correspondence generated by the executive's trip. Follow-up letters and thank-you letters may be sent as a result of the business contacts and activities encountered on the trip. Another important follow-up activity is the completion of reports that the executive needs to submit regarding the trip.

QUESTIONS FOR REVIEW

1. What points should you clarify with the executive or manager in order to be able to maintain calendars effectively and efficiently?

2. What guidelines should you follow in scheduling appointments?

3. Describe the duties of the office assistant prior to a formal business meeting.

4. What items generally appear in minutes of a meeting?

5. What guidelines should you follow when it is your responsibility to prepare the minutes of a meeting?

6. After the meeting, what duties will the office assistant be expected to complete?

7. What duties might an office assistant be asked to complete in order to prepare for a teleconference?

8. Identify and describe three common forms of executive travel.

9. Identify and describe the procedures an office assistant should follow to complete travel arrangements for the executive.

10. What are the office assistant's duties while the executive is away from the office? When the executive returns?

MAKING DECISIONS

Megan's employer, Mr. Burrell, is meeting with union labor leaders to discuss delicate labor-management relations pending the renewal of the employees' contract. The meeting has been underway for about half an hour when Mr. Burrell's brother appears in the office and asks to speak to Mr. Burrell. Even after Megan tells him that Mr. Burrell is in a very important meeting, the brother still insists on speaking with him. He is becoming upset with Megan for attempting to prevent him from entering his brother's office.

What You Are To Do: Write a paragraph explaining how Megan might handle this situation. How could this situation have been avoided?

EXTENDING YOUR ENGLISH COMPETENCIES

In this exercise, you will be reviewing pronouns. The following are sentences taken from reports keyed by an office assistant.

1. The executive (that, who) directed the meeting is considered an effective business leader.

2. Neither Jack nor Jim feels that (his, their) itinerary should be changed.

3. The executives said that (them, they), along with a group from another company, would attend the seminar in Paris.

4. Office workers who take the minutes of meetings need a parliamentary procedures resource available to (them, they).

5. The committee has promised to have (its, their) findings ready for review at the departmental meeting next week.

6. The executives traveling on business from that office often use (its, their) company's credit cards.

7. The executive and her associate were uncertain how (she, they) should reschedule the trip.

8. The members of the group attending the meeting wanted (its, their) opinions aired before a final vote was taken.

9. The oval table (that, who) was placed in the meeting room will be there only a short time.

10. Joy and Wendy reviewed the meeting agenda before (it, they) was sent to the participants.

What You Are To Do: Key the sentences, selecting the proper pronoun. Your teacher may wish to review the identification and use of pronouns with you. Basically, pronouns are words that serve as substitutes for nouns. They take the place of nouns. They must agree with their **antecedents** (nouns for which they stand) in person, number, and gender.

APPLICATION ACTIVITIES

Activity 1

As the assistant to Ms. Moyer, planning director for the city, you are responsible for scheduling appointments. Ms. Moyer is preparing a briefing that she must give tomorrow at the state capitol. She has asked not to be interrupted except for previously scheduled appointments or for any critical business that requires her official input. "Just take my messages, but bring in the mail after you've opened it," she says as she closes the door to her office.

Word processing equipment can be used to complete this activity.

What You Are To Do: On a plain sheet of paper, center the heading HANDLING APPOINTMENT REQUESTS. Key a short paragraph telling how you would handle each appointment situation. Number each paragraph to match the situation numbers given. Ms. Moyer prefers to confirm all appointments. Generally, she prefers not to have appointments before 9 a.m.

WEDNESDAY, OCTOBER 1

The following situations arise during the day:

1 8:30 a.m. You open a letter from the City Beautification Council asking Ms. Moyer to speak at its luncheon five weeks from today.

2 9:45 a.m. The mayor's secretary telephones to set a time for Ms. Moyer to meet with the mayor when she returns from tomorrow's briefing at the state capitol. The meeting will be held in the mayor's office down the hall. You check your calendar and note that Ms. Moyer does not have an appointment scheduled until 1 p.m. on Friday when she returns.

3 10:25 a.m. A staff member comes by to set up an appointment. "I'd like to see her sometime tomorrow, if possible. We need to discuss the Riverfront Development Project. If tomorrow isn't convenient, then it will have to wait until next week when I return from my Baltimore trip."

4 11:10 a.m. Ms. Moyer buzzes you and asks you to reschedule her 3:15 p.m. appointment with Mr. Bellevue for the same time next week. "By the way, do I have any messages?" she asks.

5 1:30 p.m. A staff member comes by to see Ms. Moyer about arranging neighborhood group meetings to discuss the new city zoning plan. "No rush," she says to you. "Anytime within the next two or three days is fine. If she likes the idea, our meeting could take about an hour."

6 3:45 p.m. A salesperson without an appointment wants to see Ms. Moyer about a new office copier.

Activity 2

You work in Atlanta as an office assistant to Ernest L. Fogg, Director of Marketing. Mr. Fogg is in the process of finalizing arrangements for a teleconference with regional marketing vice presidents located in five different regional offices. The teleconference will originate in Atlanta.

Mr. Fogg hands you an edited copy of the on-line agenda for the teleconference and says, "Please key this agenda in final form. Open up the spacing as I've indicated and list the participants in alphabetic order according to city. Proofread very carefully. It's vital that all times and telephone numbers are correct."

What You Are To Do: Use plain paper to key the final agenda. Follow Mr. Fogg's oral and written instructions.

Word processing equipment can be used to complete this activity.

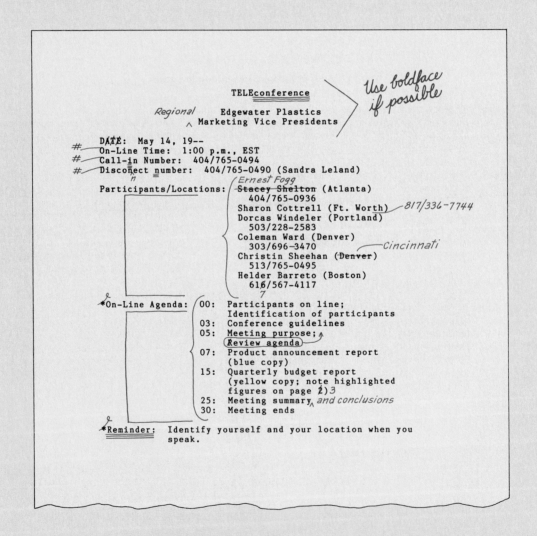

BUSINESS REPORTS AND GRAPHICS

When you have completed your study of this topic, you will be able to:

- identify the parts of a formal business report and describe the function of each part

- prepare business reports and financial statements

Business reports represent an important method of communication for a business. They are a source of information for many of the decisions affecting a business organization. For example, if the owners of a firm are considering expanding their firm's product markets, much of the information they need to make their decision will be presented to them in the form of reports. Some reports, such as those including financial statements, are of interest to outsiders. A potential stockholder, for example, will spend time studying the financial reports of the business before investing money in that business.

In this topic you will be introduced to formal business reports including some commonly prepared financial reports. The extent of your involvement in the preparation of business reports will vary. It will depend not only on the size and type of your organization, but also on the nature of the report. Generally the smaller the organization, the more likely you are to be involved personally with preparing, assembling, and distributing business reports. Whatever the extent of your involvement, as an office worker you will want to have a basic understanding of the business reports your employer prepares.

You are already familiar with the short, informal business report from your study of Chapter 6. In this topic, you will study the function and purpose of both the formal business report and the major financial reports used on a regular basis.

A formal business report includes standard parts that readers find valuable in understanding such a report. Generally an explanation of the reason for the report is given, the types and sources of information used, the meaning of the information, and the conclusions. In this topic, you will be introduced to the parts of a formal report and to your role in helping to prepare such reports.

Parts of a Formal Business Report

The common parts of a business report that are covered in this topic are:

- title page
- table of contents
- summary
- body
- references
- appendices

A formal business report may contain all or some of the common report parts. An informal business report may contain only a heading and the body of the report. Several acceptable formats are available for keying a business report. However, your company may have a preferred format which you can determine from previous reports or from the company procedures manual. The formats presented to you in this topic represent acceptable business report formats for keying documents.

Business reports may be single- or double-spaced. Double spacing provides copy that is easier to read. Single spacing, however, reduces the volume of paper required. Report formats are identified as unbound, leftbound, or topbound:

- The *unbound report* is fastened together (generally in the upper left-hand corner) with a fastening device such as a paper clip or staple. No extra space is provided in the margin of the unbound report for fastening the report together.
- The *leftbound report* format moves the left margin a half inch beyond the margin for the unbound report, making the left margin one and one-half inches. This margin allows room to bind the report at the left. All other margins are the same as those of the unbound report.
- The *topbound report* format moves the top margin down a half inch below the top margin for the unbound report. This margin allows room for the report to be fastened at the top of the pages.

Title Page

The title page contains the report title, the writer's name, the name of the organization, and the report date (month, day, and year). The title page is double-spaced, as shown in Illus. 11-15 on page 478.

Table of Contents

The table of contents presents an overview of the material covered in the report by listing chapter titles or main topics with their page numbers. (Refer to Illus. 11-15.) The final copy of the table of contents is prepared after the entire report has been completed. This allows you to verify the titles and page numbers, particularly if any last-minute changes were made in the report.

The heading, TABLE OF CONTENTS, is centered according to the format you have selected (unbound, leftbound, or topbound). Quadruple space after the title to the first entry.

Leaders (periods and spaces alternated) extend across the page to guide the reader in finding the page number. The periods in the leaders are aligned vertically (each directly over the other) by keying all periods at either the even or odd numbers on the horizontal line scale.

preliminary: before the main part

The pages **preliminary** to the body of the report are numbered with lowercase Roman numerals. If a table of contents follows the title page, it is numbered *ii.* If, however, the table of contents is the only preliminary page to the body of the report, the page may not be numbered. Although the title page is considered the first of the preliminary pages, it is never numbered.

Summary

The summary is a brief description that gives the reader an overview of the report. In the business office, you may hear the summary called by a variety of names, including *executive summary* or *abstract*. An executive summary highlights the reports findings, conclusions, and recommendations. An abstract, however, is shorter and simply states the report's contents. The summary is a preliminary page to the body of the report and is numbered with lowercase Roman numerals.

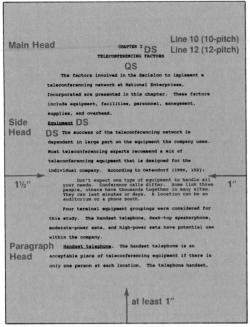

Leftbound, page 1

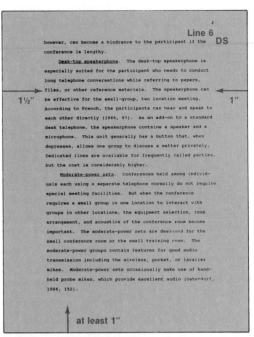

Leftbound, page 2

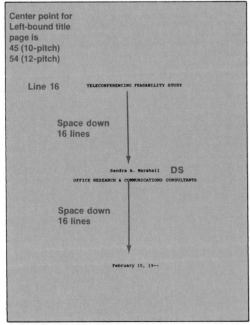

Leftbound, Title Page

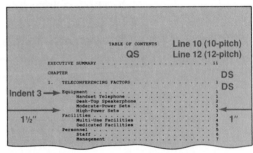

Leftbound, Contents page

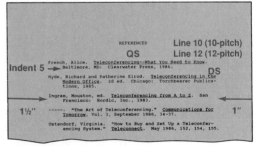

Leftbound, References

Illus. 11-15. Leftbound report formats for formal business reports.

Body

In longer reports, the body of the report will be divided into chapters or sections. The main heading of each of these divisions should begin on a new page with the word "Chapter" or "Section" typed in all capital letters, followed by the Roman numeral for that division. (Refer to page 478.) Double-space before and after all side heads. Underscore all side heads and all paragraph heads. Refer to Illus. 11-16 for information regarding margins and page numbers in formal reports.

FORMAL BUSINESS REPORTS

PLACEMENT/SPACING		UNBOUND		LEFTBOUND		TOPBOUND	
CENTERPOINT		Pica 42	Elite 51	Pica 45	Elite 54	Pica 42	Elite 51
TOP MARGIN	FIRST PAGE Place heading on.................. QS below heading. No page number is necessary.	line 10	line 12	line 10	line 12	line 12	line 14
	SECOND AND SUCCEEDING PAGES Place page number on	line 6 at right margin	line 6	line 6 at right margin	line 6	line 62 bottom center	line 62
	Continue body of report on line.................................	8	8	8	8	10	10
BOTTOM MARGIN	ALL PAGES	1" 6 lines	1"	1" 6 lines	1"	1" 6 lines	1"
LEFT MARGIN	ALL PAGES Inches..................................... Spaces....................................	1" 10	1" 12	1 1/2" 15	1 1/2" 18	1" 10	1" 12
RIGHT MARGIN	ALL PAGES	All report styles use a 1" right margin.					
SPACING MODE		Body of a report is usually DS, but may be SS.					

Illus. 11-16. Format guidelines for setting up formal business reports.

Your supervisor may include quotes from sources of information used to prepare the report. *Quotations*, which are excerpts from other sources, are identified in the body of the report. A quotation of more than three lines is set off from the rest of the text. Single-space the quotation, and indent it five spaces from the left margin. Giving credit to the sources of information used in a report is called **documentation**. Common methods of documentation are footnotes, endnotes, and textual citations.

Footnotes. When the **footnote method** is used, a superior (raised) reference figure is placed at the appropriate point in the copy with a matching numbered footnote at the bottom of the same page.

```
The most commonly found keyboard design is the familiar Qwerty

keyboard.¹
DS _____  1½ inch line
DS
¹ James F. Clark and Beverly Oswalt, Computer Confidence:  A
Challenge for Today (Cincinnati:  South-Western Publishing
Company, 1991), p. 447.

               (At least 1 inch bottom margin)
```

Endnotes. When the **endnote method** is used, a superior (raised) reference figure is placed at the appropriate point in the copy, the same as the footnote method does. The matching numbered references, however, are listed at the end of the report. The endnote method of documentation relieves the office worker of having to consider footnote placement at the bottom of individual pages.

```
The most commonly found keyboard design is the familiar Qwerty

keyboard.¹
```

Textual Citations. When the **textual citations method** is used, the source information is placed in parentheses within the text. This information includes author(s), date of publication, and page number(s).

```
The most commonly found keyboard design is the familiar Qwerty

keyboard (Clark and Oswalt, 1991, 447).
```

If the source is identified by name within the report copy, only the publication date and page number are used.

```
According to Clark and Oswalt (1991, 447), the most commonly
found keyboard design is the familiar Qwerty keyboard.
```

References

The reference section follows the body of the report and identifies the sources used in preparing the report. These include the sources for direct quotes, **paraphrased** sources, and sources your supervisor used to obtain ideas or background information.

paraphrased: expressed in another form

The title and format of the reference section depend upon the methods of documentation used in the body of the text:

- For footnotes, title the reference section BIBLIOGRAPHY. List the footnote references in alphabetic order in appropriate bibliographic format. Consult a style manual, an office handbook, or a previously prepared report which you know has an acceptable format.
- For endnotes, title the reference section ENDNOTES. Number and list each endnote in bibliographic format in the order presented in the body of the report.
- For textual citations, title the reference section REFERENCES. List the textual citations in alphabetic order in bibliographic format. If a reference does not show the author's name, list it alphabetically by the first important word in the title. Illustration 11-15 on page 478 shows one acceptable form for textual citation references.

Appendices

An **appendix** provides more detailed data (usually in the form of a chart, graph, table, or text) to support the body of the report. The appendix (or *appendices* if several are included) is placed at the end of the report for the benefit of interested readers. If more than one appendix is included, number or letter each in sequence. Center the heading APPENDIX (plus the appropriate number or letter, if needed) according to the report format (unbound, leftbound, or topbound).

Information Services

external: not located within the company

By using a computer, modem, and communications software, a business office can connect with ***external*** on-line information services. **Information services** provide electronic means of gaining access to accurate and timely information that otherwise may not be available to a business. An information service usually charges a connect fee, then bills according to time used or the number of ***searches*** made. Many businesses find an external information service such as CompuServe is less costly than maintaining expensive journal subscriptions and more efficient than using staff time to search for information in libraries. By using an information service, volumes of information can be searched quickly. Over 1,000 on-line databases provide many subscription services, such as financial and investment analysis, text of magazines and journals, and airline schedules.

searches: on-line database inquiries

Illus. 11-17. This office assistant has accessed an external information service to obtain up-to-the-minute information on stock quotations to include in a report.

Guidelines for Preparing Business Reports

A responsible office worker can be a helpful assistant in preparing a report. If you are asked to assist with a report, you will be expected to use your research skills to locate and process information quickly, accurately, and with attention to detail. The following guidelines will help you work efficiently:

1. During the information gathering stage, you may be able to key some information directly into your computer. If information must be collected manually, use note cards.
2. Scanners can reduce the amount of time you need to enter large quantities of previously keyed information or technical material into the report. If scanning is not possible, photocopy the material (such as tables) to be sure the details are accurate. Photocopying is faster and more accurate than copying the material by hand.
3. Record complete source details for all information you locate. (For example, title of publication, author, publisher, date, and page.)

FINANCIAL REPORTS

Many reports relate to financial aspects of businesses. Some financial reports are for internal use only. Others are provided to those outside the company, including shareholders in publicly owned corporations. In this section you will examine two commonly prepared financial reports—the income statement and the balance sheet. You will also be given guidelines for keying these important financial reports (also known as *financial statements*).

resources: available wealth

Financial statements provide information about a company's economic **resources** and results of operations. Publicly owned companies must provide financial statements to shareholders at the end of each quarter and at the end of the fiscal year.

Income Statement

An **income statement** is a financial report that details the results of operations for a specified period of time. It answers the question, "How successful was the business during the time period?" In this report you will find **revenues**, expenses, and the net income or net loss of a business for the reporting period.

revenues: earnings realized for goods and services

The income statement lists the amounts and sources of revenues, as well as expenses, for the reporting period. A *net income* results if revenues are greater than expenses. A *net loss* results if expenses are greater than revenues. Illustration 11-18 on page 484 shows Dandy's Delights (a single proprietorship) income statement for the recently ended fiscal year.

```
                        Dandy's Delights
                        Income Statement
                 For Year Ended December 31, 19--

                             QS

          Sales                                          $200,000
            DS
          Cost of Goods Sold                    100,000
          Gross Profit on Sales                          $100,000
            DS
          Operating Expenses
              Advertising Expense          $    500
Indent 5 ──►  Delivery Expense                1,000
              Office Supplies Expense           800
              Payroll Taxes Expense           4,500
              Salaries Expense               58,200
              Utilities Expense               3,500
              Miscellaneous Expense             500
Indent 10 ────────► Total Operating Expense              69,000
          Net Income from Operations                     $ 31,000
            DS
          Other Expense
              Interest Expense                            2,000
          Net Income Before Income Tax                   $ 29,000
              Less Income Tax                             8,200
          Net Income After Income Tax                    $ 20,800
```

Illus. 11-18. An income statement reflects the results of operating the company during a specific time period.

Samantha is the office assistant to Dan Burls, the owner of Dandy's Delights. Mr. Burls' cookies and baked goods are sold in most local supermarkets, and he is planning to expand soon into nearby towns. One of Samantha's duties is to key the final copy of financial statements. (Refer to Illus. 11-18 and Illus. 11-19.) Note the format and content of the two statements.

Balance Sheet

A **balance sheet** is a report that presents the financial condition of a company as of a specific date. The balance sheet reports the assets, liabilities, and owner's equity or capital. You will recall that the *assets* of a company include all the goods and property owned by the firm as well as the amount due the company from others. *Liabilities* are the debts of the company—what the company owes. The **owner's equity** or *capital* is the

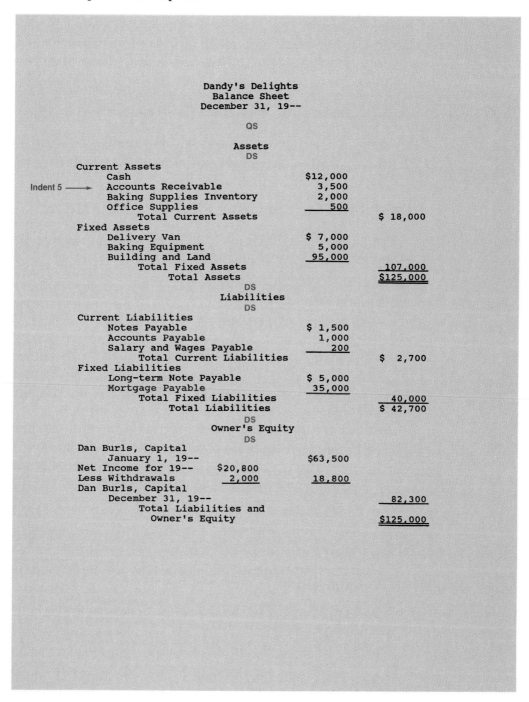

```
                          Dandy's Delights
                           Balance Sheet
                          December 31, 19--

                                QS

                              Assets
                               DS
           Current Assets
              Cash                           $12,000
Indent 5 ───▶ Accounts Receivable              3,500
              Baking Supplies Inventory        2,000
              Office Supplies                     500
                 Total Current Assets                     $ 18,000
           Fixed Assets
              Delivery Van                   $ 7,000
              Baking Equipment                 5,000
              Building and Land               95,000
                 Total Fixed Assets                        107,000
                    Total Assets                          $125,000
                               DS
                           Liabilities
                               DS
           Current Liabilities
              Notes Payable                  $ 1,500
              Accounts Payable                 1,000
              Salary and Wages Payable           200
                 Total Current Liabilities                $  2,700
           Fixed Liabilities
              Long-term Note Payable         $ 5,000
              Mortgage Payable                 35,000
                 Total Fixed Liabilities                    40,000
                    Total Liabilities                     $ 42,700
                               DS
                          Owner's Equity
                               DS
           Dan Burls, Capital
              January 1, 19--                $63,500
           Net Income for 19--    $20,800
           Less Withdrawals         2,000     18,800
           Dan Burls, Capital
              December 31, 19--                            82,300
                 Total Liabilities and
                    Owner's Equity                        $125,000
```

Illus. 11-19. A balance sheet represents the financial condition of a company as of a specific date.

owner's share or the worth of the firm—the excess of assets over liabilities. On every balance sheet, the total assets must equal the total liabilities plus the owner's equity. Thus, the accounting formula

$$\text{Assets (A)} = \text{Liabilities (L)} + \text{Owner's Equity (E)}$$

applies to every balance sheet, whether the balance sheet is for a giant corporation or a small, individually owned business.

Guidelines for Preparing Financial Statements

The following guidelines will help you to prepare financial statements accurately and with confidence:

1. Study the report formats of earlier copies of the income statement and the balance sheet before you key the financial statements. Continuing to use the same report formats helps executives compare data from year to year. Format guidelines may be included in a company's procedures manual.

2. Check the accuracy of all calculations *before* preparing the statements. Use a calculator or your computer to check the addition and subtraction required on the statements.

3. Although the financial statement formats may vary, the following format guidelines represent the generally accepted style of presenting financial statements:

   - Leave at least a one-inch margin at the top and bottom and on both sides.

   - Center the lines in the statement heading—company name, statement name, and the date(s) covered by the statement.

   - Double-space before and after headings in the body of the statement.

   - Key headings and titles in upper- and lowercase letters.

   - Use a single line (extending the width of the longest item in the column) keyed underneath the last figure to indicate addition or subtraction.

   - Use double lines underneath the final figure in a column.

- Use the dollar sign with the first figure of each *new* column of figures to be added or subtracted or with every sum or difference if the figure is keyed directly underneath a single line.

4. Proofread the copy slowly and carefully. Give attention to detail. If another worker is available to help you, proofreading can be made easier with one person reading aloud from the original document while the other person proofreads the prepared copy. In addition to the words and figures, the person reading aloud should indicate details such as capitalization, punctuation, underscores, vertical spacing, indentions, and dollar signs. Be particularly alert to **transposing** figures (for example, keying $1,245,385 for $1,254,385). As a final proof, recalculate or **prove** all totals.

transposing:
changing the order of

prove:
check the correctness of

Illus. 11-20. One effective method of proofreading is to have one person read aloud from the original document while the other person proofreads the prepared copy.

COMPUTER APPLICATIONS

A microcomputer will be a valuable tool as you prepare business reports. You are familiar with using word processing software to prepare text. Spreadsheet software packages enable you to use electronic worksheets to help perform calculations and analyze data to be included in reports. Additionally, the graphs used in formal and informal business reports may be generated through spreadsheet or graphics software. When color is available, graphs can be in color both on the screen and on the printout.

Spreadsheets

A **spreadsheet** is an electronic worksheet for analyzing numerical problems. Some spreadsheet programs contain hundreds of columns and rows. Spreadsheets are commonly used to report "what is" (an income statement, for example) or "what might be" (projections of costs or sales, for example). Once the information is displayed on the screen, calculations can be made and results can be analyzed. Decisions can then be made based upon the projections made by the computer. For example, an executive might use a spreadsheet program to forecast sales over the next five years or to determine whether to rent or buy new equipment.

Spreadsheets can be used for administrative tasks as well as for executive decision making. For example, you might be asked to use a spreadsheet program to calculate figures for a report your supervisor is submitting.

> *Brad, Audrey's supervisor, stopped at her workstation and said, "Please figure 7-percent, 10-percent, and 12-percent price increases for our 10 varieties of Valentine's Day candy boxes. Once I have that information, I can complete my report and have it in the sales manager's hands by Friday morning."*
>
> *Audrey used her spreadsheet software program to determine the projected price increases for the ten types of candy. (The data that appears in red in Illus. 11-21 on page 489 was entered by Audrey. After she entered the sample formulas, the computer automatically made the calculations that resulted in the information shown in blue.) Within minutes, Audrey was able to produce a computer printout showing the needed information. Brad then was able to complete his report.*

Graphs

You are familiar with graphs found in newspapers, magazines, and textbooks. Graphs make the copy more interesting, and in some cases graphs are easier to interpret than are columns of figures or blocks of text. Graphs, therefore, are used frequently in business reports to display supporting information.

As an office assistant, you may be expected to key or assemble documents which require the preparation of graphs. Three commonly used graphs are the *line graph*, the *bar graph*, and the *circle graph*. Refer to Illustrations 11-22, 11-23, and 11-24 on page 490 as you read about each graph.

```
   :  A   ::   B   ::   C   ::   D   ::   E   ::   F   ::   G   :

 1                          ZAMBERNELLI CHOCOLATES
 2                             Price Increases
 3
 4      ===============================================================
 5
 6      Candy        Current
 7        ID          Price
 8      Number       (Pound)      7%          10%          12%
 9                               Increase    Increase     Increase
10      ===============================================================
11
12      1041          4.89        5.23         5.38         5.43
13      1050          3.45        3.69         3.80         3.86
14      1053          2.25        2.40         2.48         2.52
15      1057          5.15        5.51         5.67         5.78
16      1063          5.98        6.40         6.58         6.70
17      1075          6.50        6.96         7.15         7.28
18      1147          3.98        4.26         4.38         4.46
19      1148          2.22        2.38         2.44         2.49
20      1150          5.49        5.87         6.04         6.15
21      1151          5.51        5.90         6.06         6.17
```

Illus. 11-21. Using a spreadsheet software program, Audrey entered the data that appears in red. The computer made the calculations that resulted in the information shown in blue.

Circle Graph

The circle graph (also called a *pie chart* because of the way in which the graph is divided into wedges like pieces of a pie) is used to show how part of something contributes to the whole. The whole circle represents 100 percent, and each wedge represents a portion of the whole. Each wedge should be identified with an appropriate label, color, or pattern, as shown in Illus. 11-22 on page 490. Software programs are available which will take the figures you key into the system (or the data already in the system), convert the figures into percentages, and prepare the pie chart for you.

Bar Graph

A bar graph can be used to show comparisons, as seen in Illus. 11-23. When preparing a bar graph, use bars of equal width. Space the bars equally across the graph. If you are using a graphics software package, the spacing probably will be determined automatically for you from the graphic specifications you entered into the computer.

Line Graph

The line graph, as shown in Illus. 11-24, is used to display trends that emerge over a period of time. Monthly sales, for example, are frequently represented in line graph form. In preparing such a graph, place the time categories across the bottom and the amounts along the side.

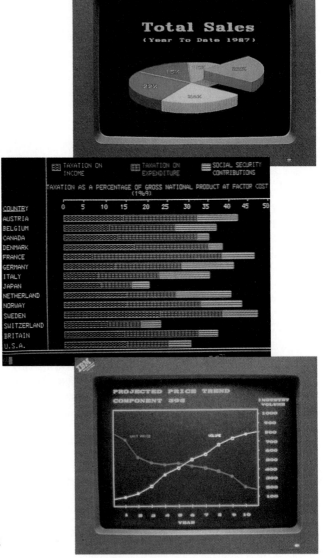

Illus. 11-22. Circle graphs show the relationship of a part to a whole. Color helps distinguish the individual parts of the chart.

Illus. 11-23. Bar graphs are used to show comparisons. A bar graph can have vertical or horizontal bars.

Illus. 11-24. Line graphs are excellent for showing changes over a period of time.

Guidelines for Preparing Graphs

The following general guidelines will be helpful to you as you keyboard and assemble a business report which contains graphs:

1. Study previous reports from the company to determine style preferences.
2. If the graph is half of a page or less in size, include it in the body of the text. Leave enough space before and after the graph to separate it visually from the text. Position the graph as near as possible to the portion of the text in which it is mentioned, ideally on the same page.
3. If the graph is larger than half of a page, place it on a separate page. That portion of the text in which the graph is mentioned should include a reference to the specific page on which the graph can be found.
4. Center the graph title in capital letters at the bottom or top of the graph.

QUESTIONS FOR REVIEW

1. Name six common parts of a formal business report.
2. Describe the formats of unbound, leftbound, and topbound reports.
3. What is report documentation? Name the three common methods of report documentation.
4. Describe how the titles and formats of the three report documentation methods differ in the reference section of a business report.
5. What guidelines should you follow to increase your effectiveness as you assist with preparing business reports?
6. Identify and describe two common financial reports.
7. What format guidelines should you follow when preparing financial statements?
8. What is a spreadsheet? Describe one purpose for which a spreadsheet might be used.
9. Identify three common graphs. What is the primary function of each kind of graph?
10. What guidelines should you follow in preparing graphs?

INTERACTING WITH OTHERS

Beth is the new office assistant to Mr. Hope, supervisor of the Customer Service Division. This morning Mr. Hope called Beth into his office and asked her to arrange for dinner reservations for himself and two clients at a local restaurant. When Beth returned from Mr. Hope's office, she looked upset. "I don't think I was hired to be a social secretary," she said. "I guess rank has all the privileges. Don't you agree?"

What You Are To Do: Prepare a brief response to Beth's question. What is Beth's professional responsibility in this situation?

EXTENDING YOUR MATH COMPETENCIES

As an office worker, you will be expected to deal with common measurements (such as seconds, hours, feet, yards, ounces, and pounds). Sometimes you may be asked to convert measurements into their equivalent values in another measurement form. For example, a project with the final report is scheduled to be completed in 217 days. How many weeks will it take to complete the project? The following exercise requires you to convert measurements into equivalent values.

What You Are To Do: On plain paper, number from 1 through 15. Convert the measurements in Column A into the equivalent measurements in Column B. (Use scratch paper for figuring.) Write the answers on your numbered paper; show any remainder as a fraction.

Column A	Column B		Reference
1. 390 seconds =	6 1/2	minutes	60 seconds = 1 minute
2. 1,230 minutes =	?	hours	60 minutes = 1 hour
3. 1,008 hours =	?	days	24 hours = 1 day
4. 371 days =	?	weeks	7 days = 1 week
5. 1,095 days =	?	years	365 days = 1 year
6. 723 months =	?	years	12 months = 1 year
7. 728 weeks =	?	years	52 weeks = 1 year
8. 485 pints =	?	quarts	2 pints = 1 quart
9. 628 quarts =	?	gallons	4 quarts = 1 gallon
10. 528 dozen =	?	gross	12 dozen = 1 gross
11. 88 ounces =	?	pounds	16 ounces = 1 pound
12. 10,500 pounds =	?	tons	2,000 pounds = 1 ton
13. 768 inches =	?	feet	12 inches = 1 foot
14. 105 feet =	?	yards	3 feet = 1 yard
15. 26,400 feet =	?	miles	5,280 feet = 1 mile

APPLICATION ACTIVITY

Your employer hands you the two handwritten drafts on page 494 and says, "Please prepare final copies of these two financial statements. I've checked the totals once, but you'd better verify them before you begin to key."

What You Are To Do:
1. Use a calculator or paper and pencil to prove the totals on both statements. (Refer to Reference Section D for instructions for verifying totals.)
2. Using sheets of plain paper, key final copies of the income statement and balance sheet for Energy Enterprises. Use the format guidelines presented on pages 483-487.
3. Clip together the final copies of the income statement and the balance sheet. Also include the paper tape or sheet of paper showing the verification of the totals (if a paper form was used).

CHAPTER SUMMARY

In this chapter, you were introduced to the important role office assistants play in management support activities. Much of the executive's decision making is based upon information received from the support staff. These are key points you will want to keep in mind:

1. As an office worker, you may help executives complete their responsibilities by your efficient and responsible handling of reminder systems, business meetings, travel arrangements, and the preparation of business reports.
2. The office calendar is the most widely used reminder system for scheduling the activities and resources of the business office. You will be expected to maintain office calendars and to manage appointment requests.
3. Executives spend a significant portion of their time in meetings and traveling on business. Your ability to complete meeting and travel arrangements efficiently and accurately adds to the executive's effectiveness. Such arrangements typically involve procedures that must be completed before, during, and after the event.
4. Business reports represent an important form of communication within a business. Formal business reports and financial reports are prepared using standard formats for these reports. Using spreadsheets, graphics, and other computer-related resources, such as information services, can be helpful in preparing business reports.

ENERGY ENTERPRISES
INCOME STATEMENT
FOR YEAR ENDED DECEMBER 31, 19--

Operating Revenue	328 50000	
Cost of Merchandise Sold	203 47000	
Gross Profit on Operations		125 03000
Operating Expenses		
Delivery Expense	4 53000	
Sales Salary Expense	23 82000	
Warehouse Supplies Expense	15 17000	
Office Salary Expense	22 80000	
Administrative Expense	3 29000	
Total Operating Expenses		69 61000
Net Income from Operations		55 42000
Other Expense		
Interest Expense		40000
Net Income Before Income Tax		55 02000
Less Income Tax		19 25700
Net Income After Income Tax		35 76300

BALANCE SHEET
DECEMBER 31, 19--

Assets		
Current Assets		
Cash	15 23000	
Accounts Receivable	25 50000	
Merchandise Inventory	85 49000	
Total Current Assets		126 22000
Plant Assets (Net)		251 00000
Total Assets		377 22000
Liabilities		
Current Liabilities		
Notes Payable	3 27000	
Interest Payable	37300	
Accounts Payable	19 54000	
Federal Income Tax Payable	4 50000	
Total Current Liabilities		27 68300
Long-term Liability		
Mortgage Payable		15 48000
Total Liabilities		43 16300
Owner's Equity		
John Jones, Capital		
January 1, 19--	322 29400	
Net Income for 19-- 35 763.00		
Less Withdrawals (24 000.00)	11 76300	
John Jones, Capital		
December 31, 19--		334 05700
Total Liabilities and		
Owner's Equity		377 22000

KEY CONCEPTS AND TERMS

reminder systems	footnote method
electronic calendar	endnote method
tickler file	textual citations method
agenda	appendix
minutes	information services
teleconference	income statement
on-line agenda	balance sheet
itinerary	owner's equity
documentation	spreadsheet

INTEGRATED CHAPTER ACTIVITY

You work as an office assistant for East Coast Office Consultants. Mrs. Neida B. Mashuda, your supervisor, is in the process of preparing a report on legal documents. She comes to your workstation and says, "Although this report is far from complete, I'd like you to key a draft of the title page and the first chapter. That way, I'll have some idea of how it will look in final form."

Word processing equipment can be used to complete this activity.

What You Are To Do: Keyboard the leftbound report on page 496 using plain paper. Refer to page 478 for proper document format. Prepare a title page that gives (a) the title of the report, LEGAL DOCUMENTS; (b) your supervisor's name, (c) the name of the company; and (d) the current date. Then prepare the pages for Chapter I of the report. Side heads are indicated by an underscore. There are no paragraph heads.

OPTIONAL COMPUTER APPLICATION ACTIVITY
See Computer Application Activity 11
in your Information Processing Activities workbook.

OPTIONAL CRITICAL THINKING ACTIVITY
See Critical Thinking Activity 4
in your Information Processing Activities workbook.

CHAPTER I
PREPARING LEGAL DOCUMENTS

(P) Legal documents are official papers which may be keyed by office assistants. Typical documents include contracts, powers of attorney, affidavits, wills, and acknowledgments. While each legal document has its own requirements, there are some general guidelines which apply to most documents. Legal Papers Legal documents may be prepared using standard 8 1/2 by 11-inch paper or special legal-size paper which is 8 1/2 by 14 inches. This paper may have printed left and right margin lines. Preprinted Legal Forms Some legal documents are prepared by keying the necessary information on a printed legal form. Standard forms for bills of sale, deeds, leases, mortgages, and wills may be purchased from office supply stores. However, important legal documents, even though they are on a printed form, should be checked carefully by a lawyer. Legal Backs or Covers A single backing sheet (called a legal back or cover) is used to protect a legal document. The sheet is usually a high-grade, heavy-quality paper that is wider and longer than the legal document itself. According to Tilton, Jackson, and Popham (1987, 644), backing sheets may be color coded to differentiate types of documents. Margins Minimum margins of two inches at the top and one inch at the bottom are usually allowed. When typing on legal paper with printed margin rules, margin stops are set so that margins of the typewritten material will be one or two spaces within the printed rules. If paper without margin rules is being used, a 1 1/2-inch left margin and a 1/2-inch right margin is allowed. Spacing and Paragraphs Legal documents are usually double-spaced, and paragraphs are indented ten spaces. Acknowledgments and quoted material are single-spaced. Erasures and Corrections A legal document states the rights or privileges or obligations of the parties who sign it and later may be submitted in a court of law as evidence. Therefore, it is imperative that there be no erasures or corrections on key details (such as names, amounts, and dates). Such corrections are forbidden in most states. Errors of only one or two letters in a relatively unimportant word are usually allowed. If the legal document has already been signed when an error is discovered, the change on that page must be initialed by the signers. Signature Lines Signature lines for the maker or makers of the document should be placed on the right side of the page. Lines for the signatures of witnesses (if any) are placed on the left side of the page. The first signature line is placed a quadruple space below the last line of the document. If there is more than one line, double spacing is used. The actual lines should be approximately three inches in length.

PRODUCTIVITY CORNER

Kathy Malenky
OFFICE SUPERVISOR

IS IT ANY OF MY BUSINESS?

DEAR MS. MALENKY:

I have been worrying about something that happened last week, and I still am not sure what I should have done. You see, I work as an assistant in the office of one of the division managers in our company. One of the staff members asked me to prepare a draft of the monthly income statement. I left the draft on the staff member's desk. A few hours later, the division manager called me into his office. He said, "I've just reviewed the figures in this draft. These revenues aren't right; the profit isn't high enough. Some of these figures must be changed. Please prepare another draft." I said nothing. I took the draft and changed the figures as indicated.

Now I wonder what I should have done. Did the division manager dishonestly change numbers to reflect false profits? Should this have been done? Did I have any responsibility?—LYNN IN LITCHFIELD

DEAR LYNN:

As an office assistant, it was your job to prepare the drafts as instructed. From what you say, I am guessing that you did not keep the records from which the staff member prepared the initial income statement. Therefore, it is possible the staff member had to use some *estimates* for the figures because final figures for the month were not available. The division manager may have had access to the final figures and used this information to revise the estimated numbers. The figures you were asked to use in the revision may have given a more accurate presentation of the month's activity than the figures you had keyed initially. Of course, there is the possibility that the manager was deliberately distorting the figures in order to show a more favorable performance record.

I would advise you not to worry about having done the wrong thing. You were not in a position to challenge the manager. However, in the future:

- Become familiar with your company's ethical standards. There may be a printed code of ethics available to all employees. Ask about such a code and read it carefully.
- Be careful to understand a situation fully before you make judgments about the ethical behavior of others.
- Always strive to reflect high ethical standards in all aspects of your own work.

Lynn, companies need employees with high ethical standards. Your sensitivity to such matters is a valuable trait.—KATHY MALENKY

RECORDS ADMINISTRATION
AND TECHNOLOGY

CHAPTER 12

Records Management

In Chapter 5 you learned how important information is to the successful operation of a company. However, a large amount of information in itself is not enough to insure that an organization will be productive. It is necessary to have a system for organizing, storing, and retrieving records. Equally necessary is a system for removing outdated records and disposing of them.

As an office worker in a small company or in the records management department of a large company, you will need to follow carefully the procedures for organizing, storing, retrieving, removing, and disposing of records. As you will learn in this chapter, businesses keep records on a variety of media, such as paper, magnetic media, and microfilm. You should be knowledgeable about these media so that you can maintain records properly.

Records management is a growing and changing field. It is important that you understand the need for good records management systems and that you remain informed about changes in office technology that may affect your job.

In this chapter, you will gain an overview of the ways in which businesses manage records and the ways in which office workers contribute to the efficiency of the existing records management system.

The objectives of the chapter are to:

- describe how a company's records management system can improve total office efficiency

- present the filing systems used to organize records

TOPIC 1

MAINTAINING OFFICE RECORDS

When you have completed your study of this topic, you will be able to:

- explain the objectives of records management

- identify the benefits of records management

- describe types of media on which information is kept

- identify the cost factors involved in a records management system

- describe the phases of a record life cycle

A company cannot operate without records. Each time an item is purchased or sold by a company, a record of the transaction is kept in the files. You will keep a copy of every letter you mail. You may even keep a written record of important telephone conversations. You will also keep items that you receive from other individuals or companies, such as letters, memos, reports, advertisements, and printouts.

Records are kept so that you can refer to the information at a later date or use the information to complete another task. That is why many businesses have a records management system. An effective records management system will help you store and retrieve records efficiently and keep the files current.

As an office worker, you need to realize how vital an efficient records management system is to the smooth operation of a business. In this topic, you will learn how businesses use a records management system to maintain office records.

A **record** is any information—text, data, image, or voice—kept for future reference. A **records management filing system** is a set of procedures used to organize, store, retrieve, remove, and dispose of records.

The main purpose of a records management system is to make sure records are available when needed so the business can operate efficiently. A records management system fulfills this purpose in several ways: by choosing appropriate storage media, by providing proper storage equipment and supplies, by outlining procedures for filing, by developing an efficient retrieval procedure, and by setting up a record retention and disposition policy.

Choosing Appropriate Storage Media

medium: singular of media

A company may keep records on a variety of media: paper, magnetic media, and microfilm. A good records management system includes a program for analyzing the needs of the company to determine which storage *medium* or combination of media is best. As an office worker, you may be expected to work with all of these media. Each medium has particular advantages and disadvantages, and you will learn more about these in this topic.

Providing Proper Storage Equipment and Supplies

Storage equipment, such as filing cabinets, should be chosen with specific storage media in mind. For example, if your records are on paper, you might use a filing cabinet similar to the one shown in Illus. 12-1. But this cabinet would not be appropriate for filing microfilm records. You may use supplies such as file folders to hold paper records, but you would not use them for storing computer tapes. Chapter 13 discusses the types of equipment and supplies appropriate for each type of storage medium.

You should keep certain records in fireproof cabinets or vaults. A records management system includes policies that help you determine which records require special protection. For example, you may be instructed to protect original copies of contracts by storing them in a fireproof vault.

Illus. 12-1. An efficient records management system provides for the proper storage of records. Filing cabinets are ideal for storing paper records.

Establishing Procedures for Filing

Filing is the process of storing office records in an orderly manner within an organized system. The procedure you follow to file records will vary according to the storage media used and the manner in which the files are organized. Chapter 13 will present specific filing procedures.

You may file records alphabetically according to name, subject, or geographic location. Or you may file them by number or date. Topic 2 of this chapter explains these systems in more detail.

Developing an Efficient Retrieval Procedure

You need an orderly way to retrieve records. An efficient retrieval procedure will include specific instructions for removing or *charging out* records. Charging out a record usually means that the following information is written down when the record is removed from the file: the name and department of the worker who is taking the record, the date the record was retrieved, and the date the record will be returned. This information is kept on file in case someone else must locate the record. A retrieval procedure also would indicate whether all workers had free access to the records or whether only designated staff members could retrieve the records. Chapter 13 will explain retrieval procedures in more detail.

Setting up a Record Retention and Disposition Policy

policy: rule

Each record has a life cycle. A records management system should include a statement of the *policy* on how long records are kept and how they are to be disposed of. Most companies use a *retention schedule*, which lists how long each type of record should be kept. You should keep the files free of outdated or unnecessary records so that you can work efficiently. Later in this topic, you will learn more about this aspect of records management.

BENEFITS OF AN EFFECTIVE RECORDS MANAGEMENT SYSTEM

An effective records management system benefits the company in two ways. First, workers are more productive. Second, customer *goodwill* is maintained.

Greater Productivity

goodwill: positive relationship

compile: put together

To make an intelligent decision or complete a task well, you need accurate, current information. To *compile* a monthly sales report, you need to have the sales figures for each sales representative. Before you pay an invoice, you should check your records to be sure the charge is correct. Before you can mail a package, you need to know the recipient's complete address.

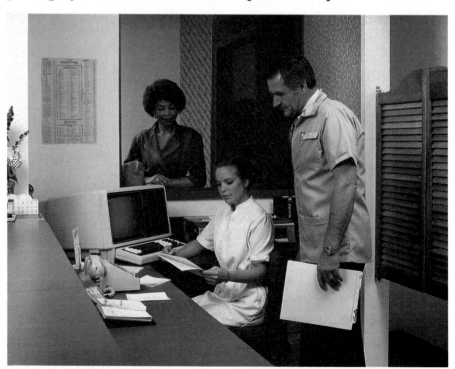

Illus. 12-2. Because current information is readily available, this medical assistant can perform office tasks without wasting valuable time.

You must be able to access needed records easily and quickly. An effective records management system will enable you to be more productive since you will not waste valuable time searching for information that should be easily available.

Customer Goodwill

Customers and business associates may not fully appreciate efficient records management in your company even though they like the results of such management. They are pleased when you retrieve pertinent information quickly. Yet they may take the smooth operation of the records management system for granted.

eroded: made less; worn away

Imagine a customer's reaction if he or she called to ask a question, and after several minutes the customer services representative reported that there was no record of the account! The customer would be furious and probably would tell others about this frustrating event. Customer goodwill and confidence would have been **eroded**. On the other hand, if a customer called and received a prompt and courteous response to questions, he or she would be pleased. Goodwill between the customer and the business would be maintained or even improved.

An effective records management system will specify procedures for accessing records quickly and for keeping records current. If you follow these procedures, the records management system will help you maintain customer goodwill.

STORAGE MEDIA FOR RECORDS

Businesses typically store records on a variety of media. The most common storage medium continues to be paper. But businesses are recording more and more information on magnetic media and microfilm because less space is required to store the records and because the records can be accessed more quickly.

Paper

Each time you print a copy of a letter, record an address on an index card, complete a telephone message form, or command the computer to print out a statistical report or complicated graph, you are recording information on paper. These paper records are referred to as *hard copy*.

The advantage of paper is that you can immediately read the information recorded. With magnetic media, on the other hand, you need a display screen or printer to read the information recorded. Two disadvantages of storing records on paper are that paper records take up a great deal of space and they can easily be misfiled.

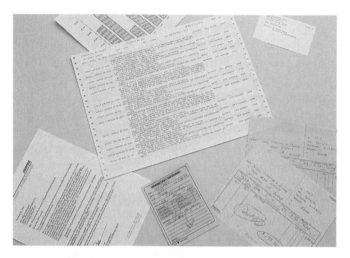

Illus. 12-3. A record is any information kept for future reference. This includes paper records (left) and records stored on magnetic media (right).

Magnetic Media

You were introduced to magnetic media in Chapter 5. You will recall that magnetic media are reusable media that store information electronically. The most frequently used forms of magnetic media are flexible (floppy) disks, hard disks, and tapes.

Advantages of Using Magnetic Media

Four major advantages to the use of magnetic media are:

● Records can be retrieved quickly and easily.
● The storage space required for housing records on magnetic media is much less than that required for paper media.
● Records stay in the same sequence on the magnetic media even after being retrieved several times.
● Records can be updated easily.

Disadvantages of Using Magnetic Media

Three disadvantages to using magnetic media to store records are:

● An output device such as a monitor or printer is needed to read the information recorded on the magnetic media.

alter: change
- Electrical power surges and failures can erase and/or ***alter*** the information recorded on magnetic media.
- Magnetic media require special protection from extremely hot or cold temperatures and should be kept away from magnetic fields.

> *When Joyce walked by Ken's workstation, she noticed that several floppy disks were out of their protective jackets and lying on top of the monitor. Ken was working at the computer and seemed unconcerned about the situation:*
>
> *Joyce:* *Ken, did you know you could be destroying all your hard work right now?*
>
> *Ken:* *What do you mean?*
>
> *Joyce:* *Floppy disks are sensitive to magnetic forces such as those found in the computer and even the telephone. You should never place them on top of the monitor! And by leaving them out of their jackets you risk scratching them or dropping something on them that will mar the surfaces.*
>
> *Ken:* *I guess you're right. (He removes the floppy disks from the top of the monitor and places them in their jackets.) I'd hate to lose everything I just worked on.*

Microfilm

Microfilm is similar to motion picture film and is available in different widths. The most common widths are 16 millimeter (mm), 35 mm, and 105 mm. **Microimaging systems**, also called *micrographics*, are systems that photographically reduce documents to a fraction of their original size to fit on film. You will want to understand the equipment, supplies, and procedures used to record information on microfilm. The following steps are involved in the microimaging process:

1. Records are gathered so they can be recorded on microfilm. (Chapter 13, Topic 2, describes methods of organizing records for storage on microfilm.)
2. A microimaging camera is used to take pictures of the hard copies.
3. The microfilm is developed. Each record then appears as a tiny picture—a *microimage*—on the film, as shown in Illus. 12-4 on page 508.
4. A device called a *reader* is used to display the microimage for reading. Some readers, referred to as *reader/printers*, will also print a hard copy of the microimage.

Computer Output Microfilm (COM) is the process of transferring images from magnetic media directly to microfilm. The computer reads information recorded on magnetic media and outputs it as microimages on film rather than as paper printouts. Microfilm takes less space to store than paper and will not deteriorate after long periods of time.

Microforms

You may use microfilm in different forms. These different forms of microfilm are referred to as **microforms**. The most frequently used microforms are described here:

Roll Microfilm. Roll microfilm is a roll of 16-mm or 35-mm film which contains a series of pictures or images much like movie film. The film, which usually comes in 100- or 215-foot lengths, is the most inexpensive microform. A 100-foot roll can hold up to 4,000 images. Typically, roll microfilm is used to store records that are not used frequently or records that do not require changes. Roll microfilm is usually housed in a protective cassette or cartridge.

Aperture Cards. The most commonly used aperture card is a card that contains one microimage from 16-mm or 35-mm film. You may be asked to keep images of large-format drawings, such as engineering drawings or land surveys, on aperture cards. Identifying information about the microimage can be printed on the card itself.

Illus. 12-4. Roll microfilm is an inexpensive record storage medium.

Illus. 12-5. An aperture card contains one microimage.

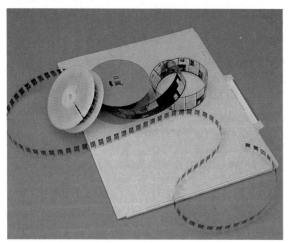

Microfiche. Microfiche is a small rectangular sheet of microfilm which contains a series of microrecords arranged in rows and columns. Although microfiche is available in a variety of sizes, the 6″ x 4″ size is the most commonly used. You might be asked to store directories or manuals on microfiche. Identifying information about the microrecords appears at the top of each microfiche, as shown in Illus. 12-6.

Microfilm Jackets. A microfilm jacket is a plastic holder for strips of 16 mm or 35 mm microfilm. The most common jacket size is 4″ x 6″. Strips of microfilm or single microimages are inserted into sleeves or pockets, as shown in Illus. 12-7. You can easily update a microfilm jacket by removing a microimage or an entire strip of film from a sleeve and replacing it with another. Some companies use microfilm jackets to store personnel records. With a microfilm jacket, records can be added easily. Space at the top of the jacket is reserved for identifying the contents.

Illus. 12-6. Microfiche is a popular, economical, and practical medium for storing records.

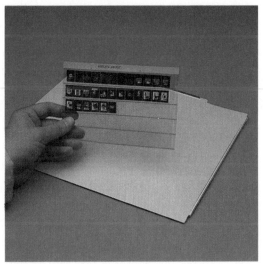

Illus. 12-7. A microfilm jacket is used to hold strips of microfilm or single microimages.

Advantages of Using Microfilm

Six advantages of storing records on microfilm are:

- A microimage takes up less space than a record stored on paper.
- In a microimaging system, the image is viewed but not removed from the film. The microimages are always in the

same sequence on the same microform, regardless of how often the microform is retrieved and filed. In a paper storage system, the record is usually removed from the folder for reference and then returned later.

- Hard copies of microimages can be produced on reader/printers when needed.

- Microimaging is an inexpensive way to **archive** important records. Microimages are accepted in courts as legal evidence just as paper records are.

- Retrieval devices available for use with microfilm make it easy to access needed records.

- Microfilm can be easily duplicated and stored in a separate, protected location.

> During their break, Mario and Carolyn began discussing the new microimaging system their company had recently implemented:
>
> Mario: At first I wasn't sure that microimaging would be helpful. But now I'm glad we have the system.
>
> Carolyn: I was looking forward to having our records on microfilm! Our file cabinets were so crowded and the file drawers so high that I had difficulty just filing and retrieving records.
>
> Mario: What I've enjoyed is being able to refer to a record without cluttering my workstation with more paper. But if I need a hard copy, I can make one by using the microfilm reader/ printer.

Disadvantages of Using Microfilm

Two disadvantages of storing records on microfilm are:

- The initial cost may seem high, since a camera, reader/printer(s), and microfilm must be purchased to record information on film.

- Office workers must be given special training so they can operate the microimaging equipment.

COST FACTORS ASSOCIATED WITH RECORDS MANAGEMENT

Costs are **inevitable** with any records management system. The cost factors involve buying equipment and supplies, leasing storage space, and paying office workers to file and retrieve records.

Equipment and Supplies

Major equipment purchases such as filing cabinets and shelves, as well as periodic purchases of filing supplies, contribute to the cost of maintaining a records management system.

conservative: not
wasteful

Proper care of equipment and ***conservative*** use of supplies on your part will help control costs.

Storage Space

When businesses lease office space, they lease by the square foot. The company pays for the space occupied by records every time it writes a rent check. By keeping the space required to house records to a minimum, the space available for work is increased. Using microfilm to store records is one way to reduce the amount of space required to house records.

Personnel

Workers are a key element in an effective records management system. Efficient procedures are worthless unless they are put into practice by workers. The salaries a company must pay personnel to manage records are a cost factor of records management.

Illus. 12-8. As a tape librarian for the Census Bureau, this office worker contributes to the efficiency of the overall records management system.

Large companies often have an entire staff of records management personnel. There may be a records manager who is in charge of the records management department. The staff may include a records management analyst, a records center supervisor, and several records clerks. Since records management is a field growing in importance, more and more businesses are looking for workers who specialize in managing records. Records management is a major career opportunity.

Use of Cost-Saving Techniques

Professional office workers eagerly search for ways to reduce costs. Even as a beginning office worker, you can be on the lookout for ways to improve the existing records management system such as:

streamline: make more efficient

- ***Streamline*** the filing and retrieval process.
- Reduce the storage space required for records.
- Be cost-conscious.

RECORD LIFE CYCLE

Records come from many sources. Some records originate from outside the organization (correspondence from other businesses and industry surveys, for example). Other records originate within the organization (interoffice memorandums; records of sales and purchases; computer printouts; and copies of outgoing correspondence, for example).

The usefulness of each record has a beginning and an end. Therefore, each record has a life cycle. The phases of the record life cycle are the same regardless of whether the records are kept on paper, magnetic media, or microfilm. A record life cycle is shown in Illus. 12-9. Refer to this illustration as you read the following brief description of each phase.

Phase 1: Collect the Records

The cycle begins when you collect the records. The two arrows at the top of Illus. 12-9 indicate the source of the records—either from outside the company or within the company.

Phase 2: Categorize the Records

categorize: assign to a group on the basis of certain characteristics

Next, you need to ***categorize*** the records as to how important they are to the operation of the company. A records management policy will help you do that. How records are categorized will affect how you store the records and how long you keep them. Refer to Illus. 12-10 on page 514.

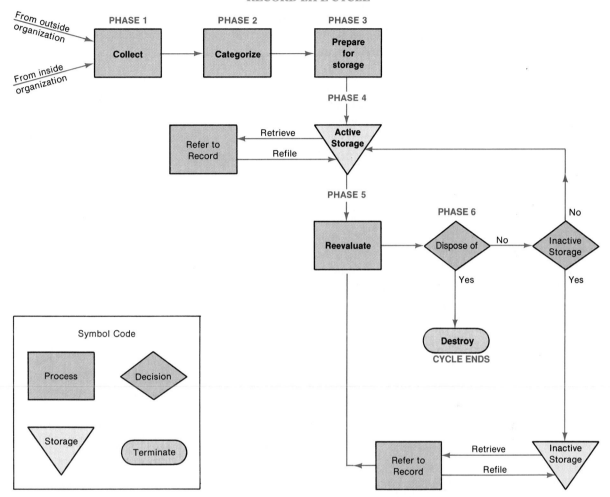

RECORD LIFE CYCLE

Illus. 12-9. These six phases make up the life cycle of records, whether the records are kept on paper, magnetic media, or microfilm.

Phase 3: Prepare the Records for Storage

The procedure you use in this phase will vary. The specifics of the procedure will depend on whether the record is on paper, magnetic media, or microfilm. You also need to know whether the record should be filed alphabetically, numerically, or chronologically.

Phase 4: Maintain the Records in Active Storage

When a record is in active storage, you probably will file and retrieve it many times. A good records management system will specify procedures for retrieving records and for returning them to the files efficiently.

Phase 5: Reevaluate the Records

Each record's importance should be reevaluated regularly. Some records may remain in active storage while others are transferred to inactive storage. Some records may be removed from the files altogether and destroyed. Records in inactive storage are still retrieved and refiled, but not as frequently as records in active storage.

Phase 6: Dispose of the Records

Disposing of a record involves transferring it to inactive storage or destroying it. When a record is no longer needed, you should destroy it to make room for current records. The cycle ends when a record is destroyed.

Illus. 12-10.
Records must be categorized as to their importance to the company. Into which category do canceled checks fall?

RECORD CATEGORIES		
Category	**Description**	**Examples**
Vital Records	Essential for the company to survive	Original copies of: deeds, copyrights, mortgages, trademarks
Important Records	Needed for business to operate smoothly; expensive to replace	tax returns, personnel files, cancelled checks
Useful Records	Convenient to have, yet replaceable	correspondence, purchase orders, names and addresses of suppliers
Nonessential Records	Has one-time or very limited usefulness	meeting announcements, advertisements

REMOVING RECORDS FROM ACTIVE STORAGE

When records are outdated, or needed only infrequently, you should remove them from the active storage area. An effective records management system will include a policy for removing records from active storage.

Retention Schedule

A **retention schedule**, shown in Illus. 12-11, is a valuable records management tool that identifies how long particular types of records should be kept. The retention schedule has columns for a description of the type of record, the retention period (how long the record should be kept), and the authority who regulates how long the record should be kept. Government authority dictates how long you should keep certain records such as tax returns. Company executives may also establish policies for keeping records such as bank statements, expense reports, and budgets.

Illus. 12-11. Can you determine from this retention schedule how long bank statements must be kept?

RECORDS RETENTION SCHEDULE		
Record Description	**Retention Period**	**Authority**
ACCOUNTING RECORDS		
Accounts Payable Ledger	5 years	Company Policy
Accounts Receivable Ledger	5 years	Company Policy
Balance Sheets	Permanent	Company Policy
Bank Statements	3 years	Company Policy
General Ledger Records	Permanent	Code of Federal Regulations
Payroll Registers	3 years	Fair Labor Standards Act

Inactive Storage

Records that are needed by the company, but are not often referred to, are *inactive*. Inactive records should be stored separately from active records. For example, assume you are required to keep company bank statements for three years. Since it is not likely that you will often refer to the past years' statements, you should remove them from active storage. You do not want inactive records to take up valuable active storage space. It is easier to retrieve and file active records when the inactive ones are in a separate location.

Archives

Special records of historical value are stored apart from active records. An **archive** is a storage area that is dedicated to organizing and preserving such historical records.

QUESTIONS FOR REVIEW

1. Why do companies keep records?

2. Why is an effective records management system vital to the smooth operation of a company?

3. How does an effective records management system result in greater productivity by office workers?

4. List one advantage and one disadvantage of using paper to store information.

5. What are the three most frequently used forms of magnetic media?

6. Identify four types of microforms.

7. List four advantages of storing records on microfilm.

8. What are three cost factors that affect the efficiency of a records management system?

9. List the six phases of the record life cycle.

10. What is a retention schedule?

INTERACTING WITH OTHERS

An important folder is missing from the central files. Your supervisor asks if you have it or know where it is. After quickly searching your workstation, you inform your supervisor that you do not have the missing folder. The next day as you are looking through a stack of materials on the table behind your workstation, you find the missing folder. What should you do or say now? How could you have prevented this awkward situation?

What You Are To Do: Prepare a response to the questions asked.

EXTENDING YOUR MATH COMPETENCIES

Activity 1

Seven departments have requested additional file folders. Folders are ordered from the supply company in boxes, each containing 25 folders. The number of folders each department needs is given in the following list:

```
Accounting                20
Finance                   45
Human Resources          100
Marketing                130
Production               175
Public Relations          95
Word Processing          250
```

How many folders are needed to meet the needs of the seven departments? How many boxes of folders should be ordered? How many folders will be left after each department has received the number of folders it requested?

What You Are To Do: Calculate the answers to the above questions. Show your calculations. Refer to Reference Section D, if necessary.

Activity 2

A single file drawer contains 75 folders. Fifteen of these were transferred to inactive storage. Of the remaining active folders, six had their contents divided into two folders each.

What You Are To Do: Calculate how many active folders are now in the file drawer. Show your calculations. Also, calculate the percentage of decrease in the number of folders in the active file. Refer to Reference Section D, if necessary.

APPLICATION ACTIVITY

Word processing equipment can be used to complete this activity.

Your supervisor, Mrs. Suzuki, is responsible for updating the records management section of the company office manual. She approaches your workstation and says: "Here is my edited draft of the updated material for the company office manual. Please key a final copy, making the changes I've indicated on the draft. Correct any errors I may have overlooked."

What You Are To Do: Using plain paper, key a final copy of the draft, which follows.

JOB DESCRIPTION FOR POSITIONS IN RECORDS MANAGEMENT   *use two lines for the heading*

RECORDS MANAGEMENT DIRECTOR

     Minimum of
    Education: Bachelor's Degree with intensive course work in business administration; ~~minimum~~ advanced degree helpful.

    Duties: ~~Responsible for~~ developing and implementing all company records management policies and practices; coordinates personnel and resources.

    Experience: Five years experience as a records management supervisor or consultant.

     center
RECORDS SUPERVISOR

    Education: Two years of college or vocational training in business.
 #   Experience: Two to five years in records center.
 #   Duties: Maintain and oprate corporate records center; hire and supervise staff; ~~responsible~~ for protection, storage, and disposal of ~~vital~~ records.   *establish and monitor procedures*

MICROIMAGING TECHNICIAN
                              stet
    Education: High school diploma plus ~~technical~~ training in
lc Microfilming.
 #   Experience: Previous experience helpful but not necessary.
 #   Duties: Operate cameras and film processors; test developed film for quality; ~~conform~~ operations ~~to meet~~ production standards.
    maintain   *in conformity with*

RECORDS CLERK
                                       and keyboarding
    Education: High school diploma with courses in office procedures.
 #   Expereince: Entry-level position; experience not required.
 #   Duties: Sort, file, and retrieve records; classify materials and records; transfer records to inactive storage.
  to company policy.   *; dispose of records according*

TOPIC 2

PAPER RECORDS SYSTEMS

When you have completed your study of this topic, you will be able to:

- identify the components of a filing system

- describe four alphabetic filing systems

- explain how a numeric filing system is organized

- explain how a chronologic filing system is organized

In Topic 1 you learned that each record has a life cycle. In this topic you will become acquainted with systems for organizing paper files while the records are in the storage phase of the record life cycle.

Although there is a definite move toward computerized filing systems, paper filing systems continue to be the most common. In today's rapidly changing offices, it is not unusual for a company to use both computers and paper filing systems. Systems for organizing magnetic media and microfilm files will be presented in detail in Chapter 13. Here you will concentrate on paper filing systems.

In a filing system for paper records, individual records are stored in folders. The folders are labeled and organized alphabetically according to names of individuals or businesses, subjects, or geographic locations. You can also organize files numerically and by date.

As a beginning office worker, you will be expected to understand your company's filing system so you can file and retrieve records efficiently. You may even have an opportunity to suggest improvements for an existing filing system.

Some companies use only one filing system for all their paper records. Other companies may use more than one. For example, purchase orders may be filed numerically by order number, while records about customers are filed alphabetically. You will learn how each type of paper filing system is organized and used.

house: store

A filing system requires equipment, procedures, and supplies. You will need to understand the various types of each.

Equipment

Various types of equipment—cabinets and shelves—are used to *house* paper records. Lateral file cabinets like those shown in Illus. 12-12 are used in many offices. In this topic we will assume that all records in your company are stored in a lateral file cabinet. Chapter 13, Topic 1, describes other equipment used in a paper filing system.

Illus. 12-12. Lateral files are frequently used to store medical records.

Procedures

Before placing records in folders, you should index and code each record. Chapter 13 will explain procedures for indexing, coding, and filing in detail. However, a brief introduction is included here to help you understand why these procedures are an important component of a filing system.

Indexing

Indexing is the process of deciding how to identify each record to be filed—either by name, subject, geographic location, number, or date. In a name file, for example, you would index a record by a specific individual or company name. In a numeric file, on the other hand, you would index a record by a specific number.

Coding

Coding is the process of marking a symbol or other identification on the record to indicate how it was indexed. Colored pencils often are used for coding.

You may code a record by circling the appropriate name, subject, geographic location, or number which appears on the record. Or you may write the identification in the upper right corner of the record.

As you learned in Topic 1, you may retrieve and refile a record many times while it is in active storage. By coding a record, you help ensure that the record will be filed correctly each time it is returned to the files.

Supplies

Each drawer in a file contains two different kinds of filing supplies: guides and file folders. The *guides* divide the drawer into sections and serve as *signposts* for quick reference. They also provide support for the folders and their contents. File folders hold the papers in an upright position in the file drawer and serve as containers to keep the papers together. *Labels* are attached to file folders to identify the contents of the folders. Labels are also attached to file cabinet drawers to identify the contents of each drawer.

Guides

Guides are heavy cardboard sheets which are the same size as the file folders. A *tab* extends over the top of each guide, and a notation is marked or printed on the tab. This notation on the tab of a guide is called a *caption*. By reading the captions, you can quickly identify divisions within the file. For example, a guide may carry the caption A, which tells you that only material starting with the letter A is found between that guide and the next one.

Guides are classified as primary or special. *Primary guides* indicate the major divisions, such as letters of the alphabet, into which the filing system is separated. *Special guides* indicate subdivisions within these major divisions. Illus. 12-15 on page 525 shows how primary and special guides are arranged in an alphabetic filing system. Behind primary guide "C" you may have a special guide such as Cooper Temporaries. Try not to have more than 10 folders behind a guide, and try to have only about 15 to 25 guides in a file drawer.

Labels

You need labels on file drawers so you can identify the contents of each drawer without opening the drawer. You also need labels on file folders.

Drawer Labels. The information on the drawer label should be specific, easy to read, and current. When the contents of a cabinet are changed in any way, the drawer label must be corrected immediately.

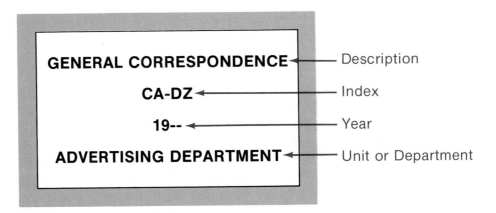

Folder Labels. Folder labels are gummed strips of paper you attach to the folder tabs. The caption on the label identifies the contents of the folder. It is important to format the captions in a consistent manner, usually at the top, left corner of the label.

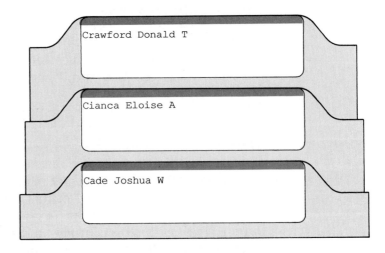

Color-Coded Labels. Many companies use color-coded labels to improve filing efficiency. There are several ways to use color-coded labels. One way simply involves assigning a specific color to each alphabetic or numeric section of the files. On page 525 notice that all the fourth/fifth position folders in the drawer labeled CA-DZ have labels coded with the same color.

A more complex coding system is shown in Illus. 12-13. You can see the color pattern formed by the labels. Such a pattern helps you file and retrieve records quickly and accurately. If a folder were misfiled, you would know immediately because the color pattern would be interrupted.

Illus. 12-13. A color-coded filing system is designed to help office workers file and retrieve records efficiently. Can you see the pattern formed by the folder labels?

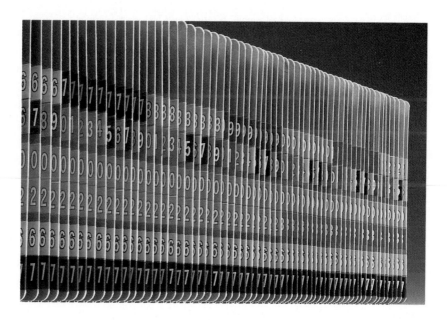

Folders

A folder is made of strong, durable paper called *manila*. Folders are larger than the papers they contain so that they will protect the papers. Standard folder sizes are designed for papers that are 8 ½" x 11" and for papers that are 8 ½" x 13" or 8 ½" x 14".

Folder Cuts. Folders are cut across the top so that the back has a tab that projects above the top of the folder. You attach labels to the folder tabs to identify the contents of the folders. Folder tabs vary in width and position, as shown on page 524. Sometimes the tab is the full width of the folder. This is called a full-cut or straight-cut folder. Half-cut tabs are half the width of the folder and have two possible positions. Third-cut folders have three positions, each tab occupying a third of the width of the folder. Another standard tab has five positions and is called a fifth-cut folder. Some folders hang from metal frames placed inside the file drawer. Removable tabs can be attached to these folders at appropriate positions.

Illus. 12-14.
Standard folder cuts. Notice that the folder tabs vary in width and position.

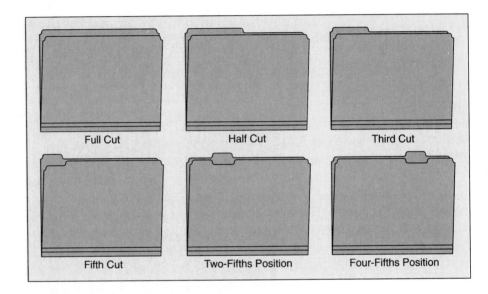

Full Cut	Half Cut	Third Cut
Fifth Cut	Two-Fifths Position	Four-Fifths Position

Position of Guides and Folders

There exists in offices today a variety of filing systems. Some systems (especially color-coded systems) are purchased from commercial manufacturers of filing supplies; other systems are developed **in-house**. Therefore, the positioning of guides and folders within filing systems will vary from company to company. Regardless of the system used, the guides and folders should be arranged in such a way that they are easy to see and in a logical order. You can see that the arrangement in Illus. 12-15 allows your eye to move easily from left to right.

in-house: within the company

Primary Guides

When you open a file drawer, you look first for the appropriate primary guide. Since you read from left to right, the tab on the primary guide should be at the far left *(first position)* where it will be easy to locate. Usually companies use guides with fifth-cut tabs. Tabs on primary guides are most often in the first position.

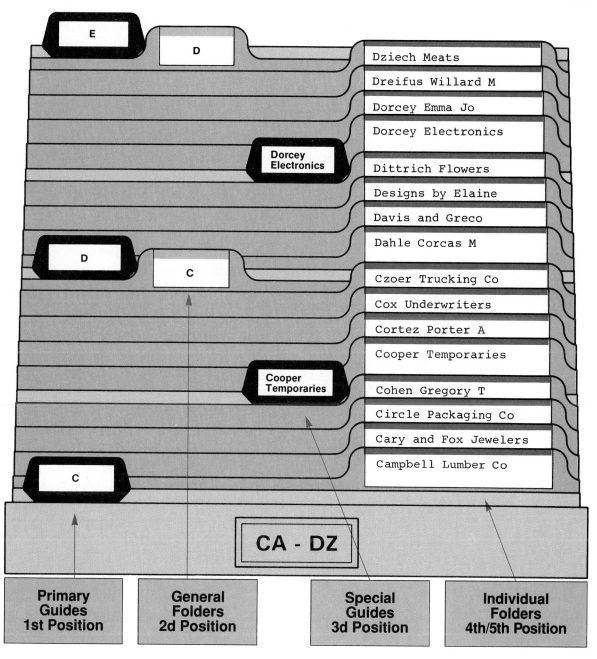

Illus. 12-15. Portion of a name file. Notice the positions of the guides and folders.

General Folders

There is usually a general folder for each primary guide. This second position folder bears the same alphabetic caption as the one shown on the primary guide. For example, the general folder that goes behind the primary guide "C" also will bear the caption "C." These folders are given the name *general* because they are used to accumulate records that do not justify the use of an individual folder. When you accumulate five or more records relating to one name or subject, prepare an individual folder for those records.

Special Guides

On page 525, special guides are located in the *third position*. Special guides are used to pinpoint the location of a specific *fourth/fifth position* individual folder. For example, the special guide "Dorcey Electronics" was added because of frequent requests for the Dorcey Electronics folder. Because of the special guide, this folder can easily be located.

Sometimes a special guide is used to pinpoint the location of a single folder or a series of folders relating to a specific subject. On page 529 for example, the special guide "Film" marks the location of two individual folders relating to the subject, film.

Individual Folders

In the illustration on page 525, individual folders are shown in the combined *fourth/fifth position*. Using individual folders helps you locate records more quickly. Notice the width of the tabs on the individual folders. This extra width allows ample space for labeling personal, company, or subject names.

ALPHABETIC FILING SYSTEMS

In an alphabetic filing system, letters and words (names, subjects, or geographic locations) are used as captions on the guides and folders. You arrange the guides and folders in alphabetic order according to the captions. Reference Section F presents rules for filing alphabetically. Refer to Reference Section F to complete the end-of-topic activities.

Four common alphabetic filing systems use name, subject, a combination of name and subject, and geographic location.

Illus. 12-16. A records management system is efficient only if records can be retrieved quickly and easily when needed.

Filing by Name

If a name file is used, you will index records according to the name of an individual or a company. The folders are arranged in alphabetic order within the file drawer.

Guides and Folders

The illustration on page 528 shows how alphabetic primary and special guides are used in a name file to help you file and retrieve records efficiently. If you were looking for a folder labeled "Burns Jewelers," you would find the primary guide "B," then scan the special guides until you found "Bu." Then you would search for the individual folder of Burns Jewelers. By using the guides, you would be able to locate the folder quickly without having to thumb through all the folders.

If you do not find an individual folder for the record, file the record in the appropriate general folder.

Carrie:	*Roy, there is no folder in the file labeled "Burton Real Estate." Where do I file this letter?*
Roy:	*If there is no individual folder for Burton Real Estate, file it in the general folder behind the "Bu" secondary guide. When we have several more letters to or from Burton Real Estate, we will set up an individual folder for those records.*

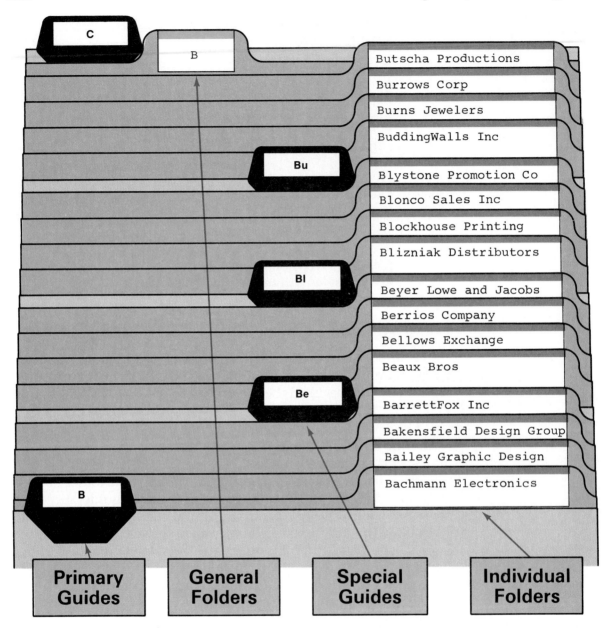

Primary Guides	**General Folders**
Special Guides	**Individual Folders**

Illus. 12-17. Portion of a name file. Can you locate the alphabetic primary and special guides?

Filing by Subject

When a subject filing system is used, you index records according to particular subjects, such as marketing, office machines, and public relations. A subject file is used when you request records by their contents more often than by the names of individuals or companies.

Guides and Folders

Use subject titles as captions for primary guides. In Illus. 12-18 you can see that the primary guides are Advertisers, Applications, and Audiovisual Equipment.

You may use special guides to identify subdivisions within the main subjects. In Illus. 12-18 the main subject "Audiovisual Equipment" is divided by special guides into subdivisions of "Film" and "Overhead Projectors." You may use names, geographic locations, numbers, or subjects as captions for special guides.

Illus. 12-18. Portion of a subject file. The special guides are used to identify subdivisions within the main subjects.

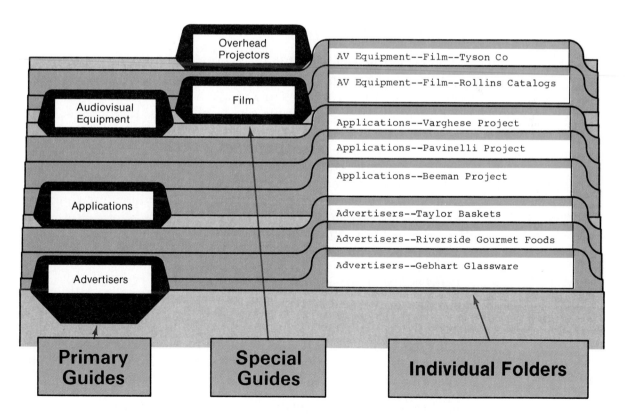

As you can see on page 529, the label for an individual folder behind a primary guide includes the following information:

- the primary guide caption (Advertisers, for example)
- the caption for the folder (Gebhart Glassware, for example)

The label for an individual folder behind a special guide should include the following information:

- the primary guide caption (AV Equipment, for example)
- the secondary guide caption (Film, for example)
- the caption for the folder (Rollins Catalogs, for example)

Filing by Combination Name and Subject

Many offices do not have enough file space for separate name and subject files. When this is true, you may file name and subject folders together.

Filing by Geographic Location

When using a geographic file, you index records according to geographic location. You may base a geographic file upon sales territories, states, or cities in a single state.

Typical users of geographic filing are publishing houses, mail-order houses, radio and television advertisers, real estate firms, and organizations dealing with a large number of small businesses scattered over a wide area. The personnel in these small businesses may change frequently. Therefore, the name of each individual owner or manager is often less important than the location of the business.

Refer to Illus. 12-19 as you read about the components of a geographic filing system.

Guides and Folders

The primary guides in a geographic file are named for the largest geographic divisions. For example, in Illus. 12-19 the primary guides are based on cities. The key unit (Alabama) appears on a *location name guide* positioned in the center front of the file. The special guide *(Capitol)* is used to **pinpoint** the location of certain individual folders.

pinpoint: identify

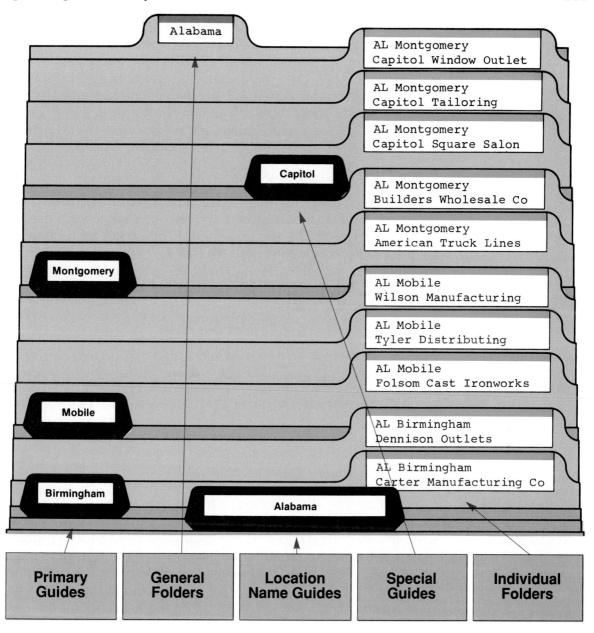

Illus. 12-19. Portion of a geographic file. Notice that the primary guides identify the largest geographic divisions.

You need a general folder behind each location name guide. In the illustration, the general folder and the location name guide bear the same caption (Alabama). When you prepare labels for individual folders, give the geographic location on the first line (*AL Birmingham*, for example). On the second line, indicate the caption for the individual folder (*Carter Manufacturing Co*, for example). These complete labels tell you behind which primary and special guide to refile the folder.

Index Card Control File

To retrieve a specific record in a geographic file, you must know the geographic location of each person or business. Since you may not remember all this information, you will find it helpful to keep an *index card control file*. This is usually a 5″ x 3″ card file that includes a card for each individual or business record in the geographic file. The cards containing the names and addresses are filed alphabetically.

pertaining: relating to

*The firm where Carlota works uses a geographic filing system based on states. This morning her supervisor needed a record **pertaining** to Wonderland Toy Company. To retrieve the record, Carlota first checked the card index. She learned the toy company was located in Richmond, Virginia. She scanned the drawer labels and opened the drawer labeled Virginia. She then searched through the primary guides until she came to the city of Richmond. It was then easy to locate the individual folder for Wonderland Toy Company. Carlota's supervisor appreciated her ability to locate the record so quickly.*

NUMERIC FILING SYSTEMS

In a numeric filing system, records are indexed by number. This method of filing is frequently used when records are already arranged in numeric order. For example, insurance companies may arrange their records according to policy number. Utility companies often index customers' accounts by account number. The Internal Revenue Service indexes tax returns by social security number.

Some companies may ask you to index records numerically even though they are not already numbered. For example, you may be asked to assign a number to each name or subject in a file. The caption on the individual folder would then be a number (i.e., 3877 for Global Security Systems or 8551 for West Coast Development Project) rather than a name or a subject.

Guides

The guide captions in a numeric system are numbers instead of letters or words. Look at the numeric file shown in Illus. 12-20. Notice how the numbered special guides highlight divisions within the primary guide category. This helps you retrieve records quickly.

Illus. 12-20. Portion of a numeric file. Insurance companies, for example, often arrange their records according to policy number.

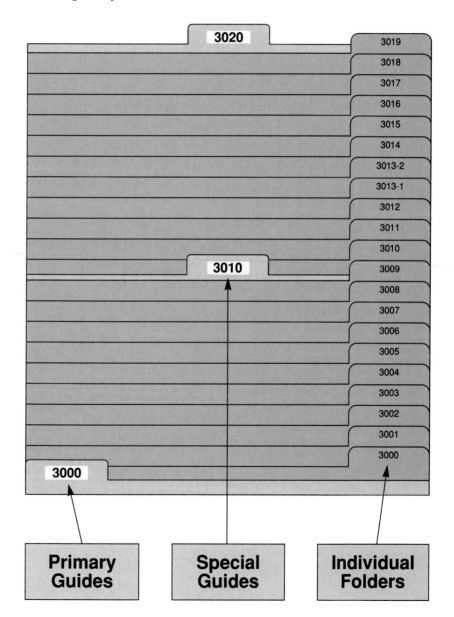

General Folders

In a numeric system, you do not provide a general folder behind each numeric guide. Instead, you maintain a separate *alphabetic general file*. Records that do not have an individual numeric folder are filed in the general alphabetic file by name or subject. When you collect enough records related to one name or subject, you create an individual numeric folder.

Individual Folders

To set up an individual folder, you first refer to the accession book. An **accession book** is a record that lists in numeric order the file numbers already assigned and the name or subject related to each number. In Illus. 12-21 you can see that the last number, 3877, was assigned to Global Security Systems. The next number you assign will be 3878. By keeping an accession book, you avoid assigning the same number to more than one name or subject.

Illus. 12-21. Portion of an accession book. Can you identify the file number assigned to the Joseph E. Fuline Co.?

NUMBER	NAME	DATE
3873	Payroll Register	Jan. 1, 19--
3874	Joseph E. Fuline Co.	Jan. 3, 19--
3875	Monthly Production Reports	Jan. 3, 19--
3876	Rogers Collection Agency	Jan. 4, 19--
3877	Global Security Systems	Jan. 10, 19--

Index Card Control File

After you have assigned a number to an individual folder, you need to record both the name or subject of the folder contents and the folder number on a 5″ x 3″ card. Just as you need an alphabetic index with a geographic file, you need one with a numeric file as well. It is extremely difficult to remember the number for each name or subject in the files. When you must retrieve a record, you refer to the index card control file to learn the correct file folder number. Illus. 12-22 shows how the card index corresponds to individual records.

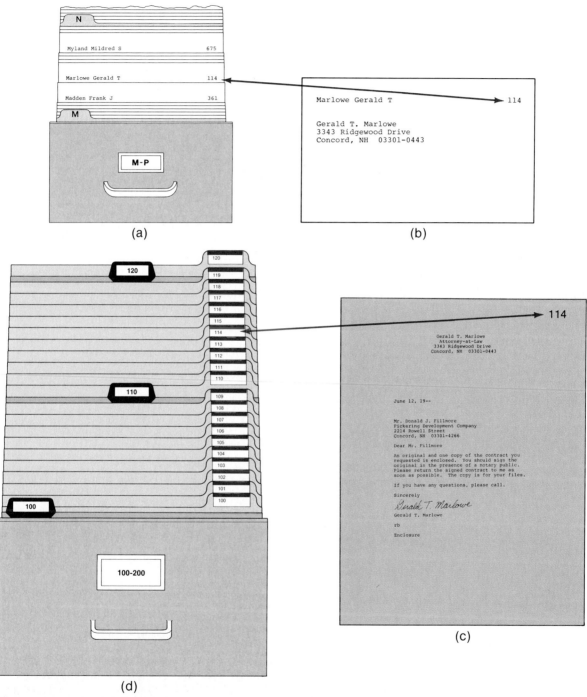

Illus. 12-22. An alphabetic index must be used in conjunction with a numeric file. (a) index card control file, (b) individual alphabetic index card, (c) incoming letter with numeric code, and (d) numeric file.

Also prepare a 5″ x 3″ card for each name or subject in the general alphabetic file. Instead of including a folder number on the card, type the letter "G" as shown in Illus. 12-23. The G indicates you filed the record in the general alphabetic file instead of in an individual numeric folder.

An advantage to a numeric system is that it helps you keep records confidential. Scanning the numeric captions on folders will not tell an **intruder** much about the contents.

intruder: unwelcome or uninvited person

Today is Carlos' first day of work. Mimi Dibbern, Carlos' supervisor, briefed him on the filing system they use: "Carlos, the records in our department are confidential. We use a numeric filing system so unauthorized people cannot locate specific records easily. To keep these files secure, we have a policy which allows only workers in our department to have access to the index card control file and the accession book."

Illus. 12-23. If a name or subject has been assigned an individual numeric folder, the alphabetic index card will have the number recorded on it. Otherwise, the card will only have a "G" indicating that the record has been filed in the general folder.

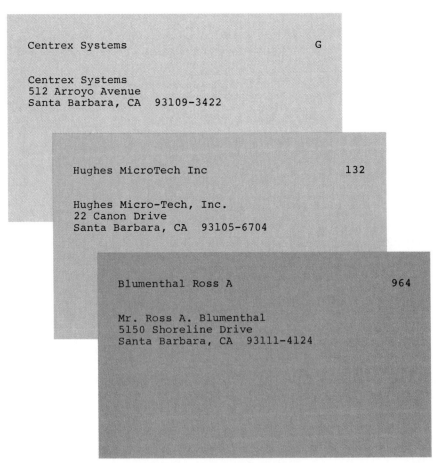

```
Centrex Systems                                    G


Centrex Systems
512 Arroyo Avenue
Santa Barbara, CA   93109-3422
```

```
Hughes MicroTech Inc                               132


Hughes Micro-Tech, Inc.
22 Canon Drive
Santa Barbara, CA   93105-6704
```

```
Blumenthal Ross A                                  964


Mr. Ross A. Blumenthal
5150 Shoreline Drive
Santa Barbara, CA   93111-4124
```

CHRONOLOGIC FILING SYSTEMS

In a chronologic filing system, you file according to date. A few companies may choose to use a chronologic system for filing all records. But most often you will use a chronologic file to help you keep track of tasks you need to complete each business day.

As you learned in Chapters 9 and 11, a desk calendar and a tickler file are two kinds of chronologic files.

QUESTIONS FOR REVIEW

1. What are the three components of a filing system?

2. What are two methods of coding a record? Why is coding helpful?

3. Why are guides used in a filing system?

4. What is a caption?

5. Describe an advantage of using color-coded labels.

6. Where should the tabs on primary guides be located? Why?

7. What are four frequently used alphabetic filing systems?

8. Why do you need an index card control file in a geographic filing system?

9. What is an accession book? Why is it necessary to use an accession book?

10. When would you most often use a chronologic file?

MAKING DECISIONS

For three months, you have worked in the office of Davis-Rider, Inc.—a company with 12 employees. When you began the job, your supervisor, Mr. Davis, told you that you would be "generally in charge of the files" as well as have transcribing and light bookkeeping duties. While everyone has access to the files, he explained that you need to make sure the files are neat and that materials do not stack up.

Although the task seemed simple when Mr. Davis explained it to you, it has become a source of frustration. Some employees remove records and do not return them for several weeks. Other employees open file drawers and place folders on top of the other folders instead of inserting them in their proper places. Needless to say, the files are not being managed well.

Since you are "generally in charge of the files," you are being held accountable for the situation.

What You Are To Do: Remembering that you are a relatively new employee, how would you handle this problem? Prepare a written description of the steps you would take.

EXTENDING YOUR ENGLISH COMPETENCIES

Knowing when to use "it's" (contraction) and when to use "its" (possessive) can be difficult. To help you know which term to use, ask yourself: "Could I substitute the words 'it is' or 'it has' in the sentence and have it make sense?" If you can, use "it's"; if not, use "its."

What You Are To Do: Rewrite the following eight sentences, inserting either "it's" or "its," whichever is appropriate.

1. You need to put the folder back in _____ place.
2. _____ time to remove the inactive files from active storage.
3. He replied, "_____ necessary to charge out each record."
4. This folder has lost _____ label.
5. _____ been returned to the files.
6. Please let me know when _____ ready.
7. The company improved _____ image.
8. _____ on the top shelf of the bookcase.

APPLICATION ACTIVITY

You work for a management consulting firm in Miami, Florida. In order to keep the records confidential, a numeric file system is used. You find that enough records have accumulated in the general files to necessitate creating individual folders for the following Miami businesses:

Rosewood Import Company, 2699 South Bayshore Drive, 33133-0630

Peninsula Savings & Loan, 100 South Biscayne Boulevard, 33131-1221

Fuline's Delivery Service, 10039 Little River Drive, 33147-0330

Nico's Fine Seafood Restaurant, 1502 Coral Way, 33129-1202

Gomez, Jackson & Associates, 1680 Meridian Avenue, 33139-0930

Trade Winds Travel Agency, 2121 Ponce De Leon Boulevard, 33134-3056

Citrus Growers' Association, 8808 Collins Avenue, 33154-0228

Executive Helicopter Service, 550 NW Le Jeune Road, 33126-1027

What You Are To Do:
- For each business, key an index card for the alphabetic card index. Use the illustration on page 536 as a guide. (If index cards are not available, use blank pieces of 5″ x 3″ paper.) Consult the accession book shown below to find which number to key on each card at the upper right corner.
- Arrange the cards alphabetically according to business name. If necessary, refer to Reference Section F.

ACCESSION BOOK   Page 10

NUMBER	NAME	DATE
1009	Rosewood Import Company	Dec. 3, 19--
1010	Peninsula Savings & Loan	Dec. 3, 19--
1011	Fuline's Delivery Service	Dec. 3, 19--
1012	Nico's Fine Seafood Restaurant	Dec. 3, 19--
1013	Gomez, Jackson & Associates	Dec. 3, 19--
1014	Trade Winds Travel Agency	Dec. 3, 19--
1015	Citrus Growers' Association	Dec. 3, 19--
1016	Executive Helicopter Service	Dec. 3, 19--

CHAPTER SUMMARY

In this chapter you learned that an effective records management system improves office efficiency and customer goodwill. You also learned about the equipment, procedures, and supplies used in paper filing systems. As an office worker, you will probably be involved in some aspect of records management. You should be knowledgeable about the following key points:

1. A records management system is the manner in which a company chooses to organize, store, retrieve, remove, and dispose of its records.

2. You may be called upon to manage records on various media such as paper, magnetic media, and microfilm.
3. The phases of the record life cycle are as follows:
   Phase 1: Collect the records.
   Phase 2: Categorize the records.
   Phase 3: Prepare the records for storage.
   Phase 4: Maintain the records in active storage.
   Phase 5: Reevaluate the records.
   Phase 6: Dispose of the records.
4. Records can be filed alphabetically by name, subject, combination name and subject, or geographic location. Records can also be filed numerically or chronologically.
5. Each company will choose a filing system that best suits its individual needs.

KEY CONCEPTS AND TERMS

record	retention schedule
records management filing system	archive
filing	indexing
microimaging systems	coding
computer output microfilm (COM)	accession book
microforms	

INTEGRATED CHAPTER ACTIVITIES

Activity 1

You work for Midwestern Mutual Life Insurance Company. Records of policyholders are placed in an alphabetic name file and also in a chronologic file set up according to the dates the policies are accepted. Your supervisor has given you the following list of names, addresses, and policy dates for new policyholders whose records must be added to both filing systems.

What You Are To Do: For the two exercises which follow, key in the upper right corner of each card the item number given in parentheses on the list of policyholders. This will aid your instructor in checking your work.

1. *For the name file*, key a 5″ x 3″ index card for each policyholder. (If index cards are not available, use blank sheets of paper approximately 5″ x 3″.) List the last name first with the address and policy date underneath. Arrange the cards alphabetically.
2. *For the chronologic file*, key a 5″ x 3″ card for each policyholder. List the policy acceptance date on the first line with the name and address underneath. Arrange these cards chronologically.

```
Cohen Jessica P Ms                          1

Ms. Jessica P. Cohen
5414 Highland Drive
Denver, CO  80215-5632
11/21
```

```
11/21                                       1

Ms. Jessica P. Cohen
5414 Highland Drive
Denver, CO  80215-5632
```

(1) Ms. Jessica P. Cohen
5414 Highland Drive
Denver, CO 80215-5632
Policy: 11/21

(2) Mr. Thomas Parker Hill
253 Gary Court
Stockton, CA 95212-2131
Policy: 1/20

(3) Miss Kathleen A. Young
34 East Mercer Place
Denver, CO 80237-7114
Policy: 1/29

(4) Miss Susan J. Caldwell
8254 Willow Road
Syracuse, NY 13212-2023
Policy: 8/14

(5) Mr. Christopher Thomas Privett
6333 South Hudson Street
Seattle, WA 98108-2184
Policy: 6/12

(6) Ms. Felicia M. Rodriguez
8731 First Avenue
Memphis, TN 38109-8830
Policy: 2/10

(7) Mr. Miles C. Ulberg
3212 West 53rd Street
Little Rock, AR 72209-2433
Policy: 5/18

(8) Mr. Ryan Baker
3600 Linden Avenue
Pittsburgh, PA 15234-2770
Policy: 10/2

(9) Mr. Clayton W. Ingraham
334 Madrid Lane
Santa Fe, NM 87501-3434
Policy: 9/4

(10) Mrs. Jolene C. Ward
122 Oak Street
Rutherford, NJ 07075-8122
Policy: 2/15

Activity 2

Word processing
equipment can be used
to complete this activity.

The president of Brooks Advertising Agency has appointed a committee to determine whether or not to establish a separate records management department. The committee has drafted a survey designed to identify how hard-copy records are currently being managed. The chairperson hands you a draft of the survey instrument and says, "Please key this questionnaire in final form. Use your judgment regarding spacing so that the questionnaire does not appear so 'tight.' Lines for answers should be added after each question. Also, make sure the questionnaire fits on one page."

What You Are To Do: Key a final copy of the survey instrument.

Records Management Survey

1. How many filing cabinets are in your particular department?
    a. How many letter size drawers are used?
    b. How many legal size drawers are used?
2. How are records organized in your department?
    alphabetically   numerically   chronologically
3. Do you house records in locations other than file cabinets?
    If yes, how do you house them?
4. Do you follow a schedule for removing inactive files and destroying outdated records?
5. Do you use a standardized procedure for charging out records?
    If yes, what procedure do you use?
6. What percentage of your active records would you classify as:
    vital?   important?   useful?   nonessential?
7. How frequently do you refer to active files?
8. How frequently do you refer to inactive files?
9. What method is most often used to destory records?
10. Who in your department has responsibility for managing the files?
    is responsible

Department
Name and title of person completing the survey   Date

OPTIONAL COMPUTER APPLICATION ACTIVITY
See Computer Application Activity 12
in your Information Processing Activities workbook.

PRODUCTIVITY CORNER

Blake Williams
OFFICE SUPERVISOR

LOOKING TO THE FUTURE

DEAR MR. WILLIAMS:

I recently graduated from high school and found a job at a local insurance agency. A good deal of my time on the job is spent filing and retrieving customer records. From my experience, I see that management puts a high priority on maintaining good records. I wonder, therefore, if there would be any future for me in the records management field?—KARLA IN PORTLAND

DEAR KARLA:

You have made a good observation. Even though you are a new employee, you are able to see the value of the customer records you handle each day. Records management is a vital part of *every* company, not just the insurance agency for which you work. If a business is to operate efficiently, up-to-date records must be available when needed.

I heartily recommend that you pursue your interest in the records management field. The practical experience you are getting on the job today will provide a firm foundation upon which to build a career in this rapidly growing field.

There are several professional organizations for records management personnel that you might wish to contact for additional information. One organization is the Association of Records Managers and Administrators (ARMA). Another is the Institute of Certified Records Managers (ICRM). The ICRM administers a professional exam. If you pass the exam and meet the qualifications, you earn the title of Certified Records Manager.

Approximately 90 percent of all office workers perform some records management tasks. So, whether or not you plan to pursue a records management career, your interest in maintaining good records and your desire to learn more about the field of records management will be a definite aid to you on this job or any job you hold in the future. Best wishes.—BLAKE WILLIAMS

CHAPTER 13

Managing Records

As you learned in Chapter 12, office records are stored on a variety of media. These storage media include paper, floppy disks, hard disks, magnetic tape, and microfilm. Some companies use only one storage medium for records. Most offices, however, use a combination of several different media. For example, a small accounting firm may store tax returns on paper in file folders but keep customer account records on disks. A large bookstore may keep its inventory records on microfiche but maintain other records on paper or magnetic media.

With technology becoming more affordable to businesses, it is very probable that you will work in an office that uses a variety of media for storing records. Different media have different storage requirements. For example, magnetic media must be protected from other magnetic sources that could erase or change the stored information. Therefore, equipment and supplies specially designed to protect magnetic media should be used. Special storage equipment and supplies also are available for microfilm files as well as for paper records.

All records that relate to a particular topic, regardless of the storage media used, are often stored together. For example, a floppy disk containing a project proposal and the paper correspondence relating to the project are placed in a file folder that is stored in a file cabinet.

This chapter describes the principles, procedures, equipment, supplies, and technology available to help you manage various forms of records efficiently.

The objectives of the chapter are to:

- describe principles and procedures for managing paper storage systems

- describe principles and procedures for managing records stored on magnetic and microimaging media

MANAGING HARD-COPY RECORDS

When you have completed your study of this topic, you will be able to:

- explain how to prepare records for filing
- apply efficient filing procedures
- list three charge-out procedures
- describe how inactive files are transferred and stored

Wherever you work—whether it be in a small advertising agency or in a large manufacturing company—you probably will store some records on paper. Even in offices where magnetic media and microfilm are used extensively, there often is a need for certain paper (hard copy) records.

Kerry works for O'Roark & Sullivan, a law firm of four attorneys. Kerry keeps form documents such as leases and wills on floppy disks. But for a legal transaction to be valid, the document must be signed. These signed paper documents are stored so that the signatures can be kept on file.

Because paper is a major medium for storing records, it is important that you understand how to maintain paper files. Once you have a clear understanding of the principles and procedures for managing paper files, you can easily adapt this knowledge to maintaining records stored on other media.

545

You already know rules for organizing records alphabetically, numerically, and chronologically. In this topic you will learn about preparing individual records for storage. You will learn methods for locating and removing individual records as well as entire folders. You also will become acquainted with the equipment used to store paper records.

PREPARING RECORDS FOR STORAGE

Before filing a record for the first time, you need to prepare it properly for storage. By doing so, you speed the actual filing process and insure that the record is filed correctly. Follow these five steps to prepare paper records for storage:

1. Collect the records.
2. Inspect the records.
3. Index/code the records.
4. Cross-reference the records.
5. Sort the records.

Illus. 13-1. To file and retrieve records, this office worker must be thoroughly familiar with the procedures for managing paper files. Here, he is preparing records for storage.

Collect Records

accumulate: gather or collect

designated: set apart for a specific purpose

Throughout the workday, you will **accumulate** records that need to be filed. Instead of preparing and filing each record as you are finished with it, collect the records in a **designated** place such as a tray labeled *TO BE FILED*. Then at scheduled times, such as after lunch or at the end of the day, you can prepare a batch of records for storage at one time. You will not need to index, code, or cross-reference records that have been filed before. But you will still need to inspect and sort them before they can be refiled.

Inspect Records

After you collect a batch of records to prepare for storage, you next need to inspect each record. Inspect the records by following these procedures:

- When you are preparing a record for the first time, look for a release mark to make sure the record has been officially released for filing. A **release mark** is an authorization to file a record. One person usually has the responsibility for releasing records to be filed. Often this person's initials, written in the upper left corner of the record, serve as the release mark.
- Remove all paper clips or rubber bands from the records.
- Staple all related materials together.

transparent:
see-through

- Repair any torn records with *transparent* tape.
- Attach small records to 8 ½″ x 11″ paper or 8 ½″ x 14″ paper so they will not be lost or crumpled in the file. Alternatively, you may copy the small record onto 8 ½″ x 11″ paper or 8 ½″ x 14″ paper.

Illus. 13-2. These are the five steps to take when preparing paper records for storage.

STEPS INVOLVED IN PREPARING PAPER RECORDS FOR FILING	
COLLECTING	COLLECTING means gathering records in a designated place such as a tray labeled TO BE FILED.
INSPECTING	INSPECTING means observing a record to be sure that it has a release mark, paper clips are removed, materials are stapled together, and tears are repaired.
INDEXING/CODING	INDEXING means deciding how to identify a record. CODING means marking on the record how it was indexed.
CROSS-REFERENCING	CROSS-REFERENCING means providing a way to retrieve a record by more than one name or subject.
SORTING	SORTING means arranging all the records in alphabetic, numeric, or chronologic order before placing them in the files.

Index/Code Records

As you learned in Chapter 12, indexing a record means deciding how to identify it. The name, subject, geographic location, or number used to identify a record is called the **filing segment**. You should code the record by the filing segment for two reasons:

- You can quickly tell how to file a record by glancing at it.
- You will file the record the same way each time it must be refiled.

Some companies prefer that you code records with a blue, non-reproducing pencil. This way, if you must copy the record, the code markings will not copy.

To code a record indexed by subject, geographic location, or number, write the filing segment in the upper right corner of the record.

Coding a record indexed by individual or company name involves three steps:

1. Identify the filing segment. Underline or circle the name the first time it appears on the record. If the name is not contained in the record, write it in the upper right corner of the record.
2. Identify the indexing units. The **indexing units** of a name include each word, initial, or abbreviation within a name. For example, there are three indexing units in the name Grady P. Hill. Use slash marks to divide the filing segment into separate indexing units:

Grady/P./Hill

3. Number the units in proper indexing order. **Indexing order** is the order in which units are considered when a record is filed alphabetically. For example, individual names are filed alphabetically by last names, not by first names. So in the case of Grady P. Hill, you would number the indexing units this way:

2   3   1
Grady/P./Hill

Reference Section F presents standard rules for identifying indexing units and for alphabetizing names. You will use these rules to complete the activities at the end of this topic. Illus. 13-3 shows a record properly indexed and coded.

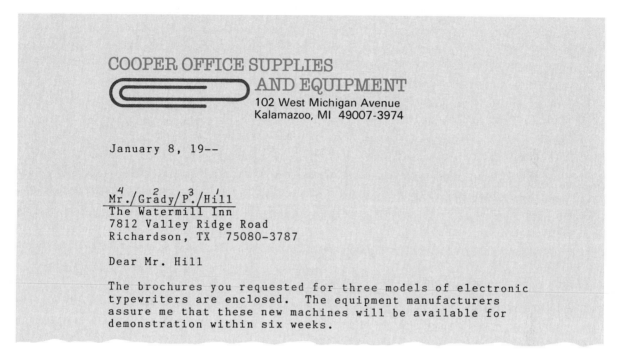

COOPER OFFICE SUPPLIES AND EQUIPMENT

102 West Michigan Avenue
Kalamazoo, MI 49007-3974

January 8, 19--

Mr./Grady/P./Hill
The Watermill Inn
7812 Valley Ridge Road
Richardson, TX 75080-3787

Dear Mr. Hill

The brochures you requested for three models of electronic typewriters are enclosed. The equipment manufacturers assure me that these new machines will be available for demonstration within six weeks.

Illus. 13-3. This letter has been indexed and coded for filing. Coding eliminates the need for rereading the record each time it is filed.

Cross-Reference Records

Some records may be requested by more than one name or subject. For example, on page 550 the record may be indexed by the name of the company sending the letter or by the subject of the letter. In this case, you would first index and code the record by the name or subject of *primary importance*, which is Boyer Wholesale Groceries (the name of the company sending the letter). Then you would code the name or subject of *secondary importance*, which is SPRING BONANZA OF VALUES (the subject of the letter). Note that you code the subject by underlining it, numbering the indexing units if appropriate, and placing an X in the margin. The X is a signal that the record is cross-referenced under that particular subject.

Illus. 13-4. This letter has been properly indexed and coded by name and also by subject. The X is a signal that the letter is cross-referenced under the subject, SPRING BONANZA OF VALUES.

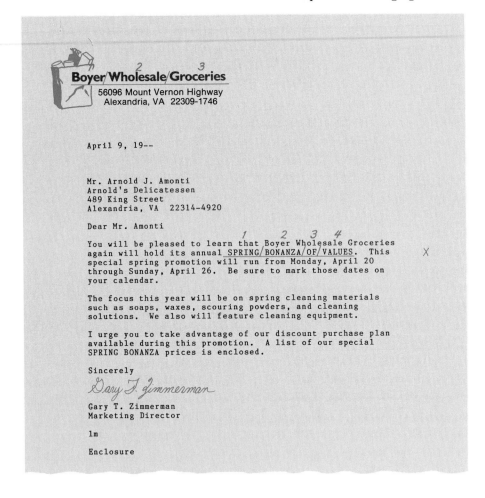

Cross-Reference Sheet

A *cross-reference sheet* includes information about the record and is filed in the cross-referenced folder. The following information is recorded on the cross-reference sheet shown in Illus. 13-5:

a. the name or subject under which the record was cross-referenced
b. the date the record originated
c. a brief description of the record
d. the location of the record in the files
e. the name of the authorized person who released the record and the date the record was released

Illus. 13-5. Cross-reference sheet for the letter in Illus. 13-4.

CROSS-REFERENCE SHEET

a. Name or (Subject)   *Spring Bonanza of Values*

b. Date of Item   *April 9, 19--*

c. Regarding   *Discount purchase plan*

SEE

d. (Name) or Subject   *Boyer Wholesale Groceries*

e. Authorized by   *Glenda A. Ackinclose*   Date *4/21/--*

File the cross-reference sheet in the SPRING BONANZA OF VALUES folder and the record in the BOYER WHOLESALE GROCERIES folder.

Copies of Records

Some companies do not use cross-reference sheets. Instead, they copy the original record and place the copy in the cross-referenced folder. This speeds retrieval since a complete copy of the record is available at each file point. If you are instructed to use this method, be sure to code the copy for cross-referencing so you will file it in the proper folder.

Cross-Reference Guides

If a permanent cross-reference is desired, you will need to prepare a *cross-reference guide.* A cross-reference guide is a stiff board the same size as a file folder. A typical situation requiring a permanent cross-reference guide might occur when a company with which you do a great deal of business changes its name. You would first label a folder using the new company name and place in the folder all materials from the old folder. Then you would replace the old folder with a permanent cross-reference guide showing the necessary retrieval information on the tab. The cross-reference guide remains in the file as long as the name or subject is still active.

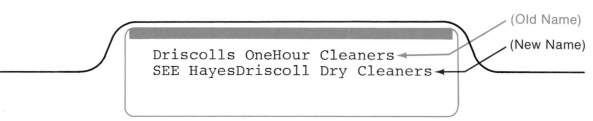

(Old Name)

(New Name)

Driscolls OneHour Cleaners
SEE HayesDriscoll Dry Cleaners

When To Cross-Reference

As a general rule, you should cross-reference a record if doing so will save you time when you need to retrieve the record later. Too much cross-referencing, however, will hinder your ability to retrieve records quickly. An effective records management program will include guidelines to help you know when to cross-reference a record.

You usually will cross-reference only records filed in name or subject filing systems. Geographic and numeric filing systems have alphabetic card indexes that lead you directly to the needed record.

Sort Records

After you have coded the records and cross-referenced them, if necessary, you are ready to sort them. **Sorting** is the process of arranging the records alphabetically or numerically before placing them in the folders.

Sorting serves two important purposes. First, it saves you actual filing time. Since records are in proper sequence, you are able to move quickly from file drawer to file drawer as you place the records in folders. Second, if records are requested before you file them, you can find them quickly.

Charlotte is training Henry, a new office worker. This afternoon they are preparing the records collected that day for storage. They have already indexed, coded, and cross-referenced the records that had never been filed before. Henry thinks they are ready to place the records in the folders. But Charlotte explains they have one more step to complete first:

Charlotte: Henry, we need to sort these records alphabetically before we file them.

Henry: It will take forever to sort this stack of records. Let's just file them in the order they are already in.

Charlotte: Sorting doesn't take that long. First we'll rough sort.

Henry: What does that mean?

Charlotte: It means we'll group all the "A" records together, all the "B" records together, and so forth. Then we'll fine sort. That means we'll place all the "A" records in alphabetic order, then all "B" records, and so on.

(Charlotte and Henry quickly sort the records and begin to file. Their supervisor, Miss Foster, approaches them and asks a question.)

Miss Foster: Charlotte, I placed the Norris letter in the TO BE FILED tray, but I need it again. Have you filed it yet?

Charlotte: No, Miss Foster. We've only filed up to the "C's." (Charlotte flips through the records which are in alphabetic order and quickly retrieves the Norris letter.)

Charlotte (after Miss Foster leaves): Well, Henry, now you see why I believe sorting is worth the time it takes!

FILING RECORDS

clogged: cluttered; overloaded

You need to set aside time each day to file. This may seem simple to do, but it is not. Many other tasks often seem more important than filing. But if the rest of your tasks are to go smoothly, the records management system cannot become **clogged** with stacks of unfiled records. If you have followed the five steps for preparing records for storage, you can file the records easily and quickly by following these procedures:

1. Locate the proper file drawer by reading the drawer labels.
2. Search through the guides in the drawer to locate the desired alphabetic or numeric section.
3. If an individual folder has been prepared for the record, place the record in the folder with the front of the record facing the front of the folder and the top of the record at the left side. You should arrange records in an individual folder according to date, with the most recent record in front.
4. If no individual folder is available, file the record in the general folder for that section. You should arrange records in a general folder alphabetically by name or subject. If there are two or more records for the same name or subject, they are arranged according to date with the most recent record in front.

Using Special Folders

Some companies use special folders as well as general and individual folders. A *special folder* is a type of general folder that is used for a variety of "special" purposes. For example, you may remove all the records coded *Smith* from the general folder and place them in a special folder, thus permitting material filed under *Smith* to be found more quickly. You also may prepare special folders to collect miscellaneous information about a particular subject or project, such as *ARMA Convention Travel Plans*. You arrange records alphabetically in a special folder. Within each group of names or subjects, arrange the records by date.

Avoiding Overcrowded Files

Never allow folders to become overcrowded. Usually a folder has *score lines* at the bottom. Creasing the score lines widens the folder and increases its capacity. But a folder should not contain more than an inch of filed material.

subdivide: break into smaller parts

When a folder becomes too full, **subdivide** the records into two or more folders. The folder labels should accurately reflect the contents of the new folders. For example, the folders could be labeled by date or subject:

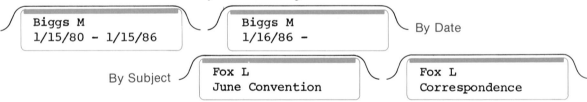

Biggs M
1/15/80 – 1/15/86

Biggs M
1/16/86 –

By Date

By Subject

Fox L
June Convention

Fox L
Correspondence

Be sure to examine general folders often so you can prepare individual and special folders when necessary. It is best not to fill a file drawer to capacity. You should have enough room in the drawer so that you can move the folders easily.

STORAGE EQUIPMENT

Paper is the oldest and most commonly used storage medium, so equipment and supplies for filing paper are plentiful. The following descriptions will give you a general idea of the equipment that is available to help you maintain paper files.

Vertical File Cabinets

Vertical file cabinets are used in many offices and contain one to five drawers. Five-drawer cabinets use storage space most economically since more filing space is available for the same amount of floor space used for a cabinet with fewer drawers. Vertical file cabinets must be arranged so there is space in front of the cabinet to allow each drawer to be opened fully.

Lateral File Cabinets

Lateral file cabinets are also popular storage equipment. Fully opened drawers in a lateral file cabinet do not open as far out into the room as do drawers in a vertical file cabinet. Lateral file cabinets are manufactured in a variety of drawer heights, widths, and depths to fit different office needs.

Illus. 13-6. (Left) Vertical file cabinets are standard equipment in many offices.

Illus. 13-7. (Right) Lateral file cabinets are available in a variety of sizes to meet the specific needs of your office.

Horizontal (Flat) Files

Horizontal files (as shown in Illus. 13-8 on page 556) are used in offices that store large-format documents. Such documents include architectural plans, advertising layouts, engineering drawings, and geographic surveys.

Shelf Files

Shelf files store records on open shelves instead of in cabinets. Central file departments often use shelf files to conserve space. When cabinets are used, the amount of room needed to open the drawers fully must be included in planning the area layout.

Records on open shelves are immediately accessible, as you can see in Illus. 13-9. No drawers need to be opened. Shelf filing is most appropriate for filing and retrieving entire folders and is ideally suited for numeric filing systems. Since folders on open shelves are visible, many companies use color-coded folder labels to improve filing efficiency.

Illus. 13-8. (Left) Horizontal files come in a variety of drawer depths and widths and are used to store large-format documents such as architectural plans.

Illus. 13-9. (Right) Rotary shelf files provide easy access to office workers. The model shown here is made of five tiers which turn independently of each other.

Mobile Files

Mobile shelf files (as shown in Illus. 13-10) have many shelves but only one aisle. The shelves are arranged next to each other on a track. To form the aisle in front of the desired shelf, the shelves are moved along the track manually or electronically. Mobile files take up less floor space than either fixed shelf files or cabinets holding the same number of records.

Card Files

Card files (as shown in Illus. 13-11) are used in many offices. Office workers keep card files containing the names, addresses, and telephone numbers of the people with whom they communicate regularly. Card files can be used in many ways depending on the needs of particular offices.

The devices for housing card files are varied. Cards can be stored vertically in plastic or metal boxes. They can also be stored in vertical file cabinets designed to house cards. When information on cards is referred to often, an open card file is used. The cards are on special trays or wheels that make it easy to locate specific cards quickly.

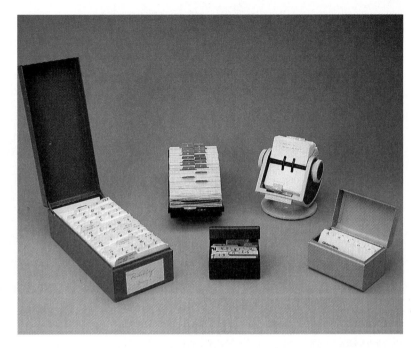

Illus. 13-10. (Left) The file sections of a mobile file are mounted on rollers and can be moved quickly and quietly.

Illus. 13-11. (Right) A variety of card files are used in many offices.

Printout Storage

With the increasing use of computer information processing, more and more computer printouts are being generated. Printouts vary in size, but they usually are too bulky to store in traditional filing cabinets. Most companies prepare printouts for storage by placing them in binders made of thick cardboard or plastic. The binders have thin, flexible metal posts that fit through the holes on the sides of the printouts. When the posts have been threaded through the printout, the remaining portion is folded over so the binder can be closed. Binders can be stored in several ways. They can be:

- placed on shelves horizontally.
- hung on racks or cabinets using binders with special hooks or handles.
- filed in a frame which accommodates hanging binders.

Some storage units for printouts are mobile in that they can be rolled from one location to another. Most binders are indexed by tabs or labels that attach to the binder. Color-coded binders (as shown in Illus. 13-12 on page 558) are frequently used to help you locate specific groupings of printouts.

Illus. 13-12. Bulky materials such as computer printouts are often stored in binders and hung on racks.

RETRIEVING RECORDS

In Chapter 12, you learned about the record life cycle. Once records are in active storage, you may retrieve and refile them many times. An effective records management program will include charge-out procedures that help you keep track of records when workers remove them from the files.

Requisition Cards

Many companies that use central files have a staff of trained records management personnel to file and retrieve records. In companies using this arrangement, other office workers do not have direct access to the files. To retrieve records, you must fill out a requisition card. A **requisition card** is a card that has space for all the charge-out information needed. A member of the records management staff will read the information on the card and retrieve the record for you.

If you work in the central files, you will keep a copy of each requisition card in a card tickler file. When a record has not been returned by the expected date, you need to take appropriate follow-up action. Taking such action is an important part of an effective records management program. A records manager also may use requisition cards to analyze how often the files are used and which records are most active.

Out Guides

When you remove a record from the files, you must replace it with a record of the charge-out information. This can be accomplished by using an out guide. An **out guide** is a sheet of thick cardboard that has the word OUT printed on the tab. On some out guides, you write the charge-out information on ruled lines. On other out guides, there is a pocket where you insert the completed requisition card. You usually use out guides when individual records within a folder are removed.

OUT			
NUMBER, NAME, OR SUBJECT	**CHARGE OUT DATE**	**NAME OF BORROWER**	**DUE DATE**
Forest Park Florist	4/22/--	Ruth Carson	5/1/--
Spanish Village Apartments	5/6/--	Jerry Ahmed	5/14/--

Illus. 13-13. (Left) Ruled out guide and (Right) out guide with pocket containing a requisition card.

Out Folders

An out folder is used when an entire folder is removed from the file. When an out folder is used, you may temporarily file additional records in the out folder until the regular folder is returned.

When Marcy removed the Brandon-Mills folder from the files, she provided the charge-out information on the printed lines of an out folder. Later, when Peter was filing, he placed two letters in the Brandon-Mills out folder. If Marcy had not provided the out folder, Peter would not have been able to file the two letters. This way, Peter could file the records. Marcy then would insert those records into the Brandon-Mills folder when she returned it to the files.

REMOVING RECORDS FROM ACTIVE STORAGE

An efficient records management system will have a retention schedule that identifies which records should be removed from active storage and on which dates. Records that are kept in inactive storage usually are kept in cardboard storage files rather than metal cabinets. The boxes are sturdy and provide a place to identify the contents. Some storage boxes are stackable, which saves space. Color-coded storage boxes can help you locate inactive records quickly. Some companies store inactive records in off-site locations. These locations range from rented storage space to underground vaults.

Illus. 13-14. Inactive records frequently are stored in cardboard boxes designed for that purpose.

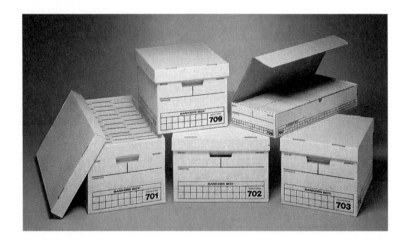

QUESTIONS FOR REVIEW

1. List the five steps involved in preparing paper records for storage.

2. What is the purpose of a release mark?

3. How would you code a record indexed by name?

4. Why is it necessary to cross-reference some records?

5. Give two reasons for sorting records before filing them.

6. How should you arrange records in an individual folder?

7. What is a special folder and how might it be used?

8. What is an advantage of mobile files?

9. Under what circumstances might a requisition card be used?

10. What is the difference between an out guide and an out folder?

MAKING DECISIONS

Professional Support Services, Inc. is a small personnel agency that places workers in both permanent and temporary jobs. The office is staffed by two placement officers and one general office worker, Eileen. The office is a busy place, and Eileen has many responsibilities. She greets the clients who visit each day, answers the telephone, prepares correspondence, handles incoming and outgoing mail, orders office supplies, and files records. Although Eileen is considered a competent office worker, she sometimes gets behind in her filing. This morning, one of the placement officers says to her, "I can't even see the top of the filing cabinet because it's so cluttered with file folders. Don't you think you should take time to file them?" Eileen thought to herself, "I don't even have time to take a coffee break during the day. When am I going to find time to file all these folders?"

Why do you think Eileen puts filing so low on her priority list of things to do? How might she find time to file and fulfill her other responsibilities as well?

What You Are To Do: Prepare a response to the questions raised.

EXTENDING YOUR ENGLISH COMPETENCIES

For written communication to be clear to the reader, you must use commas correctly. Test your skill on the following sentences:

1. Records can be organized alphabetically numerically and chronologically.

2. You will however be responsible for preparing paper records for storage.

3. As a general rule you should cross-reference a record if doing so will save you time when you need to retrieve the record later.

4. Before filing a record for the first time you need to prepare it properly for storage.

5. An out guide is used when an individual record is removed from the files and an out folder is used when an entire folder is removed from the files.

What You Are To Do: Prepare a copy of the sentences, inserting commas in the correct positions. Refer to Reference Section B, if necessary.

APPLICATION ACTIVITY

This activity involves placing the following 25 names of individuals and organizations in alphabetic order. Reference Section F presents rules for placing names in alphabetic order. Rules 1-7 apply to the names listed in this activity. Consult these rules as you work this activity. (The Integrated Chapter Activity will cover the remaining rules in Reference Section F.) You will need twenty-five 3″ x 5″ cards or twenty-five pieces of plain paper cut to that size.

What You Are To Do: 1. Key each name at the upper left corner of the card, placing the units in correct indexing order (see the sample card which follows). Also key the number of each name in the upper right corner of the card. (These numbers will help your instructor check your work.)
2. Arrange the cards alphabetically. (**NOTE:** *Save* these cards to use with the Integrated Chapter Activity at the end of this chapter.)

```
Cooper Janet R Miss                                              13
```

(1) Albert P. Sweeney
(2) The Art Center
(3) Nico's Italian Restaurant
(4) Clayton J. Pierce, Jr.
(5) Javier Gomez, M.D.
(6) Mrs. Angela T. Lightner
(7) Del Norte Manufacturing
(8) Melissa K. Jackson
(9) Grayson Oil & Gas Company
(10) Jefferson, Riggs & Associates
(11) Sister Margaret
(12) Papa's Pizzas
(13) Miss Janet R. Cooper
(14) O'Reilley Motors
(15) Albright Aviation
(16) Clayton J. Pierce, Sr.
(17) Miss Petite Dress Shop
(18) Mrs. Thomas G. Ramirez
(19) Gerald M. Von Hagen
(20) Allied Builders
(21) Bonnie's Bakery
(22) S&D Marina
(23) Sweeney & Sons, Inc.
(24) Wm. S. De Palma
(25) Dependable Pest Control

TOPIC 2

MANAGING MAGNETIC AND MICROIMAGING MEDIA

When you have completed your study of this topic, you will be able to:

- explain how to store individual records on magnetic media
- describe supplies used to store and organize magnetic media
- explain why databases are useful in businesses
- describe two ways to produce microfilm files
- explain how computer-assisted retrieval systems are used to speed the record retrieval process

Advancements in technology affect almost every aspect of office work, including records management. As an office worker, you will need to know how to store and access information recorded on magnetic media such as tapes, floppy disks, hard disks, and optical disks.

Unlike paper files, files stored on magnetic media are not "readable" to the human eye. You cannot tell what information is stored on a disk or tape by looking at the disk or tape. For this reason, it is especially important to properly organize and manage information stored on magnetic media. The procedures presented in this topic are used in business to store and access information recorded on magnetic media.

Companies that keep many records for an extended period of time frequently use microforms to store records conveniently and safely. Many companies use microforms for active records as well. Microfilm is a medium that not only meets today's storage and retrieval needs, but also is part of the advancing office technology of the future. As an office worker, you should know how microfilm records are created and maintained and how to use computer-assisted retrieval systems.

Executives know that stored information is useful only if it can be accessed when needed. They realize that a records management system is the basis for the efficient operation of the entire company.

This topic provides an overview of the technology, procedures, and supplies used to manage magnetic media and microfilm files.

You will recall that information stored outside the internal memory of a computer system or a word processing system is referred to as *auxiliary* or *secondary storage*. Each collection of related information treated as a unit is called a **file**. Common auxiliary media used for storing files include magnetic tape, floppy disks, and hard disks.

Illus. 13-15. A variety of secondary storage media is available, including floppy disks (5 1/4-inch), floppy microdisks (3 1/2-inch), and magnetic tape.

Illus. 13-16. The hard disk is a popular storage medium and provides much greater storage capacity than floppy disks.

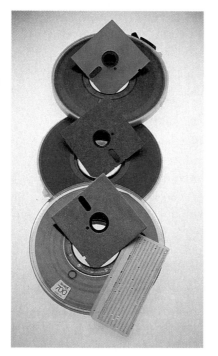

The Importance of Secondary Storage

The internal storage medium for most systems is usually a hard disk. It is used primarily to (1) store programs that run the system and (2) store files temporarily as they are being created and processed. While it is possible to store files permanently in internal storage, the capacity to do so is limited. Therefore, files that have been created or processed usually are stored on a secondary storage medium.

If an electronic records management system is to be efficient, it is crucial that the directory of files stored in the internal memory of the system be examined. Files that are no longer needed in internal memory are saved onto a secondary storage medium. After files have been copied, they are deleted from the internal memory of the system.

Naming a File

One company stores its mailing list for the city of Austin, Texas, on a floppy disk. This mailing list is considered to be a file, and it must be assigned a name so that it can be identified and accessed when needed. Any combination of letters, numbers, and symbols (with some exceptions) can be used for a filename. However, many operating systems limit the length of the filename to eight characters. Some systems allow you to add a three-character *extension* (such as *DOC* for *document*) to further identify your file. Naturally you will want to assign a name that reflects the type of information stored in the file. For example, the name assigned to the Austin mailing list file could be *AUSTINML.DOC*.

A directory of the files that you store on magnetic media is easily accessed and displayed on the screen. If you are using a microcomputer system, you key a command that causes a directory of files stored on secondary storage media to be displayed on the screen. A **command** is a word or abbreviated word that instructs the system to perform a function or operation.

Illus. 13-17. This directory reveals much about the files stored on the disk in drive B. Column 1 identifies the filename, and Column 2 is the filename extension. Column 3 identifies the amount of disk memory the document uses. Columns 4 and 5 identify the date and time the document was created or revised.

Directory of B: \				
DOUGLASS	DOC	19456	04-18-91	8:10a
ADAMS	DOC	5120	04-24-91	10:30a
HART	DOC	3072	05-08-91	2:19p
SWETTS	DOC	7680	06-15-91	8:11a
ADAMS	002	4096	06-22-91	9:39a
FRANKLIN	DOC	3584	06-30-91	12:26p
HART	002	16904	08-14-91	11:13a
SWETTS	002	3446	10-23-91	3:04p
DOUGLASS	002	1415	11-02-91	11:44a
RYAN	DOC	10240	01-17-92	10:16a
HART	003	1027	01-24-92	4:12p
FRANKLIN	002	712	02-18-92	3:56p

12 File(s)   285744 bytes free

Common commands for displaying a file directory are DIR (for directory), FILES, and CATALOG. Page 565 shows a list of the files stored on the floppy disk in disk drive B of a microcomputer system. The user keys the proper command, and the filenames saved on the disk are displayed. The name assigned to each file in this case is the last name of the person to whom the document is being sent.

Prompts and Menus

Application software is available to help you perform records management tasks. Some software provide *prompts* which aid you in assigning filenames and in storing files on secondary storage media. The prompt may be in the form of a directive (for example, "Enter filename: _____ ") or a question (for example, "Delete what?"). Other software provide a series of *menus*. Once the menu is displayed on the screen, you select from the options listed the specific activity you wish to complete. Illus. 13-18 shows a typical menu for creating and maintaining a mailing list.

The menu in the illustration offers you several options. You can view a directory of all the files, create a new file, add to an existing file, read/print a file, change/delete a record, or return to the records management menu. You can use the arrow keys to highlight the desired option, then strike the Enter key to **execute** the option. To create a new mailing list, for example, you would highlight *Create New File* and strike Enter. The prompt "Enter filename:" will appear on the screen, and you then will key in the name of the new file.

execute: carry out; perform

Next, you will see the prompts asking for specific information regarding the names, addresses, and telephone numbers of the individuals to be included on the new mailing list. (Refer to Illus. 13-19.) Respond to each prompt by providing the necessary information.

After all data has been keyed, you will be given an opportunity to make any necessary changes. The information then is stored automatically under the filename that you selected. A prompt then will appear asking if additional records are to be entered. If you respond by entering *Y* for *yes*, a new record can be keyed. If you enter *N* for *no*, the Mailing List Menu again will be displayed.

As you can see from this brief illustration, applications software provide prompts and menus designed to help you in carrying out records management tasks.

Illus. 13-18. A typical menu for creating and maintaining a mailing list. Note that the *Create New File* option is highlighted.

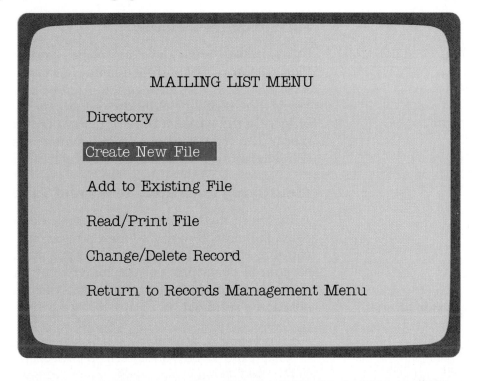

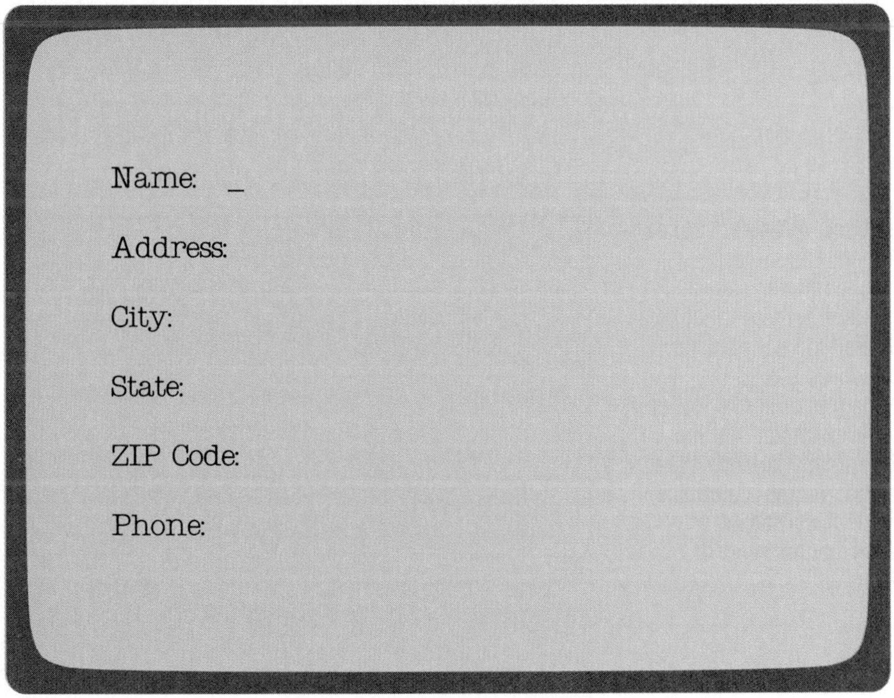

MAILING LIST MENU

Directory

Create New File

Add to Existing File

Read/Print File

Change/Delete Record

Return to Records Management Menu

Illus. 13-19. These screen prompts aid you by asking for specific information. The cursor following *Name* is prompting you to provide the name of an individual to be included on the mailing list.

Name: _

Address:

City:

State:

ZIP Code:

Phone:

Policies and Procedures

Businesses must develop policies and procedures for storing files on secondary storage media. For example, will all letters be stored on one disk? All mailing lists on another? All business forms on another? Will documents be stored in chronologic order? By the name of the originator? By the name of the department? The type of records management system a company uses will determine which files go on which storage medium.

Identifying Individual Disks and Tapes

Magnetic media can be organized alphabetically or numerically. Label each disk and tape so you can locate it quickly. Use captions that are as descriptive as possible, just as a folder label caption is descriptive of the folder's contents. Often, the labels are color coded to indicate how long the data on the disk or tape should be ***retained***.

retained: kept

> *The Petro-Davis Company has classified all information placed on its floppy disks as permanent, semi-permanent, or temporary in nature. The chart shown in Illus. 13-20 further describes these categories. To aid in distinguishing the disks by their retention category, disk labels are color coded. Permanent disks are labeled with a red felt-tipped pen; semi-permanent, with blue; and temporary, with green. Look at the disks shown in Illus. 13-21. Label A identifies the type of information that will be placed on the disk. Label B tells what Disk Operating System (DOS) and computer program were used and the retention category.*

Illus. 13-20. Just as there is a retention schedule for paper records, there must be a retention schedule for records stored on magnetic media. Notice, for example, that the company balance sheet and income statement are classified as permanent records.

Retention Category	Label A Information on Disk	Label B Disk Operating System Computer Program Retention Category
Permanent	Balance Sheet 12/31/-- Income Statement 12/31/--	DOS 5.0 WordText Permanent
Semi-Permanent	Expense Forecast 5/8/-- Alcorn Proposals 5/10/--	DOS 5.0 MaxiCalc Semi-Permanent
Temporary	Correspondence	DOS 5.0 WordText Temporary

Making Backup Copies

It is a good practice to make a *backup* (duplicate) copy of each disk or tape if the loss of the disk or tape or the accidental erasure of the data would have serious consequences. *Backing up a tape* or *disk* means making a copy of all the data on another tape or disk. *Backing up a file* means making a copy of an individual file on a different tape or disk. Most word processing systems and computer systems provide easy-to-follow procedures for making backup copies of tapes and disks. On many systems, the command COPY begins the backup process. Prompts and messages then appear on the screen to tell you what to do next. Backup disks should be labeled the same as their original with the word "backup" added to Label B.

Applications software is fragile and expensive to replace. Therefore, it is common practice to make a backup copy of all applications software, such as records management, spreadsheet, and word processing software. Backup copies are also made of important data files such as customer, payroll, and personnel records. Backup copies of tapes and disks should be stored in a separate, safe location.

Illus. 13-21. These 5 1/4-inch and 3 1/2-inch disks are properly labeled for storage and retrieval.

Controlling File Security

The security of confidential files stored on magnetic media is a concern to you as an office worker. You would not want a competitor to have access to a customer mailing list or a sales report that you keyed. As you learned in Chapter 5, some companies use security measures such as access logs and passwords which allow authorized employees to access certain files. You should, however, take steps to safeguard all files you use. For example, clear a document from the computer screen when you are not working on it, and store disks in a concealed location rather than on the surface of your workstation.

STORING MAGNETIC MEDIA

You know that magnetic media require special care to protect the valuable information they contain. By becoming familiar with the wide variety of equipment and supplies available, you can adequately protect the media that you handle and organize.

Floppy Disk Storage

Floppy disks can be organized and stored in a variety of ways. The way selected will depend on the number of disks you need to store, the size of the disks (standard 5 $\frac{1}{4}$-inch or micro 3 $\frac{1}{2}$-inch), the frequency with which you use the disks, and the storage space available. Many companies color code their floppy disk labels to *expedite* the storage and retrieval process. The flexible protective covers for floppy disks also are available in various colors. Some examples of floppy disk storage are described in the following paragraphs.

expedite: speed up

Containers for Standard 5 $\frac{1}{4}$-Inch Disks

Standard floppy disks often are filed in plastic boxes, cases, or trays designed to protect the disks. Within the case are guides to aid you in filing and retrieving the floppy disks.

Floppy disks also are stored in pockets that are attached to a stationary post or a disk stand. The disks are stored and retrieved easily by rotating the pockets around the center post.

Illus. 13-22. Disks are a very popular storage medium. These 5 ¼-inch disks are easily stored in plastic trays.

Floppy disks also are stored in plastic pockets punched to fit a ring binder. The floppy disk slips into the clear plastic pocket, where it is protected. Each pocket has space for some type of disk identification. Some plastic pockets can hold hard copy as well as the floppy disk. Other pockets are designed so that you can file floppy disks in a standard file drawer.

Containers for 3 ½-Inch Microdisks

More and more businesses are using *microdisks*, also called minidisks, as storage media in much the same way standard disks are used. Because of their smaller size, 3 ½-inch floppy disks require less storage space and are, therefore, more cost efficient. They are also more **durable** than standard disks because they have a rigid, plastic protective casing.

durable: sturdy; strong

A variety of containers is available for storing microdisks. One type of container is shown in Illus. 13-23 on page 572.

Reel Tape Storage

Reels of tape are stored in round, protective cases. These cases usually are hung for easy access or are stored on wire racks. Sometimes the cases have handles or hooks that allow the reels to be attached to frames or cabinets. Other times, the cases rest on a backward-slanting shelf. Labels on the protective cases can be color coded for easy reference, as shown on page 572.

Illus. 13-23. The smaller 3 ¹/₂-inch disks can be stored in containers similar to those used for 5 ¹/₄-inch disks, such as plastic trays.

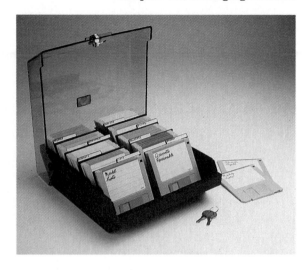

Illus. 13-24. Magnetic tapes are stored in protective cases. Notice the color-coded numbering system used by this company.

RETRIEVING FILES ON MAGNETIC MEDIA

Files stored on secondary storage media are considered to be *off line* when they are removed from the disk drive or tape drive of the computer system. In order to access the information on a secondary storage medium, the medium must be returned to the disk drive or tape drive so that it is once again *on line* with the system.

You must complete the following three steps in order to retrieve a file stored on a secondary storage medium:

1. Locate the proper disk or tape in its storage facility by reading the labels.
2. Insert the disk into the disk drive or mount the tape onto the tape drive.

3. Select the appropriate menu option or initiate the proper command to access the file.

Databases

A *database* is any collection of related items stored in computer memory. Databases are useful to businesses because a manager or office assistant can search through thousands of files in only a few seconds in order to locate the specific information needed. If you had to search through the same number of files stored on paper, the search would be overwhelming! Also, the use of a database helps remedy the problem of having information filed in several different departments within the company. Software is available that allows a company to **devise** its own database designed to meet the needs of that particular organization.

devise: create

Database Management Systems

The more efficiently you can retrieve files from a database, the more productive you will be. A **database management system (DBMS)** organizes and manipulates large numbers of files in a database. A major advantage of a DBMS is information can be compared and shared among the files in the database. For example, the Internal Revenue Service uses a DBMS to compare information on a person's current income tax return with information on past tax returns.

A DBMS also is able to keep database files up to date. If you change information in one file, the system will update all files affected. Suppose you work in a company that uses a DBMS to manage its personnel and payroll files. If an employee's last name changes, you need only make the change in the personnel file and the system will update automatically the payroll file.

A DBMS eliminates repetition in the database. Because the system can automatically locate information requested, the information needs to be stored only once. Another advantage of a DBMS is file security. Access to parts of the database can be limited to authorized employees who have been issued passwords.

IMAGE PROCESSING SYSTEMS

Manufacturers continue to research and develop new products in order to satisfy the ever-changing needs of business and industry. One technological development that has affected records management is image processing. An **image processing system** uses software and special equipment, including

enormous: giant

scanners and optical disks, to store an exact reproduction of a document. These systems are like *enormous* electronic filing cabinets linked together that allow the user to quickly access and review the actual images of original documents. An office worker uses a computer to display a document on the screen or to print a hard copy of the document.

Optical disks, which are an important component of image processing systems, offer large storage capacity and are available in various sizes. The smaller, 5-inch optical disk can store about the same number of documents contained in two file drawers. The larger, 14-inch disk can store about the same number of documents contained in six four-drawer file cabinets.

Illus. 13-25.
Technology makes it possible to store documents on optical disks. This large-capacity storage medium holds great promise for high tech offices.

For ease of access, disks can be stored in a retrieval system called a *jukebox*. An image processing jukebox consists of many optical disks of varying sizes. By entering the proper commands at a computer terminal, the office worker is able to quickly store, retrieve, and read images of documents. Image processing jukeboxes can be linked together electronically, which further increases storage capacity and speed of record retrieval.

Image processing is an effective way to store documents that must be seen in their original form to verify information. For example, American Express utilizes image processing to store the individual charge slips received from businesses. Copies of the charge slips are merged with the monthly statements that are mailed to cardholders.

Sharmane is a customer service supervisor at a savings and loan company. All questions and comments from customers regarding their mortgage accounts are directed to her. The company stores all its customer accounts on optical disks. Sharmane is describing the features of the image processing system to Dewey, a new employee.

Sharmane: Our new image processing system lets me retrieve documents quickly. When customers call with questions about a mortgage payment, I just key in the customer's name at my computer. The system almost instantaneously locates the account and displays it on my screen. I can even get a printout, if I want!

Dewey: That's certainly efficient.

Sharmane: Right! Before, it took so long to locate customers' files that I'd have to tell customers that I'd call them later after I'd pulled the folder.

CREATING MICROFILM FILES

You will recall from your study of Chapter 12 that the space required to keep records on microforms is greatly reduced from the space needed to keep the same number of records on paper. You also will recall that images on microfilm can be created in two ways:

- Paper records are photographed and are developed as images on roll microfilm, microfiche, or aperture cards.
- A computer is used to convert information stored on magnetic media into images on microfilm. Microfilm produced by computer is *computer output microfilm,* usually referred to as COM. The most common form of COM is microfiche.

Photographing Records

A company that chooses microfilm as a storage medium may purchase photographic equipment so the microfilm can be produced in-house. Some businesses offer microimaging services and will photograph a company's records for a fee.

Special cameras are used to reduce records onto film. **Reduction ratio** is a term used to describe how small the microimage is compared to the original record. For example, if the reduction ratio is 48:1 (also written as 48x), the microimage is 48 times smaller than the original record.

Computer Output Microfilm (COM)

Illus. 13-26. Follow the flow of the computer-produced magnetic tape as it is converted into images on microfiche.

You learned in Chapter 12 that computers are also used to create microfilm files. By using a COM recorder in ***conjunction*** with a computer, information stored on magnetic media is converted directly into readable images on roll microfilm or microfiche. Illus. 13-26 shows how records on computer-produced magnetic tape are converted into images on microfiche. When a record is needed, it can be retrieved quickly and viewed on a microfilm reader.

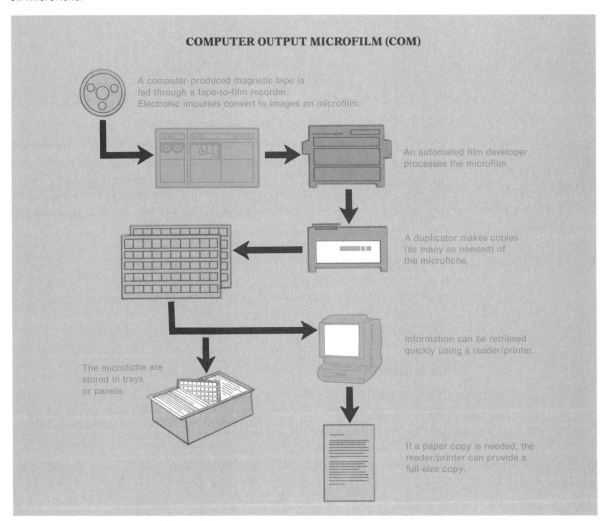

COMPUTER OUTPUT MICROFILM (COM)

A computer-produced magnetic tape is fed through a tape-to-film recorder. Electronic impulses convert to images on microfilm.

An automated film developer processes the microfilm.

A duplicator makes copies (as many as needed) of the microfiche.

Information can be retrieved quickly using a reader/printer.

The microfiche are stored in trays or panels.

If a paper copy is needed, the reader/printer can provide a full-size copy.

**ORGANIZING
MICROFORMS**

In a paper system, you file individual records in folders. You label each folder so you can identify the contents of the folder and file the folder alphabetically, numerically, or chronologically with other folders. A microform is similar to a folder because it contains many records. It is important to label and organize microforms alphabetically, numerically, or chronologically so that they can be retrieved easily. How you label and organize the microforms will depend on the particular filing system used in your company.

Organizing Microfiche

You will recall that a microfiche is a transparent sheet of film containing several rows of microimages. At the top of each microfiche (or *fiche*) is space to label the contents of that particular microform. The caption on a microfiche is similar to the caption used on a folder in a paper filing system. Microfiche labels are frequently color coded for easy retrieval.

Microfiche is the microform commonly used for active (frequently used) storage. Fiche can be stored efficiently in panels. A panel is a page of paper or vinyl that has several slots into which you insert the microfiche. The slots are deep enough to protect the fiche, yet shallow enough to allow the microfiche caption to be read easily.

Illus. 13-27. Microfiche are easily stored in plastic trays (left) and in packets attached to a rotary stand (right).

Microfiche can also be stored in trays where guides and color-coded labels are used to organize the media, just as in a diskette tray or card file.

Organizing Roll Microfilm

Roll microfilm is kept in protective cases or boxes. A label is attached to the case or box to identify that particular roll of microfilm. The roll is filed alphabetically, numerically, or chronologically with other rolls in a drawer or cabinet.

Organizing Aperture Cards

You will recall that the most commonly used aperture card contains only one microrecord or image. Because identifying information can be printed along the top edge of the card, you may file and retrieve aperture cards much as you would file and retrieve paper records. Aperture cards are often housed in trays.

Illus. 13-28. This aperture card is labeled for storage.

RETRIEVING RECORDS ON MICROFILM

When you find it necessary to refer to a record on microfilm, you must know on which roll, fiche, or aperture card the record is stored. If the record is on roll microfilm or microfiche, you also must know the specific location of the record on the film. An index provides you with the information you need by listing an *address* for each microfilm record. Therefore, the first step in retrieving a specific record is to consult the index to determine the exact location of that record. You then would use a reader to view the record. If a hard copy of the record is needed, many readers are equipped with printers that allow you to make a full-size copy of the record.

Illus. 13-29. This office worker is using a microfilm reader/printer to retrieve the records he needs.

Computer-Assisted Retrieval (CAR) Systems

Computer-assisted retrieval (CAR) is the process of locating records on film by using computer-stored indexes. A CAR system may be very simple or very sophisticated.

Simple CAR Systems

A simple CAR system uses an off-line computer and a reader/printer. When you need to refer to the index, you command the computer to print the index on paper, display it, or print it on film. Then you consult the index and manually locate and load the proper microform into the reader.

Database Indexes

Some CAR systems use computer software to maintain an index that is similar to a database. You will recall that a database is a collection of related information or data maintained in computer memory. A database can be accessed in many ways. An advantage of a database index is that you can search for a record by name, subject, or date. The address of the needed record will be displayed on the screen. Then you place the microform into the reader/printer and view the record. Some CAR systems automatically locate the correct image and display it on the reader screen.

Illus. 13-30. An advanced computer-assisted retrieval system.

Advanced CAR Systems

More advanced CAR systems are created as new technologies become available and as existing technologies are integrated with one another. For example, when the ability to transmit data over telephone lines was combined with the need to view microimages from a ***remote*** location, an advanced CAR system became available. The following steps outline how you would use an advanced CAR system to view from a remote location a record stored on microfilm.

remote: distant

1. Use the computer keyboard to access the database index; search the index for the appropriate record address.
2. Use the computer to command the film autoloader to load the proper roll of film and scan the film until the specific image you need is located. The *film autoloader* is a piece of equipment that not only loads and scans the film but also houses the microfilm rolls until they are needed.
3. As the image is being scanned, it is converted into electrical impulses which travel through a *local area network* (LAN) or over telephone lines to your remote computer terminal. You then can view the enlarged image on the screen.
4. If a hard copy of the record is needed, a printer can quickly produce one.

The Paperless Office

Some forecasters predict there will be no paper in the electronic office of the future. Think of it! An office without printed memos circulated among employees, without filing cabinets full of paper records, without envelopes and outgoing mail, without WHILE YOU WERE OUT message forms.

In a paperless office, information would be stored only on microforms, magnetic media, or optical disks. Information would be transmitted from one location to another over telephone lines, by microwaves, or by satellite. Each workstation would have a terminal to view and transmit information.

While the idea of a paperless office is appealing to many office workers, most industry experts do not believe that paper will be obsolete, even with all the advances in technology predicted for the future. Still, there is no doubt that computer technology has dramatically altered how office tasks are performed. Therefore, we can look forward to even more exciting changes—and challenges—in the future.

QUESTIONS FOR REVIEW

1. How are individual files on magnetic media identified?

2. When labeling individual disks or tapes, what descriptive information should appear on Label A? on Label B?

3. Why is it considered a good practice to make backup copies of disks and tapes?

4. What are the three steps you must complete in order to retrieve a record stored on a magnetic medium?

5. Why are databases useful to businesses?

6. What is one major advantage of using optical disk storage?

7. Describe two ways in which images are created on microfilm.

8. What does the reduction ratio 48x tell you about the size of the microimage?

9. Describe how an advanced CAR system enables you to view a microform record from a remote location.

10. Describe what a paperless office might be like.

INTERACTING WITH OTHERS

You and two of your coworkers, Tom and Paula, are working late one evening. All the other workers have gone for the day. During a brief break, Tom says to you: "I hear the company is about to close some pretty big real estate deals. Since you know the access code for the financial database, let's look and see what's going on." Paula agrees, saying, "Sure! No one else is here. What difference will it make? We won't tell anyone you let us see the information." How would you react in this situation? What would you say to your coworkers?

What You Are To Do: Prepare a response to the questions asked.

EXTENDING YOUR MATH COMPETENCIES

Activity 1

Your company estimates that the time it takes you to file each day using folders with color-coded file labels is 20 minutes less than the time it takes to file using folders without color-coded file labels.

What You Are To Do: Calculate how much time the use of color-coded file labels saves you (1) each week, (2) each 4-week month, and (3) each year (52 weeks). Show your calculations.

Activity 2

There are 8 file folders with captions that have Randolph as the first indexing unit, 6 with Reynolds as the first unit, and 2 with Rogers as the first unit. There are 130 folders filed under the letter R.

What You Are To Do: Of the total R folders, calculate which percentage are Randolph folders, which percentage are Reynolds folders, and which percentage are Rogers folders. Round your answers to the nearest whole percentages. Show your calculations.

APPLICATION ACTIVITY

The Cookie Jar, a well-known producer of 34 varieties of cookies, uses a computer system for word processing tasks. Copies of documents prepared on the company's system are classified as follows:

Permanent   Documents that will be revised or used indefinitely (for example, an office manual) are stored on floppy disks with red labels bearing the caption PERMANENT.

Semipermanent   Documents that will be kept only for several weeks or months before being deleted (for example, a price list) are stored on floppy disks with blue labels bearing the caption SEMIPERMANENT.

Temporary   Documents that are saved for a very limited period of time (for example, routine correspondence) are stored on floppy disks with green labels bearing the caption TEMPORARY. These documents will be deleted after the document has been fully processed and a photocopy has been made.

What You Are To Do: Use a plain sheet of paper. In a column at the left side of the paper, list the following ten items. In a column at the right side of the paper, write the appropriate storage classification (permanent, semipermanent, or temporary) for each item.

1. company procedures manual
2. letter to a customer
3. distributor's price list
4. ten-page training manual for the position of customer service representative
5. sales presentation for a new line of cookies
6. legal document
7. thank-you letter to a distributor
8. inventory records
9. advertising copy
10. memorandum about a sales meeting

CHAPTER SUMMARY

In this chapter you learned about the procedures, equipment, supplies, and technologies available to help you manage records stored on paper, magnetic, and microimaging media. You should be knowledgeable about the following key points:

1. Use these five steps to prepare paper records for storage: collect, inspect, index/code, cross-reference (if necessary), and sort the records.
2. Vertical and lateral file cabinets are used most frequently in offices to house folders. Other equipment includes horizontal (flat) files, fixed shelf files, and mobile files.

3. Supplies such as requisition cards, out guides, and out folders are used to manage records efficiently.
4. Many businesses store records on magnetic disks and tapes. Since you cannot read the information on magnetic media without using a reader, it is necessary to identify individual records appropriately and to organize the media carefully.
5. A company that has many records to maintain may use a database. A database management system simplifies and speeds up the retrieval process by organizing and manipulating large numbers of files in a database.
6. Image processing systems allow users to quickly access and review actual images of original documents. The documents are stored on optical disks, a recent alternative for storing information. Advantages of optical disk storage are high storage capacity and speedy record retrieval.
7. Records may be stored on microfilm. Microimages produced by a computer are referred to as computer output microfilm (COM).
8. Many companies use computers to retrieve microimages. A computer-assisted retrieval (CAR) system can be very simple or very sophisticated.

KEY CONCEPTS AND TERMS

release mark	file
filing segment	command
indexing units	database management system (DBMS)
indexing order	image processing system
sorting	reduction ratio
requisition card	computer-assisted retrieval (CAR)
out guide	

INTEGRATED CHAPTER ACTIVITY

At the end of Topic 1, you completed an application activity that involved indexing names of individuals and organizations and placing them in correct alphabetic order. That application activity dealt with Rules 1-7 of Reference Section F. The names presented in this activity relate mainly to Rules 8-14. You will need thirty-five 3" x 5" cards or thirty-five pieces of plain paper cut to that size.

What You Are To Do: 1. Key each name at the upper left corner of a card, placing the units in correct indexing order (see the sample card in Topic 1, page 562). Refer to Reference Section F, Rules 8-14. Also key the number of each name in the upper right corner of the card. (These numbers will help your instructor check your work.)
2. Arrange the cards alphabetically, combining them with the cards you prepared in Topic 1.

(26) North Side Florist Shoppe
(27) McCullum Printing Co., Augusta, Georgia
(28) Collin County Department of Human Services
(29) Lightner & Bagwell, Inc.
(30) 39 and Holding Club
(31) Republic National Bank
(32) Louann D. Grayson
(33) The First Bank of Topeka
(34) Parker-Smith Real Estate
(35) Northside Dry Cleaners
(36) Saint John's Hospital
(37) Omaha Savings and Loan
(38) California Department of Public Safety
(39) Bonny Brite Industries
(40) Carl Michael Collin
(41) Carrollton Department of Engineering and Planning
(42) East Texas State University
(43) North Trails Inn

(44) Strickland-Hall Photography
(45) United States Government Department of Labor
(46) X-Cel Interiors
(47) Lou Ann Grayson
(48) Health Science Center
(49) 16th Street Cafe
(50) Anderson Paint Store, Paris, Tennessee
(51) McCullum Printing Co., Atlanta, Georgia
(52) American Institute of Architects
(53) Clarence C. Bonner
(54) 16th and Grand Shoe Repair
(55) City of Richardson Department of Parks & Recreation
(56) E-Z-Rest Motel
(57) 18th Avenue Apartments
(58) McCullum Printing Co., Savannah, Georgia
(59) 39 Palms Hotel
(60) Anderson Paint Store, Paris, Texas

PRODUCTIVITY CORNER

Kathy Malenky
OFFICE SUPERVISOR

HALTING HACKERS

DEAR MS. MALENKY:

I am a computer operator for a large chemical company that manufactures prescription drugs. My supervisor constantly stresses the need to keep the files confidential. Each week we use a different password to access the files. Only those who are authorized to use the files are told the new password.

Recently on the news I've been hearing about hackers—those who gain access to computer files without permission. What other types of security measures besides passwords are available to keep hackers out?—ERNEST IN SANTA FE

DEAR ERNEST:

You might be surprised at the variety of security systems that are used. For example, an access control may use fingerprints, voice recognition, or even palm geometry to verify your identity.

One interesting access control is referred to as Random Personal Identification. Stored with the computer are personal history questions about each authorized user. When you try to access files, the computer will randomly choose several personal history questions to ask such as, "Where did you live in 1983?" "What is your mother's maiden name?" or "When did you begin working for the company?" It is very unlikely that someone other than the person seeking access could successfully answer these questions.

Another access control is an *error lockout*, which means that after a certain number of unsuccessful attempts to gain access, the terminal's power shuts off. A company may also choose a *time lock*. A time lock restricts the use of the computer to regular office hours.

These are only a few of the security control measures available. As technology advances, even more sophisticated methods of security control probably will be invented. But the best security "device" of all is people who recognize and respect the need for companies to maintain confidential files. I'm glad *you* realize the importance of protecting your company's files!—KATHY MALENKY

AT WORK AT DYNAMICS: *Simulation 3*

Miss Branigan telephones to say that your next assignment will be in the Finance and Administration Division of DYNAMICS. This division prepares the financial and managerial reports necessary for planning, budgeting, reviewing, and reporting purposes. Because this time of the year is always a peak period for the Finance and Administration Division, several temporary employees are being called to help out.

"As a temporary worker in this division," Miss Branigan says, "you will find that two qualities are very important to getting the work done: *flexibility* and *cooperation*. The employees in the Finance and Administration Division all gladly pitch in to help one another whenever possible." Miss Branigan further explains that this division handles all the accounting, management information services, business planning, and purchasing.

A key component of the Finance and Administration Division is the Management Information Services (MIS) Department. This department is responsible for overseeing all computer operations within the company. Additionally, the MIS department develops software to meet the information needs of the total company. "Your experiences in the Finance and Administration Division will be varied, and you will find that all phases of the company's activities are involved in what you do. I know you will find your work challenging," says Miss Branigan.

Turn to your *Information Processing Activities* workbook to learn more about your assignment in the Finance and Administration Division of DYNAMICS.

MAIL AND TELECOMMUNICATION SYSTEMS

CHAPTER 14

Processing Mail

As you learned in Chapter 3, workers frequently use written messages to communicate with coworkers as well as individuals outside the company. For example, Joan, a worker in the marketing department, sends a memo to Darrell, in the research & development department, requesting information about a new product. Shawn Fields, an architect, sends a set of plans to Gayle Minton, an electrical engineer, to have them approved. Juan Ramirez, the advertising director for a furniture store, sends announcements of an upcoming sale to all customers. In all these situations, information may be sent and received by mail. Mail must be processed as efficiently as possible so that communication is not delayed.

The size of a company and the amount of automated equipment available affect the procedures used for processing incoming and outgoing mail. In a small company, one worker may handle incoming and outgoing mail (as well as perform other office tasks) using limited automated equipment. In a large company, a full-time mailroom staff often uses specialized equipment to process mail. Even in large companies, workers outside the mailroom may have certain mail-handling responsibilities.

In this chapter you will learn procedures for processing incoming and outgoing mail in both small and large companies. You also will learn about the equipment available to process mail with maximum efficiency. The objectives of the chapter are to:

- present procedures for processing incoming mail

- explain procedures for preparing outgoing mail and acquaint you with the various services provided by the United States Postal Service

INCOMING MAIL PROCEDURES

When you have completed your study of this topic, you will be able to:

- apply procedures for sorting and distributing mail

- handle incoming mail for your supervisor(s)

Incoming mail includes mail from outside the company as well as **interoffice mail**—messages exchanged by workers within a company. Office workers often need to take action promptly in response to items received in the mail. There may be checks to deposit, orders to fill, invoices to pay, literature to read, reports to review, and correspondence to answer. Mail must be accurately sorted and promptly distributed to the appropriate people so necessary actions can be taken without delay.

You may be responsible for sorting and distributing incoming mail for the entire company. You may help your supervisors process their mail after another worker has distributed it. Your role in processing incoming mail will depend on the size of the company, the volume of incoming mail, and the preferences of your supervisor(s).

This topic is divided into two sections. The first section will present procedures for processing mail from the time it is delivered until it is distributed to the appropriate people in the company. In the second section, you will learn specific ways to help your supervisor with the processing of incoming mail.

SORTING AND DISTRIBUTING MAIL

precedence: priority of importance

When delivered to an organization, mail for various individuals and departments is all mixed together. Most companies want all mail sorted quickly so that it can be delivered promptly. Special delivery letters, mailgrams, registered mail, and insured mail are delivered to the addressee immediately upon receipt. In fact, the delivery of such letters takes *precedence* over the processing of ordinary mail. The method used for sorting mail will depend upon the size of the company and how the incoming mail processing function is organized.

In Small Companies

In a small company, you can easily sort the mail at your workstation by making a stack of mail for each employee or department. In a small company, one person may process incoming mail as well as perform other office tasks.

To distribute the mail, you hand deliver each stack of mail to the appropriate person or department. If you have several stacks or bundles of mail to deliver, you may need to carry them in a

Illus. 14-1. This mail clerk is responsible for delivering mail at regularly scheduled times throughout the workday.

pouch, alphabetized expanding folder, lightweight mail basket, or mail cart as you make your rounds through the office. You should arrange the bundles according to the route you will take.

When Brad is finished sorting the mail, he places rubber bands around each stack, creating a separate bundle for each worker. Then he places the bundles in a mail cart in the order he will deliver them. Since Julia Wesley's workstation is his first stop, Brad places her mail bundle at the front of the cart. Using this procedure, Brad can distribute the mail quickly.

In Large Companies

Many large companies have mailrooms. A **mailroom** is a designated area where large volumes of incoming mail are processed. Mailrooms are easily accessible to postal workers who deliver the mail to the company. You are likely to find specialized equipment to aid mailroom workers in following procedures for opening, sorting, and delivering the mail. Such equipment typically includes electric envelope openers, sorting units, and automated delivery systems.

Procedures and equipment for processing incoming mail are described here. In Topic 2, you will learn about procedures and equipment for processing outgoing mail.

Illus. 14-2. This mailroom worker is sorting incoming mail from the post office and from private mail services.

Opening Envelopes

In some companies, mailroom workers open all the mail (except envelopes marked *Personal* or *Confidential*) before delivering it. An electric envelope opener often is used for this task.

An electric envelope opener trims a narrow strip off one edge of each envelope. The amount trimmed off is very small so that there is little risk that the contents of the envelope will be damaged. To reduce the chances of cutting the contents, tap each envelope on the table before placing it in the opener, so the contents will fall away from the edge that you are trimming.

Sorting Mail

A wide variety of sorting units are used to sort the mail. Each compartment is labeled with the name of an individual or department within the organization. To sort the mail, you place each piece of mail in the appropriate compartment.

Companies with a huge amount of incoming mail have found that they can save time and effort by using a rotary unit. The unit turns easily, and the worker can remain in one place as he or she sorts the mail.

Distributing Mail

Once the mail has been sorted, it is ready for distribution. Procedures for delivering mail within the organization vary from company to company. For example:

- A worker from each department comes to the mailroom to pick up the department's mail.
- A mailroom employee carries the mail in a basket or cart from the mailroom to the departments.

automated:
automatic

- An **automated** delivery system transports mail to the various departments.

**HANDLING
INCOMING
MAIL FOR
YOUR
SUPERVISORS**

Some office workers are asked to process the mail before giving it to their supervisors. Some supervisors, however, prefer to process their own mail.

Becky is the receptionist in a small real estate office. For each of her supervisors she opens the mail, removes the contents, and stamps the date and time on each item.

Todd works in a florist shop where he only sorts and distributes the mail. His supervisors then process their own mail.

Illus. 14-3. Mobile mail carts are used in some large companies to distribute the mail. This robot-like cart follows a chemical path on the floor and is programmed to stop at certain locations throughout the building. Employees can then pick up incoming mail and deposit outgoing mail.

Typical procedures for processing incoming mail are described next. Your supervisors will tell you which procedures they want you to follow.

Opening Mail

If the mail is not opened when it reaches you, use a letter opener to open all envelopes except those marked *Personal* or *Confidential.* If you mistakenly open an envelope marked *Personal* or *Confidential,* write on the envelope, "Sorry, opened by mistake," and add your initials. Check the outside of each envelope carefully before you open it to avoid making that error.

If your supervisor wants you to remove the contents from the envelopes, be sure to verify that all enclosures referred to in the correspondence are actually enclosed. If an enclosure is missing, you should note the ***omission*** in the margin of the letter. You may need to keep a record on file of the missing enclosure if it is a check, money order, cash, or stamps.

omission: something left out

Check each letter for the signature and the address of the sender before you discard the envelope. If either is missing on the letter, attach the envelope to the letter, since the envelope usually has a return address on it. Sometimes the envelope is stapled to a document because the mailing date may be important.

Dating and Time-Stamping Mail

Illus. 14-4.

Each incoming mail item should be marked with the current date and time. You can do this with a pen or pencil, a rubber stamp, or a time-stamp machine.

Separating Mail

inquiries: questions

As you inspect the mail, put aside the letters that you can answer or handle yourself if your supervisor has instructed you to do so. These would include communications that could be answered by a form letter, circular, or advertisement. Requests for catalogs or price lists can usually be handled this way. However, your supervisor may wish to see all *inquiries* that are received.

Underlining and Annotating Mail

annotating: writing comments

If your supervisor requests, you may further assist in handling correspondence by underlining and *annotating*. However, good judgment is necessary here, since too many markings can be annoying.

First, underline the key words and phrases in the correspondence that will help your supervisor understand the content quickly. Note the key phrases underlined in Illus. 14-5. Then determine the answers to questions you can answer and to which your supervisor must respond. Where appropriate, make related comments on the letter. Write the clearly worded answers and/or comments in the margin in legible handwriting. Note the annotations in the margin of the letter shown in Illus. 14-5.

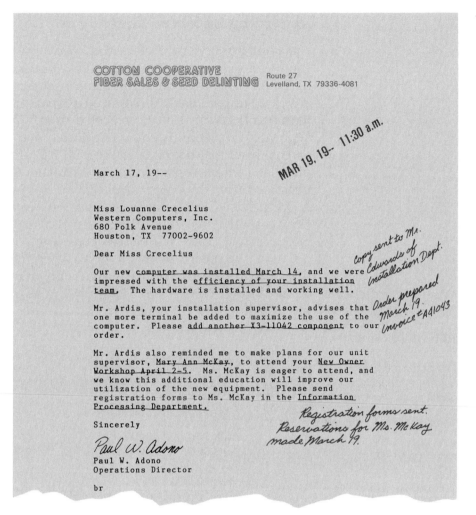

Illus. 14-5. The date-time stamp, underlined words and phrases, and annotations indicate that this incoming letter is ready for presentation to the supervisor.

COTTON COOPERATIVE
FIBER SALES & SEED DELINTING   Route 27
Levelland, TX 79336-4081

MAR 19, 19-- 11:30 a.m.

March 17, 19--

Miss Louanne Crecelius
Western Computers, Inc.
680 Polk Avenue
Houston, TX 77002-9602

Dear Miss Crecelius

Our new computer was installed March 14, and we were
impressed with the efficiency of your installation
team. The hardware is installed and working well.

Copy sent to Mr. Edwards of Installation Dept.

Mr. Ardis, your installation supervisor, advises that
one more terminal be added to maximize the use of the
computer. Please add another X3-11042 component to our
order.

Order prepared March 19. Invoice # A41043

Mr. Ardis also reminded me to make plans for our unit
supervisor, Mary Ann McKay, to attend your New Owner
Workshop April 2-5. Ms. McKay is eager to attend, and
we know this additional education will improve our
utilization of the new equipment. Please send
registration forms to Ms. McKay in the Information
Processing Department.

Sincerely

Paul W. Adono

Paul W. Adono
Operations Director

br

Registration forms sent. Reservations for Ms. McKay made March 19.

Attaching Related Materials to Mail

Copies of previous correspondence, reports, and other related documents may help your supervisor respond to the mail. For example, you may attach the file copy of a letter written to Ms. McKay to the reply you receive from her. Or you may place related items where your supervisor can find them easily. For example, you might retrieve from the files a folder related to an inquiry and place it with the incoming letter on your supervisor's desk.

Recording Expected Mail

If your supervisor prefers that you remove the contents from the envelopes and process the mail, you may learn of promises by senders to mail materials *under separate cover* (in another envelope or package). You should keep a record of these expected items to be sure that you receive them. One type of record for separate cover mail is shown in Illus. 14-6. Notice that the entry on the first line was made on August 2 (Date of Entry). The article promised was a report from Reid Brothers. The correspondence indicated that the report was mailed on August 1 (Date Sent) to A. Weir (For Whom). It was received on August 4 (Date Received). Notice on the last line of the record that the tickets mailed on September 22 have not been received yet.

Check the record at least twice a week to see which items have not been received. That way, you can take follow-up action on delayed mail. Workers in the mailroom usually do not keep such records since they do not read the contents of the mail.

Illus. 14-6. Keep a record of mail you expect to receive in another envelope or package.

EXPECTED MAIL					
Date of Entry	Article	From Whom	Date Sent	For Whom	Date Received
8-2	Report	Reid Bros.	8-1	A. Weir	8-4
8-5	Micro-cassettes	Foxworth Supply	8-3	J. Tyler	8-10
8-15	Computer Printouts	Lehman & Bennett	8-12	A. Weir	8-18
9-3	Catalog	Cole Mfg. Co.	9-1	H. Rice	9-7
9-25	Benefit Tickets	Jack Hill	9-22	H. Rice	

Documenting Receipt of Important Mail

document: make a written record of

Whether you process incoming mail in a small company or in the mailroom of a large company, you should **document** the receipt of mail sent by special postal services. For example, you should record the receipt of special delivery, insured, registered, or Express Mail. You may use a form similar to that shown in Illus. 14-7.

Illus. 14-7. Use a mail register to document the receipt of special mail.

MAIL REGISTER					
Received		From Whom		For Whom	Kind of Mail Received
Date	Time	Name	City/State		
4-5	3:20 p.m.	T. J. McIntosh	St. Louis, MO	B. Rudd	Insured
4-6	9:15 a.m.	Bates Mfg. Co.	Memphis, TN	S. Norwell	Special Delivery
4-9	10:45 a.m.	Ken Stewart	Des Moines, IA	M. Jones	Registered
4-12	3:15 p.m.	Haskins & Associates	Erie, PA	W. Yeager	Express Mail

Referring Mail to Others

facilitate: speed the process of

Your supervisor may decide to refer certain items to an assistant or associate to handle. To **facilitate** this referral, a *referral slip* is attached to the item. The referral slip shown in Illus. 14-8 lists a series of instructions from which the supervisor may choose. A check mark is used to indicate the specific instruction to be followed.

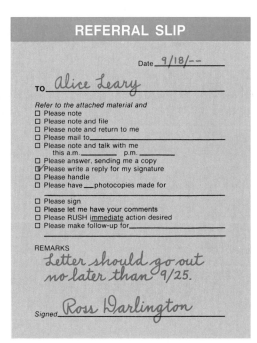

Illus. 14-8. Supervisors frequently forward a piece of mail to an associate. In some cases, it is for the associate's information only; in other cases, an action is requested.

When action is requested of another individual, you may be asked to keep a record of the referral. You should note the date the item was referred, the name of the person to whom it was referred, the subject, the action to be taken, and a follow-up date if one is necessary.

Routing Mail

route: send on a particular path

There are times when items such as correspondence and important magazine articles should be read by more than one person in the company. You may be asked to make a copy for each person who should read the item. Or you may be asked to **route** the item through the office. To do so, attach a *routing slip* like the one shown in Illus. 14-9 to the item. Indicate with check marks the individuals who should read the item.

FROM

Ryan Eft, Director

Public Relations Department

DATE *3/25/--*

ROUTING SLIP

		Date Forwarded
_____	Everyone	_____
_____	Baker, D.	_____
✓	Gossett, S.	*3/25*
_____	Ianowski, B.	_____
_____	Lansing, T.	_____
✓	Nussbaum, S.	*3/25*
✓	Rhea, J.	*3/28*
_____	Stevens, L.	_____
✓	Tomes, S.	*3/28*
_____	Waugh, H.	_____
✓	York, M.	*3/28*

Please:

_____	Read and keep
_____	Read and pass on
_____	Read and return
✓	Read, pass on, and return

Illus. 14-9. A routing slip is attached to mail to be distributed to others.

Prioritizing Mail

The mail should be prioritized according to your supervisor's preference. As a general rule, mail is categorized in the order of its importance. The following arrangement is usually satisfactory, moving from the top to the bottom of the stack:

1. unopened personal and confidential letters
2. business letters of special importance to your supervisor; interoffice correspondence
3. letters containing checks or money orders
4. other business letters
5. letters containing orders
6. letters containing bills, invoices, or other requests for payment
7. advertisements
8. newspapers and magazines

Place the mail, properly arranged, on your supervisor's desk. The supervisor can then easily process the mail in priority order. Prioritizing the mail is an example of being sensitive to others' tasks as well as your own. When you facilitate the work of others, you contribute to the overall efficiency of the company.

QUESTIONS FOR REVIEW

1. What is interoffice mail?

2. What three factors affect your role in processing incoming mail?

3. What is a mailroom?

4. What equipment is used in mailrooms to process incoming mail?

5. What should you do if you open a confidential letter by mistake?

6. When you remove contents from an envelope, what should you verify?

7. How might your annotating a letter save your supervisor time?

8. What is the purpose of keeping a record of expected mail?

9. Give an example of when a routing slip might be used.

10. What is the generally accepted order for prioritizing a supervisor's mail?

INTERACTING WITH OTHERS

You are a general clerk in a small medical clinic. Kelly, the receptionist, is responsible for sorting and distributing all incoming mail. Mail addressed to the three physicians is opened before it is delivered; mail addressed to the general office staff is to be delivered unopened. Today, however, Kelly delivers a letter addressed to you that *has* been opened. The letter includes salary information that is both personal and confidential in nature. You are concerned that Kelly may have read the letter.

Should you ask Kelly why the letter was opened? Should you ask her if she read the letter? How would you handle this situation?

What You Are To Do: Prepare a response to the questions raised.

EXTENDING YOUR MATH COMPETENCIES

Based on records kept by the mailroom supervisor, about 3,000 pieces of incoming mail are sorted and distributed each month in your company. Additionally, the volume of mail is expected to increase by 6 percent next year.

What You Are To Do:
- Calculate how many pieces of mail will be processed this year.
- Calculate how many pieces of mail are expected to be processed next year.
- Calculate how many more pieces of mail will be processed next year than will be processed this year.
- Calculate how many pieces of mail per month the mailroom will handle next year.

APPLICATION ACTIVITY

You work in the general office of Sterling Enterprises. Because the company receives many items under separate cover, you have been asked to keep a record of these expected items to be sure they are received.

What You Are To Do: Use the Expected Mail form provided in *Information Processing Activities* or prepare a form similar to the one shown on page 598. Fill in the form using the following information:

May 2	A letter from Kevin Bradshaw refers to an office procedures manual he sent to Carolyn Sachs on April 29.
May 2	In a letter dated April 29, Joan Murray states she mailed a catalog to Larry Pokowski.
May 5	In her May 1 letter, Meagan Czander states she sent five copies of a marketing research analysis in another package to Roger Wilcox.
May 6	A letter dated May 3 from Stanley Johnson states he returned a briefcase by parcel post to Elizabeth Koenig.
May 8	The office procedures manual from Kevin Bradshaw arrives.
May 8	The marketing analysis from Meagan Czander arrives.
May 11	A letter from Roy Almondson states he sent twelve copies of his company's annual report to Nico Mirandos on May 8.
May 12	The briefcase from Stanley Johnson arrives.
May 12	A notice dated May 9 from Jerrod's Office Supply states that supplies were shipped by parcel post on the same day to Larry Pokowski.
May 13	A letter dated May 11 from Ulin Mitchell states he sent three copies of this year's budget in another envelope to Carolyn Sachs.
May 13	The annual reports from Roy Almondson arrive.
May 14	The budgets from Ulin Mitchell arrive.
May 16	In her May 12 letter, Maria Gonzales states she sent two copies of a proposal in another package to Paul Harrington.
May 17	The catalog from Joan Murray arrives.

TOPIC 2

OUTGOING MAIL PROCEDURES

When you have completed your study of this topic, you will be able to:

- apply procedures for preparing outgoing mail

- identify the classes of domestic mail

- explain the various services provided by the USPS

- arrange for courier service

- send materials through an interoffice mail system

Throughout a working day, many forms of communication are sent to those outside the company. For example, you may be asked to send purchase orders to customers, letters to business organizations, and advertisements to potential customers. It is important that outgoing mail be properly prepared.

You have prepared letters for mailing and are acquainted with addressing envelopes, inserting documents, and affixing proper postage. However, you will find that companies have developed specific procedures for completing these tasks in order to handle outgoing mail efficiently.

The way outgoing mail is processed will depend on the size of your company and the procedures designated by the company. If you work in a small office, you probably will be responsible for all the details involved with processing outgoing mail. However, if you work in the mailroom of a large company, you may weigh and seal, apply postage to, and mail envelopes that have been prepared and stuffed by workers in other departments.

The *United States Postal Service* (USPS) processes over 530 million pieces of mail each day! Businesses all across the country use the varied services of the USPS to send such items as letters, financial reports, computer printouts, architectural drawings, invoices, manuscripts, newsletters, and merchandise to their intended destinations. In some cases, the items are destined for delivery in the same city; in other cases, delivery is to be made to an individual or an organization in a city halfway around the world.

courier: messenger

Although most outgoing mail is sent through the USPS, there also are local, national, and worldwide *courier* services available that deliver envelopes and packages. Most courier services guarantee their delivery times. You also may send mail through an *interoffice mail system.* As an office worker, you need to be acquainted with the mailing options available to you. This topic will help you learn about procedures for processing outgoing mail efficiently.

PROCESSING OUTGOING MAIL IN A SMALL COMPANY

In a small organization you may be responsible for processing all the outgoing mail, as well as handling other office tasks.

Linda is the receptionist in a small real estate office. On her workstation is an out basket where all the workers place their outgoing mail. A postal carrier usually picks up and delivers the mail about 10:30 a.m. At 10:00 a.m., Linda prepares an envelope for each item in the out basket. Then she stuffs the envelopes, seals them, weighs them, and applies the appropriate postage. By 10:30 a.m., the mail is ready to be picked up by the postal carrier.

Illus. 14-10. This office worker places outgoing mail in a small mail rack on her desk. The mail is then collected by a mail clerk making regularly scheduled pickups and deliveries.

The USPS picks up and delivers mail to some organizations twice a day. In other organizations, a postal carrier may come in the morning, but an office worker may take outgoing mail to a

drop box: mail box

post office or *drop box* in the afternoon. You need to know the scheduled times for pickup so you can have the mail ready on time. The USPS recommends mailing as early in the day as possible for the fastest service.

Folding and Inserting Mail

Once a document is ready to mail, it is a good idea to give it a final check before inserting it in the envelope. Be sure that:

- copies have been made, if necessary
- your initials appear below your supervisor's signature on any letter you have signed for your supervisor
- any enclosures noted at the bottom of a letter are actually enclosed in the envelope
- the address on the envelope agrees with the address on the letter
- the ZIP Code appears on the last line of both the envelope address and the return address

You usually will insert documents into standard or window envelopes. Folding business documents correctly to fit into envelopes is a simple, but important, task. You should take care that the creases are straight and neat. A document should be inserted in an envelope so that it will be in a normal reading position when it is removed from the envelope and unfolded.

Standard Envelopes

The most common sizes of standard envelopes are 9 $\frac{1}{2}$″ x 4 $\frac{1}{8}$″ (No. 10) and 6 $\frac{1}{2}$″ x 3 $\frac{5}{8}$″ (No. 6 $\frac{3}{4}$). Illus. 14-11 shows how to fold a letter and insert it into a No. 10 envelope.

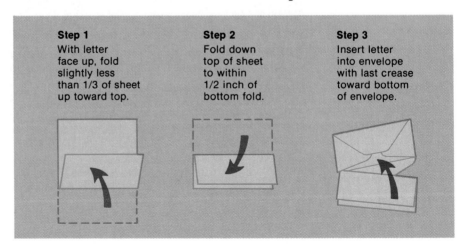

Step 1
With letter face up, fold slightly less than 1/3 of sheet up toward top.

Step 2
Fold down top of sheet to within 1/2 inch of bottom fold.

Step 3
Insert letter into envelope with last crease toward bottom of envelope.

Illus. 14-11. Follow these steps to fold an 8 $\frac{1}{2}$″ x 11″ letter to insert into a No. 10 envelope.

Illus. 14-12 shows how to fold a letter and insert it into a No. 6 ³/₄ envelope. The enclosures that accompany a document should be folded with the document or inserted so that they will come out of the envelope when the document is removed.

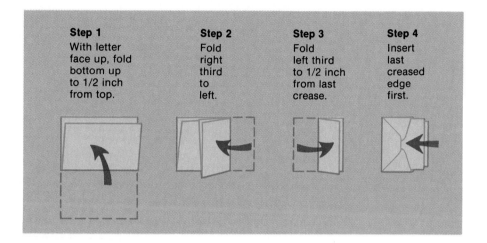

Illus. 14-12. Follow these steps to fold an 8 ¹/₂" x 11" letter to insert into a No. 6 ³/₄ envelope.

Step 1
With letter face up, fold bottom up to 1/2 inch from top.

Step 2
Fold right third to left.

Step 3
Fold left third to 1/2 inch from last crease.

Step 4
Insert last creased edge first.

Window Envelopes

A window envelope has a see-through panel on the front of the envelope. A window envelope eliminates the need to address a standard envelope since the address on the letter or form is visible through the see-through panel, or *window*. The address on the letter or form must be positioned so that it can be seen through the window after the letter is folded and inserted into the envelope.

Window envelopes are available as No. 10 and No. 6 ³/₄ envelopes. No. 6 ³/₄ window envelopes are used mostly for forms or statements that are designed to fit with only a single fold. Illus. 14-13 on page 608 shows how to fold an 8 ¹/₂" x 11" page to fit correctly into a No. 10 window envelope.

Sealing and Weighing Envelopes

Envelopes must be sealed before they are mailed. When you need to seal more than one or two envelopes, you probably will want to use a moist sponge or moistener. To quickly seal many envelopes at once, spread about ten envelopes on a table or desk. Place them address-side down, flap open, one on top of the other

Illus. 14-13. Follow these steps to fold an 8 ½" x 11" letter to insert into a No. 10 window envelope.

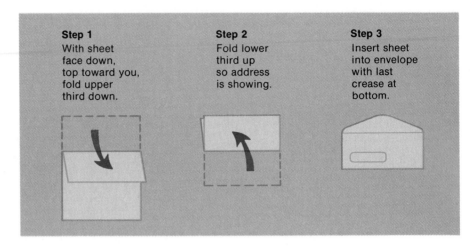

Step 1
With sheet face down, top toward you, fold upper third down.

Step 2
Fold lower third up so address is showing.

Step 3
Insert sheet into envelope with last crease at bottom.

with the gummed edges showing. Note in Illus. 14-14 (left) how the worker has done this. Brush over the gummed edges with a sponge or moistener. Starting with the top envelope, quickly fold the flaps down one at a time until all the envelopes are sealed.

It is important to weigh each piece of outgoing mail accurately so you can apply the proper amount of postage. Electronic scales are available that automatically calculate the correct amount of postage for each piece of mail. You simply place the item to be mailed on the scale and indicate which postal class you wish to use. The amount of the postage is displayed on a small screen. When postal rates change, you update the scale by inserting a new computer memory unit.

Illus. 14-14. (Left) A moistener can be used to quickly seal several envelopes at once.

Illus. 14-15. (Right) An electronic postage scale.

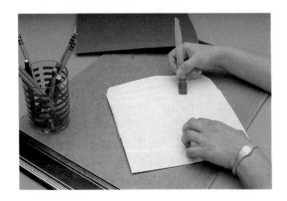

Stamping/Metering Mail

Postage must be paid for all mail before it can be delivered. There are various methods of purchasing postage.

Stamps

You may purchase postage stamps in sheet, booklet, or rolled form. Rolled stamps often are used in business because they can be placed quickly on envelopes and packages and they are less likely than individual stamps to be lost or damaged.

Stamped Envelopes and Cards

lots: things considered as a group

The post office sells envelopes and cards which already have the correct postage printed on them. You can buy them one at a time or in quantity **lots**. First-class postal cards may be purchased in single or double form. The double form is used when a reply is requested on the attached card.

Postage Meter

A **postage meter** is a machine that prints postage in the amount needed. It prints the postage either directly onto the envelope or onto a pre-moistened label that you apply to the envelope. You can use the numeric keys on the postage meter to set it to print postage for a letter weighing one ounce and easily reset it to print postage for a letter weighing three ounces. The postage meter prints the date as well as the postage amount. Always be sure the correct date is set on the meter. Some meters also print a business slogan or advertisement next to the postmark.

To buy postage, you take the meter with you to the post office. The postal worker will reset the meter for the amount of postage purchased. As you use the postage meter, the meter setting decreases, showing you how much postage is left. Do not let the postage get too low before buying more. The meter locks when the postage paid for has been used.

Pitney-Bowes, a company specializing in mailroom equipment, has a postage system called *Postage-by-Phone*. To purchase postage, you simply call a toll-free number and use the keys of your touch-tone telephone to enter required information (including an assigned resetting number). You are then assigned a new resetting number, which you enter into the meter. Using Postage-by-Phone, you can reset your meter in less than two minutes.

Illus. 14-16. An electronic postage meter prints the postmark and the postage.

Illus. 14-17. A company that has a Postage-by-Phone system can "buy additional postage" by calling a toll-free number.

Because metered mail is already dated and postmarked, it can be processed faster than stamped mail.

PROCESSING OUTGOING MAIL IN A LARGE COMPANY

You have just learned that in a small company, an office worker may be responsible for all the steps of processing outgoing mail. In a large company, however, these steps may be divided between mailroom workers and workers in other departments.

Jenner Industries is a large corporation with many departments. Office workers in each department address the envelopes and insert the correspondence into the envelopes. Each department has a central location for collecting outgoing mail. A mailroom worker picks up the mail and takes it to the company mailroom. The mailroom workers then seal, weigh, and affix postage to the mail in time for scheduled pickups from the post office.

If you are an office worker in a large company, the extent of your mail-handling duties will be determined by company policy.

Sending the same items to many people at the same time is a **volume mailing**. For example, a marketing research company may send a questionnaire to all residents in a city to determine their preferences with regard to particular products, such as televisions or breakfast cereals.

Mailing Lists

current: up to date

forward: send on

Mailing lists for volume mail may contain addresses for customers, prospective customers, subscribers, or those who live in certain geographic areas. Mailing lists should always be **current**. That means you should delete, correct, and add addresses as soon as you learn about any changes. The post office recommends having the words FORWARDING AND ADDRESS CORRECTION REQUESTED printed on all envelopes. Then the post office will **forward** mail with an old address to the new address. For a small fee, the post office will send you a card giving the new address.

As companies expand their mailing lists, many are choosing to use computer-generated mailing lists. A **computer-generated mailing list** is a mailing list that is created and updated on computer storage media. Some of the advantages of using computer-generated mailing lists are:

- You can quickly retrieve, change, or delete addresses.
- You can easily avoid duplicate addresses.
- Most software allows you to select addresses from a master list to create a smaller list for a special mailing.
- Some software allows you to print not only address labels but also letter addresses and salutations on form letters.

Preparing Address Labels

One method of preparing labels is to type all the addresses on paper in a format that will allow you to photocopy the addresses onto sheets of labels. Each time you have a mailing, you simply photocopy the addresses, peel the labels off the backing sheets, and apply them to the envelopes.

Many companies use computers to print address labels. On page 612, you can see an computerized addressing/labeling/folding/inserting system. With such a system, addresses stored on a disk can be printed onto sheets of pressure-sensitive labels. *Pressure-sensitive labels* can be peeled from backing sheets and affixed to envelopes, using light pressure. Some printers can print as many as 7,000 address labels per hour.

You can apply computer-generated address labels to envelopes manually or automatically, using an automatic labeling device.

Illus. 14-18. Large companies may have an addressing/labeling/folding/inserting system to speed up the processing of volume mail. Note that "four-up" refers to the number of labels printed across a page.

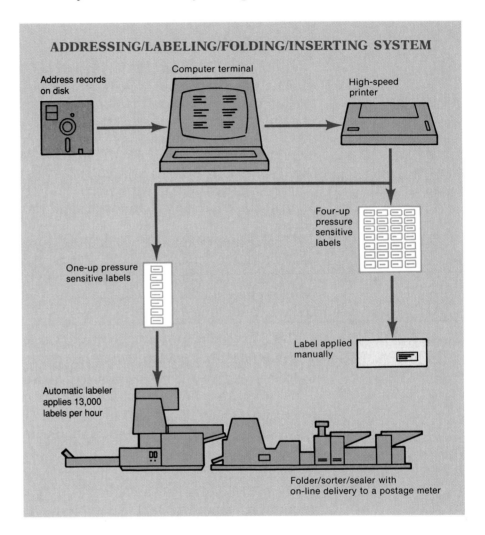

ADDRESSING/LABELING/FOLDING/INSERTING SYSTEM

Address records on disk

Computer terminal

High-speed printer

Four-up pressure sensitive labels

One-up pressure sensitive labels

Label applied manually

Automatic labeler applies 13,000 labels per hour

Folder/sorter/sealer with on-line delivery to a postage meter

ADDRESS REQUIREMENTS FOR AUTOMATED MAIL HANDLING

The USPS uses high-speed electronic mail-handling equipment in many of its postal centers in order to speed mail to its destination. This equipment includes optical character readers and bar code sorters. An **optical character reader (OCR)** is electronic equipment that quickly scans or "reads" the address on an envelope and prints a bar code at the bottom of the envelope.

During the sorting process, the bar codes are "read" by a bar code sorter and the mail is quickly routed to its proper destination. Not all postal centers are equipped with OCR equipment and bar code sorters; therefore, not all mail you receive will have a printed bar code on the envelope.

If the optical character reader is unable to read an address, the envelope is routed to a manual letter-sorting machine. This, of course, increases the processing time. Some of the reasons why an OCR may be unable to read an address are listed here:

- The address is handwritten.
- The address is not printed or typed in the proper format.
- The envelope may be too small or too large for the OCR equipment to handle. (To avoid this problem, use rectangular envelopes no smaller than 3 1/2" x 5" and no larger than 6 1/8" x 10 1/2".)
- The address is not within the OCR read area.
- The complete address is not visible through the panel of a window envelope.

Address Format

The address should be typewritten or machine printed on the envelope or label. It is very important that the characters be dark, even, and clear. As you learned in Chapter 6, the address is typed or machine printed according to the following format:

- Use all capital letters.
- Block the left margin of the address.
- Omit all marks of punctuation (except the hyphen in a nine-digit ZIP Code).
- Use the standard two-letter abbreviation for the state (see Reference Section E for a list of these abbreviations).
- Leave two spaces between the state abbreviation and the ZIP Code.

The post office has an approved list of abbreviations for cities and other words commonly used in addresses. You should use these approved abbreviations if the address is too long to fit on a label.

Illus. 14-19. Use the proper address format and abbreviations for mailing labels as recommended by USPS.

```
MS EMMA JO BERMAN
132 CANNON GREEN TOWERS APT 6A
SANTA BARBARA CA 93105-2233


MR ARTURO FUENTES
VICE PRESIDENT MARKETING
ROSSLYN WHOLESALE COMPANY
1815 N LYNN STREET
ARLINGTON VA 22209-6183


ATTN THOMAS W THIESEN
BATES MICROWAVE COMPANY
4025 EASTWAY DRIVE
CHARLOTTE NC 28205-2736
```

ZIP Codes

To assure prompt delivery of your mail, always use the nine-digit ZIP Code, if known. **ZIP + 4** is a voluntary nine-digit ZIP Code system recommended by the USPS.

You are already familiar with the five-digit ZIP Code. The first three digits indicate a major geographic area or post office, while the last two digits designate a local post office. A hyphen and four digits are added to the existing five-digit ZIP Code to help the post office sort the mail more specifically. The first two digits after the hyphen indicate a delivery *sector.* A sector is several blocks within a city, a group of streets, several office buildings, or another small geographic area. The last two digits represent a delivery *segment,* which can indicate one side of a street, one floor in an office building, or specific departments in a firm.

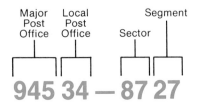

ZIP Code directories for both the five-digit and nine-digit codes can be purchased from the post office. If a directory is not available in the office where you work, you can call the post office to obtain a particular ZIP Code.

CLASSES OF DOMESTIC MAIL

Domestic mail is distributed within the United States and its territories (such as Puerto Rico, the Virgin Islands, and Guam.) Domestic mail is divided into various classes, which are described in the following paragraphs.

First-Class Mail

expeditiously: with maximum efficiency

The post office will handle and transport first-class mail *expeditiously*. The USPS requires that you send the following items first-class:

- personal correspondence
- handwritten and typewritten messages, including copies
- bills and statements of account
- post cards (privately purchased mailing cards which require postage) and postal cards (cards sold by the post office with postage imprinted on them)
- canceled and uncanceled checks
- printed forms filled out in writing
- business reply mail

Illus. 14-20. Various classes of domestic mail must be sorted by postal workers each day.

There is a minimum charge for all first-class mail weighing up to one ounce. An additional charge is made for each additional ounce or fraction of an ounce. If you are sending material in an oversized envelope that does not bear a pre-printed FIRST CLASS notation, be sure to print or stamp FIRST CLASS on the envelope. It is illegal to open first-class mail without a federal search warrant.

Priority Mail

First-class mail that weighs over 11 ounces is referred to as *Priority Mail.* The maximum weight for priority mail is 70 pounds. Priority mail is usually delivered within two to three days. The amount of postage for priority mail is based on the weight of the item and its destination.

Second-Class Mail

Second-class mail consists of publications such as newspapers and periodicals. To mail material second class, you need authorization from the USPS and must pay a special fee. Second-class mail must bear a notice that it is second class, and it must be mailed in bulk lots (volume mailings).

Third-Class Mail

Third-class mail is material that is not classified as first-class mail or second-class mail and that weighs less than 16 ounces. Advertising brochures and catalogs often are sent third class. Third-class mail sent in 200-piece quantities or in 50-pound batches may be eligible for reduced postage rates. Third-class mail that is sealed must bear the notation THIRD-CLASS MAIL.

Fourth-Class Mail (Parcel Post)

Fourth-class mail is also known as *parcel post.* It includes packages, printed matter such as books, and all other mailable matter that weighs 16 ounces or more and is not included in first-, second-, or third-class mail. Parcel post rates are based on the weight of the item and the distance it must travel to be delivered.

A *library rate* may be used by some mailers who send books, printed music, academic papers, and other similar items. The material must be clearly labeled LIBRARY RATE. Library rate is usually used by organizations such as schools, libraries, non-profit organizations, and veterans' groups.

Mixed Classes of Mail

Sometimes it is better to send two pieces of mail of different classes together as a single mailing to make sure they both arrive at the same time. For example, you may attach a first-class invoice to the outside of a large package sent fourth class, or you may enclose a first-class letter in a large envelope or parcel. When a first-class letter is *attached*, the postage is affixed to each part separately. When a first-class letter is *enclosed*, its postage is added to the parcel postage on the outside of the package. You should write or stamp the words FIRST-CLASS MAIL ENCLOSED below the postage and above the address. A piece of mixed mail is not treated as first-class mail. The class of mail that the larger piece falls into determines how the mixed mail is handled.

SPECIAL POSTAL SERVICES

In addition to the regular delivery of first-, second-, third-, and fourth-class mail, special postal services also are available. You must pay a fee for each of these special services. As a worker who processes outgoing mail, you need to know the different services that are available so you can choose the one best suited to your mailing needs.

Express Mail

Express Mail offers the fastest delivery service. It guarantees delivery the next day, and sometimes even the same day. All Express Mail travels by regularly scheduled airline flights; therefore, only cities with airports are able to participate in the Express Mail service.

You may send any mailable item weighing up to 70 pounds by Express Mail. Express Mail rates are based on the weight of the item and the distance it must travel. The rates include insurance coverage, record of delivery, and a receipt. If the item is not delivered on time, the sender receives a refund.

Special Delivery and Special Handling

Special delivery mail is handled with the same promptness given to first-class mail. In addition, it is given immediate delivery within prescribed hours and distances. The fees charged are in addition to the regular postage and vary according to the weight of the letter or parcel. The mail must be marked SPECIAL DELIVERY and is available for all classes of mail.

Illus. 14-21. The United States Postal Service, as well as many private courier services, offer guaranteed delivery by a certain day or specific time.

For a fee in addition to regular third- or fourth-class postage, packages may receive a *special handling* service. Packages marked SPECIAL HANDLING travel with first-class mail between cities. At the post office, special handling packages are processed before regular third- and fourth-class mail, but after priority mail. They are delivered on regularly scheduled trips.

Registered Mail

Mail can be *registered* to give protection to valuable items such as money, checks, jewelry, stock certificates, and bonds, as well as important papers including contracts, bills of sale, leases, mortgages, deeds, wills, and other vital business records. All classes of mail may be registered, but the first-class rate must be paid.

Mail may be registered for any amount. The post office, however, will only pay claims up to $25,000, regardless of the amount for which the package was registered.

You will be given a receipt showing that the post office has accepted your registered mail for transmittal and delivery. For an additional fee, you may obtain a *return receipt* to prove that the mail was delivered.

Insured Mail

Third- or fourth-class mail may be insured for up to $500 against loss or damage. A receipt is issued to the sender of insured mail. You should keep the receipt on file until you know that the insured mail has arrived in satisfactory condition. If an insured parcel is lost or damaged, the post office will **reimburse** you for the value of the merchandise or the amount for which it was insured, whichever is smaller.

reimburse: pay back

Certificate of Mailing

An inexpensive way to obtain proof that an item was taken to the post office for mailing is to purchase a *Certificate of Mailing.* The certificate is *not* proof of delivery; it serves only as proof that the item was mailed.

Certified Mail

If any first-class mail (such as a letter, a bill, or an important notice) has no dollar value of its own, yet you want proof of mailing and delivery, send it by *certified mail.* Certified mail provides a receipt for the sender and a record of delivery. However, no insurance coverage is provided for certified mail.

COD Mail

As a seller of goods, a company may send an order to a buyer and collect payment for the item when it is delivered. Mail sent in this manner is referred to as COD—*collect on delivery.* The seller may obtain COD service by paying a fee in addition to the regular postage. Since fees and postage must be **prepaid** by the seller, the seller often specifies that the total COD charges to be collected from the buyer include the postage and the collect-on-delivery fee. The maximum amount collectible on one package is $500. If the company you work for did not order an item that arrives COD, do not accept the package.

prepaid: paid in advance

INTERNATIONAL MAIL

Many companies today send mail to cities in other countries. A company may have branch offices or customers in cities throughout the world. Postage for letters and postal cards mailed to Mexico is the same as that for letters and cards mailed within the United States. Rates for mail going to all other countries are

Illus. 14-22.
Certified mail receipt. To whom was the item sent? Where specifically was the item delivered?

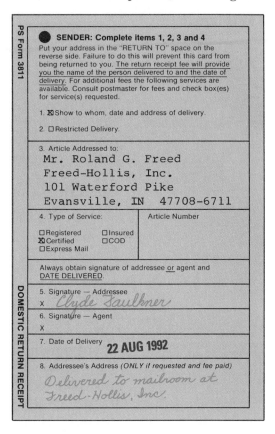

higher and the weights are limited. Contact your local post office for current rates and weight limitations. Overseas parcel post packages must be packed very carefully to ensure safe delivery. A customs declaration form that accurately and completely describes the contents must be attached to each parcel.

ARRANGING FOR COURIER/ DELIVERY SERVICE

Many companies use a private courier/delivery service rather than the USPS when a guaranteed delivery time is required. Most large cities have several companies that deliver both locally and nationwide. Check under *Delivery Service* in the Yellow Pages of the telephone directory for a listing of companies in your area. You will want to ask about services and fees in order to identify the courier that best meets your needs. When the messenger arrives, you will be asked to fill out a delivery form. If you use the courier often, the courier may provide you with forms that you can fill out before the messenger arrives.

INTEROFFICE MAIL

In a small company, processing interoffice mail may involve hand delivering a memo from one worker to another. In a large company, however, interoffice mail is collected from the departments, sorted in the mailroom, and redistributed to the appropriate department or individuals. Interoffice mail envelopes usually differ in color and size from envelopes used for mail going outside the company. That way, interoffice mail will not be sent to the post office accidently.

ELECTRONIC MAIL SERVICES

viable: workable

Telecommunications technology makes it possible to transmit text electronically from one location to another. As a result, you may work in an office where electronic mail services are used as a *viable* alternative to traditional mail services. In the following paragraphs, you will learn about several electronic mail services available through Western Union. Electronic mail will be discussed in detail in Chapter 15.

Telegrams and Mailgrams

A **telegram** is a message transmitted by Western Union over telephone lines. The two types of telegrams delivered within the United States are the *full-rate telegram* and the *overnight telegram.* Full-rate telegrams are delivered by phone within two hours or by messenger within five hours. Overnight telegrams, as the name implies, are sent during the night. Delivery is guaranteed by 2 p.m. the next day. Charges for messages are based on a minimum number of words, with an extra charge for each additional word.

A **mailgram** is a message transmitted by Western Union to the post office that serves the ZIP Code of the addressee. At the post office, the mailgram is printed, inserted in an envelope, and delivered with the regularly scheduled mail. Mailgrams are a speedy and economical way to send longer messages. Charges are based on groups of 50 words. A mailgram is less expensive than a telegram, and delivery is guaranteed by the next day.

Telex

Telex is a Western Union service used primarily to transmit messages to foreign countries via telephone lines, fiber optic cables, microwave dishes, and space satellites. A **teletypewriter**, which is a terminal with a printer, is used to send and receive Telex messages.

EasyLink

EasyLink, another Western Union service, is a worldwide business communication network. Both EasyLink and Telex are used largely for communicating overseas. However, EasyLink is fast replacing Telex because EasyLink offers more services and also allows different types of equipment to communicate with each other. Companies subscribing to EasyLink have access to Western Union services such as telegrams, mailgrams, Telex, and facsimile messages. Also available are more than 900 databases, including current news reports and airline schedules.

EasyLink makes it possible for subscribers to use word processors, personal computers, teletypewriters, and facsimile machines worldwide to exchange messages. If you work in a company that subscribes to EasyLink, you may use your computer to send product information to a client (also an EasyLink subscriber) who may receive the information with a teletypewriter. Or a branch office may use a facsimile machine to send a sales report to your computer.

QUESTIONS FOR REVIEW

1. How is a window envelope different from a standard envelope?

2. When would a volume mailing be used?

3. What is an optical character reader (OCR)?

4. What address format does the postal service recommend for use on outgoing envelopes?

5. Name the various classes of domestic mail.

6. What is priority mail? What is its weight restriction?

7. What is the difference between special delivery and special handling?

8. Under what circumstances would you use COD mail?

9. Why should interoffice mail be placed in envelopes distinctly different from those used to send mail by the postal service?

10. Describe two electronic mail services available through Western Union.

INTERACTING WITH OTHERS

You work in an office where the mail is picked up by postal workers twice a day, at 10:30 a.m. and 2:45 p.m. Monday afternoon you receive a call from the regional vice president in a branch office. He needs six copies of the company's annual report by Wednesday. If the reports are in the 2:45 p.m. mail today, they will be delivered on Wednesday. You gather the annual reports, place them in a large envelope, and take them to the mailroom. You explain to Gayle, a mailroom worker, that the envelope must go with the 2:45 p.m. pick-up. Gayle says she understands.

Later in the day, you call Gayle to verify that the annual reports were sent. Gayle sheepishly replies that she was on break at 2:45. When she returned, she noticed that the postal carrier had overlooked the copies. They were not mailed.

You are very annoyed. Should you tell Gayle how you feel? If so, what should you tell her? Should you report this incident to Gayle's supervisor? How can you and Gayle work together to solve this problem?

What You Are To Do: Prepare a response to the questions raised.

EXTENDING YOUR MATH COMPETENCIES

An envelope has been prepared for each address on a mailing list of 18,000 names. The mailing machine can feed, seal, meter stamp, count, and stack 200 envelopes a minute. Of the 18,000 envelopes being processed, 20 percent are being sent to Minnesota, 30 percent to Wyoming, 15 percent to Wisconsin, and 35 percent to Nebraska.

What You Are To Do: ● Calculate how long it will take to process all the envelopes using the mailing machine.
● Calculate how many envelopes will be sent to each state.

APPLICATION ACTIVITIES

Activity 1

You work in a small office. You have been given the following items to mail.

a. A package weighing 4 $^3/_4$ pounds to be sent parcel post to Ann Arbor, Michigan

b. A letter weighing 3 ounces to be sent by Express Mail (post office to addressee) to Camden, Maine

    c. A twelve-ounce package containing a printed report to be sent by first-class mail to Santa Barbara, California

    d. A two-ounce letter to be sent by first-class certified mail to Denver, Colorado

    e. A ten-ounce letter to be sent to a local bank

What You Are To Do: Figure the amount of postage needed to send each item listed. Use your town as the origin point in figuring the postage. Consult current USPS rate charts, or call your local post office and ask for assistance. On a plain sheet of paper, list item to be mailed and the correct postage.

Activity 2

You are responsible for inserting outgoing mail into envelopes before delivering them to the mailroom to be sealed and stamped. Today you have mail that must be inserted into No. 6 3/4 envelopes, No. 10 envelopes, and No. 10 window envelopes.

What You Are To Do:
- Fold a blank sheet of paper properly to fit into a No. 10 standard envelope.
- Fold a blank sheet of paper properly to fit into a No. 6 3/4 envelope.
- Fold a blank sheet of paper properly to fit into a No. 10 window envelope.

CHAPTER SUMMARY

In this chapter, you learned the procedures for processing both incoming and outgoing mail. You should be knowledgeable about the following key points:

1. The extent of your mail-related tasks will depend on the size of the company, the volume of mail handled, and the preference of your supervisor.
2. To expedite the processing of incoming mail, some companies use electric envelope openers, rotary units to help sort mail, and automated delivery systems.
3. Classes of domestic mail include: first-class, priority, second-class, third-class, and fourth-class (or parcel post). Special postal services are available such as express mail, registered mail, insured mail, and certified mail.

4. To expedite the processing of outgoing mail, some companies use electronic postage scales, postage meters, computer-generated mailing lists, and automated addressing/labeling/folding/inserting systems.

5. The USPS uses electronic equipment such as optical character readers and bar code sorters to speed mail to its destination. You can help speed the process by following USPS address format guidelines and by using nine-digit ZIP Codes.

6. Telecommunications technology makes it possible to electronically transmit messages from one location to another. Telegrams, mailgrams, Telex, and EasyLink are examples of electronic mail.

KEY CONCEPTS AND TERMS

interoffice mail	ZIP + 4
mailroom	telegram
postage meter	mailgram
volume mailing	Telex
computer-generated mailing list	teletypewriter
optical character reader (OCR)	EasyLink

INTEGRATED CHAPTER ACTIVITY

Word processing equipment can be used to complete this activity.

You work as an office assistant at Chaparral Cheese Company. Your supervisor approaches your workstation and says, "Here is a list of this month's new mail-order customers. When you key the names and addresses, please group them by state. Use alphabetic order to arrange the customers within each state. Use the all-caps, no punctuation format recommended by the USPS and the appropriate two-letter state abbreviations."

What You Are To Do: Key the customer list on page 626. Use the labels provided in *Information Processing Activities* or a sheet of plain paper. Refer to Reference Section E for a listing of standard two-letter state abbreviations and to page 614 for an example of the address format recommended by the USPS.

Mail-Order Customers

Mr. Jerry M. Osterman
1906 N. Market Street
Shreveport, Louisiana 71107-4568

Miss Linda A. Wood
301 Rue Dauphine
New Orleans, Louisiana 70112-4688

Mr. Richard ^{C.} Wiegand
12 Roderick (St.)
Morgan City, Louisiana 70380-1233

Mrs. Sherri E. Sempf
101 Pinckney Place
Howell, Michigan 48843-2638

Ms. Sandra B. Sholl^c
301 Centerville Road
Sturgis, Michigan 49091-8244

Mrs. Susan ^{A.} Curlovich
927 (Mt.) Royal Circle   Apt. 16-G
Apartment 16-G
Roanoke, Virginia 24014-7634

Dr. Ralph D. Narcissi
95 Staples Mills Road
Richmond, Virginia 23230-4433

Mr. Robert J. Caldwell
373 Pleasant Valley Road
Harrisonburg, Virginia
              22801-6624

Ms. Debe M. Behun
61 Jefferson Avenue
Newport News, Virginia
              23605-7124

Mr. Darryl M. Brandon
50 Sand Dunes Drive
Monterey, California
              93940-4524

Miss Karen S. Bentz
2563 La Paz Road
Laguna Beach, California
              92653-4179

Dr. Diane C. Arnold
111 Colorado (Ave.)
Santa Monica, California
              90401-3679

Miss Judi ^{W.} Nalitz
7911 St. Armonds Way
Sarasota, Florida
              33577-3912

Ms. Kiki L. Mashusa
555 Sailfish Drive
St. Augustine, Florida
              32084-1143

PRODUCTIVITY CORNER

Blake Williams
OFFICE SUPERVISOR

OVERWHELMED!

DEAR MR. WILLIAMS:

Last month I was hired as a mailroom worker by a growing company that had recently created a separate mail department. I want to be an efficient worker, yet I feel overwhelmed by all the postal regulations and services that are available. There is so much to learn so fast! How will I ever learn it all?—DENNIS FROM TUCSON

DEAR DENNIS:

I have good news. You do not have to learn it all! Even postal workers must look up answers to questions from time to time.

There are two postal publications that are excellent references: the *Post Office Directory* and the *ZIP Code Directory*. You might suggest to your supervisor that the company buy these publications. Those who work in a small company that does not have a mailroom can also benefit from having these publications on hand.

You and your coworkers can stay current on postal matters by subscribing to the "Postal Bulletin" (a weekly publication) or to the "Memo to Mailers" (a monthly publication). There is even a Postal Customer Council your company can join. You also might plan to attend USPS-sponsored seminars which cover such topics as ZIP + 4 and cost-saving ideas for bulk mail.

You can save your company money by being aware of the full range of postal services. The initiative you show on your job in the mailroom will surely be noticed and rewarded.

Take advantage of this opportunity to learn the names of all the workers in your company. Practice your organizational skills. Since your mail department is newly formed, there will be "glitches" in the system that must be worked out. Exercise your problem-solving abilities in dealing with such situations. Both you and the company will benefit. Good luck.—BLAKE WILLIAMS

CHAPTER 15

Using Telecommunication Systems

Communicating over distances is not new. Indians, for example, used smoke signals to communicate. This early form of long-distance communications had obvious limitations. Today's worldwide communication networks, however, use a variety of equipment (computers, FAX machines, photocopiers, printers, for example) to make possible rapid and reliable transmission of information.

At Music Mart (a national distributor of musical instruments), a telecommunications network makes it possible to ship 98 percent of all orders on the day received. A customer service worker is able to determine immediately if a musical instrument is available and from which regional distribution center it will be shipped. Within minutes, the order is processed and a packing list is printed at the distribution center. Soon the musical instrument is on its way to the customer. Without the network, it could take five days to process an order!

Telephones play a key role in modern telecommunications. As a result, the capabilities of telephone systems continue to be enhanced. State-of-the-art technology enables data, text, images, and voice to be transmitted across the country or around the world.

As an office worker, you will use telecommunications equipment and services. You will find it useful to have a general understanding of the equipment and procedures commonly used in offices today.

The objectives of this chapter are to:

- acquaint you with the equipment, technology, and procedures for common forms of telecommunications

- present techniques for responding effectively to incoming telephone calls

- present procedures for placing outgoing telephone calls

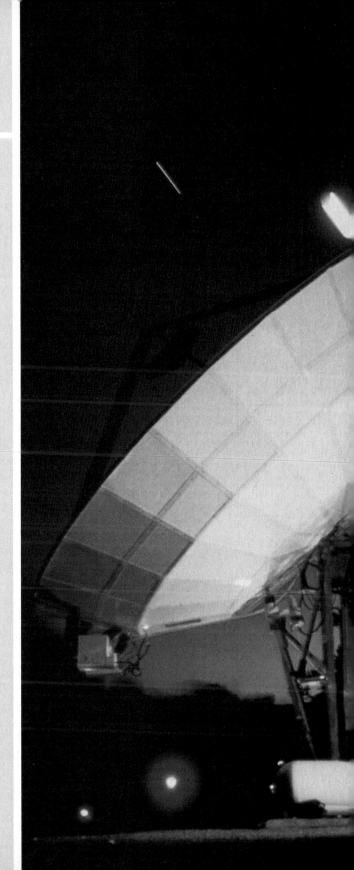

TOPIC 1

TELECOMMUNICATION TECHNOLOGY

When you have completed your study of this topic, you will be able to:

- identify methods of transmitting voice, data, text, and images

- explain common features of telephone and voice messaging systems

- describe electronic mail procedures

- follow common procedures for using FAX

Telecommunications is one of the fastest growing technologies in the office today. As a result, advancements in the telecommunications industry will continue to change the way millions of Americans work.

Information today can be transmitted more easily and quickly than ever before. Live television news broadcasts, originating from locations around the world, give millions of people instant information. In the same way, many companies have equipment that enables office workers to transmit documents and exchange information with coworkers across the corridor or with customers 10,000 miles away. The telecommunications a particular company chooses will be determined by its communications needs.

629

Telecommunications technology plays a vital role in the "Information Age" in which we live and work. Workers in offices rely on the ability to access and transmit up-to-date information quickly. **Telecommunications** is the electronic transfer of information over a distance. All forms of information (voice, data, text, and images, such as maps, graphs and pictures) can be sent electronically.

Today's information technologies are *integrated*, which means that machines that in the traditional office performed only one function now can be linked together to expand their capabilities and speed the flow of information. For example, office workers use computers to electronically transmit information to printers, photocopiers, facsimile machines, and other computers. As telecommunications technology continues to evolve, businesses will acquire new equipment and implement new procedures in order to improve their communications capabilities. As an office worker, you will want to learn about the many time-saving features of the equipment available for your use.

TRANSMITTING INFORMATION

Methods of sending information across the country or around the world include telephone lines, communication satellites, microwave towers, and radio signals. Telephone lines and communication satellites will be discussed here.

Telephone Lines

When an office worker places a telephone call, uses a facsimile machine, or transfers information from one computer to another, the information likely will travel as *digital* signals over telephone lines. Most companies are replacing *analog* lines with digital lines because digital signals can transmit larger quantities of information at faster speeds. What this means to you as an office worker is that your transmission (an electronic message, a five-page report, or a chart) is received quickly and reliably.

Some communication networks continue to use only analog signals. In such cases, a modem is needed. A **modem** is a device used to **convert** the digital output of a computer into analog signals that can be transmitted over a telephone line. A modem can be a separate device or it can be **housed** within the computer.

convert: change

housed: installed

Communication Satellites

Earth-orbiting satellites play an important part in worldwide communication systems. A *communication satellite* is a transmitter/receiver relay station positioned in space. A *satellite dish* is a transmitter/receiver relay station on the ground. Satellite dishes bounce voice, video, and data communications in the form of microwave signals to a satellite station in space and receive the microwaves bounced to earth from space satellite.

Kim must send a price list from her office in Miami to a branch office in London, England. Using the company FAX machine, she sends the price list to London in minutes via a worldwide satellite communication network.

Communication Networks

You may work in a company that uses networks to enhance its communications capabilities. Because communication networks link or interconnect many types of electronic office equipment, growth in the popularity of networks will continue to impact how workers complete office tasks. Two common types of networks, LANs and WANs, are discussed here.

Local Area Network

A **local area network** (LAN) is a communication network that links or interconnects electronic equipment within a limited area such as a single room or a single building or several rooms or *adjacent* buildings. With a LAN, several computer users share data files, software, and equipment such as a printer. LANs allow

adjacent: next to

Illus. 15-1. In this LAN, workers at these computers share one laser printer.

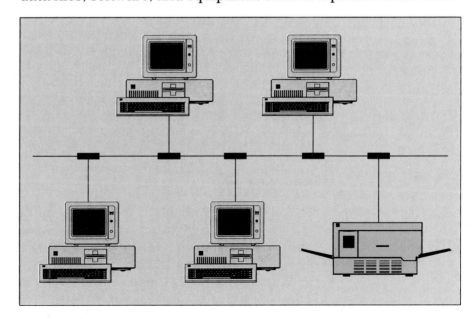

users to exchange information rapidly over specially installed, privately owned cables. Universities, hospitals, and corporate headquarters are typical users of local area networks. However, remember that an organization's communication needs—rather than its size—determine if a LAN is desirable.

If you work in an office with a local area network, you and other workers may share printers and other devices, software, or information stored in memory on any computer in the network. You likely will be provided with a network users' manual that details all procedures to be followed. Common procedures included in this kind of manual relate to logging on and off the network, exchanging files, and viewing network printer **queues**.

queues: items waiting to be printed

Wide Area Network

Local area networks can be expanded into long distance networks called wide area networks. A **wide area network** (WAN) is a communication network that links electronic equipment separated by long distances. WANs, which make use of microwave and satellite transmission methods, enable office workers to send information from one city to another or across continents! A WAN for a small company may cover several cities or states. WANs for a large multinational company may cover several countries. When Kim sent the revised list from Miami to London, England, she used her company's wide area network.

VOICE COMMUNI-CATION SYSTEMS

You know that telecommunications technology is used to transmit and receive voice communications. You also are familiar with the most frequently used voice communication device—the telephone. Businesses may choose from a wide variety of equipment and features to meet their specific needs. While some common systems and equipment will be discussed here, you must be prepared to become acquainted with new telephone equipment and features as they become available.

Key Systems

A telephone system found in many small- to medium-size companies is the key system. A **key system** is a small capacity, multi-line system that allows the user to select a line by pressing a key or pushbutton on the telephone console. A typical key system provides up to 120 extensions and two or more outside lines.

When there is an incoming call, one of the keys (pushbuttons) flashes to indicate which line is ringing. You depress the appropriate key to answer the call.

Key systems may be purchased from telephone vendors or leased from a local telephone company.

Private Branch Exchange Systems

Large businesses often purchase high-capacity, private telephone systems called **private branch exchanges** (PBXs). These systems can handle more than 25 outside lines and up to 10,000 internal extensions. The three main functions of a PBX system are to receive incoming calls from outside the firm, place outgoing calls, and handle all internal calls.

Some PBX systems require the assistance of a switchboard operator. Incoming calls are routed through a central switchboard, where an operator answers the calls and transfers them to the appropriate department or individual. Outgoing calls, however, can be placed directly without calling the operator.

Private automatic branch exchanges (PABXs) typically do not require operator assistance. Many of these systems feature *direct inward dialing* (DID). With DID, each telephone extension has its own seven-digit telephone number. This means that an outside caller can dial the person or department direct.

Illus. 15-2. Two telephone systems: (Left) a PABX system, (Right) a key system.

It is common practice for companies to replace older, operator-based PBX systems with computer-based systems called **computerized private branch exchanges** (CPBXs). Most new systems being installed today are computerized systems.

Centrex Systems

Companies may choose to lease the services and equipment from a local telephone company. In this case, a **centrex system** provides telephone service through the facilities located at the telephone company's central office. The company pays the telephone company a monthly service fee for using the equipment and providing service.

Common Telephone Features

customize: adapt to
your specific needs

Many of the same features are available on key, PBX/PABX, and centrex telephone systems. Illus. 15-3 describes common telephone features designed to increase your efficiency in handling telephone communication. These and other features may be available so that you will be able to **customize** your telephone, depending on your duties and responsibilities. The needs of the company and the size of the system needed will determine the features available.

activate: turn on

deactivate: turn off

You likely will be provided with a users' manual that details procedures to be followed to use your telephone keypad to **activate** and **deactivate** all features available. To activate *call forwarding*, for example, you may be instructed to lift the handset, push the * and 4 keys, listen for a tone, dial the extension number to which you want all incoming calls routed, and hang up. Your incoming calls will be forwarded and will ring automatically at that extension.

Cellular Telephones/Pagers

Many businesspersons today use *cellular phones* and *pagers* to keep in touch with their offices or customers. Cellular phones may be classified as mobile, transportable, or portable. Mobile phones are used primarily in automobiles. Transportable phones are designed to be carried in a briefcase. Portable telephones are small, hand-held units which may fit in a shirt pocket (see Illus. 15-4 on page 636). Cellular phones may have familiar telephone

COMMON FEATURES OF TELEPHONE SYSTEMS	
Auto redial	Redials automatically the last number dialed by pressing one key.
Call block	Restricts callers from making telephone toll calls or calls for which an extra charge is made.
Call forwarding	Forwards calls automatically to another telephone extension.
Caller ID	Records or displays the telephone number of the caller.
Call queuing/ Camp on	Reestablishes the connection after a busy signal when both parties are free. The caller does not have to remain on the phone while waiting.
Call return	Redials the number of the last call received for up to half an hour.
Call waiting	Signals (often a beep) an incoming call is waiting while a call is in progress. The first call can be placed on hold while the second call is being answered.
Conferencing	Lets you set up conversations with three or more people at the same time.
Memory	Lets you store and dial numbers at the touch of one button.
Speakerphone	Lets you speak with your hands free.

Illus. 15-3. Telephone systems offer many efficient features.

Illus. 15-4. A mobile cellular phone allows this executive to contact her office while traveling.

features, such as call forwarding, call waiting, and automatic redial.

expedited: moved forward

You may work in an office where your tasks are **expedited** by the use of cellular telephones. Radio frequencies are used to transmit the voice across geographic segments called *cells*. When you dial a mobile telephone number to reach a supervisor or a manager, the radio signal "switches" from cell to cell until the right number is reached.

Pagers use radio signals to transmit short, one-way messages to individuals who work in areas where telephone contact is limited. If you work in an organization where pagers are used to keep in contact with supervisors or managers, you will use your telephone to dial the pager number. The message (received by voice, digital readout, or beeper signals) will prompt the recipient to respond to the "page" by finding the nearest telephone to call the number on the readout or to call the office.

Voice Mail Systems

Voice mail is a messaging system that uses computers and telephones to record, send, store, and retrieve voice messages. Voice messaging systems are growing in popularity because they eliminate the time lost in playing "telephone tag" or trying to place calls to individuals in different time zones.

Each user of a voice messaging system has a voice mailbox. A *voice mailbox* is on-line computer storage space designated to hold voice messages. Messages are delivered electronically to the person's mailbox, where they remain stored until the recipient chooses to access them. The sender and the receiver use special features on pushbutton telephones to activate and use voice mail. You can see how Lila uses voice mail to communicate needed information efficiently:

> *Taledine Corporation recently installed a voice messaging system in all its regional offices. Lila works in the Los Angeles office. It is 5 p.m. and she must relay important sales information to Ed Dugan in the Boston office. Because of the difference in time zones, she knows Ed has already gone home. But thanks to voice mail, she still can place her call. When Ed's telephone is automatically answered by the voice mail system, Lila hears the following message: "Hello, this is Ed Dugan. I am not available to take calls right now; but, if you will leave your name, telephone number, and a short message, I will return your call." Lila then uses the buttons on her telephone to send and store her message in Ed's voice mailbox.*
>
> *When Ed arrives at work the next morning (three hours before the Los Angeles office opens), he uses the pushbuttons on his telephone to access Lila's message. Then he uses voice mail to send Lila a message thanking her for her help. Ed's message is waiting for Lila that same morning when she arrives at work.*

Unless a message is deleted, it remains in storage and can be accessed later for reference. Some systems have a message tracking capability that lets the sender know when the message was received. Because of the ability to store and forward messages, voice mail is sometimes called a *store and forward voice messaging system.*

DATA/TEXT COMMUNI-CATION SYSTEMS

You have learned how telecommunications technology is used for voice transmission. Similar technology also can be used to transmit data and text from a computer in one location to a computer in another location. The difference is the method of transmission. With voice communication, you use the telephone. With data and text transmission, you use a computer keyboard.

In Chapter 14, you learned that Telex and EasyLink are forms of electronic text communication. Electronic mail is discussed in detail here.

ELECTRONIC
MAIL
SYSTEMS

Electronic mail, or E-mail, is the electronic transfer of information. E-mail is similar to receiving and sending traditional mail in that it is addressed, received, opened, read, and—if necessary—answered and filed. The major advantage of electronic mail systems over traditional mail systems is that information (in the form of messages, data, and documents) can be sent and received almost **instantaneously** on the computer screen. The use of local area networks and wide area networks enables electronic messages to be sent easily to persons in the same office as well as those in different countries.

instantaneously:
immediately

Each user of an electronic mail system is assigned an electronic mailbox. An *electronic mailbox* is on-line computer storage space designated to hold electronic messages. Because messages are stored until accessed by the owner of the mailbox, messages may be sent to individuals even though they are not at their workstations. You can see how easily Mark uses his company's electronic mail system to respond to an urgent request from a coworker.

Mark works in a Records Center. When he sits down to begin work at his computer, he sees the MAIL WAITING message on his screen. This tells him that he has mail in his electronic mailbox. After he keys in the command to RECEIVE MESSAGES, a list of his messages in priority order appears on the screen. He sees that he has an urgent message from a coworker. Mark selects the READ MAIL option and reads the urgent message requesting a copy of a report he distributed yesterday. He immediately chooses the SEND MAIL option and keys the commands to access his coworker's mailbox to send the report.

Options

Electronic mail systems offer many options. For example, a message may be printed or filed for future reference. More urgent messages can be labeled as "urgent" and **prioritized** accordingly. Many systems include a directory option. This feature enables the user to locate the appropriate mailbox designation for any other user on the network. With some systems, confidential messages may be protected with passwords. One of the most time-saving features of an electronic mail system involves a distribution list. This means that a message can be keyed once and sent automatically to everyone on the distribution list.

prioritized: ranked
in order of importance

Illus. 15-5. An electronic mail system enables you to use a computer to send and receive messages.

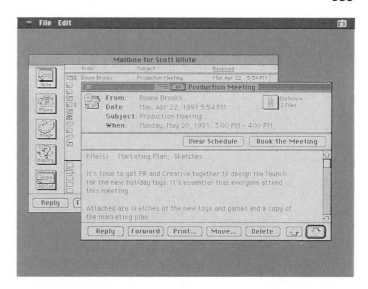

Procedures

If you work in an office with an electronic mail system, you likely will be provided with a users' manual that details all procedures to be followed. Common procedures involve entering and leaving the electronic mail system, opening and reading mail, sending mail, and safeguarding system security.

You will find the following suggestions helpful when sending and receiving electronic mail:

- Check regularly for E-mail messages.
- Plan your message ahead of time.
- Before sending the message, check the E-mail address of the recipient to be sure it is correct.
- Use the electronic mail system for company business only.
- Create single-subject messages; use words that are clear and concise.
- Observe proper etiquette; do not use profanity.
- Save only those messages that you need.
- Honor the rights of privacy; do not use another person's password.

IMAGE
COMMUNI-
CATION
SYSTEMS

Telecommunications technology also is used to transmit and receive images in the form of data, text, photographs, diagrams, blueprints, drawings, and statistical information. Two common applications of image communication systems, facsimile and videoconferencing, are discussed here.

Facsimile

Facsimile (FAX) transfers images (data, text, pictures, drawings, photographs) electronically using telephone lines. FAX technology has been accepted so rapidly that FAX machines in offices are as commonplace as photocopiers. Self-service *FaxMail* terminals are found in many post offices.

FAX machines are an easy-to-use, quick way to transmit and receive information. As long as the sending and receiving machines are **compatible**, facsimiles can communicate with each other. Businesses with branch locations find this form of communication convenient and inexpensive.

compatible: capable of working together

FAX technology combines scanning technology and telephone technology. The sending facsimile machine scans a page and encodes (electronically "takes a picture of") the information to be sent. The information is transmitted over telephone lines to a receiving facsimile machine. In seconds, the page (including text, drawings, logos, and signatures) is reproduced as an exact copy or "facsimile."

> *Luisa works for an engineering design firm in Miami that has branch offices in Atlanta, Houston, and Louisville. This morning she receives a typical assignment. An engineer needs to send a copy of several design changes to a supervisor in Houston as soon as possible. The engineer also has a handwritten note that is to accompany the design changes. Using the FAX machine, Luisa is able to send both the design changes and the handwritten note to the supervisor in Houston within minutes.*

A company, depending on its needs, may have one or more FAX machines. In addition to the desktop FAX machine, portable FAX machines may be used by business people to transmit and receive documents while they are away from the office. This size FAX can be carried in a briefcase as shown in Illus. 15-6.

Features

Facsimile machines offer many features, such as laser or full-color printing, store-and-forward capability, automatic dialing

Illus. 15-6. A portable facsimile machine (left) and a desktop facsimile machine (right) are pictured here.

and answering; auto feed; activity-reporting of date, time, and number of pages received; and indicator lights that tell when the message has been received. The automatic answering feature makes some FAX systems almost completely self-operating.

Procedures

Procedures for using facsimile machines will vary from office to office and from machine to machine. If you work in an office where you will use an auto-feed FAX to transmit information, here are some common procedures you may follow:

1. Prepare a facsimile transmission cover sheet showing the current date and time, the total pages that are being sent, the name and company of the recipient of the message, and the FAX number. (See Illus. 15-7 on page 642.) If the message is confidential, indicate this on the transmission cover sheet, also.
2. Count the number of pages to double check the accuracy on the transmission cover sheet.
3. Place the pages to be transmitted in the carrier.
4. Dial the FAX number where the material is being sent. (Some FAX machines digitally display the number dialed.)
5. When connected (designated usually by a tone), press the SEND or START button.
6. After the last page has been transmitted, a series of beeps will designate the end of the transmission.

7. Enter the name and department of the sender and the time of transmission in the FAX log, if necessary.

8. If a report form is printed after each transmission, attach it to the FAX cover sheet and return it and the original materials to the sender. In Illus. 15-7, the transmission report includes the date, start time of the message, the FAX number, total number of pages sent, and the time it took to transmit the pages. The report notes that the results were "OK"— the transmission was received.

Illus. 15-7. The FAX transmission cover sheet (top) and the transmission report (bottom) provide important information regarding the pages transmitted.

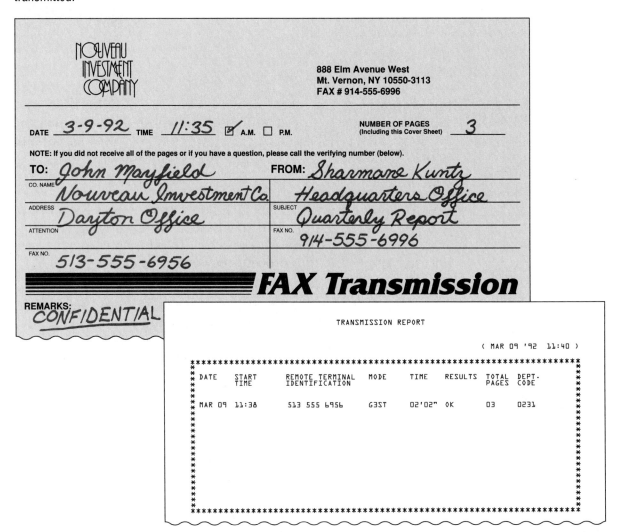

NOUVEAU INVESTMENT COMPANY

888 Elm Avenue West
Mt. Vernon, NY 10550-3113
FAX # 914-555-6996

DATE _3-9-92_ TIME _11:35_ ☑ A.M. ☐ P.M.   NUMBER OF PAGES (Including this Cover Sheet) _3_

NOTE: If you did not receive all of the pages or if you have a question, please call the verifying number (below).

TO: _John Mayfield_   FROM: _Sharmane Kuntz_
CO. NAME _Nouveau Investment Co._   _Headquarters Office_
ADDRESS _Dayton Office_   SUBJECT _Quarterly Report_
ATTENTION   FAX NO. _914-555-6996_

FAX NO. _513-555-6956_

FAX Transmission

REMARKS: _CONFIDENTIAL_

TRANSMISSION REPORT

(MAR 09 '92 11:40)

DATE	START TIME	REMOTE TERMINAL IDENTIFICATION	MODE	TIME	RESULTS	TOTAL PAGES	DEPT. CODE
MAR 09	11:38	513 555 6956	G3ST	02'02"	OK	03	0231

If your responsibilities include maintaining the FAX machine, you may be asked to do any or all of the following:

- Complete the log of messages transmitted and received.
- Keep the machine supplied with paper.
- Make copies of FAX messages received, since the print will fade over a period of time.
- Deliver FAX messages received.
- Keep an adequate supply of paper on hand (at least 2 rolls).
- Report the need for maintenance or repairs of equipment.

Videoconferencing

Videoconferencing is an image communication system that allows people at two or more locations to have two-way voice and video communication using a wide area network. A special conference room equipped with television cameras, TV screens, and microphones is used to conduct meetings in which data, text, voice, and pictures may be exchanged. For example, managers in Baltimore could "meet" with top management in St. Louis and be able to see and hear each other and exchange information using a FAX machine. This type of conferencing is very expensive to use. Procedures for videoconferencing, also known as teleconferencing, were discussed in Chapter 11.

Illus. 15-8.
Videoconferencing enables persons in different locations to "meet" and exchange information.

INTEGRATED COMMUNI-CATION SYSTEMS

interface:
connection

The digital revolution now taking place in the telecommunications industry has as its goal the complete integration of previously separate technologies through a standardized, integrated all-digital network. **Integrated Services Digital Network** (ISDN) is not an actual network, but a set of *interface* standards. These standards will be common to the design and operation of all communication equipment. The end result will be the ability of any type of computer or electronic device to communicate with any other device. It then will be possible to talk with someone on the telephone and send data to that person at the same time over one ISDN telephone line.

Business continues to upgrade its telecommunications technology. As technological innovations become available, additional benefits will be realized. As an office worker, you will want to be alert to developments in telecommunications that will make your job easier and improve your efficiency.

QUESTIONS FOR REVIEW

1. Describe three methods used to transmit voice, data, text, or images over distances.

2. Why are modems needed to send data from one computer to another via telephone lines?

3. How are companies using local area networks to enhance their communications capabilities?

4. Describe a key telephone system, a PBX telephone system, and a centrex telephone system.

5. How is voice mail different from simply speaking on the telephone?

6. How is electronic mail different from voice mail? How is electronic mail similar to voice mail?

7. How is electronic mail similar to traditional mail? How is it different?

8. Explain how facsimile is used to transmit information.

9. List four responsibilities in maintaining a FAX machine.

10. What is the purpose of an Integrated Services Digital Network?

MAKING DECISIONS

The legal office where you work has a telephone system with four telephone lines. As the receptionist, you know who receives telephone calls. Brian, a coworker, receives calls from his friends frequently throughout the day. Sometimes his conversations last 15 or 20 minutes.

This morning Ms. DuBois, one of the lawyers, tries to place an outgoing call. No line is available. She asks you if all the lines are busy or if there is a problem with the phones. You tell her that all the lines are busy. You know that Brian has been on the phone for 10 minutes. His personal call is making it impossible for Ms. DuBois to place her business call. There have been other times when Brian's personal calls have tied up the lines. Should you talk to Brian about this problem? Should you go directly to your supervisor, or should you simply keep silent about it?

What You Are To Do: Prepare a response to the questions raised.

EXTENDING YOUR ENGLISH COMPETENCIES

As office worker, your knowledge of punctuation rules will be an asset. Ten sentences follow that will test your ability to use proper punctuation marks. Use Reference Section B: Punctuation to help you complete this exercise.

What You Are To Do: Write each sentence, inserting the proper punctuation.

1. She sent a report from Cheyenne Wyoming to Tuscon Arizona on the FAX machine
2. Both accounts were credited with two months interest
3. Melvin said that its your turn next
4. On Monday July 8 1991 we began using our new computerized telephone system
5. Has a limit been set asked Maria
6. To qualify you must have five years experience
7. Whoever goes goes at his or her own expense
8. It was a pleasure to show you our new voice mail system we look forward to showing it again in the near future
9. We prefer hard disks not floppy disks
10. Do you use single sided or double sided disks

APPLICATION ACTIVITY

You work as an office assistant at the headquarters office of Hughes Development Corporation, 800 Martin Luther King Blvd., Austin, TX 78765-0800. The FAX number is 512-555-4028. Marjorie Franklin (your supervisor) hands you an 8-page draft to fax to Edwin Stoddard, Manager, Hughes Development Corporation in Denver, CO. The FAX number is 303-555-3199. She also asks you to compose a short memo to send as part of the transmission. "Tell him you are sending the latest draft of my proposal to institute a company-wide telecommunications network. Ask him to write any comments on the proposal and return it to me within five days."

Word processing equipment may be used to complete this activity.

What You Are To Do: A. Compose the memo (to Edwin Stoddard from you). Follow the simplified memo format shown on page 234. Use the letterhead provided in *Information Processing Activities* or a sheet of plain paper.

B. Complete a FAX transmission sheet to send the memo and proposal (refer to page 642, if necessary). Use the form provided in *Information Processing Activities* or a sheet of plain paper.

INCOMING TELEPHONE COMMUNICATIONS

When you have completed your study of this topic, you will be able to:

- create a favorable first impression over the telephone

- apply telephone techniques and procedures that will enable you to handle incoming calls courteously and efficiently

As you might expect, the telephone is the most universal form of voice communication. Think of the many calls received each day by employees at various levels of the company. Executives receive calls from other executives wishing to discuss common concerns. Customers call to place orders or request information. Office assistants receive calls from persons wishing to set up or cancel appointments or leave messages. Because the telephone is such an important communication tool, all office workers should be able to use proper telephone techniques to answer incoming calls courteously and efficiently.

From the telephone calls you place to various businesses, you realize that your first impression of an organization is often based on how you are treated by the person answering the phone. If the person is pleasant, courteous, and interested in helping you, you probably form a good impression of the company. If the person is abrupt or rude and unwilling to help, you probably form a negative impression.

Many companies have a receptionist or a switchboard operator whose main responsibility is to answer all incoming calls. This person identifies the company and then routes the call to the appropriate department or individual. In large organizations, each department may have its own receptionist.

Other office workers also may be expected to answer incoming calls. For example, a primary responsibility of customer service personnel is to respond to incoming calls. Secretaries or administrative assistants usually answer incoming calls for executives and take messages when the executives are not available. When answering the phone, you will want to give callers a positive impression of your company not only by what you say, but by how you say it.

Advancements in telephone technology continues to change how incoming telephone calls are handled. Many companies use answering machines, voice messaging systems, as well as switchboard operators, to process incoming telephone calls. The new technology, however, does not replace the need for good manners, courtesy, and efficiency when handling telephone calls. Regardless of whether you are recording a message on an answering machine or a voice messaging system or answering the telephone in person, it is important to remember that the caller will form an impression of you, your department, and your organization. The message and the impression you leave should be positive and professional.

In this topic, you will learn about incoming telephone communications and how to use proper telephone techniques and procedures to handle incoming calls courteously and effectively.

MAKING A GOOD FIRST IMPRESSION

It is important to greet and respond to callers properly. Your voice, your speech patterns, your vocabulary, and your attitude all contribute to the first impression you make on callers.

Your Voice

When you communicate with visitors in person, you help them feel welcome by smiling—or perhaps by shaking hands. You show interest and alertness by maintaining eye contact with them during the conversation. When you communicate by telephone, you must use your voice to convey the interest, alertness, and courtesy normally exhibited in face-to-face conversations.

Visualize the Caller

visualize: see in your mind

To help you respond to callers on the phone as effectively as you would in person, try to **visualize** the caller. You may not know exactly what the other person looks like, but you can form a mental picture from the caller's voice. The caller is already forming an impression of you (and the company you represent) based on *your* voice.

Illus. 15-9. When you answer the telephone, you want to make a positive, professional impression.

Communicate Positively

animated: full of life

monotonous: one tone

How do you communicate positively with your voice? The easiest way is to speak with enthusiasm. An ***animated*** voice reflects interest in the caller. A ***monotonous*** voice suggests indifference and inattention.

Your Speech Patterns

project: send out

Your speech patterns affect the impression you ***project*** to callers. While you may have a pleasant tone of voice, communication is difficult if the caller cannot understand your words. Follow these suggestions for good telephone speech:

Pronounce Each Word Distinctly

Try not to mumble or run words together. For example, say "what do you" instead of "whaddaya."

Speak at a Proper Speed

You have probably called a company where the receptionist said the company name so quickly that you wondered whether or not you had reached the correct number! Speak slowly enough so that the caller can understand what you are saying. This is especially true if you are giving detailed or technical information.

Your Vocabulary

State your ideas in simple terms and use standard English to express yourself. Choose words that are tactful and positive. When you do not understand a caller, do not respond with "Huh?" or "What?" Instead, ask the caller, "Would you please repeat your last statement?"

Your Attitude

You learned in Chapter 4 that a positive attitude is a key to success. Your success in being able to handle incoming calls courteously will depend on your ability to maintain a positive attitude. If one of your main responsibilities is to answer the telephone, do not regard the phone as an interruption. Instead, view it as an opportunity to be helpful, thereby giving callers a favorable impression.

PROPER TELEPHONE TECHNIQUES

You know that your voice, your speech patterns, your vocabulary, and your attitude all affect a caller's impression of you and your company. To strengthen that positive impression still further, you should use the telephone techniques described in the following paragraphs.

Answer Promptly

Answer all incoming calls promptly and pleasantly. If possible, answer the telephone after the first ring. At the same time you reach for the receiver, reach for your pen or pencil and a notepad or message form. You must be ready to take messages immediately.

Identify Yourself

A telephone conversation cannot begin until the caller knows that the correct number has been reached. Immediately identify your company, department or office, and yourself:

Not Proper: *"Hello," or "Yes?" (These greetings do not give any identification.)*

Proper: *"Global Electronics, Linda Perkins." (Use this greeting when you are answering an outside call.)*

Proper: *"Advertising Department, Dewey DiMarco." (Use this greeting when you are answering an inside or outside call in a company where all calls are routed through a switchboard operator or a receptionist who has already identified the company.)*

Proper: *"Mrs. Yamaguchi's office, Lisa Stein." (Use this greeting when you are answering the phone for a supervisor.)*

Illus. 15-10. Always be prepared to take a message when you answer the telephone.

Assist the Caller

Your job is to help the caller as efficiently as you can. Be careful not to *assume* you know what the caller wants. Instead, listen **attentively** to the caller's questions and comments. If you believe it will take more than a minute or two to find the information the caller needs, do not keep the caller waiting. Ask if you may call back when you locate the information. It is important that you **conscientiously** follow through on any promise you make to return a telephone call.

Make sure that you give accurate information to callers. If you do not know the answer to a question, admit that you do not know. Then either transfer the call to someone who can answer the question or tell the caller that you will obtain the information and call back.

attentively: considerately; courteously

conscientiously: with a sense of duty

Illus. 15-11. This office worker is assisting the caller by providing accurate information in response to the questions asked.

Conclude the Call

As a general rule, the person who places a call is the one who should end it and hang up first. By following this rule, you avoid making the caller feel as if the conversation were "cut off" before he or she was ready to hang up.

It is also a good habit to use the caller's name as you end the conversation. For example: "Yes, Mrs. O'Sullivan, I'll be sure to put the catalog in the mail today," or, "Thank you for calling, Mr. Salzen. I'll be sure to give Ms. Driscoll the information." Such a practice personalizes the conversation.

EFFECTIVE TELEPHONE PROCEDURES

As you answer incoming calls, you may find it necessary to screen calls, give information, take messages, transfer calls, place callers on hold, or handle a disconnected call. Effective procedures for managing each of these situations are presented here.

Screening Calls

In some offices, you may be asked to *screen* the incoming calls. **Screening** is a procedure used to determine who is calling and, at times, the purpose of the call. Screening can save you and the caller time because you will be able to transfer the call immediately to the proper person. You can learn the caller's name by asking questions such as *"May I say who is calling?"* or *"May I tell Ms. Grayson who is calling?"*

Sometimes callers refuse to give their names. If it is the policy of your company to identify each caller by name before transferring the call, you must be courteous, yet firm:

> *Office Worker:* *"Hartford, Grayson, and Thatcher—Mary Timms speaking."*
>
> *Caller:* *"I want to speak to Ann Grayson."*
>
> *Office Worker:* *"May I say who is calling?"*
>
> *Caller:* *"My name is **irrelevant**. Just let me talk with Ann."*
>
> *Office Worker:* *"I'm very sorry, sir, but I am unable to transfer a call without first identifying the caller."*
>
> *Caller:* *"I understand. I'm Jess Evans, Ann's uncle."*

irrelevant: unimportant

Giving Information

There may be times when executives are out of the office for several days. In these situations, you must tactfully communicate to the caller that the executive is not available:

> *Caller:* *"May I please speak with Mr. Lesinski? This is Henry Robbins from Central Realty."*
>
> *Office Worker:* *"I'm sorry, Mr. Robbins, but Mr. Lesinski is out of the office until Friday. I'm Mr. Lesinski's secretary. Perhaps I could help you, or may I ask him to call you when he returns?"*

When executives are unavailable to receive calls, give the caller enough information to explain the executive's absence without **divulging** unnecessary details.

divulging: revealing

> *Not Proper:* *"Mrs. Fox is at a prospective customer's office."*
>
> *Proper:* *"Mrs. Fox is out of the office until tomorrow morning. May I take a message or ask her to call you then?"*

Taking Messages Using Printed Forms

You probably will have a pad or printed message forms for recording telephone messages. When you record a message, be sure that it is accurate and complete. Verify names and telephone numbers with the caller. Write the message in legible handwriting so you do not waste time rewriting it later. Each message should include the following:

- the date and exact time of the call
- the name of the caller and the caller's company (Check the spellings of any names about which you are uncertain.)
- the telephone number, including the area code if it is a long distance call (Repeat the number to verify it with the caller.)
- the details of the message
- the initials of the person who wrote the message

Illus. 15-12. Printed forms are used in many offices for taking telephone messages. It is important that telephone messages be recorded legibly and accurately.

```
To   Mr. Landry
Date  8/21        Time  1:30 p.m.
          WHILE YOU WERE OUT
M  r. Kinsel
of  Maintenance Dept.
Phone                              2581
     Area Code      Number        Extension

TELEPHONED        ✓  | PLEASE CALL          ✓
CALLED TO SEE YOU    | WILL CALL AGAIN
WANTS TO SEE YOU     | URGENT
          RETURNED YOUR CALL

Message  Wants to discuss
      the safety report
      for August.


          By  D.R.
```

Taking Messages Using a Computer

You may work in an office where software makes it possible to use an on-screen message form rather than a preprinted message form to record telephone messages. A typical message screen is shown in Illus. 15-13. Using a computer message screen offers these advantages:

- Less time is needed to key a message than to write it.
- The number of lost messages is reduced since messages can be transferred immediately to the intended receiver.
- Printed message forms are not needed.

Illus. 15-13. The receptionist, MJJ, has taken this message for Mirella Ewing.

```
FROM:   MJJ
                              DATE:   09-13
   TO:   MIRELLA EWING      TIME:   10:30
   CC:
   SUBJECT:   CALL FROM DON BAKER
   PRIORITY:   URGENT
   ATTACHMENTS:
   --------------------------------------
   NEEDS SALES FIGURES FOR AUGUST THAT
   WERE DISCUSSED AT LAST STAFF MEETING.
   CALL HIM AT 555-7226.
```

Each computer message you key should include the same basic information as a handwritten message. As you key the message, make sure that it is accurate and complete. Verify names and telephone numbers of the caller. You do not need to key the current date and time since they are entered automatically into the on-screen message form. Include your name or initials if you take the message. You will transfer the computer message to the receiver's computer screen by keying in the correct extension number. A reminder will appear on the receiver's screen showing that a message is waiting.

Transferring Calls

Calls are usually transferred when the caller has reached a wrong extension, when the caller wishes to speak with someone else, or when the caller's request can be answered more effectively by another person or office. Always tell the caller why the transfer is necessary. For example, you may say:

"I'm going to transfer your call to Mr. Rooke. He will be able to provide you with the information you need."

Placing a Caller on Hold

There will be times when you must place a caller on *hold*. If another incoming call comes through while you are on the phone and there is no one else available to answer the second call, you may need to place the first caller on hold while you answer the other line. Ask the first caller if you may place her or him on hold. Then answer the second call. Ask permission to place the second caller on hold while you complete your conversation with the first caller.

Sometimes you will need to place a caller on hold while you look up information in order to answer a question. Politely inform the caller that you are putting him or her on hold. If you believe it will take you several minutes to find the answer, ask the caller if you should call back or if the caller would prefer to hold. If the caller chooses to hold, check back frequently to reassure the caller that you have not forgotten him or her.

Handling a Disconnected Call

Occasionally you will be disconnected while you are talking on the telephone. The general rule is that the person who placed the call should call back immediately after the disconnection. That person has the telephone number of the party being called and should therefore be able to redial the call quickly.

The caller should report a disconnected long-distance call to the telephone company. An adjustment will then be made in the long-distance charge.

PERSONAL TELEPHONE CALLS

You must understand your company's policy regarding personal telephone calls. Some companies permit a limited number of personal calls; others discourage such calls or ask that a pay phone located on the premises be used. Generally, brief, urgent, or emergency calls are permitted.

TELEPHONE ANSWERING EQUIPMENT AND SERVICES

Many companies use answering machines or an answering service to handle incoming calls after business hours or when the business phones are unattended. Rather than let incoming calls go unanswered after business hours or when phones are unattended, it is to a company's advantage to ask callers to leave a message on an answering machine. Some answering machines ask the caller to leave a message, while others only provide information. A prerecorded message might say:

"Thank you for calling Newsom Insurance. I'm sorry, but the office is closed now. Our business hours are from 8:30 a.m. to 5:00 p.m., and we are eager to serve you. Please leave your name and phone number when you hear the tone. Your call will be returned promptly at the beginning of the next business day."

-or-

"Thank you for calling Stern's Department Store. The office is closed now. Our business hours are from 9:00 a.m. to 6:00 p.m. Please call again during business hours."

Your responsibilities may include playing back messages received on answering machines. On some machines, a blinking light on the answering machine indicates messages have been received. To access the messages, you will press the PLAYBACK button.

Some companies subscribe to a telephone answering service. An answering service is more effective than an answering machine, but it is far more expensive. Calls are forwarded from the business to the answering service, where operators answer the calls and take messages. You may call the service to collect messages or access messages sent from the answering service to a special computer screen at your business.

Whether you are taking messages from an answering machine or answering service, you should record them in the same way you record messages when a caller reaches you directly.

QUESTIONS FOR REVIEW

1. Describe four factors that influence the first impression you make when you respond to a telephone call.

2. How can you communicate positively with your voice?

3. What must a caller know before the conversation can begin?

4. Why should you use the caller's name as you end the conversation?

5. How can screening calls save time for you and the caller?

6. What questions might you ask to learn a caller's name?

7. What information should you include when you take a telephone message?

8. Describe two situations in which you might place a caller on hold.

9. When a call has been disconnected, who is responsible for calling back? Why?

10. What are two alternatives a company might use to handle incoming calls after business hours or when company phones are unattended?

MAKING DECISIONS

Two weeks ago, you began working as a receptionist for an architectural firm. You were told that Minerva, the marketing secretary, would sit at the reception desk and answer the telephone during your breaks and lunch hour. Minerva is scheduled to go to lunch from 11:30 a.m. to 12:30 p.m. Your lunch period is from 12:30 p.m. until 1:30 p.m. You both get two 15-minute breaks each day.

At first, the arrangement seemed to work well. Monday, Tuesday, and Wednesday of this week, however, Minerva went to lunch at 11:30 a.m. but did not return until almost 1:00 p.m. Yesterday, Minerva did return on time, and you were able to go to lunch at 12:30 p.m. as scheduled. But when you returned from lunch at 1:30 p.m., there was no one at the reception desk— Minerva had already gone on a break!

You believe Minerva is being totally uncooperative. Yet you hesitate to complain since you are new to the firm. Should you ask someone else to cover the phone for you? Should you talk with Minerva about being more responsible? Should you talk with your supervisor?

What You Are To Do: Prepare a response to the questions raised. Make any suggestions you believe would be helpful in working out a solution to this problem.

EXTENDING YOUR ENGLISH COMPETENCIES

Receptionists spend much of their time talking with individuals, both by telephone and in person. As company representatives, they try to present a positive image to everyone they meet. The language they use in their conversations with others can go far in projecting a positive image. Following are some statements made by a number of different receptionists. These statements contain grammatical errors that limit the receptionist's ability to make a good impression on the listener.

Word processing
equipment can be used
to complete this activity.

What You Are To Do: Key a copy of the receptionists' statements, correcting all grammatical errors.

Receptionist A: "Whom shall I say is calling?"

Receptionist B: "Mr. Crouch has went with Mr. Posey to a downtown meeting."

Receptionist C: "No one in Human Resources are in."

Receptionist D: "Copies of the report was sent to them who was at the staff meeting."

Receptionist E: "Between you and I, them reports will be printed in time."

Receptionist F: "I weren't told about the FAX machine."

Receptionist G: "Each employee is supposed to turn in their expenses to Mrs. Parrack."

Receptionist H: "Was you supposed to get a copy of that report?"

Receptionist I: "All of the Purchasing Department is gone."

Receptionist J: "Most all of the reports has been mailed."

APPLICATION ACTIVITY

You work at the headquarters office of Wodehouse Chemicals, Inc., a company that distributes chemical supplies. In addition to the company officers (Elaine Shewbart and Levi Weathers) and one administrative assistant, there are two office assistants and an information processing specialist. As one of the office assistants, you answer incoming calls for Ms. Shewbart and Mr. Weathers when the administrative assistant is unable to do so.

At 8:30 a.m. you are told that Ms. Shewbart and the administrative assistant will attend a motivational seminar until noon. They should be back in the office by 1:30 p.m. Mr. Weathers is making a presentation to a new customer and expects to be unavailable until 11:00 a.m. Mr. Weathers has asked that you record the advertising figures that Les Clark will provide when he calls.

Word processing equipment can be used to complete this activity.

What You Are To Do: Use the message forms provided in *Information Processing Activities* or prepare forms similar to the one shown on page 654. Record the messages for Elaine Shewbart and Levi Weathers. Use today's date.

8:45 a.m.   Caller: "I need to speak with Elaine Shewbart, please."
            You: "Ms. Shewbart is out of the office now. May I take a message?"
            Caller: "This is John Abbott with Petro Chemicals. Please ask her to call me when she returns."
            You: "May I take your number?"
            Caller: "555-3235."
            You: "Thank you, Mr. Abbott. I'll give Ms. Shewbart your message when she returns."

9:15 a.m.   Caller: "I'd like to speak with Levi Weathers. This is Paul
                      Osmond from the Pittsburgh office."
             You: "I'm sorry, Mr. Weathers is with a customer right now.
                      May I take a message?"
             Caller: "No...tell him I'll call back around three this afternoon."
             You: "May I take a number where you will be in case he is able
                      to return your call before three?"
             Caller: "No, I'm calling from a pay phone at the airport. My flight
                      leaves within an hour. Just tell him that I called about the
                      Evans account and I'll call back this afternoon."

9:45 a.m.   Caller: "This is Les Clark from the Chicago office. Levi Weathers
                      called yesterday and asked for advertising costs that I
                      did not have available. He said I could give the figures to
                      you."
             You: "Yes, Mr. Clark. I was told you would be calling."
             Caller: "Good. Here are the figures: $5,624 in advertising costs
                      for March; $8,518, for April; $3,526, for May; $10,594, for
                      June; $7,882, for July; and $9,988, for August."
             You: (You verify all amounts by repeating the figures to Mr.
                      Clark.) "May I have your number in case Mr. Weathers
                      has any questions?"
             Caller: "Of course. My direct line is Area Code 312-555-8379."

10:20 a.m.   Caller: "This is Sharon Montgomery with Hercules & Son. I'd like
                      to speak with Elaine Shewbart, please."
             You: "I'm sorry, Ms. Shewbart is out of the office until 1:30
                      p.m. May I take a message?"
             Caller: "Please ask her to call me as soon as possible. My
                      number is 555-9764. Tell her that I want to discuss the
                      recent order we received from you."

OUTGOING TELEPHONE COMMUNICATIONS

When you have completed your study of this topic, you will be able to:

- describe telephone directories you will find useful

- use proper telephone techniques to place local and long-distance domestic and international calls

- use proper telephone techniques and procedures to place outgoing calls

Office workers make outgoing calls for many reasons. For example, calls often are placed to request information, confirm appointments, or give instructions. A telephone call to a coworker or to another business may be less time-consuming than a memo or a letter.

Local telephone service may be provided by a Bell Operating Company or an independent telephone company. Long-distance calls placed outside the service area of the local telephone company will be handled by a long-distance company, such as AT&T, MCI, GTE, Sprint, or others. Businesses have an opportunity to select the long-distance company, the telephone services, and the equipment that can best meet their needs.

As an office worker, you likely will place outgoing calls to arrange with a delivery service to pick up a package or make airline reservations for an executive. You may be asked to check on an order for office supplies or place local and long-distance calls to customers. You may be asked to place calls to companies or individuals in other countries.

In order to make outgoing calls efficiently and economically, you should be aware of the services offered by the telephone companies that provide local and long-distance service to your office. You also should be able to use the many time-saving features available on the telephone system in use in the office.

Local telephone companies usually provide directories to their customers free of charge. If your office makes frequent calls to certain large cities, you also may have access to some out-of-town directories. Most directories include a *Customer Guide*, complete with a table of contents. You should become familiar with this contents page so that you can find needed information rapidly. You also may keep a personal directory or a listing of frequently used telephone numbers.

These directories are valuable references. You should keep them close at hand so that you can use them efficiently.

Local Telephone Directory

You will use this directory when you want to find the telephone number of a business or an individual in your local area. Unless a local business or individual has an unlisted number or has recently moved into the area, you should be able to find the number listed. Otherwise, you may call the operator for assistance.

White Pages

This directory lists in alphabetic order the names and telephone numbers of individuals, businesses, and government agencies. In some cities, the white pages may be divided into two sections. The first section lists personal names and numbers only, while the second section lists only business names and numbers. Sometimes these sections are each contained in separate books. When personal and business numbers are divided, another section called the *Blue Pages* also may be included. The Blue Pages serve as an easy reference for locating telephone numbers of government offices and other helpful numbers such as those of the chamber of commerce, consumer protection, and weather service.

Government agencies are listed in the directory according to their level of government—federal, state, county, and city. For example, to find the telephone number for the Occupational Safety and Health Administration, you would first turn to *U.S. Government*. (See Illus. 15-14.) There, you will find listed alphabetically the various departments, bureaus, and agencies of the federal government. To locate a state agency, you would first look under the name of the state, as in *Florida, State of*. County and city government telephone numbers are listed under the appropriate county or city name, as in *Allegheny, County of* and *New York, City of*.

Illus. 15-14.
Government agency
listings from a local
telephone directory.

```
UNITED STATES GOVERNMENT—

INTERIOR DEPARTMENT OF—
   Fish & Wildlife Service Division Of Law
      Enforcement . . . . . . . . . . . . . . . . . 555-7273
JUSTICE DEPARTMENT OF—
   Federal Bureau Of Investigation
      1205 Texas 79401 . . . . . . . . . . . . . . . 555-8571
      If No Answer Call . . . . . . . . . . . 214 555-2200
   United States Attorney's Office
      1205 Texas 79401 . . . . . . . . . . . . . . . 555-7351
   United States Border Patrol
      1205 Texas 79401 . . . . . . . . . . . . . . . 555-7355
   United States Marshall
      1205 Texas 79401 . . . . . . . . . . . . . . . 555-7655
LABOR DEPARTMENT OF—
   Bureau of Apprenticeship Training
      1205 Texas Av 79401 . . . . . . . . . . . . . 555-7650
   Employment Standards
      Administration-Wage & Hour Field
      Station 1205 Texas Av 79401 . . . . . . . . . 555-7666
   Occupational Safety & Health
      Administration 1205 Texas 79401 . . . . . . . 555-7681
MARINE CORPS—
   Marine Corps Officer Selection Office
      4206-B 50th St
      Toll Free-Dial 1 & Then . . . . . . . . . . 800 555-2600
```

Yellow Pages

The Yellow Pages contain an alphabetic listing of businesses only. The businesses are arranged according to the services they provide or the products they sell. For example, to find a telephone number for a company that repairs computers, you would look under *Computers—Service and Repair*. If you wanted to find the names and telephone numbers of businesses in the area that might **cater** your company's 50th anniversary dinner, you would look under *Caterers* (as shown on page 664). To find a listing for a company which sells briefcases, you would look under *Luggage*.

Included in the Yellow Pages is an index that lists the headings under which all businesses are categorized. The Yellow Pages can be in the same directory as the white pages or in a separate directory.

cater: supply food

Directory Assistance

If you are unable to locate a telephone number, call the directory assistance operator for help. Turn to the *Directory Assistance* section of your directory to find the operator's number. Be sure to have a pad and pencil ready to record the information the directory assistance operator will give you. Be prepared to tell the operator the city, exact name and street address (if known) of the person or business you wish to call.

Illus. 15-15. The Yellow Pages can help you find out where to obtain a particular product or service.

Personal and Company Directories

extensive: lengthy

To save time and improve efficiency, you may want to keep a personal directory of frequently called telephone numbers. If you have only a few numbers to record, tape the list to the telephone or post it at your workstation. If your list is **extensive**, you may use a card file or a small directory with alphabetic tabs.

highlight: underline or mark with color

You may be given a company telephone directory of employees working at a particular location. The directory also may include procedures for using the features of the company's telephone system. You may wish to **highlight** the numbers you call most often, as well as the features you use most frequently.

LONG-DISTANCE SERVICE

Long-distance calls are made to numbers outside the service area of your local telephone company. Several factors determine the cost of long-distance service, including the time of day the call is placed, the type of call, and the length of the conversation. To place calls efficiently and economically, you must be familiar with the various long-distance services available.

Several types of long-distance service are available from AT&T and other carriers such as MCI and Sprint. Four common services (direct-dial calls, operator-assisted calls, wide-area telecommunication service, and 800 Service) are described here.

Direct-Dial Calls

Direct-dial calls are those placed without assistance from an operator. To make a direct-dial call, first dial *1*, which gives you access to a long-distance line. Then dial the area code and the number you are trying to reach. (In some places, it is not necessary to dial the area code if it is the same as yours.) If, for example, you work in Lincoln, Nebraska, and wish to call Barkley Distributors in Sacramento, California, you dial 1-916-555-3094:

1 (for a long-distance line)
916 (the area code for Sacramento)
555-3094 (the telephone number for Barkley Distributors)

Charges for direct-dial calls begin as soon as the telephone is answered. If you make a direct-dial call and the person you need to speak with is unavailable, your company still will be charged for the call.

Operator-Assisted Calls

Calls that require the help of an operator to complete them are known as **operator-assisted calls**. These calls are more expensive than those you dial direct. Person-to-person calls, collect calls, and conference calls are all types of calls which require the assistance of an operator. Each of these is explained here.

Illus. 15-16. In addition to helping you place operator-assisted calls, telephone operators also can be of help when problems arise. For example, an operator can credit your account if you accidentally reach a wrong number or call the police in case of an emergency.

Person-to-Person Calls

Person-to-person calls are the most expensive type of operator-assisted calls. To place a person-to-person call, dial 0 (operator), the area code, and the telephone number of the individual or business you are calling. When you have finished dialing, the operator will come on the line:

Operator: *"How may I help you?"*

Caller: *"I want to make this a person-to-person call to Andrew Verreng, spelled V as in Victor, e-r-r-e-n-g."*

Operator: *"One moment, please."*

Charges for the call begin only after the person you have asked for is on the line. If that person is not available, you will not be charged for the call. If you wish, you may ask the operator to continue trying to complete the call. The operator will call to inform you when your call can be completed.

Collect Calls

The charges for a **collect call** are billed to the telephone number being called, not to the number from which the call was placed. To place a collect call, dial the operator, the area code, and the number you are calling. When the operator comes on the line, state that you want to place a collect call and give your name. The operator will complete the call and ask the recipient if she or he will accept the charges.

Traveling executives frequently make collect calls to their offices. In some cases, businesses will give their customers or clients permission to call collect.

Conference Calls

simultaneously: at the same time

A **conference call** is placed when it is necessary to talk ***simultaneously*** with persons at several different locations. With some telephone systems, you can use the special features of your office telephone to arrange these calls. But in many cases, conference calls are set up in advance with a *conference operator*. Dial the operator and say that you want to place a conference call. You will be connected with a conference operator who will arrange the call. Be prepared to give the conference operator the names, telephone numbers, and locations (city and state) of the persons who will participate in the call and the exact time the call is to be made. At the designated time, the conference operator will call you and indicate that the other parties are on the line.

Bank vice president in **Washington** whose bank is financing the PARAGON MALL PROJECT.

Advertising executive in **San Diego** whose company is planning the major campaign to announce the PARAGON MALL PROJECT.

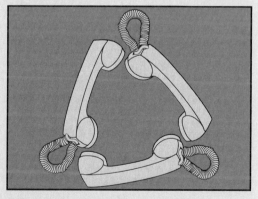

Executive in **New York City** who is in charge of the PARAGON MALL PROJECT and who initiated the conference call.

Illus. 15-17. Conference calls make it possible to conduct business without the expense of face-to-face meetings.

Wide Area Telecommunication Service (WATS)

A company that makes many long-distance calls may find it economical to lease one or more WATS lines. Instead of charging a regular long-distance rate for each call placed, the telephone company charges a set monthly fee plus a discounted rate for each outgoing call. The geographic service area covered will vary.

800 Service

interstate: between two or more states

intrastate: within one state

As a convenience to customers who call long-distance, a company may subscribe to 800 Service. This discounted service applies to incoming calls only, and there is no charge to the caller. 800 Service is available on either an *interstate* or *intrastate* basis. For example, a company which services customers from Maine to Florida may subscribe to 800 Service that includes all the states along the East Coast. A company with customers in California only may subscribe to 800 Service for that one state. To determine whether a company in the United States has an 800 number, dial 800 directory assistance at 1-800-555-1212.

DIFFERENCES IN TIME ZONES

It is important that you be aware of time zone differences when placing long-distance calls. The continental United States and parts of Canada are divided into five standard time zones: *Atlantic, Eastern, Central, Mountain,* and *Pacific.* (See Illus. 15-18.) As you move west, each zone is one hour earlier. For example, when it is 1 p.m. in Washington, D.C. (Eastern zone), it is noon in Dallas (Central zone), 11 a.m. in Denver (Mountain zone), and 10 a.m. in Los Angeles (Pacific zone). If you are in San Diego and need to speak to a coworker in the New York regional office, you will need to place the call before 2 p.m. Pacific time (which is 5 p.m. Eastern time). Otherwise, the New York office may be closed.

INTERNATIONAL CALLS

Satellites and undersea cables make it possible to place direct calls to over 150 countries. There are 24 time zones throughout the world. You need to be aware of time differences when placing international calls, just as you do when placing long-distance calls within the United States.

To place a call to London, England, you would direct dial the following sequence of numbers: *011* (international access code) + *44* (country code) + *71* (city code) + *seven-digit phone number.* Consult the *Directory Assistance* section in your local directory

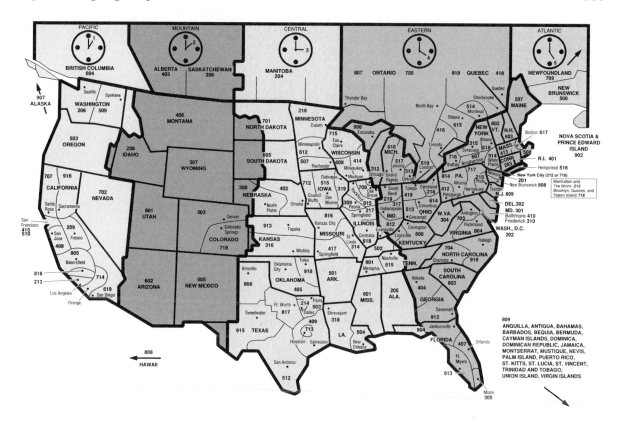

Illus. 15-18. This map shows telephone area codes and time zones in the continental United States and parts of Canada.

or call 1-800-874-4000 for additional information or country codes.

CONTROLLING TELEPHONE COSTS

As an office worker, you will be expected to help control telephone costs. Some suggestions are listed here.

- Make operator-assisted calls only when necessary.
- Plan your conversation so the time spent during a long-distance call is used efficiently.
- If possible, call when long-distance rates are least expensive. (See Illus. 15-19 on page 670.)
- Save on directory assistance fees by keeping a current telephone directory at or near your workstation.
- Keep a personal directory of frequently called numbers.
- Notify the operator immediately after reaching a wrong number so you can receive credit for the call.

Illus. 15-19. Chart showing one long-distance carrier's rate periods for direct-dial calls. Notice that the most expensive calls are those placed Monday through Friday between the hours of 8 a.m. and 5 p.m.

LONG DISTANCE RATE PERIODS		
Rates	Hours	Days
Weekday full rate	8 a.m. to 5 p.m.	Monday through Friday
Evening discount rate	5 p.m. to 11 p.m.	Monday through Friday and Sunday
Night and weekend discount rate	11 p.m. to 8 a.m.	Every day
	All day	Saturday
	8 a.m. to 5 p.m.	Sunday

QUESTIONS FOR REVIEW

1. Which types of listings are included in the White Pages? in the Yellow Pages? For what purpose are the Blue Pages used?

2. If you need to find the telephone number of the nearest post office, under which level of government would you look?

3. Identify four types of long-distance service available from long-distance carriers.

4. When do charges for direct-dial calls begin? for person-to-person calls?

5. What is a collect call?

6. How would you arrange for a conference call with a conference operator?

7. What is the advantage of WATS Service?

8. How does 800 Service benefit a company's customers?

9. The continental United States and parts of Canada are divided into how many time zones? Name them.

10. If you placed a long-distance call at 8:15 a.m. on Tuesday, which rate would apply? at 5:05 p.m. on Friday?

INTERACTING WITH OTHERS

As switchboard operator for EcoLand Services, Ruth Ramirez' job is to screen all calls. She recently received a call from a caller who refused to identify herself. The conversation went like this:

> *Ruth:*   "*EcoLand Services. Ruth Ramirez speaking.*"
> *Caller:*   "*Let me speak with Mr. Whitaker right now.*"
> *Ruth:*   "*May I ask who is calling?*"
> *Caller:*   "*No, I do not wish to give my name. I want to speak with Mr. Whitaker right away!*"

Ruth was stunned by the woman's rudeness. How should she have responded?

What You Are To Do: Answer the above question by composing an ending to the conversation.

EXTENDING YOUR MATH COMPETENCIES

You work as an office assistant for Carlson-Greer, Inc., which has offices in Seattle, Houston, and St. Louis. Your supervisor, Mr. Penrod, is responsible for monitoring the costs of the various forms of telecommunications used by the company. As part of his analysis, he prepares a report showing the monthly long-distance telephone charges for each regional office for a period of six months. Mr. Penrod hands you some figures (which appear at the top of page 672) and asks for your help.

What You Are To Do: Prepare a copy of the chart on page 672 or use the form provided in *Information Processing Activities*. Show all calculations and prove all totals.
  A. Calculate the total charges for each regional office for the six-month period.
  B. Calculate the total charges for each of the six months for all regional offices.
  C. Calculate the total charges for the six-month period for all regional offices.
  D. Calculate the average monthly charges for each regional office. *Do NOT round off your answers.*
  E. Calculate the average of the total charge determined in B. *DO round off your answer.* (To cross-check your work, add the average monthly charges determined in D. That total should equal the six-month total.)

APPLICATION ACTIVITY

You have been working for two weeks as a secretary for an insurance agency. You find you are wasting time looking up the same telephone numbers, so you decide to prepare a personal directory of frequently called and emergency numbers. Include the telephone numbers of the companies or organizations identified at the bottom of page 672.

LONG-DISTANCE CHARGES				
Months	**Regional Offices**			**Total**
	Seattle	**Houston**	**St. Louis**	
January	$201.56	$58.67	$250.76	?
February	190.45	75.34	277.68	?
March	175.66	68.90	265.90	?
April	188.34	59.12	288.10	?
May	205.44	61.36	272.89	?
June	198.17	74.77	259.29	?
TOTAL	?	?	?	?
AVERAGE	?	?	?	?

Word processing
equipment can be used
to complete this activity.

What You Are To Do: Using your local telephone directory, find telephone numbers and addresses for the companies or organizations to be included in your personal directory. If the telephone directory lists more than one choice for a particular company or organization, choose the one that is located nearest your school.

A. On lined paper, record the name, address, and telephone number of each company or organization.

B. From the listing you prepared in Step A, key your personal directory. Use FREQUENTLY CALLED AND EMERGENCY NUMBERS as the title. Key the list in what you consider to be "priority" order. Use your own judgment with regard to format.

C. Suggest two places at your workstation where you could post your personal directory.

fire department/EMS
   (emergency medical service)
bank
post office
photocopying service
newspaper

police department
office supply store
overnight delivery service
florist
advertising agency
Chamber of Commerce

CHAPTER SUMMARY

Telecommunications continues to play a vital role in today's business world. As an office worker, you should be eager to learn how new and improved technologies will help you do your job better. After reading this chapter, you should be able to discuss these points:

1. Telecommunications refers to the electronic transfer of information over considerable distances.
2. LANs and WANs provide the means by which information can be transferred locally or over distances.
3. Key, PBX/PABX/CPBX, and centrex telephones are voice communication systems that offer a variety of features and equipment.
4. Cellular phones and pagers enable businesspersons to stay in touch with their offices.
5. Voice mail and electronic mail systems allow for electronic storage and retrieval of spoken and written messages.
6. Facsimile is an extremely popular way of transmitting data and images to other locations quickly.
7. Office workers who answer the telephone give callers their first impression of the company. It is important for workers to use proper telephone procedures in order to handle all incoming and outgoing calls courteously and efficiently.
8. Telephone companies provide directories and operator assistance to help you place local and long-distance calls. Long-distance calls can be direct-dial calls or operator-assisted calls. It is important to remember that there are different time zones throughout the United States and the world.

KEY CONCEPTS AND TERMS

telecommunications	videoconferencing
modem	ISDN
local area network	screening
wide area network	long-distance calls
key system	direct-dial calls
PBX/PABX/CPBX	operator-assisted calls
centrex system	person-to-person calls
voice mail	collect call
electronic mail	conference call
facsimile	

INTEGRATED CHAPTER ACTIVITY

To complete the following role-playing activity, you will need the assistance of a classmate. Your teacher will divide your class into learning teams of two students each. Once the assignments have been made, decide who will play the role of the caller and who will play the role of the person who answers the call in the telephone situation.

What You Are To Do: A. You and your learning partner will work together to create a script for the telephone situation that follows. Key the dialogue on plain paper. Both you and your learning partner should have a copy.

B. Role-play the situation, following the script.

C. Evaluate your partner's telephone techniques. Use the forms provided in *Information Processing Activities* or follow your teacher's instructions for writing your comments on plain paper. (**NOTE:** *While you are evaluating your partner, your partner will be evaluating you.) Then exchange evaluation sheets and review the evaluation of your telephone techniques.*

D. Role-play a second situation, if time permits. Complete the evaluation process as you did in Step C. Have you improved any poor techniques that were identified while role-playing the first situation?

Word processing equipment can be used to complete this activity.

Situation

The receptionist at Shuman Brothers department store receives a call from Timothy Wolinsky, who wishes to speak to Miss Holthaus, the store manager. The receptionist is aware that Miss Holthaus is visiting several departments throughout the store and is not in her office. The receptionist also knows that Mr. Wolinsky works for Lee, Wolinsky, and Jones—the accounting firm that handles the department store's tax records. The receptionist puts Mr. Wolinsky on hold while she uses the in-house paging system to try to locate Miss Holthaus. Another employee answers the page and informs the receptionist that Miss Holthaus has left the store but will return after 2:00 p.m. Mr. Wolinsky says he will call back at 2:30 p.m.

OPTIONAL COMPUTER APPLICATION ACTIVITY
See Computer Application Activity 15
in your Information Processing Activities workbook.

OPTIONAL CRITICAL THINKING ACTIVITY
See Critical Thinking Activity 6
in your Information Processing Activities workbook.

PRODUCTIVITY CORNER

Kathy Malenky
OFFICE SUPERVISOR

THE TELEPHONE'S RINGING —AGAIN!

DEAR MS. MALENKY:

Last month I was hired as an office worker in an auto parts supply store. My duties include keying invoices and correspondence, keeping the books, and answering the phone. I am interrupted *often* by the phone. To compound the problem, my supervisors always seem to misplace the messages I leave. Mr. Parra is especially bad about losing messages. More than once he has said something like, "Sylvia, I can't find that message from Peter Torres. Please look up his number in the phone book." So I'm interrupted twice about the same matter!—SYLVIA IN SHREVEPORT

DEAR SYLVIA:

Did you notice the contradiction in your letter? You said that your job *includes* answering the telephone, but then you said that you are *interrupted* by the telephone. Remember, answering the telephone contributes to the smooth functioning of your office just as much as the other tasks you perform. If you regard telephone calls as interruptions, you probably feel annoyed each time the phone rings. You may even communicate that annoyance through your voice while you talk with a caller. Feeling annoyed also can reduce your willingness to work efficiently. Your overall productivity suffers as a result.

Suppose you are keying a letter when the telephone rings. Instead of resenting the call, remember that answering the telephone is a high work priority for you. The telephone does not keep you from doing your job—it *is* your job! Giving attention to incoming calls is an important task. When the telephone rings, mentally note where you are with the letter you are keying. Then, switch your full attention to the caller. When you have completed the conversation, return to keying the letter you had put aside.

You must be helpful when your supervisors request information about a particular telephone message. Consider buying a spiral-bound pad of telephone message forms that includes duplicate-copy forms. Each time you record a message, you also record a copy of it. When you give the original to your supervisor, a copy remains in your spiral pad. If one of the supervisors loses a message, you can quickly refer to your own copy.—KATHY MALENKY

PERSONAL AND CAREER DEVELOPMENT

CHAPTER 16

Planning and Advancing Your Career

In this final chapter, the spotlight shifts to you and to the tasks of job seeking and career planning. In addition to valuable office skills, your personality goes with you when you enter the office as an employee. Knowing your own personality, including your strengths and weaknesses, will be of critical importance to you as you consider job possibilities.

You learned how important good human relations are in the office when you studied Chapter 4. You learned that your behavior contributes to the atmosphere of the office in which you choose to work. In this chapter, you will be asked to step back and think of yourself in a somewhat more basic manner. You will be asked to consider the value of self-acceptance, the process of self-assessment, and the nature of mature behavior. Knowing yourself and your potential for growth will be invaluable strengths as you enter the world of work on a full-time basis.

Attention also will be given to the practical tasks of developing a career strategy and getting a job. Common job application procedures will be outlined for you. Job-seeking knowledge will help you make decisions about your job choice with confidence and competence. Also, you will be introduced to how you can guide your own professional growth on the job.

The objectives of this chapter are to:

● help you to understand and assess your own personality

● introduce you to the practical tasks of career planning and job hunting

FOCUS ON YOU

When you have completed your study of this topic, you will be able to:

- explain why self-acceptance is important to personal growth

- describe the value of self-assessment

- identify key components of one's personality

- explain the value of a mature personality

Psychologists talk of a person "becoming" as a way of emphasizing the limitless possibilities for personal growth. The unique combination of characteristics that distinguishes one person from another is called **personality**. You may or may not be aware of your own ability to change your personality. There is nothing absolutely fixed about who you are, what you believe, and how you behave. There is perhaps no more magical characteristic of human beings than that which allows them to shape their own personalities.

You *can* change your personality if you want to. Some people, however, deny the possibility of change. You have probably heard comments such as, "Well, that's just the way I am; I can't change me," or "I wish I could be different, but it is too late now to try to change."

Such comments are made by individuals who do not realize the power they have to make changes or who, in truth, do not want to change. Individuals who insist that change is beyond their control are not likely ever to become the persons they are capable of becoming. On the other hand, individuals who know that they possess the power to change can quietly and sensibly modify their attitudes, beliefs, and behaviors to attain their own goals for a satisfying life. Human beings can make deliberate efforts to improve aspects of their personalities.

SELF-ACCEPTANCE

scornful: filled with disrespect

At the core of your mental health is your attitude toward yourself. When you accept yourself, you have respect for yourself as a person. You are not **scornful** of who you are or what you do. It is generally believed that individuals cannot have a positive view of the world if they do not accept themselves.

Perceiving Yourself

perception: mental image

To learn self-acceptance, you must first have a proper **perception** of yourself. People who accept themselves have adopted certain basic attitudes that help them understand themselves. To learn self-acceptance, you must:

deceive: keep hidden, lie

- be honest with yourself and not **deceive** yourself about your behavior and beliefs.
- understand that while you are a unique individual, you also share many of the same wants, needs, and fears with other persons.
- develop a deep-seated belief in your own worthiness yet respect the **uniqueness** of others.

uniqueness: the quality of being the only one

Being Honest with Yourself

You cannot be accepting of yourself if you are unable to view yourself honestly. Facing yourself honestly means admitting your weaknesses and acknowledging your strengths.

Don believed that he was a hardworking student who studied carefully before every examination. When he performed poorly on an examination, however, he blamed the teacher for giving an unfair examination. He had convinced himself that he was hardworking and was unwilling to admit that he simply had not studied for the examination.

Kevin wanted to be a good student, but he knew that from time to time he didn't apply sufficient effort to his studies. When he did poorly on an examination, he admitted that he had neglected studying. He concluded that if he really wanted to be a good student, he would have to change his study habits.

Can you guess how Don's performance differed from Kevin's on later examinations? Don continued to blame others for his poor grades while maintaining the false belief that he was hardworking. Kevin, on the other hand, began to behave like a hardworking student. Don's performance never improved; Kevin earned a high grade in the course.

Illus. 16-1. Time alone to reflect on one's own behavior in an honest way is time well spent.

Being Aware of Others

It is very easy to believe that you are the only person in the world with deficiencies or weaknesses. Others sometimes don't seem to have the problems that you face, you think. Such thoughts, however, will not solve your problems. Besides, they are usually not a clear perception of reality.

Marie was deeply unhappy because she always felt so shy. She resented how her classmates talked with one another and answered questions the teacher raised in class. She wondered why it was so easy for them to interact. She could not understand her fear of others and thought life was unfair.

Elsie had suffered from shyness; but by talking with others, she learned that she was not alone in being shy. She also noted that others did not give in to their shyness—they reached out to people. Elsie decided to put aside thoughts of her own shyness and began thinking of others instead. She soon found it much easier to talk with people.

An awareness that others face problems and overcome them can help you accept yourself. You are not likely to impose unrealistic standards on yourself when you understand that everyone has both strengths and weaknesses in their personalities.

Being Aware of Your Own Worthiness

Self-acceptance means that you are willing to live with yourself, faults and all. With such a basic belief, you are able to feel confident and secure. Good emotional health depends, to a considerable extent, on your sense of worthiness as reflected in your confidence and feelings of security.

Illus. 16-2. The young woman is looking directly into the eyes of the person to whom she is talking. She reflects self-confidence.

Carol is highly self-critical and anxious. She feels worthless and conveys her feelings through her unkind behavior toward others. Carol often complains that no one can be trusted, that people aren't nice, and that others reject her.

Betsy, on the other hand, believes that every person is valuable, including herself. She assumes that others are as trusting, secure, and confident as she is. Her behavior toward others reflects these attitudes. In most cases, other persons respond with a reflection of the same attitudes as those Betsy has.

How you behave toward others influences how others behave toward you. Your own sense of worthiness seems to be a basic factor in determining your behavior. You should strive to develop a realistic, yet positive, attitude about yourself.

Recognizing Your Separateness

When you accept yourself, you become an individual with choice-making opportunities. You have a *sense of person*—you are able to make decisions uninfluenced by pressures from others. This does not mean that you have a closed mind to what others suggest or recommend. It means that although you consider what others are saying, in the end you come to an independent decision that you believe is best. An individual with a sense of person does not justify a decision or a choice by saying, "Well, everyone else was doing it and I didn't want to be different from others." You are able to develop your own awareness of what is right and what is wrong.

gait: manner of walking

ridiculed: mocked; make the object of laughter

*Four friends were seated on a park bench one afternoon after school. An elderly man who was having difficulty walking came into sight. Three in the group began to laugh at the man's strange **gait**. The fourth one was surprised at the laughter and thought it was unjustified. She did not laugh, and she did not think it was proper for her friends to poke fun at the elderly gentleman. She turned to her three friends and said, "Why are you laughing? That man should be admired, not **ridiculed**. He is trying to get someplace despite his problem."*

The young woman did not feel the need to follow the group. She took a risk when she communicated her feelings to the others. In this instance, the three friends listened and realized that their behavior could have been different. However, they could have judged their friend's comment to be ridiculous.

Often your beliefs will match those of your friends and acquaintances; sometimes they will not. Nevertheless, you must treasure your own individuality so that you have a clear sense of who you are. Others generally respect **authentic** persons.

authentic: genuine

SELF-ASSESSMENT

paradox: contradiction

It may seem something of a **paradox** that you are told that you must accept yourself and then told that you must assess yourself. Remember, though, that accepting yourself does not mean there is no need to improve your personality. In fact, accepting yourself is necessary before you can profit from a self-assessment.

The Value of Assessing Yourself

As you know, you must give conscious attention to anything you want to accomplish. This also applies to changing yourself in ways that will make you happier. You are undoubtedly familiar with the popular tradition of making New Year's resolutions, but have you ever thought about their significance? Frequently, they deal with the hope of improving one's personality. A typical resolution might be, "I am going to be more considerate of my brother and sister this year," or "I am going to be fair to my friends and not talk behind their backs," or "I'm going to take more initiative on my part-time job."

Resolutions demonstrate that individuals believe they can do better. They want to establish, in effect, a contract with themselves to change their behavior. Clearly identifying what you do not like gives you clues as to what you must do. Self-assessment implies that you care about how you behave and are willing to make changes.

Components to be Assessed

There are many components to one's personality. Only a few of the key components, as related to one's behavior at work, will be discussed here.

Disposition

One of the most basic components of personality is disposition. Disposition is defined as "one's attitudes and moods in reacting to life around oneself."

There are great variations in dispositions. Some people have "sunny" dispositions, as observed by others. Such persons tend to see the bright side of any situation; they are optimistic about the future; and they are likely to see the good qualities in others first. This does not mean that a person with a "sunny" disposition cannot be objective or critical in evaluating others. It does mean that there is a tendency to be positive initially in responding to others. In general, individuals at work prefer to associate with those who have good dispositions. If you try to discover what is meant by "good," you may elicit such comments as these:

> *"A person with a good disposition is calm, friendly, not moody or uncooperative when interacting with me during our workday."*
> *"I think a good disposition means that you enjoy associating with others and can consider other persons' points of view."*

Illus. 16-3. When you look at yourself in the mirror, you can be looking deep into your inner self.

Confidence

A firm belief in oneself and one's abilities is what is meant by *confidence*. It is very important that you strive to develop confidence in yourself. Of course, self-confidence must be based on realistic assessment, not fantasy.

Ken studies for all of his courses in a very thorough manner. One day, a teacher asked him to explain to the class some techniques for using time wisely when studying. Ken was so frightened at the teacher's request that he responded, "I'm sorry, I do not know any time management techniques." The teacher was surprised because she knew that Ken was an excellent student. She sensed that Ken did not feel confident when he had to talk before the class. After class, the teacher found a chance to talk with Ken privately. She tried to convince Ken that he did know what he was asked to discuss. After some discussion, Ken promised to speak before the class very soon. The teacher said to Ken, "We must build up your confidence. You are cheating yourself if you don't face life with confidence."

Margarita studies in much the same fashion as Ken but does not have Ken's problem. When she is asked to speak to the class, she quickly assesses her knowledge of the topic. If she decides that she has studied the topic carefully, she accepts the teacher's offer to speak to the class. Margarita has confidence when she talks because she has learned to make an accurate evaluation of her own level of knowledge.

Isn't Ken robbing himself of an opportunity to participate in class? Is he being fair to himself? He undoubtedly knew something worthwhile to communicate to his fellow students. Would he not feel happier if he could respond positively to his teacher's request?

Margarita is fortunate to have self-confidence, which she bases on an accurate assessment of her knowledge. Margarita has developed an objective way of viewing herself and is able to determine whether or not she can manage her teacher's requests.

Character

The basic values and principles that are reflected in the way you live your life are referred to as *character*. Basic values, such as honesty and sincerity, are implied when someone speaks of a "person's character." A person of good character is one who observes the ethical standards of society. For example, an employee whose work hours end at 5 p.m. is expected to continue working until 5 p.m. even if the supervisor or manager is out of the office. An office worker who leaves the office at 4:30 because the manager is out of town would be considered a person of questionable character. A person of good character is one who knows the difference between right and wrong when situations require a *moral* judgment. Persons of good character can be

moral: determining right from wrong

trusted because their behavior reflects what they actually believe.

Sandy and Eileen became good friends by working together in the same office. When Sandy was asked, "Why do you consider Eileen your best friend?" Sandy answered, "Eileen never lies to me. She is always truthful. She is a good person, and I like knowing her and being her friend."

Achievement

Interest and behavior that is guided by a wish to accomplish something is what is meant by *achievement*. Your personality is influenced by your attitude toward achievement. If you have an **intrinsic** wish to do something well, you are likely to develop characteristics of a good employee. Among the key characteristics are:

intrinsic: basic, natural

- willingness to take initiative
- acceptance of responsibility
- persistence in maintaining high work standards

Illus. 16-4. A job well done is valued by your supervisor.

Persons who choose *not* to achieve encounter many problems. For example, students who do not give attention to their studies fail courses. If they accept jobs, they are often dismissed because they cannot meet the minimum requirements for employment. Furthermore, such persons often are unhappy because they seem to be failing in many ways. An assessment of their own attitudes, though, can sometimes aid in redirecting their behavior.

How to Assess Yourself

It is a common human reaction to reflect on something you said or did and make a judgment about your behavior. It is also a common human reaction not to face your own evaluation—to hide from or ignore it—when it is not favorable. You will find it valuable, though, to make a deliberate effort to think about your behavior at times. You may choose to reflect on specific aspects of your behavior that you want to change in some way. A simple strategy to help you change your behavior follows:

1. Identify something that is less than satisfactory in your own personality.
   Example: I wish I were doing better in class. I don't use the most efficient techniques to complete assignments and study for exams.

2. Think of circumstances or situations that give you clear evidence of the problem.
   Example: I submitted two assignments late. I didn't study for the last test and I failed it.

3. Think of the reasons why you behaved as you did.
   Example: I had a shortsighted view of how I wanted to spend my time. I thought it was more important to spend time with my friends.

4. Think about the different ways you could have behaved.
   Example: I could have begun the assignments earlier if I had refused to go to the ball game. I could have turned down the invitation to play tennis by explaining that I had to study for a test.

5. Devise a plan to change your behavior, and promise yourself to stay with it.
   Example: I'll draw up a schedule. I'll establish priorities and adhere to them.

reflection:
thoughtful
consideration

Self-assessment can be a quiet, personal type of **reflection**. However, there may be times when it is more beneficial to discuss your plans and goals with another person. Just as you would be willing to help someone who wanted to talk with you, remember that there are others who have the same feelings for you. Reflecting on your behavior and acting on what you learn will be very helpful to you. It will help you to become the type of worker who enjoys interacting with others.

MATURE BEHAVIOR

Even though there is potential for growth as long as there is life, a person in our society is expected to behave in a mature manner by the end of adolescence. Of course, many people reflect maturity at a younger age. To be mature, as the dictionary states, is "to have or express the emotional and mental qualities that are considered normal to a socially adjusted adult human being." To be mature means that you see beyond the moment, that you understand the consequences of your choice, that you consider the rights of others, and that you make a decision based on such understanding.

> Marilyn, a high school senior, is a part-time office assistant. Her department manager thinks Marilyn is an exceptionally mature young woman. When the manager was asked why he considered Marilyn mature, he replied: "Seldom do we get a beginning worker, especially one who is part-time, who accepts responsibility as Marilyn does. When she has been here alone, she has used excellent judgment in responding to customer inquiries. She is absolutely dependable; she never leaves without turning off all equipment and locking doors. We feel fortunate to have her here; we hope she will join us full-time when she graduates."

inevitable: cannot
be avoided

As you know, the business office is a place where individuals must work cooperatively. You can understand that if coworkers are mature individuals, the **inevitable** problems and conflicts that arise will be resolved in ways satisfactory to everyone. However, it is unrealistic to expect that all of your coworkers will be mature. In any group, there likely will be persons at different stages of growth. What your goal should be is to behave in as mature a manner as possible. One person reflecting a quiet, sincere type of maturity can at times positively influence the group's behavior. Your efforts to influence the group may not always succeed, but such efforts are often rewarded.

Illus. 16-5. Maturity is something you can develop.

You Are Mature When You Are Willing To:

- accept criticism

- acknowledge that you do not understand

- admit that you made a mistake

- learn from your mistakes

- face your weaknesses and strive to overcome them

- be kind and helpful to others

- be objective and fair in your relationships with others

- put aside any inclination to appear superior to another human being

QUESTIONS FOR REVIEW

1. Why should a person believe that one's personality can be changed?

2. Why is it important for a person to be self-accepting?

3. What does it mean to be honest with yourself?

4. Why should a person be aware of others?

5. Describe how a person reflects a sense of worthiness.

6. Why should a person be interested in self-assessment?

7. Explain why character is considered a valuable component of personality.

8. What are some key characteristics that you are likely to observe in a person who is interested in achieving?

9. Describe the strategy that you might use to reflect on an aspect of your behavior that you would like to change.

10. Choose one of the characteristics of maturity listed in Illus. 16-5. For the characteristic you chose, describe a situation that illustrates behavior that would be considered immature.

MAKING DECISIONS

Joyce and Penny work in the same office. From time to time they have lunch together. During lunch one day Joyce said to Penny: "I really think we shouldn't work so hard at our jobs. The supervisor doesn't seem to notice what we do. I sometimes take a half-hour break and nothing is said. I notice that you always rush back in 15 minutes. Today Mrs. Wallace will be away all afternoon at a seminar downtown. She will go directly home at the end of the seminar. I don't have anything at my desk that must get done today, and I doubt if you have either. Let's not go back to the office; let's go to see a new movie."

What You Are To Do: If you were Penny, what decision would you make about how to spend the afternoon? What would you say to Joyce about her attitude toward work?

EXTENDING YOUR ENGLISH COMPETENCIES

You have been introduced in this topic to some aspects of personality that are important at work. However, there are other personality traits that influence your behavior. You may have learned about these in other high school courses. Listed below are some traits that have been introduced in this topic, and others that were not. You will find it useful to understand the meaning of each of these traits.

- ambitious
- assertive
- confident
- cooperative
- friendly

- honest
- outgoing
- resourceful
- shy
- studious

What You Are To Do: (1) Write a definition for each trait in relation to personality. You may need to consult a dictionary. (2) Choose three of the traits. For each, write a brief description of behavior you might observe at work that reflects either a positive or negative aspect of the trait.

APPLICATION ACTIVITIES

Activity 1

As you learned in this topic, self-assessment is important to becoming mature. In this activity, you are asked to review each characteristic indicated in Illus. 16-5 and make a judgment about your present level of maturity.

What You Are To Do: A. Make a list of the eight characteristics shown in Illus. 16-5 on page 690.

B. Determine your maturity level for each characteristic on a scale from 1 to 10. (10 is the highest level of maturity; 1, the lowest.)

C. Choose the one characteristic which you would like to improve. Write a brief paragraph discussing what you think would help you raise your level of maturity.

Activity 2

Assume that you are a supervisor in a large office. One of your employees is being considered for a promotion to a position that involves a great deal of interacting with people. Ms. Ruth Ann Wellins, Director of Human Resources, asks for your assessment of the employee's personality.

What You Are To Do: A. Assume that a personal friend (someone you know well enough to make judgments about that person's personality) is the employee who has been recommended for promotion.

B. Consider the person's personality in relation to the characteristics included in this topic. Make notes from which you will be able to write a reference.

C. Compose a memo to Ms. Wellins. In the memo, give your assessment of the strengths and weaknesses of the person. Be as specific as possible. Key the memo in final form on a sheet of plain paper. Use the simplified memorandum format shown on page 234.

Word processing equipment can be used to complete this activity.

FOCUS ON YOUR CAREER

When you have completed your study of this topic, you will be able to:

- devise a career plan
- prepare a resume
- compose a letter of application
- explain what is expected of a candidate during a job interview
- identify steps for advancing at work

You have been introduced to a wide range of office jobs. Demand for office employees continues. You will now turn your attention to considering a career strategy, getting a job, and thinking ahead to ways of advancing at work.

Your present skills and knowledge have vocational value in a variety of jobs. Remember that any decision about a job that you make now does not have to determine your work for the rest of your adult life. You will have opportunities to reassess what you have chosen to do and make changes that seem proper to you. At this point, though, focus is on considering an office position based on your high school education and on any work experience you have had while a student.

Several candidates are likely to apply for a specific job. A prospective employer must evaluate the strengths and weaknesses of each candidate and make a decision about which candidate is to be offered the job. In general, employers in reviewing resumes and talking with candidates are looking for the following qualities and abilities:

- specific skills and knowledge required for the job
- desire to do the job with initiative, commitment, and enthusiasm
- willingness to interact cooperatively with coworkers and others with whom they associate
- positive attitude toward work
- flexibility in meeting changing work demands

You will want to keep these factors in mind as you explore job possibilities and as you talk with prospective employers. You will want to choose a job that will give you a chance to use your skills and to learn while you work.

Life at work in the United States has changed markedly in recent years. Among the reasons for the changes are:

displace: to remove from a job or office

1. Technological developments continue to make some jobs obsolete. Workers are **displaced** and must make job changes, and in some instances career changes, during their working lives.

prohibit: not allow

2. Recent laws **prohibit** automatic retirement at age 65 in many occupations. Some workers, therefore, are remaining members of the labor force for many more years than was true in earlier decades.
3. Women have entered the workforce in increasingly greater numbers and are continuing to work for most of their adult lives.

So, you undoubtedly will be at work for many years and may change jobs—or careers—several times. Therefore, what you learn now about the skills and attitudes needed to make wise career decisions will be of continuing value to you.

PRESENT YOUR QUALIFICATIONS

Prospective employers are not likely to know you. Yet, they must evaluate your qualifications. You, therefore, have the task of presenting yourself effectively. This is one of the pleasant challenges you face as you enter the world of work.

Think about a Career Strategy

Your interest at this point may be in your first full-time job. You may ask: "Why should I consider anything more?" Thinking ahead may help you make a wiser decision about your first job. Thinking ahead to what you see as a career goal and devising realistic steps to meet that goal is known as a **career strategy**. With a career goal in mind, you can evaluate beginning job offers in relation to that goal.

paralegal: technically trained to assist lawyers

*Laurel eventually wants to work in a law office as an assistant to an attorney. After completing high school, she plans to continue her education on a part-time basis at a local community college where there is a specialized program for **paralegal** workers. Therefore, when considering office positions shortly before her high school graduation, she accepts a position as a word processing worker for a large law firm.*

unexpected: not planned

reconsider: to think about something again

Remember, though, that career planning is not a one-time event. The world is changing too rapidly and your own circumstances may change in ***unexpected*** ways for career goals established at high school graduation to be appropriate for a lifetime. As you gain experience and become better acquainted with alternatives for your interests and talents, you will want to ***reconsider*** what you planned as your career. Of course, a reconsideration may establish once again that your earlier career goal is still appropriate.

Set a Career Goal

As you know from talking with other students, some have clear ideas of the kind of work they want to do and what their career goals are while others have no idea of what they want to do. Those who have career goals can begin now to determine the steps that will help them meet their goals. To establish realistic steps in the pursuit of a career goal, you will want to get acquainted with job qualifications as well as common educational requirements. Some research in the school or local public library about a field of interest will be valuable to a person designing a career plan.

Illus. 16-6.
Reference books about job qualifications are available at school or public libraries.

Consider a Job Without a Career Goal

Many students are not sure what career is most appealing to them. Such students can still enter the work world and perform successfully. There are some useful options. Assume that a high school student has no idea of what career is best.

That student, however, studied business courses in high school, including office procedures. The student is well qualified to be an office worker. Such a student as an office worker can find work rewarding by keeping in mind objectives such as the following:

- to perform every task assigned according to instructions.
- to constantly strive to improve performance of each task and to learn as much as possible about activity related to each task.
- to be aware at all times of his/her own attitude toward each task as a means of becoming better acquainted with his/her own interests and preferences.
- to be alert to what is happening in the organization and especially what the work of others is like as a means of broadening understanding of career possibilities.
- to use off-the-job time to explore career opportunities through talking with friends and reading articles and books about careers that seem interesting.

Another option, commonly pursued, is to continue one's education at a postsecondary school. Often such schools allow a student to take courses from a variety of fields. Careful, thoughtful reflection on experiences during the first years of college may help in choosing a career.

PLAN YOUR JOB SEARCH

Whether you have a career goal or not, you can effectively plan your search for a job. The success you experience in meeting job requirements need not be related to whether or not you have a career goal. Common steps in a job search include:

1. Become acquainted with the types of jobs you wish to consider. You may want to reread Chapter 2.
2. Explore job opportunities related to the types of jobs in which you have an interest.
3. Prepare a resume.
4. Prepare a letter of application.
5. Send letters of application with resumes to companies which have job openings.
6. Accept interviews with companies who wish to talk with you about job openings.
7. Follow up all job interviews.
8. Accept a job.

Job openings for qualified office workers usually are plentiful. There are a number of sources available to help you locate specific jobs in which you may be interested. Friends, relatives, or former employers often know of good job opportunities. You may also find job openings by talking with counselors at your school, reading the newspaper, contacting employment agencies, or watching for government announcements. After planning your career, you will know more specifically which job openings interest you most.

School Placement and Counseling Services

You will want to become familiar with the placement and counseling services your school may provide. In some schools, for example, there may be a placement counselor to help students find part-time employment while enrolled in school or full-time employment upon graduation. Job openings may be posted regularly on a bulletin board as a service to students. In schools where there is no placement counselor, prospective employers often inform school guidance counselors or business teachers about job opportunities in their organizations.

You may find it helpful to discuss your career plans—as well as current job opportunities—with a school counselor or business teacher.

Newspapers

The classified ads section of the newspaper lists many job openings. Some employers advertise directly, asking you to call or write their companies for an appointment. Other employers use **blind advertisements** which do not identify the employer and request that applications be sent to a box number address.

Employment Agencies

Employers submit job openings to employment agencies, and counselors at the agencies help match your qualifications and goals with the jobs available. *Private employment agencies* charge a fee for their services. Sometimes you may have to pay the fee; other times, the employer who hires you pays it. The fee is usually a percentage of your first year's salary. *State employment agencies* provide placement services at no charge to the job applicant or the employer.

Temporary employment agencies hire you to fill temporary jobs that may last anywhere from one day to several months. The employer pays the temporary employment agency an hourly fee, and you receive a percentage of that fee for your work. Many businesses use temporary workers. By working in temporary jobs, you can gain valuable job experience while still looking for a permanent position. Some temporary jobs ***evolve*** into permanent positions.

evolve: change

Government Announcements

Many different types of office employees are required in governmental offices at the local, county, state, and federal level. You will be able to get information from your state employment office about job opportunities at the state and federal levels. In many states bulletins are issued on a regular basis that list jobs with qualifications required. Candidates for state and federal office jobs generally must satisfactorily complete job-related examinations. Examinations are given periodically and the dates announced in advance.

You can secure information from your local government employment office. If there is not one locally, call 800 information for the number for your state employment service or the federal Office of Personnel Management. Another source for information is to write to the Office of Personnel Management, 1900 E. Street, NW, Washington, DC 20415.

Personal Inquiry

If you have a special interest in working for a particular organization, you may want to write a carefully worded letter inquiring about job possibilities. In your letter you should explain the reason for your interest in being an employee, describe the kind of job you wish, and briefly outline your qualifications. You need not include a resume with such a letter, but you may want to state that you would be willing to send a detailed resume, if one is requested.

You may also want to call the personnel office of a company in which you are interested to ask if there are job openings. Some companies are willing to send you applications that should be returned for consideration. A common practice is to invite candidates with the best qualifications, as indicated on the applications, to come for job interviews.

```
                        Maria T. Herandez
                        2113 Mindon Road
                    Albuquerque, NM  87112-0341
                        (505) 555-8997


JOB INTEREST

A word processing position in a growth-oriented company.

EDUCATION

Will graduate from Southwest High School, May 19--
Grade Average:  3.2
Class standing: 97th in class of 572

Business subjects studied:

Business Math
Keyboarding
Accounting
Office Procedures
Advanced Word Processing

Special skills:

62 words per minute on a microcomputer
110 strokes per minute on an electronic calculator

School activities:

Office Education Association, Vice President
Senior Class Chorus

WORK EXPERIENCE

Office assistant (part-time) at Desert Ice Cream Company,
3424 Highway 85 NW, Albuquerque, NM  87112-3434 (May 19-- to
present).  Duties include preparing letters at a microcomputer
and answering the telephone.

Student assistant (part-time) in the Attendance Office, Hayes
Junior High School, 3100 Mountain Road NW, Albuquerque, NM
87104-3131 (August 19-- to May 19--).  Duties included recording
attendance, answering the telephone, filing, and making
photocopies.

REFERENCES

Furnished upon request.
```

Illus. 16-7. A resume aids a prospective employer in becoming acquainted with your qualifications.

A **resume** (also called a data sheet or vita) is a concise, well-organized presentation of your qualifications for a job. The prospective employer usually will see your resume before interviewing you. Your resume should make the best possible impression. Proofread your resume carefully. You may print it on a laser printer or have it duplicated on a high-quality copier. Whichever method you use, however, be sure that the copies are clean and sharp.

Categories of a Resume

competencies: skills

A resume usually has five categories: personal information, job interest, education, work experience, and references. You may include additional categories, such as office *competencies* and scholastic honors, if appropriate. There is no standard resume format. Therefore, a prospective employer may consider your resume to be a representation of your organizational ability. You may wish to prepare several variations of your basic resume, each one highlighting information *appropriate* for the job you seek. A general guideline is to list the most important information first. Refer to page 699 as you read about common resume categories.

appropriate: fitting

Personal Information

marital: relating to marriage

List the mailing address and telephone number where you can be reached. You need not provide information such as age, date of birth, or *marital* status. However, you may volunteer such information if you choose to do so.

Job Interest

Briefly state the job for which you are applying. A prospective employer will then be able to assess your qualifications in relation to a specific position.

Education

You should list the name and address of the high school you are attending and the date you will graduate. List the courses that prepared you for an office job. You may also list any scholastic honors or awards you have earned.

You may want to list any out-of-class activities in which you participated, such as membership in special interests clubs.

Work Experience

List in chronologic order the jobs you have had, beginning with the most recent job. For each job, list the name and address of the company, your job title, a brief description of the tasks you performed, and the dates of your employment.

At this stage in your career, your job experience may be quite limited. If you have had limited or no work experience, list volunteer work you may have done.

References

References are those people who know your academic ability and/or work habits and are willing to recommend you to a prospective employer by letter or telephone. You should get permission from all your references before you list them or provide them to a prospective employer. You may list references on a resume or include a statement that references will be provided upon request. If you list references, be sure to include complete name, position, and address for each one. Sometimes it is appropriate to include telephone numbers, too. Three references are generally sufficient.

REQUEST AN INTERVIEW

At this stage in your search, you have planned your career, prepared your resume, and identified potential job opportunities. Now you must ask prospective employers for an interview. A technique used frequently to request an interview is to send the company a letter of application and a copy of your resume.

Letter of Application

A **letter of application** introduces you to a prospective employer and includes a request for an interview. While your resume may be a photocopy, the letter of application, which accompanies each resume, must be an original. The tone of the letter should convey your interest and ability in a job. Remember, the reader is interested in you only in terms of your qualifications for a job in the company. Follow these guidelines when composing a letter of application:

● Address the letter to a person, not a department or company position. If necessary, call the company and ask for the name and correct spelling of the person who is responsible for hiring.

2113 Mindon Drive
Albuquerque, NM 87112-0341
April 23, 19--

Ms. Leslie W. Langan
Human Resources Director
Walker-Phibbs, Inc.
1015 Tijeras Avenue NW
Albuquerque, NM 87102-1015

Dear Ms. Langan

Your advertisement in the April 23 issue of the Albuquerque
Times describes a word processing position at your company.
I am interested in such a job and believe I am qualified to
fill it. Enclosed is a copy of my resume.

I am currently completing my senior year at Southwest High
School. I work part-time as an office assistant at a local
company. The business subjects I have studied, such as
keyboarding, office procedures, and advanced word processing
help me adapt quickly to on-the-job tasks and procedures.
My education and practical experience will help me learn new
procedures and perform the tasks of a word processing
operator effectively.

I would like very much to have an opportunity to talk with
you about the position you wish to fill. I can be reached
at 555-8997.

Sincerely

Maria T. Herandez
Maria T. Herandez

Enclosure

Illus. 16-8. A letter of application clearly identifies the job in which the writer is interested.

- In the first paragraph, explain why you are writing the letter. State specifically which position you are applying for and explain how you learned of the job opening.

- Next, indicate why you believe you are qualified for the position. Briefly refer to specific classes, experience, and/or interests you have that make you a good **candidate** for the job. Indicate that a resume is enclosed.

- Limit the letter to one page in length. At the end of the letter, request an interview and specify when you are available. After proofreading the letter carefully, sign the letter in black or blue ink.

candidate: applicant

Illus. 16-9. Most companies request that job applicants complete an employment application form like the one shown here.

| APPLICATION FOR EMPLOYMENT | | | Please print or use typewriter. | DATE: APRIL 23, 19— |

Employment Application Form

Many companies request that you complete an *employment application form*, even if you have submitted a resume. A completed application form provides information the company needs about you in a format that is easy for them to process.

Before filling out an application form, read all of the instructions carefully. If a question or blank does not apply to you, write N/A (not applicable) or draw a line in the blank space. On some application forms, you are asked to state the salary you expect to receive. If you had no full-time experience, you may want to write "open" to this request. Give the complete mailing address for each reference listed. Proofread the form carefully.

Illus. 16-10. Before filling out an application form, read it thoroughly. Look for special instructions and plan how you will complete each item on the form.

Interviewing successfully means that you communicate clearly and remain ***poised*** during the interview. Even if you do not receive a job offer, you might make such a favorable impression that the interviewer will remember you later when another, perhaps more appealing, position becomes available.

INTERVIEW SUCCESSFULLY

poised: calm; at ease

Before Your Interview

To interview successfully, you MUST be prepared. If you take the time to prepare before the interview, you have more confidence and make a better impression during the interview. Here are several ways in which you can prepare.

Plan to Make a Good First Impression

Since your appearance makes such a vivid impression on an interviewer, you should take time before the interview to plan what you will wear and to handle personal grooming details. Choose conservative, businesslike attire, even though you may know that some employees wear casual clothing—you are not an employee yet! Women should choose a business dress, conservative suit, or coordinated skirt, blouse, and jacket. Men should choose a dark suit or dress slacks and appropriate jacket.

The night before the interview, spend the necessary time to be sure the clothes you want to wear are clean and in good repair. Try to get a good night's rest so you will look rested and feel energetic the next day.

Learn about the Company

Use your school or community library resources to find out as much as possible about the company. What is the company's primary product or service? Does the company have branch offices? Does the company sponsor community events? If you are

Illus. 16-11. You will want to choose conservative, businesslike attire for the interview so that you make a good first impression.

unsure about the proper pronunciation of the company name or the name of the interviewer, call ahead of time and ask for clarification.

Anticipate Questions

During the interview, you will be asked many questions. You will want to listen carefully to each question and answer it thoughtfully. Therefore, it is wise to anticipate probable questions and think about appropriate responses. Some questions interviewers frequently ask are:

- Why does this job interest you?
- What would you like to know about this company and its products?
- Why do you think you would enjoy working in this company?
- What do you believe are your primary qualifications for this job?
- What types of activities at school required your working in a group? Did you enjoy team assignments?
- Do you have a career goal at this point?

In our country, laws have been established to safeguard your right to an equal opportunity for employment. Therefore, questions regarding age, marital status, ethnic background, religious beliefs, and physical and emotional disabilities (unless job-related) are considered illegal. If you encounter questions on these points, you are not legally required to answer. You may respond simply: "I prefer not to answer that question." However, you are free to answer if you like.

You may want to role play an interview situation by having a friend ask you questions. Role playing gives you an opportunity to practice responding and to evaluate those responses. You must remember, though, to listen closely to the interviewer. Prepared answers may not match the questions; you want to respond directly to the interviewer's questions.

Prepare Questions

Interviewers sometimes ask, "Do you have any questions about the company or the position?" Therefore, before the interview you may prepare a list of appropriate questions you might ask. Some of the questions would naturally pertain to the job for which you are applying: "What would my specific duties be? Is a training program available? Are there promotional opportunities for beginning workers?" Other questions could cover a broad range of subjects, such as the company's product line and fringe benefits provided by the company. You should not, however, make salary and other benefits the *focal point* of your questions.

focal point: center of attention

If you do, the interviewer may think you are interested only in what you will receive from the company instead of what you can contribute to it.

Be on Time

Arriving late for a job interview should be avoided. Plan to arrive early enough so you can relax and gather your thoughts before the appointment. A calm, composed job applicant will make a better impression than a rushed, *frenzied* one. Go to the interview *alone*; do not take friends or relatives with you.

frenzied: disorderly and ill at ease

Illus. 16-12. The interviewer, by talking with you, forms an opinion of you as a prospective employee. In some companies, you complete an application form and see an interviewer during the same visit.

During Your Interview

It is natural to be nervous before a job interview, especially your first one. But instead of dwelling on how apprehensive you may be, think instead about the measures you have taken to prepare for the interview. By keeping a positive attitude, you will increase your confidence and have a better interview. Concentrate on the information the interviewer gives you and the

JOB INTERVIEW DOS AND DON'TS

DO	DON'T
Dress appropriately.	Bring a friend or relative to the interview.
Greet the interviewer with a smile and a firm handshake.	Display nervousness by tapping a pencil on the desk, twirling your hair, or any other annoying habit.
Remain standing until you are asked to have a seat.	Slouch in your chair.
Use good posture when standing or sitting.	Answer questions with "yeah," "nope," or "uh huh."
Listen attentively.	Lie about your strengths or your accomplishments.
Answer questions honestly and clearly.	Smoke, chew gum, or complain.
Use good grammar.	Criticize past employers or your teachers.
Exhibit a positive attitude.	Ask questions only about the company's benefit package (what the company will do for you).
Ask questions about the company and its products.	Stand at the door after the interview is over and continue to talk.
Keep good eye contact with the interviewer.	

questions you are asked. Remember that the interview is a two-way communication process. The interviewer is learning more about you, and you are learning more about the company. Be sure to follow the job interview "Dos and Don'ts" shown above.

Do not expect a job offer during the interview. Most of the time, other applicants will be interviewed before a choice is made. It is reasonable, though, to expect the interviewer to tell you when you can expect a letter or telephone call regarding the decision made.

Some companies administer *pre-employment tests*. Such tests often give you an opportunity to exhibit your competencies in keyboarding, spelling, or calculating. If you are to be tested on a piece of equipment such as a typewriter, word processor, or calculator, you will likely be given time to practice briefly on the machine. Remain calm and follow all instructions. Do not be afraid to ask questions. If you have time, review your work before submitting the completed test.

Following up Your Interview

Review the interview in your mind and jot down notes to yourself that will help you in future interviews. Take time to write the interviewer a brief follow-up letter. This extra effort will demonstrate your willingness to follow through on a job, thereby enhancing the impression you made during the interview.

If the interviewer does not communicate with you within the time period mentioned in the interview, call the interviewer to express your continued interest in the job. If you receive a job offer and decide to take the job, accept the offer in writing. If you decide not to accept the job offer, you should write a brief letter stating your decision and expressing thanks for the offer.

START OFF RIGHT

Make just as favorable a first impression on your new coworkers as you did on the interviewer. Report to work on time. Listen carefully to instructions and suggestions offered by supervisors and coworkers. Take notes. Make a concentrated effort to learn coworkers' names as quickly as possible. It may take you a few weeks to feel totally comfortable in your new work environment. But, if you exhibit a genuine desire to learn and improve, you will be accepted by your new coworkers.

RECOGNIZE OPPORTUNITIES FOR GROWTH

You will have many opportunities both on your job and on your own after your work hours to become a more proficient office employee and to extend your competencies. You will find it worthwhile to plan for continued learning.

On-the-Job Learning

Take advantage of opportunities available to you every day to learn and to improve. Keep informed about new office technology and procedures. Be flexible and willing to adapt to the changes taking place in offices today. Be open to suggestions that can increase your productivity. Learn as much as you can about your job, the company, and the business environment.

Illus. 16-14. Small groups of office workers are discussing a case at a professional seminar.

Professional Organizations

Persons with common professional interests often belong to professional organizations. Some secretaries and administrative office workers, for example, belong to Professional Secretaries International (PSI). Such an organization provides a *forum* for exchanging ideas and for establishing standards for performance.

forum: a place for discussion

Professional Periodicals

The organization in which you work may subscribe to magazines and newspapers related to the company's business activities. You may find it worthwhile to read some from time to time to extend your understanding of the work of your organization. Also there are many publications related to office technology and procedures that you may find interesting as you strive to improve your performance. Your company and your local public library are likely to have periodicals of this nature which you are free to read.

Courses and Seminars

Companies encourage further learning through several means. Some offer training programs through their own human resource department. Others grant workers time off and the funds to attend workshops and courses offered by various groups or local colleges. Some companies have a tuition reimbursement program for employees who want to earn a college degree on a part-time basis.

Professional Certificates of Proficiency

criteria: standards

rigorous: demanding

Some professional associations (PSI, for example) have programs that certify an individual's level of knowledge and experience. The **criteria** for being certified vary for each association. Work experience, or a combination of formal education and work experience, is a common requirement. You also may be required to pass a **rigorous** examination.

PROFESSIONAL COMMITMENT

Your own commitment to professional behavior is critical to your future success in the workplace. Performing all job responsibilities, completing tasks properly and on a timely basis, and evaluating the quality of what you have done reflect your commitment. Additionally, striving to learn more about your job and your organization conveys a level of professional commitment that makes you a valuable employee.

PROFESSIONAL IMAGE

Because you will undoubtedly work with people who do not know you well, it is important that the image you project reflects your professional commitment. Your dress, your general behavior, your responsiveness in interactions with others all should be in harmony with your professional commitment.

RESPONSE TO CHANGE

There are many new and challenging job opportunities in office occupations. THE OFFICE: PROCEDURES AND TECHNOLOGY has given you a broad understanding of the business world you will soon be entering, either as a part-time or a full-time worker. The basic skills and knowledge you now have will help you to learn new procedures and adapt to new technologies. Change is inevitable, so you should be reassured to know that you now have a firm foundation upon which to build your career.

Preparation for a Job Change

As you become proficient in your job, you may begin to see other opportunities that are appealing to you. You may want to consider a job change. Think ahead by doing the following:

- maintain a file of information about job opportunities and qualifications for future reference.

● maintain a file of your work experience and accomplishments to aid you in updating your resume when you decide to consider new jobs. You may actually want to keep your resume updated.

Think carefully of your career strategy when you make a decision to consider jobs with other organizations. You may want to explore possibilities quietly without informing your employer. If you accept a new position, you will want to set a beginning date that allows you to leave your current job on good terms. Companies request that employees notify their supervisors a specified number of weeks in advance of their last day at work. A minimum of two weeks is common. Many firms conduct *exit interviews* with employees who resign. Such an interview provides the human resources department a chance to learn about the employee's experience in the company and to end the association pleasantly. Sometimes, at such an interview, an employee is invited to consider returning to the company at some future date.

When Employment Is Terminated

In today's rapidly changing business world, there is no guarantee that a job will be yours as long as you want it. Your job may be eliminated and your employment terminated. In such instances, some companies provide assistance in helping you find another position. At times, companies use **outplacement services**, which are specialized organizations that provide displaced employees with professional assistance in locating new jobs. Remember that while one company no longer needs your services, there are likely to be other companies who need the skills and abilities you can offer.

There are instances when employment is terminated because of failure to meet job demands as judged by a supervisor or manager. If you should face such a situation, you must be honest about the assessment that was made of your performance. You can learn from such an honest assessment. Plan to give attention to any deficiencies identified. You may need to study or practice skills on your own or take additional courses in a local school. If the inadequacies are related to such factors as punctuality, cooperation, and responsibility, you will want to reconsider your work attitudes and attempt to change them.

Some persons lose their jobs because their interests were not related to a particular job. In such cases, it is important that prospective positions be carefully assessed. Failure in one job does not necessarily mean failure in your next position. How well you perform when given another opportunity is up to you.

THE CHALLENGE OF TOMORROW

dynamic: constantly changing

At this point in your life you may not fully realize the contribution that you can make as a worker in our society. However, you should have a general idea of your capabilities and of your value to the organization you choose to join as an employee.

You live in a *dynamic* world—it is everchanging. To realize your potential, you must be ready at all times to meet new challenges with confidence and optimism.

Illus. 16-15. There will be challenges for you in the future. A positive and confident attitude will help you meet these challenges.

QUESTIONS FOR REVIEW

1. What qualities and abilities is an employer likely to assess to determine your qualifications for a job?

2. How has life at work in the United States changed in the last several decades?

3. How does a career strategy help you plan for your first job?

4. What objectives might guide a beginning worker who has not identified a career goal?

5. Where can you find information about job opportunities?

6. How does a resume help an employer to become acquainted with a candidate for a job?

7. Describe the information that you should include in a letter of application.

8. Identify three ways to make a good first impression during an interview.

9. What are two ways in which you can learn on the job?

10. Describe what you should do to be prepared for future job opportunities.

INTERACTING WITH OTHERS

You are applying for an entry-level position as a word processing operator at City Republic Gas Company. Ms. Pauline Lewis, director of human resources, is conducting the interview. Ms. Lewis introduces herself, shakes your hand, and asks you to be seated in the chair in front of her desk. She explains what is required for the job by saying: "The person filling the job must be able to work with limited supervision, manage time so that all deadlines are met, evaluate all work produced, and use good judgment in making decisions." Ms. Lewis then asks you: "Why do you believe you can meet the demands of this job?"

What You Are To Do: Prepare a brief response to the question Ms. Lewis raised.

EXTENDING YOUR MATH COMPETENCIES

The manager of your department has a meeting scheduled with the budget director for the next day. The manager wants to present an estimate of the cost of sending eight administrative assistants to a national office technology seminar. The manager gives you the following information. The manager says: "Could you calculate the total cost for eight staff members?"

SEMINAR ON THE HIGH-TECH OFFICE
Rochester, New York
August 5-6

AIRLINE TRAVEL — per person, round trip, $379.00
TAXI — per person, $16.50 each way, home to airport and return
AIRPORT BUS — per person, $7.50 each way, airport to hotel and return to airport
HOTEL — single occupancy, $110.00 per night; needed for two nights;
        NOTE: add 11% room tax to room rate
MEALS — per person, per day, $40; need for 2 1/2 days.

What You Are To Do: Calculate the cost per person for each item of the budget as well as the total cost for sending eight staff members to the seminar. Prepare the information in an attractive format that is easy to read.

APPLICATION ACTIVITY

Your friend, Paul Martinez, works as an accounting clerk at the headquarters office of Northeast Insurance Corporation. Paul informs you that the company is opening a new office in your area and will soon hire several beginning office workers. He suggests that you send a resume and a letter of application to Mr. Erwin L. Schell, Director of Human Resources, Northeast Insurance Corporation, 400 Thornfield Road, Baltimore, MD 21229-3472.

Word processing equipment can be used to complete this activity.

What You Are To Do: Assume that a beginning office job in which you are interested is one of the jobs available. Using plain paper, prepare a resume and a letter of application.

CHAPTER SUMMARY

You have learned about the relationship between personal growth and development and career development. Among the key points that you should be able to discuss are:

1. You can grow professionally if you have an honest perception of yourself and assess your strengths and weaknesses realistically.

2. Mature behavior is important on the job.
3. A career strategy is thinking ahead to a career goal and considering your first job in relation to that goal.
4. It is possible to choose a job and be successful in meeting its demands without having a career goal.
5. A carefully prepared resume and a letter of application will aid in communicating your qualifications for a position.
6. An interview is a critical step in getting a job.
7. Advancing in the work world is aided by taking advantage of opportunities for further learning and training.
8. A rapidly changing business world means that some jobs may be eliminated from time to time. Outplacement services are often provided to help employees find other positions.

KEY CONCEPTS AND TERMS

personality	blind advertisement
career strategy	letter of application
resume	outplacement services

INTEGRATED CHAPTER ACTIVITIES

Word processing equipment can be used to complete this activity.

Activity 1

Talk by telephone or in person with someone who accepted a job in the past year. Record the person's responses to the following questions: (1) What is your current job title? (2) What do you think were the most important reasons you were hired? (3) What advice would you give inexperienced interviewees about their conduct during an interview?

What You Are To Do: Prepare a report in which you present the responses to the questions. Include the experience the person had when hired and the type of company in which the person is employed.

Activity 2

Situation: A bank in your community is considering candidates for a position as general office worker. The person employed will maintain customer accounts and respond to telephone inquiries. An interviewer in the human resources department is soon to interview the first candidate for the job.

Participants: One student is to act as interviewer for the bank and another student is to act as candidate for the available position.

What You Are To Do: The two students assigned the roles are to present the interview before the class. All others in the class are to evaluate the candidate using the form provided in the *Information Processing Activities* or prepare a form similar to the one below. After the interview, there should be discussion of the strengths and weaknesses of the candidate's performance.

Candidate evaluated _____

Student completing evaluation _____

Did the candidate	Yes	No	Did the candidate	Yes	No
Bring a friend or relative to the interview?	___	___	Dress appropriately?	___	___
Display nervousness by tapping a pencil on the desk, twirling his/her hair, or any other annoying habit?	___	___	Greet the interviewer with a smile and a firm handshake?	___	___
Slouch in his/her chair?	___	___	Remain standing until asked to have a seat?	___	___
Answer questions with "yeah," "nope," or "uh huh"?	___	___	Use good posture when standing or sitting?	___	___
Lie about his or her strengths or accomplishments?	___	___	Listen attentively?	___	___
Smoke, chew gum, or complain?	___	___	Answer questions honestly and clearly?	___	___
Criticize past employers or teachers?	___	___	Use good grammar?	___	___
Ask questions only about the company's benefit package (what the company will do for him/her)?	___	___	Exhibit a positive attitude?	___	___
Stand at the door after the interview was over and continue to talk?	___	___	Ask questions about the company, its products sold, or services provided?	___	___
			Keep good eye contact with the interviewer?	___	___

OPTIONAL COMPUTER APPLICATION ACTIVITY
See Computer Application Activity 16
in your Information Processing Activities workbook.

OPTIONAL CRITICAL THINKING ACTIVITY
See Creative Thinking Activity 7
in your Information Processing Activities workbook.

PRODUCTIVITY CORNER

Blake Williams
OFFICE SUPERVISOR

WILL I BE PREPARED FOR THE YEAR 2000?

DEAR MR. WILLIAMS:

I just read a newspaper article titled: "The Office Worker in the Year 2000." According to this article, the office is going to be a very different place from what it is today. The author stated that executives will call their offices while en route by air to another country as easily as calling from their cars or homes. Office workers will be constantly communicating via telecommunications networks with other offices and their customers. Office workers will need to understand the business of their organizations and make decisions quickly and wisely.

It isn't clear to me that the skills I have been learning in high school will be of much value to me in the office of the future. Will they?—LESLIE FROM BOSTON

DEAR LESLIE:

You have raised an interesting question. I can give you a quick answer. Any skills and knowledge you have learned will be valuable in the year 2000. The predictions are that there will continue to be great need for basic skills such as keyboarding, office proce-dures, and record keeping. It is true that the equipment in offices may, in many organizations, be quite different from what is common now. The ways of applying your skills may also be different. However, in addition to the skills you now have, Leslie, you have the ability to learn—which will be of critical importance as you face changes. Furthermore, you have basic competencies in communications and math. You have learned to think, to solve problems, to manage time, and to make decisions. Your total high school education has given you the foundation upon which to build further competencies.

I must tell you, though, that a trend toward the need for higher skill levels is having a profound impact on business. But higher-level skills can be developed on the foundation of your basic literacy and math skills. You will have much opportunity to improve your competencies on the job. You will want to consider further education, too. You are thinking ahead, which is wise. You will undoubtedly seek opportunities to continue developing new competencies of value at work. Best wishes.—BLAKE WILLIAMS

AT WORK AT DYNAMICS: *Simulation 4*

The vice president of the Research and Development Division has asked Miss Branigan for a responsible temporary worker to fill in for her executive assistant during the days the executive assistant is on jury duty. Throughout much of the day, several full-time office assistants within the division will be answering the telephone, completing correspondence, and processing the mail. Miss Branigan is counting on you to fill in during the late afternoons after your classes have ended.

Miss Branigan discusses with you the importance of this assignment, "Remember, this is the office of a top-level manager. You are expected to act professionally at all times," Miss Branigan says. "You already act in a profession manner, so you will do just fine. As this is research and development, you will see and hear about emerging plans for new equipment and product designs. These plans are confidential and are not yet known by others in the company. You will be expected to keep all information in strict confidence. You never know how even a seemingly simple comment about a new product, for example, can be used to a competitor's advantage."

The vice president's executive assistant will try to complete as many of his current projects as possible before he leaves. However, you will be expected to follow his notes to complete any project left unfinished. Of course, you will need to exercise judgment with regard to your work. But with the experiences you have had already at DYNAMICS, you will be able to complete this assignment successfully.

Turn to your *Information Processing Activities* workbook to learn more about your assignment in the office of the vice president of the Research and Development Division at DYNAMICS.

SYMBOL	REVISION	EDITED COPY	CORRECTED COPY
∽	Transpose letters or words	to efficiently keyboard for a long period	to keyboard efficiently for a long period
ℰ	Delete copy	Send ~~two or~~ three copies	Send three copies
/	Cross out the misstroke and and write correct letter above it	the majer problem	the major problem
—	Change copy as indicated	Your ~~The~~ copy ~~will be sent~~ was mailed	Your copy was mailed
⌒	Close up horizontal space	the letter head	the letterhead
∧	Insert copy (caret)	When ∧we receive the ∧edited copy	When we receive the edited copy
⊙	Insert period	Donald P⊙ Miller	Donald P. Miller
?/	Insert question mark	Are you sure?/ I am.	Are you sure? I am.
!/	Insert exclamation point	No/ I refuse . . .	No! I refuse . . .
⌄⌄∧∧∧	Insert punctuation mark	Mary's comment was The project must be completed by 130 otherwise it will be of no value.	Mary's comment was, "The project must be completed by 1:30; otherwise, it will be of no value."
#	Insert space	The text on the shelf	The text on the shelf
lc or /	Use lowercase letters	THE MAIN Event lc	The Main Event
caps or ≡	Capitalize single letters or words	eastern; pacific	Eastern; Pacific
DS	Double-space (Leave one blank line.)	DS> Dear Miss Schindler Thank you for . . .	Dear Miss Schindler Thank you for . . .
SS	Single-space (Leave no blank lines.)	SS< We are happy to announce that . . .	We are happy to announce that . . .
QS	Quadruple-space (Leave three blank lines.)	June 30, 19-- QS< Walter E. Fening, Manager	June 30, 19-- Walter E. Fening, Manager
stet or ····	Let it stand; ignore correction	Our ~~proposed~~ conference will ~~probably~~ be held . . .	Our proposed conference will probably be held . . .
⊓⊔ ⊏⊐	Move copy in the direction of the bracket.	Sincerely yours Andrew Carl Manager jt	Sincerely yours Andrew Carl Manager jt
⌗	Begin new paragraph. Run paragraphs together.	. . . at the last meeting. ⌗Beginning on December 18 . . . No ⌗ Our next . . .	. . . at the last meeting. Beginning on December 18 . . . Our next . . .
— or ital	Underline or italicize	All requests _must_ be	All requests _must_ be
//	Align copy	1. Call to order 2. Approval of minutes	1. Call to order 2. Approval of minutes
(sp)	Spell out word or number	1945 N Water St sp	1945 North Water Street
=/or ⩟	Insert hyphen	Her father/in/law	Her father-in-law

SECTION B: *PUNCTUATION*

Punctuation makes written communication clearer and easier to read. The proper use of the most commonly used punctuation marks is explained in this section.

APOSTROPHE (')   An apostrophe is used

1. **To form possessives.**

   (a) **The possessive of singular and plural common and proper nouns not ending with the *s* or *z* sound (except *ce*) usually is formed by adding an apostrophe and *s*.**

student's book	women's rights
Ted's paintings	Alice's workstation

   (b) **The possessive of singular common and proper nouns ending with the *s* or *z* sound is formed by adding an apostrophe and *s* if the *s* is to be pronounced as an extra syllable. If not, add only the apostrophe.**

class's assignment	business' benefits
Chris's paper	Hopkins' proposal

   (c) **The possessive of plural common nouns ending with the *s* or *z* sound is formed by adding an apostrophe only.**

secretaries' salaries	members' dues

   (d) **The possessive of compound nouns is formed by adding an apostrophe or an apostrophe and *s* (according to Rules a, b, and c) to its final word or element.**

   chief executive officer's visit
   City of New York's ordinance

   (e) **The possessive of a series of names denoting joint ownership is formed by adding an apostrophe or an apostrophe and *s* to the final name in the series.**

   Bennington and Morris' proposal
   Farber and Galbrieth's store

   (f) **The possessive of a series of names denoting separate ownership is formed by adding an apostrophe or an apostrophe and *s* to each name in the series.**

   Adam's, Fred's and Tony's suggestions
   Ringman's and Turner's stores

   (g) **The possessive of abbreviated words is formed by adding an apostrophe and *s* to the last letter of the abbreviation.**

USA's resources	the CEO's office

721

(h) **The apostrophe is not used to form the possessive of personal pronouns or of the relative pronoun who.**

mine	his	ours	its
yours	hers	theirs	whose

2. **To show the omission of letters (in a contraction) or the omission of figures.**

won't (will not)   the '92 edition (1992)

3. **To form the plurals of figures, lowercase letters, signs, and words.**

The bonds were available in denominations of *50's* and *100's*.
Her *i*'s and *e*'s were written poorly.
Use /'s to indicate division and *'s to indicate multiplication when you write computer programs in BASIC.
He wanted to hear no *if*'s, *and*'s, or *but*'s.

4. **To form the past tense of arbitrarily created verbs; the apostrophe is followed by a *d*.**

She *OK*'d the final draft.   She *x*'d out several words.

COLON (:)   The colon is used

1. **To introduce formally a word, a list, a statement, a question, a series of statements or questions, or a long quotation.** The colon should be followed by two spaces.

Only one thing matters to her: success.
Please follow these steps for inserting a diskette into the disk drive: open the disk drive door; grasp the diskette by its label; insert the diskette into the drive as far as it will go; and close the disk drive door.

2. **Between hours and minutes whenever they are expressed in figures.**

8:15 a.m.   2:45 p.m.

3. **After salutations in some styles of business letters.**

Dear Mrs. Conrad: Ladies and Gentlemen:

COMMA (,)   The comma is one of the most commonly used forms of punctuation. Errors in its use are frequent. The comma is used

1. **To set off a subordinate clause preceding a main clause.**

If you complete all four letters with no errors, you will receive an "A."

2. **To set off a nonrestrictive (nonessential) phrase or subordinate clause.**

James Macintosh, author of *Your Career Path*, will present a lecture.

3. **To separate a compound sentence joined by the coordinating conjunctions *and, but, for, so, yet, neither, nor,* and *or.***

   Mary was asked to keyboard the manuscript, and Bill was asked to keyboard the tables.

4. **To set off introductory words or phrases.** (This use of the comma varies from writer to writer.)

   Therefore, you should mail the check.
   By the way, the meeting was cancelled.

5. **To separate words, phrases, or clauses in a series.** A comma is placed after each item in the series, except the last.

   You will need a pen, paper, and calculator for the exam.
   Please turn off the lights, lock the door, and return the key.

6. **To separate two or more adjectives, provided they each modify the same noun. No comma is used between the two adjectives, however, if one adjective modifies a combination of the noun and the other adjective.**

   The harried, frustrated secretary was overworked.
   Ms. Bickers was an important national figure.

7. **To set off words and phrases used in apposition.**

   John Roberts, president of the company, presented the award.

8. **To set off parenthetical words, phrases, or clauses.**

   I did, however, make a contribution.
   She will, in spite of his argument, vote for the proposal.

9. **To set off words in direct address.**

   John, please turn off the lights.

10. **To set off the names of a city and state.**

    I worked in Chicago, Illinois, for three years.

11. **To separate the day of the month from the year, and to set off the year when used with the month.**

    We met on April 1, 1992, in San Francisco.

12. **To set off a participial expression used as an adjective.**

    Walking slowly, he approached the deserted building.

13. **To separate unrelated numbers.**

    In 1990, 300 students were enrolled in the microcomputer course.

14. **To divide a number of four or more digits into groups of three, counting from right to left.**

    8,246,301 $12,500

15. **To set off phrases that denote residence or position.**

> Dr. Evelyn Sanchez, from Colombia, has accepted the office.

16. **To indicate the omission of a word or words readily understood from the context of the sentence.**

> The electric bill in January was $380; in June, $110.

17. **Before a short, informal, direct quotation.**

> Mr. Collins asked, "Will Diane accept the position?"

18. **To separate elements which might be misread if the comma were omitted.**

> Though I called, Anne had left her desk.

DASH (--)   In keyboarding, the dash consists of two hyphens placed together, with no space preceding or following them. The dash is used

1. **To indicate a change in the sense or construction of a sentence.**

> When the executive arrived--she had almost missed her flight--the meeting began.

2. **Instead of a comma, semicolon, colon, or parentheses, when strong emphasis is desired.**

> His suggestion--and I think it is the most sound--is the best option.

HYPHEN (-)   The hyphen is used

1. **To divide a word between syllables at the end of a line.**

The supervisor indicated that everyone would have to work overtime if the project was to be completed on time.

2. **To show compound words.**

> She ordered double-sided, high-density diskettes.

PARENTHESES ()   Parentheses are used

1. **To enclose figures or letters that mark a series of enumerated elements.**

He made these points: (1) our profit margin is too low, (2) our gross sales have decreased, and (3) our distribution system is inadequate.

2. **To enclose figures confirming a number which is written in words.**

> fifty (50) dollars   eighty-seven dollars ($87)

3. **To enclose material that is indirectly related to the main thought of a sentence.**

> The schedule (as it stands now) is incomplete.

4. **To enclose matter introduced as an explanation.**

> The microcomputer software (software for John's computer) arrived this morning.

PERIOD (.)   The period is used

1. **After a sentence that makes a statement or gives a command.**

> There are basic guidelines for spacing after punctuation marks.
> Complete it now.

2. **After initials in a name.** Space once after each period.

> Dr. N. R. Evans   Ms. Robin E. Cook   Fifth Ave. Market

3. **Within some abbreviations.** Do not space after these periods.

> p.m.   Ph.D.   M.D.   f.o.b.

4. **After many abbreviations.**

> St.   Co.   Inc.

The following abbreviations usually are written without periods:

(a) News and broadcasting organizations: UPI, KDKA, NBC
(b) Business abbreviations: IBM, YWCA, COD
(c) Data processing terminology: BASIC, LED, VDT
(d) Geographic abbreviations: USA, USSR, NM, NC, CA
(e) Government agencies: FBI, CIA, IRS
(f) Shortened words: memo, photo

5. **In decimal numbers, and between dollars and cents when expressing figures.** Do not space after a period that is used as a decimal point.

> $18.33   5.8%   16.227

QUESTION MARK (?)   The question mark is used

1. **After a direct question, but not after an indirect question or a polite request.**

> Will you accept the position?
> She asked who was hired for the position.
> Will you please take these materials to Mr. Jones.

2. **After each question in a series, if special emphasis is desired.** When the question mark is used in this way, it takes the place of the comma, and each element in the series begins with a lowercase letter.

> What is the scheduled starting date? the duration? the completion date?

QUOTATION MARKS ("") Quotation marks are used

1. **To enclose direct quotations.** Single quotation marks are used to enclose a quotation within a quotation.

> The supervisor said, "This report must be completed by 2:30 p.m."
> Andrea whispered, "I heard the director say, 'Don't be late'; then she left the office."

2. **To enclose the titles of articles, lectures, reports, and so forth; and the titles of sections of publications (parts, chapters, and so forth).** The titles of books and periodicals are not enclosed in quotation marks, but are italicized, underscored, or keyed in all capital letters.

> The chapter was titled "Effective Letter Writing."

3. **To enclose unusual, peculiar, or slang terms.**

> The television "news blurb" interrupted the regularly scheduled programming.

4. **To enclose words used in some special sense, or words to which attention is directed in order to make a meaning clear.**

> The word is "picture," not "pitcher."
> The "efficient" secretary lost the executive's report.

Quotation Marks with Other Punctuation

At the end of quoted material, a quotation mark and another mark of punctuation often are used together. The rules governing the placement of these marks are not entirely logical, but since they are well established and generally accepted, you should follow them.

1. **A period or comma should precede the closing quotation mark, even though it may not be a part of the quotation.**

> "I'll be back in ten minutes," he said, "and will sign the letters then."

2. **A semicolon or colon should *follow* the closing quotation mark, even when it is part of the quotation.**

> Susan Hutchinson was named "Employee of the Month"; Dennis Jacobs was named "Employee of the Year."

3. **Other marks of punctuation should precede the closing quotation mark if they apply to the quotation only, and should follow the mark if they apply to the sentence as a whole and not just to the quotation.**

> Mr. Stern asked, "Have you completed the report?"
> Did you read the article "Controlling Office Expenses"?

SEMICOLON (;) The semicolon is used before a connective joining two independent clauses. (A comma follows the connective only if the connective is to be emphasized.) Some commonly used connectives are *consequently, however, in fact, nevertheless, therefore,* and *thus.*

Our earnings were up 15 percent in March; however, our earnings were down 5 percent in April.

SECTION C: *CAPITALIZATION*

Capitalization (the use of uppercase letters) is used primarily to indicate the importance of certain words. Unnecessary capitalization should be avoided. When in doubt about a specific capitalization principle, consult a dictionary or other reference book.

BASIC RULES

1. **Capitalize the first word of a sentence.**

   > He was eager to begin work as a receptionist.

2. **Capitalize proper nouns (names of particular persons, places, or things) and proper adjectives derived from these nouns.**

Monica	West Virginia	the Liberty Bell
America (n.)		American (adj.)

3. **Capitalize the first word of the salutation of a letter and the first word of the complimentary close.**

   > Dear Mr. Stevensen   Sincerely yours

4. **Capitalize the days of the week, the months of the year, and holidays.**

   > Friday   February   Christmas

5. **Capitalize all significant words in the names of companies, organizations, and main government agencies.**

Delta Air Lines	Future Business Leaders of America
the Utah Tax Commission	Department of Justice

6. **Capitalize the first word of a direct quotation.**

   > The sales manager stated, "We will honor our commitment."

7. **Capitalize principal words in the titles of books, articles, magazines, newspapers, reports, and so forth. Do not capitalize articles (*a, and,* and *the*), short prepositions (*of, in, to,* and *but*), or short conjunctions (*and, but, or,* and *nor*).**

An Introduction to Computers and Data Processing	*Time*
"The Key to Success with Graphics"	*The New York Times*

BUSINESS TITLES AND POSITIONS

1. **Capitalize titles when they immediately precede individual names and are directly related to them.** Generally, titles that follow personal names are not capitalized. When known, it is always correct to follow the preferences of specific companies.

   > It was Ambassador Young who delivered the proposal.
   > Janet Turner was appointed president of Woodrow College.

2. **Do not capitalize business titles when they do not refer to specific persons.**

A regional manager of the company spoke to us.
The chairperson will be appointed at the next meeting.

GEOGRAPHIC NAMES

1. **Capitalize the names of countries, regions of countries, cities, and sections of cities. The names of mountains, islands, bodies of water, and other such geographic places and sections are also capitalized.**

Egypt	Appalachian Mountains
Paris	Bahama Islands
Montego Bay	the East Coast
Mississippi River	Greenwich Village

2. **A geographic term such as river, ocean, country, city, and street that precedes a proper name, or a geographic term that is used in the plural and follows a proper name, should not be capitalized.**

the river Thames   the Antarctic and Indian oceans

NOTE: If the term is part of the legal name, it should be capitalized.

the City of New York

3. **Capitalize points of the compass designating specific geographic sections of the country.**

the North	the South
the Northeast	the Southwest

Points of the compass used to indicate direction are not capitalized.

Miami is south of Atlanta.   The storm moved west to east.

4. **Capitalize proper names denoting political divisions.**

Allegheny County   Sixth Precinct

INDIVIDUAL NAMES

1. **Capitalize all units in the name of an individual (except some surname prefixes such as *du, de, van,* and *von*, which are capitalized or left lowercase according to the practice of the individual).**

DeKoven	deGaulle
Demille	deSoto

2. **When a surname with a prefix that is usually lowercase begins a sentence, capitalize the prefix.**

DeGaulle was known for his speeches.

SECTION D: *MATH*

Numbers are used by almost everyone who works in offices. This math review covers basic math skills and will help you complete the Extending Your Math Competencies activities included in this text.

ADDITION

1. **In addition, two or more numbers (called addends) are combined to get a sum, or total.**
2. **If the sum of one column exceeds 9 (6 + 7 = 13), carry the excess digit (1) to the next column; then add the digits in that column (1 + 2 + 5 = 8).**

$$
\begin{array}{r}
1 \leftarrow \text{carry} \\
26\ \} \\
+\,57\ \} \text{addends} \\
\hline
83 \text{ sum (total)}
\end{array}
$$

3. **Decimal points must be aligned one above the other before addends can be added correctly.**

Decimals Not Aligned	Decimals Aligned
71.16	1 1 ← carry
9.5	71.16 }
+ .872	9.5 } addends
	+ .872 }
	81.532 sum (total)

4. **Prove the sum (total) of an addition problem by calculating the addends in opposite directions.**

Add Down
$$
\begin{array}{r}
71.16 \\
9.5 \\
+\quad .872 \downarrow \\
\hline
81.532 \text{ sum (total)}
\end{array}
$$

Add Up
$$
\begin{array}{r}
\underline{81.532} \text{ sum (total)} \uparrow \\
71.16 \\
9.5 \\
+\quad .872
\end{array}
$$

SUBTRACTION

1. **In subtraction, one number (the subtrahend) is deducted from another number (the minuend) to get a difference.**
2. **If a digit in one column (the 4 in 24) is too large to be subtracted from a digit in the same column, (the 2 in 62), borrow 10 from the next column to the left (60 − 10 = 50, and the 2 becomes 12).**

$$
\begin{array}{r}
5\ 1 \\
\cancel{6}2 \text{ minuend} \\
-\,24 \text{ subtrahend} \\
\hline
38 \text{ difference}
\end{array}
$$

3. **Prove a subtraction problem by adding the subtrahend to the difference; the total should be the minuend.**

$$
\begin{array}{r}
1 \\
38 \text{ difference} \\
+\,24 \text{ subtrahend} \\
\hline
62 \text{ minuend}
\end{array}
$$

MULTIPLICATION

1. **In multiplication, the multiplicand is multiplied by the multiplier to get a product.**

$$
\begin{array}{r}
5 \text{ multiplicand} \\
\times \ 3 \text{ multiplier} \\
\hline
15 \text{ product}
\end{array}
$$

2. **Determine the number of decimal places in a product by adding the number of decimal places in the multiplicand to the number of decimal places in the multiplier.**

$$
\begin{array}{r}
2.41 \text{ multiplicand} \\
\times \quad 5.6 \text{ multiplier} \\
\hline
13.496 \text{ product}
\end{array}
\qquad
\begin{array}{r}
(2 \text{ decimal places}) \\
+ \ (1 \text{ decimal place}) \\
\hline
(3 \text{ decimal places})
\end{array}
$$

3. **Prove a multiplication problem by multiplying the original multiplier by the original multiplicand.**

$$
\begin{array}{r}
5.6 \text{ original multiplier} \\
\times \quad 2.41 \text{ original multiplicand} \\
\hline
13.496 \text{ product}
\end{array}
$$

DIVISION

1. **In division, the dividend is divided by the divisor to get a quotient.**

$$
\text{divisor } 5 \overline{)\ 15 \text{ dividend}} \quad {}^{3 \text{ quotient}}
$$

2. **If a decimal is in the dividend only, a decimal point is aligned in the quotient above the one in the dividend.**

$$
\text{divisor } 5 \overline{)\ 1.5 \text{ dividend}} \quad {}^{.3 \text{ quotient}}
$$

3. **If decimals are in both the dividend and the divisor, move the decimal point in the divisor all the way to the right (.5). Then move the decimal point in the dividend (1.5) the same number of places to the right. Align the decimal point in the quotient with the decimal point in the dividend.**

$$
\text{divisor } .5 \overline{)\ 1.5 \text{ dividend}} \quad {}^{3. \text{ quotient}}
$$

   If necessary, add a zero (0) to the right of the dividend so the decimal point can be moved the proper number of places to the right.

$$
.5 \overline{)\ 15.0} \quad {}^{30.}
$$

4. **Prove a division problem by multiplying the divisor by the quotient to get the dividend.**

$$
\begin{array}{r}
.5 \text{ divisor} \\
\times \ 30 \text{ quotient} \\
\hline
15.0 \text{ dividend}
\end{array}
$$

ROUNDING DECIMALS

Decimals are rounded so the number contains only as many decimal places as are actually necessary. For example, if a number with four decimal places is being used to represent a money amount, round the number to two decimal places for the cents.

If the third decimal place is 5 or more, the number in the second decimal place is increased by 1. If the third decimal place is 4 or less, the number in the second decimal place is not changed. Decimals can be rounded at any number of places using this procedure.

$$\begin{array}{r} 1.24 \\ \times\ \ .08 \\ \hline .0992 \end{array} = .10\ (10\cancel{c})$$

$$\begin{array}{r} 6.21 \\ \times\ \ .02 \\ \hline .1242 \end{array} = .12\ (12\cancel{c})$$

CONVERTING FRACTIONS AND PERCENTAGES TO DECIMALS

Fractions, percentages, and decimals are all different ways of expressing parts of a whole. For example, a part of $1 can be expressed as:

a fraction	$1/4$ (one quarter)
a percentage	25% (25 percent)
a decimal	$.25 (25 cents)

1. **To convert a fraction to a decimal, divide the numerator (the upper number) by the denominator (the lower number).**

$$\frac{\text{(numerator)}}{\text{(denominator)}} \quad \frac{1}{4} = 4\overline{)1.00}\ ^{.25}$$

2. **To convert a percentage to a decimal, delete the percent sign (%) and move the decimal point two places to the left.**

$25\% = 25.\% = .25$

$25.5\% = 25.5\% = .255$

$148\% = 148.\% = 1.48$

$12^1/2\% = 12.5\% = .125$

$1/2\% = 00.5\% = .005$

CONVERTING DECIMALS TO PERCENTAGES

To convert a decimal to a percentage, move the decimal point two places to the right and add a percent sign.

$.25 = .25 = 25\%$

$.255 = .255 = 25.5\%$

$1.48 = 1.48 = 148\%$

$.125 = .125 = 12.5\%$ or $12^1/2\%$

$.005 = .005 = .5\%$ or $1/2\%$

CALCULATING PERCENTAGES

1. **To find the percentage of one number in relation to another, divide the part by the whole and show the quotient as a percentage.**

    1 is what percentage of 4?

    $$\begin{array}{r} .25 \text{ quotient } = 25\% \\ 4\overline{)\ 1.00} \text{ part} \end{array}$$

2. **To find a specific percentage of a single number, change the percentage to a decimal and multiply the number by that decimal.**

    What is 2% of 150?

    $$\begin{array}{r} 150 \\ \times\ .02 \text{ percentage to a decimal} \\ \hline 3.00 = 3 \end{array}$$

PERCENTAGE OF INCREASE OR DECREASE

The percentage of increase or decrease compares numbers from two different time periods. To find the percentage of increase or decrease, determine the amount of change between the first and second periods. Then divide this amount of change by the first period, which is called the "base period."

second period sales	= $75
first period sales	= 50
amount of increase	= $25

$$\underset{\text{increase}}{\overset{(\$25)}{\text{amount of}}} \div \underset{\text{period}}{\overset{(\$50)}{\text{first}}} = \underset{\text{increase}}{\overset{(50\%)}{\text{percentage of}}} \qquad 50\overline{)\ 25.00}^{\;.50}$$

Change the decimal to a percentage by moving the decimal point two places to the right and adding a percent sign.

$$.50 = 50\%$$

MULTIPLYING AND DIVIDING BY 10 AND MULTIPLES OF 10

1. **To multiply by 10 or any multiple of 10, mentally move the decimal point one place to the right for each zero in the multiplier.**

    $$47 \times 10 = 47.0 = 470 \qquad 47 \times 1{,}000 = 47.000 = 47{,}000$$

    $$47 \times 100 = 47.00 = 4{,}700$$

2. **To divide by 10 or any multiple of 10, mentally move the decimal point one place to the left for each zero in the divisor.**

    $$1{,}362 \div 10 = 1362. = 136.2 \qquad 1{,}362 \div 1{,}000 = 1362. = 1.362$$

    $$1{,}362 \div 100 = 1362. = 13.62$$

AVERAGES

An average is obtained by dividing the total of the addends by the number of addends.

$$\left.\begin{array}{r} 13 \\ 7 \\ +\ 4 \\ \hline 24 \end{array}\right\} 3 \text{ addends} \qquad \underset{\text{addends}}{\text{number of }} 3\overline{)\ 24}^{\;8 \text{ average}} \text{ total}$$

TEN-KEY NUMERIC TOUCH METHOD

The ten-key numeric touch method means striking the 0 through 9 keys without looking at the keyboard. The keys are located by keeping the index, middle, and ring fingers over the 4, 5, and 6 keys, which are called the home row. Strike each key with a quick, rhythmic stroke.

The correct placement of your fingers is shown below.

Finger	Left Hand Operation	Right Hand Operation
Index	6, 9, 3	4, 7, 1
Middle	5, 8, 2, 00	5, 8, 2, 00
Ring	4, 7, 1	6, 9, 3
Little	0	Plus Bar
Thumb	Plus Bar	0

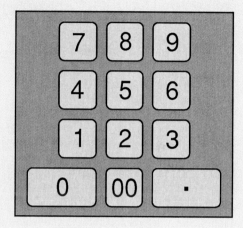

Ten-Key Keyboard

METRIC EQUIVALENTS

There are two methods of measurement, metrics and English. The metric system is a decimal system, which means that you can convert from one measuring unit to another by moving a decimal point. For example, 10 decimeters = 1 meter. By moving the decimal point one place to the left, you have converted decimeters into meters.

Length and weight measurements are illustrated below.

LENGTH MEASUREMENTS

Metric System	English System	Equivalencies
10 millimeters = 1 centimeter	12 inches = 1 foot	1 inch = 2.540 centimeters
10 centimeters = 1 decimeter	3 feet = 1 yard	1 foot = 30.48 centimeters
10 decimeters = 1 meter	5,280 feet = 1 mile	39.37 inches = 1 meter
10 meters = 1 decameter		1 mile = 1.609 kilometers
10 decameters = 1 hectometer		
10 hectometers = 1 kilometer		

WEIGHT MEASUREMENTS

Metric System	English System	Equivalencies
10 milligrams = 1 centigram	16 ounces = 1 pound	1 ounce = 28.35 grams
10 centigrams = 1 decigram	100 pounds = 1 hundredweight	1 pound = 453.6 grams
10 decigrams = 1 gram	2,000 pounds = 1 ton	1 ton = 907.2 kilograms
10 grams = 1 decagram		
10 decagrams = 1 hectogram		
10 hectograms = 1 kilogram		

SECTION E: *TWO-LETTER STATE ABBREVIATIONS*

U.S. State, District, Possession, or Territory	Two-Letter Abbreviation	U.S. State, District, Possession, or Territory	Two-Letter Abbreviation
Alabama	AL	North Carolina	NC
Alaska	AK	North Dakota	ND
Arizona	AZ	Ohio	OH
Arkansas	AR	Oklahoma	OK
California	CA	Oregon	OR
Canal Zone	CZ	Pennsylvania	PA
Colorado	CO	Puerto Rico	PR
Connecticut	CT	Rhode Island	RI
Delaware	DE	South Carolina	SC
District of Columbia	DC	South Dakota	SD
Florida	FL	Tennessee	TN
Georgia	GA	Texas	TX
Guam	GU	Utah	UT
Hawaii	HI	Vermont	VT
Idaho	ID	Virgin Islands	VI
Illinois	IL	Virginia	VA
Indiana	IN	Washington	WA
Iowa	IA	West Virginia	WV
Kansas	KS	Wisconsin	WI
Kentucky	KY	Wyoming	WY

U.S. State, District, Possession, or Territory	Two-Letter Abbreviation	Canadian Province, Possession, or Territory	Two-Letter Abbreviation
Louisiana	LA		
Maine	ME		
Maryland	MD	Alberta	AB
Massachusetts	MA	British Columbia	BC
Michigan	MI	Labrador	LB
Minnesota	MN	Manitoba	MB
Mississippi	MS	New Brunswick	NB
Missouri	MO	Newfoundland	NF
Montana	MT	Northwest Territories	NT
Nebraska	NE	Nova Scotia	NS
Nevada	NV	Ontario	ON
New Hampshire	NH	Prince Edward Island	PE
New Jersey	NJ	Quebec	PQ
New Mexico	NM	Saskatchewan	SK
New York	NY	Yukon Territory	YT

Address	Abbreviation	Address	Abbreviation
Avenue	AV & AVE	Heights	HTS & HGTS
Boulevard	BLVD	Highway	HWY & HGWY
Center	CTR	Lane	LN & LA
Circle	CIR	Parkway	PKY & PKWY
Court(s)	CT(S)	Place	PL
Drive	DR	Plaza	PLZ
Expressway	EXPY & EXPWY	Road	RD
		Rural	R
Extension	EXT	Square	SQ
Freeway	FWY & FRWY	Street	ST

SECTION F: *ALPHABETIZING PROCEDURES*

1. **Alphabetically compare the Key Unit (Anderson in Elizabeth Anderson) of one filing segment (a complete name such as Elizabeth Anderson is a filing segment) with the Key Unit (Brown in Thomas Brown) in another filing segment.** File Anderson before Brown because A is before B in the alphabet. An underscore is placed below the letter that determines the filing order.

Key Unit	Unit 2
Anderson	Elizabeth
Brown	Thomas

2. **Alphabetically compare parts in the same filing unit of two names.** File Anderson before Andress because alphabetically the e in Anderson is before the r in Andress. All punctuation is disregarded when indexing personal and business names.

Key Unit	Unit 2
Anderson	Elizabeth
Andress	M

3. **When the first unit of two names being compared are identical, determine the filing order by comparing the next unit in the filing order.** The first filing unit, Anderson, is identical for both names. Anderson, Elizabeth is filed before Anderson, Thomas, because the E in Elizabeth is before the T in Thomas in the alphabet.

Key Unit	Unit 2
Anderson	Elizabeth
Anderson	Thomas

4. **When a name is the same as the first part of a longer name, the shorter name is filed first. In filing, "nothing comes before something."** When comparing Anders and Anderson, there is nothing after the s in Anders which precedes the something (o-n) in Anderson.

Key Unit	Unit 2
Anders	Elizabeth
Anderson	Elizabeth

735

Other applications of the "nothing before something" rule are:

Key Unit	Unit 2	Unit 3
Anderson	T	
Anderson	Thomas	
Anderson	Thomas	L
Anderson	Thomas	Lawrence

INDEXING RULES

Rule 1: Order of Indexing Units

A. PERSONAL NAMES. A personal name is indexed in this manner: (1) the surname (last name) is the key unit, (2) the given name (first name) or initial is the second unit, and (3) the middle name or initial is the third unit. Unusual or obscure (often foreign) names are indexed in the same manner. If it is not possible to determine the surname in a name, consider the last name as the surname. Cross-reference unusual or obscure names by using the first written name as the key unit.

Index Order of Units

Name	Key Unit	Unit 2	Unit 3
Elizabeth Anderson	Anderson	Elizabeth	
Elizabeth R. Anderson	Anderson	Elizabeth	R
M. M. Andress	Andress	M	M
Thomas James Ansley	Ansley	Thomas	James
John Anthony	Anthony	John	
Ann B. Arthur	Arthur	Ann	B
J. Brett Austin	Austin	J	Brett
Isheanyl Awambu	Awambu	Isheanyl	

B. BUSINESS NAMES. Business names are indexed *as written** using letterheads or trademarks as guides. Business names containing personal names are indexed as written. Newspapers and periodicals are indexed as written. For newspapers and periodicals having identical names that do not include the city name, consider the city name as the last indexing unit. If necessary, the state name may follow the city name.

* "As written" means the order of the words or names *as written or printed* on the person's, organization's, or publication's signature, letterhead, or title.

Index Order of Units

Name	Key Unit	Unit 2	Unit 3
Action Appliance Store	Action	Appliance	Store
Dallas Morning News	Dallas	Morning	News
Evening Times (Duluth)	Evening	Times	(Duluth)
Evening Times (Houston)	Evening	Times	(Houston)
John Baker Company	John	Baker	Company

Rule 2: Minor Words and Symbols in Business Names

Each complete English word in a business name is considered a separate indexing unit. Prepositions, conjunctions, symbols, and articles are included; symbols (&, cts, $, #, %) are considered as spelled in full (and, Cent, Dollar, Number, Percent). All spelled-out symbols except "and" begin with a capital letter.

When the word "The" appears as the first word of a business name, it is considered the last indexing unit.

Index Order of Units

Name	Key Unit	Unit 2	Unit 3	Unit 4
The Baker Company	Baker	Company	The	
Baker $ Store	Baker	Dollar	Store	
For You Shop	For	You	Shop	
John Baker & Sons	John	Baker	and	Sons
John the Baker	John	the	Baker	

Rule 3: Punctuation and Possessives

All punctuation is disregarded when indexing personal and business names. Commas, periods, hyphens, and apostrophes are disregarded, and names are indexed as written. (For example, Smith's Playhouse would be filed after Smiths' Bakery.)

Index Order of Units

Name	Key Unit	Unit 2	Unit 3	Unit 4
Samuel B. Church	Church	Samuel	B	
Church, Wilson, and Jones	Church	Wilson	and	Jones
Church's Fried Chicken	Churchs	Fried	Chicken	
Church-Town Bookstore	ChurchTown	Bookstore		

Rule 4: Single Letters and Abbreviations

A. PERSONAL NAMES. Initials in personal names are considered separate indexing units. Abbreviations of personal names (Wm., Jos., Thos.) and brief personal names or nicknames (Liz, Bill) are indexed as they are written.

B. BUSINESS NAMES. Single letters in business names are indexed as written. If there is a space between single letters, index each letter as a separate unit. An acronym (a word formed from the first, or first few, letters of several words) is indexed as one unit. Abbreviations are indexed as one unit regardless of punctuation or spacing (AAA, Y M C A, Y.W.C.A.). Radio and television station call letters are indexed as one word. Cross-reference spelled-out names to their acronyms or abbreviations if necessary. For example: American Automobile Association SEE AAA.

Index Order of Units

Name	Key Unit	Unit 2	Unit 3
A M Motors	A	M	Motors
Billy Bob Adams	Adams	Billy	Bob
J. B. Adams	Adams	J	B
Robt. Adams	Adams	Robt	
KLYO Radio	KLYO	Radio	
PAWS Assoc.	PAWS	Assoc	
SHOWS, Inc.	SHOWS	Inc	

Rule 5: Titles

A. PERSONAL NAMES. A personal title (Miss, Mr., Mrs., Ms.) is considered the last indexing unit when it appears. If a seniority title is required for identification, it is considered the last indexing unit in abbreviated form, with numeric titles (II, III) filed before alphabetic titles (Jr., Sr.). When professional titles (D.D.S., M.D., CRM, Dr., Mayor) are required for identification, they are considered the last units and filed alphabetically as written. Royal and religious titles followed by either a given name or a surname only (Father Leo) are indexed as written. When all units of identical names, including titles, have been compared and there are no differences, filing order is determined by the addresses.

B. BUSINESS NAMES. Titles in business names are indexed as written. See Rules 1 and 2.

Index Order of Units

Name	Key Unit	Unit 2	Unit 3	Unit 4
Miss Anila Armstrong	Armstrong	Anila	Miss	
Mrs. Mason's Bakery	Mrs	Masons	Bakery	
Travis Parker, II	Parker	Travis	II	
Travis Parker, Jr.	Parker	Travis	Jr	
William Porter, M.D.	Porter	William	MD	
A. B. Price, Mayor	Price	A	B	Mayor
Princess Margaret	Princess	Margaret		
Sister Jeanice	Sister	Jeanice		
Rev. Charles Tyson	Tyson	Charles	Rev	

Rule 6: Married Women

A married woman's name is indexed as she writes it. It is indexed according to Rule 1. If more than one form of a name is known, the alternate name may be cross-referenced. For example: Atwill Doris C Mrs SEE Atwill James T Mrs.

Note: A married woman's name in a business name is indexed as written and follows Rules 1B and 5B.

Index Order of Units

Name	Key Unit	Unit 2	Unit 3	Unit 4
Mrs. Karen Lynn Cole *(Mrs. Keith J. Cole)	Cole	Karen	Lynn	Mrs
Mrs. Kathy Jones Cole **(Ms. Kathy Jones)	Cole	Kathy	Jones	Mrs
Mrs. Keith J. Cole	Cole	Keith	J	Mrs
Ms. Kathy Jones	Jones	Kathy	Ms	
Karen Cole's Jewelry	Karen	Coles	Jewelry	

*These names are the alternate names and are also listed at their alphabetic locations as cross-references.

Rule 7: Articles and Particles

A foreign article or particle in a personal or business name is combined with the part of the name following it to form a single indexing unit. The indexing order is not affected by a space between a prefix and the rest of the name, and the space is disregarded when indexing. Examples of articles and particles are: a la, D', Da, De, Del, De la, Della, Den, Des, Di, Dos, Du, El, Fitz, II, L', La, Las, Le, Les, Lo, Los, M', Mac, Mc, O', Per, Saint, San, Santa, Santo, St., Ste., Te, Ten, Ter, Van, Van de, Van der, Von, Von der.

Index Order of Units

Name	Key Unit	Unit 2	Unit 3
Mary M. D'Andro	DAndro	Mary	M
D'Anglo's Dairy	DAnglos	Dairy	
Andrew Del Gado	DelGado	Andrew	D
A. D. du Boise	duBoise	A	Inc
Duboise Medical Inc.	Duboise	Medical	
Sharon Fitz Henry	FitzHenry	Sharon	A
John A. MacGeorge	MacGeorge	John	
George Saint Thomas	SaintThomas	George	

Rule 8: Identical Names

When personal names and names of businesses, institutions, and organizations are identical, filing order is determined by the addresses. Cities are considered first, followed by states or provinces, street names, house numbers or building numbers in that order.

Note 1 When the first units of street names are written as figures, the names are considered in ascending numeric order and placed together before alphabetic street names (19 Street, 34 Street, Acuff Road, Dobbins Avenue).

Note 2 Street names with compass directions are considered as written. Numbers after compass directions are considered before alphabetic names (East 8 Street, East Main Street, Sandusky, SE Eighth, Southeast Eighth).

Note 3 House and building numbers written as figures are considered in ascending numeric order and placed together before alphabetic building names (308 Temple Avenue, 575 Temple Avenue, 624 Wayside Terrace, The Wayside Terrace). If a street address and a building name are included in an address, disregard the building name. ZIP Codes are not considered in determining filing order.

Note 4 Seniority titles are indexed according to Rule 5 and are considered before addresses.

Index Order of Units

Name	Key Unit	Unit 2	Unit 3	Unit 4	Address
Names of cities used to determine filing order					
Abington School Harrisburg, Pennsylvania	Abington	School			Harrisburg Pennsylvania
Abington School Lancaster, Pennsylvania	Abington	School			Lancaster Pennsylvania
Names of states and provinces used to determine filing order					
First Federal Bank Decatur, Georgia	First	Federal	Bank		Decatur Georgia
First Federal Bank Decatur, Illinois	First	Federal	Bank		Decatur Illinois
Gould's Clothiers Windsor, Connecticut	Goulds	Clothiers			Windsor Connecticut
Gould's Clothiers Windsor, Ontario	Goulds	Clothiers			Windsor Ontario
Names of streets used to determine filing order					
Saving Markets 2680 42 Street Salem, Oregon	Saving	Markets			2680 42 Street
Saving Markets 1479 63 Street Salem, Oregon	Saving	Markets			1479 63 Street
Saving Markets 7832 Abbott Ave. Salem, Oregon	Saving	Markets			7832 Abbott Ave
Saving Markets 5403 East Abbott Ave. Salem, Oregon	Saving	Markets			5403 East Abbott Ave
House and building numbers used to determine filing order					
Furniture Mart 3204 14 Street Norfolk, Nebraska	Furniture	Mart			3204 14 Street
Furniture Mart 6062 14 Street Norfolk, Nebrasks	Furniture	Mart			6062 14 Street
Pizza Palace 219 Kingston Building Denver, Colorado	Pizza	Palace			219 Kingston Building
Pizza Palace The Kingston Building Denver, Colorado	Pizza	Palace			The Kingston Building

Index Order of Units

Name	Key Unit	Unit 2	Unit 3	Unit 4	Address
Seniority titles used to determine filing order before addresses					
Dennis B. Davis 5207 Vicksburg Boise, Idaho	Davis	Dennis	B		
Dennis B. Davis II 1607 Albany Avenue Des Moines, Iowa	Davis	Dennis	B	II	
Dennis B. Davis III 1001 University Avenue Des Moines, Iowa	Davis	Dennis	B	III	
Dennis B. Davis, Jr. 1001 University Avenue Des Moines, Iowa	Davis	Dennis	B	Jr	Des Moines Iowa
Dennis B. Davis, Jr. 4420 Marshall Drive Ogden, Utah	Davis	Dennis	B	Jr	Ogden Utah

Rule 9: Numbers in Business Names

Numbers spelled out in a business name are indexed as written and filed alphabetically. Numbers written in digit form are considered one unit. Names with numbers written in digit form as the first unit are indexed in ascending order before alphabetic names. Arabic numerals (2, 3) are filed before Roman numerals (II, III). Names with inclusive numbers (33-37) are arranged by the first number only (33). Names with numbers appearing in other than the first position (Pier 36 Cafe) are filed alphabetically and immediately before a similar name without a number (Pier and Port Cafe).

    Note: When indexing numbers written in digit form containing *st, d,* and *th* (1st, 2d, 3d, 4th), ignore the letter endings and consider only the digits (1, 2, 3, 4).

Index Order of Units

Name	Key Unit	Unit 2	Unit 3	Unit 4
2 By 4 Lumber	2	By	4	Lumber
2 Circle Ranch	2	Circle	Ranch	
2-20 Circle Shopping Center	220	Circle	Shopping	Center
2d Street Cafe	2	Street	Cafe	
4 Seasons Restaurant	4	Seasons	Restaurant	
IV Seasons Motel	IV	Seasons	Motel	
Four Seasons Shop	Four	Seasons	Shop	
Four-Hundred Club	FourHundred	Club		
Fourth Street Shops	Fourth	Street	Shops	
Route 40 Motel	Route	40	Motel	
Route 44 Motel	Route	44	Motel	

Rule 10: Organizations and Institutions

Banks and other financial institutions, clubs, colleges, hospitals, hotels, lodges, motels, museums, religious institutions, schools, unions, universities, and other organizations and Institutions are indexed and filed according to the names written on their letterheads. *The* **used as the first word in these names is considered the last filing unit.**

Index Order of Units

Name	Key Unit	Unit 2	Unit 3	Unit 4
The Art Association	Art	Association	The	
Austin Bank & Trust	Austin	Bank	and	Trust
Bank of Berkley	Bank	of	Berkley	
Center of Technology	Center	of	Technology	
Christopher Columbus High School	Christopher	Columbus	High	School
Foundation for the Blind	Foundation	for	the	Blind
National Land Studies Department	National	Land	Studies	Department
Political Science Club	Political	Science	Club	
South Plains Christian Church	South	Plains	Christian	Church
University of South Carolina	University	of	South	Carolina

Rule 11: Separated Single Words

When a single word is separated into two or more parts in a business name, the parts are considered separate indexing units. If a name contains two compass directions separated by a space (South East Car Rental), each compass direction is a separate indexing unit. Southeast and south-east are considered single indexing units. Cross-reference if necessary. For example: South East SEE ALSO Southeast, South-East.

Index Order of Units

Name	Key Unit	Unit 2	Unit 3	Unit 4
South West Telestar	South	West	Telestar	
Southwest Telestar	Southwest	Telestar		
South-West Vending Company	SouthWest	Vending	Company	
Sun Shine Car Wash	Sun	Shine	Car	Wash
Sunshine Tanning Salon	Sunshine	Tanning	Salon	

Rule 12: Hyphenated Names

A. PERSONAL NAMES. Hyphenated personal names are considered one indexing unit and the hyphen is ignored. *Jones-Bennett* is a single indexing unit—*JonesBennett*.

B. BUSINESS NAMES. Hyphenated business names are considered one indexing unit and the hyphen is ignored. *Dial-a-Meal* is a single indexing unit—*DialaMeal*.

Index Order of Units

Name	Key Unit	Unit 2	Unit 3
Laura Armstrong-Jones	ArmstrongJones	Laura	
Browning-Ferris Ind.	BrowningFerris	Ind	
Dial-a-Gardener	DialaGardener		
D-Signer's Shop	DSigners	Shop	
Northeast Realtors	Northeast	Realtors	
North-East Service Station	Northeast	Service	Station

Rule 13: Compound Names

A. PERSONAL NAMES. When separated by a space, compound personal names are considered separate Indexing units. *Mary Lea Gerson* is three units.
Note: Although *St. John* is a compound name, *St.* (Saint) is a prefix and follows Rule 7 which considers it a single indexing unit.

B. BUSINESS NAMES. Compound business names with spaces between the parts of the name follow Rule 11, and the parts are considered separate units. New Jersey and Mid America are considered two indexing units each.

Index Order of Units

Name	Key Unit	Unit 2	Unit 3	Unit 4
Miss Anna Mae Abbott	Abbott	Anna	Mae	Miss
Miss Annamae Abbott	Abbott	Annamae	Miss	
East West Travel Agency	East	East	Travel	Agency
East-West Trucking Co.	EastWest	EastWest	Co	
Pre Fab Housing Sales	Pre	Pre	Housing	Sales
Pre-Fabricated Designers	PreFabricated	PreFabricated		
Prefabricated Products	Prefabricated	Prefabricated		
St. Martins Home	StMartins	StMartins		

Rule 14: Government Names

A. FEDERAL. The name of a federal government agency is indexed by the name of the government unit (United States Government) followed by the most distinctive name of the office, bureau, department, etc., as written (Internal Revenue Service). The words "Office of," "Department of," "Bureau of," etc., are added only *if needed* for clarity and if part of the official name. These words are considered separate indexing units.
Note: if "of" is not a part of the official name as written, it is not added.

B. STATE AND LOCAL. The names of state, province, county, parish, city, town, township, and village governments/political divisions are indexed by their distinctive names. The words "State of," "County of," "City of," "Department of," etc., are added only *if needed* for clarity and if part of the official name. These words are considered separate indexing units (Wisconsin/Transportation/Department/of).

C. FOREIGN. The distinctive English name is the first indexing unit for foreign government names. This is followed, *if needed* and if part of the official name, by the balance of the formal name of the government. Branches, departments, and divisions follow in order by their distinctive names. States, colonies, provinces, cities, and other divisions of foreign governments are followed by their distinctive or official names as spelled in English (Canada; Poland; France, Paris). Cross-reference the written foreign name to the English name, if necessary.

Name	Index Form of Name

Department of Public Safety
State of Arizona
Phoenix, Arizona
	Arizona State of
	  Public Safety Department of
	  Phoenix Arizona

Administrative Division
Department of the Secretary of State
Dominion of Canada
Montreal, Quebec
	Canada Dominion of
	  State Secretary of Department of the
	  Administrative Division
	  Montreal Quebec

Department of Health
Laramie, Wyoming
	Laramie
	  Health Department of
	  Laramie Wyoming

Lubbock County
Tax Assessor Collector
Lubbock, Texas
	Lubbock County
	  Tax Assessor Collector
	  Lubbock Texas

Food Safety and Inspection Service
Compliance Division
U.S. Department of Agriculture
	United States Government
	  Agriculture Department of
	  Food Safety and Inspection Service
	  Compliance Division

SECTION G: *LEGAL RIGHTS OF EMPLOYEES*

Employees in the U. S. are assured employment rights and benefits by federal and state laws. Employees can act to correct violations of these rights and benefits without being disciplined by employers. Many organizations provide procedures for fair review. Employee manuals often include such procedures.

Some important employee rights and benefits are briefly identified below.

FAIR WAGES, OVERTIME PAY, AND EQUAL PAY

The Fair Labor Standards Act (FLSA) sets the minimum wage that employees covered by the law must receive. Requirements related to overtime are also specified. An amendment makes it unlawful to pay different wages to members of the two sexes in cases where jobs are equal in skills required, effort, responsibility, and working conditions. The Equal Pay Act is enforced by the Equal Employment Opportunity Commission (EEOC).

FREEDOM FROM DISCRIMINATION

Title VII of the 1964 Civil Rights Act, which makes it illegal to discriminate in employment on the basis of a person's race, color, religion, sex, or national origin, is the principal federal employment discrimination law. Later acts specify that discrimination is illegal against handicapped individuals; against women because of pregnancy, childbirth, or other related medical conditions; or against anyone 40 years of age or older.

FREEDOM FROM SEXUAL HARASSMENT

An amendment of Title VII of the Civil Rights Act of 1964 makes harassment in the workplace unlawful. The EEOC has issued "Guidelines on Discrimination Because of Sex," which describes sexual harassment as unwelcome sexual advances, requests for sexual favors, and other verbal or physical conduct when: a. submission to such conduct is made a term or condition of employment; b. submission to or rejection of such conduct is used in making employment decisions; and c. such conduct has the purpose or effect of unreasonably interfering with an individual's work performance or creating an undesirable working environment.

SAFE AND HEALTHY WORKPLACE

The Occupational Safety and Health Administration (OSHA) requires that employers maintain safe working conditions for workers.

UNEMPLOYMENT INSURANCE

Persons who have worked for a required time and who are dismissed through no fault of their own are entitled to payments for a stated period of time.

SOCIAL SECURITY ACT BENEFITS

The federal Social Security Act, also known as the Federal Insurance Contribution Act (FICA), provides for the following:

- retirement income
- benefits for spouses of retired or disabled workers
- survivor benefits
- disability benefits
- health Insurance

FOLLOW UP

If employees fail to get satisfactory resolution of a violation within their companies, they should report the violation to the closest office of the agency responsible for enforcing the particular law. The local telephone directory will include the number for the closest office under "United States Government," and then the name of the agency.

Application software Software that directs the computer to carry out specific tasks.

Auxiliary storage Storage that is external to the processor but that can be made available to the processor as needed.

Block format Letter format in which all lines begin at the left margin.

Boilerplate Prestored text combined to form a finished document.

Central Processing Unit (CPU) Hardware device that receives and stores instructions and data, performs arithmetic calculations and logical comparisons, and directs the actions of the input and output devices.

Command A word or abbreviated word that instructs the system to perform a function or operation.

Computer assisted retrieval (CAR) The process of locating records on film by using computer-stored indexes.

Computer Output Microfilm (COM) The process of transferring images from magnetic media directly to microfilm.

Computerized private branch exchange (CPBX) A high-capacity, private computer-based telephone system.

Data processing The collecting, organizing, and summarizing of data, generally in numeric form.

Database A collection of related items stored in computer memory.

Database management system (DBMS) A system that organizes and manipulates large numbers of files in a database.

Deadline A specific time or date by which a project, task, or assignment must be completed.

Defaults Preset format settings.

Desktop Publishing (DTP) Creating of computer-generated publications that appear to have been professionally typeset.

Display Screen Known also as monitor. Most commonly used output device.

Download Transfer files from the central computer.

EasyLink A world-wide business communication network.

Editing The process of making changes to a document.

Electronic calendar A calendar maintained on a computer.

Electronic clip art Predrawn art available on disk.

Electronic funds transfer (EFT) The use of a computer and a telecommunications network to move funds.

Electronic mail (E-Mail) Electronic transfer of information (messages, data, documents, blocks of text).

End User The person who uses computer equipment and software.

Ergonomics Study of the effects of work environments on the health and well-being of employees.

Facsimile (FAX) Transfer of images (data, text, pictures, drawings, photographs) electronically using telephone lines.

Flowchart A diagram showing step-by-step progress through a system.

Font Complete alphabet (upper- and lower-case), numbers, and symbols of one typeface in one size and one style.

Formatting Process of adjusting equipment or software to achieve the desired layout or arrangement of text on the page.

Graphics Software that can create charts, drawings, or pictures.

Image processing system System that uses software and special equipment, including scanners and optical disks, to store an exact reproduction of a document.

Impact Printer Printer that makes impressions by the printing device striking a ribbon for each character and transferring the image onto a sheet of paper.

Information Flow The movement of information in an organization.

Information Processing System The organization and procedures used to transform facts into a meaningful and useful form.

Information Processing The transformation of facts into a meaningful and useful form.

Information services Provide electronic access to timely information.

Input Device Hardware that allows the computer to accept data for processing.

Integrated Electronic System A computer setup whereby computer-based equipment is linked electronically so that information may be exchanged between the electronically connected units.

Integrated Services Digital Network (ISDN) Digital interface standards that will eventually become common to the design and operation of all communication equipment.

Integrated Software Software that combines several applications.

Local area network (LAN) A communication network that links or interconnects electronic equipment within a limited area.

Macro A file created to represent a series of keystrokes.

Magnetic ink character recognition (MICR) A machine that reads and converts the amount of a check into electronic signals to be recorded on magnetic tape or entered directly into computer memory.

Mail merge A function on a software program that combines information stored in a database with a word processing document.

Menu A listing of available options.

Messages Self-explanatory, on-screen statements that guide you in completing the task or that acknowledge that the task is being performed.

Microforms Common forms of microfilm, including roll microfilm, aperture cards, microfiche, and microfilm jackets.

Microimaging systems Systems that photographically reduce documents to a fraction of their original size to fit on film.

Modem A device used to connect a computer to a telephone system.

Mouse Small input device designed to fit in the palm of your hand. When moved across a flat surface, the mouse controls cursor movement on the screen.

Nonimpact Printer Printer that produces output without striking images through a ribbon.

Operating System Software Software that controls the operation of the computer and provides the means for communicating with devices connected to the computer.

Optical character reader (OCR) Electronic equipment that quickly scans or "reads" the address on an envelope and prints a bar code at the bottom of the envelope.

Output Device Hardware that prints, displays, or records information.

Pagination Process of dividing the document into individual pages for printing.

Password A preassigned number or term designed to keep unauthorized people from accessing files.

Pen PCs Computers that can recognize words and numbers written on a screen and convert them to computerized data.

Productivity Level of accomplishment.

Prompts One-line statements or questions that provide additional instructions or request specific detail.

Record Any information—text, data, image, or voice—kept for future reference.

Records management filing system A set of procedures used to organize, store, retrieve, remove, and dispose of records.

Scanners Input devices that convert characters, images, and printed code into a form the computer can process.

Software A set of instructions or programs that directs the computer to perform specific actions.

Spell Checker An electronic dictionary.

Spreadsheet An electronic worksheet made up of columns and rows of data.

Standard format The layout pattern of a document on the page.

Stylesheets Preset formats used to automate document formatting.

Submenu Detailed listings under each of the options in the main menu.

Telecommunications Electronic transfer of information over a distance.

Telecommuting Working at home and communicating with the office by electronic devices.

Teleconference A meeting of people who are geographically separated but who are connected by a telecommunications system.

Text memory Internal memory within the electronic typewriter that is erased once the typewriter is turned off, unless a battery provides current to maintain the memory.

Touch screen An input method that allows the user to select functions or enter limited data by merely touching the computer screen.

Trackball Input device that performs the same function as a mouse without being moved across a surface.

Tutorial Program to help the user get started quickly and shows how to use software features.

Typeface Specific type design

Typography Style, shape, or appearance of printed alphabetic and numeric characters.

Upload Transfer files to the central computer.

Utility Software Software that carries out "housekeeping" duties, such as formatting a disk or making backup copies of data.

Videoconferencing Image communication system that allows people at two or more locations to have two-way voice and video communication using a wide area network.

Voice mail A messaging system that uses computers and telephones to record, send, store, and retrieve voice messages.

Wide area network (WAN) Long distance networks used to link electronic equipment that is separated by long distances.

Windows A feature used to split the screen into two or more sections horizontally or vertically. This allows the user to view two or more programs or several portions of the same application at the same time.

Workflow The sequence of operations followed to complete an activity.

WYSIWYG An acronym for "What you see is what you get," which means that the document on-screen appears the same as on the printed page.

INDEX

Utility software, 169; defined, 752

ACKNOWLEDGEMENTS

COVER PHOTOS: Jim Zuckerman/Westlight
Computer Graphics/Westlight

SECTION OPENERS

G. Glod/SUPERSTOCK, x-1
G. Glod/SUPERSTOCK, 68-69
T. Rosenthal/SUPERSTOCK, 154-155
David Clark Wendt, 388-389
R. Chen/SUPERSTOCK, 498-499
© 1991 Mittermiller, 588-589
K. Moan/SUPERSTOCK, 676-677

CHAPTER OPENERS

Storm Photo © Eric Meola/The Image Bank, 3
Mark Segal/Tony Stone Worldwide, 37
Photo Courtesy of Bull HN Information Systems Inc., 121
Stephen Johnson/Tony Stone Worldwide, 305
1985 by Ira Wexler, 449
Courtesy of Eastman-Kodak Company, 501
Courtesy of Federal Express Corporation. All rights reserved., 629
Courtesy of United Technologies Corporation, 679

THE OFFICE IN THE BUSINESS WORLD: Courtesy of International Business Machines Corporation, 22; Courtesy of Xerox Corporation, 41; Photo Courtesy of Unisys Corporation, 43; Photo Courtesy of Hewlett Packard Company, 45; Photo Courtesy of Unisys Corporation, 55.

THE SKILLS OF WORKING TOGETHER: CATHY Copyright 1984 Cathy Guisewite. Reprinted with permission of Universal Press Syndicate. All rights reserved., 95; (left) John Waterman/Tony Stone Worldwide, 109.

INFORMATION PROCESSING: Photo courtesy of Hewlett-Packard Company, 158; Courtesy of International Business Machines Corporation, 169; (left) Photo Courtesy of Apple Computer, Inc., 185; (right) Photo courtesy of Hewlett-Packard Company, 185; (left and right) Courtesy of International Business Machines Corporation, 186; (bottom) Photo Courtesy of Apple Computer, Inc., 186; From THE WALL STREET JOURNAL - Permission Cartoon Features Syndicate., 187; NeXT Computer, Inc., 189; Photo courtesy of Hewlett-Packard Company, 191; Dictaphone Corp., 240; Dictaphone Corp., 241; Reprinted with permission of Compaq Computer Corporation. All rights reserved., 242; Photo courtesy of Hewlett-Packard Company, 253; Photo courtesy of Hewlett-Packard Company, 256; Courtesy of International Business Machines Corporation, 260; Courtesy of International Business Machines Corporation, 261; (right) DFI, Inc., 263; (left) Photo courtesy of Hewlett-Packard Company, 263; (left) Photo Courtesy of Apple Computer, Inc., 264; (right) Photo Courtesy of Abaton, 48431 Milmont Dr., Tremont, CA 94538, 264; Courtesy of International Business Machines Corporation, 275; Photo courtesy of Hewlett-Packard Company, 292; © Robert McElroy, Woodfin Camp., 329; Photo Courtesy of INTERMEC Corporation, 332; Photo Courtesy of Hewlett-Packard Company, 336; Photo courtesy of Xerox Corporation, 376.

TIME AND TASK MANAGEMENT: Photo Courtesy of MAGNA VISUAL, INC., 401; Photo Courtesy of Xerox Corporation, 411; Photo Courtesy of Xerox Corporation, 412; Photo courtesy of Agfa Corp., 423; Photo courtesy of Apple Computer, Inc., 424; (left) Photo courtesy of Identifications Systems, Inc., 439; (right) Photo courtesy of Figgie International Inc., 439; John Coletti/Stock Boston, 440; Courtesy of AT&T Archives, 463; Location courtesy of AAA World Wide Travel, Cincinnati, Ohio, 465; Avis, Inc., 467; Courtesy of International Business Machines Corporation, 482; (top, middle, and bottom) Courtesy of International Business Machines Corporation, 490.

RECORDS ADMINISTRATION AND TECHNOLOGY: Courtesy of Tandy Corporation/Radio Shack, 504; Courtesy of the Census Bureau, 511; TAB Products Co. Unit Spacefinder, 520; Courtesy of Wright Line, Inc. Worcester, MA, 523; (left and right) Kardex Systems, Inc., 555; Photo courtesy of Datum Filing Systems, Inc., 556; (left) Kardex Systems, Inc., 557; Courtesy of Wright Line, Inc. Worcester, MA, 558; Fellowes Manufacturing Co., 560; (right) BASF Corporation-Information Systems, 564; (top) Fellowes Manufacturing Co., 572; SUPERSTOCK Four By Five, 572; 3M Optical Recording, 574; (right) Fellowes Manufacturing Co., 577; Eastman Kodak Company, 580.

MAIL AND TELECOMMUNICATION SYSTEMS: Haworth, Inc., 593; Bell & Howell Mailmobile Company, 595; CATHY, by Cathy Guisewrite. Copyright, 1983, Universal Press Syndicate. Reprinted with permission. All rights reserved., 596; (right) Pitney Bowes, Inc., 608; (left and right) Pitney Bowes, Inc., 610; United States Postal Service, 615; (left and right) Courtesy of AT&T Archives, 633; Picture provided by Ameritech Mobile Communications, Inc., 636; Electronic Mail from Microsoft Corporation, 639; (left) Pitney Bowes, Inc., 641; P. Rivera SUPERSTOCK, 643; Courtesy of AT&T Archives, 665; Cincinnati Bell Directory, 669.

PERSONAL AND CAREER DEVELOPMENT: Pamela Monfort, 695; SUPERSTOCK, 713.